COLLEGE ALGEBRA WITH TRIGONOMETRY

Joseph B. Rosenbach
Edwin A. Whitman
Carnegie Institute of Technology

Bruce E. Meserve
University of Vermont

Philip M. Whitman
Rhode Island College

XEROX

XEROX COLLEGE PUBLISHING
Lexington, Massachusetts • Toronto

PREFACE

This book is written for a unified course in College Algebra and Trigonometry.

The algebra material is based on the authors' *Essentials of College Algebra*, second edition,* with modifications to facilitate meshing with trigonometry and to adapt the presentation to the types of students commonly taking such a course. In particular, many of the topics are rearranged and much of the material is rewritten in detail. Some topics (such as mathematical induction and the slide rule) are included which did not appear in the *Essentials of College Algebra*, whereas statistics is omitted since there is not likely to be time for it in such a combination course. The material on matrices has been reoriented and the work on determinants collected in one place. A much earlier treatment of interpolation brings out the basic idea of this topic without the specialized connotations of its usual location with logarithms or the theory of equations.

In accordance with current trends, there is some decrease in the degree of attention to drill and computation. Moreover, the book is designed to be quite flexible in this and other respects. Thus, it permits the teacher to select to a considerable degree the variation of emphasis which he judges suitable for a particular class. The needs of students who do not have a full command of elementary algebra (for instance, after their work in algebra has been dormant for some time) are met by a comprehensive review of elementary algebra, mainly in the early chapters but with some mixing of old and new topics for variety. The review material is however written for students at the stage of maturity that may be expected of first-year college students.

The material on trigonometry has been written from scratch to fit the present needs. In such a familiar subject, naturally there is little that is basically novel. However, the emphasis is radically different from the traditional computational approach, as befits the present day use of

* For a still more extensive treatment, see the authors' *College Algebra*, fourth edition (Ginn, Boston, 1958).

computing machines in place of extensive hand computations. Attention is directed primarily to functional aspects and to relationships with algebra. Just enough computation is utilized to give some insight into the uses of the trigonometric functions and their properties and into the inherent problems of computation which transcend any mechanization.

The major features of this series of books have been retained. Illustrations, warnings, and historical notes are numerous. Most of the exercise lists have been revised. The chief aim of the authors has been to write a thoroughly teachable textbook. No attempt has been made to save space at the expense of clarity and thoroughness.

In the text, the illustrations and illustrative examples are carefully selected to anticipate the difficulties of the student and at the same time to set before him applications of basic principles and properly arranged solutions of problems. The abundance of carefully graded exercises affords the instructor a different selection in succeeding years. A star ($\star$) is used to mark exercises which require special caution in assignment: either the exercise is more difficult than might be expected from its position in the list (for example, it may have been advisable to deviate from the order of difficulty so as to group similar exercises) or the exercise involves new concepts or concepts from other chapters which may have been omitted or deferred by some classes.

Answers are provided in this book for the odd-numbered exercises. Thus the student is enabled to check his work in some of the exercises, but is placed on his own resources in others. Answers to the even-numbered exercises are available in a separate pamphlet, but are furnished to students only at the request of the instructor.

The "Warnings" in the text, by showing the results obtained by incorrect applications of the principles under discussion, are designed to put the student on guard against certain common errors. The "Historical Notes" link the subject with its rich historical background and should stimulate some students to read one or more of the excellent general histories of mathematics.

Thanks are due the many teachers whose suggestions provided much of the background for the present work.

CONTENTS

GREEK ALPHABET

Letters	Names		Letters	Names		Letters	Names
A α	Alpha		I ι	Iota		P ρ	Rho
B β	Beta		K κ	Kappa		Σ σ s	Sigma
Γ γ	Gamma		Λ λ	Lambda		T τ	Tau
Δ δ	Delta		M μ	Mu		Υ υ	Upsilon
E ε	Epsilon		N ν	Nu		Φ φ	Phi
Z ζ	Zeta		Ξ ξ	Xi		X χ	Chi
H η	Eta		O o	Omicron		Ψ ψ	Psi
Θ θ	Theta		Π π	Pi		Ω ω	Omega

LIST OF SYMBOLS

$\pm$	plus or minus.	sin	sine
$=$	is equal to.	cos	cosine
$\equiv$	is identically equal to.	tan	tangent
$\neq$	is not equal to.	ctn	cotangent
$<$	is less than.	sec	secant
$>$	is greater than.	csc	cosecant

$\leq$ is less than or equal to.

$\geq$ is greater than or equal to.

$\approx$ is approximately equal to.

$|a|$ absolute value of a.

a_n a subscript n, or, a sub n.

a^n a to the nth power, or, a exponent n.

$\sqrt{a}$ square root of a.

$\sqrt[n]{a}$ nth root of a.

$f(x)$ f-function of x, or, f of x.

(x, y) point whose coordinates are x and y.

x' and x'' x prime and x second respectively.

$°, ', ''$ degrees, minutes, and seconds, respectively.

$n \to \infty$ as n increases without bound.

$n!$ n factorial, or, factorial n.

... and so on.

log common logarithm, $\log_{10}$

ln natural logarithm, $\log_e$

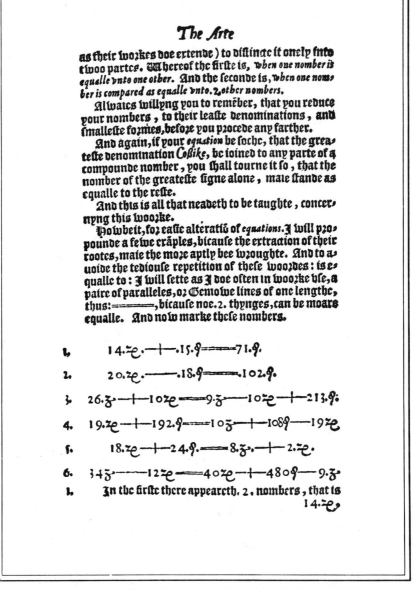

The Arte

as their woꝛkes doe extende) to diſtincte it onely into two partes. Whereof the firſte is, *when one number is equalle vnto one other.* And the ſeconde is, *when one nom̄ber is compared as equalle vnto.2.other nombers.*

Alwaies willyng you to remēber, that you reduce your nombers, to their leaſte denominations, and ſmalleſte foꝛmes,befoꝛe you pꝛocede any farther.

And again,if your *equation* be ſoche, that the greateſte denomination *Coſſike,* be ioined to any parte of a compounde nomber, you ſhall tourne it ſo, that the nomber of the greateſte ſigne alone, maie ſtande as equalle to the reſte.

And this is all that neadeth to be taughte, concernyng this wooꝛke.

Howbeit,foꝛ eaſie alteratiō of *equations.*J will pꝛopounde a fewe exāples, bicauſe the extraction of their rootes,maie the moꝛe aptly bee wꝛoughte. And to auoide the tedtouſe repetition of theſe wooꝛdes: is equalle to: J will ſette as J doe often in wooꝛke uſe,a paire of paralleles,oꝛ Gemowe lines of one lengthe, thus:=====,bicauſe noe.2. thynges,can be moare equalle. And now marke theſe nombers.

1. $14.\overline{z}e. \longaftermid .15.9 ====== 71.9.$

2. $20.\overline{z}e. \longrule .18.9 ==== .102.9.$

3. $26.\mathfrak{z} \longaftermid 10\overline{z}e === 9.\mathfrak{z} \longrule 10\overline{z}e \longaftermid 213.9.$

4. $19.\overline{z}e \longaftermid 192.9 ==== 10\mathfrak{z} \longaftermid 108\mathfrak{9} \longrule 19\overline{z}e$

5. $18.\overline{z}e \longaftermid 24.9. ==== 8.\mathfrak{z}. \longaftermid 2.\overline{z}e.$

6. $34\mathfrak{z} \longrule 12\overline{z}e ==== 40\overline{z}e \longaftermid 480\mathfrak{9} \longrule 9.\mathfrak{z}.$

1.   In the firſte there appeareth. 2. nombers, that is
     $14.\overline{z}e,$

A Page of the First Algebra Published in England (1557)

A reproduction of page f. Ff 1 of Recorde's *Whetstone of witte*, the page on which the equality sign $=$ is first found in print. In modern notation, equation 3 above would be written in the form $26\,x^2 + 10\,x = 9\,x^2 - 10\,x + 213$. The symbol after 213 in the original indicates the absence of the unknown.

CHAPTER 1

RATIONAL NUMBERS

1-1 Introduction

This book continues from the student's previous experience in algebra, taking up more advanced or more complicated problems and subjects. To an even greater extent than in elementary algebra, the richer returns come from understanding the processes and ideas involved rather than from acquiring skills in mechanical manipulations. However, without some of the elementary procedures, further work in algebra and in many other sciences is retarded or even prevented. For this reason attention to basic facts and operations, even if mainly in the nature of a review, constitutes an important part of this chapter and some subsequent chapters.

Algebra developed out of arithmetic through extension and generalization of operations on numbers to wider classes or kinds of numbers and number symbols. It is with these arithmetical numbers that our discussions start. In trigonometry, algebra is applied to treat numerically some geometric configurations and the more abstract ideas generated thereby, but this part of our subject matter will come only in later chapters.

Historical Note. The word algebra comes to us from the Arabic *al-jabr* in the title *ilm al-jabr w'al muqâbalah* of a work published early in the ninth century by MOHAMMED IBN MÛSÂ AL-KHOWÂRIZMÎ. The word *al-jabr* means "a restoration," and refers to the fact that after any number has been added to one member of an equation, the same number must be added to the other member to restore the equality between the members. Trigonometry was first developed as a tool for astronomy and later for surveyors; the name means "triangle measurement". Among the originators of this subject were the Greek astronomers HIPPARCHUS (about 140 B.C.) and PTOLEMY (about 150 A.D.).

1-2   Rational Numbers and Literal Number Symbols

The numbers of arithmetic provide a basis for the numbers and letters of algebra. The four fundamental operations of arithmetic (addition, subtraction, multiplication, and division) provide a basis for the processes of algebra. Accordingly, our initial tasks are to summarize properties of the numbers and operations of arithmetic and to extend these properties to letters as generalized number symbols.

Our present number system is the result of a long process of evolution. At the beginning, the need for counting led to the introduction of **natural numbers,** or **positive integers,** such as 1, 2, 3, etc. Strictly speaking, these printed symbols are **numerals** rather than numbers. However, we shall follow common practice and say "the number 5" as an abbreviation for "the number represented by the numeral 5".

The positive integers can be used in many ways. They also have shortcomings, many of which were overcome by the introduction of **positive fractions** such as $\frac{3}{4}$, $\frac{16}{75}$, and $\frac{28}{9}$. The positive integers and the positive fractions together constitute the **positive rational numbers.** Since any positive integer, such as 5, can be identified with a quotient, such as $\frac{5}{1}$, an alternative description is that a positive rational number is a number which can be expressed as the quotient of two positive integers. The positive rational numbers collectively have many of the same properties as the positive integers; for example, the sum of any two such numbers is again a number of the same type. The positive rational numbers also have an important property which does not hold for the integers: the quotient of any two positive rational numbers is a positive rational number.

It is convenient to consider next (though this is not the historical order) zero and negative numbers. The number zero, 0, is needed to denote, for instance, the number of apples left if three apples are taken away from three apples. It has many special properties, which are to be noted in due course. The enlarged system which includes the negative* rational numbers (such as -1 and $-\frac{3}{4}$) is called the **rational number system.**

---

* For the early use and development of negative numbers, see D. E. Smith's *History of Mathematics* (Ginn, Boston, 1925), Vol. II, pp. 257–260. In this context a distinction can be made between natural numbers and positive integers. The natural numbers are the integers obtained by counting, while the positive integers are the opposites of the negative integers. The distinction is of some importance logically, but practically they may be taken as synonymous, as was done in the previous paragraph.

The number system can be further extended to include positive and negative **irrational** (that is, nonrational) numbers, such as $\sqrt{2}$, $\sqrt[3]{7}$, $-\sqrt{2}$, and $-\pi$; this system is called the **real number system.*** The real numbers are so called in contrast to the imaginary numbers which are to be considered in § 3-9 and more extensively in Chapter 8.

The numbers in the number systems just described are **explicit numbers;** that is, each number symbol represents a single specific number. In arithmetic these numbers are represented by numerals, usually Arabic numerals, except for some very special cases such as π. In algebra, numbers, and even sets of numbers, may be represented by letters, called **literal number symbols.** For example, in the formula $A = bh$ for the area of a rectangle, the symbols b and h represent the number of units of length in the base and altitude, respectively. The formula may be used for any rectangle and, implicitly, the symbols A, b, and h represent numbers. The symbol "$=$" (read "equals") is used to indicate that the symbol A and the expression bh represent the same number. As another example, we may say that the rational number system consists of the numbers which can be written as $\dfrac{m}{n}$, where m and n are integers and n is not zero. The rational numbers, and operations of a corresponding character, are emphasized in this chapter and the next.

A letter with different subscripts may be used to represent different numbers; then the letter with its subscript constitutes a single symbol. For example, the area of a trapezoid with altitude h and bases b_1 (read "b sub one") and b_2 is given by the formula $A = \frac{1}{2}h(b_1 + b_2)$.

It is customary to think of a number symbol as either a constant or a variable. A **variable** is a symbol which may represent different numbers during a discussion. A **constant** represents the same number, usually an explicit number, throughout a discussion. All variables and many constants are represented by literal number symbols. From a slightly different point of view a literal number symbol which represents a number or numbers to be determined is often called an **unknown.** A constant which remains fixed throughout a given discussion but, unlike π, may take on different values in different applications is called an **arbitrary constant.** Thus in $(ax^2 + bx + c)$, a, b, and c customarily are

---

* For a further discussion of the number system, see B. E. Meserve's *Fundamental Concepts of Algebra* (Addison-Wesley, Reading, Mass., 1953), G. E. Bates and F. L. Kiokemeister's *The Real Number System* (Allyn and Bacon, Boston, 1960), or B. W. Jones's *Elementary Concepts of Mathematics* (Macmillan, New York, 1947).

arbitrary constants and x a variable. The use of letters near the beginning of the alphabet as constants, and letters near the end of the alphabet as variables and unknowns, is common.

We often refer to a **set** of elements, such as the set of positive integers, the set of real numbers, or the set of fingers on a certain person's right hand. In this concept, the collection of all the elements described is considered as a single entity. The individual elements are called **members** of this set.

Whenever a literal number symbol is used, one should specify the set of numbers which the symbol may represent. However, when the same type of number is under consideration throughout a study, it may more conveniently be specified once and for all instead of being repeatedly stated. Usually this set is the real numbers, or the complex numbers after the latter have been studied.

Historical Note. Symbols for positive integers and fractions appear on Babylonian cuneiform tablets (about 2000–1800 B.C.) and in early Egyptian papyrus manuscripts (about 1650 B.C.). The discovery of irrational numbers is credited to PYTHAGORAS (about 540 B.C.) and they were used extensively by EUCLID (about 300 B.C.). Many symbols have been used to represent unknowns. AHMES (about 1650 B.C.) used the word 'h'w, usually translated "heap". Our present usage dates back only to the seventeenth century.

EXERCISES

1. Indicate which of the following represent **(a)** integers; **(b)** rational numbers; **(c)** irrational numbers; **(d)** real numbers: 3, -3, $\frac{1}{3}$, $\frac{4}{3}$, $\sqrt{3}$, 3π, $\sqrt[3]{27}$, $\sqrt[3]{25}$, $\sqrt[3]{-8}$, $\sqrt[3]{\frac{27}{8}}$, and $\sqrt[4]{16}$.

Indicate which of the statements in Exercises 2 through 4 are true; correct each false statement by changing or replacing the italicized phrase.

2. The **(a)** sum, **(b)** product, **(c)** difference, **(d)** quotient, of any two positive integers is always *a positive integer.*

3. The **(a)** sum, **(b)** product, **(c)** difference, **(d)** quotient, of any two positive rational numbers is always *a positive rational number.*

4. The **(a)** sum, **(b)** product, **(c)** difference, **(d)** quotient, of any two real numbers different from zero is *a real number.*

5. Assume that m and n represent positive integers, and specify the types of numbers which may be represented by **(a)** $m + n$; **(b)** $m - n$; **(c)** $m \times n$; **(d)** m/n.

6. Repeat Exercise 5, assuming that m may represent any rational number and n may represent any rational number different from zero.

7. Repeat Exercise 5 assuming that m and n may each represent any positive real number.

8. Suppose that, instead of ordinary positive integers, a, b, and c denote hours as shown on a clock face. The sum of two such quantities is defined to be the hour reached after both times have elapsed successively, starting at noon; for instance, $(11 + 2)$ is defined to be 1 since the first time expires at 11 o'clock and 2 hours later it is 1 o'clock. Multiplication is defined by repeated addition; for instance, on the clock $3 \cdot 5 = 5 + 5 + 5 = 10 + 5 = 3$. The numbers 1 to 12 with these operations are called "integers modulo 12". **(a)** What is $(2 - 5)$ in this system? **(b)** Is division always possible in this system? Tell which quotients m/n exist, and try to find a way of describing these without listing them or their denominators.

*9. Repeat Exercise 8 for integers modulo 5 (as though clock numbers only read up to 5 instead of 12).

1-3   A Number Scale

The set of real numbers x may be represented geometrically as the set of points P_x on a line. Let $X'X$ designate a straight line extended indefinitely in both directions, as in Figure 1.1. Then select on the line an arbitrary initial point as the **zero point** or **origin,** O, and another point as the **unit point** P_1 preferably to the right of O. The points O and P_1 are called the **reference points** on the line. The selection of the two reference points determines the unit of length, OP_1, and also determines the direction from O to P_1 as the **positive direction** on the line.

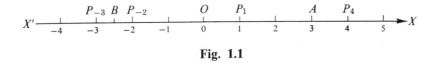

Fig. 1.1

The reference points O and P_1 on any line determine a **number scale** on that line. The positive integers are represented by points obtained

---

* Suggested further reading: Oystein Ore's *Number Theory and its History* (McGraw-Hill, New York, 1948), pages 209–258 or B. W. Jones's *Elementary Concepts of Mathematics* (Macmillan, New York, 1947).

by marking off successive units of length OP_1 from O along the line in the positive direction; the negative integers, by points obtained by marking off successive units from O along the line in the **negative direction** (that is, in the direction opposite to the positive direction). The points represented by rational numbers can be located by constructions with compass and straightedge; for instance, bisecting the segment between P_{-2} and P_{-3} locates the point B corresponding to $-2\frac{1}{2}$ in Figure 1.1. The points represented by irrational numbers can be approximately located in accordance with their decimal expansion. We shall assume, without formal proof, that:

After the two reference points have been selected on a line, there is on the line exactly one point, P_x, corresponding to each real number x, and, conversely, there is exactly one real number corresponding to each point on the line.

We indicate the correspondence between a real number x and a point P_x on a number scale by calling the real number the **coordinate** of the point; the point, the **graph** of the real number. In this notation, A in Figure 1.1 would be P_3. The use of coordinates as subscripts is common but not universal. Other notations, such as P_1 for "first point" and P_2 for "second point," regardless of their coordinates, are also used.

Applications of number scales include ordinary rulers, yardsticks, thermometer scales, and representation of gains and losses.

On any number scale the points on the positive side of the origin have positive numbers as coordinates; the points on the negative side of the origin have negative numbers as coordinates; and the origin has coordinate 0, which is neither positive nor negative. Thus the coordinate of any point P on a number scale indicates both the length of the segment OP and the direction (positive or negative along the line) from O to P. For example, in Figure 1.1 the line segment OA has length 3 and the direction from O to A is positive; the line segment OB has length $2\frac{1}{2}$ and the direction from O to B is negative.

The **length** of a line segment OP (that is, the number of units from the origin to the point P, regardless of the direction from O to P) is called the **absolute value,** or the **numerical value,** of the coordinate of P. Then *the absolute value of a positive number or of zero is the number itself; the absolute value of a negative number is the given number with its sign changed.* The symbol $|a|$ is used to represent the absolute value of any real number a, and is read "the absolute value of a."

ILLUSTRATIONS. $|5| = 5; |-5| = 5; |-\pi| = \pi; |0| = 0$. If a is positive, then $|a| = a$ and $|-a| = a$; if a is negative, then $|a| = -a$ and $|-a| = -a$.

On a number scale there are also line segments not starting at O. Any line segment P_rP_s may be considered as a **directed line segment** (from P_r to P_s) of length $|r - s|$. The direction on the line segment may be positive (as in the case of P_1P_4) or negative (as in the case of P_1B) relative to the direction on the number scale. The length $|r - s|$ will always be a nonnegative number.

EXERCISES

In Exercises 1 and 2, graph on a number scale the points having the given numbers as coordinates:

1. (a) 5; **(b)** -5; **(c)** $-\frac{1}{5}$; **(d)** -1.5; **(e)** 0.5.

2. (a) 3; **(b)** -3; **(c)** $\frac{1}{3}$; **(d)** -3.1; **(e)** 0.3.

3. State the direction and length of each of the following segments, where the subscript of P denotes the coordinate of P: **(a)** OP_1; **(b)** OP_6; **(c)** OP_{-4}; **(d)** P_1P_3; **(e)** $P_{-3}P_2$; **(f)** P_2P_{-1}; **(g)** $P_{-1}P_{-5}$; **(h)** $P_{-5}P_{-1}$; **(i)** P_5P_π.

4. Suppose that on a vertical line, O is chosen and P_1 is taken as the point two inches higher than O. What is the coordinate of the point **(a)** eight inches above O? **(b)** eight inches above P_1? **(c)** five inches below O?

5. Express each of the following as an integer:

(a) $|3|$;   **(c)** $|0|$;   **(e)** $-|16|$;   **(g)** $\sqrt{|-16|}$;
(b) $|-5|$;   **(d)** $|-16|$;   **(f)** $-|-16|$;   **(h)** $-|0|$.

6. Express each of the following without using the absolute-value symbol $|\ \ |$: **(a)** $|1|$; **(b)** $|-\frac{5}{3}|$; **(c)** $|\sqrt[3]{8}|$; **(d)** $|\sqrt[3]{-8}|$.

7. On five successive days, the temperature at 8 A.M. was respectively $40°$, $10°$, $-2°$, $29°$, $32°$. Use a signed number to specify the degrees by which each day's temperature differed from the normal seasonal temperature of $30°$.

8. Consider the following yardages made on successive plays in a football game: 4, 1, 7, 25, -8, 13, 11, 0, -2, -12, 16. List these numbers in order **(a)** as they would appear on a number scale such as that of Figure 1.1; **(b)** of increasing absolute value.

1-4 Order Relations

Real numbers may be arranged in order in two ways: numerically and algebraically. The numerical ordering is based only upon the absolute (or numerical) values of the numbers; the algebraic ordering is based upon both the signs and the absolute values of the numbers. These order relations may be conveniently stated using the **inequality symbols**

$<$ (read "is less than"),
$>$ (read "is greater than"),
$\leq$ (read "is less than or equal to"), and
$\geq$ (read "is greater than or equal to").

Given a number scale with its positive direction to the right, any two real numbers a and b may be **algebraically ordered** according to the positions of their corresponding points on the line, as in the following definitions:

$$a < b \quad \text{and} \quad b > a \quad \text{if } P_a \text{ is on the left of } P_b;$$
$$a \leq b \quad \text{and} \quad b \geq a \quad \text{if } P_a \text{ is not on the right of } P_b.$$

The **numerical ordering** of a and b may be formally defined in terms of the lengths of the line segments OP_a and OP_b:

$$|a| < |b|, \quad \text{and} \quad |b| > |a|, \text{ if } OP_a \text{ is less than } OP_b;$$
$$|a| \leq |b|, \quad \text{and} \quad |b| \geq |a|, \text{ if } OP_a \text{ is not greater than } OP_b.$$

Note that $a < b$ if and only if $b > a$. Given any two real numbers a and b, the relation $a < b$ holds if and only if $b - a > 0$; therefore (since each real number is negative, zero, or positive) exactly one of the relations

$$a > b, \quad a = b, \quad a < b$$

must hold.

ILLUSTRATIONS. $3 > 2$; $-1 > -3$; $0 < 5$; $-5 < 0$; $-3 < -2$.
If $x > 0$, then $-x < 0$. If $x > y$, then $-x < -y$.

The set of real numbers satisfying the condition $x > 0$ is the set of coordinates of the points on the positive side of O on the number scale (Figure 1.1). A detailed discussion of elementary order relations will be given in Chapter 12.

EXERCISES

1. Replace "and" by the proper inequality sign in each case:

(a) 3 and 5;   (c) -5 and 2;   (e) 0 and -2;
(b) -3 and -5;   (d) 2 and 0;   (f) -1 and -2.

2. Draw a number scale (§ 1-3) and find the coordinates of the points P_x such that the specified segments are equal in length and direction:

(a) P_1P_4, OP_x;   (c) P_3P_x, P_1P_{-2};

(b) P_1P_6, P_2P_x;   (d) P_xP_{-2}, P_4P_3.

3. During the month of June the batting averages of five baseball players changed as follows: .027 increase, .030 decrease, .053 increase, .004 decrease, and .100 decrease. Choose appropriate signs and arrange these changes in (a) algebraic order; (b) numerical order.

4. Give three numbers (a) between -3 and -2; (b) not between -5 and 15; (c) serving as coordinates of points on the line segment P_3P_4; (d) serving as coordinates of points on the segment $P_{-3}P_{-5}$.

5. List the following numbers in their algebraic order:

(a) 3, $-\frac{2}{3}$, 0, $\frac{22}{7}$, 1.62, $-\sqrt{6}$;   (b) 4, -3, -5, 6, $\sqrt{10}$, $-\sqrt{13}$.

6. List in their numerical order the numbers given in Exercise 5.

7. Describe by inequalities the sets of real numbers x that serve as coordinates of the following sets of points P_x:

(a) the points on the positive side of P_a;

(b) the points on the negative side of P_b;

(c) the points between P_a and P_b where $a < b$; and

(d) the points that are not on the segment P_aP_b where $a < b$.

8. Assume that x represents a positive number and insert the proper inequality sign between each of the following:

(a) x and $x + 1$;   (c) x and x^2 when $x < 1$;

(b) x and x^2 when $x > 1$;   (d) x and $1/x$ when $x < 1$.

9. Describe the possible positions of the point P_c on a number scale under each of the following conditions:

(a) $|c| = c$;   (b) $3c = c$;   (c) $3c > c$;   (d) $3c < c$.

10. Use a number scale to explain why, without further information, it is not possible to assert which number is greater in each of the following pairs:

(a) n or $-n$;   (b) n or $3n$;   (c) n or $-2n$.

11. Identify the points P_x, if any, on a number scale such that

(a) $x = x^2$;   (c) $x > x^2$;   (e) $x < -x$;

(b) $x < x^2$;   (d) $x = -x$;   (f) $x > -x$.

12. Identify the points P_x, if any, on a number scale such that

(a) $|x| > 1$;   (c) $|-x| < 1$;   (e) $|x| > 0$;

(b) $|-x| = 1$;   (d) $|-x| = 0$;   (f) $|-x| < 0$.

1-5 Fundamental Operations

The fundamental operations of arithmetic are addition, subtraction, multiplication, and division. Given any two numbers a and b, there exist unique numbers (exactly one for each pair of values for a and b) $a + b$, $a - b$, $a \times b$, and, if b is not 0, $a \div b$. Also, numbers are raised to specified powers (involution) and roots of numbers are extracted (evolution). In algebra the fundamental operations of arithmetic are used for more extensive sets of numbers, namely, for rational numbers, for real numbers, for complex numbers, and also for literal number symbols.

The symbols for the operations of addition and subtraction in arithmetic carry over into algebra, but in algebra they are used in two senses. In the difference $(8 - 5)$, the minus sign is a sign of an operation; but in -2, it is a sign of quality, or of direction on a number scale. As signs of operations, the plus and minus signs are always expressed, but the plus sign as a sign of quality is commonly omitted. Thus, negative seven is written -7, but positive seven is written 7.

The symbols for the operations of multiplication and division in arithmetic also carry over into algebra, but other ways of indicating these two operations are more generally used. For example, ten times five is written $10 \cdot 5$, and the product of a and b is written $a \cdot b$ or ab. The quotient of one number by another is commonly written as a fraction with the dividend as the numerator and with the divisor as the denominator. Thus, $a \div b$ is written $\dfrac{a}{b}$ or a/b. Note that the indicated quotient a/b implies that b is *not equal to zero* (written $b \neq 0$). The reason for this restriction is discussed in § 2-4 and can readily be seen if one attempts to perform a division with zero as a divisor.

In order to extend the fundamental operations to numbers generally, certain fundamental laws governing the use of numbers are necessary. These are in the nature of assumptions, since it is not possible to prove them; indeed, they play much the same role in algebra as the postulates do in geometry. Specifically, they assert that the basic properties of numbers in arithmetic—which are familiar, although perhaps not by name—hold also for literal number symbols. They are known as the **fundamental assumptions of algebra.**

I. Addition is commutative, that is, *the sum of two numbers is the same in whatever order they are added.*

Illustration 1. $2 + 7 = 7 + 2$; $a + b = b + a$.

II. Addition is associative, that is, *the sum of three or more numbers is the same in whatever manner they are grouped in adding.*

ILLUSTRATION 2. $(4 + 9) + 5 = 4 + (9 + 5) = 4 + 9 + 5$;
$$(a + b) + c = a + (b + c) = a + b + c.$$

III. Multiplication is commutative, that is, *the product of two numbers is the same in whatever order they are multiplied.*

ILLUSTRATION 3. $6 \times 11 = 11 \times 6$; $ab = ba$.

IV. Multiplication is associative, that is, *the product of three or more numbers is the same in whatever manner they are grouped.*

ILLUSTRATION 4. $8 \times (3 \times 7) = (8 \times 3) \times 7 = 8 \times 3 \times 7$;
$$a(bc) = (ab)c = abc.$$

V. Multiplication is distributive with respect to addition, that is, *the product of a number by the sum of two or more numbers is equal to the sum of the products of the first number by each of the numbers of the sum.*

ILLUSTRATION 5. $12(3 + 6) = 36 + 72$; $a(b + c) = ab + ac$.

The fundamental assumptions of algebra and the order relations which we have previously considered provide the basis for the following procedures, known as the **laws of signs.** They are stated for real numbers. We recall that all positive numbers and all negative numbers are also real numbers.

1. *To* **add** *two real numbers which have the* **same** *signs, add their absolute values and prefix their common sign to the result.*

2. *To* **add** *two real numbers which have* **opposite** *signs, subtract the smaller absolute value from the larger and prefix to the result the sign of the number with the larger absolute value.*

3. *To* **subtract** *one real number (the* **subtrahend**) *from another (the* **minuend**), *change the sign of the number to be subtracted and proceed as in addition.*

4. *To* **multiply** (*or* **divide**) *one real number by another, multiply (or divide) their absolute values, and, if the numbers have like signs, take this result as the answer; if the numbers have unlike signs, take the negative of this result as the answer.*

The procedure for subtraction is based upon the following important relationship between addition and subtraction:

$$a - b = a + (-b).$$

Each of the numbers b and $-b$ is called **the negative of** the other.

The real number zero is neither positive nor negative and thus does not have a sign. For any real number b, $b + 0 = b$, $b - 0 = b$, $b \times 0 = 0$, and, if $b \neq 0$, $0 \div b = 0$.

ILLUSTRATION 6. $5 - 3 = 5 + (-3) = 2$; $0 - 3 = 0 + (-3) = -3$;
$$0 - (-3) = 0 + [-(-3)] = 0 + 3 = 3;$$
$$5 - (-3) = 5 + 3 = 8.$$

The procedure for multiplication and division is often considered as a rule for associating signs with products and quotients of more general expressions, although "their absolute value" should then be read as "the symbols without any prefixed sign." In particular, we have

$$a(b) = (ab) = (-a)(-b), \quad \text{and} \quad a(-b) = -(ab) = (-a)b,$$

where the symbols a and b may represent any real numbers (positive, negative, or zero) or any algebraic expressions.

ILLUSTRATION 7. $5(2) = 10 = (-5)(-2)$; $5(-2) = -10 = (-5)(2)$;
$$3(x - 5) = 3x - 15; \quad (-3x)(-5x) = 15x^2.$$

Historical Note. The generalization of the operations of arithmetic and the development of the necessary algebraic symbolism were largely the work of mathematicians of the sixteenth and seventeenth centuries, particularly VIETA (about 1590), DESCARTES (1637), and WALLIS (1693). Many of the problems now solved by algebra originated at least three thousand years ago, but even as late as the time of CARDAN (1545) the solutions were stated in words, as rules, with at most a few lines of symbols appearing incidentally.

EXERCISES

Perform the indicated operations:

1. $6 + (-2)$.

2. $-6 + 2$.

3. $-6 + (-2)$.

4. $6 - (-2)$.

5. $6(-2)$.

6. $(-6)(2)$.

7. $(-6)(-2)$.

8. $(-6)/2$.

9. $(-6)/(-2)$.

10. $2/(-6)$.

11. $-6 - (-2)$.

12. $\frac{6}{35} \div (-\frac{7}{2})$.

13. $(-\frac{6}{35}) \div \frac{2}{7}$.

14. $(-\frac{16}{15})(-\frac{5}{6})$.

15. $(-\frac{16}{15})/(-\frac{5}{6})$.

16. $(-\frac{16}{15})(0.3)$.

17. $(-\frac{16}{15})/(0.3)$.

18. $(-3)(x - 2)$.

19. $(-x)(y - z)$.

20. $(-\frac{2}{3})(x - 6)$.

21. $(-1)(-x + 8)$.

22. $8 + (-5) + (-7)$.

23. $(-7) + (-6) - 3$.

24. $\frac{3}{4}(-\frac{2}{3})(-\frac{5}{6})$.

25. $(-\frac{3}{5})(-\frac{2}{3})/(-\frac{5}{4})$.

26. Give the negative of **(a)** 4; **(b)** -4; **(c)** 1.4; **(d)** x; **(e)** $-x$.

27. Write each of the following as sums:

(a) $5x - 2$;

(b) $4 - y$;

(c) $2 - (5 + \sqrt{2})$;

(d) $a - (b - c)$.

28. What is the sign of the product (a) of an even number of negative numbers? (b) of an odd number of negative numbers?

29. Determine whether the following are true or false:

(a) $(a + b)c = ac + bc$;

(b) $(a + b) \div c = \dfrac{a}{c} + \dfrac{b}{c}$;

(c) $c(a + b) = ac + bc$;

(d) $c \div (a + b) = \dfrac{c}{a} + \dfrac{c}{b}$.

30. Give an example illustrating the fact that (a) subtraction is not commutative; (b) subtraction is not associative; (c) division is not commutative.

31. State conditions upon the real numbers which may be used to replace the symbols x and y if $-xy$ is to be (a) positive; (b) zero; (c) negative.

32. A man runs 200 yards and walks 2000 yards. Find the total number of *feet* that he travels. This can be done either by converting both distances and then adding, or by adding first and then changing the units. Do the two answers agree, and, if so, is this fact related to any of the fundamental assumptions stated in this section?

33. Using the fundamental assumptions of algebra, and showing all steps, prove:

(a) $(ab)c = (cb)a$;

(b) $(a + b)c = cb + ca$.

$\star$**34.** For the integers modulo 5 (Exercise 9 of § 1-2), (a) is addition commutative? (b) is addition associative? (c) is multiplication commutative?

1-6 Powers and Exponents

If two or more quantities are multiplied together, then each of them, or the product of any number of them, is called a **factor** of the product. If a quantity is the product of factors which are equal to each other, the quantity is called a **power** of the repeated factor. The symbol a^2 is used to represent the product $a \cdot a$; a^3 to represent $a \cdot a \cdot a$; and, in general, a^m for any positive integer m is used to represent the product of m factors each equal to a. We read a^2 as "a squared," "the square of a," or "the second power of a"; the symbol a^3 as "a cubed," "the cube of a," or "the third power of a"; and a^m as "the mth power of a." The number a

is called the **base,** a^m the **mth power of the base a,** and m the **exponent** of the power.

ILLUSTRATIONS. $3^5 = 3 \cdot 3 \cdot 3 \cdot 3 \cdot 3 = 243$;

$$(-2)^3 = (-2)(-2)(-2) = -8;$$

$$a^2 \cdot a^3 = (a \cdot a)(a \cdot a \cdot a) = a \cdot a \cdot a \cdot a \cdot a = a^5;$$

$$\frac{a^5}{a^2} = \frac{\not{a} \cdot \not{a} \cdot a \cdot a \cdot a}{\not{a} \cdot \not{a}} = \frac{a \cdot a \cdot a}{1} = a^3;$$

$$(-x)^3 = (-x)(-x)(-x) = (-1)(-1)(-1)(x)(x)(x) = -x^3.$$

An oblique stroke, as used above, indicates the common factors by which the numerator and the denominator of the fraction have been divided. It is called a **cancellation mark.**

These results suggest the following laws, known as the **laws of exponents.**

Law I. $\mathbf{a^m \cdot a^n = a^{m+n}}$, *where* m *and* n *are any two positive integers.*

Proof.
$$a^m \cdot a^n = (a \cdot a \cdot a \cdots a, m \text{ factors } a)(a \cdot a \cdot a \cdots a, n \text{ factors } a)$$
$$= a \cdot a \cdot a \cdots a, (m + n) \text{ factors } a$$
$$= a^{m+n}.$$

ILLUSTRATIONS. $a^3 \cdot a^7 = a^{3+7} = a^{10}$; $c^{3p} \cdot c^{2p} = c^{3p+2p} = c^{5p}$.

Warning 1. $a^m b^n \neq (ab)^{m+n}$;

$$2^3 \cdot 3^2 = 8 \cdot 9 = 72 \quad \text{but} \quad 2^3 \cdot 3^2 \neq (2 \cdot 3)^5.$$

Law II. $\mathbf{(a^m)^n = a^{mn}}$, *where* m *and* n *are any two positive integers.*

Proof.
$$(a^m)^n = a^m \cdot a^m \cdot a^m \cdots a^m, n \text{ factors } a^m$$
$$= a^{m+m+m+\cdots+m}, n \text{ terms } m$$
$$= a^{mn}.$$

ILLUSTRATIONS. $(2^2)^3 = 2^6 = 64$; $(2^a)^3 = 2^{3a}$; $(b^{3p})^{4q} = b^{12pq}$.

Warning 2. $(a^{m^2})^3 = a^{3m^2}$ but $(a^{m^2})^3 \neq a^{m^6}$.

Law III. $\mathbf{(ab)^n = a^n b^n}$, *where* n *is any positive integer.*

Proof.
$$(ab)^n = (ab)(ab)(ab) \cdots (ab), n \text{ factors } (ab)$$
$$= (a \cdot a \cdot a \cdots a, n \text{ factors } a)(b \cdot b \cdot b \cdots b, n \text{ factors } b)$$
$$= a^n b^n.$$

ILLUSTRATIONS. $(a^n c^2)^3 = (a^n)^3 (c^2)^3 = a^{3n} c^6$;
$$(abc)^m = (ab)^m c^m = a^m b^m c^m.$$

Law IV. $\left(\dfrac{a}{b}\right)^n = \dfrac{a^n}{b^n}$, *where* n *is any positive integer, and* b $\neq$ 0.

Proof.

$$\left(\frac{a}{b}\right)^n = \frac{a}{b} \cdot \frac{a}{b} \cdot \frac{a}{b} \cdots \frac{a}{b}, \; n \text{ factors } \frac{a}{b}$$

$$= \frac{a \cdot a \cdot a \cdots a, \; n \text{ factors } a}{b \cdot b \cdot b \cdots b, \; n \text{ factors } b} = \frac{a^n}{b^n}.$$

ILLUSTRATIONS. $\dfrac{2^5}{2^3} = 2^2 = 4$; $\left(\dfrac{x^2}{y^a}\right)^m = \dfrac{x^{2m}}{y^{am}}.$

Law V$_1$. $\dfrac{a^m}{a^n} = a^{m-n}$, *where* m *and* n *are two positive integers such that* m > n, *and* a $\neq$ 0.

In § 1-7, the restriction $m > n$ in Law V$_1$ and the restriction $m < n$ in Law V$_2$ will be removed. The requirement $a \neq 0$ cannot be removed.

Proof of Law V$_1$.

$$\frac{a^m}{a^n} = \frac{a \cdot a \cdot a \cdots a, \; m \text{ factors } a}{a \cdot a \cdot a \cdots a, \; n \text{ factors } a}$$

$$= \frac{[a \cdot a \cdot a \cdots a, \; n \text{ factors } a][a \cdot a \cdot a \cdots a, \; (m-n) \text{ factors } a]}{a \cdot a \cdot a \cdots a, \; n \text{ factors } a}$$

$$= a \cdot a \cdot a \cdots a, \; (m-n) \text{ factors } a$$

$$= a^{m-n}.$$

ILLUSTRATIONS. $(-2)^8 \div (-2)^5 = (-2)^3$;
$$a^{3c} \div a^{2d} = a^{3c-2d}, \quad \text{if} \quad 3c > 2d.$$

Warning 3. $\dfrac{27^6}{3^4} = \dfrac{(3^3)^6}{3^4} = \dfrac{3^{18}}{3^4} = 3^{14}$ but $\dfrac{27^6}{3^4} \neq \left(\dfrac{27}{3}\right)^2.$

Law V$_2$. $\dfrac{a^m}{a^n} = \dfrac{1}{a^{n-m}}$, *where* m *and* n *are two positive integers such that* m < n, *and* a $\neq$ 0.

The proof is similar to that for Law V$_1$.

ILLUSTRATIONS. $a^{3c} \div a^{2d} = \dfrac{1}{a^{2d-3c}}$ if $2d > 3c.$

These laws are particularly useful in simplifying or changing the form of complicated formulas. In appropriate cases, a numerical answer can be obtained from the simplified form. Table I, pages 446 and 447, shows the answers for some common cases; namely, the squares and cubes of integers from 1 to 100 inclusive are shown in the columns headed "N^2" and "N^3" respectively.

EXERCISES

Write as powers:

1. $3^2 \cdot 3^3$.   **5.** x^2/x^6.

2. $3^5 \div 3^3$.   **6.** $(3^5)^2$.

3. $x^2 \cdot x^5$.   **7.** $(3^2)^5$.

4. x^6/x^2.   **8.** $(x^3)^3$.

9. $\dfrac{2^3 \cdot 2^5}{2^2 \cdot 2^4}$.

10. $\dfrac{3^3 \cdot 3}{3^2 \cdot 3^5}$.

11. $\dfrac{x^6 \cdot x^5}{x^2 \cdot x^7}$.

12. $\dfrac{x \cdot x^6}{x^5 \div x^2}$.

Find the value from Table I:

13. 17^2.   **14.** 36^2.   **15.** 73^2.   **16.** 26^3.   **17.** 98^3.

Perform the indicated operations and simplify:

18. $r^4 \cdot r^3 \cdot r^2$.   **20.** $(xy)^4$.   **22.** $(a^2b)^4$.   **24.** $(-x^2)^5$.

19. $a \cdot a^3 \cdot a^6$.   **21.** $(2u)^3$.   **23.** $(-x)^5$.   **25.** $-(x^2)^5$.

26. $[(-x)^2]^5$.   **32.** $(\frac{2}{3})^4$.   **38.** $(x^2y^3) \div (x^5y^2)$.

27. $(x^2y^3) \cdot (x^5y^2)$.   **33.** $(-\frac{4}{3})^3$.   **39.** $(uv^2w^5) \div (uv^4w^2)$.

28. $(a^3b^2) \cdot (ab^4)$.   **34.** $(\frac{1}{3})^3 \cdot (\frac{1}{3})^2$.   **40.** $(\frac{1}{2})^4 \cdot (100)^4 \cdot (0.02)^4$.

29. $(a^3b^2)^4$.   **35.** $(-0.5)^3 \cdot (-2)^4$.   **41.** $x^a \cdot x^b$.

30. $(4x^3)^3$.   **36.** $(-1.5)^2 \cdot (\frac{2}{3})^4$.   **42.** $(x^a)^b$.

31. $(-x^6)^2$.   **37.** $(a^3b^2) \div (ab^4)$.   **43.** $(ba)^x$.

Write in terms of a power of 2:

44. $8 \cdot 4^2 \cdot 16$.

45. $2^6 \cdot 16^2 \cdot 64$.

46. $2^3 \cdot 4^2 \cdot \frac{1}{2}$.

47. $\dfrac{(-2)^5 \cdot 2^4}{2^3 \cdot (-2)^2}$.

48. $\dfrac{2^{10}}{4^2 \cdot 8}$.

49. $\dfrac{8^4 \cdot (\frac{1}{4})^3}{2^7}$.

50. $\dfrac{(-\frac{1}{2})^2}{(-\frac{1}{8})^2}$.

51. Prove Law V_2.

52. A cubical pile is made of 27 blocks; each block is a cube, one centimeter on a side. Find the number of cubic millimeters of volume in the pile, where one centimeter equals ten millimeters, **(a)** by first converting each dimension of the pile to millimeters; **(b)** by first finding the volume of the pile in cubic centimeters. Show how the equivalence of these methods illustrates one of the laws of exponents.

In Exercises 53 through 56, m *represents a positive integer.*

53. If a represents an integer, will a^m always represent an integer? Explain.

54. State the conditions on a and m for which **(a)** $a^m > 0$; **(b)** $a^m = 0$; **(c)** $a^m < 0$. Explain (prove) your statements.

55. If $a > 0$, what is implied about a and m by **(a)** $a^m > a$? **(b)** $a^m = a$? **(c)** $a^m < a$? Explain your statements.

56. State the conditions on a and m for which **(a)** $a^m > a$; **(b)** $a^m = a$; **(c)** $a^m < a$. Explain your statements.

57. The positional decimal notation that we now use to represent numbers in terms of powers of ten, such as

$$1962 = 1(10)^3 + 9(10)^2 + 6(10) + 2,$$

was introduced by the Hindus and Arabians. Several other notations were developed in other cultures. Modern electronic computing machines make use of the **binary** number notation, in which numbers are expressed in terms of powers of 2; only two digits, usually written 0 and 1, are required. For example,

$$13 = 1(2)^3 + 1(2)^2 + 0(2) + 1 = 1101_2,$$

where the subscript 2 denotes the use of binary digits. **(a)** Write 3, 6, 11, and 20 in binary notation. **(b)** Write 10_2, 101_2, 1011_2, and 11011_2 in decimal notation.

1-7   Zero and Negative Integral Exponents

The laws of exponents in the previous section were based upon the definition of a^m for positive integers m. We next define a^m for zero and negative integral exponents so that the laws of exponents continue to hold. Indeed, with these definitions, Laws V_1 and V_2 hold regardless of whether $m > n$, $m = n$, or $m < n$.

If zero, as an exponent, is to obey Law I of the laws of exponents, it is necessary that

$$a^0 \cdot a^n = a^{0+n} = a^n \tag{1}$$

for any positive integer n. If $a \neq 0$, we may divide by a^n and obtain $a^0 = a^n/a^n = 1$. Hence, we **define** a^0 as follows:

$$a^0 = 1, \quad \text{if } a \neq 0.$$

When $a = 0$, the symbol a^0 may take on many values in (1) above, and its value cannot be uniquely chosen to satisfy (1). Accordingly, the symbol 0^0 is undefined.

ILLUSTRATIONS. $5^0 = 1$; $(2a)^0 = 1$; $3b^0 = 3 \cdot 1 = 3$.

Now let $m = -n$, where n is a positive integer. If $-n$, as an exponent, is to obey Law I of the laws of exponents, it is necessary that we have $a^{-n} \cdot a^n = a^{-n+n} = a^0 = 1$, if $a \neq 0$. Hence we **define** a^{-n} by the equality

$$a^{-n} = \frac{1}{a^n}, \quad \text{if} \quad a \neq 0.$$

ILLUSTRATIONS. $3ab^{-2} = 3a \cdot \dfrac{1}{b^2} = \dfrac{3a}{b^2}$; $\dfrac{2}{5}(ab)^{-1} = \dfrac{2}{5} \cdot \dfrac{1}{ab} = \dfrac{2}{5ab}$.

Warnings. $2a^{-1} = 2 \cdot \dfrac{1}{a} = \dfrac{2}{a}$ but $2a^{-1} \neq \dfrac{1}{2a}$; $(2a)^{-1} = \dfrac{1}{2a}$.

$a^{-1} - b^{-1} = \dfrac{1}{a} - \dfrac{1}{b} = \dfrac{b-a}{ab}$ but $a^{-1} - b^{-1} \neq \dfrac{1}{a-b}$.

EXAMPLE.   Write $\dfrac{2ab^{-1}}{c^2 d^{-2}}$ in a form free from negative exponents.

Solution.

$$\frac{2ab^{-1}}{c^2 d^{-2}} = \frac{2a \cdot \dfrac{1}{b}}{c^2 \cdot \dfrac{1}{d^2}} = \frac{\dfrac{2a}{b}}{\dfrac{c^2}{d^2}} = \frac{2a}{b} \cdot \frac{d^2}{c^2} = \frac{2ad^2}{bc^2}.$$

The **reciprocal** of a is $1/a$, that is, a^{-1}.

EXERCISES

Express in a form free from zero and negative exponents, and simplify if possible:

1. 2^{-3}.	**9.** $2^2 \cdot 2^{-5}$.	**17.** $(3^{-4})^3$.	**25.** $(2^3 \cdot 3^{-4})^2$.
2. 3^{-2}.	**10.** $3^2 \cdot 3^{-6}$.	**18.** $(2^{-3})^2$.	**26.** $(5^2 \cdot 2^{-3})^4$.
3. -2^3.	**11.** $2^2/2^{-5}$.	**19.** $(3^3)^{-4}$.	**27.** $(\frac{1}{2})^{-1}$.
4. 2^0.	**12.** $3^2/3^{-6}$.	**20.** $(2^2)^{-3}$.	**28.** $(\frac{1}{2})^{-3}$.
5. 3^0.	**13.** $3^{-6}/3^2$.	**21.** $(3^{-3})^4$.	**29.** $(\frac{1}{2})^0$.
6. 0^2.	**14.** $2^{-5}/2^2$.	**22.** $(2^{-2})^3$.	**30.** $(\frac{2}{3})^{-3}$.
7. 0^3.	**15.** $2 \cdot 2^{-4}$.	**23.** 4^{-1}.	**31.** $x^4 \cdot x^{-3}$.
8. $0/2$.	**16.** $3^{-4} \cdot 3$.	**24.** 1^{-4}.	**32.** $y^{-2} \cdot y^7$.

33. $a^2 \cdot a^{-5} \cdot a$.

34. $a^{-2}a^{-5}a^0$.

35. $b^3c^{-2}d^0$.

36. $x^4x^{-1}x$.

37. $(2a^{-1}b^2)^3$.

38. $(3x^3y^{-1})^2$.

39. $(-5c^3d^{-1})^{-1}$.

40. $(-4xy^{-1})^4$.

41. $(-xy^2z^{-3})^2$.

42. $(-x^{-1})^2$.

43. $(-x^{-1})^{-1}$.

44. $8^2 \cdot 2^{-5}$.

45. $(6x^2)^0$.

46. x^4/x^{-3}.

47. y^2/y^{-5}.

48. z^{-2}/z^5.

49. $a^2 \cdot a^{-5} \div a$.

50. $r^{-4} \cdot r \div r^5$.

51. $(a^2b^4)^0x^2$.

52. $x \div (x^2 \cdot x^{-3})$.

53. $b^3 \div (b^{-1} \cdot b^2)$.

54. Find the reciprocal of (a) n; (b) $\frac{3}{2}$; (c) $\frac{3}{4}$; (d) x^2.

From the definitions, and using the laws for the case of positive integers as exponents, prove the laws of exponents (§1-6) in the following cases:

55. Law I, if $m < 0$ and $n > 0$.

56. Law I, if $m < 0$ and $n < 0$.

57. Law I, if $m = 0$ and $n > 0$.

58. Law II, if $m > 0$ and $n < 0$.

59. Law III, if $n < 0$.

60. Law III, if $n = 0$.

61. Law IV, if $n < 0$.

62. Law II, if $m = n = 0$.

63. Law V_1, if $m > 0$ and $n < 0$.

1-8 Scientific Notation

Integral exponents have a very useful application in the writing of a positive number in **scientific notation**, that is, as an integral power of 10 or as the product of an integral power of 10 and a number between 1 and 10. This notation is particularly convenient when handling very large or very small numbers, or when a wide variety of magnitudes occur in problems on a computing machine.

ILLUSTRATION 1. $2,700,000 = 2.7 \cdot 10^6$; $0.523 = 5.23 \cdot 10^{-1}$;
$0.000165 = 1.65 \cdot 10^{-4}$; $25 = 2.5 \cdot 10^1$;
$275 = 2.75 \cdot 10^2$; $3.3 = 3.3 \cdot 10^0$.

From the definition of scientific notation, any positive number N in our ordinary decimal notation can be rewritten in scientific notation as $p \cdot 10^k$, for some integer k, as follows:

(*i*) p is the number formed by rewriting the digits in N with a decimal point after the first nonzero digit counting from the left;

(*ii*) k is the number of places the decimal point has been moved from its position in the decimal notation for N to its position in p, and is positive if the decimal point has been moved to the left, zero if not moved, negative if moved to the right.

In particular, $p = 1$ if N is an integral power of 10. In all other cases $1 < p < 10$. The integer k is negative in case $0 < N < 1$, zero if $1 \leq N < 10$, positive if $N \geq 10$.

Scientific notation, or a form similar to it, is useful in such instances as applying Table I, pages 446 and 447, to find squares, cubes, and reciprocals of certain numbers not listed in the table but differing only in the location of the decimal point.

ILLUSTRATION 2. $(510)^3 = (51 \cdot 10)^3 = 51^3 \cdot 10^3$ by Law III
$$= 132651 \cdot 10^3 \quad \text{by Table I}$$
$$= 132,651,000.$$

$$(0.51)^3 = (51 \cdot 10^{-2})^3 = 51^3 \cdot 10^{-6} = 0.132651.$$

$$\frac{1}{0.51} = \frac{1}{51 \cdot 10^{-2}} = \frac{1}{51} \cdot 10^2$$
$$= 0.01961 \cdot 10^2 = 1.961,$$

by last column of Table I.

EXERCISES

Write in scientific notation:

1. 324.   **3.** 46,000.   **5.** 0.00092.   **7.** $634 \cdot 10^4$.

2. 0.32.   **4.** 40,600,000.   **6.** 0.000 000 44.   **8.** $0.063 \cdot 10^{-3}$.

Find, using Table I:

9. $(260)^2$.   **11.** $(7400)^3$.   **13.** $(0.043)^2$.   **15.** $\frac{1}{4300}$.

10. $(2.6)^2$.   **12.** $(0.74)^3$.   **14.** $(0.034)^3$.   **16.** $\frac{1}{0.043}$.

Write in ordinary decimal notation:

17. The distance from the earth to the moon, $2.4 \cdot 10^5$ miles.

18. One light year (that is, the distance light travels in a year), $5.88 \cdot 10^{12}$ miles.

19. The distance from the earth to the sun, $9.3 \cdot 10^7$ miles.

20. The distance to the nearest star, $24.5 \cdot 10^{12}$ miles.

21. The speed with which an object must be shot upward if it is to escape from the earth, $2.5 \cdot 10^4$ miles per hour.

22. The number of electrons passing any point in an electrical circuit each second, per ampere of current, $6.25 \cdot 10^{18}$.

23. A typical factor of increase in light intensity, 10^{10}, when a star explodes and becomes a supernova.

24. The charge on an electron, $1.602 \cdot 10^{-19}$ coulomb.

25. An energy of $1.60 \cdot 10^{-12}$ erg ("one electron volt," the energy possessed by an electron under an electrical potential difference of 1 volt).

Write in scientific notation:

26. The temperature, 3,800,000,000° absolute, at which the equilibrium abundance of the various chemical elements is approximately that observed in the solar system.

27. The estimated population of the United States in 1970, about 209.5 million persons.

28. One hundred-millionth of a centimeter, the smallest linear unit in common use today, equaling 1 angstrom, used in expressing the length of light waves. Write also in decimal notation.

29. The largest linear unit in common use today, 1 megaparsec, 19.2 quintillion miles. Write also in decimal notation.

1-9   Significant Digits

We shall distinguish between numbers developed theoretically from positive integers and numbers obtained as approximations or as measures of magnitudes. The numbers based upon the integers are called **exact** numbers; the numbers based upon approximations or measurements are called **approximate** numbers. Approximations are also common in the sense of decimal approximations for numbers such as $\frac{1}{3}$ and $\sqrt{2}$. We shall use the symbol "$\approx$" (read "is approximately equal to") to indicate that one number is used as an approximation for another. Thus $\frac{1}{3} \approx 0.33333$, $\sqrt{2} \approx 1.414$, and $\pi \approx 3.1416 \approx \frac{22}{7}$. All numbers used in the formal definitions of units are exact. For example, the number 12 in the relationship between an inch and a foot is exact.

We consider next a measure of the accuracy of approximate numbers. The digits required in writing p for an approximate number N expressed in scientific notation are called the **significant digits** or **significant figures** of the number. Thus 25 (considered as an approximate number) has two significant digits; 0.000165 has three significant digits, namely, 1, 6, and 5; the zeros merely serve to locate or emphasize the decimal point. Indeed, 165 and 0.165 likewise each have three significant digits.

A number with two significant digits is said to have **two-digit accuracy**; a number with three significant digits is said to have **three-digit accuracy**, and similarly for other accuracies.

The use of scientific notation for a number avoids certain ambiguities about significant digits which sometimes accompany decimal notation when the unit of measurement is not specified. For example, if the population of a town is stated as 40,000, this may be a "round" number stated to the nearest thousand ($40 \cdot 10^3$ or better $4.0 \cdot 10^4$, with two significant digits) or perhaps to the nearest hundred ($4.00 \cdot 10^4$, with three significant digits) or it may be an actual census count for a certain date, subject only to the errors inherent in taking a census. When a number is given in decimal notation, the choice among such meanings may have to be judged from the context, since usually it cannot be determined from the notation for the number whether the zeros are significant or merely serve to locate the decimal point. On the other hand, for 32.20 there is no ambiguity: the zero must be significant; otherwise, it need not and should not be written. Thus while 32.2 and 32.20 have the same value as exact numbers, they are distinct from each other as approximate numbers, having respectively three and four significant digits.

When numbers such as $\sqrt{2}$ and $\sqrt[3]{5}$ occur in a problem, they are often replaced by decimal approximations, and the question arises as to the accuracy that should be used in the decimal forms. This depends upon the problem under consideration. For example, a surveyor may need to use very precise measurements and computations, especially in surveying valuable city property, whereas a leader planning a hike for a group of boys will need only a rough estimate of its length, perhaps to the nearest mile.

When it is impractical or undesirable to write all of the available decimal places for a number N, it must then be **"rounded off"** to, or approximated by, a number with fewer significant digits, say n significant digits. This is done by taking the n-digit number which is closest to N. For example, π is rounded to five significant digits as 3.1416, to three significant digits as 3.14. The rounding off should be done all in one step, not digit by digit. For example, 1.2748 is rounded to four significant digits as 1.275; to three significant digits as 1.27.

The above procedure may be described for numbers in decimal form as follows: the last remaining digit is retained unchanged if the first digit dropped is less than five; the last remaining digit is increased by 1 if the first digit dropped is 5 or greater, unless it is 5 followed only by zeros. In this last case there are two numbers equally close to the given number, and we shall adopt the convention of rounding off to the nearest *even* digit.

ILLUSTRATIONS. The following represent rounding off to three significant digits:

$$3.14159 \approx 3.14; \qquad 4.085 \approx 4.08;$$
$$1.732 \approx 1.73; \qquad 0.026457 \approx 0.0265;$$
$$4.795 \approx 4.80; \qquad 1274.5 \approx 1270 \quad \text{or} \quad 1.27 \cdot 10^3.$$

In performing computations with approximate numbers, it is frequently important to know the accuracy of the answer. This problem results from the fact that when computations are performed on approximate numbers, the results are necessarily only approximate. The following rules of thumb apply:

A product or quotient of numbers has as many significant digits as the least accurate of these numbers.

A sum or difference of numbers is as precise (is correct to the same number of decimal places) as the least precise of these numbers.

These rules are obtained by observing how much spread in the answer is possible from the specified uncertainty of the given numbers. For example, the approximate number 4.31 is entirely uncertain in the third decimal place. Thus $4.31 + 17.121 \approx 21.43$. In the case of a product, the limitation concerns the number of significant digits rather than decimal places; $4.31 \times 17.121 \approx 73.8$. The reason for this rule is illustrated by the following: $2.7 \times 100.0 \approx 270$, $2.8 \times 100.0 \approx 280$, where both answers are uncertain in the third digit.

In all calculations with approximate numbers, the answer should be rounded off to the proper number of significant digits. In the intermediate steps of a calculation, it is customary to carry one or two extra digits, rounding off fully only at the final answer, in order to avoid compounding the rounding-off approximations.

EXERCISES

Round off to (**a**) *two significant digits;* (**b**) *three significant digits:*

1. 2.973.   **3.** 3.453.   **5.** 0.00149.   **7.** 209.98.

2. 0.36764.   **4.** 7392.   **6.** 0.07348.   **8.** 31.550.

Use scientific notation and three-digit accuracy to represent:

9. The distance sound travels in one microsecond (10^{-6} sec) if its speed in 1087 feet per second (speed in dry air at $0°$ centigrade).

10. The diameter, 0.000 000 031 5 centimeter, of a molecule of the chemical element nitrogen.

11. The number of cubic centimeters in a cube 2.00 meters on a side. (One meter equals 100 centimeters.)

12. The number of grams in a ton. (One pound is 453.5924 grams.)

13. The distance light travels in 24 hours if its speed is 186,000 miles per second (speed in a vacuum).

14. The wave length, in inches, of blue light with wave length 4500 angstroms. (One angstrom equals 10^{-8} centimeter, and one centimeter equals 0.3937 inch.)

15. The wave length, in inches, of yellow light with wave length 6000 angstroms (see Exercise 14).

16. The proper length, in feet, of a half-wave dipole on a television antenna, which is given by $468 \cdot 10^6 f^{-1}$, where f is the frequency in cycles per second, if the frequency is 69,000,000 cycles per second (69 megacycles, Channel 4).

Assume that each of the following numbers is approximate, and round off the results to the appropriate number of significant digits:

17. $(2.3)(0.4) = 0.92.$

18. $6.0 \div 2.0 = 3.000.$

19. $4.3 - 0.3 = 4.00.$

20. $6.8 + 0.2 = 7.000.$

21. $(2.43)^2 = 5.9049.$

22. $(23.91)(1.4) = 33.474.$

23. $\sqrt{9.0} = 3.000.$

24. $\sqrt{0.56} \approx 0.748331.$

25. $8275.34 \div 0.56 = 14777.39285.$

26. $(2356.14)^2 = 5551395.6996.$

27. $17 \div 0.027 \approx 629.6296296.$

28. $(0.634)(7125.68) = 4517.68112.$

29. $47.286 - 37.28 = 10.006.$

30. $291.627 - 291.624368 = 0.002632.$

31.
$$
\begin{array}{r}
16.431 \\
9.2 \\
540. \\
26.00 \\
\hline
591.631
\end{array}
$$

32.
$$
\begin{array}{r}
284.3 \\
0.0310 \\
\hline
284.3310
\end{array}
$$

33.
$$
\begin{array}{r}
28.64 \\
0.0225 \\
6.25 \\
83.2 \\
\hline
118.1125
\end{array}
$$

34. $2.8 \cdot 10^3 + 4.1 \cdot 10^6 = 4,102,800.$

35. $600.0(3.1416 - 3.1245) = 10.2600.$

36. $3.1416(2.51 + 1.757840) = 13.4078461440.$

37. $3.1416(2.51 + 21.757840) = 76.2398461440.$

From Table I, find the value **(a)** *if the given number is exact;* **(b)** *if the given number is approximate:*

38. $(6.4)^2$.

39. $(0.76)^2$.

40. $(140)^3$.

41. $(2800)^3$.

42. $(0.094)^3$.

43. $\dfrac{1}{29{,}000}$.

44. $\dfrac{1}{0.38}$.

45. $\dfrac{1}{0.0018}$.

46. $\dfrac{1}{0.00180}$.

47. $\dfrac{1}{73.00}$.

★48. $\dfrac{4.00}{6.70}$.

49. A certain clock for use in a scientific experiment is required to have a maximum error E of one second in T days. If $T = 30$, express E and T in the same units and write E/T in scientific notation to one significant digit.

50. A guided missile is required to land within distance d, namely one mile, from its target which is R miles away. If $R = 3000$, express d/R in scientific notation to two significant digits.

CHAPTER 2

RATIONAL EXPRESSIONS

2-1 Rational Expressions; Polynomials

Any combination of symbols for explicit numbers or literal number symbols by the four fundamental operations—addition, subtraction, multiplication, and division—is called a **rational expression.** Rational expressions and expressions involving radicals are special cases of **algebraic expressions.**

If an algebraic expression consists of distinct parts connected by plus and minus signs, it is called an **algebraic sum,** and each part, together with the sign preceding it, is called a **term** of the expression. If the expression is not a sum or difference, then the whole expression is called a term. An algebraic expression consisting of just *one* term is called a **monomial,** one consisting of just *two* terms is called a **binomial,** and one of just *three* terms a **trinomial.**

ILLUSTRATION 1.   When x, y, and r represent numbers, $(2x - 3y^2 + 6)$, $2\pi r$, $(8x - 6)$, and $7x/(5x - 4)$ are rational expressions and also algebraic expressions. In $(2x - 3y^2 + 6)$, $2x$ is one term, $-3y^2$ is another term, and 6 is a third term; the entire expression is a trinomial. The expression $2\pi r$ has only one term and is a monomial; $(8x - 6)$ is a binomial; $7x/(5x - 4)$ is a monomial since the minus sign does not separate the whole expression into two parts.

Suppose that an algebraic expression involves certain literal number symbols and that for each such symbol a particular number is specified as the number represented by that symbol. Then the algebraic expression represents the result of the specified operations on the particular numbers. This result is called the **value** of the expression for the particular values of the literal number symbols.

ILLUSTRATION 2.   When $x = 2$ and $y = 5$, then $(3x^2 + xy^2 - 2)$ has the value $3 \cdot 2^2 + 2 \cdot 5^2 - 2$, or 60. Note that for any one symbol, such as x, the same value must be used throughout the expression.

Any factor of a term of an algebraic expression is called the **coefficient**

26

of the remaining part of the term; the product of all the factors of the term that are explicit numbers is called the **numerical coefficient.** When a term is a constant or is the product of a constant and variables or unknowns, the constant is called **the coefficient** of the term.

Two or more terms which differ only in their coefficients are called **like,** or **similar,** terms. Any algebraic sum of like terms can be combined into a single term; doing so is called **combining like terms.**

ILLUSTRATION 3. In $12xy^2$, the numerical coefficient is 12, the coefficient of y^2 is $12x$, the coefficient of x is $12y^2$, and the coefficient of the term is 12. The coefficient of a^3b is 1 and of $-a^3b$ is -1; the coefficient of -5 is -5; the coefficient of $2\pi r$ is 2π. In

$$4x^2y^3 - 3x^3y^2 - 5x^2y^3 + 7x^3y^2$$

the first and third terms are like terms and the second and fourth terms are like terms. After combining like terms, we obtain $(4x^3y^2 - x^2y^3)$ for the algebraic sum, by the distributive law.

An algebraic term is **integral and rational** in certain literal number symbols if either (i) it does not contain the symbols or (ii) it is a product of positive integral powers of those symbols and a factor which does not contain them. An algebraic sum of terms, or a single term, is called a **polynomial** (or integral rational expression) if each term is integral and rational. Thus for any nonnegative integer n,

$$a_0 + a_1x + a_2x^2 + \cdots + a_nx^n$$

is a polynomial in x. The expression is called a polynomial in x even when all the a's, or all but a_0, are zero. "Monomial," "binomial," and "trinomial" are mainly used for polynomials, though they are defined for algebraic expressions in general.

ILLUSTRATION 4. The terms 5, $-\sqrt{2}x^3$, and $\frac{3}{4}xy^2$ are integral and rational in x and y; $(5 - \sqrt{2}x^3 + \frac{3}{4}xy^2)$ is a polynomial in x and y. However, $-6/x^2$ is not integral in x, $7\sqrt{x}$ is not rational in x, and $(7\sqrt{x} - 6/x^2)$ is neither integral nor rational in x; $4x^2/y$ is integral in x but not integral in y.

The **degree of a term** of a polynomial in certain literal number symbols is the sum of the exponents of those symbols. The **degree of a polynomial** in certain literal number symbols is the degree of the term or terms that are of *highest* degree in those symbols. A term of the first degree is called **linear,** for reasons which will appear in Chapter 4; a term of the second degree is called **quadratic;** a term of the third degree is called **cubic.**

ILLUSTRATION 5.   The term $3x^3yz^2$ is of the third degree (that is, cubic) in x, of the first degree (that is, linear) in y, of the second degree (that is, quadratic) in z, of the fourth degree in x and y, of the fifth degree in x and z, and of the sixth degree in x, y, and z. The polynomial $(2x^5 - a^8x^2y^2 - 3x^2yz^4)$ is of the fifth degree in x, of the second degree in y, of the fourth degree in z, and of the seventh degree in x, y, and z. The term $2x^5$ is of degree zero in y.

EXERCISES

In Exercises 1 through 6, evaluate (find the value of):

1. $10x^3$ when **(a)** $x = 4$; **(b)** $x = \frac{3}{2}$; **(c)** $x = -2$.

2. $-5a^2$ when **(a)** $a = 2$; **(b)** $a = -1$; **(c)** $a = \pi$.

3. $(2x^2 - 4y^3 - 3)$ when **(a)** $x = 3$, $y = 2$; **(b)** $x = 5$, $y = -2$; **(c)** $x = -\frac{1}{2}$, $y = -\frac{3}{4}$; **(d)** $x = \sqrt{3}$, $y = -\frac{3}{2}$.

4. $(2x - 3x^3y^2 - 4y^5)$ when **(a)** $x = 2$, $y = -1$; **(b)** $x = \frac{2}{3}$, $y = 3$.

5. $\left[\dfrac{a^2(x^2 - y^2)}{a^3x^2(-y)^3}\right]^3$ when **(a)** $a = 3$, $x = 2$, $y = -1$; **(b)** $a = \frac{1}{2}$, $x = 2$, $y = -2$.

6. $\dfrac{3xy^3}{8a^3b^2}$ when $x = \dfrac{1}{16}$, $y = \dfrac{2}{3}$, $a = -\dfrac{3}{4}$, $b = -2$.

7. Tell which of the following are **(a)** monomials; **(b)** binomials; **(c)** trinomials; **(d)** polynomials in x, y, and z:

$$3x + 4; \qquad 3a^2 - 2a + 1; \qquad 3x^2 - 5xy + 6y^2;$$
$$3x^4; \qquad ax + b; \qquad x^2 - y^2 + x - y + 2;$$
$$3xyzw; \qquad ax^2 + bx + c; \qquad 2x^2y^2/z.$$

8. In $\pi r^2 h$, what is **(a)** the numerical coefficient? **(b)** the coefficient of r^2? **(c)** the coefficient of h?

9. Tell which of the terms $2xy^2$, $2x$, $2x^2y$, $3x^2/y$, $3xy^2$, πxy^2 are similar to $3xy^2$.

10. For each of the following, tell whether or not it is **(a)** a rational expression; **(b)** a polynomial in x; **(c)** a polynomial in y; **(d)** integral and rational in x and y: (*i*) $4xy$; (*ii*) $4x$; (*iii*) $4xz$; (*iv*) $4xy + z$; (*v*) $4xz^2/y$; (*vi*) $4xy^2\sqrt{z}$; (*vii*) $4xz^2\sqrt{y}$.

11. Write an expression similar to $3x^4y^5$ but with its coefficient **(a)** 2 larger; **(b)** 2 less; **(c)** 7 less; **(d)** twice as large; **(e)** a times as large; **(f)** half as large.

12. Give the degree of each term of the polynomial

$$3xy^2z^3 - 4x^2yz^4 + 5y^5 + 4x - 1$$

(a) in x; **(b)** in x and y; **(c)** in y and z; **(d)** in x, y, and z.

13. Give the degree of $(5x^3yz^2 - b^3y^3z^2 - z^5 - b + 5x^5y^2)$ **(a)** in x; **(b)** in y; **(c)** in z; **(d)** in x and y; **(e)** in x, y, and z.

Give, if possible, at least one example of a polynomial in two literal number symbols, x *and* y, *satisfying the specified conditions:*

14. Linear in x and y.

15. Quadratic in x and cubic in y.

16. Linear in x, linear in y, quadratic in x and y.

17. Quadratic in x, cubic in y, of fourth degree in x and y.

18. Quadratic in x, cubic in y, of sixth degree in x and y.

19. Linear in x, linear in y, cubic in x and y.

2-2 Symbols of Grouping

In an algebraic expression several parts are often grouped together to indicate that they are to be considered together as a single number. For this purpose the following symbols of grouping are used: the **parentheses,** ( ); the **brackets,** [ ]; the **braces,** { }; and the **bar** or **vinculum,** $\overline{}$. The vinculum is seldom used except as the horizontal bar with the radical sign $\sqrt{}$ in expressions such as $\sqrt{x + 1}$.

ILLUSTRATION. The problem of subtracting $(3x^2 + 7xy - y^2)$ from $(x^2 - xy - 2y^2)$ may be written as the problem of simplifying

$$(x^2 - xy - 2y^2) - (3x^2 + 7xy - y^2).$$

When the only indicated operations within an expression that is to be simplified are those of addition and subtraction, parentheses and other symbols of grouping may be removed—or inserted—by use of the following rules:

Parentheses, or other symbols of grouping, preceded by a **plus** *sign may be removed, or inserted, by rewriting the enclosed terms each with its original sign.*

Parentheses, or other symbols of grouping, preceded by a **minus** *sign may be removed, or inserted, if the sign of each of the enclosed terms is changed.*

The directive "simplify" means that, as far as possible, one shall remove all symbols of grouping and combine like terms.

EXAMPLE.   Simplify:

$$(6x - 2y) - \{2x - [2(y - 3x) - (x - 5y)]\}.$$

Solution. $(6x - 2y) - \{2x - [2(y - 3x) - (x - 5y)]\}$
$$= 6x - 2y - \{2x - [2y - 6x - x + 5y]\}$$
$$= 6x - 2y - \{2x - 7y + 7x\}$$
$$= 6x - 2y - 9x + 7y$$
$$= 5y - 3x.$$

Warning. $x - 2(a - x^2 + 3y) = x - 2a + 2x^2 - 6y$
but $x - 2(a - x^2 + 3y) \neq x - 2a - x^2 + 3y.$

EXERCISES

Simplify:

1. $(2x - y) + z.$

2. $2x - (y + z).$

3. $(4x + 1) - (x - 3).$

4. $(5x - 2) - (2x + 3).$

5. $5x - 2(2x + 3).$

6. $ab - b(c - a).$

7. $3[(\frac{1}{2} + \frac{1}{3}) + 2(\frac{1}{3} - \frac{1}{2})].$

8. $4\{\frac{1}{2} + 2[\frac{1}{6} - (\frac{2}{3} - \frac{1}{4})]\}.$

9. $\frac{2}{3}(\frac{1}{2} + \frac{1}{16}) + \frac{5}{2}(\frac{1}{4} - \frac{1}{5}).$

10. $3x - [2x - (5x - 3)].$

11. $-3(x - 2) - [3x - (x + 1)].$

12. $-3\{x - 2[3x - (x + 1)]\}.$

13. $a + \{a - [a + (a - 1) - 1] + 1\}.$

14. $(c - 4) - 2\{3c - 5[\frac{1}{2}c - (2c - 5)]\}.$

15. $(2x^2 - 5xy + 3y^2) - (3x^2 + 6xy - 5y^2).$

16. $(5x^2 + 3xy - 7y^2) - (-3x^2 + 3xy - y^2).$

Using parentheses, write each of the following as a polynomial in x *and* y *subtracted from a polynomial in* a *and* b*:*

17. $a + b - x + y.$

18. $a - b - x - y.$

19. $3(a - x) + 2(y + b).$

20. $a^2 - x^2 + 2xy - y^2.$

Simplify:

21. $2 + 3b^0.$

22. $2 + (3b)^0.$

23. $(2 + 3b)^0.$

24. $2/(3b^0).$

25. $(2^{-2} - 3^{-1})^{-1}.$

26. $(2^{-2})^{-1} - 3^{-1}.$

27. $(5^{-1} \div 2)(0.1x)^{-1}.$

28. $[\frac{1}{2} + (-2)^{-1}]^5.$

29. $(3x^{2n})^4.$

30. $3(x^{2n})^4.$

31. $3(x^{2n})^{-4}.$

32. $\{[(3x^{2n})^{-4}]^2\}^5.$

2-3   Operations on Polynomials

Problems in addition and subtraction were solved in the preceding section as problems in the removal of parentheses. However, especially in long addition problems, it is often more convenient to collect terms by a systematic arrangement, namely, to arrange the various polynomials in vertical columns with like terms in the same columns.

To **add** *two or more polynomials, find the algebraic sum of like terms.*

To **subtract** *one polynomial from another, change the sign of each term of the subtrahend and add to the minuend.*

EXAMPLE 1.   Find the sum of $(a^3 + 3a^2b + 2ab^2 + b^3)$, $(2a^3 + ab^2 - 3b^3)$, $(4a^2b - 3ab^2 - 5b^3)$, and $(b^3 - 6a^2b)$.

Solution.   Arrange in columns of like terms:

$$
\begin{array}{l}
a^3 + 3a^2b + 2ab^2 + b^3 \\
2a^3 + ab^2 - 3b^3 \\
 4a^2b - 3ab^2 - 5b^3 \\
 - 6a^2b + b^3 \\
\hline
\end{array}
$$

Add by columns: $3a^3 + a^2b - 6b^3$ **(sum)**

EXAMPLE 2.   Find the remainder when $(3x^3 - 6x^2 + 7x + 4)$ is subtracted from $(x^3 + 3x^2 + 3x - 2)$.

Solution.

$$
\begin{array}{ll}
x^3 + 3x^2 + 3x - 2 & \text{(minuend)} \\
3x^3 - 6x^2 + 7x + 4 & \text{(subtrahend)} \\
\hline
-2x^3 + 9x^2 - 4x - 6 & \textbf{(remainder)}
\end{array}
$$

Change signs *mentally* and add by columns:

The product of two polynomials is given by the following rule based on the distributive law (§ 1-5) which reduces it to the sum of products of monomials. The latter can then be found by using the laws of exponents (§ 1-6) and signs (§ 1-5) together with the commutative and associative laws for multiplication (§ 1-5).

To find the **product** *of two polynomials, multiply each term of one polynomial* (called the **multiplicand**) *by each term of the other* (called the **multiplier**) *and add these results.*

In applying this rule it is desirable to arrange both multiplicand and multiplier in either descending or ascending powers of one literal number symbol. The results may be checked by division or by assigning numerical values to the literal number symbols and performing the multiplication on these *numerical* values. The latter is not a complete check, but it will usually reveal any error, especially if the numbers 0 and 1 are avoided in assigning values to the literal number symbols.

EXAMPLE 3.   Find the product of $2x^3y^2$ and $(5x^4 - 3x^2y - 4)$.

Solution.   Multiplying each term of the polynomial by the single term of the monomial and adding, we have

$$2x^3y^2(5x^4 - 3x^2y - 4) = 2x^3y^2 \cdot 5x^4 - 2x^3y^2 \cdot 3x^2y - 2x^3y^2 \cdot 4$$
$$= 10x^7y^2 - 6x^5y^3 - 8x^3y^2.$$

EXAMPLE 4.   Multiply $(a^2 - 2ab - b^2)$ by $(2a^2 + b^2 - ab)$.

Solution.   Arrange the polynomials in descending powers of a:

$$a^2 - 2ab - \quad b^2 \quad \text{(multiplicand)}$$
$$2a^2 - \quad ab + \quad b^2 \quad \text{(multiplier)}$$

Multiply by $2a^2$: $\overline{2a^4 - 4a^3b - 2a^2b^2}$

Multiply by $-ab$: $\quad - \quad a^3b + 2a^2b^2 + \quad ab^3$

Multiply by b^2: $\qquad\qquad\quad a^2b^2 - 2ab^3 - b^4$

Add: $\overline{2a^4 - 5a^3b + \quad a^2b^2 - \quad ab^3 - b^4}$ **(product)**

Check.   If $a = 3$ and $b = 2$, the multiplicand is $(9 - 12 - 4)$, or -7; the multiplier is $(18 - 6 + 4)$, or 16; and, from the last line of the solution, the product is $(162 - 270 + 36 - 24 - 16)$, or -112. Since -7 (the multiplicand) times 16 (the multiplier) also equals -112 (the product), the multiplication is presumed to be correct.

Division of polynomials will be considered in the next section.

EXERCISES

Perform the indicated operations:

1. $(x^3 - 3x^2 + 4x - 5) + (3x^3 - 6x - 7)$.
2. $(x^2 + 5x + 3) + (2x^2 - 8x - 1) + (4 - 5x^2)$.
3. $(2y^3 - 7y^2 - 5) - (5y^3 + 2y^2 - 2y + 1)$.
4. $(x^3 - x^2) + (4x^2 - 5x + 2) + (x^3 - 5) - (2x^3 - 1)$.
5. $(a^3 - a) - (3ab - b^2) - (a + 4) + (a^2 + 3ab + b^2)$.
6. $x(x^2 - 3x + 4)$.   9. $2z^3w(w^2 + 3zw - 4z^2)$.
7. $3a(1 + a - a^3)$.   10. $ab^2c^3(a^4b^2 + a^3c - 2bc^2)$.
8. $\frac{1}{2}r^2s(r - s + rs)$.   11. $\frac{2}{3}x^2yz^4(z - 2xy^2 + 3x^2z^3)$.
12. $(x + 4)(x + 3)$.   14. $(y - 3)(y + 2)$.   16. $(2x + 1)(3x - 2)$.
13. $(x + 5)(x - 2)$.   15. $(a - 6)(a - 8)$.   17. $(5x - 2)(3x + 4)$.

18. $(2 + 3x)(4 - x)$.   **20.** $(a + 2b)(a - 2b)$.   **22.** $(2x - 3)^2$.

19. $(3 - 2n)(2 - 3n)$.   **21.** $(c + d)(c + d)$.   **23.** $(x + 2y)^2$.

24. $(4x - 3a)(4x + 3a)$.   **34.** $(x - 1)(x^2 + 2x + 3)$.

25. $(3a - 5b)(3a + 5b)$.   **35.** $(2x + 1)(3x^2 - x + 5)$.

26. $(xyz + 6)(xyz - 2)$.   **36.** $(3x + 4y)(x^2 - 2xy + y^2)$.

27. $(x + 3)(3 - x)$.   **37.** $(ax - b)(a^2x^2 + abx + b^2)$.

28. $(4x - 1)(1 - 4x)$.   **38.** $(x - 3y)(x^2 + 3xy + 9y^2)$.

29. $(2r + 3s)(3r - 2s)$.   **39.** $(3 - 2x^2 - 5x)(x^2 - 2x + 3)$.

30. $(x + \frac{1}{2})(2x - 3)$.   **40.** $(5k^2 + 1 - 2k)(2k - k^2 - 3)$.

31. $(\frac{1}{2}y - 1)(\frac{1}{3}y - \frac{1}{4})$.   **41.** $(a - 4)(2 + 3a)(1 + a)$.

32. $(x + 2y - 3)^2$.   **42.** $(x + 3y)(x + 2y)(x - 3y)$.

33. $(2u - v + 5)^2$.   **43.** $(x + 2y - 3z)(2x - 5y + 4z)$.

44. $(a - b + 2c)(2a - 3b - c)$.

Find the remainder when **(a)** *the second polynomial is subtracted from the first;* **(b)** *the first polynomial is subtracted from the second:*

45. $2x^2 - 3x + 5$; $3x^2 + x - 4$.

46. $x^2 + 6x - 7$; $2x^2 - 4x - 3$.

47. $y^2 - 3xy + x^2$; $xy - x^2 + y^2$.

Explain with regard to Exercises 45 through 47:

48. The relationship between the answer to part (*a*) and the answer to part (*b*).

49. An easy method for obtaining the answer to part (*b*) after the answer to part (*a*) is known.

2-4 Division of Polynomials

To divide a number a *by a number* b *is to find a number* q *such that* a = b · q. Here *a* is called the **dividend,** *b* the **divisor,** and *q* the **quotient** of *a* and *b*. The symbols $a \div b$, $\dfrac{a}{b}$, and a/b are used to denote this quotient. The operation of division in algebra, as in arithmetic, is the inverse of multiplication.

Let us examine the reason for the well-known restriction that the divisor must not be zero. If *b* were zero in the above definition, then $a = 0 \cdot q$. If also $a = 0$ then $a = 0 \cdot q$ holds regardless of the value of *q*, and so no *unique* value can be assigned to the quotient; whereas, if $a \neq 0$ then $a = 0 \cdot q$ does not hold for any *q* since $0 \cdot q = 0 \neq a$. Thus, in either case, b must be different from zero, and *division by zero is excluded*. Whenever the divisor contains literal number symbols, the assumption that the divisor is different from zero may imply a restriction upon the values which may be assigned to these symbols.

From the definition of division as the inverse of multiplication, and from the properties of multiplication, one gets the following rules:

To **divide a polynomial by a monomial,** *divide each term of the polynomial by the monomial and add these results.*

To **divide one polynomial by another,** *first arrange both in descending powers of some common letter. Divide the first term of the* **dividend** *(the polynomial to be divided) by the first term of the* **divisor.** *The result is the first term of the* **quotient.** *Then multiply the whole divisor by the first term of the quotient and subtract the product from the dividend. Consider the remainder thus obtained as a new dividend and repeat the operation. Continue in this manner until a* **remainder** *is obtained which is either zero or an expression whose first term does not contain the first term of the divisor as a factor.*

When the remainder is zero, the division is said to be **exact** and the divisor is an **exact divisor** or **factor** of the dividend. As in the case of other operations, a numerical check (though imperfect) can be made by assigning values to the literal number symbols.

If the division is not exact, the division of one polynomial by another leads to a result in the form of a polynomial plus a fraction with the remainder as numerator and the divisor as denominator. In advanced algebra it is customary, as at the beginning of this section, to define the complete result (polynomial plus fraction) to be the quotient. However, especially when the remainder is specifically mentioned, the word "quotient" is also sometimes used to denote the integral or polynomial part of the result obtained. This is done in Example 2. In this form, the definition at the beginning of the section becomes $a = b \cdot q + r$. Thus an absolute check is provided by multiplying the quotient by the divisor and then adding the remainder; the result should be the dividend.

EXAMPLE 1.   Divide $(12a^2x^4 - 7a^7x^6 - 42ax^9)$ by $-14a^2x^6$.

Solution.

$$\frac{12a^2x^4 - 7a^7x^6 - 42ax^9}{-14a^2x^6} = \frac{12a^2x^4}{-14a^2x^6} - \frac{7a^7x^6}{-14a^2x^6} - \frac{42ax^9}{-14a^2x^6}$$

$$= -\frac{6}{7x^2} + \frac{a^5}{2} + \frac{3x^3}{a}.$$

EXAMPLE 2.   Divide $(3x^4 - x^2 + 1)$ by $(x^2 + x)$.

Solution.

$$
\begin{array}{r}
3x^4 \quad\quad - x^2 \quad\quad + 1 \\
\underline{3x^4 + 3x^3} \\
- 3x^3 - x^2 \quad\quad + 1 \\
\underline{- 3x^3 - 3x^2} \\
2x^2 \quad\quad + 1 \\
\underline{2x^2 + 2x} \\
- 2x + 1
\end{array}
$$

$x^2 + x$ (**divisor**)

$3x^2 - 3x + 2$ (**quotient**)

$- 2x + 1$ (**remainder**)

Hence $\dfrac{3x^4 - x^2 + 1}{x^2 + x} = 3x^2 - 3x + 2 + \dfrac{1 - 2x}{x^2 + x}.$

Check.   If $x = 3$,

$$(3 \cdot 3^2 - 3 \cdot 3 + 2)(3^2 + 3) + 1 - 2 \cdot 3 = 20 \cdot 12 - 5 = 235;$$
$$3 \cdot 3^4 - 3^2 + 1 = 243 - 9 + 1 = 235.$$

Warning.   The **oblique line** used to indicate division applies only to those numbers before and after it up to any indicated addition or subtraction. Thus, $a + b/c$ is equal to $a + (b/c)$ but *not equal* to $(a + b)/c$, and $a/b + c$ is equal to $(a/b) + c$ but *not equal* to $a/(b + c)$.

EXERCISES

Find the following quotients, including remainders if any:

1. $\dfrac{6x^3y^2}{2xy}.$

2. $\dfrac{63ay^2}{21y}.$

3. $\dfrac{-36x^6y^4z^5}{3(2y)z^3x^6}.$

4. $\dfrac{24a^2b^3c^5}{20ab^3c^2}.$

5. $\dfrac{8x^3 - 6xy}{2x}.$

6. $\dfrac{x^4 + x^2y + y^3}{x^2}.$

7. $\dfrac{10uv^2 - 15uv + 6v}{15uv}.$

8. $\dfrac{x^2 + 4xy + 4y^2}{x + 2y}.$

9. $\dfrac{a^3 - 7a + 6}{a - 2}.$

10. $(3x^2 - 13x - 4) \div (x - 4)$.

11. $(3y^2 + 7y + 4) \div (3y + 1)$.

12. $(6x^2 + 5xy - 6y^2) \div (2x + 3y)$.

13. $(12x^2 - 3 + 5x) \div (2 + 3x)$.

14. $(2m^2 + 7m) \div (2m + 1)$.

15. $(x^4 - 3x^2 + 2x + 1) \div (x^2 - 1)$.

16. $(6x^3 - 5x^2 + x + 3) \div (2x - 3)$.

17. $(19a^2 - 16a + 15a^3 + 1) \div (3a^2 + 5 + 5a)$.

18. $(6x^5 - 13x^3 + 5x + 3x^4 + 3 - 4x^2) \div (3x^3 - 1 - 2x)$.

19. $\dfrac{x^3 - 1}{x - 1}$.   **20.** $\dfrac{8x^3 + 27}{2x + 3}$.   **21.** $\dfrac{x^4 - 81}{x + 3}$.   **22.** $\dfrac{x^5 + 32}{x + 2}$.

Find the value of:

23. $(x + y)/(2x - y)$ when $x = 3$ and $y = -1$.

24. $(3x + y)/(x^2 - y^2)$ when $x = -1$ and $y = 5$.

25. $2a - 8b/(a + 4b)$ when $a = 4$ and $b = 2$.

26. $c + 2k/(c + k^2)$ when $c = 2$ and $k = -2$.

2-5 Factors

Factoring an expression is the process of finding two or more expressions (factors) whose product is the given expression. This is a generalization of the process of factoring an integer, which most students have encountered in arithmetic and which we shall discuss in some detail as an introduction to the factoring of expressions.

Factoring an integer n is the process of finding two or more integers whose product is n. This is done by trial and error, though the order of trials may be systematic. The factor 1 is not usually stated; the factor -1 is used whenever the given number is negative. Thereafter we need consider only the factoring of positive numbers. The factors of an integer n are required to be integers, since n can always be expressed as a product of rational numbers—thus, for example, $5 = \frac{2}{3} \cdot \frac{15}{2}$—so that it would not be meaningful to admit fractions as factors of an integer.

A positive integer n is called a **prime** number if $n \neq 1$ and if the expression of n as a product of positive integers, $n = bc$, requires that one of the integers b and c be equal to 1. The integers

$$2, \quad 3, \quad 5, \quad 7, \quad 11, \quad 13, \quad 17, \quad 19, \quad \cdots$$

are primes. Any positive integer which is not 1 and is not a prime is called a **composite** number. The integers 4, 6, 8, 9, $\cdots$ are composite numbers. Each positive integer can be expressed in essentially only one way as a product of primes. A positive integer is said to be completely factored when it is expressed in terms of its prime factors.

More generally, factoring a given member of a class of expressions is the process of finding two or more expressions in the class, whose product is the given expression.

The factoring of algebraic expressions is usually limited to the factoring of polynomials into products of polynomials with specified types of coefficients, since any polynomial, and more generally any rational expression, can be written in many ways as a product of rational expressions. A polynomial which cannot be factored without violating these restrictions is called a **prime polynomial** or **irreducible polynomial.** Each polynomial can be expressed in essentially only one way as a product of prime polynomials. The factorization is considered complete when each factor is prime. For the present we shall write a polynomial with rational coefficients as the product of a rational number and a polynomial with integral coefficients, the latter to be factored into prime polynomials with integral coefficients.

ILLUSTRATION. $\frac{2}{3}x^2 + 4x = \frac{1}{3}(2x^2 + 12x) = \frac{2}{3}x(x + 6)$.

Factoring should not be regarded as a new operation, but rather as the reverse of multiplication in that the product of two or more expressions is given and the expressions are to be found. Thus from Example 3 of § 2-3 we see that $2x^3y^2$ and $(5x^4 - 3x^2y - 4)$ are factors of $(10x^7y^2 - 6x^5y^3 - 8x^3y^2)$. Success in factoring depends largely on the ability to recognize in given polynomials the products of certain factors.

The following type products occur frequently, and students should be able to state the products for special cases of these types without resort to the general process of multiplication.

> **I.** $a(b + c) = ab + ac.$
> **II.** $(a + b)(a - b) = a^2 - b^2.$
> **III.** $(a + b)^2 = a^2 + 2ab + b^2.$
> **IV.** $(a - b)^2 = a^2 - 2ab + b^2.$
> **V.** $(a + b)(a^2 - ab + b^2) = a^3 + b^3.$
> **VI.** $(a - b)(a^2 + ab + b^2) = a^3 - b^3.$
> **VII.** $(x + a)(x + b) = x^2 + (a + b)x + ab.$
> **VIII.** $(ax + b)(cx + d) = acx^2 + (ad + bc)x + bd.$
> **IX.** $(a + b + c)^2 = a^2 + b^2 + c^2 + 2ab + 2ac + 2bc.$
> **X.** $(a + b)^3 = a^3 + 3a^2b + 3ab^2 + b^3.$
> **XI.** $(a - b)^3 = a^3 - 3a^2b + 3ab^2 - b^3.$

The products given above can be verified by actual multiplication. Ordinarily the student is encouraged to depend on understanding rather than memorization, but these type products are encountered so frequently that one should learn to recognize immediately both the product from the factors and the factors from the product.

EXERCISES

1. List **(a)** the prime numbers, **(b)** the composite numbers, in the following set of numbers: 9, 10, 11, 12, 30, 31, 32.

2. List the prime numbers between **(a)** 1 and 20; **(b)** 20 and 40.

3. Explain why 2 is the only prime even number.

Find the following products by inspection:

4. $-3(4x + 5)$.

5. $2x(5 - 3x)$.

6. $(x + 3)(x - 3)$.

7. $(2 - 3x)(2 + 3x)$.

8. $(3a - 4b)(3a + 4b)$.

9. $2(y - 2a)(2y + 4a)$.

10. $x(4y - z^2)(4xy + xz^2)$.

11. $(n + 4)^2$.

12. $(2y - 5)^2$.

13. $(3a + 8b)^2$.

14. $(5a^2 - 2bc)^2$.

15. $2(2x + y)^2$.

16. $(x - y)(x + y)(x^2 + y^2)$.

17. $(x + 5)(x - 2)$.

18. $(x - 6)(x - 1)$.

19. $(x - y)(5x + 2y)$.

20. $(3x - 7y)(4x + 5y)$.

21. $(2a - 3b^2)(3a - 2b^2)$.

22. $(2x - \frac{1}{3}y)(\frac{1}{4}x - \frac{2}{3}y)$.

23. $(\frac{1}{3}a - \frac{1}{2}b)(\frac{1}{6}a + \frac{1}{4}b)$.

24. $(-4x + 3y)(5x + 2y)$.

25. $(-2r - 3s)(3r - 2s)$.

26. $[(a - 3b)(a + 3b)]^2$.

27. $(x + y)^2(x - y)^2$.

28. $(x + 2)(x^2 - 2x + 4)$.

29. $(a - 2b)(a^2 + 2ab + 4b^2)$.

30. $(2x + y^2)(4x^2 - 2xy^2 + y^4)$.

31. $(x + 2y + 3)^2$.

32. $(3x - 2y - z)^2$.

33. $(3x - 2)^3$.

34. $(x + 2y)^3$.

35. $[(x + 2) + a][(x + 2) - a]$.

36. $(x + y - z)(x - y + z)$.

37. $(x^2 + x^{-1})^2$.

38. $(a^2 + a^{-2})^2$.

39. $(x^n + 3)^2$.

40. $(a + b + c + d)(a - b + c - d)$.

41. The relation $(a - b)(a + b) = a^2 - b^2$ provides a basis for arithmetic procedures such as

$$(78)(82) = (80 - 2)(80 + 2)$$
$$= (80)^2 - 2^2 = 6400 - 4 = 6396.$$

Find the following products by inspection:

    (a) $(8)(12)$;   **(c)** $(2.9)(3.1)$;   **(e)** $(9.7)(10.3)$;

    (b) $(19)(21)$;   **(d)** $(25)(35)$;   **(f)** $(0.195)(0.205)$.

42. The relation $(a + b)^2 = a^2 + 2ab + b^2$ suggests a convenient method of squaring certain numbers. Find by inspection the squares of **(a)** 102; **(b)** 97; **(c)** 0.99.

2-6 Some Methods of Factoring

The products in the preceding section enable us to factor, by inspection, certain types of polynomials. The more common types are:

I. Expressions whose terms have a common factor.
II. Differences of two squares.
III. Perfect square trinomials.
IV. Sums and differences of two cubes.
V. Some trinomials not perfect squares.

ILLUSTRATIONS.

I.a. $6x - 9y + 12z = 3(2x - 3y + 4z)$.
  b. $3ab^2 - 6a^2x^2 + 9ay^3 = 3a(b^2 - 2ax^2 + 3y^3)$.
  c. $x(y + z) - 5y(y + z) = (x - 5y)(y + z)$.

II.a. $81p^2 - 4q^2 = (9p + 2q)(9p - 2q)$.
  b. $(2x - y)^2 - 9c^2 = [(2x - y) + 3c][(2x - y) - 3c]$
          $= (2x - y + 3c)(2x - y - 3c)$.

III.a. $25a^2 - 30ab + 9b^2 = (5a - 3b)^2$.
  b. $3x^2 + 6xy + 3y^2 = 3(x^2 + 2xy + y^2)$
          $= 3(x + y)^2$.

IV.a. $27x^3 + 8y^3 = (3x + 2y)(9x^2 - 6xy + 4y^2)$.
  b. $2ax^3 - 54a^4 = 2a(x^3 - 27a^3)$
          $= 2a(x - 3a)(x^2 + 3ax + 9a^2)$.
  c. $a^6 - b^6 = (a^3)^2 - (b^3)^2 = (a^3 + b^3)(a^3 - b^3)$
          $= (a + b)(a^2 - ab + b^2)(a - b)(a^2 + ab + b^2)$.

V. $x^2 + 3xy - 10y^2 = (x - 2y)(x + 5y)$.

Note that Illustrations IIIb, IVb, and IVc were factored into two or more expressions as one of the above types and then one or more of the factors was, in turn, factored. *All such polynomials should be factored as completely as possible.* In other words, each polynomial should be factored into its prime factors.

When the trinomials are of Type V above, it is usual to consider pairs of binomials and to test these by multiplication until the factors are found or, by trying all possible pairs of binomials, it is established that there are no factors. From the Type VIII product in § 2-5, the conditions that the pair of binomial factors must satisfy are as follows: the first term of the trinomial equals the product of the first terms of the binomials; the last term of the trinomial equals the product of the last terms of the binomials; and the middle term of the trinomial equals the algebraic sum of the remaining two products of terms of the binomials.

EXAMPLE 1.   Factor: $6x^2 + 13xy - 5y^2$.

Solution.   The coefficient 6 is the product of 2 and 3 or of 1 and 6, and the two numbers in each combination must be alike in sign. Likewise, 5 is the product of 1 and 5, and these two numbers must be unlike in sign. Now consider the following products:

$$(3x + 5y)(2x - y) = 6x^2 + 7xy - 5y^2;$$
$$(3x - 5y)(2x + y) = 6x^2 - 7xy - 5y^2;$$
$$(3x + y)(2x - 5y) = 6x^2 - 13xy - 5y^2;$$
$$(3x - y)(2x + 5y) = 6x^2 + 13xy - 5y^2.$$

Hence $\qquad 6x^2 + 13xy - 5y^2 = (3x - y)(2x + 5y).$

In § 12-2 we shall show a general method for factoring trinomials of the form $(ax^2 + bx + c)$ which are not perfect squares. We shall also show the necessary relationship between a, b, and c for the trinomials to have factors.

Many polynomials can, by proper grouping, be placed in one of the type forms listed in the preceding section. Even though no general rule can be given, it is usually helpful to remove common monomial factors first and then to consider grouping one of the following sets of terms:

1. Terms involving the same letter or letters.
2. Terms of the same degree.
3. Terms forming a trinomial square.
4. Pairs of terms having a common binomial factor.

ILLUSTRATIONS.   1. $\begin{aligned}[t] ac + d - c - ad &= (ac - c) + (d - ad) \\ &= c(a - 1) - d(a - 1) \\ &= (a - 1)(c - d). \end{aligned}$

2. $\begin{aligned}[t] x^2 - x - y^2 + y &= (x^2 - y^2) - (x - y) \\ &= (x - y)(x + y) - (x - y) \\ &= (x - y)(x + y - 1). \end{aligned}$

3. $\begin{aligned}[t] a^2 - b^2 + 2bc - c^2 &= a^2 - (b^2 - 2bc + c^2) \\ &= a^2 - (b - c)^2 \\ &= [a + (b - c)][a - (b - c)] \\ &= (a + b - c)(a - b + c). \end{aligned}$

4. $\begin{aligned}[t] 4x^3 - 8x^2 - x + 2 &= (4x^3 - 8x^2) - (x - 2) \\ &= 4x^2(x - 2) - (x - 2) \\ &= (x - 2)(4x^2 - 1) \\ &= (x - 2)(2x + 1)(2x - 1). \end{aligned}$

A polynomial which has another polynomial as a factor is said to be a **multiple** of the latter polynomial. A polynomial which is a multiple of two or more polynomials is called a **common multiple** of these polynomials. A common multiple which has the smallest possible number of prime factors (not necessarily distinct) is a **lowest common multiple** (L.C.M.) of the given polynomials.

To find an L.C.M. of two or more polynomials, first factor each polynomial into its prime factors. Then the product of all the different prime factors, with each prime factor appearing to the highest power with which it appears in any of the given polynomials, is an L.C.M. of the given polynomials.

EXAMPLE 2.   Find an L.C.M. of $(2x^2 - 8)$, $(x^2 + 4x + 4)$, and $(x^3 - 8)$.

Solution.
$$2x^2 - 8 = 2(x + 2)(x - 2).$$
$$x^2 + 4x + 4 = (x + 2)^2.$$
$$x^3 - 8 = (x - 2)(x^2 + 2x + 4).$$

The prime factors are 2, $(x + 2)$, $(x - 2)$, and $(x^2 + 2x + 4)$. The product $2(x + 2)^2(x - 2)(x^2 + 2x + 4)$ is an L.C.M. of the given polynomials. The product $2(x + 2)^2(2 - x)(x^2 + 2x + 4)$ is also an acceptable L.C.M. of the given polynomials.

A special device for factoring is sometimes of use, especially in more advanced work. This device consists of adding and subtracting the same quantity, namely a quantity which puts the expression in a factorable form such as the difference of two squares.

ILLUSTRATION 5.

$$x^4 + 2x^2y^2 + 9y^4 = (x^4 + 6x^2y^2 + 9y^4) - 4x^2y^2$$
$$= (x^2 + 3y^2)^2 - (2xy)^2$$
$$= (x^2 + 3y^2 + 2xy)(x^2 + 3y^2 - 2xy)$$
$$= (x^2 + 2xy + 3y^2)(x^2 - 2xy + 3y^2).$$

EXERCISES

Factor:

1. $3x + 6xy$.

2. $12a^2b - 8ax$.

3. $a(x + y) - b(x + y)$.

4. $(a - 2b)x - (a - 2b)y$.

5. $x^2 - 4y^2$.

6. $9a^2 - 4b^2$.

7. $25x^2 - 16y^2$.

8. $x^2y^2 - 25a^2$.

9. $(a - b)^2 - c^2$.

10. $(p + 2q)^2 - 4r^2$.

11. $a^2 + 4ab + 4b^2$.

12. $x^2 - 6x + 9$.

13. $4u^2 - 12uv + 9v^2$.

14. $9x^2 + 24x + 16$.

15. $49 + 28y + 4y^2$.

16. $x^3 - 8y^3$.

17. $27 + x^3$.

18. $z^3 + 64$.

19. $125a^3 - 8b^3$.

20. $27p^3 + 64q^6$.

21. $a^2 - 5a + 6$.

22. $x^2 + x - 6$.

23. $x^2 - 10x + 16$.

24. $y^2 - 3y - 10$.

25. $7 - 8c + c^2$.

26. $2x^2 - 11x + 5$.

27. $3x^2 - 8x + 4$.

28. $8x^2 + 14xy - 9y^2$.

29. $6x^2 - 5ax - 4a^2$.

30. $x + y + xy + y^2$.

31. $ab - a - b + 1$.

32. $x^3 + ax^2 + ax + a^2$.

33. $a^2 + a + b - b^2$.

34. $a^2 + 2ab + b^2 - c^2$.

35. $x^2 - y^2 + 2yz - z^2$.

36. $x^4 - 8x^2y^2 - 9x^2 + 16y^4$.

37. $2a^3 + 8a^2 - 3a - 12$.

38. $x^3 + y^3 + x^2y + xy^2$.

39. $6x^2 - 7x - 20$.

40. $8x^2y^2 - 18y^2$.

41. $0.36m^2 - 0.49n^2$.

42. $10x - 25 - x^2$.

43. $x^4 - y^4$.

44. $a^6 - b^6$.

45. $x^6 + 7x^3 - 8$.

46. $108x^2 - 90xy - 108y^2$.

47. $16x^4 + 24x^2yz^3 + 9y^2z^6$.

48. $x^{2k} + x^k - 6$.

49. $x^{2n} + 3x^n + 2$.

50. $x^6 + 26x^3 - 27$.

51. $3(x - 1)^2(x - 2) + 2(x - 1)(x - 2)^2$.

52. $3(x + 1)^{n+1}(x + 4)^2 - 5(x + 1)^n(x + 4)$.

53. $a^4 + 9a^2 + 25$.

54. $x^4 - 3x^2y^2 + y^4$.

55. $4x^4 + 16b^4$.

56. $a^8 - 16b^8$.

For each of the following sets of polynomials, find an L.C.M.; leave the results in factored form:

57. $18x, 28x, 21x$.

58. $27b, 6b, 52b$.

59. $4y^3, 15x^2y, 48xy^2$.

60. $5a^4b^3, 4a^2b^4c, a^5b^2c^3, 6a^3$.

61. $56xy^3z^2, 18ax^2yz^2, 49bx^3$.

62. $x^2 - y^2, x - y, x^2 + y^2$.

63. $x + 3, 9 - x^2, 2x - 6$.

64. $2x^2 - 128, 3x - 24$.

65. $a^2 - 2ab + b^2, a^2 - b^2$.

66. $4x^2 - 4, x^2 + 3x + 2, x^2 - 10 - 3x$.

67. $9z^2 + 12z + 4, 12z^2 - z - 6, 18z^2 - 8$.

68. $16 - x^4, 4x^4 - 64$.

69. Show that for any integer m greater than one, $(m^3 + 1)$ represents a composite number.

70. Factor $(x^{3k} - y^{3k})$ when k is **(a)** 2, **(b)** 3.

71. If possible, find an integer n such that $(n^2 - n + 41)$ represents a composite number.

72. Show that $(n^3 - n)$ represents a multiple of 6 when n represents an integer greater than 1.

73. Show that if a represents a prime integer and k represents a positive integer, then a^k cannot represent a number having a final digit zero in our usual number notation.

2-7   Fractions

An indicated quotient of two algebraic expressions, a/b, where b does not stand for the constant zero, is called an **algebraic fraction,** or simply a **fraction.** The dividend a is the **numerator** of the fraction, and the divisor b is the **denominator.**

For example,

$$\frac{3x - 4}{15}, \quad \frac{2x}{x^2 + 1}, \quad \text{and} \quad \frac{x + 3}{x - 2}$$

are fractions; the first two of them represent real numbers whenever x represents a real number, while the third fraction has meaning only if $x \neq 2$ since division by zero is excluded (§ 2-4).

In general, a fraction is said to be **defined** when its denominator is different from zero, **undefined** when its denominator takes on the value zero. Whenever a fraction is used in this text, we shall assume that the set of numbers which may be used to replace the literal number symbols involved has been restricted so that the denominator cannot be zero. There is no restriction against the numerator being zero.

The operations on fractions follow the same laws as in arithmetic. These operations are based on their definitions and the following **fundamental principle of fractions:**

The value of a fraction is not changed when its numerator and denominator are both multiplied or both divided by the same number, zero excluded.

Arithmetic expressions are said to be equivalent if they represent the same number. For example,

$$\frac{12}{-4}, \quad \frac{6}{-2}, \quad \frac{-6}{2}, \quad \text{and} \quad -3$$

are equivalent. Two algebraic expressions, and in particular two fractions, are said to be **equivalent** if both expressions are defined for at least one set of values of the literal number symbols and if, for each set of values of the literal number symbols for which both expressions are defined, the expressions represent the same number. Any expression may be replaced by an equivalent expression when both expressions are defined for the values of the literal number symbols under consideration.

The equivalence of two expressions may be indicated either by the symbol "$\equiv$" (read "is identically equal to") as in $x^2 \equiv xx$ or (less explicitly) by the symbol "$=$" as in $x^2 = xx$. Except where special emphasis is desired, we shall use the latter symbol.

ILLUSTRATION 1.   The expressions

$$\frac{x^2 - y^2}{x + y} \quad \text{and} \quad x - y$$

are equivalent and may be used interchangeably whenever $x \neq -y$.

By the law of signs for division and the fundamental principle of fractions,

$$\frac{a}{b} = \frac{-a}{-b} = -\frac{a}{-b} = -\frac{-a}{b} \quad \text{and} \quad \frac{-a}{b} = -\frac{a}{b} = \frac{a}{-b}.$$

Likewise, changing the sign of an even number of *factors* (not *terms*), in the numerator or denominator or both, does not change the sign of a fraction, whereas changing the sign of an odd number of factors does change the sign of the fraction.

ILLUSTRATION 2.

$$\frac{3x + y}{(a^2 + b^2)(2y - x)} = -\frac{3x + y}{(a^2 + b^2)(x - 2y)}.$$

$$\frac{(-a^3)(b^2)(b - a)}{(-3a^2)(-b^3)(a + b)} = \frac{a^3b^2(a - b)}{3a^2b^3(a + b)}.$$

Warning. $\dfrac{1}{a - b} = -\dfrac{1}{b - a}$ but $\dfrac{1}{a - b} \neq -\dfrac{1}{a + b}.$

The laws already stated, and factoring as discussed in § 2-6, assist in the reduction of a fraction to **lowest terms,** that is, in the replacement of a fraction by an equivalent fraction whose numerator and denominator have no common factors (excepting, of course, 1 and -1). A fraction can be reduced to lowest terms by first factoring the numerator and denominator and then dividing both of them by all their common factors. This division by a common factor is an application of the fundamental principle of fractions.

EXAMPLE. Reduce $\dfrac{4b^3 - 9a^2b}{3a^3b + a^2b^2 - 2ab^3}$ to lowest terms.

Solution. $\dfrac{4b^3 - 9a^2b}{3a^3b + a^2b^2 - 2ab^3} = \dfrac{b(2b + 3a)(2b - 3a)}{ab(3a - 2b)(a + b)}$

$$= -\dfrac{\cancel{b}(3a + 2b)\cancel{(3a - 2b)}}{a\cancel{b}\cancel{(3a - 2b)}(a + b)}$$

$$= -\dfrac{3a + 2b}{a(a + b)}.$$

Warning. $\quad 1 = \dfrac{2x - y}{2x - y} \neq 0, \quad \dfrac{a + b}{a + c} \neq \dfrac{b}{c}, \quad \dfrac{2a + b}{2c + d} \neq \dfrac{a + b}{c + d}.$

EXERCISES

Multiply both numerator and denominator of:

1. $\dfrac{12}{3x + 9}$ by (a) 2; (b) -1; (c) $\tfrac{1}{3}$; (d) x.

2. $\dfrac{3x - 1}{x - 1}$ by (a) $x + 3$; (b) $x - 3$; (c) $3x$.

3. $\dfrac{a^2 + ab + b^2}{a + b}$ by (a) ab; (b) $a - b$.

4. $\dfrac{(x + z)^2}{x^2 - z^2}$ by $\dfrac{1}{x + z}$.

Specify the real values, if any, of the variables for which the expression is undefined:

5. $\dfrac{x + 2}{x + 3}.$ **6.** $\dfrac{x - 4y}{x + 1}.$ **7.** $\dfrac{x}{x^2 + 1}.$ **8.** $\dfrac{x + y}{x^2 + y^2}.$

Find the value of the fraction when x $= 1$, y $= 2$, z $= -3$:

9. $\dfrac{x + y}{x + z}.$ **10.** $\dfrac{3x + z}{z - 3x}.$ **11.** $\dfrac{x + 3y}{x + 3z}.$ **12.** $\dfrac{3x - 5y + z}{3x + 5y - z}.$

Write equivalent fractions having no minus signs in the numerator and denominator:

13. $\dfrac{-ab}{c}$.   **15.** $\dfrac{p(-q)}{-r}$.   **17.** $\dfrac{-(a+b)}{-a-b}$.   **19.** $\dfrac{a(-b)^3}{(-c)^2}$.

14. $\dfrac{ab}{-c}$.   **16.** $-\dfrac{(-x)y}{z}$.   **18.** $-\dfrac{a(-b)}{-a-b}$.   **20.** $\dfrac{(-x)^2y^3}{x^2(-y)^3}$.

Using the fundamental principle of fractions, write as a fraction with denominator 12:

21. $\frac{1}{4}$.   **22.** $\frac{18}{24}$.   **23.** $\dfrac{3x+5}{6}$.   **24.** $\dfrac{x^2-y^2}{2}$.

Write as a fraction with denominator 18xy:

25. $\dfrac{x}{9}$.   **26.** $\dfrac{9}{x}$.   **27.** $\dfrac{2b}{3xy}$.   **28.** $\frac{1}{3}$.   **29.** 1.

Reduce to lowest terms:

30. $\dfrac{15x}{5y}$.   **32.** $\dfrac{24xy}{16y^2}$.   **34.** $\dfrac{15x^2y^2}{12(xy)^2}$.   **36.** $\dfrac{40a^2(-b)^2}{16a(-b)}$.

31. $\dfrac{6a}{12ax}$.   **33.** $\dfrac{16x^2y^3}{64x^3y}$.   **35.** $\dfrac{8(xy)^3}{18(x^2)^3}$.   **37.** $\dfrac{18(-x)^3y^2}{4(-x)^2(-y)^2}$.

38. $\dfrac{(x+1)(x+2)^3}{(x+1)^3(x+2)^2}$.   **41.** $\dfrac{(y-x)^2}{x^2-y^2}$.   **44.** $\dfrac{a^2-b^2}{a^6-b^6}$.

39. $\dfrac{(x+y)(y-x)^3}{(x+y)^2(x-y)^3}$.   **42.** $\dfrac{(y+x)^2}{x^2-y^2}$.   **45.** $\dfrac{(a-b)^2}{a^3-b^3}$.

40. $\dfrac{x^2-(y^2-z^2)}{x^2+z^2-y^2}$.   **43.** $\dfrac{y^2-x^2}{y^4-x^4}$.   **46.** $\dfrac{(a+b)^2-4ab}{(a-b)^2}$.

Criticize the outline of each alleged solution. That is, if the solution is correct, fill in the details; if the solution is incorrect, point out where it is wrong and why, and replace it by a correct solution:

47. Problem: Simplify $\dfrac{4-5x^4y}{4-2x^3z}$.

Proposed outline of solution:

$$\frac{4-5x^4y}{4-2x^3z} = \frac{4-5xy}{4-2z} = \frac{-5xy}{-2z} = -\frac{5}{2}\,xy/z.$$

48. Problem: Find the value of $\left(4x + \dfrac{x+y^2}{x^2-y^4}\right)$ when $x=0$ and $y=1$.

Proposed outline of solution:

$$4x + \frac{x + y^2}{x^2 - y^4} = 4x + \frac{x + y^2}{(x + y^2)(x - y^2)}$$

$$= 4x + x - y^2 = 5x - y^2.$$

When $x = 0$ and $y = -1$, this equals -1, which is the answer.

2-8 Operations on Fractions

The algebraic sum of two or more fractions having the same denominator
*is the fraction whose numerator is the algebraic sum of their numerators
and whose denominator is the common denominator.*

Symbolically,

$$\frac{a}{c} + \frac{b}{c} = \frac{a + b}{c} \quad \text{and} \quad \frac{a}{c} - \frac{b}{c} = \frac{a - b}{c}.$$

From this definition it follows that the first step in addition or subtraction of fractions is to replace the given fractions by equivalent
fractions having a common denominator. We assume that the given
fractions are in lowest terms. Then for the common denominator we use
a lowest common multiple of the given denominators and call it the
lowest common denominator (L.C.D.) of the fractions.

EXAMPLE 1.   Combine into one fraction: $\dfrac{2}{x + 3} - \dfrac{4x - 1}{x^2 - 9} + \dfrac{2}{x}$.

Solution.   The L.C.D. may be taken as $x(x + 3)(x - 3)$.

$$\frac{2}{x + 3} - \frac{4x - 1}{x^2 - 9} + \frac{2}{x} = \frac{2 \cdot x(x - 3)}{(x + 3)x(x - 3)} - \frac{x(4x - 1)}{x(x^2 - 9)} + \frac{2(x^2 - 9)}{x(x^2 - 9)}$$

$$= \frac{2x(x - 3) - x(4x - 1) + 2(x^2 - 9)}{x(x + 3)(x - 3)}$$

$$= \frac{2x^2 - 6x - 4x^2 + x + 2x^2 - 18}{x(x + 3)(x - 3)}$$

$$= \frac{-5x - 18}{x(x + 3)(x - 3)} = -\frac{5x + 18}{x(x + 3)(x - 3)}$$

$$= \frac{5x + 18}{x(9 - x^2)}.$$

Check. Since the resulting fraction is not defined if $x = 0$, $x = -3$, or $x = 3$, we must avoid using these values for x. It is also desirable to avoid using $x = 1$. If we let $x = 2$,

$$\frac{2}{x+3} - \frac{4x-1}{x^2-9} + \frac{2}{x} \quad \text{becomes} \quad \frac{2}{2+3} - \frac{8-1}{4-9} + \frac{2}{2}$$

$$\text{or} \quad \frac{2}{5} + \frac{7}{5} + 1 \quad \text{or} \quad \frac{14}{5};$$

$$\frac{5x+18}{x(9-x^2)} \quad \text{becomes} \quad \frac{10+18}{2(9-4)} \quad \text{or} \quad \frac{28}{10} \quad \text{or} \quad \frac{14}{5}.$$

EXAMPLE 2.   Write $a + b - \dfrac{2ab}{a+b}$ as a single fraction.

Solution. $a + b - \dfrac{2ab}{a+b} = \dfrac{a+b}{1} - \dfrac{2ab}{a+b} = \dfrac{(a+b)(a+b) - 2ab}{a+b}$

$$= \frac{a^2 + 2ab + b^2 - 2ab}{a+b} = \frac{a^2 + b^2}{a+b}.$$

Warning. $\dfrac{a}{b} + \dfrac{c}{d} = \dfrac{ad + bc}{bd}$ but $\dfrac{a}{b} + \dfrac{c}{d} \neq \dfrac{a+c}{b+d}.$

$$\frac{a}{b+c} \neq \frac{a}{b} + \frac{a}{c} \text{; the fraction is already in simplest form.}$$

The product of two fractions *is the fraction whose numerator is the product of their numerators and whose denominator is the product of their denominators.*

Symbolically,

$$\frac{a}{b} \cdot \frac{c}{d} = \frac{ac}{bd}.$$

As always, it is required that all denominators be different from zero. Any quotient of fractions can also be written as a product,

$$a \div b = a(1/b).$$

The reciprocal of any number is 1 divided by that number (§ 1-7); thus $1/b$ is the reciprocal of b. The reciprocal of a fraction b/c is given by

$$\frac{1}{\dfrac{b}{c}} = \frac{1}{\dfrac{b}{c}} \cdot \frac{c}{c} = \frac{1 \cdot c}{\dfrac{b}{c} \cdot \dfrac{c}{1}} = \frac{c}{b}.$$

Hence the reciprocal of a fraction is the fraction obtained by inter-changing the numerator and denominator of the given fraction. The process of obtaining the reciprocal of a fraction is often called **inverting the fraction**. Thus we have the familiar rule for division: **Invert the divisor and proceed as in multiplication**. Symbolically,

$$\frac{a}{b} \div \frac{c}{d} = \frac{a}{b} \cdot \frac{d}{c} = \frac{ad}{bc}.$$

EXAMPLE 3.   Find $\dfrac{2a + b}{a^2 - 2ab} \cdot \dfrac{a^3 - 2a^2b}{4a^2 - b^2}$.

Solution.

$$\frac{2a + b}{a^2 - 2ab} \cdot \frac{a^3 - 2a^2b}{4a^2 - b^2} = \frac{\cancel{2a + b}}{\cancel{a}(a - 2b)} \cdot \frac{\overset{a}{\cancel{a^2}}(a - 2b)}{(2a + b)(2a - b)} = \frac{a}{2a - b}.$$

EXAMPLE 4.   Simplify: $\left(\dfrac{a^2 - 2ax + x^2}{a^2 - x^2} \div \dfrac{a^2 + x^2}{a + x}\right) \cdot \dfrac{x}{x - a}$.

Solution.

$$\left(\frac{a^2 - 2ax + x^2}{a^2 - x^2} \div \frac{a^2 + x^2}{a + x}\right) \cdot \frac{x}{x - a} = \frac{(a - x)\overset{-1}{\cancel{(a - x)}}}{\cancel{(a + x)}\cancel{(a - x)}} \cdot \frac{\cancel{a + x}}{a^2 + x^2} \cdot \frac{x}{\cancel{x - a}}$$

$$= -\frac{x}{a^2 + x^2}.$$

Warnings. $a \cdot \dfrac{b}{c} = \dfrac{a}{1} \cdot \dfrac{b}{c} = \dfrac{ab}{c}$ but $a \cdot \dfrac{b}{c} \neq \dfrac{ab}{ac}$.

$\dfrac{a}{b} \div c = \dfrac{a}{b} \cdot \dfrac{1}{c} = \dfrac{a}{bc}$ but $\dfrac{a}{b} \div c \neq \dfrac{ac}{b}$.

$\dfrac{ab + bc}{b - bd} \div b = \dfrac{\cancel{b}(a + c)}{\cancel{b}(1 - d)} \cdot \dfrac{1}{b} = \dfrac{a + c}{b(1 - d)}$ but $\dfrac{ab + bc}{b - bd} \div b \neq \dfrac{a + c}{1 - d}$.

A fraction that contains one or more fractions in either its numerator or its denominator, or in both, is called a **complex fraction** or **compound fraction**. In such cases the main rule (dividing line) in the fraction is usually made heavier than the other rules.

The simplification of a complex fraction is essentially a problem in the division of fractions, the main rule (dividing line) in the fraction serving as a division sign. Thus any complex fraction may be simplified by *first reducing the numerator and the denominator to single fractions, and then performing the division*. The following equivalent procedure is based upon the fundamental principle of fractions (§ 2-7) and is preferred by many persons:

To simplify a complex fraction *first multiply its numerator and its denominator by the L.C.D. of all fractions occurring in either its numerator or its denominator, then reduce the fraction obtained.*

EXAMPLE 5.   Simplify: $\dfrac{a - \dfrac{1}{a}}{1 + \dfrac{1}{a}}$.

First Solution. $\dfrac{a - \dfrac{1}{a}}{1 + \dfrac{1}{a}} = \dfrac{\dfrac{a^2 - 1}{a}}{\dfrac{a + 1}{a}}$

$$= \frac{(a - 1)(a + 1)}{a} \cdot \frac{a}{a + 1} = a - 1.$$

Second Solution. $\dfrac{a - \dfrac{1}{a}}{1 + \dfrac{1}{a}} = \dfrac{\left(a - \dfrac{1}{a}\right)a}{\left(1 + \dfrac{1}{a}\right)a} = \dfrac{a^2 - 1}{a + 1}$

$$= \frac{(a - 1)(a + 1)}{a + 1} = a - 1.$$

EXERCISES

Find the expression by which the numerator and denominator of the given fraction should be multiplied to obtain an equivalent fraction with the specified new denominator:

1. $\frac{1}{2}$, to have denominator $(6x + 4y)$.

2. $\dfrac{2x}{5x + 5}$, to have denominator $5(x^2 - 1)$.

3. $\dfrac{a - b}{a + b}$, to have denominator $(ab^3 + b^4)$.

4. $\dfrac{x + yz^2}{xy + xz}$, to have denominator $(x^3y^2 - x^3z^2)$.

Write as a set of fractions with a common denominator:

5. $\dfrac{2}{a}, \dfrac{3}{b}, \dfrac{15}{ab^2}$.   **6.** $\dfrac{x}{y}, \dfrac{y}{x}, \dfrac{1}{2}$.   **7.** $\dfrac{x - y}{x + y}, \dfrac{x^2 + y^2}{x - y}, \dfrac{3}{x^2 - y^2}$.

Combine into a single fraction, and check numerically:

8. $\dfrac{x - 2y}{16} + \dfrac{3x + y}{12}$.

13. $\dfrac{5a + 1}{a^2 - 1} - \dfrac{3}{a - 1} + \dfrac{2}{a + 1}$.

9. $\dfrac{10}{a + 2b} - \dfrac{6}{a - 2b}$.

14. $\dfrac{1 + 2x}{3x - 3} - \dfrac{5 - x}{x^2 - 5x + 4}$.

10. $\dfrac{x}{2x - 3y} - \dfrac{y}{2x + 3y}$.

15. $\dfrac{x + 1}{2x^2 - 18} + \dfrac{x + 2}{9x + 3x^2}$.

11. $\dfrac{x - y}{3} - \dfrac{x + y}{2} + x$.

16. $\dfrac{2}{x - 3} - \dfrac{2}{x + 3} - \dfrac{1}{x}$.

12. $\dfrac{3}{3z - 2} - \dfrac{1 - 2z}{9z^2 - 4}$.

17. $\dfrac{2}{x + 1} - \dfrac{3}{x} - \dfrac{2}{x^2} + \dfrac{1}{x^3}$.

18. $\dfrac{1}{(a - b)(a - c)} + \dfrac{1}{(b - a)(c - b)} - \dfrac{1}{(a - c)(b - c)}$.

19. $\dfrac{x}{(y - x)(z - x)} - \dfrac{y}{(y - x)(z - y)} + \dfrac{z}{(x - z)(y - z)}$.

Find (a) $y_1 + y_2$, (b) $y_1 - y_2$, (c) $y_2 - y_1$, when:

20. $y_1 = \dfrac{2}{1 - 3(x + t)}$, $y_2 = \dfrac{2}{1 - 3x}$.

21. $y_1 = \dfrac{3}{2 - (x + t)^2}$, $y_2 = \dfrac{3}{2 - x^2}$.

Find the reciprocal of:

22. $\dfrac{2}{3}$.   **23.** $4\frac{1}{2}$.   **24.** $\dfrac{5x}{y}$.   **25.** $\dfrac{x + y}{z}$.   **26.** $\dfrac{3}{5}(x - 4)$.

Perform the indicated operations and simplify:

27. $\dfrac{8a^2}{9b^2} \cdot \dfrac{12b^3}{5a}$.

32. $\dfrac{x^2 + 2x - 15}{x^2 - 9} \cdot \dfrac{x^2 + 6x + 9}{3y + xy}$.

28. $\dfrac{2x^3y}{19xy^3} \cdot \dfrac{38y}{x}$.

33. $\dfrac{x^3}{y^2} \cdot \dfrac{xy - y^2}{x^2 + xy} \div \dfrac{x^2 - y^2}{x^2 + y^2}$.

29. $\dfrac{r^2st}{rst^2} \div \dfrac{rs^2t}{rt}$.

34. $\left(1 - \dfrac{x + 1}{x^2 + 1}\right) \div \dfrac{(x - 1)^2}{x^4 - 1}$.

30. $\dfrac{a - 1}{a^2 + 1} \div \dfrac{(a - 1)^2}{a^4 - 1}$.

35. $1 - \dfrac{x + 1}{x^2 + 1} \div \dfrac{(x - 1)^2}{x^4 - 1}$.

31. $\dfrac{2x + 3}{x^2 - 1} \cdot \dfrac{2x^2 - x - 3}{4x^2 - 9}$.

36. $\dfrac{a^2 - b^2}{a^3 - b^3} \cdot \dfrac{a^2b + ab^2 + b^3}{a^2 - 4ab - 5b^2}$.

Simplify:

37. $\dfrac{\frac{1}{3} + \frac{1}{5}}{\frac{1}{5} - \frac{2}{3}}$.

38. $\dfrac{\frac{2}{7} - \frac{1}{3}}{\frac{1}{3} - \frac{4}{7}}$.

39. $\dfrac{\dfrac{9}{x} - x}{1 + \dfrac{3}{x}}$.

40. $\dfrac{1 - \dfrac{1}{a}}{1 - \dfrac{1}{a^2}}$.

41. $\dfrac{\dfrac{1}{x} - \dfrac{1}{y}}{\dfrac{1}{x^2} - \dfrac{1}{y^2}}$.

42. $\dfrac{4x^2 - 9y^2}{1 - \dfrac{y - x}{x - 2y}}$.

43. $\dfrac{\dfrac{1}{a^3} + \dfrac{2}{a^2 b} + \dfrac{1}{ab^2}}{\dfrac{b}{a} - \dfrac{a}{b}}$.

44. $\dfrac{1 - \dfrac{1}{1 - \dfrac{1}{x}}}{1 - x}$.

45. $\dfrac{\dfrac{x - y}{x + y} + \dfrac{y}{y - x}}{1 - y\left(\dfrac{3}{x - y} - \dfrac{2}{x + y}\right)}$.

MISCELLANEOUS EXERCISES

Simplify:

1. $\left(3x - \dfrac{x + 2}{3}\right) + x - \left(\dfrac{x - 3}{2} + 3x\right)$.

2. $(r + 3) + 4r + 5\{2r - 3[r + 2(2r - 3) + 3] - 3\}$.

3. $\dfrac{\dfrac{a^2 - 4}{a^2 - 3a + 2}}{\dfrac{a^2 - a - 6}{a^2 - 1}}$.

4. $\left(\dfrac{z}{3} - \dfrac{3}{z}\right)\left(\dfrac{1}{z + 3}\right)$.

5. $\dfrac{z}{3} - \dfrac{3}{z} + \dfrac{1}{z + 3}$.

6. $\dfrac{x^2 - 3}{x - \dfrac{2}{x - \dfrac{1}{x}}}$.

7. $\dfrac{a^3 b^2 - a^2 b^3}{a^2 b^4 - a^4 b^2}$.

8. $\dfrac{2x^2 y^3 - 2xy^4}{x^3 y - x^2 y^2}$.

9. $\dfrac{(u + v)^2 - w^2}{u^2 - (v - w)^2}$.

10. $\dfrac{(a - b)^2 - c^2}{(a - c)^2 - b^2}$.

11. $\dfrac{12x^2 + 5x - 3}{3x^2 - 13x + 4}$.

12. $\dfrac{6x^2 - 18x - 60}{2x^2 + 2x - 4}$.   **13.** $\dfrac{6a^2 - 13ab + 6b^2}{(3b - 2a)^2}$.   **14.** $\dfrac{20 - k^2 - k}{6k - 8 - k^2}$.

15. $\dfrac{x^2 + y^2}{x + \sqrt{3}} \cdot \dfrac{x^2 - 3}{x^2 - y^2} \div \dfrac{x - \sqrt{3}}{x - y}$.

16. $\dfrac{\left(b + \dfrac{1}{b}\right)^2 - 4}{\left(b - 1 + \dfrac{1}{b}\right)\left(1 + \dfrac{1}{b}\right)} \div \dfrac{\dfrac{1}{b^2} - b^2}{\dfrac{1}{b^2} + b}$.

17. $a^{-2}(-2a) \div 6(-a)^{-1}$.
18. $(a^{-1} - b^{-1})^{-1}$.
19. $(x^{-1} - x)^{-2}$.

20. $-(4^{-1} - x)^{-1}$.
21. $x^{-3}(-4x) + 6(-x)^{-1}$.
22. $[x(-4x)]^{-3} + (6 - x)^{-1}$.

23. $(5x^{-1})^3[3x^5(x^{-3} + x^{-4})^2]^0$.
24. $(3x)^{-1} \div [2x^3(x^{-3} - 2x^{-2})^0]^{-1}$.
25. $(y + 1)^{-1} - (y - 1)^{-1} + 1$.
26. $a^{-1}b^2 + (ab^{-2})^{-3}$.
27. $(x + 1)^{-1}(x - 1)^{-3}(x^2 - 1)^2$.

28. $\dfrac{x - y^{-1}}{(x - y)^{-1}}$.   **30.** $\dfrac{4n^{-1} + 9nk^{-2}}{16n^{-2} - 81n^2k^{-4}}$.

29. $\dfrac{x^{-2} - y^{-2}}{x^{-1} + y^{-1}}$.   **31.** $\dfrac{a^{-1} + b^{-1}}{ab^{-2} + a^{-2}b}$.

32. $\dfrac{x - y}{x^{-1} - y^{-1}} + \dfrac{x^2 + y^2}{x^{-2} + y^{-2}} - \dfrac{x^{-1}y}{x^{-3}y^{-1}}$.

33. $(3 \cdot 10^6) \cdot (2 \cdot 10^{-2})$.   **35.** $(1.00 \cdot 10^{-7}) \div (2.0 \cdot 10^{-4})$.
34. $(16 \cdot 10^5) \div (2 \cdot 10^{-4})$.   **36.** $6.0000 \cdot 10^2 + 1.60 \cdot 10^1$.
37. $(6.000 \cdot 10^2)(20.0)/(4.00 \cdot 10^0)$.

Find the reciprocal of each of the following, using Table I:

38. 46.0.   **40.** 460.0.   **42.** 0.380.   **44.** 0.0002800.
39. 4.60.   **41.** 7,500.   **43.** 0.069.   **45.** 0.00490.

46. A temperature of $C°$ centigrade corresponds to a temperature of $F°$ Fahrenheit where $C = \frac{5}{9}(F - 32)$. Find the centigrade temperatures corresponding to Fahrenheit temperatures of **(a)** 50°; **(b)** 60°; **(c)** 20°; **(d)** 0°; **(e)** −40°; **(f)** 212°.

47. If $y = \dfrac{x - 1}{1 - 2x}$, find $\dfrac{y - 1}{1 - 2y}$ in terms of x.

48. If a side of one triangle is n times as long as the corresponding side of a second triangle which is similar, then the area of the first triangle is n^2 times the area of the second triangle. How many times the area of the second is the area of the first if **(a)** $n = 23$? **(b)** $n = 1\frac{1}{2}$? **(c)** $n = a/b$? **(d)** $n = a^3b/c^2$?

49. The "light-gathering power" of an optical telescope is a^2/b^2, where a is the diameter of the telescope lens and b is the diameter of the pupil of the eye (taken as $\frac{1}{3}$ inch since it is used at night). What is the light-gathering power of **(a)** a 4-inch telescope? **(b)** a $3\frac{1}{2}$-inch telescope? **(c)** a 100-inch telescope?

50. Suppose a man's net income I is taxed at the rate of $r\%$; that is, his tax is $\frac{1}{100} rI$. Represent **(a)** the amount of his income after taxes; **(b)** his income after taxes, as a fraction of his income before taxes; **(c)** his tax as a fraction of his income after taxes.

51. The number n of waves per centimeter in the Balmer lines of the spectrum of light from hydrogen is given by $n = R\left(\dfrac{1}{2^2} - \dfrac{1}{m^2}\right)$ where $m = 3$ for the first line, $m = 4$ for the second line, $m = 5$ for the third line, and so on, and $R = 109{,}678$. Find n for $m = 3$, $m = 4$, $m = 5$, $m = 6$, and $m = 7$ to three significant digits, and plot these values of n on a number scale.

52. If several wires, with electrical resistances $R_1, R_2, \cdots, R_n$ ohms respectively, are connected in parallel, then the resistance, R ohms, of the combination is given by

$$R = \frac{1}{\dfrac{1}{R_1} + \dfrac{1}{R_2} + \cdots + \dfrac{1}{R_n}}.$$

Find R if **(a)** $n = 2$, $R_1 = 100$, $R_2 = 400$; **(b)** $n = 3$, $R_1 = 1$, $R_2 = 1000$, $R_3 = 200$; **(c)** $n = 3$, $R_1 = x$, $R_2 = 3x$, $R_3 = 4x + 3$.

53. If two planets revolve around the sun with periods ("sidereal periods") P_1 and P_2, then the "synodic period" (the period between successive times at which the two planets are in a straight line with the sun and on the same side of the sun) is

$$\left| \frac{1}{\dfrac{1}{P_1} - \dfrac{1}{P_2}} \right|.$$

The earth's sidereal period is $365\frac{1}{4}$ days, that of Venus is 224.7 days, and that of Mars is 687.0 days. Without using Table I, find the synodic period of **(a)** Venus as seen from the earth; **(b)** Mars as seen from the earth; **(c)** the earth as seen from Mars; **(d)** two planets if they have sidereal periods p and $4p$.

54. Use the relation given in Exercise 53 to find the synodic period of two satellites circling the earth in the same direction in **(a)** 23 hours and 24 hours respectively; **(b)** 1 hour 40 minutes and 1 hour 45 minutes respectively.

55. The weight of an object on the surface of a celestial body is $\dfrac{m}{m_e} \cdot \dfrac{r_e{}^2}{r^2}$ times the weight the same object would have on the surface of the earth, where m_e and r_e are the mass and the radius of the earth respectively, and m and r are the mass and the radius of the other celestial body, respectively. If a person or object weighs **(a)** 150 pounds, **(b)** x pounds, on the surface of the earth, what would be the weight on the surface of the moon, which has mass 0.012 times that of the earth and radius 1080 miles while the earth's radius is 3957 miles? on the surface of Jupiter, with radius 42,900 miles and mass 318.4 times that of the earth? on a planet with mass k^2 times that of the earth and radius $\frac{5}{4}k$ times that of the earth?

CHAPTER 3

REAL NUMBERS AND RADICALS

3-1 Real Numbers

In § 1-2 it was mentioned briefly that other numbers were needed besides the rationals. This is evident since points on a number scale correspond to decimals but not necessarily to repeating decimals (see § 14-6) such as

$$\tfrac{12}{55} = 0.2181818\cdots \quad \text{or} \quad \tfrac{5}{4} = 1.25000\cdots$$

Consequently the rational number system is extended so that every decimal represents a real number, and every real number is represented by a decimal. The rational numbers are represented by repeating decimals; the irrational numbers, by nonrepeating decimals. Any real number is either rational or irrational.

Numbers such as $\sqrt{2}$, $\sqrt{3}$, $\sqrt{5}$, and $\sqrt[3]{2}$ are irrational. Some real numbers, such as π, cannot even be represented in terms of radicals. However, radicals suffice to represent many important numbers, and so will be considered next.

Historical Note. Though π was well known to the ancients in connection with circles, the fact that π cannot be represented by radicals was not proved until 1766–1794, by LAMBERT and LEGENDRE. In 1882, LINDEMANN proved that π cannot even be a solution of a polynomial equation (§ 5-1) with rational coefficients.

3-2 Roots

If a *is a number whose* nth *power,* n *being any positive integer, is equal to a given number* b, *then* a *is called an* **nth root**, *or* **root of order** *n*, **of the number** *b*. Thus, if $a^2 = b$, a is a **square root** of b; if $a^3 = b$, a is a **cube root** of b; and, in general, if $a^n = b$ and n is a positive integer, a is an **nth root** of b.

ILLUSTRATION 1.   3 is a fourth root of 81, -2 is a fifth root of -32, -2 is a sixth root of 64, and 10^3 is a fourth root of 10^{12}.

The process of extracting roots is known as **evolution**. However, special methods for extracting square and cube roots were developed independently of any general theory of evolution. Although the process of raising any number to an integral power, known as **involution**, leads to a single result, evolution does not necessarily lead to a single result. Either $+3$ or -3 satisfies the definition of a square root of 9, since $3 \cdot 3 = 9$ and $(-3)(-3) = 9$. In general, if b is positive, it has two square roots, numerically equal but opposite in sign.

In § 8-7 it will be shown that when imaginary numbers (§ 3-9) as well as real numbers are accepted as roots, then *every number, except zero, has exactly n distinct nth roots.* At present we are primarily concerned with real numbers as roots. For any positive *odd* integer n, every real number b has exactly one real number as an nth root; this root is positive if b is positive, negative if b is negative. For any positive *even* integer n, every *positive* number b has exactly two real numbers as nth roots; these numbers are numerically equal and opposite in sign. For any positive *even* integer n, a *negative* number b cannot have any real number as nth root; thus, b has only imaginary numbers as nth roots. Prior to a more detailed study of imaginary numbers in Chapter 8, we shall assume that all literal number symbols which occur are such that the indicated operations do not involve even roots of negative numbers, unless otherwise indicated.

The **principal nth root** of b is defined as the positive nth root of b when b is positive, and the negative nth root of b when b is negative and n is odd. If all the nth roots of b are imaginary, we do not define the principal nth root of b.

ILLUSTRATION 2.   The principal cube root of 27 is 3 and of -27 is -3. The real fourth roots of 16 are $+2$ and -2; the principal fourth root is $+2$. The two square roots of -25 are imaginary numbers, and we do not define the principal square root of -25.

The symbol $\sqrt[n]{b}$, for n a *positive integer*, is called a **radical** and is read "the nth root of b." It is used to denote the *principal* nth root of b if there is a real nth root, and to denote *any one* of the n distinct nth roots of b if all of these nth roots are imaginary. The symbol "$\sqrt{}$" is called the **radical sign**, the positive integer n the **index** or **order** of the radical, and the number b the **radicand**. In a square root it is customary to omit the index 2. From the preceding discussion, if b is positive then $\sqrt[n]{b}$ is positive; if b is negative and n is odd, then $\sqrt[n]{b}$ is negative; and if b is negative and n is even, then $\sqrt[n]{b}$ is imaginary.

ILLUSTRATION 3. $\sqrt{16} = 4$; $-\sqrt{16} = -4$; $\pm\sqrt{16} = \pm 4$; $\sqrt[3]{125} = 5$; $\sqrt[3]{-125} = -5$; $\sqrt[4]{81} = 3$; $\sqrt[4]{-81}$ is   imaginary; $\sqrt[5]{32} = 2$; $\sqrt[5]{-32} = -2$; $-\sqrt[5]{-32} = -(-2) = 2$.

The number $\sqrt[n]{b}$ is rational if b is the nth power of a rational number. If, however, $\sqrt[n]{b}$ is *real* and b is *not* the nth power of a rational number, then $\sqrt[n]{b}$ is irrational and is called a **surd of order n**. A surd of order *two* is called a **quadratic surd** and one of order *three* a **cubic surd**.

ILLUSTRATION 4.   The numbers $\sqrt{49}$, $\sqrt[5]{-32}$, and $\sqrt[4]{81/16}$ are rational since $49 = 7^2$, $-32 = (-2)^5$, and $81/16 = (3/2)^4$. The numbers $\sqrt{2}$, $\sqrt[3]{-5}$, and $\sqrt[4]{14}$ are irrational.

For positive two-digit integers, the principal value of the square root and cube root can be found in Table I. For numbers similar to this except for the location of the decimal point, Table I can still be used by writing the number in a form resembling scientific notation except that the power of 10 is chosen to be a multiple of 2 in the case of square roots and a multiple of 3 for cube roots, and the columns headed "$\sqrt{N}$", "$\sqrt{10N}$", "$\sqrt[3]{N}$", "$\sqrt[3]{10N}$", and "$\sqrt[3]{100N}$" are used.

ILLUSTRATION 5.   Assuming the given numbers are exact, $\sqrt{23} \approx 4.796$ by column "$\sqrt{N}$"; $\sqrt{230} \approx 15.166$ by column "$\sqrt{10N}$"; $\sqrt{230{,}000} = \sqrt{23 \cdot 10^4} = \sqrt{23} \cdot 10^2 \approx 479.6$ by column "$\sqrt{N}$"; $\sqrt{0.023} = \sqrt{230 \cdot 10^{-4}} = \sqrt{230} \cdot 10^{-2} \approx 0.15166$ by column "$\sqrt{10N}$"; $\sqrt[3]{0.0023} = \sqrt[3]{2300 \cdot 10^{-6}} = \sqrt[3]{2300} \cdot 10^{-2} \approx 0.13200$ by column "$\sqrt[3]{100N}$".

EXERCISES

1. Find the positive and the negative square roots of each of the numbers

(a) 1, 4, 16, 81;   (c) 121, 400, 676;

(b) $\frac{1}{4}$, $\frac{1}{16}$, $\frac{1}{144}$;   (d) $9 \cdot 10^4$, $36 \cdot 10^{10}$, $1.6 \cdot 10^5$, $8.1 \cdot 10^{-5}$.

2. Find the real cube roots of

(a) 27, −27, 125, −216, −1000;

(b) $27 \cdot 10^{12}$, $6.4 \cdot 10^{10}$, $-1.25 \cdot 10^8$.

3. Find the principal fourth roots of (a) 16; (b) 256; (c) $\frac{1}{625}$; (d) 0.0016; (e) $81 \cdot 10^{20}$.

Express as rational numbers:

4. $\sqrt[3]{-8}$.

5. $\sqrt[3]{\frac{1}{125}}$.

6. $\sqrt[5]{-32}$.

7. $\sqrt[4]{\frac{81}{256}}$.

8. $\sqrt{0.0036}$.

9. $\sqrt[4]{0.0625}$.

10. $\sqrt[8]{256}$.

11. $\sqrt[5]{-0.00032}$.

12. $\sqrt[6]{729 \cdot 10^{-6}}$.

Use Table I and find (a) *the square,* (b) *the principal square root,* (c) *the cube, and* (d) *the principal cube root, of each of the following numbers considered as an exact number:*

13. 6.

14. 60.

15. 0.6.

16. 0.06.

17. 370.

18. 3700.

19. 3.7.

20. 7.3.

21. 0.85.

22. 69,000.

23. 0.0044.

24. 0.00048.

25. $2.8 \cdot 10^6$.

26. $2.8 \cdot 10^5$.

27. $9.2 \cdot 10^{-6}$.

28. $5.6 \cdot 10^{-4}$.

Round each of the following square roots to four significant digits and note, by comparing the results obtained for the numbers in each pair, the effect of rounding before using a table of square roots:

29. $\sqrt{337} \approx 18.35756$; $\sqrt{340} \approx 18.43909$.

30. $\sqrt{114} \approx 10.67708$; $\sqrt{110} \approx 10.48809$.

Determine whether the following are true or false:

31. $\sqrt{x} < x$ whenever $1 < x$.

32. $\sqrt{x} < x$ whenever $0 < x$.

33. $\sqrt[3]{x} < x$ for any real number x.

34. $x < \sqrt[5]{x}$ whenever $x < -1$.

Find to two significant digits:

35. The length of an edge of a cube whose volume is 5,700,000 cubic inches.

36. The distance along one side of a square city block having an area of ten acres (1 acre = 43,560 square feet).

37. The length in meters of a square field if its area is 4.5 square kilometers (1 kilometer = 1000 meters).

38. The distance to the "radio horizon" in miles, $\sqrt{2h}$, where h is the antenna height in feet, for (a) $h = 100$; (b) $h = 400$; (c) $h = 20$. (d) Find the sum of the answers for transmitting antenna height 400 feet and receiving antenna height 20 feet.

3-3   Fractional Exponents

Let $m = 1/q$, where q is any positive integer. If $1/q$, as an exponent, is to obey Law I of the laws of exponents (§ 1-6), it is necessary that

$$a^{\frac{1}{q}} \cdot a^{\frac{1}{q}} \cdot a^{\frac{1}{q}} \cdots a^{\frac{1}{q}}, \text{ } q \text{ factors } a^{\frac{1}{q}} = a^{\frac{1}{q}+\frac{1}{q}+\frac{1}{q}+\cdots+\frac{1}{q}, \text{ } q \text{ terms} \frac{1}{q}} = a^{\frac{q}{q}} = a.$$

Hence $a^{\frac{1}{q}}$ **is defined as a** q**th root of** a**, and is taken to represent the principal root** if there is one. Thus $a^{\frac{1}{q}}$ has the same meaning as $\sqrt[q]{a}$.

If the exponent is a rational number p/q with q a positive integer and p an integer (not necessarily positive), we define

$$a^{\frac{p}{q}} = (a^{\frac{1}{q}})^p$$

in accordance with Law II of exponents, thus extending the definition of exponent to all rational numbers. Under this definition, and with the same restriction as in § 3-2 regarding even roots of negative numbers, the symbol $a^{\frac{p}{q}}$ satisfies all of the laws of exponents, except that roots other than the principal root may have to be considered if p/q is not in lowest terms. In particular, again by Law II of exponents, $(a^p)^{\frac{1}{q}} = a^{\frac{p}{q}}$.

Thus,
$$a^{\frac{p}{q}} = \sqrt[q]{a^p} = (\sqrt[q]{a})^p.$$

Each of these forms has its own advantages in manipulation.

ILLUSTRATIONS. $125^{\frac{1}{3}} = \sqrt[3]{125} = 5;$
$81^{\frac{3}{4}} = (\sqrt[4]{81})^3 = 3^3 = 27.$

EXAMPLE 1.   Simplify: $\left[\dfrac{9^{\frac{3}{2}} - 2 \cdot 8^{-\frac{2}{3}}}{2b^0 + (\frac{1}{4})^{-2}} \right]^{-1}$

Solution.

$$\left[\frac{9^{\frac{3}{2}} - 2 \cdot 8^{-\frac{2}{3}}}{2b^0 + (\frac{1}{4})^{-2}} \right]^{-1} = \left[\frac{(9^{\frac{1}{2}})^3 - 2\left(\dfrac{1}{8^{\frac{2}{3}}}\right)}{2 \cdot 1 + 4^2} \right]^{-1} = \left[\frac{27 - \dfrac{2}{4}}{18} \right]^{-1} = \left[\frac{53}{36} \right]^{-1} = \frac{36}{53}.$$

The use of literal number symbols as exponents poses additional problems unless the symbols are restricted to representing rational numbers. These problems will be discussed further in § 6-1; meanwhile we shall assume that the laws of exponents hold for literal number symbols.

EXAMPLE 2. Simplify: $\left[a^{\frac{1}{n+1}} \div a^{\frac{1}{n-1}}\right]^{\frac{1-n}{2}}$.

Solution.

$$\left[a^{\frac{1}{n+1}} \div a^{\frac{1}{n-1}}\right]^{\frac{1-n}{2}} = \left[a^{\frac{1}{n+1} - \frac{1}{n-1}}\right]^{\frac{1-n}{2}} = \left[a^{\frac{(n-1)-(n+1)}{(n+1)(n-1)}}\right]^{\frac{1-n}{2}}$$

$$= \left[a^{\frac{-2}{(n+1)(n-1)}}\right]^{\frac{1-n}{2}} = a^{\frac{-2}{(n+1)(n-1)}\left(-\frac{n-1}{2}\right)} = a^{\frac{1}{n+1}}.$$

Historical Note. The use of exponents to indicate positive integral powers was introduced by DESCARTES (1637). Fractional and negative powers, although not expressed in modern symbols, were known in theory to such men as ORESME (about 1360). JOHN WALLIS (1655) was the first to explain with any completeness the meaning of fractional and negative exponents. ISAAC NEWTON (1642–1727) made use of such exponents, and since his time the present symbolism has been generally recognized.

EXERCISES

Find the value of each of the following, using tables when necessary:

1. $16^{\frac{1}{2}}$.
2. $8^{\frac{1}{3}}$.
3. $64^{\frac{1}{3}}$.
4. $64^{\frac{1}{2}}$.
5. $64^{\frac{1}{6}}$.
6. $9^{-\frac{1}{2}}$.
7. $27^{-\frac{1}{3}}$.
8. $27^{\frac{2}{3}}$.

9. $8^{\frac{2}{3}}$.
10. $\left(\frac{1}{81}\right)^{\frac{3}{4}}$.
11. $\left(\frac{1}{8}\right)^{-\frac{2}{3}}$.
12. $\left(\frac{1}{8}\right)^{-\frac{4}{3}}$.
13. $\left(\frac{1}{81}\right)^{-\frac{5}{4}}$.
14. $\left(\frac{27}{64}\right)^{-\frac{1}{3}}$.
15. $\left(\frac{25}{4}\right)^{-\frac{1}{2}}$.
16. $\left(\frac{5}{4}\right)^{0}$.

17. $(-64)^{-\frac{5}{3}}$.
18. $\left(-\frac{1}{8}\right)^{-\frac{2}{3}}$.
19. $(0.0016)^{\frac{1}{2}}$.
20. $(0.008)^{\frac{1}{3}}$.
21. $(25 - 3^2)^{\frac{1}{2}}$.
22. $(1^{\frac{1}{2}} + 0.25^{\frac{1}{2}})^2$.
23. $(2^2 + 3^2)^{\frac{1}{2}}$.
24. $(4^2 - 3^2)^{\frac{1}{2}}$.

25. $(17^2 - 8^2)^{-\frac{1}{2}}$.
26. $[8^{\frac{1}{3}} + (-8^{\frac{1}{3}})]^2$.
27. $[32^{\frac{1}{5}} - (-32)^{\frac{1}{5}}]^{-3}$.
28. $40,000^{\frac{3}{2}}$.
29. $(0.125)^{-\frac{1}{3}}$.
30. $(-8000)^{-\frac{2}{3}}$.
31. $(-0.064)^{\frac{2}{3}}$.
32. $(-1)^{\frac{1}{17}}$.

Express with positive exponents and simplify whenever possible:

33. $(x^6)^{\frac{1}{3}}$.
34. $(x^{\frac{1}{3}})^6$.
35. $(x^3)^{\frac{1}{6}}$.
36. $(a^{\frac{1}{4}})^6$.
37. a^{-4}.
38. $\dfrac{1}{x^{-2}}$.
39. $\dfrac{3}{b^{-3}}$.

40. $b^{-\frac{2}{3}}$.
41. $x^{-\frac{3}{2}}$.
42. $a^2 b^{-3} c^{\frac{1}{3}}$.
43. $a^{\frac{2}{3}} a^{-\frac{1}{2}}$.
44. $x^{\frac{1}{2}} x^{-\frac{3}{4}}$.
45. $z^{-1} z^{\frac{1}{4}}$.
46. $(a^{-\frac{2}{3}})^{\frac{1}{2}}$.

47. $(-x^{-\frac{3}{5}})^{-\frac{1}{3}}$.
48. $a^{-5} \div a^{-2}$.
49. $x^{\frac{2}{3}} \div x^{\frac{3}{4}}$.
50. $c^3 \cdot c^{-5} \div c^2$.
51. $-(x^{12} y^4)^{\frac{1}{4}}$.
52. $(a^3 b^6 c^9)^{\frac{2}{3}}$.
53. $(x^2 y^{-\frac{1}{3}} z^{\frac{1}{6}})^2$.

54. $(x^{\frac{1}{6}}y^{-\frac{1}{4}}z^{\frac{1}{3}})^{-3}$.

55. $(a^{-\frac{3}{4}} \div a^{\frac{5}{4}})^{-\frac{1}{6}}$.

56. $(8x)^{-\frac{2}{3}} \div (9x)^{-\frac{3}{2}}$.

57. $\dfrac{2x^3}{5y} \cdot \dfrac{y}{2x^{-3}}$.

58. $5/x - 3x^{-1}$.

59. $\dfrac{2x^3}{x^2} + \dfrac{3}{x^{-1}}$.

60. $\dfrac{x^{-1} + 1/y}{x^{-2} - y^{-2}}$.

61. $(x^{-1} - y^{-1})^2$.

62. $xy^{-1} - x^{-1}y$.

63. $(r^{-2} + s^{-2})^{-1}$.

64. $(r^{\frac{1}{2}} - s^{\frac{1}{2}})^2$.

65. $(r^{\frac{1}{2}} - r^{-\frac{1}{2}})^2$.

66. $(a^{-\frac{2}{3}} - 1/b^{\frac{2}{3}})^3$.

67. $(x^{\frac{1}{2}} - y^{\frac{1}{2}})(x^{\frac{1}{2}} + y^{\frac{1}{2}})$.

68. $(x^{\frac{1}{3}} - 1)(x^{\frac{2}{3}} + x^{\frac{1}{3}} + 1)$.

69. $[(x^{\frac{1}{2}} - x^{-\frac{1}{2}})^2 + 4]^{\frac{1}{2}}$.

70. $[(x^{\frac{2}{3}} + x^{-\frac{2}{3}})^2 - 4]^{\frac{1}{2}}$.

71. $\left[x^{\frac{1}{2n+3}}x^{\frac{1}{2n-3}}\right]^{\frac{1}{4n}}$.

72. $\left[a^{1-x} \div a^{x^2+1}\right]^{\frac{1}{x+1}}$.

73. $[y^{a^2-1} \div y^{a+1}]^{\frac{1}{a}}$.

74. $[5 + 8^{\frac{2}{3}} - 125^{-\frac{4}{3}}]^0 + 125^{\frac{2}{3}}$.

Find the value of:

75. $(9 \cdot 10^6)^{-\frac{1}{2}}$.

76. $(2.7 \cdot 10^7)^{-\frac{2}{3}}$.

77. $(6.4 \cdot 10^{-11})^{-\frac{1}{6}}$.

78. $(6.4 \cdot 10^{-5})^{-\frac{2}{3}}$.

Simplify:

79. $x^{a+1}x^2$.

80. $x^{a-1}x^{a+1}$.

81. $(x^{a+1})^{a-2}$.

82. $(ab^x)(ab)^x$.

83. $b^{3x} \div b^x$.

84. $(2z)^3/(3z)^n$.

85. $(a^x)^{x-2}$.

86. $(2b)^3 \div (3b^x)$.

87. $y^{k(k+2)} \div y^k$.

88. $x^{a(a-b)}x^{b(a+b)}x^{a^2-b^2}$.

89. $x^{3a+b}x^{a-2b} \div x^{4(a-b)}$.

90. $(a^n + b^n)^2$.

91. $(a^n - b^n)(a^n + b^n)$.

92. $x^{2h-3}y \div [x^{h-4}(y^{5-h})^2]$.

93. $2^x \cdot 4^{x-1} \cdot 8^{x+1}$.

94. $[(9^x)^{2x-1} \cdot 27^{x+2}]/81^{x^2+1}$.

95. $(x^{4a} - 3y^{5b})^2$.

96. $(x^n - y^{2s})^3$.

97. $\dfrac{(y^{m-4n})^m}{y^{m(m-5n)}y^{n(m-6n)}}$.

98. $\dfrac{9^{b-1}}{(3^{b+1})^b} \div \dfrac{(27^{b+2})^{b-3}}{(81^{b-2})^{b+3}}$.

99. $\left(\dfrac{x^{m+3n}}{x^{2n}}\right)^n \div \left(\dfrac{x^{5n}}{x^{m+4n}}\right)^{m+n}$.

100. $\left(\dfrac{x^a}{x^b}\right)^{a-b}\left(\dfrac{x^c}{x^b}\right)^{b+c} \div \left(\dfrac{x^a}{x^c}\right)^{a-c}$.

101. $(\frac{4}{3})^{2n} - (\frac{1}{3})^{2n}$.

The following exercises are similar to some that arise in many calculus courses:

102. Show that $\sqrt{1 + m^2}$ reduces to $\dfrac{e^{\frac{2x}{a}} + 1}{2e^{\frac{x}{a}}}$ when $m = \frac{1}{2}\left(e^{\frac{x}{a}} - e^{-\frac{x}{a}}\right)$.

103. Show that the fraction $-\dfrac{x^{\frac{1}{2}}(\frac{1}{2}y^{-\frac{1}{2}}m) - y^{\frac{1}{2}}(\frac{1}{2}x^{-\frac{1}{2}})}{x}$ reduces to $\dfrac{a^{\frac{1}{2}}}{2x^{\frac{3}{2}}}$ when $m = -\dfrac{y^{\frac{1}{2}}}{x^{\frac{1}{2}}}$ and $x^{\frac{1}{2}} + y^{\frac{1}{2}} = a^{\frac{1}{2}}$.

3-4 Changes in Radical Form

By reason of the definition of a radical, any change in the form of a radical must be made in conformity with the laws of exponents. In practice, we need especially the following:

I. $(\sqrt[n]{a})^n = a,$ **III.** $\sqrt[m]{\sqrt[n]{a}} = \sqrt[mn]{a},$

II. $\sqrt[n]{a}\sqrt[n]{b} = \sqrt[n]{ab},$ **IV.** $\dfrac{\sqrt[n]{a}}{\sqrt[n]{b}} = \sqrt[n]{\dfrac{a}{b}},$

where the symbols are assumed to represent real numbers. Procedures for handling imaginary numbers are considered in § 3-9.

The first of these equalities follows from the definition of an nth root; the others follow directly from the laws of exponents. For example,

$$\sqrt[n]{a}\sqrt[n]{b} = a^{\frac{1}{n}}b^{\frac{1}{n}} = (ab)^{\frac{1}{n}} = \sqrt[n]{ab}.$$

The four ways in which radicals are ordinarily changed are:
1. Removing factors from the radicand;
2. Introducing coefficients under the radical sign;
3. Reducing a radical with a fractional radicand to an equivalent radical with an integral radicand;
4. Reducing to a radical of lower order.

EXAMPLE 1.   Remove all possible factors from the radicand in $\sqrt{108a^3}$.

Solution. $\sqrt{108a^3} = \sqrt{36a^2 \cdot 3a} = 6a\sqrt{3a}.$

EXAMPLE 2.   Change $4b\sqrt[3]{7a}$ to a radical whose coefficient is 1.

Solution. $4b\sqrt[3]{7a} = \sqrt[3]{(4b)^3}\sqrt[3]{7a} = \sqrt[3]{64b^3}\sqrt[3]{7a} = \sqrt[3]{448ab^3}.$

EXAMPLE 3.   Reduce $\sqrt{\frac{2}{3}}$ to a form where the radicand is integral.

Solution. $\sqrt{\dfrac{2}{3}} = \sqrt{\dfrac{2}{3} \cdot \dfrac{3}{3}} = \dfrac{\sqrt{6}}{\sqrt{9}} = \dfrac{\sqrt{6}}{3}$,   or $\frac{1}{3}\sqrt{6}$.

EXAMPLE 4.   Reduce $\sqrt[6]{8}$ to a radical of lower order.

Solution. $\sqrt[6]{8} = (2^3)^{\frac{1}{6}} = 2^{\frac{3}{6}} = 2^{\frac{1}{2}} = \sqrt{2}$.

The process shown in Example 3 is also known as **rationalizing the denominator**, and is considered further in § 3-5.

If the operations above, except that of introducing coefficients under the radical sign, have been performed wherever possible, the resulting radical is said to be in **simplest form**. By making a few trials, the student will see that the simplest form, as here defined, is usually the form from which an approximate value in decimal form can most easily be found.

Warning. $\sqrt{a^2 + b^2} \neq a + b$ when $ab \neq 0$. The radical is already in simplest form.

EXERCISES

Write in simplest radical form:

1. $6^{\frac{1}{3}}$.   **4.** $4x^{\frac{3}{4}}$.   **7.** $2x^{\frac{1}{2}} - (3y)^{\frac{1}{2}}$.   **10.** $(\frac{1}{9}x - 2)^{-\frac{1}{2}}$.

2. $5^{\frac{2}{5}}$.   **5.** $2^{\frac{3}{2}}a^{\frac{5}{2}}$.   **8.** $(9a^2 + 4b^2)^{\frac{1}{2}}$.   **11.** $x^{\frac{1}{2}}y^{-\frac{1}{2}}$.

3. $x^{\frac{2}{3}}$.   **6.** $x^6 y^{\frac{6}{5}} z^{\frac{3}{5}}$.   **9.** $5^{-\frac{1}{2}}$.   **12.** $(a^2 + 2ab + b^2)^{-\frac{1}{4}}$.

Write with fractional exponents:

13. $\sqrt[3]{5^4}$.   **15.** $\sqrt[4]{16x^3}$.   **17.** $\sqrt[4]{x}\sqrt[5]{y^2}$.   **19.** $\sqrt{a^2 - x^2}$.

14. $\sqrt{a^3}$.   **16.** $\sqrt[3]{4x^6y^2}$.   **18.** $\sqrt{a^7}\sqrt[3]{x^4}$.   **20.** $\sqrt[3]{(r^3 + s^3)^2}$.

Change to simplest radical form:

21. $\sqrt{8}$.   **28.** $\sqrt[3]{27 \cdot 10^{-4}}$.   **35.** $\sqrt{12x^5y^2}$.   **40.** $\sqrt[3]{4x^{-2}y^{-3}}$.

22. $\sqrt{98}$.   **29.** $\sqrt[3]{0.54}$.   **36.** $\sqrt{\dfrac{5x}{8a}}$.   **41.** $\sqrt[6]{16}$.

23. $\sqrt[3]{432}$.   **30.** $\sqrt{0.8}$.   **42.** $\sqrt[6]{8a^3}$.

24. $\sqrt[3]{-810}$.   **31.** $\sqrt{\frac{3}{5}}$.   **37.** $\sqrt[3]{\dfrac{3z^2}{4x}}$.   **43.** $\sqrt[4]{36x^{2n}}$.

25. $\sqrt[3]{-32}$.   **32.** $\sqrt[3]{\frac{3}{5}}$.   **44.** $\sqrt[8]{81x^{12}y^6}$.

26. $\sqrt[5]{-128}$.   **33.** $\sqrt[3]{-\frac{5}{9}}$.   **38.** $\sqrt{28x^4y^3}$.   **45.** $\sqrt{x^3\sqrt[3]{x^2}}$.

27. $\sqrt{16 \cdot 10^8}$.   **34.** $\sqrt{\frac{27}{8}}$.   **39.** $\sqrt{9x^8y^{-7}}$.

46. $\sqrt[3]{x^3\sqrt{y}}$.   **47.** $\sqrt[3]{x\sqrt[5]{y\sqrt{z}}}$.   **48.** $\sqrt[3]{a^{-5}\sqrt[5]{a^4\sqrt{a^{-7}}}}$.

Write as radicals with coefficient 1:

49. $5\sqrt{3}$.   **51.** $a\sqrt[3]{b}$.   **53.** $\dfrac{9c^3}{d^2}\sqrt{\dfrac{d^2}{9c^3}}$.

50. $\dfrac{2}{x}\sqrt[3]{5}$.   **52.** $\dfrac{x}{y}\sqrt{\dfrac{y}{x}}$.   **54.** $\frac{2}{3}x^2\sqrt[n]{a^2b^{2n}}$.

Change to radicals of the same order:

55. $\sqrt{a}$, $\sqrt[3]{b}$, $\sqrt[6]{c}$.   **58.** $\sqrt[4]{\frac{1}{3}x^3}$, $\sqrt[3]{\frac{1}{2}x^2}$, $\sqrt[6]{\frac{1}{5}x^5}$.

56. $\sqrt{2}$, $\sqrt[3]{3}$, $\sqrt[4]{5}$.   **59.** $3a^{\frac{1}{4}}$, $(3a)^{\frac{1}{2}}$, $\frac{1}{2}a^{\frac{1}{3}}$.

57. $\sqrt[6]{\frac{5}{4}}$, $\sqrt[3]{\frac{4}{3}}$, $\sqrt{\frac{3}{2}}$.   **60.** $2x^{\frac{5}{6}}$, $(3x)^{\frac{4}{3}}$, $x^{\frac{1}{2}}$.

Evaluate, first removing as many factors as possible from under the radicals:

61. $\sqrt{3240}$.   **63.** $\sqrt[3]{135}$.   **65.** $\sqrt{7290}$.   **67.** $\sqrt{0.441}$.

62. $\sqrt{2420}$.   **64.** $\sqrt[3]{686}$.   **66.** $\sqrt{0.4356}$.   **68.** $\sqrt[3]{4.48}$.

69. A freely falling body in a vacuum falls s feet in $t = \sqrt{2s/g}$ seconds where $g \approx 32$ feet per second per second. Find t when s is **(a)** 50 feet; **(b)** 100 feet; **(c)** 1000 feet.

70. In analyzing alternating current electricity, the maximum voltage E must be divided by $\sqrt{2}$ to obtain the average voltage $\bar{E}$. Find $\bar{E}$ if E is 155 volts.

71. The speed of a sound wave is $\sqrt{E/p}$ where E is the elasticity and p the density of the medium through which it is passing. Find the approximate speed of sound in centimeters per second **(a)** in water with $E = 2.25 \cdot 10^{10}$ and $p = 1.0$; **(b)** in alcohol with $E = 1.32 \cdot 10^{10}$ and $p = 0.79$.

72. According to Einstein's special theory of relativity, the relation between the mass m of a moving object and its mass m_0 when at rest is given by $m = m_0/\sqrt{1 - v^2/c^2}$ where v is the speed of the object and c is the speed of light. Find m/m_0 if an object is moving at **(a)** one-half, **(b)** one-tenth, of the speed of light.

73. Show that Law III of radicals in the text of this section is a consequence of the laws of exponents in § 1-6.

74. Show that Law IV of radicals in the text of this section is a consequence of the laws of exponents in § 1-6.

3-5   Operations on Radicals

Radicals having the **same index** and the **same radicand** are called **like radicals,** and can be added or subtracted in the same way as any other like expressions. The algebraic sum of **unlike radicals** can only be indicated. When radicals are reduced to simplest form, they can immediately be recognized as like or unlike.

EXAMPLE 1.   Find the algebraic sum $\sqrt{24} - \sqrt{\frac{2}{3}} - \sqrt[3]{\frac{2}{9}}$.

Solution.

$$\sqrt{24} - \sqrt{\tfrac{2}{3}} - \sqrt[3]{\tfrac{2}{9}} = \sqrt{4 \cdot 6} - \sqrt{\tfrac{2}{3} \cdot \tfrac{3}{3}} - \sqrt[3]{\tfrac{2}{9} \cdot \tfrac{3}{3}} = 2\sqrt{6} - \tfrac{1}{3}\sqrt{6} - \tfrac{1}{3}\sqrt[3]{6}$$

$$= (2 - \tfrac{1}{3})\sqrt{6} - \tfrac{1}{3}\sqrt[3]{6} = \tfrac{5}{3}\sqrt{6} - \tfrac{1}{3}\sqrt[3]{6}.$$

When a decimal approximation for the value of a sum of radicals is desired, it is usually easier to reduce the radicals to simplest form first, to combine like radicals, and then to consult the necessary tables.

The product of two radicals of the same order (that is, with equal indices) is found directly from the identity $\sqrt[n]{a}\sqrt[n]{b} = \sqrt[n]{ab}$, where $a > 0$ and $b > 0$. The product of two or more radicals of different orders can be found in the same way after the radicals have been expressed as equivalent radicals of the same order.

ILLUSTRATIONS. $\sqrt{14}\sqrt{\tfrac{2}{3}} = \sqrt{14 \cdot \tfrac{2}{3}} = \sqrt{\tfrac{28}{3}} = \sqrt{4 \cdot \tfrac{7}{3} \cdot \tfrac{3}{3}} = \tfrac{2}{3}\sqrt{21}.$

$$\sqrt[3]{12}\sqrt{10} = 12^{\frac{1}{3}} \cdot 10^{\frac{1}{2}} = 12^{\frac{2}{6}} \cdot 10^{\frac{3}{6}} = \sqrt[6]{12^2 \cdot 10^3}$$

$$= \sqrt[6]{(2^2 \cdot 3)^2 \cdot (2 \cdot 5)^3} = \sqrt[6]{2^4 \cdot 3^2 \cdot 2^3 \cdot 5^3}$$

$$= \sqrt[6]{2^6 \cdot 2 \cdot 3^2 \cdot 5^3} = 2\sqrt[6]{2 \cdot 9 \cdot 125} = 2\sqrt[6]{2250}.$$

$$(\sqrt{3} + 2\sqrt{2})(3\sqrt{3} - \sqrt{2}) = \sqrt{3} \cdot 3\sqrt{3} - \sqrt{3}\sqrt{2} + 6\sqrt{2}\sqrt{3} - 2\sqrt{2}\sqrt{2}$$

$$= 3 \cdot 3 - \sqrt{6} + 6\sqrt{6} - 2 \cdot 2$$

$$= 5 + 5\sqrt{6}.$$

The quotient of one radical by another is generally expressed in fractional form, and fractions involving radicals are considered to be in simplest form when the denominators are free of radicals. Hence the process of division generally becomes one of changing a fraction to an equivalent form where the denominator is free of radicals. This latter process is called **rationalizing the denominator.**

If the product of two radical expressions is free of radicals, each is called a **rationalizing factor** of the other. Thus $\sqrt{2}$ is a rationalizing factor of $\sqrt{8}$, and $a\sqrt{x} + b\sqrt{y}$ is a rationalizing factor of $a\sqrt{x} - b\sqrt{y}$. In rationalizing the denominator of a fraction, we multiply both numerator and denominator of the fraction by a rationalizing factor of the denominator.

EXAMPLE 2. Divide $\sqrt{2}$ by $3\sqrt{3}$.

Solution. $\quad \dfrac{\sqrt{2}}{3\sqrt{3}} = \dfrac{\sqrt{2}}{3\sqrt{3}} \cdot \dfrac{\sqrt{3}}{\sqrt{3}} = \dfrac{\sqrt{6}}{3 \cdot 3}$, or $\frac{1}{9}\sqrt{6}$.

EXAMPLE 3. Divide $\sqrt[3]{2}$ by $\sqrt[4]{27}$.

Solution. $\quad \dfrac{\sqrt[3]{2}}{\sqrt[4]{27}} = \dfrac{2^{\frac{1}{3}}}{3^{\frac{3}{4}}} = \dfrac{2^{\frac{4}{12}}}{3^{\frac{9}{12}}} = \sqrt[12]{\dfrac{2^4}{3^9}} = \sqrt[12]{\dfrac{2^4}{3^9} \cdot \dfrac{3^3}{3^3}} = \dfrac{\sqrt[12]{432}}{3}$, or $\frac{1}{3}\sqrt[12]{432}$.

EXAMPLE 4. Rationalize the denominator of $\dfrac{\sqrt{2} - 3\sqrt{3}}{2\sqrt{2} - \sqrt{3}}$.

Solution. $\quad \dfrac{\sqrt{2} - 3\sqrt{3}}{2\sqrt{2} - \sqrt{3}} = \dfrac{\sqrt{2} - 3\sqrt{3}}{2\sqrt{2} - \sqrt{3}} \cdot \dfrac{2\sqrt{2} + \sqrt{3}}{2\sqrt{2} + \sqrt{3}}$

$$= \dfrac{4 - 5\sqrt{6} - 9}{8 - 3} = \dfrac{-5 - 5\sqrt{6}}{5} = -1 - \sqrt{6}.$$

EXERCISES

Express the following in simplest radical form and in decimal form to the accuracy allowed by Table I:

1. $3\sqrt{3} - 5\sqrt{12} + 5\sqrt{27}$.

2. $2\sqrt{5} + \sqrt{45} - \sqrt{125}$.

3. $5\sqrt{\frac{1}{2}} + \frac{3}{2}\sqrt{18} + \sqrt{98}$.

4. $5\sqrt{\frac{3}{10}} - 2\sqrt{\frac{5}{6}} - 6\sqrt{\frac{15}{32}}$.

5. $\sqrt[3]{32} + 5\sqrt[3]{\frac{1}{16}} - 3\sqrt[3]{-\frac{1}{2}}$.

6. $3\sqrt[3]{54} - 7\sqrt[3]{-32} - \sqrt[3]{\frac{1}{2}}$.

7. $\frac{3}{2}\sqrt{24}\sqrt{72}$.

8. $\frac{1}{3}\sqrt[3]{18} \cdot 4\sqrt[3]{24}$.

9. $2\sqrt{6} \div \sqrt{12}$.

10. $3\sqrt{5} \div 5\sqrt{2}$.

11. $2\sqrt{3} \div 3\sqrt{2}$.

12. $\sqrt{\frac{3}{5}} \div \sqrt{\frac{5}{3}}$.

13. $\sqrt{\frac{3}{2}}(\sqrt{\frac{2}{3}} - \sqrt{\frac{3}{2}})$.

14. $\sqrt{\frac{5}{3}}(\frac{1}{5}\sqrt{5} - \frac{1}{3}\sqrt{3})$.

15. $(5\sqrt{3} + \sqrt{2})(5\sqrt{3} - \sqrt{2})$.

16. $(3\sqrt{5} + 5\sqrt{3})^2$.

17. Find the simplest rationalizing factor for each of the following:
(a) $\sqrt{5}$; (b) $\sqrt{12}$; (c) $\sqrt{\frac{1}{3}}$; (d) $\sqrt{\frac{3}{8}}$; (e) $\sqrt{0.08}$.

18. Note that $a\sqrt{x} + b\sqrt{y}$ is a rationalizing factor for $a\sqrt{x} - b\sqrt{y}$, and find the simplest rationalizing factor for:

(a) $2 - \sqrt{3}$;   **(b)** $2\sqrt{3} - 1$;   **(c)** $2\sqrt{5} + \sqrt{6}$;   **(d)** $\sqrt{12} - \sqrt{3}$.

Perform the indicated operations and simplify:

19. $a\sqrt{a} - \sqrt{ab^4} - b\sqrt{a^3}$.

21. $\sqrt{\dfrac{2x}{y}} - 4\sqrt{\dfrac{y}{2x^3}} - 3\sqrt{\frac{1}{8}x^3y}$.

20. $x\sqrt{2y} - \sqrt{8x^2y^3} + \frac{1}{3}x\sqrt{18y}$.

22. $\frac{3}{2}\sqrt[3]{16} - \frac{2}{3}\sqrt[3]{4\frac{1}{2}} - \frac{1}{4}\sqrt{72}$.

23. $\frac{5}{6}\sqrt{\frac{15}{7}}\sqrt{12}\sqrt{\frac{7}{8}}$.   **30.** $(\frac{1}{2}\sqrt[3]{9}\sqrt{3})^4$.

37. $\sqrt{x}(y\sqrt{x} - x\sqrt{y})$.

24. $\frac{1}{3}\sqrt{\frac{63}{10}} \cdot \frac{5}{6}\sqrt{\frac{6}{7}}$.   **31.** $\sqrt{10}(2\sqrt{5} - 5\sqrt{2})$.

38. $\sqrt[3]{4x^2} \div \sqrt[3]{\frac{1}{2}x}$.

25. $\frac{1}{10}\sqrt[3]{20x}\sqrt[3]{50x^2}$.   **32.** $\sqrt{6}(3\sqrt{2} - 2\sqrt{3})$.

39. $\sqrt[4]{x^3y^5} \div 3\sqrt[4]{xy}$.

26. $\frac{1}{6}\sqrt[3]{3x^2}\sqrt[3]{54x^4}$.   **33.** $\sqrt{\frac{2}{3}}(\frac{1}{2}\sqrt{3} - \frac{1}{3}\sqrt{2})$.

40. $\sqrt[4]{2a} \div \frac{1}{3}\sqrt[4]{8a^5}$.

27. $(7\sqrt{3})^2$.   **34.** $(3 + \sqrt{2})^2$.

41. $\sqrt[3]{3x^2y} \div \sqrt[3]{81x^5y^4}$.

28. $(2\sqrt[3]{13})^3$.   **35.** $\sqrt{\frac{3}{5}}(\sqrt{1\frac{2}{3}} + \sqrt{\frac{3}{5}})$.

42. $\sqrt{x^3\sqrt[3]{x}} \div \sqrt{y}$.

29. $(\frac{4}{5}\sqrt{5}\sqrt[3]{4})^2$.   **36.** $(x + y\sqrt{z})^2$.

43. $\sqrt{ab} \div \sqrt[3]{b\sqrt{a}}$.

44. $(2\sqrt{3} + 5)(2\sqrt{3} - 2)$.

50. $\dfrac{\sqrt{3}}{4 - \sqrt{3}}$.

45. $(2\sqrt{3} - 5)(2\sqrt{3} + 5)$.

51. $\dfrac{\sqrt{7} - \sqrt{2}}{\sqrt{7} + \sqrt{2}}$.

46. $(\sqrt{x} - 3\sqrt{y})(2\sqrt{x} + \sqrt{y})$.

47. $(x\sqrt{6} - 2y\sqrt{2})(3x\sqrt{6} - 5y\sqrt{2})$.

52. $\dfrac{x\sqrt{3} - 4y\sqrt{5}}{2x\sqrt{5} + 3y\sqrt{3}}$.

48. $\sqrt{3 + 2\sqrt{2}} \cdot \sqrt{3 - 2\sqrt{2}}$.

53. $\dfrac{3x\sqrt{2} + y\sqrt{6}}{4x\sqrt{2} - 3y\sqrt{6}}$.

49. $\sqrt{\sqrt{21} + \sqrt{5}} \cdot \sqrt{\sqrt{21} - \sqrt{5}}$.

54. $(\sqrt{5} - \sqrt{3})(\sqrt{7} - 2)(\sqrt{5} + \sqrt{3})$.

55. $(1 + \sqrt{2} - \sqrt{3})(1 + \sqrt{2} + \sqrt{3})$.

56. $(3 - \sqrt{2} - \sqrt{5})(3 - \sqrt{2} + \sqrt{5})$.

57. $\sqrt{\dfrac{x - y}{x + y}} + 2\sqrt{\dfrac{x + y}{x - y}} - \sqrt{\dfrac{36x^2}{x^2 - y^2}}$.

58. Find the value of $(3x^2 - 2x - 1)$ when x is

   (a) $\sqrt{5}$;   **(b)** $1 + \sqrt{2}$;   **(c)** $\frac{1}{2}(2 - \sqrt{3})$.

59. The resonant frequency f, in cycles per second, of an oscillatory electric circuit with resistance R ohms, inductance L henrys, and capacitance C farads is given by

$$f = \frac{1}{4\pi} \sqrt{\frac{4}{LC} - \frac{R^2}{L^2}}.$$

Find the value of f to the accuracy permitted by Table I if $R = 5$, $C = 35 \cdot 10^{-12}$, and $L = 5 \cdot 10^{-6}$.

3-6   Simple Equations

Two expressions are **equal** if they stand for the same number. Thus $2(x + 4) = 2x + 8$ by the distributive law (§ 1-5); $\frac{16}{12} = \frac{4}{3}$ by the fundamental principle of fractions (§ 2-7). Such a statement of equality is called an **equation** if (unlike the above examples) the two expressions are not always equal but rather are equal only for some of the values of the literal number symbols involved. The two expressions are called **members** of the equation. Equations will be studied further in Chapter 5. Meanwhile some simple ones will be considered.

The equation $x = 4$ is an assertion that the literal number symbol x stands for the number 4. If we multiply that number by 2, the result is 8 and may be represented either by $2x$ or by 2×4. In other words, if $x = 4$ then $2x = 2 \times 4$. Similar reasoning may be used to establish each of the following principles for equations:

If $a = b$, and c is any number, then

$$a + c = b + c \quad \text{and} \quad a - c = b - c.$$

If $a = b$, and $c \neq 0$, then

$$ac = bc \quad \text{and} \quad a \div c = b \div c.$$

Note that for division, $c \neq 0$ is required by § 2-4; for multiplication, the statement as made would be true even if $c = 0$ but this is to be avoided for reasons which will be discussed in § 5-4.

These principles may be stated in words:

(i) If the same number is added to (or subtracted from) both members of an equation, the sums (or differences, respectively) are equal.

(ii) If both members of an equation are multiplied (or divided) by the same number different from zero, the products (quotients) are equal.

These principles are used to **solve** simple equations; that is, to find the values of the literal number symbol for which the expressions are indeed equal. (In this context, a literal number symbol is often called an *unknown*, as in § 1-2.) This is done by rewriting the equation in the form $x = k$.

EXAMPLE 1.   Find x if $3x = 7$.

Solution.   Dividing both members by 3, we have

$$\frac{3x}{3} = \frac{7}{3},$$

or

$$x = \frac{7}{3}.$$

EXAMPLE 2.   Solve $2x + 5 = 7x + 8$.

Solution.   Subtracting $7x$ and 5 from both members, we get all terms involving the unknown in one member of the equation and the constant terms in the other member. Then like terms are combined as in § 2-1:

$$2x + 5 - 7x - 5 = 7x + 8 - 7x - 5;$$
$$-5x = 3;$$
$$x = \frac{3}{-5} = -\frac{3}{5}.$$

When an answer has been obtained, its correctness can be checked by substituting this value for the unknown in the original equation and by seeing then whether the two members have the same value.

EXAMPLE 2 (*continued*).

Check.   If $x = -\frac{3}{5}$, then

$$2x + 5 = 2(-\tfrac{3}{5}) + 5 = -\tfrac{6}{5} + \tfrac{25}{5} = \tfrac{19}{5},$$
$$7x + 8 = 7(-\tfrac{3}{5}) + 8 = -\tfrac{21}{5} + \tfrac{40}{5} = \tfrac{19}{5}.$$

Thus the answer $-\frac{3}{5}$ checks.

EXERCISES

Solve and check:

1. $3x = 12$.

2. $4x = 20$.

3. $2x = -10$.

4. $5x = -5$.

5. $2x = \frac{1}{3}$.

6. $\frac{1}{2}x = 5$.

7. $\frac{3}{4}y = -\frac{4}{5}$.

8. $\frac{3}{2}z = -\frac{6}{7}$.

9. $3x + 5 = 0$.

10. $3u - 7 = 0$.

11. $5x + 2 = 8x - 6$.

12. $4x + 5 = 7x - 17$.

13. $3x - 1 = x + 5.$ **18.** $x\sqrt{6} = 5\sqrt{2}.$ **23.** $c^2dw = cd^3.$

14. $4 - y = 10 - 3y.$ **19.** $x/\sqrt{2} = 3/\sqrt{10}.$ **24.** $y - \sqrt{2} = 1 - \sqrt{2}y.$

15. $6 - 5y = 7 + y.$ **20.** $ax = b.$ **25.** $z\sqrt{5} - 3 = z + 1.$

16. $3n + 2 = 2n.$ **21.** $cy = -d.$ **26.** $\frac{3}{4}x - \frac{1}{6} = 2 + \frac{4}{3}x.$

17. $x\sqrt{2} = 3\sqrt{10}.$ **22.** $a^2x = a^5.$ **27.** $\frac{1}{2}y + \frac{1}{8} = \frac{2}{3} - \frac{1}{4}y.$

28. The curved (or lateral) surface S of a right circular cylinder with altitude h and base of radius r is given by $S = 2\pi rh$. Solve for r.

29. A retailer sells at a price R in dollars which is n percent greater than the wholesale price W in dollars. Represent **(a)** R in terms of W and n; **(b)** W as a fraction of R; **(c)** his gross profit G as a fraction of W; **(d)** his gross profit as a fraction of R; **(e)** his net profit N per item in terms of W if his selling costs are $5 per item.

3-7   Proportion

The **ratio** *of a number* a *to a second number* b *is the quotient* a/b. The ratio of *a* to *b* is also sometimes denoted by $a : b$, which is read "*a* is to *b*." Since a ratio may be expressed as a fraction, the rules applying to fractions also apply to ratios.

Every measurement is a ratio of the magnitude of the quantity measured to the unit of measure. For example, when we speak of the wheelbase of a certain automobile as 125 inches, we mean that the ratio of the distance between the centers of the front and the rear axle to the unit of length used, the inch, is $125 : 1$.

A **proportion** *is a statement of the equality of two ratios.* Thus

$$a : b = c : d, \quad \text{also written in the form} \quad a/b = c/d,$$

is a proportion. It is read "*a* is to *b* as *c* is to *d*." Since proportions are equations, the rules and operations that apply to equations also apply to proportions.

In the proportion $a : b = c : d$, the terms *a* and *d* are the **extremes,** *b* and *c* the **means,** and *d* is the **fourth proportional** to *a*, *b*, and *c*. In the proportion $a : b = b : c$, the term *c* is the **third proportional** to *a* and *b*, and *b* is a **mean proportional** between *a* and *c*.

By means of the operations of algebra it is possible to transform a proportion into a variety of forms. One of the properties of proportions is derived in Example 2. Other properties are illustrated in the exercises.

EXAMPLE 1.   Find the fourth proportional to 3, 6, and 9.

Solution.   Given $3:6 = 9:x$; that is, $\dfrac{3}{6} = \dfrac{9}{x}$.

Multiplying both members by $6x$, we have

$$3x = 54,$$
$$x = 18.$$

EXAMPLE 2.   Given $a:b = c:d$, prove that $(a + b):b = (c + d):d$.

Proof.   Given: $\dfrac{a}{b} = \dfrac{c}{d}$.

Add 1 to each member: $\dfrac{a}{b} + 1 = \dfrac{c}{d} + 1$.

Reduce to fractional form: $\dfrac{a + b}{b} = \dfrac{c + d}{d}$.

Change the form: $(a + b):b = (c + d):d$.

This new proportion is said to be obtained from the original proportion by **composition.** This proportion and the proportions in Exercises 16 through 21 of the following set of exercises are often considered as theorems in plane geometry. Further problems in proportion will arise as exercises on equations, Chapter 5.

EXERCISES

1. Test whether 4 is (**a**) the fourth proportional to 1, 2, and 3; (**b**) the fourth proportional to $\frac{1}{2}$, 1, and 2; (**c**) a mean proportional between 2 and 8.

Solve for x:

2. $x:4 = 5:8$.   **8.** $0.02:0.1 = x:64$.

3. $x:2 = -8:3$.   **9.** $0.007:0.01 = x:3.4$.

4. $x:a = a^4:b$.   **10.** $x:1 = 8:64$.

5. $b:c = x:c^3$.   **11.** $x:0.1 = 7:12$.

6. $0.2:1 = x:64$.   **12.** $x:(a + b) = (a - b):(a^2 - b^2)$.

7. $0.7:1 = x:3.4$.   **13.** $x:(a^2 + ab) = (ab - b^2):ab$.

14. Find the third proportional to (**a**) 5 and 10; (**b**) 6 and 8; (**c**) r and s; (**d**) x^2y and xy.

15. Find the fourth proportional to (**a**) 3, 4, and 5; (**b**) $\frac{1}{2}$, $\frac{1}{4}$, and $\frac{1}{12}$; (**c**) a, b, and c; (**d**) a^2b, ab, and ac.

If a : b = c : d, *and if each denominator involved is different from zero, prove the following propositions:*

16. $ad = bc$; product of the means equals product of the extremes.

17. $b : a = d : c$; proportion by inversion.

18. $a : c = b : d$; proportion by alternation.

19. $(a + b) : a = (c + d) : c$; a form of proportion by composition.

20. $(a - b) : b = (c - d) : d$; proportion by division.

21. $(a + b) : (a - b) = (c + d) : (c - d)$; proportion by composition and division.

22. On a certain map $\frac{1}{5}$ inch represents 1 mile. (**a**) What distance represents 2.5 miles? (**b**) How many miles does 10 inches represent?

23. Two cities 450 miles apart are represented by points 6.0 inches apart on a certain map. How far apart are sites which are represented by points 3.5 inches apart on the map?

24. In similar triangles, corresponding sides are proportional. One triangle has sides 12, 9, and 5. A similar triangle has corresponding sides 16, x, and y. Find x and y.

25. A vertical yardstick has a shadow 18 inches long at the same time that a certain tree has a shadow 24 feet long, both on level ground. Find the height of the tree.

★26. The ratio of the surfaces of two cubes is $50 : 8$. Find the ratio of (**a**) their edges; (**b**) their volumes.

3-8   Interpolation

It has already been seen (§ 1-6 and § 3-2) that Table I yields values of certain powers and roots of two-digit numbers. We next consider a method which yields, to a good approximation, values of these same powers and roots of numbers with one more digit. The method is widely applicable; it will be encountered again in § 4-8, and in Chapters 6 and 7 in connection with logarithmic and trigonometric functions.

In this method, called **linear interpolation,** it is assumed that the change in the value of the power or root of N is proportional to the change in N, in the following sense. Suppose N_1, N_2, N_3 are three values of N, and k is some exponent (an integer or fraction). Then when we change N from N_1 to N_2, the algebraic amount of the change in N is

$(N_2 - N_1)$ while the change in the power is $(N_2{}^k - N_1{}^k)$. Similarly if N is changed from N_1 to N_3 the change in N is $(N_3 - N_1)$ and in the power is $(N_3{}^k - N_1{}^k)$. Suppose N_1, N_2, and N_3 are nearly equal; then, approximately,

$$(N_2{}^k - N_1{}^k) : (N_3{}^k - N_1{}^k) \approx (N_2 - N_1) : (N_3 - N_1). \qquad (1)$$

If N_1, N_2, and N_3 are given, and if $N_1{}^k$ and $N_3{}^k$ are known (for instance, from a table), then $N_2{}^k$ can be found as shown in the following illustration. The difference (in this case, $N_3{}^k - N_1{}^k$) between the adjacent tabulated values is called the **tabular difference**. A geometric interpretation of interpolation will be considered in § 4-8.

ILLUSTRATION.   To find $\sqrt{60.6}$ from Table I, first note the nearest square roots obtainable directly from Table I: $\sqrt{60} \approx 7.746$ and $\sqrt{61} \approx 7.810$. Then $\sqrt{60.6}$ is to be found and will be denoted by x. However, x is found indirectly by first finding c where $c = \sqrt{60.6} - \sqrt{60}$; that is, $x - \sqrt{60} = c$ or, equivalently, $x = c + \sqrt{60}$. The facts are shown in tabular form in the box. The tabular difference d is 0.064.

Changes in N	N	$\sqrt{N}$	Changes in $\sqrt{N}$
$1 \left[0.6 \left[\right. \right.$	60	7.746	$\left. \left. \right] c \right] d = 0.064$
	60.6	$7.746 + c$	
	61	7.810	

Then the proportion (1) becomes

$$c : 0.064 \approx 0.6 : 1$$

or

$$\frac{c}{0.064} \approx \frac{0.6}{1} = 0.6.$$

Then, as in § 3-6,

$$c \approx 0.6 \cdot 0.064 = 0.0384, \qquad (2)$$

$$x \approx 7.746 + 0.0384 \approx 7.784.$$

From more extensive tables, a more accurate answer is 7.7846. Linear interpolation gives only an approximately correct answer. It is usually only safe to interpolate for one more digit of N than appears in the table; thus c is treated as having only one significant digit. Accordingly, in this illustration, x should be rounded off to the nearest hundredth:

$$\sqrt{60.6} \approx 7.78.$$

With practice, interpolation to this accuracy can be done mentally or at least with very little of the detailed writing which is shown for clarity in the illustration. Alternatively, a table of **proportional parts,** Table X on pages 468 and 469, can be used. This table shows, for various tenths such as 0.6, the product of such a factor (denoted by n) and various numbers by which n may be multiplied. Thus in Table X, in the column headed "64" and the row labeled "0.6" we find $0.6 \cdot 64 = 38.4$; by adjusting the decimal point one obtains the product needed in (2).

EXERCISES

Verify by linear interpolation in Table I:

1. $(3.82)^2 \approx 14.6.$　　**3.** $\sqrt{32.1} \approx 5.67.$　　**5.** $\sqrt[3]{2790} \approx 14.08.$

2. $(0.516)^3 \approx 0.137.$　　**4.** $\sqrt{8.45} \approx 2.907.$　　**6.** $1/2790 \approx 0.000358.$

Find by linear interpolation in Table I:

7. $(4.38)^2.$　　　　**14.** $\sqrt{0.0176}.$　　　　**21.** $1/1.88.$

8. $(0.483)^2.$　　　　**15.** $\sqrt[3]{0.0162}.$　　　　**22.** $1/273.$

9. $(39.4)^3.$　　　　**16.** $\sqrt[3]{0.288}.$　　　　**23.** $1/0.457.$

10. $(2.86)^3.$　　　　**17.** $\sqrt[3]{70.9}.$　　　　**24.** $1/0.0524.$

11. $\sqrt{21.1}.$　　　　**18.** $\sqrt[3]{0.000\ 008\ 17}.$　　**25.** $1/0.00371.$

12. $\sqrt{20.9}.$　　　　**19.** $\sqrt[3]{9410}.$　　　　**26.** $1/(-13,900).$

13. $\sqrt{1.67}.$　　　　**20.** $\sqrt[3]{84,500}.$　　　　**27.** $1/(-3.46).$

28. In an evolving language, the fraction p of words which remain substantially unchanged after n millenia (thousands of years) is given approximately by $p \approx (0.864)^n$. Find p after (**a**) 2000 years; (**b**) 3000 years.

★29. Discuss whether the statements about significant digits in this section, related to equations (1) and (2), give the same results as the rule of thumb about significant digits stated in § 1-9, and why. Suggested examples: $(0.516)^3$; $\sqrt[3]{2710}$; $\sqrt[3]{2790}$.

3-9　Complex Numbers

In problems involving radicals we often meet symbols of the form $\sqrt{-b}$ where $b > 0$. The square of a number represented by such a symbol must be negative:

$$(\sqrt{-b})^2 = [(-b)^{\frac{1}{2}}]^2 = (-b)^1 = -b.$$

However, the square of any real number (positive, negative, or zero) must be a positive number or zero. Accordingly, we must extend our concept of a number beyond that of a real number if symbols of the form $\sqrt{-b}$, $b > 0$, are to represent numbers.

The symbol $\sqrt{-1}$, called the **imaginary unit** and usually designated by *i*, represents a new kind of number with the property that

$$i^2 = (\sqrt{-1})^2 = -1.$$

Then for any positive real number *N* we have

$$\sqrt{-N} = \sqrt{i^2 N} = i\sqrt{N};$$

that is, the square root of any negative number can be expressed as the product of a real number and the number *i*. Any number of the form $\pm bi$ (or $\pm ib$), where *b* is a real number, is called a **pure imaginary number.**

ILLUSTRATION 1. $-\sqrt{-9} = -\sqrt{9(-1)} = -\sqrt{9} \cdot \sqrt{-1} = -3i$;

and $\pm\sqrt{-5} = \pm\sqrt{5(-1)} = \pm\sqrt{5} \cdot \sqrt{-1} = \pm i\sqrt{5}.$

Therefore $-\sqrt{-9}$ and $\pm\sqrt{-5}$ are pure imaginary numbers.

The sum of a real number and a pure imaginary number—that is, *a number of the form* (a + bi) *where* a *and* b *are real numbers*—*is called a* **complex number.** The number *a* is called the **real part** and *bi* is called the **imaginary part** of the complex number. The name **imaginary number** (or **mixed imaginary number**) is given to the complex number (*a* + *bi*) when $b \neq 0$. When $a = 0$ but $b \neq 0$, (*a* + *bi*) reduces to the form *bi* and, as above, is called a pure imaginary number. When $b = 0$, (*a* + *bi*) reduces to the real number *a*. Thus it can be seen that real numbers, pure imaginary numbers, and imaginary numbers are all particular kinds of complex numbers. They are numbers in the complex number system.

ILLUSTRATION 2. $(3 - 5i), (-\sqrt{3} + 2i)$, and $(-\sqrt{5} - i\sqrt{2})$ are imaginary numbers, $-3i$ and $2i\sqrt{7}$ are pure imaginary numbers, 5, $\sqrt[3]{-3}$, and $-\sqrt{2}$ are real numbers; all these are complex numbers.

Complex numbers that differ only in the signs of their imaginary parts are called **conjugate complex numbers,** and either one is called the conjugate of the other.

ILLUSTRATION 3. $(a + bi)$ and $(a - bi)$ are conjugate complex numbers, as are also bi and $-bi$. A real number is its own conjugate.

If i is raised to successive positive integral powers, we obtain

$$i = \sqrt{-1}; \quad i^2 = -1; \quad i^3 = i^2 \cdot i = (-1)i = -i;$$
$$i^4 = i^2 \cdot i^2 = (-1)(-1) = 1; \quad i^5 = i^4 \cdot i = (1)i = i;$$
$$i^6 = i^4 \cdot i^2 = (1)(-1) = -1; \quad \text{and so on.}$$

Thus the successive positive integral powers of i have only four different values: i, -1, $-i$, 1, repeating in regular order.

Warning.   In all problems involving imaginary numbers each imaginary number should first be expressed in the form $(a + bi)$. Then proceed according to the usual rules of algebra and substitute $i^2 = -1$. For example, if a and b are positive real numbers,

$$\sqrt{-a}\sqrt{-b} = i\sqrt{a} \cdot i\sqrt{b} = i^2 \cdot \sqrt{ab} = -\sqrt{ab},$$

but $\qquad\qquad \sqrt{-a}\sqrt{-b} \neq \sqrt{(-a)(-b)}, \quad \text{or} \quad \sqrt{ab}.$

Thus, the law of radicals, $\sqrt{a}\sqrt{b} = \sqrt{ab}$, holds only when either a or b is not negative; $\sqrt{a}\sqrt{b} = \sqrt{ab}$ *if, and only if, either* $a \geq 0$ *or* $b \geq 0$.

EXAMPLE 1.   Simplify: $(i^4 - 2i^3 + 3i^2 - 5i + 4)^2$.

Solution.

$$
\begin{aligned}
(i^4 - 2i^3 + 3i^2 - 5i + 4)^2 &= [i^2 \cdot i^2 - 2i^2 \cdot i + 3(-1) - 5i + 4]^2 \\
&= [(-1)(-1) - 2(-1)i - 3 - 5i + 4]^2 \\
&= (1 + 2i - 3 - 5i + 4)^2 \\
&= (2 - 3i)^2 = 4 - 12i + 9i^2 \\
&= 4 - 12i + 9(-1) \\
&= -5 - 12i.
\end{aligned}
$$

EXAMPLE 2.   Simplify: $(3 - 2\sqrt{-2})(-1 + 5\sqrt{-2})$.

Solution.

$$
\begin{aligned}
(3 - 2\sqrt{-2})(-1 + 5\sqrt{-2}) &= (3 - 2i\sqrt{2})(-1 + 5i\sqrt{2}) \\
&= -3 + 15i\sqrt{2} + 2i\sqrt{2} - 10i^2(2) \\
&= -3 + 15i\sqrt{2} + 2i\sqrt{2} + 20 \\
&= 17 + 17i\sqrt{2}.
\end{aligned}
$$

EXAMPLE 3. Simplify: $\dfrac{3 - \sqrt{-5}}{3 + \sqrt{-5}}$.

Solution.

$$\frac{3 - \sqrt{-5}}{3 + \sqrt{-5}} = \frac{3 - i\sqrt{5}}{3 + i\sqrt{5}} \cdot \frac{3 - i\sqrt{5}}{3 - i\sqrt{5}}$$

$$= \frac{9 - 6i\sqrt{5} + 5i^2}{9 - 5i^2} = \frac{9 - 6i\sqrt{5} - 5}{9 + 5}$$

$$= \frac{4 - 6i\sqrt{5}}{14} = \frac{2 - 3i\sqrt{5}}{7} = \frac{2}{7} - \frac{3}{7}i\sqrt{5}.$$

EXERCISES

Simplify:

1. i^7.   **5.** i^{20}.   **9.** $(2 - i)^2$.   **13.** $(2 + 3i)(3 - 2i)$.

2. i^8.   **6.** i^{30}.   **10.** $(2 + 3i)^2$.   **14.** $(2 + 3i)/(3 - 2i)$.

3. i^9.   **7.** i^{71}.   **11.** $(1 - i)^3$.   **15.** $\sqrt{-i^6}$.

4. i^{14}.   **8.** i^{101}.   **12.** $i^3(2 + 3i)$.   **16.** $\sqrt[3]{-i^8}$.

Write in the form (a + bi) *and simplify:*

17. $3 + \sqrt{-2}$.   **21.** $-\sqrt{-16}$.

18. $3(1 - \sqrt{-5})$.   **22.** $\sqrt{-9a^2}$.

19. $-2(3 - \sqrt{-3})$.   **23.** $-9\sqrt{-\frac{25}{12}}$.

20. $\sqrt{-20}$.   **24.** $(\sqrt{-1} + \sqrt{3})^2$.

Perform the indicated operations and simplify to the form (a + bi):

25. $\sqrt{4} - \sqrt{-9} + \sqrt{-25}$.   **35.** $(4 - 5i)^2$.

26. $\sqrt{-81} + \sqrt{36} - \sqrt{16}$.   **36.** $(5 + \sqrt{-3})^2$.

27. $\sqrt{-3} + \sqrt{-12} - 5\sqrt{-18}$.   **37.** $(\sqrt{3} - \sqrt{-2})^2$.

28. $\sqrt{-27} - \sqrt{121} + \sqrt{12}$.   **38.** $(\sqrt{2} + i\sqrt{3})^2$.

29. $\sqrt{-2}(4 - \sqrt{-6})$.   **39.** $(2 - 3\sqrt{-5})(-3 + 2\sqrt{-5})$.

30. $\sqrt{-3}(3 + \sqrt{-12})$.   **40.** $(\sqrt{6} - \sqrt{-7})(2\sqrt{6} + \sqrt{-7})$.

31. $5\sqrt{-5}\sqrt{-10}\sqrt{-8}$.   **41.** $(i^3 - 4i^2)(3i^4 + i^7)$.

32. $-2\sqrt{-28}\sqrt{7}\sqrt{-14}$.   **42.** $(3i^4 - i^2 + 3)(5i - i^3)$.

33. $(3i\sqrt{5})^2$.   **43.** $(i^4 + 2i^3 - i^2 - 3)^2$.

34. $(-5i\sqrt{3})^2$.   **44.** $(1 + 2i + 3i^2 - 4i^5)^3$.

                45. $(6i^7 + 5i^5 - 4i^4 - 3i^3 + i^2 - 2i + 1)^4$.

Find the value of:

46. $3x^2 - x - 2$ when $x = 1 - i$.

47. $5x^2 + 7 - 2x$ when $x = -3 + 2i$.

48. $5 - 3x - 2x^2$ when $x = \frac{1}{2}(1 - i\sqrt{12})$.

49. $60x - 6 - 35x^2$ when $x = \frac{1}{5}(1 - i\sqrt{2})$.

Use the general form (a + bi) *to demonstrate:*

50. The sum of any complex number and its conjugate is a real number.

51. The product of any complex number and its conjugate is a real number.

*52. If a complex number and its conjugate are equal, the number is real.

CHAPTER 4

FUNCTIONS AND GRAPHS

4-1 Functions

As a direct consequence of the introduction of letters and other symbols to represent numbers, the various rules of arithmetic may be replaced by formulas in algebra. In these formulas, and in the other formulas of mathematics, physics, engineering, and other branches of science, some of the literal number symbols (§ 1-2) are constants and some are variables. Each formula expresses a relationship among the constants and variables involved.

In the formula $A = \pi r^2$, giving the area A of a circle in terms of its radius r, π is a constant, but r and A are variables, since they may have different values for different circles. This formula expresses a relationship between r and A, since to each value assigned to r there corresponds a definite value of A. For example, if $r = 1$ inch, then $A = \pi$ square inches; if $r = 3$ feet, then $A = 9\pi$ square feet; and so on. To specify such relationships, we make the following definition:

A variable y *is said to be* **a function of** *a variable* x *if corresponding to each value of* x *there is one and only one value of* y. *Then* x *is called the* **independent variable** *and* y *the* **dependent variable.**

The above discussion shows that the area of a circle is a function of its radius. Similarly, the circumference of a circle is a function of its diameter, the area of an equilateral triangle is a function of its side, the volume of a cube is a function of its edge, and the elongation of a particular spiral spring is a function of the applied force.

In the above definition of a function of a variable, the phrase "to each value of x" does not exclude the possibility of some limitation upon the set of values which may be assigned to x. For example, when it was said that the area of a circle was a function of the radius r of the circle, it was implied that only positive numbers (and possibly 0) were to be considered for values of r, since any other values for the radius of a circle are meaningless. The set of all possible values that may be assigned to the independent variable is called the **domain of the function**. As in the case of the radius of a circle, the domain is often implied rather than explicitly stated. If the domain is neither stated nor otherwise implied, it is customarily assumed to be the set of all real numbers.

For each of the functions cited above, the relationship can be expressed by an algebraic formula. This will be the case for most of the functions that we shall consider, but there are many functions which are not so expressible. For instance, the postage on a letter is a function of the weight of the letter; for any particular weight there is just one proper amount of postage, yet this amount is not expressible by an algebraic formula.

If a function can be written in the form of an algebraic expression (§ 2-1) involving only one variable, x, then the expression is called an **algebraic function** of x. A polynomial in x is often called a **polynomial function** of x; a quotient of polynomial functions is a rational expression in x and is often called a **rational function** of x. Other common types of functions are exponential functions, such as 2^x, and trigonometric functions, such as $\sin x$; see Chapters 6 and 7.

On the other hand, not every relation, even if algebraic in form, defines a function. Thus the equation $x^2 + y^2 = 4$ certainly states a relation between the values of x and the values of y, but corresponding to most values of x there are two values of y instead of only one as is required by the definition of a function. However, in each of the equations $y = \sqrt{4 - x^2}$ and $y = -\sqrt{4 - x^2}$, both of which are derived from the above relation, y is a function of x.

The student is cautioned that somewhat different usages of the word *function* are fairly common. Thus some mathematicians consider the *relation* to be the function, rather than considering the dependent variable to be a function of the independent variable, as we have done in our definition. Others modify the definition by permitting more than one value of y to correspond to a given value of x, as in $x^2 + y^2 = 4$; in such cases, even when it is inconvenient or impossible to solve for y in terms of x, the variable y is often called a "multivalued function" of x.

One extension of the concept of function will be stated here for future use. A variable z is said to be a **function of two variables** x and y if corresponding to each pair of values of x and y, respectively, there is one and only one value of z. Similar definitions may be made of functions of three, four, or more variables.

EXAMPLE.   Express the area A of a rectangle as a function of its base x, if the perimeter of the rectangle is 24 inches.

Solution.   Let y be the altitude of the rectangle in inches.

Then $A = xy$ and $2x + 2y = 24.$

From the second equation, $y = 12 - x$, and, if y in the first equation is replaced by this value, we obtain A as the required function of x, that is,

$$A = x(12 - x),$$

where $0 \leq x \leq 12$.

EXERCISES

1. The formula $P = 0.20n$ represents the profit P from selling n copies of a certain book. Assuming that 2500 copies of the book are for sale, identify the independent variable and the domain of the function.

2. The yearly depreciation D on an automobile is often taken as 20 percent of its value v at the beginning of the year. Does this involve a functional relationship? If so, identify the independent variable and the domain of the function.

3. Write down **(a)** a function of t; **(b)** a function of v; **(c)** the sum of a function of x and a function of z.

4. The amount of postage required within the United States on a first-class letter is a function of its weight. Specify the amount of postage required for a letter having each of the following weights in ounces: **(a)** 0.2; **(b)** 1.9; **(c)** 2.1; **(d)** 2.5; and **(e)** 5.1.

Find an expression for y *as a function of* x*:*

5. $x + y = 7.$ **7.** $3x + 2y = 5.$ **9.** $2x + 3 = 3y - 2.$

6. $y - x = -4.$ **8.** $4x - 5y = \frac{1}{2}.$ **10.** $x + 2y = y + 2x.$

Express each of the following verbal relationships as an algebraic formula, and specify the domain of the resulting function of the indicated variable:

11. The area A of a square as a function of its perimeter p.

12. The area A of a circle as a function of its circumference C.

13. The cost C in cents of x rolls at 68 cents per dozen as a function of x.

14. The present age A of a person who will be n years old six years from now.

15. The amount A of a task T done each hour by a person who works steadily and completes the whole task T in t hours.

16. The area A of a rectangular field of width w that can be exactly enclosed with 600 feet of fence.

17. The volume V and the inner surface S of an open rectangular box that can be formed by cutting equal squares of side x (measured in inches) from the corners of a sheet of cardboard 14 inches square.

18. One hundred feet of woven wire fencing is available to build a rectangular pen. If a stone wall already constructed is used as one side of the pen, express the area A of the pen as a function of the side s, measured in feet, that is parallel to the wall.

19. Four hundred feet of woven wire fencing is available to enclose a rectangular field and to build a fence parallel to one end that will divide the field into two parts. Find the area A of the field in terms of the length x of the fence, measured in feet.

4-2　Functional Notation

The fact that the volume V of a sphere is a function of its radius r is conveniently expressed by the **functional notation** $V = f(r)$. This equality is read "V equals the f-function of r" or, more briefly, as "V equals f of r," and it calls attention to the fact that the value of V depends on the value of r. From geometry we know the particular form of $f(r)$ in this case, namely, $f(r) = \frac{4}{3}\pi r^3$. We may therefore write

$$V = f(r) = \tfrac{4}{3}\pi r^3.$$

The first equality states that V is a function of r, and the second specifies a particular form of the function.

Warning. The symbol $f(x)$ does *not* mean f multiplied by x.

In any one discussion, the same functional symbol, such as $f(x)$, indicates the same law of dependence between the function $f(x)$ and its variable x. If different functional relationships occur in the same discussion, different prefixed letters should be used in order to distinguish between the relationships. However, in different discussions $f(x)$ may represent different functions of x. Symbols other than f that are frequently used in the functional notation include g, F, G, f', f_1, f_2, ϕ (read *phi*), θ (read *theta*), ψ (read *psi*), etc. In some cases, especially in complicated expressions, $f(x)$ is written $f[x]$.

ILLUSTRATION 1.   If $y = ax^2 + bx + c$, where a, b, and c are constants, then y is a function of x, which fact we may express in symbols by writing $y = g(x)$. If $z = x^2 + 5$, then we may write $z = h(x)$ where $h(x) = x^2 + 5$. Note that in all cases a statement such as $z = h(x)$ indicates the existence of a relationship but gives no details as to the particular form of the relationship.

For any particular function, $f(x)$ may be thought of as the value of that function at x. Thus, if the f-function denotes that the square of a number is to be increased by 5, then $f(3) = 3^2 + 5$, $f(2) = 2^2 + 5$, and $f(x) = x^2 + 5$. In general, whenever a particular form of $f(x)$ is known and a is any value of x, then

$f(a)$ represents the value of $f(x)$ when x is replaced by a.

ILLUSTRATION 2.   When $f(x) = x^2 + 4x - 2$, then
$$f(2) = (2)^2 + 4(2) - 2 = 4 + 8 - 2 = 10;$$
$$f(-\tfrac{1}{2}) = (-\tfrac{1}{2})^2 + 4(-\tfrac{1}{2}) - 2 = \tfrac{1}{4} - 2 - 2 = -\tfrac{15}{4};$$
$$f(-3a^2) = (-3a^2)^2 + 4(-3a^2) - 2 = 9a^4 - 12a^2 - 2;$$
$$[f(-1)]^2 = (1 - 4 - 2)^2 = (-5)^2 = 25.$$

This process should seem to students to be a natural one; for if x is replaced by some number a on one side of an equality, it is also replaced on the other side of the equality by the same number. Whenever a function $f(x)$ may be expressed by a sequence of algebraic operations upon x, then $f(2)$ may be obtained by performing that same sequence of operations upon 2, $f(b)$ may be obtained by performing that same sequence of operations upon b, and so on.

Functional notation is also used for functions of several variables. Thus in the formula for the volume V of a right circular cone in terms of its altitude h and the radius r of its base, $V = \tfrac{1}{3}\pi r^2 h$ and V is a function of two independent variables, r and h. This fact is expressed in symbols by the functional notation $V = f(r, h)$. This equality is read "V equals the f-function of r and h" or, more briefly, "V equals f of r and h." The equality indicates that the value of V depends upon the values of r and h.

EXAMPLE 1.   Express symbolically in functional notation the fact that the radius r of a sphere is a function of its surface S and then give its particular form. Evaluate this function for $S = 16\pi$.

Solution.   In functional notation, we may write $r = f(S)$. Since $S = 4\pi r^2$, we obtain, upon solving for r, $r = \tfrac{1}{2}\sqrt{S/\pi}$. Hence we have

$$r = f(S) = \frac{1}{2}\sqrt{\frac{S}{\pi}} = \frac{1}{2\pi}\sqrt{\pi S}.$$

When $S = 16\pi$, $r = f(16\pi) = \dfrac{1}{2\pi}\sqrt{\pi \cdot 16\pi} = \dfrac{4\pi}{2\pi} = 2.$

EXAMPLE 2.   If $f(x) = \left(x^3 - \dfrac{2}{x^3}\right)\left(x^2 + \dfrac{1}{x^2}\right)^3$, find $f(-1)$.

Solution.   Replacing x by -1 throughout the equality, we obtain

$$f(-1) = \left[(-1)^3 - \frac{2}{(-1)^3}\right]\left[(-1)^2 + \frac{1}{(-1)^2}\right]^3$$
$$= [-1 + 2][1 + 1]^3 = 8.$$

EXERCISES

1. If $f(x) = x^2 - 3x + 5$, find **(a)** $f(2)$; **(b)** $f(-3)$; **(c)** $f(-2\frac{1}{2})$; **(d)** $f(0)$; **(e)** $f(c)$.

2. If $g(z) = 2 - z - 3z^2$, find **(a)** $g(4)$; **(b)** $g(-1)$; **(c)** $g(\sqrt{3})$; **(d)** $g(0)$; **(e)** $g(b)$.

3. If $h(y) = y - 1 - 2y^2$, find **(a)** $h(3)$; **(b)** $h(-4)$; **(c)** $h(\sqrt{5})$.

4. If $f(v) = v^2 + 2v + 1$, find **(a)** $f(-3)$; **(b)** $f(\frac{1}{2})$; **(c)** $f(\sqrt{a})$.

5. If $F(x) = x^3 + 3x^2 - 4x - 2$, find **(a)** $F(-1)$; **(b)** $F(-\sqrt{3})$; **(c)** $F(\frac{1}{2}\sqrt{2})$; **(d)** $F(y)$.

6. If $f(x) = \dfrac{1 + x}{1 - x}$, find **(a)** $f(\frac{2}{3})$; **(b)** $f(\sqrt{3})$; **(c)** $f(2 + \sqrt{3})$.

7. If $\psi(y) = \left(y^4 - \dfrac{12}{5y^3}\right)^2 - \left(3y - \dfrac{4}{y^2}\right)^3$, find **(a)** $\psi(1)$; **(b)** $\psi(-2)$.

8. If $F(x) = x^2 + 3bx - 3b^2$, find **(a)** $F(2b)$; **(b)** $F(-3b)$.

9. If $G(b) = x^2 + 3bx - 3b^2$, find **(a)** $G(2x)$; **(b)** $G(-3x)$.

10. If $f(r, h) = \frac{1}{3}\pi r^2 h$, find **(a)** $f(3, 4)$; **(b)** $f(6, 2)$; **(c)** $f(r, 24)$; **(d)** $f(9, h)$.

11. If $f(x, y) = x^2 - 10xy + 3y^2$, find **(a)** $f(2, 1)$; **(b)** $f(-1, 3)$; **(c)** $f(-3, -4)$; **(d)** $f(0, 0)$; **(e)** $f(5, 0)$; **(f)** $f(0, -5)$; **(g)** $f(x, -y)$.

12. If $f(x, y, z) = x^2 + (y + 1)^2 - (z - 2)^2$, find **(a)** $f(1, 2, 3)$; **(b)** $f(-2, 4, -1)$; **(c)** $f(0, 0, 0)$; **(d)** $f(1, -1, -2)$; **(e)** $f(0, -3, -4)$.

13. If $H(x) = \left(x^2 - \dfrac{1}{x}\right) \div \left(\dfrac{2}{x^2} - \dfrac{x}{2}\right)$, find **(a)** $H(-2)$; **(b)** $H(\frac{1}{2})$; **(c)** $H(4/x)$; **(d)** $H(-\frac{1}{4}x^2)$.

14. If $p(x) = x^2 - 2x - 1$, find **(a)** $p(i)$, **(b)** $p(3i)$, **(c)** $p(-4i)$, **(d)** $p(2 - 3i)$, **(e)** $p(-1 - i)$, where $i = \sqrt{-1}$.

15. If $f(y) = \dfrac{y^2 - 2}{y - 2}$, find **(a)** $f(\sqrt{2})$, **(b)** $f(2i)$, **(c)** $f(-\tfrac{1}{2}i)$, **(d)** $f(3 + 4i)$, where $i = \sqrt{-1}$.

16. If $g(y) = \dfrac{3 + 2y}{2 - y}$, find **(a)** $g(\tfrac{2}{3})$; **(b)** $g(2\sqrt{-1})$; **(c)** $g(2/y)$.

17. If $F(t) = t^2 - 4t$, find **(a)** $F(-t)$; **(b)** $F(a)$; **(c)** $F(a + 1)$; **(d)** $F(a + 1) - F(a)$; **(e)** $F(F(2))$.

18. If $f(x) = \dfrac{2x - 1}{x + 1}$, find **(a)** $f(1)$; **(b)** $f(x + 1) - f(x)$; **(c)** $f(4f(3))$.

In Exercises 19 through 22, express each of the specified quantities in functional notation and then give its particular form:

19. The volume V and the surface S of a box in terms of its length l, width w, and height h.

20. The volume V, the lateral surface S_1, and the total surface S_2, of a right circular cylinder in terms of its height h and the radius r of its base.

21. The length l in feet of a rectangular field in terms of its area A in acres and its width w in feet.

22. **(a)** The mass m of a solid gold bar of dimensions l, w, and h in centimeters and density 19.3 grams per cubic centimeter. **(b)** The value V of the gold bar if gold is worth \$35.00 per [troy] ounce. Assume that 1 ounce equals 31.1 grams.

23. The annual cost c, in dollars, of operating a certain automobile m miles is given by $c = 0.062m + 590$. **(a)** How many miles can be driven for an annual cost of \$2000? **(b)** Express the formula and the answer to (*a*) in functional notation. ★**(c)** Give an interpretation for the coefficients in the formula.

24. The average cost c in dollars of producing n tons of steel is given by $c = 55.7n + 182 \cdot 10^6$. **(a)** How many tons can be produced for \$800,000,000? **(b)** Express the formula and the answer to (*a*) in functional notation. **(c)** Give an interpretation for the coefficients in the formula. ★**(d)** If the orders do not use up the full capacity of the mills, what is the smallest bargain price that could be charged on some additional orders without directly losing money?

4-3   Inverse of a Function

In § 4-1 it was noted that the area of a circle is a function of its radius. But observe that also the radius is a function of the area: given the area, the radius is determined. In this case (and many others), the question of which variable is the independent variable and which is the dependent variable is not predetermined automatically, and depends upon the particular use to be made of the relationship. This observation leads to the following definition.

If y *is a function of* x, y $= f(x)$, *and* x *is also a function of* y, x $= g(y)$, *then the function* g(y) *is said to be the* **inverse** *of* f(x), *and vice versa.*

Then sometimes $g(y)$ is denoted $f^{-1}(x)$, where, however, it must be understood that "-1" notes the inverse function and is not an exponent. Note that the definition requires that $f(g(y)) = y$ for all values of y in the domain of $g(y)$ and $g(f(x)) = x$ for all values of x in the domain of $f(x)$.

ILLUSTRATION. If $y = f(x) = 3x + 4$, then (as in § 3-6) $x = \frac{1}{3}(y - 4)$. Hence $f^{-1}(x) = \frac{1}{3}(y - 4)$.

The concept of inverse function will arise again in connection with logarithms (Chapter 6) and trigonometric functions (§ 13-6). Meanwhile it is to be noted that not every function has an inverse (unless one uses the more general concept of multivalued function discussed at the end of § 4-1 or else the domain of the given function is restricted). This statement reflects the requirement in our definition of a function that a value of the independent variable shall determine just one value of the dependent variable. Thus $y = x^2$ expresses y as a function of x; but for any positive value of y there are two values of x. Thus x is not a function of y in this instance, unless (for example) x is restricted to non-negative values.

EXERCISES

Let y $= f(x)$, *and find the inverse function* x $= g(y)$, *in each exercise in which the inverse function exists:*

1. $3x + 4$.	**5.** $\frac{2}{3}x$.	**9.** x^3, x real.
2. $2x - 5$.	**6.** $4/x$.	**10.** x^5, x real.
3. $5 - x$.	**7.** 4.	**11.** x^4, $x > 0$.
4. $3 - \frac{1}{4}x$.	**8.** 0.	**12.** x^6, $x < 0$.

13. In Exercise 23 of § 4-2, **(a)** express m as a function of c; ★**(b)** give an interpretation for the coefficients in this expression.

14. In Exercise 24 of § 4-2, **(a)** express n as a function of c; ★**(b)** give an interpretation for the coefficients in this expression.

The independent variable is stated first; specify a formula for finding each dependent variable:

15. Given the circumference C of a circle, find **(a)** its radius r; **(b)** its diameter d; and **(c)** its area A.

16. Given the edge e of a cube, find **(a)** its volume V; and **(b)** its surface area S.

17. Given the area A, find the base b of a triangle of fixed altitude h.

18. Given the time t in hours required for a 300-mile trip, find the average speed of travel r.

★**19.** Given the area S of the surface of a sphere, find **(a)** its radius r; and **(b)** its volume V.

4-4   Rectangular Coordinates

The modern trend in industrial and scientific work toward graphical representation of data has brought into prominence the graphical work of algebra. Graphs offer comprehensive views of situations and reveal strikingly the relationship between the quantities involved. Many such representations are based on the **Cartesian system of rectangular coordinates** which we now consider.

Let $X'X$ and $Y'Y$ (Figure 4.1) be two arbitrarily fixed lines intersecting at right angles at the point O. In addition, let the positive direction be arbitrarily chosen toward the right when parallel to $X'X$ and upward when parallel to $Y'Y$. On each of these lines construct a number scale (§ 1-3) with an arbitrary length as a unit and O as the zero point of each scale. The line $X'X$ is called the **x-axis** and the line $Y'Y$ is called the **y-axis**; the two lines together are called the **coordinate axes.** The point O is called the **origin.** The plane in which the coordinates lie is called the **coordinate plane.**

From any given point P in the coordinate plane we may drop perpendiculars PM and PN to the axes. If the point M has coordinate x on the x-axis and N has coordinate y on the y-axis, then x is the measure of the directed line segment OM and also of its equal NP; y is the measure of the directed line segment MP and also of ON (but not of the directed

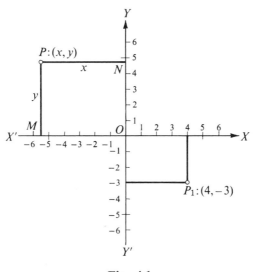

Fig. 4.1

line segment *NO*, which has the opposite direction). The numbers *x* and *y* are called the **abscissa** and **ordinate,** respectively, of *P*; both together are called the **rectangular coordinates** of *P*, or simply the coordinates of *P*.

For any two real numbers *x* and *y* the point *P*, whose abscissa is *x* and whose ordinate is *y*, is denoted by the ordered pair (x, y) or by $P: (x, y)$ where the first number in the pair (x, y) is always taken as the abscissa of the point.

The process of locating a point whose coordinates are given is called **plotting** the point, and the location may be conveniently marked by the symbol ∘. Each point on the plane of the coordinate axes has a unique ordered pair of real numbers as its rectangular coordinates, and, conversely, to each set of rectangular coordinates there corresponds one and only one point on that plane. In plotting it may be found convenient to use rectangular-coordinate paper ruled with ten small divisions to one large division. The axes should always be properly labeled and the scale indicated on each axis.

Each of the coordinates of a point may be positive, negative, or zero. When the coordinates of a point are known quantities, the proper sign must be used with the number of units. For example, the point P_1 (Figure 4.1), which is four units to the right of $Y'Y$ and three units below $X'X$, is represented by $(4, -3)$ or $P_1: (4, -3)$.

The coordinate axes divide the plane into four parts called **quadrants,** which are conventionally numbered counterclockwise I, II, III, and IV as in Figure 4.2. The abscissa is positive in the first and fourth quadrants and negative in the second and third. The ordinate is positive in the first and second quadrants and negative in the third and fourth. The signs of the coordinates of points lying in the various quadrants are shown in parentheses in Figure 4.2, with the sign of the abscissa written first. The points on the coordinate axes have at least one coordinate zero and are not in any quadrant.

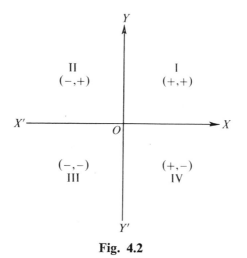

Fig. 4.2

Historical Note.   The Cartesian system of coordinates is named after RENÉ DESCARTES (1596–1650), his name in Latin being Renatus Cartesius.

EXERCISES

In Exercises 1 through 12 plot the points, at least approximately, and identify the quadrant (if any) in which each point lies:

1. (4, 3).

5. (2, 0).

9. $(-3\frac{1}{2}, -2\frac{3}{4})$.

2. (−2, 4).

6. (0, −2).

10. (−0.5, 3.6).

3. (3, −5).

7. (0, 2.5).

11. $(\sqrt{2}, -2\sqrt{3})$.

4. (−3, −1).

8. (−3.8, 0).

12. $(\pi, \frac{1}{2}\pi)$.

Draw the triangles whose vertices are as follows:

13. (2, 7), (4, −1), (−3, 5).

14. (−4, −5), (0, 10), (2, −6).

15. Draw the quadrilateral with vertices at $(-1, 3)$, $(-4, -2)$, $(4, -4)$, and $(3, 7)$.

16. Find the perimeter and the area of the quadrilateral with vertices at $(-6, -3)$, $(3, -3)$, $(3, 4)$, and $(-6, 4)$.

17. Three of the vertices of a rectangle are at $(2, -5)$, $(2, 3)$, and $(-8, 3)$. Draw the rectangle and find the coordinates of the fourth vertex and of the center.

18. Plot five points each having its abscissa equal to 2. Where are all points having 2 as abscissas?

19. Plot five points each having its ordinate equal to -5. Where are all points having -5 as ordinates?

20. (a) What is the abscissa of each point on the y-axis? (b) What is the ordinate of each point on the x-axis? (c) What are the coordinates of the point where the two coordinate axes intersect?

In Exercises 21 through 35 describe the location of all points (x, y) *with coordinates satisfying the given conditions:*

21. $x = 3$.	**26.** $x = 0$.	**31.** $x < 0, y < 0$.
22. $x = -2$.	**27.** $y > 0$.	**32.** $x = 0, y > 0$.
23. $y = -1$.	**28.** $x > 0, y > 0$.	**33.** $x = 3, y > 0$.
24. $y = 4$.	**29.** $x < 0, y > 0$.	**34.** $x = y$.
25. $y = 0$.	**30.** $x > 0, y < 0$.	**35.** $x = -y$.

36. If (a, b) is a point in quadrant IV, state the quadrant in which each of the following points lies: (a) $(-a, b)$; (b) $(a, -b)$; (c) $(-a, -b)$; (d) (b, a); (e) $(b, -a)$; (f) (b, b).

37. If $a > 0$, $b < 0$, and $c < 0$, state the quadrant in which each of the following points is located: (a) (a, c); (b) (c, a); (c) $(b, -c)$; (d) $(-b, -c)$; (e) $(-c, b)$; (f) $(c, -b)$.

38. Using (a, b) to represent one definite point in the first quadrant, plot the three points $(-a, b)$, $(a, -b)$, and $(-a, -b)$. Name the pairs of points which are (a) symmetric with respect to the x-axis; (b) symmetric with respect to the y-axis; (c) symmetric with respect to the origin.

39. In what quadrants is the ratio y/x positive? negative?

★40. The points (x, y) whose coordinates are integers are often called **integral points.** (a) On a coordinate plane mark the integral points (x, y) such that $0 < x \leq 6$ and $0 < y \leq 6$. (b) If x represents the number on the exposed face of one die and y represents the number on the exposed face of another die, then each of these points corresponds to a possible throw of a pair of dice. How many such possible throws are there? (c) The number of these points with coordinates satisfying the equation $x + y = 7$ is equal to the number of ways of throwing a seven on a pair of dice. (Explain.) In how many ways can a seven be thrown? (d) Can eleven be thrown?

4-5   The Distance Function

The length of a line segment AB on a number scale was observed in § 1-3 to be equal to $|a - b|$, the absolute value of the difference between the coordinates of the points A and B. Lengths of line segments that are on a coordinate plane and parallel to an axis may be similarly obtained. As in Figure 4.3, consider any two points $A: (x_1, y_1)$ and

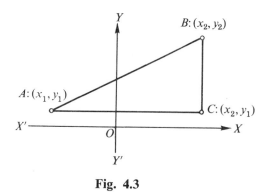

Fig. 4.3

$B: (x_2, y_2)$, together with the point $C: (x_2, y_1)$. Then the triangle ABC is a right triangle. The length of AC is given by $|x_2 - x_1|$ in terms of the units of the number scale on the x-axis, and the length of BC is given by $|y_2 - y_1|$ in terms of the units of the number scale on the y-axis. The lengths of segments which are not parallel to a coordinate axis may be obtained by using the **Pythagorean Theorem:**

For any right triangle the square of the hypotenuse equals the sum of the squares of the other sides.

Whenever the number scales on the two axes have units of equal length (as we shall assume, unless otherwise specified, whenever distances are involved), we may obtain the length d of AB by applying the Pythagorean Theorem:

$$d^2 = (x_2 - x_1)^2 + (y_2 - y_1)^2.$$

Since this formula for d also holds for line segments which are parallel to an axis, the function

$$\sqrt{(x_2 - x_1)^2 + (y_2 - y_1)^2}$$

is called the **distance function** and is used in advanced mathematics as a definition of distance on a coordinate plane.

On a plane the set of points at a given distance (radius) from a given point (center) is called a **circle.** Thus a circle of radius r and center at the origin is the set of points (x, y) whose coordinates satisfy the equation $\sqrt{x^2 + y^2} = r$ or, since we assume $r \geq 0$,

$$x^2 + y^2 = r^2.$$

Similarly, a circle of radius r and center at (h, k) is the set of the points (x, y) whose coordinates satisfy the equation

$$(x - h)^2 + (y - k)^2 = r^2.$$

EXERCISES

1. Find the distance between
   (a) $(1, 13)$ and $(8, -11)$;   (c) $(-2, -3)$ and $(2, 3)$;
   (b) $(2, -1)$ and $(2, 5)$;   (d) $(-10, -11)$ and $(-3, -4)$.

2. Find the lengths of the sides and thereby prove that the points are the vertices of an isosceles triangle:
   (a) $(4, 4), (2, 1), (-1, 3)$;   (c) $(4, 0), (14, 4), (0, 10)$;
   (b) $(1, 3), (5, 7), (5, -1)$;   (d) $(2, 1), (5, -5), (8, 1)$.

3. Assume that if the Pythagorean Theorem holds, then the triangle is a right triangle, and prove that the following points are vertices of a right triangle: (a) $(0, -2), (4, -4), (5, 8)$; (b) $(-3, 4), (-4, -7), (2, -1)$.

4. Prove that the point $(1, 1)$ is equidistant from the points $(4, 5)$, $(5, 4)$, and $(-2, -3)$.

5. (a) Prove that the points $(3, -5), (-1, -5)$, and $(-2, -4)$ are on a circle with center $(1, -2)$. (b) What is the radius of the circle?

6. Prove that the points A: (1, 5), B: (5, 1), and C: (7, -1) are on a straight line by showing that $AB + BC = AC$.

7. An automobile and a truck leave the same point at the same time traveling respectively due west at 45 miles per hour and due north at 35 miles per hour. Find an expression for their distance apart d, measured in miles, at the end of t hours.

8. In baseball the bases are at the corners of a square 90 feet on a side. Express the distance d in feet between home plate and a runner going straight from second base to third base, as a function of the time t in seconds since he left second base, if he runs 25 feet per second.

9. An airplane flying at a speed of 600 knots at an altitude of 600 feet passes over a buoy. Find an expression for its distance d, measured in feet, from the buoy t seconds later. (One knot is one nautical mile per hour; that is, 6076.1 feet per hour.)

4-6   Graph of a Function of One Variable

A **graph** is a set of points. The graph of a function $f(x)$ is the set of all points $(x, f(x))$; if $y = f(x)$, the graph may also be described as the set of all (x, y). In other words, the graph of a function is the locus of all points whose abscissas are values of the independent variable and whose ordinates are the corresponding values of the function. As in § 4-4 only real numbers are considered as coordinates; that is, only real values are assigned to the independent variable, and only real values of the dependent variable are used as ordinates. To draw the graph for any particular function, we usually plot several points and draw a smooth curve through them. Since there is no limit to the number of such points, the graph may be drawn as accurately as desired by plotting a sufficiently large number of points. Further consideration of the process of drawing the graph, also called **graphing** the function, is given later in this section; but first let us study an illustrative example.

EXAMPLE 1.   Graph the function $(2x - 3)$.

Solution.   For convenience, let $y = 2x - 3$. Next assign values for x and compute the corresponding values of y, arranging the results in the form shown in the accompanying table. Then plot the points (x, y) and, since any real number may be taken as a value of the independent variable, draw the graph proceeding from one point to another so that the values of x are taken

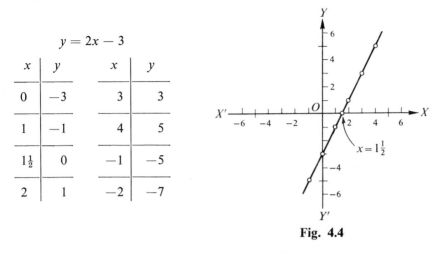

$$y = 2x - 3$$

x	y	x	y
0	−3	3	3
1	−1	4	5
1½	0	−1	−5
2	1	−2	−7

Fig. 4.4

consistently in increasing (or decreasing) order (Figure 4.4). For later reference note that when $y = 0$, $x = 1\frac{1}{2}$.

In starting the graph of any particular function the student is confronted with several questions such as: "What values of the variable x shall I use?" "How many values of x are needed?" "What unit shall I use?" Only practice in graphing will give the answers. Sometimes a preliminary graph will aid in determining the more significant parts of a graph, especially where there is no limit to the size of the numbers which may be used as abscissas. The following details deserve notice:

1. The coordinate axes should be easily recognized and should be properly labeled.

2. The scales on the coordinate axes should be as large as is consistent with showing the vital parts of the graph and should be indicated by numbering points at convenient intervals along each axis.

3. Find, when possible, the points where the curve crosses the coordinate axes. To do this, let $x = 0$ and find, if possible, the corresponding value, or values, of y. Then let $y = 0$ and find, if possible, the corresponding value, or values, of x. These values for x and y are called the **x** and **y intercepts** respectively.

4. In joining the plotted points, proceed from one point to another so that the values of x are taken in order of increasing, or decreasing, magnitude. Draw a smooth curve through (not to) the points, first lightly, then tracing over it until it appears satisfactory. If in doubt about the nature of the curve between two plotted points, determine other points in the interval.

Warnings. Most commonly-encountered functions have smooth graphs. Any sudden bumps or turns in a graph should be cause for rechecking.

If a function is not defined for some of the values of a variable, the graph must show this and must not be continued across the corresponding abscissas.

EXAMPLE 2.   Graph the function $(6 - x - x^2)$.

Solution.   Let $y = 6 - x - x^2$. Make a table of pairs of corresponding values of x and y and draw the graph (Figure 4.5).

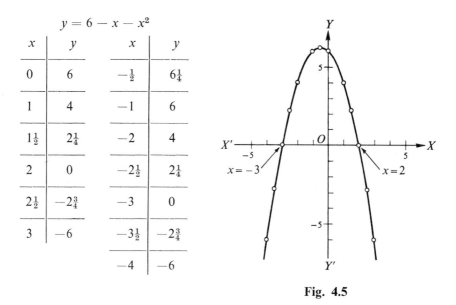

$$y = 6 - x - x^2$$

x	y	x	y
0	6	$-\frac{1}{2}$	$6\frac{1}{4}$
1	4	-1	6
$1\frac{1}{2}$	$2\frac{1}{4}$	-2	4
2	0	$-2\frac{1}{2}$	$2\frac{1}{4}$
$2\frac{1}{2}$	$-2\frac{3}{4}$	-3	0
3	-6	$-3\frac{1}{2}$	$-2\frac{3}{4}$
		-4	-6

Fig. 4.5

The graphing in Example 1 of the function $(2x - 3)$ as the set of points $(x, 2x - 3)$ and the graphing in Example 2 of the function $(6 - x - x^2)$ as the set of points $(x, 6 - x - x^2)$ illustrate how a function may also be considered as a set of pairs of numbers $(x, f(x))$ in which the first number is a value of the independent variable and the second number is the corresponding value of the dependent variable.

The general method used in graphing algebraic functions is also used in graphing data given by tables of values. However, a smooth curve should be used only when the intermediate points can be found or when they have significance in the graph. Otherwise the plotted points should be joined by a series of straight-line segments.

EXAMPLE 3.　The following table gives the maximum temperatures T, in degrees Fahrenheit, on Christmas Day from 1943 to 1960 as recorded by the United States Weather Bureau at Pittsburgh. Represent these data graphically.

Year	1943	1944	1945	1946	1947	1948	1949	1950	1951
T	43	41	45	37	40	25	47	25	41

Year	1952	1953	1954	1955	1956	1957	1958	1959	1960
T	35	36	37	59	32	43	26	46	42

Solution.　The graph is shown in Figure 4.6, where the plotted points are joined by a series of line segments since the given data have no significance for intermediate dates.

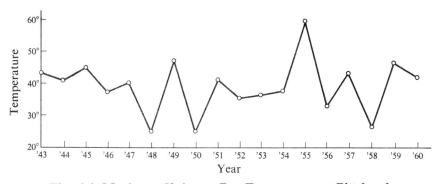

Fig. 4.6. Maximum Christmas Day Temperatures at Pittsburgh

EXERCISES

Graph the functions:

1. $x + 2$.
2. $x - 1$.
3. $2x + 3$.
4. $3x - 5$.
5. $4 - 3x$.
6. $-2x - 5$.
7. x^2.
8. $-\frac{1}{2}x^2$.
9. $4 - x^2$.
10. $x^2 + 2x$.

11. $3x - x^2$.
12. $\frac{1}{3}x^3$.
13. $-\frac{1}{4}x^3$.
14. $x^2 + 3x + 2$.
15. $x^2 - 4x - 5$.
16. $3 + x - x^2$.
17. $5 + x - x^2$.
18. $x^2 - 4x + 4$.
19. $\frac{1}{2}(1 + 3x + x^2)$.
20. $\frac{5}{3} + \frac{4}{3}x - 2x^2$.

21. $\frac{1}{10}x^4$.
22. $2(x^2 - x^3)$.
23. $x^3 - 4x$.
24. $4 + 6x - x^3$.
25. $4x^2 - x^4$.
26. $x^4 + x^3 - 1$.
27. $-1/x$.
28. $1/x^3$.
29. x^{-2}.
30. $(x + 2)^{-1}$.

Graph the relations:

31. $y = x^2 - 1$.   **35.** $y = \pm\sqrt{9 - x}$.   **39.** $y = \dfrac{5}{x^2 + 1}$.

32. $y = x^2 + 4$.   **36.** $y = \pm\sqrt{4 - x^2}$.

33. $y = \pm 3\sqrt{x}$.   **37.** $y = \sqrt{x^2 - 4}$.   **40.** $y = (x^2 - 1)^{-1}$.

34. $y = \pm\sqrt{x + 2}$.   **38.** $y = \frac{1}{2}\sqrt{16 - x^2}$.   **41.** $y = -x\sqrt{x}$.

Graph each pair of relations on the same coordinate plane and find or estimate the coordinates of the points of intersection of the graphs:

42. $y = 0$, $y = x^2 + 3x - 3$.   **45.** $y = 3x$, $y = 8 - x$.

43. $y = 1$, $y = x^2 - 2x + 1$.   **46.** $y = -4x$, $y = 10 - x$.

44. $y = -3$, $y = x^2 - 4x + 2$.   **47.** $y = x^2 - 4$, $y = 1 - x^2$.

Represent the data graphically in Exercises 48 through 52:

48. The number of years required for any given amount of money to double itself when invested at certain rates (in percent) of interest per year, compounded semiannually, is given in the following sample table:

Rate	2	3	4	5	6	7	8	9	10	11	12
Years	34.8	23.3	17.5	14.0	11.7	10.1	8.8	7.9	7.1	6.5	5.9

49. The total precipitation in New York City, in inches, in the month of April of the years stated:

1949	1950	1951	1952	1953	1954	1955	1956	1957	1958	1959	1960
3.84	2.04	2.09	5.80	5.99	2.51	2.39	3.24	5.46	6.22	2.07	3.18

50. February is sometimes mentioned as the month in which presidents are born. The actual distribution by months of the birthdays of the first thirty-four presidents of the United States is:

January–3, February–3, March–4, April–4, May–2, June–0, July–2, August–2, September–1, October–5, November–5, December–3.

51. Appropriations of the Federal government for the year stated, in billions of dollars:

1910	1919	1925	1935	1943	1945	1950	1952	1955	1959
1.0	27.1	3.7	7.5	150.8	73.1	52.9	127.8	54.8	82.1

52. The normal daily average temperatures T in degrees Fahrenheit for each month are given in the following table for **(a)** Los Angeles; **(b)** Boston; **(c)** Miami.

	Jan.	Feb.	Mar.	Apr.	May	June	July	Aug.	Sept.	Oct.	Nov.	Dec.
Los Angeles	55.0	56.4	58.9	61.5	64.8	67.8	72.5	72.9	71.0	66.6	62.1	57.3
Boston	29.1	29.2	37.6	47.2	57.8	67.2	72.2	71.5	64.3	55.0	44.4	32.8
Miami	68.5	68.7	70.8	74.1	77.1	80.3	81.6	82.1	81.0	77.6	72.3	69.5

53. In Exercise 48, read from the graph the number of years required for money to double at $4\frac{1}{2}\%$.

★54. In Exercise 49, what can you deduce from the graph as to the precipitation in 1965?

★55. At room temperature, the net current I in a "junction transistor" resulting from application of voltage V is given by $I = I_s(e^{39V} - 1)$ where $e \approx 2.718$. Compute approximate coordinates of a few points (Table VI or Table I may be helpful) and sketch the graph of I as a function of V for $I_s = 2$.

4-7 Graph of a Linear Function

The graph of $y = 2x - 3$ (Figure 4.4, page 95) appears to be a *straight line*, and indeed it is so. More generally, if $y = ax + b$ then the graph is a straight line. Conversely, if the graph is a straight line which is not parallel to the y-axis then the relationship between x and y can be expressed in the form $y = ax + b$. If $a \neq 0$, the function $(ax + b)$ is called a **linear function.**

When the graph is a straight line and (x_1, y_1), (x_2, y_2) are two distinct points on the line with $x_1 \neq x_2$, then the line is said to have **slope**

$$\frac{y_2 - y_1}{x_2 - x_1}.$$

It follows from properties of similar triangles, studied in geometry, that the slope of a line as just defined is the same no matter which two distinct points on the line are chosen, and that the graph of $y = ax + b$ is a line with slope a. Also, the line through a given point (x_0, y_0) with slope m is the graph of the relation

$$y - y_0 = m(x - x_0). \qquad (1)$$

This can be seen by rewriting (1) in the form $y = mx + (y_0 - mx_0)$, which shows it to be a straight line with slope m; also, by substitution in (1), (x_0, y_0) is a point on the graph.

ILLUSTRATIONS. The graph of $y = -2x + 5$ is a straight line with slope -2. The graph of $y = -5$ is a straight line with slope 0. A straight line with slope -4 passing through $(1, -3)$ is the graph of $y - (-3) = -4(x - 1)$; that is, $y = -4x + 1$. The graph of $x = 4$ is a straight line, namely the set of all points with abscissa 4; however, if one attempts to compute the slope it is found that the denominator is zero. The slope of this line is not defined; loosely, it is sometimes said that "the slope is infinite".

The graph of the function $(6 - x - x^2)$, shown in Figure 4.5 on page 96, is not a straight line; the function is not linear. In fact, the graph of $(ax^2 + bx + c)$, for $a \neq 0$, is a parabola (§ 12-1), and the function is called a **quadratic function.**

EXERCISES

Find the slope of the graph of each function:

1. $3x + 4$.	**5.** $2x - 1$.	**9.** $6x$.	**13.** x.
2. $4x + 3$.	**6.** $1 - 2x$.	**10.** $-7x$.	**14.** $ax - b$.
3. $-3x + 4$.	**7.** $\frac{1}{2}x + \frac{5}{2}$.	**11.** -6.	**15.** $cx + d$.
4. $-4x - 3$.	**8.** $-\frac{1}{3}x - 6$.	**12.** 7.	**16.** 0.

Find the slope of the line through:

17. $(2, 5)$ and $(6, 13)$.	**22.** $(-2, 0)$ and $(1, -4)$.
18. $(5, 2)$ and $(13, 6)$.	**23.** $(\frac{1}{2}, 2)$ and $(2\frac{3}{4}, -4)$.
19. $(1, 4)$ and $(3, 7)$.	**24.** $(1, \frac{4}{3})$ and $(-3, 0)$.
20. $(-1, -3)$ and $(2, 12)$.	**25.** $(4, 1)$ and $(-1, 1)$.
21. $(-4, -3)$ and $(-1, 1)$.	**26.** $(0, -2)$ and $(2, -2)$.

Find a function whose graph is the straight line through the given point with the given slope:

27. $(1, 2)$; 3.	**31.** $(0, \frac{2}{3})$; $\frac{3}{2}$.	**35.** $(3, -2)$; $-\frac{1}{3}$.
28. $(3, 1)$; 2.	**32.** $(0, 5)$; -2.	**36.** $(\frac{1}{2}, 1\frac{1}{2})$; -1.
29. $(1, -2)$; 4.	**33.** $(4, 0)$; -3.	**37.** $(\frac{2}{3}, -1\frac{2}{3})$; $\frac{3}{4}$.
30. $(-2, 3)$; $\frac{1}{2}$.	**34.** $(2, -1)$; $-\frac{1}{4}$.	**38.** $(4, 0)$; 1.

39. In Exercises 1 through 30 of § 4-6, which of the functions are **(a)** linear? **(b)** quadratic?

*40. Prove by similar triangles that if (x_1, y_1), (x_2, y_2), and (x_3, y_3) are distinct points on a line then the slope is the same no matter from which pair of points it is computed.

*41. Find the coordinates of the point on the graph of $y = ax + b$ with (a) abscissa 0; (b) abscissa 1. (c) Thence find the slope of this line.

4-8   More About Interpolation

Linear interpolation (§ 3-8) can be interpreted in terms of the graph of a linear function and functional notation. Moreover, it applies to other functions as well as powers and roots.

Suppose three values of x are specified, namely x_1, x_2, and x_3, and values of the function $f(x)$ are to be interpolated to obtain $f(x_2)$, knowing $f(x_1)$ and $f(x_3)$. For instance, in the Illustration in § 3-8, $x_1 = 60$, $x_2 = 60.6$, $x_3 = 61$, $f(x) = \sqrt{x}$, $f(x_1) = 7.746$, $f(x_3) = 7.810$, $f(x_2) = ?$. The proportion in formula (1) of § 3-8 becomes in the present notation

$$\frac{f(x_2) - f(x_1)}{f(x_3) - f(x_1)} \approx \frac{x_2 - x_1}{x_3 - x_1}. \tag{2}$$

The graph of a typical function is shown as a curve in Figure 4.7; ABC is a straight line which will be a good approximation to the curve if x_1 and x_3 differ only slightly from each other, as they would be chosen to do in interpolation. In the figure, they are drawn rather far apart

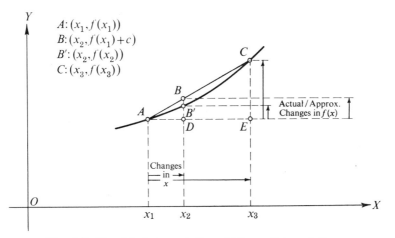

Fig. 4.7. Graphic Interpretation of Linear Interpolation

and the graph of the function is shown as sharply curved, for clarity in the drawing; this exaggerates the difference between the line and the curve. The right triangles ADB and AEC have the same acute angle A and so are similar. Hence by geometry, corresponding sides are proportional; $DB:EC = AD:AE$. With due regard to signs, $AD = x_2 - x_1$, $AE = x_3 - x_1$, $DB \approx f(x_2) - f(x_1)$, $EC = f(x_3) - f(x_1)$. Substituting, the proportion just stated becomes (2). A similar figure, leading to the same conclusions, could be drawn if the values of the function decrease when x increases, or if $x_3 < x_1$. Thus, linear interpolation is equivalent to replacing the relevant section of the graph by a straight line segment.

We now consider the use of interpolation to find a value of x instead of $f(x)$. So far, the unknown quantity in (2) has been $f(x_2) - f(x_1)$, with the other differences all known. But we can equally well be given the values of the function and interpolate to find a corresponding value x_2 of the independent variable. In other words, we can interpolate in the inverse function of $f(x)$; see § 4-3.

The necessary numerical work can be performed directly (mentally, in simple cases), or the table of proportional parts (Table X) can be used indirectly, as discussed in the following illustration.

ILLUSTRATION. To find the value of x for which $\sqrt{x} = 6.145$, note from Table I that adjacent known values are $\sqrt{37} = 6.083$, $\sqrt{38} = 6.164$. Thus $x_1 = 37$, $x_3 = 38$, $x_2 = x_1 + c$.

Changes in x		x	$f(x) = \sqrt{x}$	Changes in $f(x)$	
1	c	37	6.083	0.062	
		37 + c	6.145		0.081
		38	6.164		

$$\frac{0.062}{0.081} = \frac{c}{1}; \qquad (3)$$

$$c \approx 0.8; \qquad (4)$$

$$\sqrt{37.8} \approx 6.145.$$

The numerical work in proceeding from (3) to (4) can be done by direct arithmetic, or by applying the following reasoning to Table X: We wish to find c to the nearest tenth, so that $c \cdot 0.081 = 0.062$, hence $c \cdot 81 = 62$. In Table X, in the column headed 81, we find adjacent listings $0.7 \cdot 81 = 56.7$ and $0.8 \cdot 81 = 64.8$. Clearly 0.8 comes closest to giving the desired product, so $c \approx 0.8$.

EXERCISES

Verify by linear interpolation in Table I:

1. If $\sqrt{x} = 6.180$ then $x \approx 38.2$.   **3.** If $1/x = 0.01734$ then $x \approx 57.7$.

2. If $\sqrt{x} = 9.136$ then $x \approx 83.5$.   **4.** If $1/x = 0.02553$ then $x \approx 39.2$.

By interpolation in Table I, find x *if:*

5. $\sqrt{x} = 6.380$.   **10.** $\sqrt{x} = 96.54$.

6. $\sqrt{x} = 7.690$.   **11.** $1/x = 0.01286$.

7. $\sqrt{x} = 31.185$.   **12.** $1/x = 0.02094$.

8. $\sqrt{x} = 20.223$.   **13.** $1/x = 2.753$.

9. $\sqrt{x} = 0.5088$.   **14.** $1/x = 10.23$.

15. For the case $f(x_3) < f(x_1)$, draw Figure 4.7 and discuss the signs in the proportion given by similar triangles.

16. For $f(x) = 3x + 2$, **(a)** find $f(2)$ and $f(3)$ by substitution; **(b)** find $f(2.3)$ both by substitution and by interpolation between $f(2)$ and $f(3)$. **(c)** Why do the answers in (b) agree or disagree?

17. For $f(x) = x^2 - 5x + 3$, **(a)** find $f(1)$ and $f(3)$ by substitution; **(b)** find $f(2)$ both by substitution and by interpolation between $f(1)$ and $f(3)$. **(c)** Why do the answers to (b) agree or disagree?

4-9 Zeros of a Function; Maximum and Minimum

If a function is equal to zero for certain values of the independent variable, these values are called **zeros** of the function. Thus, a is a zero of $f(x)$ if $f(a) = 0$.

Graphically the **real zeros** (those zeros which are real numbers) of a function—as, for example, $f(x)$—are the abscissas of the points where the graph of $f(x)$ either crosses or touches the x-axis. Thus, in Figure 4.4 on page 95, $1\frac{1}{2}$ is seen to be the real zero of the function $(2x - 3)$; and in Figure 4.5 on page 96, the real zeros of $(6 - x - x^2)$ are seen to be -3 and 2. Graphs can be used to find, at least approximately, the real zeros of any function of one variable; the values for the real zeros of the functions graphed in Figures 4.4 and 4.5 are exact, as can be seen from the tables accompanying the graphs.

Some graphs have **points of relative maximum,** also called **maximum points,** and the corresponding values of these functions are said to be

maximum values of the functions. Such a point of relative maximum is a point where the ordinate is *greater* than at all other points in its *immediate* vicinity. Likewise, a curve may have a **relative minimum point** and the function a **minimum value,** at a point where the ordinate is *less* than at all other points in its *immediate* vicinity. Figure 4.5 on page 96 shows that the function $(6 - x - x^2)$ has a maximum value of about 6.2. Figure 4.4 on page 95 shows that the function $(2x - 3)$ does not have a maximum or a minimum.

EXERCISES

Graph the following functions and find the real zeros, estimating to the nearest tenth any that are not integers:

1. $x^2 + 4x - 12$.
2. $x^2 - 3x - 4$.
3. $x^2 - 2x + 1$.
4. $x^2 + 4x + 4$.
5. $6 + x - x^2$.
6. $1 + 2x - 2x^2$.
7. $2x^2 - 3x + 5$.
8. $x - x^2 - 2$.
9. $x^3 - 5x - 1$.
10. $2x^3 - 3x - 1$.
11. $x^4 - x^2 - 3$.
12. $x^3 + x^4 + 3$.

Plot the graph of each of the following functions and from the graph estimate each value of x for which the function is a maximum or a minimum:

13. $x^2 - 4x + 1$.
14. $x^2 + 2x - 5$.
15. $2 + 5x - x^2$.
16. $1 - 4x - 3x^2$.
17. $x^3 - 6x$.
18. $2x^2 + x^3$.

The following exercises illustrate the use of graphical solutions of problems.

19. An open box is to be made from a sheet of cardboard 8 inches square by cutting equal squares of side x from the corners and folding up the sides. (**a**) Find an expression for the volume V of the box as a function of x. (**b**) Use the graph of this function to estimate the dimensions of the largest box that can be made in this way.

20. Repeat Exercise 19 for a given sheet of cardboard $8\frac{1}{2}$ inches by 11 inches.

21. The function $3.09(42.1 S - S^2)$ was found to give the number of vehicles per hour passing any point in the fast lane of the Lincoln Tunnel during rush hours, as a function of their speed S in miles per hour. Graph this function and estimate the speed which should be maintained to allow the greatest number of vehicles to go through the tunnel.

22. A farmer has 1200 feet of fence to enclose completely a rectangular field. (**a**) Express the area A of such a field as a function of its width w.

(b) Estimate from the graph of this function the dimensions of the largest such field. (c) Consider the interval on which the function is positive and indicate the possible values of w.

23. The edges of two cubes differ by 2 inches. (a) Express the difference D of their volumes as a function of the edge of the smaller cube, and (b) find graphically the size of the cubes for which D is 728 cubic inches.

24. A club chartered an airplane and guaranteed that at least 35 passengers would make the trip. The usual fare is $40 per person. The airline agreed to reduce this fare (for everybody) by 25 cents for each person over the 35 required. The plane can carry as many as 85 passengers. (a) Under these conditions, is the airline's total revenue ever less than that for 35 passengers? (b) For what number of passengers does the airline have maximum revenue?

25. (a) Express three consecutive positive even integers, and the sum of their squares, each as a function of half the smallest of these integers. (b) Find, graphically, values of these integers such that the sum of their squares is 200.

26. The depth x to which a solid floating sphere of radius r and density d will sink in water is a positive number which is a zero of the function $(x^3 - 3rx^2 + 4dr^3)$. Find graphically the depth, correct to one decimal place, to which a sphere one foot in diameter will sink if it is made of ice with density 0.92.

27. Closed cylindrical tin cans are to be made to contain 54π cubic inches. Express the total external surface S of each can as a function of the base-radius r, measured in inches. Find approximately, by means of a graph, the dimensions of the can requiring the least amount of tin.

28. If the can described in the preceding exercise had one circular end open, what would be the dimensions of the can requiring the least amount of tin?

4-10 Parametric Representations

In § 4-6 it was shown how to graph a function of one variable, using values of that independent variable as abscissas. Another type of graph, less common but very important in special cases, does not depict the independent variable (which we shall often denote by t) at all. Rather the graph shows pairs of corresponding values of two dependent variables, such as x and y, each of which is given as a function of t. In this case, t is often called a **parameter,** and the two functions are said to constitute a **parametric representation** for the graph.

EXAMPLE.   Graph x and y, which are given by the parametric representation

$$\begin{cases} x = (1 - t)^2(1 + t), \\ y = (1 - t)(1 + t)^2. \end{cases}$$

Solution.   Taking values of the parameter t, we construct a table of corresponding values of x and y, and graph each such pair (x, y) as coordinates of a point. The points for successive values of t in algebraic order are connected in succession. The result appears in Figure 4.8.

t	x	y
-2	-9	3
-1.5	-3.12	0.62
-1	0	0
-0.9	0.36	0.02
-0.5	1.12	0.38
-0.1	1.09	0.89
0	1	1
0.1	0.89	1.09
0.5	0.38	1.12
0.9	0.02	0.36
1	0	0
1.5	0.62	-3.12
2	3	-9

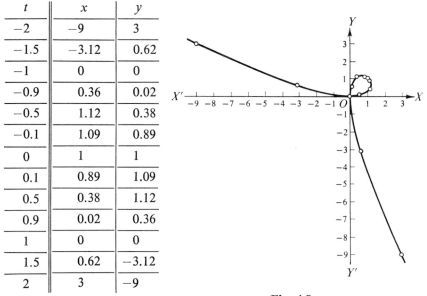

Fig. 4.8

EXERCISES

Graph the parametric representations:

1. $\begin{cases} x = t + 1, \\ y = 2t - 3. \end{cases}$

2. $\begin{cases} x = 3t - 1, \\ y = 2t. \end{cases}$

3. $\begin{cases} x = u + 2, \\ y = u^2. \end{cases}$

4. $\begin{cases} x = s^2 - 2, \\ y = s - 2. \end{cases}$

5. $\begin{cases} x = \sqrt{5 - t}, \\ y = 2\sqrt{t} - 1. \end{cases}$

6. $\begin{cases} x = t^2, \\ y = t^2 + 2. \end{cases}$

7. $\begin{cases} x = t^3, \\ y = t^3 - 1. \end{cases}$

8. $\begin{cases} x = t^2 - t + 1, \\ y = 3t^2 - 4. \end{cases}$

9. $\begin{cases} x = 3 + t^2, \\ y = 4 - t - t^2. \end{cases}$

10. $\begin{cases} x = \dfrac{t}{1 + t^2}, \\ y = \dfrac{1}{1 + t^2}. \end{cases}$

11. $\begin{cases} x = t^3 + t, \\ y = t^3 + t^2 - 1. \end{cases}$

12. $\begin{cases} x = \dfrac{1}{t} + t, \\ y = \dfrac{1}{t} - t^2. \end{cases}$

13. $\begin{cases} x = |t|, \\ y = |1 - t|. \end{cases}$

14. (a) $\begin{cases} x = 2|t|, \\ y = |t| - 3; \end{cases}$

(b) $\begin{cases} x = -2|t|, \\ y = -|t| - 3; \end{cases}$

(c) $\begin{cases} x = 2|t - 3| + 6, \\ y = |t - 3|. \end{cases}$

15. Graph $x = t + 2, y = 3t - 4$, **(a)** as a parametric representation; **(b)** by solving the first equation for t in terms of x, substituting in the second equation, and graphing as a function of one variable.

★16. Graph $x = -3|t|, y = |t| - 3$, **(a)** as a parametric representation; **(b)** by substituting $u = |t|$, solving the first equation for u, substituting in the second equation, and graphing y as a function of x. **(c)** Compare and discuss the two graphs.

4-11   Variation

Many of the laws of chemistry, engineering, physics, and other branches of science are commonly stated in the language of variation. For example, Ohm's law for a circuit states that "the current in an electric circuit varies directly as the electromotive force and inversely as the resistance." Other laws from these fields are used in the examples and exercises of this section. We consider four types of variation.

If two variables, y *and* x, *are so related that for each particular value of* x *the corresponding value of* y *is such that the ratio of* y *to* x *is always constant, then* y *is said to* **vary directly** *as* x *or to* **be proportional to** x. *That is,* y *varies directly as* x *if* y/x = k, *or* y = kx, k *being a constant.*

The constant k is called the **constant of proportionality** or the **constant of variation.** The symbols $\propto$ and $\sim$ are sometimes used to denote variation. Thus, $y \propto x$ is read "y varies directly as x."

ILLUSTRATION 1.   If a man is paid at the rate of $2.25 per hour, the amount he receives varies directly as the number of hours he works. Here the constant of proportionality is the rate per hour.

If a variable y *varies directly as the reciprocal of a variable* x, *then* y *is said to* **vary inversely** *as* x. That is, y *varies inversely as* x *if* y $= $ k$/$x, *or* xy $=$ k, k *being a constant.*

ILLUSTRATION 2.   If a man walks at a uniform rate, the time it takes him to walk a fixed distance varies inversely as his rate since $rt = d$ where d is constant.

If a variable z *varies directly as the product of the variables* x *and* y, *then* z *is said to* **vary jointly** *as* x *and* y. That is, z *varies jointly as* x *and* y *if* z $=$ kxy, k *being a constant.*

ILLUSTRATION 3.   The absolute temperature T of a perfect gas varies jointly as its pressure p and its volume v, that is, $T = kpv$, k being a constant.

Direct, inverse, and joint variations may be **combined.**

ILLUSTRATION 4.   If z varies directly as x and inversely as y, then $z = kx/y$, k being a constant.

If $w = kxy^2/\sqrt[3]{z}$, k constant, then w is said to vary jointly as x and the square of y, and inversely as the cube root of z.

The variational relations, $y = kx$, $y = k/x$, $z = kxy$, and so on, are special cases of functional relations. The solution of a problem involving variation usually has three parts:

(1) *Translating the problem into an equation involving a constant of proportionality, say* k;
(2) *Finding the particular value of* k; *and*
(3) *Applying the law to find any required unknown part.*

EXAMPLE 1.   Find the equation connecting x, y, and z if z varies directly as x and inversely as the square of y, and $z = 12$ when $x = 2$ and $y = 3$.

Solution.   Given:
$$z = \frac{kx}{y^2}.$$

Substitute for x, y, and z:
$$12 = \frac{k \cdot 2}{3^2}.$$

Solve for k:
$$k = 54.$$

Hence the required equation is $z = \dfrac{54x}{y^2}.$

EXAMPLE 2. The safe load of a horizontal beam supported at both ends varies jointly as the breadth and the square of the depth and inversely as the length between the supports. If a 2 by 10 inch beam, 10 feet between supports, can safely hold up 1 ton, how wide a beam 12 inches deep and 15 feet long should be used to carry a weight of 4200 pounds?

Solution. Let L denote the load, in pounds; b the breadth, in inches; d the depth, in inches; l the length between supports, in feet; and x the breadth, in inches, of the required beam. It is not necessary that b, d, and l in this example be expressed in the same unit of measure, since the constant of proportionality may include constant factors relating the different units. It is only necessary that each of them be used consistently throughout a solution, always in feet or always in inches, but definitely not one time in feet and another time in inches.

L (lb.)	2000	4200
b (in.)	2	x
d (in.)	10	12
l (ft.)	10	15
k	100	
law	$L = \dfrac{100bd^2}{l}$	

$$L = \frac{kbd^2}{l}.$$

$$2000 = \frac{k \cdot 2 \cdot 10^2}{10}.$$

$$k = 100.$$

$$L = \frac{100bd^2}{l}.$$

$$4200 = \frac{100 \cdot x \cdot 12^2}{15}.$$

$$x = \frac{4200 \cdot 15}{100 \cdot 144} = \frac{35}{8} = 4\tfrac{3}{8}.$$

Therefore the beam should be $4\tfrac{3}{8}$ inches wide.

EXERCISES

Write the equations expressing the relations stated between the variables, using k *as the constant of proportionality if the value of the constant is not well known:*

1. The radiant energy E of a luminous body varies directly as the fourth power of its absolute temperature A.

2. The amount A of silt carried by a stream of water varies directly as the sixth power of the speed s of the stream.

3. The number of feet s traversed by a freely falling body varies directly as the square of its time of fall t.

4. The intensity I of illumination from a given source varies inversely as the square of the distance d from the source.

5. The current I in an electric circuit varies directly as the electromotive force E and inversely as the resistance R. (Ohm's law.)

6. **(a)** The force of attraction F between two bodies varies inversely as the square of the distance d between them; **(b)** the force of attraction F between two bodies of masses m_1 and m_2 varies directly as the product of their masses and inversely as the square of the distance d between them. (Newton's law of gravitation.)

7. The number N of a certain object at P dollars each that can be bought for S dollars varies directly as S and inversely as P.

8. The distance D traveled at a constant rate R varies jointly as R and the time T.

9. The time T required for a trip varies directly as the distance D and inversely as the average rate R.

10. The volume V of an ideal gas varies directly as its temperature T and inversely as its pressure P. (General gas law.)

11. In vibrating strings the vibrating frequency, or pitch, f varies **(a)** directly as the square root of the tension t on the string; **(b)** inversely as the length l of the string; **(c)** inversely as the square root of the mass m of the string.

12. The power P required in an electric circuit varies jointly as the resistance R and the square of the current I.

13. The force F necessary to keep a car from skidding on a curve varies inversely as the radius r of the curve and jointly as the mass m of the car and the square of its speed s.

In Exercises 14 through 18 express each of the given statements in the language of variation:

14. For a circle: **(a)** $A = \pi r^2$; **(b)** $C = \pi d$.

15. For a sphere: **(a)** $S = 4\pi r^2$; **(b)** $V = \frac{4}{3}\pi r^3$.

16. For a cube: **(a)** $S = 6e^2$; **(b)** $V = e^3$; **(c)** $V = \frac{1}{36}\sqrt{6S^3}$.

17. For a cone: **(a)** $V = \frac{1}{3}\pi r^2 h$; **(b)** $S = \pi rs$.

18. For a simple pendulum: $T = 2\pi\sqrt{l/g}$.

19. If y varies directly as the square of x, and $y = 3$ when $x = 4$, find **(a)** the law connecting x and y; **(b)** the value of y if $x = 12$.

20. **(a)** If y varies inversely as x, and $y = 5$ when $x = 9$, find the law connecting x and y. **(b)** Find the law if y varies inversely as the square root of x, and $y = 5$ when $x = 9$.

21. If y varies jointly as x and the square root of z, and $y = \frac{1}{2}$ when $x = 3$ and $z = 4$, find **(a)** the law connecting x, y, and z; **(b)** the value of x when $y = 2$ and $z = 3$.

22. The current I in amperes in an electric circuit varies inversely as the resistance R in ohms when the electromotive force is constant. If in a certain circuit I is 15 amperes when R is $1\frac{1}{2}$ ohms, find I when R is 0.2 ohm.

23. If a certain amount of gas at constant temperature (see Exercise 10) occupies 600 cubic centimeters at a pressure of 2 kilograms per square centimeter, find its volume when the pressure is 3 kilograms per square centimeter.

24. The pressure p of the wind on a plane surface varies directly as the square of the speed v of the wind. If the pressure is 2 pounds per square foot when the speed of the wind is 20 miles per hour, find the pressure when the wind's speed is 75 miles per hour (hurricane force).

25. An airplane in level flight is supported by a lift which varies jointly as the angle of attack and the square of the speed. If an angle of 2° will support the weight of the plane at 600 miles per hour, what angle of attack will be required at 400 miles per hour?

26. The maximum safe load L for a horizontal beam supported at both ends varies jointly as its breadth b and the square of its thickness t and inversely as the distance d between the supports. If a 2-by-8 floor timber of a certain length will hold 2000 pounds when placed with the 2-inch side down, how much will it hold when placed with the 8-inch side down?

★27. If S varies directly as the cube of x, **(a)** what change in S results from doubling x? **(b)** What change in x is required to double S?

★28. Repeat Exercise 27 when S is proportional to the square root of x.

★29. Repeat Exercise 27 when S varies inversely as x^2.

30. The weight raised by a jack varies directly as the force applied and the length of the handle and inversely as the length of the jack arm. If the two lengths are equal, then the weight equals the force. If the jack arm is $\frac{1}{2}$ inch long and the handle is two feet long, how much force is required to raise 2400 pounds?

31. The apparent (angular) diameter of a distant object varies directly as the actual diameter and inversely as the distance from the observer. The moon and sun have apparent diameters of 31.1 and 32.0 minutes of arc respectively and are at distances from the earth of 239,000 and 92,900,000 miles respectively. The moon's diameter is 2160 miles; what is the sun's diameter?

32. In a vacuum tube, the speed of the electrons varies directly as the square root of the voltage. Under 110 volts the speed is $6.55 \cdot 10^8$ centimeters per second. What is the speed under **(a)** 220 volts? **(b)** 1100 volts?

33. The force exerted on a piston by a fluid, or vice versa, varies jointly as the fluid pressure and the area of the piston face; and the pressure is the same at all parts of a fluid. If a force of 30 pounds pushes a one-inch diameter piston against a fluid in one end of a rigid vessel, how much force does the fluid exert against a six-inch diameter piston at the other end of the vessel?

MISCELLANEOUS EXERCISES

1. John left home and drove at 40 miles per hour for two hours, then stopped for half an hour, then continued on at 50 miles per hour. **(a)** Graph his distance traveled from the start as a function of time. **(b)** Find from the graph the time when he had traveled 100 miles.

2. Two brothers, A and B, start at the same time on a direct journey from their home to a place 80 miles away. A travels 40 miles per hour, and B travels 32 miles per hour. When A reaches the destination, he immediately returns home at the same rate. **(a)** Graph the distance of each man from their home as a function of time, drawing both graphs on the same coordinate plane. **(b)** How far from their home does A meet B?

3. The distance of the visible horizon at sea, in statute miles, from certain heights in feet above sea level is given in the following table. Exhibit these data graphically. Find the distance of the horizon for heights of 25 feet, 54 feet, and 78 feet **(a)** from the graph; **(b)** by linear interpolation.

Height	10	20	30	40	50	60	70	80	90	100
Visibility	4.2	5.9	7.3	8.4	9.4	10.3	11.1	11.9	12.6	13.3

4. Write the equations expressing the relations stated between the variables, using k as the constant of proportionality if the value of the constant is not well known: **(a)** The perimeter P of a square varies directly as a side s. **(b)** The area A of a square varies directly as the square of a side s. **(c)** The wind resistance R of an automobile driven at high speed varies directly as the square of the speed v. **(d)** The square of the time t required by a planet to make one complete revolution around the sun varies directly as the cube of its average distance d from the sun. **(e)** The density D of a given mass varies inversely as its volume V.

5. The exposure time needed to make an enlargement from a photographic negative varies as the area of the enlargement. If it takes 10 seconds for a print $2\frac{1}{2}$ inches by $3\frac{1}{4}$ inches, how long will it take for a print 6 inches by 8 inches?

6. The weekly payroll P in dollars at a small factory varies jointly as the number n of men employed and the number d of days that they work. When 20 men worked 5 days each, the payroll was $3000. **(a)** Find the relation among the variables. **(b)** Give an interpretation for the constant of proportionality. **(c)** Find the payroll when 15 men work 3 days each.

7. The minimum speed v at which a motorcyclist must ride around inside a drum with vertical sides in order not to fall off varies as the square root of the radius of the drum. Under certain fixed conditions he must travel at least 30 miles per hour to stay on a drum with a radius of 40 feet. **(a)** Graph the required speed as a function of the radius. **(b)** Find both algebraically and graphically the required speed for radius 90 feet.

8. Estimate the dimensions of the largest open box that could be lined with a single sheet of aluminum foil 14 inches square (no cutting allowed).

9. A rectangular box with a square base and open at the top is to be made from 48 square feet of lumber. Express the volume V of the box as a function of a side x, measured in feet, of the square base. Find approximately, by means of a graph, the dimensions of the largest box that can be made.

10. Neglecting any atmospheric absorption, the intensity of sunlight varies inversely as the square of the distance. Mars is 1.525 times as far from the sun as the earth is. How does the intensity of sunlight on Mars compare with that on the earth?

*11. If two lines are parallel, how do their slopes compare? Explain.

*12. If two lines are perpendicular to each other, how do their slopes compare? Explain.

13. A sheet of galvanized iron is cut off and bent to form a trough with cross-section area 30 square inches. The bottom is 6 inches wide, and the two sides are equally steep. Find the required width of the sheet, before bending, as a function of the depth h of the trough.

14. Find approximately, by means of a graph, the area of the largest rectangle which can be inscribed in an isosceles triangle of base 8 inches and altitude 6 inches, where one side of the rectangle lies along the base of the triangle.

15. A rectangle with base 5 inches and altitude 3 inches is inscribed in a triangle whose base lies along the base of the rectangle. Find, at least approximately, the minimum area of such a triangle.

CHAPTER 5

EQUATIONS AND IDENTITIES

5-1 Equalities

In this chapter we treat more extensively the ideas about equations which were touched on in § 3-6.

An **equality** *is a statement that two expressions represent the same number,* the two expressions being called **members** or **sides** of the equality. Equalities are of two kinds: identical equalities, or identities; and conditional equalities, or equations.

If the two members of an equality are equal for all values of the symbols for which both members are defined, the equality is called an **identical equality,** *or simply an* **identity.**

EXAMPLES OF IDENTITIES.

$$(a + b)(a - b) = a^2 - b^2; \qquad (2x - 1)^2 + 4x = 4x^2 + 1;$$
$$(x^2 + 2x - 3)/(x - 1) = x + 3.$$

Note that the left member of the third example of an identity above is not defined for $x = 1$, since the denominator $(x - 1)$ becomes zero for this value of x. Many other examples of identities have already been met in this book. For example, the equality between any expression and the product of its factors is an identity. Likewise, when an expression has been simplified, the equality between the given expression and the simplified form is an identity.

If two members of an equality are defined but unequal for at least one set of values of the symbols involved, the equality is called a **conditional equality,** *or simply an* **equation.**

EXAMPLES OF EQUATIONS.

$$x - 3 = 2, \quad \text{true only if } x = 5;$$
$$x^2 + 2 = 3x, \quad \text{true only if } x = 1 \text{ or } x = 2;$$
$$x + 1 = x, \quad \text{not true for any value of } x.$$

Equations, such as that in the third example, which are not true for any value of x are often called **impossible equations.** The equation $\sqrt{x} + 4 = 0$ is another impossible equation, since $\sqrt{x}$ has been defined to be nonnegative.

The symbol for equality "$=$" is used for both identities and equations. However, the symbol "$\equiv$," read "is identically equal to" or "identically equals," is frequently used to emphasize that a certain equality is an identity.

An equation in one unknown, as x, is an algebraic way of describing a number by stating a condition which the number x must satisfy. For example, in the equation $x^2 + 2 = 3x$, x is described as a number whose square increased by 2 is equal to three times the number.

An equation in two unknowns expresses one condition imposed on their values in relation one to the other, but usually does not restrict either unknown to any definite value or values. For example, in the equation $y = 2x - 3$ the symbol x may represent any real number, and the equation merely restricts y to values 3 less than twice those of x.

If two polynomials in any number of unknowns are equated, the equation is called a **polynomial equation** (or **integral rational equation**) in those unknowns. The most common case is that one polynomial is the single term 0 and the other is a polynomial (not a constant) in one unknown such as x:

$$a_0x^n + a_1x^{n-1} + a_2x^{n-2} + \cdots + a_{n-1}x + a_n = 0 \qquad (1)$$

where n is a positive integer and the coefficients $a_0, a_1, a_2, \cdots, a_{n-1}, a_n$ are constants with $a_0 \neq 0$.

ILLUSTRATION 1.   The equations $2x^5 - 6x^4 + 3x^2 - 14x - 5 = 0$ and $x^3 - \frac{1}{2}x + \sqrt{3} = 0$ are integral and rational in x and are polynomial equations. The following equations are not polynomial equations:

$$x^2 + \sqrt{x} - \tfrac{1}{2} = 0 \text{ is integral but not rational in } x;$$

$$x^4 - \frac{2}{x} - 6 = 0 \text{ is rational but not integral in } x.$$

ILLUSTRATION 2. $6x^2 - 3xy - ay^3 + 5 = 0$ is a polynomial equation in x and y, and $xz^2 - bxyz + 4y = 10$ is a polynomial equation in x, y, and z.

The **degree of a polynomial equation** is the degree of the term, or terms, of highest degree; see § 2-1. Equations of the first, second, third, fourth, and fifth degrees are called **linear, quadratic, cubic, quartic** (or **biquadratic**), and **quintic equations,** respectively.

ILLUSTRATION 3.   The first equation in Illustration 1 is of degree 5 in x; that is, it is a quintic equation in x. The equation

$$2x^5 - a^2x^2y^2 - 3x^2yz^4 = b^8 - 4xz^4$$

is of the fifth degree in x, of the second degree in y, of the fourth degree in z, of the fifth degree in x and y, of the sixth degree in x and z, of the fifth degree in y and z, and of the seventh degree in x, y, and z. The term $2x^5$ is of degree zero in y.

EXERCISES

1. Give the degree of the equation

$$15x^3y^2z + xy^2z^5 - 7z^6 + 4x - 5 = 0,$$

(a) in x; **(b)** in y and z; **(c)** in x, y, and z.

2. Give the degree of the equation $s^4 + 3st - s^2t^3 = 6s^2t + 218$, **(a)** in s; **(b)** in t; **(c)** in s and t.

Give, if possible, at least one example of a polynomial equation in two unknowns, x *and* y, *which is:*

3. Linear in x and y.   **5.** Quadratic in x and cubic in y.

4. Linear in x and linear in y.   **6.** Quadratic in x and y.

7. Quadratic in x, cubic in y, cubic in x and y.

8. Linear in x, linear in y, and quadratic in x and y.

9. Linear in x, linear in y, cubic in x and y.

10. Cubic in x, cubic in y, and of degree 12 in x and y.

Assume that x *may represent any real number for which both members are defined, and classify the following equalities as identities or equations:*

11. $4(x + 3) = 4x + 12.$ **16.** $x^2 - 7x = x^2 + 7.$

12. $3(2x - 1) = 6x - 3.$

17. $\dfrac{9x^2 - 16y^2}{3x - 4y} = 3x + 4y.$

13. $7x - 3 = 9 - 5x.$

14. $(x + 2)(x - 2) = x^2 - 4.$

18. $\left(x + \dfrac{1}{x}\right)^2 - \left(\dfrac{1}{x} - x\right)^2 = 4.$

15. $(x + 1)^2 - x^2 = 1 + 2x.$

19. $(2x + 5)^2 - (2x - 5)^2 = 20x.$

20. $2(x - 3) + 8 = 3(x - 2) + 8.$

21. $(4x - 36)(3x^2 + 2x) = 4x(3x + 2)(x - 9).$

22. $9x + 6(2x + 3) = (9x + 6)2x + 3.$

23. $(12 + 8x)/4 = 12 + 8x/4.$

24. $x^2 + 4 = (x + 4)^2 - 8x.$

State, but do not solve, equations expressing each of the following conditions:

25. Twice a number m is equal to the number increased by 7.

26. The square of a number n is equal to the number decreased by 8.

27. A number x is 4 less than a number y.

28. The area of a square of side s is equal to the area of a triangle of base s and altitude h.

29. The cube of a number x is equal to the number decreased by 7.

30. The point (x, y) is at a distance of 5 from the y-axis.

31. The distance between the point $(2, -1)$ and the point (x, y) is 3.

32. The sum of the distances of the point (x, y) from the points $(4, 0)$ and $(-4, 1)$ is 10.

5-2   Algebraic Solution of an Equation

Any value of the unknown, or set of values of the unknowns, which when substituted in an equation makes its two members equal, is called a **solution** *of the equation.* Such a value, or set of values, is said to **satisfy** the equation. If the equation contains only one unknown, each solution is also called a **root** of the equation.

ILLUSTRATION.   The equation $3x^2 - 4x - 4 = 0$ has 2 as a root, since $3(2^2) - 4(2) - 4 = 0$; the equation $2x - 5y = 11$ has $x = 3$, $y = -1$ as a solution, since $2(3) - 5(-1) = 11$.

To solve an equation is to find all its solutions, and the process of finding all the solutions is called **solving the equation**. Since the number of solutions of an equation of more than one unknown is usually unlimited (see § 10-1), we shall limit our discussion of methods of solving equations in this chapter to equations in one unknown.

A method of solving certain simple equations was discussed in § 3-6. It can now be described more systematically.

The solutions of an equation are not affected by adding the same number or expression to, or subtracting it from, both members of the equation, since if the members were equal before the change, then they are still equal afterward and vice versa. Also, both members may be multiplied or divided by the same constant other than zero. By such changes, any equation of the first degree in x—that is, any **linear equation in x** (§ 5-1)—can be put in the form

$$ax + b = 0,$$

where a and b are constants. Then the equation can easily be solved.

EXAMPLE. Solve: $\frac{3}{4}x + \frac{3}{2} = \frac{1}{3}x - \frac{1}{6}$.

Solution.

Multiply both members by 12:	$9x + 18 = 4x - 2$.
Subtract $4x$ and 18 from both members:	$9x - 4x = -2 - 18$.
Combine like terms:	$5x = -20$.
Divide both members by 5:	$x = -4$.

Check. Substitute $x = -4$ in the members of the original equation:

$$\tfrac{3}{4}x + \tfrac{3}{2} = \tfrac{3}{4}(-4) + \tfrac{3}{2} = -\tfrac{3}{2};$$

$$\tfrac{1}{3}x - \tfrac{1}{6} = \tfrac{1}{3}(-4) - \tfrac{1}{6} = -\tfrac{9}{6} = -\tfrac{3}{2}.$$

The foregoing shows how to solve any particular linear equation in one unknown. However, an important part of algebra is to express things in general form so that particular problems appear as special cases of the general form.

We have already observed that any linear equation can be written in the form $ax + b = 0$; and for the equation to be actually linear, it is necessary that $a \neq 0$. Hence, an equation of the form

$$ax + b = 0, \quad a \neq 0, \tag{2}$$

where a and b are arbitrary constants, is called a **general equation of the first degree in x,** or a **general linear equation in x.**

If we subtract the constant term b from both members and then divide both members of the resulting equation by a, the coefficient of x, we obtain

$$x = -\frac{b}{a}.$$

If this value of x is substituted in (2), the equation is satisfied. Hence $-b/a$ is a root of (2). Moreover, it is the only root.

EXERCISES

By substituting in the given equation, find the answers to these questions:

1. (a) Is 1 a root of $8 - 4x = 12$? (b) Is -1 a root?

2. (a) Is -2 a root of $3x + 6 = 15$? (b) Is 3 a root?

3. (a) Is -3 a root of the equation $\frac{3}{4}(2 - 3y) + \frac{1}{2}y = 1 - y$? (b) Is $-\frac{2}{3}$ a root?

4. (a) Is 3 a root of the equation $x^2 - 2x + 3 = 0$? (b) Is -3 a root? (c) Is 1 a root? (d) Is $\frac{1}{2}$ a root? (e) Is -1 a root?

5. (a) Is $x = 4$, $y = -2$ a solution of $2x - 3y + 14 = 0$? **(b)** Is $x = -4$, $y = 2$ a solution?

6. (a) Is $x = -2$, $y = -1$ a solution of $3y - 2x = 1$? **(b)** Is $x = -3$, $y = 0$ a solution?

Substitute in the given equation to determine whether or not the equation has the given number as a root:

7. $y^3 - 7y^2 + 4y + 6 = 0$; -1.

8. $z^4 - 2z^2 + \frac{3}{2}z - 5 = 0$; -2.

9. $4s^3 - 5s^2 - 3s + 1 = 0$; $\frac{1}{4}$.

10. $2x^5 + 3x^4 - x^2 = 0$; $\frac{1}{2}$.

Solve if possible:

11. $2x + 5 = 0$.

12. $3y - 48 = 0$.

13. $2r = \frac{1}{6}$.

14. $4u = -\frac{3}{8}$.

15. $\frac{3}{2}t = -\frac{9}{5}$.

16. $\frac{7}{8}x = \frac{9}{20}$.

17. $\frac{8}{7}x = 0$.

18. $3x + 4 = 16$.

19. $3x + 16 = 4x$.

20. $2 - 3x = 10x$.

21. $2 - 3x = 10$.

22. $ax + b = c$.

23. $px - q = rx$.

24. $cx + d = 5x$.

25. $3u + 5 = -2u - 5$.

26. $5y - 2 = 2y - 8$.

27. $\frac{3}{4}x + \frac{1}{6} = x - \frac{1}{3}$.

28. $\frac{2}{3}x + \frac{3}{2} = x - \frac{5}{4}$.

29. $3x - 2 = 3x$.

30. $3x - 2 = -2$.

31. $3x - 2 = \frac{6}{2}x - \frac{12}{6}$.

32. $10^5x - 10^3 = 2 \cdot 10^4(x + 3)$.

33. $2^7x - 7 = 2^8x - 5$.

34. $2(3z - 1) + 5z = -1 - 5(z - 3)$.

35. $5^0 + \frac{1}{2}[4 - 2(x - 1)] = 3x\{1 - 7(4 - 4) + 6[-2 - 2(4^{-1})]\}$.

36. Solve $5x - 6 = 3x + 4$ **(a)** by the method of § 3-6; **(b)** by reducing to the form $ax + b = 0$ and substituting in the solution of the general linear equation in x.

Substitute in the given equation to find a value of m *such that the given number will be a root of the given equation:*

37. $x^3 - 7x^2 + 3x + m = 0$; 1.

38. $3x^3 - 3x^2 + 4 = mx$; 2.

39. $2y^2 - my = 18$; 3.

40. $8x - x^2 = m + 1$; 0.

41. $mx^2 - m^2x + 24 = 8x^2 - \frac{17}{2}x + 4m$; 0.

42. (a) Prove $x(x - 1)(x - 2) \equiv x^3 - 3x^2 + 2x$. **(b)** Verify that this identity is satisfied when $x = 3$. **(c)** Are 0, 1, 2, and 3 roots of the equation $x^3 - 3x^2 + 2x = 0$?

43. The circumference C of a circle with radius r is given by $C = 2\pi r$. Solve for r.

44. The area A of a triangle with base b and altitude h is given by $A = \frac{1}{2}bh$. Solve for **(a)** b; **(b)** h.

45. The volume V of a right circular cone with altitude h and base of radius r is given by $V = \frac{1}{3}\pi r^2 h$. Solve for h.

46. The area A of a trapezoid with altitude h and parallel bases b_1 and b_2 is given by $A = \frac{1}{2}h(b_1 + b_2)$. Solve for **(a)** h; **(b)** b_1; **(c)** b_2.

47. The net profit P on sales of n chairs (all alike) is given by the relation $P = n(p_2 - p_1) - c$, where p_2 is the selling price, p_1 the cost per chair to the seller, and c is the overhead on the n chairs. Solve for p_2.

48. The strength I of the current along a conductor is proportional to the applied electromotive force V and inversely proportional to the resistance R of the conductor: $I = V/R$. Solve for **(a)** V; **(b)** R.

5-3   Graphic Solution of an Equation

An equation in one unknown can be solved graphically—that is, by means of a graph.

ILLUSTRATION 1. To solve the equation $2x - 3 = 0$, consider the related function $(2x - 3)$. The latter is graphed in Figure 4.4 on page 95, and we see that it has just one x-intercept, $1\frac{1}{2}$; that is, $y = 0$ when $x = 1\frac{1}{2}$. But if $y = 0$, then $2x - 3 = 0$ as desired. Thus the given equation has the solution $x = 1\frac{1}{2}$.

ILLUSTRATION 2. To solve the equation $6 - x - x^2 = 0$, consider the function $(6 - x - x^2)$. By Figure 4.5 on page 96, the graph of this has x-intercepts -3 and 2. Hence the given equation has the solutions $x = -3$ and $x = 2$.

For a simple equation, as in Illustration 1, the algebraic method of solution (§ 5-2; see also § 5-4 through § 5-9, and Chapter 12) is generally preferred, but for more complicated equations the graphic method may be easier to carry out or understand. Graphic methods have one major drawback: in many cases only an approximate value for the answer can be obtained.

EXAMPLE. Solve the equation $x^3 - 4x^2 + 3x + 1 = 0$ graphically; estimate the real roots to one decimal place.

Solution. Let

$$y = x^3 - 4x^2 + 3x + 1.$$

Assigning values for x, we compute the corresponding values of y. These corresponding values of x and y are tabulated on the next page.

$$y = x^3 - 4x^2 + 3x + 1$$

x	-1	-0.5	0	0.5	1	1.5	2	2.5	3	3.5
y	-7	-1.6	1	1.6	1	-0.1	-1	-0.9	1	5.4

If these points are plotted and a smooth curve drawn through them, we obtain the curve shown in Figure 5.1. From the above table of values we note that this curve crosses the x-axis between $x = -0.5$ and $x = 0$; between $x = 1$ and $x = 1.5$; and between $x = 2.5$ and $x = 3$. From the graph we read that the three roots of $y = 0$ are approximately -0.2, 1.4, and 2.8.

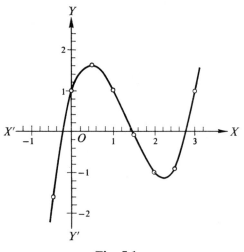

Fig. 5.1

EXERCISES

Solve each equation graphically, estimating to one decimal place any roots that are not integers:

1. $3x - 15 = 0.$
2. $4x - 24 = 0.$
3. $5x + 20 = 0.$
4. $6x + 18 = 0.$
5. $5x - 13 = 0.$
6. $6x - 13 = 0.$
7. $x^2 - 7 = 0.$

8. $x^2 - 5 = 0.$
9. $x^2 + x - 12 = 0.$
10. $x^2 - 2x - 8 = 0.$
11. $3x^2 - 4x - 4 = 0.$
12. $1 - 2x^2 + 2x = 0.$
13. $x - x^2 + 3 = 0.$
14. $x = 3 - x^2.$

15. $2 - 3x + 2x^2 = 0.$ **20.** $4 - x + x^3 + x^2 = 0.$

16. $4x = x^2 - 4.$ **21.** $x^3 + 3x^2 = 2x + 3.$

17. $x^3 + x - 3 = 0.$ **22.** $x^3 = 3x - 1.$

18. $2x^3 + 5x - 9 = 0.$ **23.** $x^4 + x^3 - 3 = 0.$

19. $4x^3 - 5x + 3 = 0.$ **24.** $x^4 - 8x^2 + 12 = 0.$

Graph $y = x^2$, $y = x^2 - 1$, *and* $y = x^2 - 4$ *on the same coordinate axes. Then:*

★25. Compare and describe the relationship between the graphs **(a)** of $y = x^2$ and $y = x^2 - 1$; **(b)** of $y = x^2$ and $y = x^2 - 4$.

★26. Tell how **(a)** the graphs of $y = x^2$ and $y = 1$ may be used to solve $x^2 - 1 = 0$; **(b)** the graphs of $y = x^2$ and $y = 4$ may be used to solve $x^2 - 4 = 0$.

27. John walked two miles from home and then was given a ride onward at a rate of 30 miles per hour. **(a)** Graph $y = 30x + 2$ and discuss the relationship between the graph and the statements in the preceding sentence. From the graph, estimate the total distance that John has traveled by the time he has ridden **(b)** $1\frac{3}{4}$ hours; **(c)** $2\frac{1}{3}$ hours. **(d)** Check algebraically.

5-4   Equivalent Equations

We now consider further a matter discussed briefly in § 5-2. We ask: "What operations of algebra are permissible in solving an equation?" What we want are operations upon the members of an equation which lead to an **equivalent equation**; that is, to a new equation containing all the roots of the original equation and no others.

The following operations always lead to equivalent equations:

Adding the same number or expression to, or subtracting the same number or expression from, both members;

Multiplying or dividing both members by the same number or expression, provided that this expression is not zero and does not contain the unknown.

This can be seen from the fact that after each of these operations the given equation could be obtained back again from the new equation by the appropriate subtraction, addition, division, or multiplication, as the case may be. In other words, the inverses of these operations are permissible operations.

ILLUSTRATION 1.   The equations $x = 4 - 3x$, $x + 3x = 4 - 3x + 3x$ (obtained by adding $3x$ to both members), and $-2x = -8 + 6x$ (obtained by multiplying both members of the original equation by -2) are equivalent, each having the root 1.

The following operations may lead to equations that are *not* equivalent to the original equation:

Multiplying or dividing both members by the same expression containing the unknown;

Raising both members to the same power.

The inverses of these operations are not always permissible; yet one or more of these operations are often necessary, as in the clearing of an equation of fractions. Whenever the new equation has roots that are *not* roots of the original equation, these roots are called **extraneous roots** of the original equation. In clearing an equation of fractions, extraneous roots may usually be avoided by using an L.C.D. (see Illustration 4, below). However, extraneous roots can always be identified by testing the roots in the original equation. Accordingly, extraneous roots can be easily handled, and it is more important to recognize operations leading to equations which *lack* one or more of the roots of the original equation. The most common operations leading to such a *loss* of roots are (1) the dividing of both members by an expression involving the unknown without recognizing the zeros of that expression as possible roots of the original equation (see Illustration 5), and (2) the taking of square roots of both members without recognizing that any number different from zero has two square roots (see Illustration 6).

ILLUSTRATION 2. The equation $x - 1 = 3$ has only one root, 4. If both members are multiplied by $(x + 4)$, we obtain the derived equation

$$x^2 + 3x - 4 = 3x + 12,$$

which has the roots ± 4. Thus the extraneous root -4 has been introduced by the multiplication of both members by the expression $(x + 4)$ having -4 as a zero.

ILLUSTRATION 3.   The equation $3x = 2x - 1$ has only one root, -1. If both members are squared, the derived equation is $9x^2 = 4x^2 - 4x + 1$, which has the two roots -1 and $\frac{1}{5}$. Thus the extraneous root $\frac{1}{5}$ has been introduced by squaring both members.

ILLUSTRATION 4.   Let us solve the equation

$$\frac{6}{x - 2} + \frac{x}{2 - x} = 3.$$

Correct method.   If both members are multiplied by $(x - 2)$, *an L.C.D.* of the fractions, we obtain the equivalent derived equation $6 - x = 3x - 6$, which has the root 3.

Improper method.   If both members are multiplied by $(x - 2)(2 - x)$, which is *not an L.C.D.* of the fractions, we obtain the derived equation

$$12 - 6x + x^2 - 2x = 12x - 12 - 3x^2,$$

which has the two roots 2 and 3. The root 2 is extraneous, since a denominator of the original equation becomes zero when $x = 2$ and this is forbidden. However, $x = 3$ satisfies the original equation; hence 3 is a root.

ILLUSTRATION 5.   The equation $x^2 - 1 = 2x + 2$ has the two roots -1 and 3. If both members are divided by $(x + 1)$, we obtain the derived equation $x - 1 = 2$, which has only the root 3. Thus the root -1 has been lost by the division of both members by the expression $(x + 1)$ which has -1 as a zero.

ILLUSTRATION 6.   The equation $x^2 = 4$ is equivalent to the equation $x^2 - 4 = 0$ and has the two roots 2 and -2. When we take the square roots of the two members, we should recognize that $\sqrt{x^2} = x$ if x is positive and $\sqrt{x^2} = -x$ if x is negative. Thus $x = 2$ if x is positive and $-x = 2$ whence $x = -2$ if x is negative.

EXAMPLE 1.   Solve: $\dfrac{x + 2}{x - 2} - \dfrac{x - 2}{x + 2} = 1 - \dfrac{x^2}{x^2 - 4}$.

Solution.   This equation is not linear. It can be transformed to an equivalent equation free of fractions by multiplying each member by $(x^2 - 4)$, an L.C.D. of the fractions. We thus obtain

$$(x + 2)^2 - (x - 2)^2 = (x^2 - 4) - x^2,$$

or $\qquad x^2 + 4x + 4 - (x^2 - 4x + 4) = x^2 - 4 - x^2.$

Upon further simplification the above equation reduces to

$$x^2 + 4x + 4 - x^2 + 4x - 4 = -4,$$

or $\qquad\qquad 8x = -4, \quad \text{or} \quad x = -\tfrac{1}{2}.$

Check.   Substitute $x = -\tfrac{1}{2}$ in the original equation:

$$\frac{x + 2}{x - 2} - \frac{x - 2}{x + 2} = \frac{(-\tfrac{1}{2}) + 2}{(-\tfrac{1}{2}) - 2} - \frac{(-\tfrac{1}{2}) - 2}{(-\tfrac{1}{2}) + 2} = \frac{16}{15};$$

$$1 - \frac{x^2}{x^2 - 4} = 1 - \frac{(-\tfrac{1}{2})^2}{(-\tfrac{1}{2})^2 - 4} = \frac{16}{15}.$$

$$\therefore \; -\tfrac{1}{2} \text{ is the root.}$$

EXAMPLE 2.   Solve: $4 + \dfrac{x+3}{x-3} - \dfrac{4x^2}{x^2-9} = \dfrac{x-3}{x+3}$.

Solution.   Clearing of fractions by multiplying each member by $(x^2 - 9)$, an L.C.D. of the fractions, we obtain

$$4(x^2 - 9) + (x + 3)^2 - 4x^2 = (x - 3)^2,$$

or $$4x^2 - 36 + x^2 + 6x + 9 - 4x^2 = x^2 - 6x + 9.$$

Upon further simplification there results

$$12x = 36, \quad \text{or} \quad x = 3.$$

Check.   If $x = 3$, a denominator of the original equation is zero. Since division by zero is not permissible, that equation is not satisfied by $x = 3$. Therefore, 3 is an extraneous root, and the original equation has no root.

EXERCISES

State whether or not the equations are equivalent. If they are equivalent, state a method for obtaining (a) the second equation from the first; (b) the first equation from the second. If they are not equivalent, tell why.

1. $3x + 2 = 8$, $3x = 6$.

2. $3x = 6$, $x = 2$.

3. $x^2 = 9$, $x = 3$.

4. $x^2 - 4 = 0$, $x = 2$.

5. $5x^2 = 15$, $x = \sqrt{3}$.

6. $\sqrt{x} = 2$, $x = 4$.

7. If both members of the equation $3x - 2 = 1$ are multiplied (a) by 6, (b) by x, (c) by $(x - 3)$, state whether the resulting equation is equivalent to the original equation, contains one or more extraneous roots, or lacks one or more of the roots of the original equation. Give a reason for each answer.

8. If both members of the equation $16y = 8y^2$ are divided (a) by 8, (b) by y, (c) by $8y$, state whether the resulting equation is equivalent to the original equation, contains one or more extraneous roots, or lacks one or more of the roots of the original equation. Give a reason for each answer.

Solve each of the following equations if possible, and check the results:

9. $\dfrac{x^2 - 4}{x} - 2 = x$.

10. $2 + \dfrac{3}{x} = \dfrac{11}{x}$.

11. $\dfrac{3}{x} = \dfrac{11}{x}$.

12. $\dfrac{x}{x-4} = \dfrac{x+4}{x}$.

13. $8(\frac{3}{4}x - \frac{1}{2}) = 15(\frac{2}{5}x + 1) - 7.$

14. $12(\frac{1}{3}y + \frac{1}{4}) = y - \frac{1}{3}(12y - 36).$

15. $(3z - 2)(3z + 2) - (3z - 2)^2 = 2z - 3.$

16. $(x - a)(x - b) = (x - c)(x - d).$

17. $\dfrac{1}{x + 1} + \dfrac{3}{x - 2} = 0.$ **20.** $\dfrac{3y}{3y + 1} + \dfrac{4}{y - 1} = 1.$

18. $\dfrac{4x - 3}{2x - 1} = \dfrac{2x + 1}{x + 3}.$ **21.** $\dfrac{x - 3}{x + 1} - \dfrac{x - 1}{x + 3} = 0.$

19. $\dfrac{3z + 2}{3} + \dfrac{z}{z + 2} = z.$ **22.** $\dfrac{2u + 3}{u^2 - 3u} = \dfrac{u + 2}{u} - \dfrac{u}{u - 3}.$

23. $\dfrac{2}{x} - \dfrac{x}{2} = \dfrac{1}{2}(x - 2)\left(1 + \dfrac{2}{x}\right).$

24. $\dfrac{2n + 3}{2n - 3} + \dfrac{6}{4n^2 - 9} - \dfrac{2n - 3}{2n + 3} = 0.$

25. If it takes h hours working steadily to complete a task, the portion w of the task that is done each hour is given by $w = 1/h$. Find h when $w = 0.125$.

26. The focal length f of a lens in terms of the distance p of an object and the distance q of its image is given by $1/f = (1/p) + (1/q)$. Solve for **(a)** f; **(b)** p; **(c)** q.

5-5   Problems

Many of the early works that were the forerunners of algebra were largely collections of problems, stated in words, among which there appeared frequently those requiring the finding of a number from certain verbal statements about it. In fact, until the invention of symbolic algebra all the problems that we now solve by algebra were of necessity stated in words. Even today many of the applied problems which arise in everyday life are expressed in words rather than in algebraic symbols.

In solving problems by means of algebraic equations, the first essential step is to translate the words in the problem into the symbolic language of algebra. Herein lies the student's main difficulty. The following general suggestions, phrased particularly for problems where one unknown is to be used, should prove helpful.*

* For a more extended discussion, see G. Polya's *How to Solve It* (Dover, New York, 1957).

1. *Read and reread carefully the statement of the problem.*

2. *Choose a letter to represent the unknown quantity in the problem, and write an accurate statement of what the letter is to represent.*

3. *Write expressions for each of the quantities in the problem which involves the unknown.*

4. *Analyze the problem until you can think of it as a statement that a certain number may be expressed in two different ways; use an equality to indicate that the corresponding expressions represent the same number.*

5. *If the equality is a conditional equation, solve it; if the equality is an identity, repeat step 4 for another choice of expressions.*

6. *Check the results obtained, that is, determine whether or not they fulfill the conditions of the problem—thus testing the accuracy of the analysis of the problem as well as the solution of the equation.*

EXAMPLE 1.   Find three consecutive integers such that four times the first plus one half the second minus twice the third is equal to 24.

Solution.   Let x represent the smallest integer. Then $(x + 1)$ and $(x + 2)$ will represent the next two consecutive integers.

From the conditions of the problem, $4x + \frac{1}{2}(x + 1) - 2(x + 2) = 24$. Solving this equation, we obtain

$$8x + x + 1 - 4x - 8 = 48, \quad 5x = 55, \quad \text{or} \quad x = 11.$$

Hence the three consecutive integers are 11, 12, and 13.

Check. $4 \cdot 11 + \frac{1}{2} \cdot 12 - 2 \cdot 13 = 44 + 6 - 26 = 24$ as required.

EXAMPLE 2.   An airplane with an air speed (that is, speed relative to the air) of 760 miles per hour requires 15 minutes longer to fly from A to B against a 40-mile-per-hour wind than from B to A with the wind. Find the distance from A to B.

Solution.   Let x represent the number of miles between A and B. The ground speed of an airplane flying 760 miles per hour against a 40-mile-per-hour wind is $760 - 40$, or 720, miles per hour. Similarly the airplane's ground speed when flying with the wind is $760 + 40$, or 800, miles per hour. Thus $x/720$ represents the time of flight (in hours) from A to B, and $x/800$ represents the time of flight from B to A. The difference between these two times was given as one-quarter hour; that is,

$$\frac{x}{720} - \frac{x}{800} = \frac{1}{4}.$$

Solving this equation, we obtain $10x - 9x = 1800$, or $x = 1800$.

Check. The time required to fly from A to B is $\frac{1800}{720}$, or $2\frac{1}{2}$, hours; the time required to fly from B to A is $\frac{1800}{800}$, or $2\frac{1}{4}$, hours. The difference in flying time checks with the conditions of the problem.

EXAMPLE 3.   The base of a triangle is 3 feet more than half its altitude, and its area is 12 square feet less than the area of the square having a side equal in length to the base of the triangle. Find the area of the triangle.

Solution.   Let x represent the number of feet in the altitude of the triangle. Then $(\frac{1}{2}x + 3)$ represents the number of feet in the base of the triangle. Hence $\frac{1}{2}x(\frac{1}{2}x + 3)$ represents the number of square feet in the area of the triangle, and $(\frac{1}{2}x + 3)^2$ represents the number of square feet in the area of the square.

From the conditions of the problem, we have

$$\tfrac{1}{2}x(\tfrac{1}{2}x + 3) = (\tfrac{1}{2}x + 3)^2 - 12.$$

Solving this equation, we obtain

$$\tfrac{1}{4}x^2 + \tfrac{3}{2}x = \tfrac{1}{4}x^2 + 3x + 9 - 12,$$

$$\tfrac{3}{2}x - 3x = -3, \quad -3x = -6, \quad \text{or} \quad x = 2.$$

Hence the area of the triangle is $\frac{1}{2}(2)(\frac{2}{2} + 3)$ square feet, or 4 square feet.

Check.   The altitude of the triangle is 2 feet; the base of the triangle is $(3 + \frac{1}{2} \cdot 2)$ feet, or 4 feet; the area of the triangle is 4 square feet; a side of the square is 4 feet; the area of the square is 16 square feet; therefore the area of the triangle is 12 square feet less than the area of the square, as required.

EXERCISES

1. Paul Jones earned $64,000, put aside $28,000 for taxes on this income, bought a house, and used the balance to pay off a debt. If the debt was $10,000 less than the cost of the house, how much was the debt?

2. The sum of the interior angles of a polygon of n sides is equal to $2(n - 2)$ right angles. How many sides must a polygon have if the sum of the interior angles is equal to **(a)** 540°? **(b)** 1620°?

3. Find three angles of a triangle such that one angle is seven times a second angle and also is one-fourth of the third angle.

4. An office boy went to the post office and bought 300 stamps, some five-cent and some eight-cent, for $18. How many five-cent stamps did he buy?

5. The sum of three consecutive integers is 111. Find the smallest of these integers.

6. Find, if possible, two consecutive positive integers whose squares differ by **(a)** 13; **(b)** 73; **(c)** $2n + 1$; **(d)** $2n + 3$.

7. The sum of three consecutive even integers is 84. Find the largest of these integers.

8. A group of six neighbors agree to contribute equally to the cost of a ladder. If an increase of two in the number in the group would reduce the cost to each by $1, what is the price of the ladder?

9. Radio waves travel at the speed of light, about $328 \cdot 10^6$ yards per second. If a signal reflected from an airplane is received by a radar $600 \cdot 10^{-6}$ second after being sent out from the same radar, how far is the airplane from the radar?

10. If sound is emitted from an approaching source, the true frequency (pitch) n and the frequency n' as heard by a stationary observer are related as in the equation $n' = \dfrac{V}{V - v} \cdot n$, where V is the speed of sound and v is the speed of the source. This is called "the Doppler effect." If $V = 1100$ feet per second, find the speed toward the observer of a source for which n' is twice n (that is, the pitch is raised one octave).

11. A gas company charges $4.25 for the first 25 cubic feet of gas used each month and 9 cents per cubic foot for the rest. Express the bill C as a function of the number n of cubic feet used, and find what gas consumption would result in a bill of $5.78.

12. An airplane is launched from an aircraft carrier traveling due east at 30 miles per hour. The plane flies due east at an air speed of 470 miles per hour and with a tail wind of 10 miles per hour. If radio communication between the plane and the ship is effective for at most 900 miles, for how long can the plane and the ship expect to be able to communicate directly by radio?

13. John has twice as much cash as Bob. If he lent Bob a dollar, they would have the same amount. How much did Bob have?

14. A messenger leaves point A for point B 50 miles distant, traveling 60 miles an hour. Fifteen minutes later a second messenger leaves B for A at 45 miles an hour. **(a)** At what point in their path will they meet? **(b)** At what point will the first messenger pass 12 minutes before the second?

15. Don usually drives from his home to the college in 12 minutes.

When rushed, he increases his average speed by 5 miles per hour and makes the trip in 10 minutes. How far does Don live from the college?

16. An airplane is flying across the ocean between two coastal cities 3000 miles apart with an air speed of 450 miles per hour and a 30-mile-per-hour headwind. Find the distance from the starting point to the "point of no return," that is, the point beyond which it is quicker to fly on to the destination than to return to the starting point.

17. An automobile radiator contains 18 quarts of a solution which is 20% alcohol and 80% water. How much of the solution must be drained off and replaced by pure alcohol to give a solution which is 30% alcohol?

18. A printer offers to furnish 10,000 copies of a certain book for $14,000, or 15,000 for $18,000. Assuming that each offer is based on a fixed price for composition and plates plus a certain price per book for printing and binding, find the price of the composition and plates.

Note. If a lever is supported at one point called the **fulcrum,** then the product of the weight *w* of any object resting on the lever and the distance *d* of the object from the fulcrum is called the **moment** of the object. A lever is in balance if the sum of the moments on one side equals the sum of the moments on the other side. Using this property, and assuming that the weight of the lever is negligible, solve Exercises 19 and 20.

19. A 50-pound weight and an unknown weight balance on a lever when they are respectively 4 feet and 6 feet from the fulcrum. Neglect the weight of the lever and find the unknown weight.

20. Two boys weigh a total of 180 pounds. They balance on a balanced teeterboard when one is 4 feet from the fulcrum and the other is 5 feet from the fulcrum. How much does each boy weigh?

21. A grocer offered for sale 25 bushels of apples at such a price as to give him a 50% gain on the cost. However, he sold only 16 bushels at this price, then four more at cost, and had to throw away the others. If he gained $6 on the transaction, find the price per bushel that he paid.

22. John can do a job alone in 4 days and Fred can do it alone in 6 days. How long do they need when working together?

23. A bullet is fired at a target 5500 feet away. Assuming that sound travels at the rate of 1100 feet per second and the bullet 1650 feet per second, find at what point along the path of the bullet the sound of its impact on the target would be heard (a) $\frac{1}{4}$ second before the report of the gun; (b) at the same time as the report of the gun; (c) $\frac{1}{4}$ second later.

24. A department store found that the increase P in weekly sales produced by opening Wednesday night was related to the total business W done Wednesday, the total weekly sales S, the ratio w of Wednesday sales to weekly sales before instituting Wednesday night openings, and the ratio r of P to business transferred from other days to Wednesdays, by $P(1 + r)/r = W - w(S - P)$. (a) Solve for P. (b) If $w = 0.16$ and $W/S = 0.23$, find P/S for $r = 0.6, 0.4, 0.2$, and for r very near 0, and graph P/S as a function of r.

5-6 Quadratic Equations

An equation of the form

$$ax^2 + bx + c = 0, \quad a \neq 0, \tag{3}$$

where a, b, and c are arbitrary constants, is called a **general quadratic equation in x**. Note that any expression which does not involve x may be considered a constant for the purposes of (3).

Any quadratic equation of the form (3) is said to be in **standard form**. If $b = 0$, the equation is called a **pure quadratic equation**; if $b \neq 0$, it is called a **complete quadratic equation**. Note that b or c, or both b and c, may be equal to zero. However, if $a = 0$, the equation would reduce to the form $bx + c = 0$, which is not quadratic but linear; this is the reason for the restriction, $a \neq 0$, in (3).

ILLUSTRATIONS.   The equations $x^2 + 5x - 6 = 0$ and $3x^2 - 4x = 0$ are complete quadratic equations in x; $9x^2 - 16 = 0$ is a pure quadratic equation in x. Each of these equations is already in standard form; for instance, in the last of them, $a = 9$, $b = 0$, $c = -16$.

The equation

$$(px + q)^2 = mx^2 + nx - q$$

is also quadratic, and it can be reduced to standard form by expanding $(px + q)^2$ and collecting like terms:

$$(p^2 - m)x^2 + (2pq - n)x + (q^2 + q) = 0.$$

A *pure* quadratic equation can be written in the form

$$ax^2 + c = 0, \quad a \neq 0, \tag{4}$$

where a and c are constants.

Equation (4) is first solved for x^2 by adding $-c$ to both members and then dividing both members of the resulting equation by a, the coefficient of x^2, giving $x^2 = -c/a$. Upon extracting the square roots of each member, we obtain

$$x = \pm \sqrt{-\frac{c}{a}}.$$

Thus, (4) has two roots, numerically equal but opposite in sign. The two roots are real when a and c are unlike in sign, and are imaginary when a and c are alike in sign.

EXAMPLE 1.   Solve $\frac{1}{3}x(9 + 2x) = 3(x - 2)$.

Solution.   Multiply each member by 3: $x(9 + 2x) = 9(x - 2)$.
Remove parentheses: $\qquad\qquad\qquad\qquad 9x + 2x^2 = 9x - 18$.
Solve for x^2: $\qquad\qquad\qquad\qquad\qquad\qquad x^2 = -9$.
Solve for x: $\qquad\qquad\qquad\qquad\qquad\qquad\; x = \pm 3i$.

Note that in extracting the square roots of each member of the equation $x^2 = 9$, the double sign $\pm$ may be prefixed to whichever member is more convenient, not necessarily to both members.

If the left member of a quadratic equation in the standard form can be factored, the equation can be solved by equating each of the two linear factors to zero and solving the resulting equations. The justification of this procedure is contained in the principle which states that *a product of two or more factors is equal to zero when and only when at least one of the factors is zero.*

EXAMPLE 2.   Solve: $10x^2 + 11x = 6$.

Solution.
Subtract 6 from each member: $\qquad 10x^2 + 11x - 6 = 0$.
Factor: $\qquad\qquad\qquad\qquad\;\; (5x - 2)(2x + 3) = 0$.
Equate each factor to zero: $\quad 5x - 2 = 0. \mid 2x + 3 = 0$.
Solve for x: $\qquad\qquad\qquad\quad x = \frac{2}{5}. \mid \quad x = -\frac{3}{2}$.

EXAMPLE 3.   Solve: $9x^2 + 6x + 1 = 0$.

Solution.
Factor: $\qquad\qquad\qquad\qquad\quad (3x + 1)^2 = 0$.
Equate each factor to zero: $\;\; 3x + 1 = 0. \mid 3x + 1 = 0$.
$\qquad\qquad\qquad\qquad\qquad\quad x = -\frac{1}{3}. \mid \quad x = -\frac{1}{3}$.

The equation $9x^2 + 6x + 1 = 0$ has *two equal roots*, $-\frac{1}{3}$ and $-\frac{1}{3}$, and $-\frac{1}{3}$ is called a **double root** of the equation.

EXERCISES

Write as many as possible of the following equalities in the standard form $ax^2 + bx + c = 0$, $a \neq 0$.

1. $x^2 - 3x + 5 = x - 3$.

2. $5x^2 - 1 = 2x^2 + 2 - 3x$.

3. $(x + 2)^2 = 3x^2 + 4x + 4$.

4. $(x - \sqrt{2})^2 + (x + \sqrt{2})^2 = 0$.

5. $x^2 + rx = sx + t$.

6. $x^2 + 2xy + y^2 - 3x + 4y = 5$.

7. $(x - y)^2 = x^2 - y^2$.

8. $(x + y)^3 = x^3 - y^3$.

Solve each of the following equations for x, r, *or* t:

9. $t^2 - \frac{16}{9} = 0$.

10. $x^2 - \frac{25}{9} = 0$.

11. $x^2 - 32 = 0$.

12. $r^2 - 125 = 0$.

13. $x^2 + 16 = 0$.

14. $x^2 + 64 = 0$.

15. $81t^2 = 169$.

16. $25x^2 = 144$.

17. $3x^2 - 5 = 0$.

18. $5x^2 - 6 = 0$.

19. $3x^2 + 4 = 0$.

20. $2x^2 + 25 = 0$.

21. $s = \frac{1}{2}gt^2$.

22. $V = \frac{1}{3}\pi r^2 h$.

23. $\frac{5}{6}x^2 - \frac{3}{4} = \frac{1}{2}x^2$.

24. $\frac{1}{4}x^2 = \frac{2}{3}x^2 - \frac{7}{4}$.

25. $9a^2x^2 - 4c^2 = 0$.

26. $4a^2s^2 + 5t^2 = 0$.

27. $x(x + 4) = 1 - 4(3 - x)$.

28. $(at + b)^2 + (at - b)^2 = c^2$.

29. $9a^2x^2 + 16b^2 = 36a^2$.

30. $\dfrac{x + 2}{3x - 4} = \dfrac{2x + 3}{x - 1}$.

31. $\dfrac{2}{r - 2} = \dfrac{3}{r + 3} - 1$.

Solve by factoring and check by substitution:

32. $x^2 - 9x = 0$.

33. $4y + y^2 = 0$.

34. $z^2 - 9 = 0$.

35. $9t^2 = 25$.

36. $9t^2 = 6t$.

37. $x^2 + 4x + 3 = 0$.

38. $r^2 - 6r + 8 = 0$.

39. $s^2 - s - 12 = 0$.

40. $s^2 + 2s - 15 = 0$.

41. $3y^2 - 8y + 4 = 0$.

42. $6x^2 - x - 2 = 0$.

43. $10z^2 = 3a^2 + az$.

44. $2t^2 - 5ct = 18c^2$.

45. $x^6 = 81x^4$.

★46. $z^4 + 81z^2 = 0$.

47. $16x^2 - (x - 1)^2 = 0$.

48. $a^2 - (w - b)^2 = 0$.

49. $(z - 3b)^2 = 25c^2$.

50. $y^2 + 2qy = p^2 - q^2$.

51. $y^5 - 5y^3 + 4y = 0$.

52. $x^6 - 8x^4 + 16x^2 = 0$.

53. $\dfrac{6}{2x - 3} = \dfrac{7}{4} - \dfrac{2x - 5}{2x + 1}$.

54. $\dfrac{y + 4}{y - 1} - \dfrac{15}{4} = \dfrac{y - 1}{y + 4}$.

In the following exercises express the answers in decimal form to three significant digits (or fewer, if clearly appropriate) using, whenever necessary, Table I and $\pi \approx \frac{22}{7}$:

55. A box with a square base has a volume of 800 cubic inches and a height of 16 inches. Find the dimensions of the box.

56. The surface S of a sphere in terms of its radius r is given by

$S = 4\pi r^2$. Find the radius r when the surface S is (a) 196π square inches; (b) 1760 square inches; (c) 512 square inches.

57. The volume V of a right circular cylinder in terms of its altitude h and base-radius r is given by $V = \pi r^2 h$. Find the radius of the base when (a) $V = 125\pi$ cubic inches and $h = 5$ inches; (b) $V = 7700$ cubic feet and $h = 7$ feet; (c) $V = 7$ cubic feet and $h = 10$ feet.

58. The distance s traveled by a freely falling body dropped from rest is given by $s = \frac{1}{2}gt^2$ where g represents the acceleration due to the force of gravity and t represents the time of the fall. Using the value $g \approx 32$ feet per second per second, find the time required for a body to fall (a) 64 feet; (b) 200 feet; (c) 1000 feet; (d) 10,000 feet.

59. The kinetic energy K, in foot-pounds, of an object with mass m pounds and speed v feet per second is given by $K = \frac{1}{2}mv^2/g$, where g is in feet per second per second. At what speed will a 3000-pound automobile have 100,000 foot-pounds of energy, taking $g \approx 32$?

60. A certain rectangle is 3 inches longer than it is wide, and the number of square inches in its area exceeds four times the number of inches in its width by 12. Find the dimensions.

61. The radius r of a circular arch of height h and span b is given by $r = (b^2 + 4h^2)/8h$. Find h when $b = 20$ and $r = 26$.

62. The rate at which a "black body" cools varies directly as the difference between the fourth power of its absolute temperature T and the fourth power of the absolute temperature T_0 of the surrounding space. If $T_0 = 300°$, and a certain black body cools 1° per second when $T = 400°$, how rapidly will it cool when $T = 500°$?

63. In a triode vacuum tube, the plate current I_b, grid (control) voltage E_c, and plate voltage E_b are related by $I_b = K(E_c + E_b/u)^{\frac{3}{2}}$, where K is a constant and u is the amplification factor of the tube; an imaginary root means that no current will flow. (a) For $u = 100$, find the relationship between E_c and E_b for which $I_b = 0$. (b) If furthermore $E_b = 250$, find the value of E_c (which is called the cutoff voltage or bias).

*64. According to Lanchester's laws, in an engagement (in war or in a game) between Red and Blue forces, initially numbering m_0 and n_0 respectively, the expected numbers m and n of the forces at any stage are related by the equation (i) $n_0 - n = E(m_0 - m)$ if the engagement consists of individual duels, or (ii) $n_0^2 - n^2 = E(m_0^2 - m^2)$ if each unit can fire at every opposing unit; E is the "exchange ratio", the ratio of the average number of Blue units lost per Red loss. If $m_0 = 1000$ and

$n_0 = 500$, find for (i) and for (ii) which side is annihilated if the engagement is carried to completion, and find the number of units then remaining on the other side, if (a) $E = 1$; (b) $E = \frac{1}{2}$; (c) $E = 2$; (d) $E = \frac{1}{4}$.

5-7 Completing the Square

The roots of a quadratic equation in one unknown can be found by a process known as **completing the square**, which is illustrated in the following examples. Before this process can be applied, the equation must be reduced to standard form (§ 5-6). The process is of most interest when the equation cannot be solved by factoring; in § 5-8 it will be applied to the general quadratic equation, and we shall obtain a general formula that can be used to find the roots of any quadratic equation in one unknown.

The process of completing the square is used not only in solving quadratic equations but also in changing certain expressions and equations into some special forms. Such uses are shown in Examples 2 and 3 below and in the exercises at the end of this section.

The process of completing the square makes use of the fact that any binomial of the form $(x^2 + mx)$ becomes a perfect square if we add to it the square of one half of the coefficient of x, that is, $(\frac{1}{2}m)^2$ or $\frac{1}{4}m^2$:

$$x^2 + mx + (\tfrac{1}{2}m)^2 = x^2 + mx + \tfrac{1}{4}m^2 = (x + \tfrac{1}{2}m)^2.$$

ILLUSTRATION.   To make $(x^2 - 5x)$ a perfect square, we add to it the quantity $(\frac{1}{2}$ of $-5)^2$, or $\frac{25}{4}$:

$$x^2 - 5x + \tfrac{25}{4} = (x - \tfrac{5}{2})^2.$$

EXAMPLE 1.   Solve by completing the square: $2x^2 - 3x - 3 = 0$.

Solution.

Add 3 to each member: $2x^2 - 3x = 3$.

Divide by coefficient of x^2: $x^2 - \frac{3}{2}x = \frac{3}{2}$.

Add $(\frac{1}{2}$ of $-\frac{3}{2})^2$, that is, $\frac{9}{16}$, to both members, thus making the left member a perfect trinomial square:

$$x^2 - \tfrac{3}{2}x + \tfrac{9}{16} = \tfrac{3}{2} + \tfrac{9}{16} = \tfrac{33}{16}.$$

Simplify: $(x - \tfrac{3}{4})^2 = \tfrac{33}{16}.$

Extract square roots: $x - \tfrac{3}{4} = \pm\tfrac{1}{4}\sqrt{33}.$

Solve for x: $x = \tfrac{1}{4}(3 \pm \sqrt{33}).$

$x = \tfrac{1}{4}(3 + \sqrt{33}).$	$x = \tfrac{1}{4}(3 - \sqrt{33}).$
Reduce to decimal form: $x \approx \tfrac{1}{4}(3 + 5.745).$	$x \approx \tfrac{1}{4}(3 - 5.745).$
In decimal form, correct to two decimal places: $x \approx 2.19.$	$x \approx -0.69.$

EXAMPLE 2. Reduce $x^2 + y^2 + 6x - 2y + 6 = 0$ to the form

$$(x - h)^2 + (y - k)^2 = r^2.$$

Solution. As this example requires completing the square in x and in y, we first write the given equation in the following form:

$$[x^2 + 6x + (\quad)] + [y^2 - 2y + (\quad)] = -6.$$

Complete the squares in x and y:

$$(x^2 + 6x + 9) + (y^2 - 2y + 1) = -6 + 9 + 1 = 4.$$

Combine terms: $\qquad (x + 3)^2 + (y - 1)^2 = 2^2.$

EXAMPLE 3. Transform $\sqrt{4 - 2x^2 + 4x}$ into an equivalent expression of the form $\sqrt{a}\sqrt{k - (x - h)^2}$.

Solution. By comparing the given form with the required form, in which the coefficient of x is 1, we observe that $a = 2$.

$$\sqrt{4 - 2x^2 + 4x} = \sqrt{2}\sqrt{2 - x^2 + 2x} = \sqrt{2}\sqrt{2 - (x^2 - 2x)}$$

Complete the square: $\qquad = \sqrt{2}\sqrt{2 - [(x^2 - 2x + 1) - 1]}$

Simplify: $\qquad = \sqrt{2}\sqrt{2 - (x - 1)^2 + 1}$

$$= \sqrt{2}\sqrt{3 - (x - 1)^2}.$$

EXERCISES

What must be added to each of the following binomials to make the resulting trinomial a constant multiple of a perfect square?

1. $x^2 + 6x.$ **3.** $u^2 - \frac{2}{3}u.$ **5.** $8w^2 + 16w.$ **7.** $\frac{1}{5}z^2 - \frac{1}{3}az.$

2. $s^2 - 10s.$ **4.** $y^2 + \frac{3}{4}y.$ **6.** $3x^2 - 18x.$ **8.** $3t^2 + 5ct.$

Solve the following equations by completing the square; express the irrational roots both in simplest radical form and as decimals correct to two decimal places:

9. $y^2 - 8y = 9.$ **12.** $s^2 + 10s = 5.$ **15.** $z^2 + 2az = 6a^2.$

10. $x^2 - 12x = 64.$ **13.** $x^2 - x - 1 = 0.$ **16.** $2w^2 - 4w = 1.$

11. $r^2 + 6r = 3.$ **14.** $u^2 + u - 4 = 0.$ **17.** $3x = 5 - 4x^2.$

18. $0.2y^2 + 0.6y + 2.1 = 0.$ **21.** $a^2x^2 - 2ax + b^2 = 0.$

19. $\frac{1}{2}z^2 - \frac{1}{3}z + \frac{7}{6} = 0.$ **22.** $x^2 + mx + n = 0.$

20. $x^2 + 2\sqrt{3}x + 2 = 0.$ **23.** $kx^2 + px + q = 0.$

The square root of a quadratic polynomial $ax^2 + bx + c$, $a \neq 0$, *may be written in the form* $\sqrt{a}\sqrt{(x - h)^2 + d}$ *if* $a > 0$ *or alternatively in the form* $\sqrt{-a} \cdot \sqrt{d - (x - h)^2}$ *if* $a < 0$. *Write each of the following in one of these forms* (*as will frequently be necessary in the integral calculus*):

24. $\sqrt{3x^2 + 6x + 81}$.   **27.** $\sqrt{12 - 8x - 4x^2}$.

25. $\sqrt{3x^2 + 12x}$.   **28.** $\sqrt{5x - 2x^2 + 9}$.

26. $\sqrt{20x - 5x^2}$.   **29.** $\sqrt{7x - x^2 - 1}$.

Any equality of a quadratic polynomial in y *with a linear polynomial in* x *may be written in the form* $(y - k)^2 = 2p(x - h)$. *This is a standard form of the equation of a parabola with vertex at* (h, k) *and the line with equation* $y - k = 0$ *as its axis. Write each of the following equations in this form, and find the coordinates of the vertex and the equation of the axis:*

30. $y^2 - 6y + 29 = 4x$.   **32.** $2x + 6y = 5 - 3y^2$.

31. $2y^2 - 16y + 30 = 3x + 4$.   **33.** $6x + 1 = 12y^2 - 12y$.

The standard form of the equation of a circle whose center is at the point (h, k), *and whose radius is* r, *is* $(x - h)^2 + (y - k)^2 = r^2$. *Write each of the following equations of circles in this standard form by completing the squares in* x *and* y, *and find the coordinates of the center and the radius:*

34. $x^2 + y^2 + 6x - 16y + 69 = 0$.

35. $4x^2 + 4y^2 - 4x - 12y - 26 = 0$.

5-8 The Quadratic Formula

By applying the process of completing the square to a general quadratic equation, we obtain a general formula for the roots of all quadratic equations. To obtain the roots of any particular quadratic equation, we need only substitute in this formula the particular values of a, b, and c. We proceed with its derivation.

In the general quadratic equation in x,

$$ax^2 + bx + c = 0, \quad a \neq 0$$

first subtract c from both members and then divide each term of the resulting equation by a, the coefficient of x^2. This gives

$$x^2 + \frac{b}{a}x = -\frac{c}{a}.$$

Upon adding the square of one half of the coefficient of x, that is, $[b/(2a)]^2$, to both members so as to make the left member a trinomial square, we obtain

$$x^2 + \frac{b}{a}x + \frac{b^2}{4a^2} = -\frac{c}{a} + \frac{b^2}{4a^2} = \frac{b^2 - 4ac}{4a^2},$$

or

$$\left(x + \frac{b}{2a}\right)^2 = \frac{b^2 - 4ac}{4a^2}.$$

Then, extracting the square roots of each member, we have

$$x + \frac{b}{2a} = \pm \frac{\sqrt{b^2 - 4ac}}{2a};$$

therefore,

$$x = \frac{-b \pm \sqrt{b^2 - 4ac}}{2a}.$$

This important formula, known as the **quadratic formula**, is used so often that it should be carefully memorized.

EXAMPLE 1. Solve by use of the quadratic formula:

$$12 - x = 6x^2.$$

Solution. Arrange the given equation in the standard form:

$$6x^2 + x - 12 = 0.$$

Here $a = 6, \quad b = 1, \quad \text{and} \quad c = -12.$

Substitute in the quadratic formula:

$$x = \frac{-1 \pm \sqrt{(1)^2 - 4(6)(-12)}}{2(6)}.$$

Simplify: $x = \dfrac{-1 \pm \sqrt{289}}{12} = \dfrac{-1 \pm 17}{12}.$

$$x = \tfrac{4}{3}. \quad \bigg| \quad x = -\tfrac{3}{2}.$$

EXAMPLE 2. Solve by use of the quadratic formula:

$$\tfrac{1}{3}x^2 = \tfrac{1}{2}x - \tfrac{5}{6}.$$

Solution. Clear the given equation of fractions, and arrange the resulting equation in the standard form:

$$2x^2 - 3x + 5 = 0.$$

Here $a = 2, \quad b = -3, \quad \text{and} \quad c = 5.$

Substitute in the quadratic formula: $x = \dfrac{3 \pm \sqrt{(-3)^2 - 4(2)(5)}}{2(2)}$.

Simplify: $x = \dfrac{3 \pm \sqrt{-31}}{4}$.

In decimal form, correct to $x = \frac{1}{4}(3 + i\sqrt{31})$. $x = \frac{1}{4}(3 - i\sqrt{31})$.
two decimal places: $x \approx 0.75 + 1.39i$. $x \approx 0.75 - 1.39i$.

EXAMPLE 3.   Solve by use of the quadratic formula:

$$x^2 + m^2 = 2mx + (nx)^2.$$

Solution.   Arrange the given equation in the standard form:

$$(1 - n^2)x^2 - 2mx + m^2 = 0.$$

Here $a = 1 - n^2$, $b = -2m$,   and $c = m^2$.

Substitute in the quadratic formula:

$$x = \frac{2m \pm \sqrt{(-2m)^2 - 4(1 - n^2)(m^2)}}{2(1 - n^2)}.$$

Simplify: $x = \dfrac{2m \pm \sqrt{4m^2 n^2}}{2(1 - n^2)} = \dfrac{2m \pm 2mn}{2(1 - n^2)} = \dfrac{m(1 \pm n)}{1 - n^2}.$

$$x = \frac{m(1 + n)}{1 - n^2}.\qquad x = \frac{m(1 - n)}{1 - n^2}.$$

$$x = \frac{m}{1 - n}.\qquad x = \frac{m}{1 + n}.$$

EXERCISES

Solve the following equations by use of the quadratic formula; express irrational roots both in simplest radical form and as decimals correct to two decimal places:

1. $x^2 - 6x + 5 = 0$.

2. $9y^2 - 6y + 1 = 0$.

3. $w^2 - 4w + 7 = 0$.

4. $7z = 6z^2 + 2$.

5. $5t^2 + 2t = 2$.

6. $3y^2 + 7y + 6 = 0$.

7. $3x^2 - \sqrt{3}x - 2 = 0$.

8. $2y^2 + 2\sqrt{5}y + 7 = 0$.

9. $z^2 + 4iz - 5 = 0$.

10. $9ix^2 + 5x + 4i = 0$.

11. $\frac{2}{3}y^2 + \frac{1}{5}y - \frac{2}{15} = 0$.

12. $\frac{5}{6}z^2 - 3z - \frac{1}{2} = 0$.

13. $0.8w^2 - 0.16w = 0.09$.

14. $0.10x^2 + 0.55x = 1.21$.

15. $3x^2 - 5ax - 12a^2 = 0.$

16. $acx^2 - axd = bcx - bd.$

17. $x^2 = b^2x^2 + 2ax - a^2.$

18. $Ay + B = \dfrac{1}{Cy}.$

19. $\dfrac{2x}{x-4} - \dfrac{2-x}{2} = x + 2.$

20. $\dfrac{2x+3}{4x-2} = \dfrac{4}{3} + \dfrac{3}{2x}.$

21. $\dfrac{7x-4}{x^2-6x+8} - \dfrac{5}{2-x} = \dfrac{x+5}{x-4}.$

22. $\dfrac{x+2}{x-4} - \dfrac{7}{4} + \dfrac{x-5}{x} = \dfrac{x+1}{x}.$

In Exercises 23 through 26, solve for x:

23. $x^2 + 2xy + y^2 = 9.$

24. $9x^2 - 6xy + y^2 - 16 = 0.$

25. $x^2 + xz + z^2 - x + 5 = 0.$

26. $x^2 - x^2z - z^2 - 4 = 0.$

27. Find the numbers which are **(a)** 72 less than their squares; **(b)** equal to their squares; **(c)** $\frac{3}{16}$ more than their squares; **(d)** 3 more than their squares.

28. Find, if possible, two positive integers such that one is double the other and their product is **(a)** 72; **(b)** 74; **(c)** 841.

29. The product of two positive integers is 224. Find the numbers if **(a)** they are consecutive even integers; **(b)** one exceeds the other by 25; **(c)** one is 250% more than the other.

30. Find, if possible, two consecutive positive integers such that **(a)** the product of their reciprocals is 0.05; **(b)** the sum of their reciprocals equals the product of their reciprocals.

31. Find the area of a right triangle with sides x inches, $(x + 1)$ inches, and $(x - 17)$ inches long.

32. Find the dimensions of a rug which will cover just 60% of the floor and be equidistant from the walls of a room 12 by 15 feet.

33. A manufacturer of circular candy disks 2.00 inches in diameter discovered that a 10% decrease in materials would enable him to make a profit instead of a loss. If he makes the new disks the same thickness as before, what would be the diameter of the disks with 10% less material?

34. What single change in either radius or height of a right circular cone will give the same change in volume when **(a)** the radius is 12 inches and the height is 4 inches? **(b)** the radius is 12 inches and the height is 8 inches?

35. If the height h of a ball t seconds after it is thrown vertically upward is given in feet by $h = 64t - 16t^2$, find when the ball will be **(a)** 40 feet high; **(b)** back on the ground.

36. The formula $s = v_0 t + \frac{1}{2}g t^2$ gives the distance s in feet passed over in t seconds by a body falling in a vacuum and having an initial velocity downward of v_0 feet per second. If g is approximately 32 feet per second per second and $v_0 = 40$ feet per second, how long will it take a body to fall **(a)** 144 feet? **(b)** 600 feet?

37. If the distance s in feet that a bomb falls in t seconds is given by $s = 16t^2/(1 + 0.06t)$, how many seconds are required for a bomb released at 2000 feet to reach its target?

5-9   Equations Involving Radicals

Certain equations where the unknowns appear under radicals may be reduced to linear or quadratic equations by squaring both members until the unknowns no longer appear under radicals. *Since the operation of squaring both members may introduce extraneous roots, it is **necessary to test** the values obtained for the unknown by substitution in the **original equation**,* as discussed in § 5-4. We recall from § 3-2 that the symbol "$\sqrt{\ }$" denotes the *positive* square root.

EXAMPLE 1.   Solve the equation $\sqrt{2x - 5} - \sqrt{x - 2} = 2$.

Solution.

Add $\sqrt{x - 2}$: $\quad\quad\quad \sqrt{2x - 5} = 2 + \sqrt{x - 2}.$

Square both members: $\quad 2x - 5 = 4 + 4\sqrt{x - 2} + x - 2.$

Combine like terms: $\quad\quad x - 7 = 4\sqrt{x - 2}.$

Square both members: $\quad x^2 - 14x + 49 = 16(x - 2).$

Subtract and combine: $\quad x^2 - 30x + 81 = 0.$

Factor: $\quad\quad\quad\quad\quad (x - 3)(x - 27) = 0.$

	$x - 3 = 0.$	$x - 27 = 0.$
	$x = 3.$	$x = 27.$
Test.		
	$\sqrt{2x - 5} - \sqrt{x - 2}$	$\sqrt{2x - 5} - \sqrt{x - 2}$
	$= \sqrt{6 - 5} - \sqrt{3 - 2}$	$= \sqrt{54 - 5} - \sqrt{27 - 2}$
	$= 1 - 1 = 0 \neq 2.$	$= 7 - 5 = 2.$
	$\therefore$ 3 *is not* a root.	$\therefore$ **27** *is* a root.

An artifice which is useful in some types of equations involving radicals, as well as in some other equations, is to make a substitution which will change the given equation to a more familiar form. If the result of the substitution is a quadratic equation, the original equation is said to be in **quadratic form.**

ILLUSTRATIONS. $x^4 - 5x^2 + 4 = 0$ is a quadratic in x^2;

$$x^{-6} - 7x^{-3} - 8 = 0 \text{ is a quadratic in } x^{-3};$$

and $2\sqrt{x-1} - 5\sqrt[4]{x-1} + 3 = 0$ is a quadratic in $\sqrt[4]{x-1}$.

EXAMPLE 2.   Solve the equation $x^{-6} - 7x^{-3} - 8 = 0$.

Solution.   Let $y = x^{-3}$: $y^2 - 7y - 8 = 0$.

Factor: $(y - 8)(y + 1) = 0$.

$y - 8 = 0$.	$y + 1 = 0$.
$y = 8$.	$y = -1$.
$\therefore x^{-3} = 8$.	$\therefore x^{-3} = -1$.
$8x^3 - 1 = 0$.	$x^3 + 1 = 0$.
$(2x - 1)(4x^2 + 2x + 1) = 0$.	$(x + 1)(x^2 - x + 1) = 0$.

$2x - 1 = 0$.	$4x^2 + 2x + 1 = 0$.	$x + 1 = 0$.	$x^2 - x + 1 = 0$.
$x = \frac{1}{2}$.	$x = \frac{1}{4}(-1 \pm i\sqrt{3})$.	$x = -1$.	$x = \frac{1}{2}(1 \pm i\sqrt{3})$.

EXAMPLE 3.   Solve the equation $2x^2 + 4x - \sqrt{x^2 + 2x + 6} - 3 = 0$.

Solution.

Add $12 - 12$: $(2x^2 + 4x + 12) - \sqrt{x^2 + 2x + 6} - 3 - 12 = 0$.

Arrange: $2(x^2 + 2x + 6) - \sqrt{x^2 + 2x + 6} - 15 = 0$.

Let $y = \sqrt{x^2 + 2x + 6}$: $2y^2 - y - 15 = 0$.

Factor: $(2y + 5)(y - 3) = 0$.

$2y + 5 = 0$	$y - 3 = 0$.
$y = -\frac{5}{2}$.	$y = 3$.
This value of y must be *rejected*, since we let $y = \sqrt{x^2 + 2x + 6}$ and this means that y *cannot* assume a negative value.	$\therefore \sqrt{x^2 + 2x + 6} = 3$.
	$x^2 + 2x + 6 = 9$.
	$x^2 + 2x - 3 = 0$.
	$(x + 3)(x - 1) = 0$.

$x + 3 = 0$.	$x - 1 = 0$.
$x = -3$.	$x = 1$.

Since both $x = -3$ and $x = 1$ satisfy the original equation, -3 and **1** are the required roots.

EXERCISES

Solve the following equations:

1. $\sqrt{x-2} = 3.$ **5.** $\sqrt{12-x} + 4 = 0.$ **9.** $y + 3 = \sqrt{y+3}.$

2. $\sqrt{2x-3} = 4.$ **6.** $\sqrt{12-z} = z.$ **10.** $z = 3 + \sqrt{z-1}.$

3. $\sqrt{x} = x - 12.$ **7.** $\sqrt[5]{3x-1} = 2.$ **11.** $2x - 5 = \sqrt{5-2x}.$

4. $\sqrt{y} = 12 - y.$ **8.** $\sqrt[3]{x-2} = -1.$ **12.** $\sqrt[4]{x^4 - 3x + 6} = x.$

13. $\sqrt{t + \sqrt{t+2}} = 2.$ **22.** $(x-1)^6 + 7(x-1)^3 = 8.$

14. $x^4 - 9x^2 + 8 = 0.$ **23.** $3\sqrt[6]{1-x} + 2\sqrt[3]{1-x} = 2.$

15. $y^4 - y^2 - 2 = 0.$ **24.** $\sqrt{x} - \sqrt[4]{x} = 2.$

16. $t^{-2} + t^{-1} = 2.$

17. $7z^{-4} - 29z^{-2} + 4 = 0.$ **25.** $y^2 + y + \dfrac{12}{y^2 + y} = 8.$

18. $9y^{-4} + 35y^{-2} - 4 = 0.$ **26.** $\dfrac{3x^2}{x+2} - \dfrac{x+2}{x^2} = 2.$

19. $3x^{-1} - 13x^{-\frac{1}{2}} + 4 = 0.$

20. $0.000001x^2 + 0.002x = 3.$ **27.** $\sqrt{7x+1} = 1 + 3\sqrt{x}.$

21. $z^6 + 9z^3 + 8 = 0.$ **28.** $\sqrt{7y+1} = 1 + \sqrt{3y}.$

29. $\sqrt{2y-3} + \sqrt{4y+9} = \sqrt{15}.$

30. $\sqrt{2y-5} - \sqrt{y+1} = \sqrt{y-2}.$

31. $x^2 + 5x + \sqrt{x^2 + 5x - 2} - 8 = 0.$

32. $y^2 - 2y - 3\sqrt{y^2 - 2y + 4} = 0.$

33. Point A has abscissa 3 and is at a distance of 13 units from the point $(8, 1)$. Find the coordinates of A.

MISCELLANEOUS EXERCISES

Solve algebraically and graphically:

1. $2 + 3x + x^2 = 0.$ **4.** $2x^2 + 4x - 5 = 0.$

2. $3x^2 + 2x - 5 = 0.$ **5.** $x^2 - x = 0.$

3. $2 + 4x - x^2 = 0.$ **6.** $x^2 + 4x + 4 = 0.$

7. (a) $\sqrt{x - \sqrt{2x}} = 2;$ (b) $\sqrt{x + \sqrt{2x}} = 2.$

8. $x(x+3)^2 + 8 = (x+2)^3.$

Solve each of the following exercises, using only one unknown:

9. Find two consecutive positive integers **(a)** whose product is 72; **(b)** the sum of whose squares is 181.

10. Find numbers such that the sum of each number and its reciprocal is **(a)** 2; **(b)** −2; **(c)** 4.

11. A projectile fired vertically upward from an initial height of s_0 with an initial velocity of v_0, and subject to an acceleration of gravity g, reaches in time t a height s which may be found by using the formula $s = s_0 + v_0 t - \frac{1}{2}gt^2$. Solve this formula for t.

12. The perimeter of one square is 24 inches longer than that of another, and its area exceeds three times that of the other by 22 square inches. Find the length of the side of each square.

13. The sum of the squares of three consecutive positive integers is 245. Find the integers, representing them by **(a)** x, $(x + 1)$, and $(x + 2)$; **(b)** $(x - 1)$, x, and $(x + 1)$.

14. A polygon of n sides has $\frac{1}{2}n(n - 3)$ diagonals. How many sides has a polygon with exactly **(a)** 65 diagonals? **(b)** 170 diagonals?

15. At one time it was said of the Greek orator Demochares that he had lived a fourth of his life as a boy, a fifth as a youth, a third as a man, and had spent 13 years in his dotage. How old was he when that was said?

16. Bill has an average of 77 on three tests. Find the grade that he must make on the fourth test in order to bring his average up to 80.

17. If a team in a baseball league wins 16 out of its first 20 games, how many additional games will it have to play where it wins only one half the time until it has a record of .700 wins?

18. The surfaces of two spheres have the ratio 25:16. What is the ratio of **(a)** their radii? **(b)** their volumes?

19. Show that for any two consecutive integers, the sum of their squares and the square of their product identically equals the square of the number which is one more than their product.

20. The square of the period a planet takes to make one revolution around the sun varies directly as the cube of the average distance of the planet from the sun. The earth's period is about 365 days and it is about 93,000,000 miles from the sun. How far from the sun is Venus, with a period of 225 days?

21. For most commodities, the quantity Q which can be sold is related to the price p per unit. For some commodities, the relationship can be expressed in this way: Starting with some base price p_0 and corresponding quantity Q_0, the increase $(Q - Q_0)$ in quantity varies directly as the decrease $(p_0 - p)$ in price. Suppose this applies to wheat within the price range considered, and that sales were 3,000,000 bushels at $2.00 per bushel and 2,800,000 bushels at $2.05 per bushel. How many bushels would be sold **(a)** at $1.96 per bushel? **(b)** at x cents per bushel?

22. Two airplanes are 1000 miles apart on routes which intersect at right angles. One plane flies 100 miles per hour faster than the other. What are their rates if each reaches the intersection in 2 hours?

23. At what time between 8 o'clock and 9 o'clock will the minute and hour hands of a watch point in the same direction?

24. A cow tied with a rope 60 feet long to a post in the middle of a field eats all the grass within reach in 2 days. How long should the rope be so that she will have just grass enough for 3 days?

25. A certain airplane is supported by a lift which varies jointly as the angle of attack and the square of the speed, up to an angle of 11°. At this angle the airplane is said to "stall" since for larger angles the lift becomes smaller again. If an angle of 2° will just support this plane at 600 miles per hour, at what speed does it stall; that is, require an angle of attack of 11°?

26. A man can row six miles down a stream and six miles back in four hours. If the stream flows two miles per hour, find his rate of rowing in still water.

27. A car goes 8 miles an hour faster than a truck and requires 1 hour and 15 minutes less time to travel 420 miles. Find the rate of each.

28. Find a man's rate of walking if, by increasing his rate by $\frac{1}{2}$ mile per hour, he can cover 30 miles in two hours less time.

29. A man paid $18,000 for a farm. He sells acre lots at $100 more per acre than they cost him, and will have received $7000 more than the farm cost him when he still has 20 acres left. Find the number of acres in the farm.

30. The illumination from any light varies directly as the intensity of the light and inversely as the square of the distance from the light. Two lamps of intensity 9 and 16 candles respectively are placed 35 inches apart. Where should a screen be placed between them in order to be equally illuminated on both sides?

31. At what distance will the illumination (see Exercise 30) be **(a)** four times the illumination at 6 feet? **(b)** one-fourth the illumination at 6 feet?

32. The wheels of an automobile are 8 feet in circumference. If they took $\frac{1}{22}$ of a second less to make one revolution, the automobile's speed would be increased 20 miles per hour. What is the present speed?

33. The gravitational attraction of an astronomical body on an object varies directly as the product of the masses of the two objects and inversely as the square of the distance between them. If the moon is 240,000 miles from the earth and the moon's mass is 0.0120 times the earth's mass, at what distance from the moon on a line joining the moon and earth do they have equal gravitational attraction on a rocket?

CHAPTER 6

EXPONENTIAL AND LOGARITHMIC FUNCTIONS

6-1 Exponential Functions and Graphs

In Chapters 1 and 3 we considered powers. There, with some exceptions, the exponent was a constant, though the base was often a variable. Now we consider the reverse case, in which the exponent is a variable and the base constant.

A function of the form cb^{kx} is called an **exponential function**. Here b, c, and k are constants different from zero. To avoid the need for complex numbers if the exponent is fractional, we consider only positive values of b. Moreover, for most purposes we want $b \neq 1$; for, if $b = 1$ then $b^{kx} = 1$ regardless of the value of x. Only rational exponents were treated in Chapters 1 and 3. A careful treatment of powers involving irrational exponents is beyond the scope of this book; here, it will be assumed that they are defined so as to fit smoothly on a graph with rational powers and so that the laws of exponents (§ 1-6) still hold. Typical graphs are shown in Figure 6.1 (for $b > 1$) and Figure 6.2 (for $0 < b < 1$). As in Chapter 1, b is called the **base**.

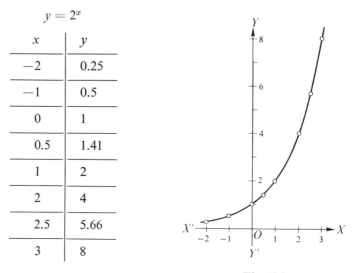

$y = 2^x$

x	y
-2	0.25
-1	0.5
0	1
0.5	1.41
1	2
2	4
2.5	5.66
3	8

Fig. 6.1

148

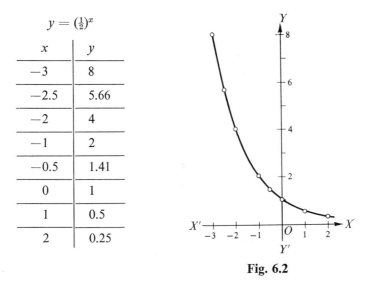

Fig. 6.2

Exponential functions arise in numerous applications, such as growth of numbers of cells in biology, compound interest, and radioactive decay.

ILLUSTRATION. Certain bacteria have the property that each cell divides into two cells about once every 15 minutes. Thus if a colony contains 500 cells initially then 15 minutes later there will be $2 \cdot 500$, that is, 1000; 30 minutes after the start there will be $2(2 \cdot 500)$, that is, $500 \cdot 2^2$; 45 minutes after the start there will be $2(500 \cdot 2^2)$, that is, $500 \cdot 2^3$; and so on. More generally, after t fifteen-minute intervals the number N of cells will be given by $N = 500 \cdot 2^t$. If the time is expressed as a number T of hours after the start, then $T = \frac{1}{4}t$ and $N = 500 \cdot 2^{4T}$.

One particular base is frequently encountered, especially in theoretical work and in certain scientific applications. This base is an irrational number, designated by e, whose value to five decimal places is 2.71828. Positive and negative powers of e are listed in Table VI. For instance, $e^{0.21} = 1.234$ and $e^{-1.63} = 0.1959$; by interpolation in the table, $e^{1.406} = 4.080$.

EXERCISES

1. From the graph of $y = 2^x$ in Figure 6.1, find approximate values of (a) $2^{1.2}$; (b) $2^{-1.5}$; (c) $2^{0.1}$; (d) $2^{\sqrt{3}}$; (e) $2^{-\sqrt{3}}$; (f) $2^{\pi/4}$.

2. From the graph of $y = 2^x$ in Figure 6.1, find approximately the values of x, if any, for which (a) $2^x = 2$; (b) $2^x = 3$; (c) $2^x = 0.3$; (d) $2^x = -3$.

3. Graph $y = (\frac{3}{2})^x$, and find approximate values of **(a)** $(\frac{3}{2})^{2.3}$; **(b)** $(\frac{3}{2})^{-0.8}$; **(c)** $(\frac{2}{3})^{-1.1}$.

4. Graph **(a)** $y = e^x$, **(b)** $y = e^{-x}$, using Table VI.

5. Find by interpolation in Table VI: **(a)** $e^{1.513}$; **(b)** $e^{-1.789}$; **(c)** $e^{0.316}$; **(d)** $e^{-0.102}$.

6. Discuss the difficulties of defining the exponential function with base -2.

Compute and plot two or three points, and sketch the rest of the graph:

7. $y = -(2^x)$.   **10.** $y = 3^{\frac{1}{2}x}$.   **13.** $y = (\frac{1}{3})^{2x}$.

8. $y = 3^{-x}$.   **11.** $y = 2^{-\frac{1}{3}x}$.   **14.** $y - 1 = 2^{x+4}$.

9. $y = x^{-3}$.   **12.** $y = (\sqrt{2})^x$.   **15.** $y + 2 = 2^{x-1}$.

16. If interest on a savings account is 3% compounded annually, then the amount of money in the account at the end of one year is 1.03 times the amount at the beginning of the year. Express the amount A at the end of n years in terms of the initial amount A_0.

17. The radioactive isotope cobalt-56 decays at such a rate that each day there is 99% as much of it as on the preceding day. If a chemist has A_0 grams of it to start, express the amount A left t days later.

18. For the radioactive isotope plutonium-239, in each 10 minutes one-fourth of the amount present at the start of that interval decays. **(a)** Express the fraction of the original amount which will be left after n minutes. **(b)** Graph this as a function of n, and find when half of it is left. (The time until half is left is called the "half-life.")

19. The population of India is increasing 2% per year. In 1959 the population was 400,000,000. **(a)** Express the population in the year n, A.D., assuming this rate continues. ⋆**(b)** Graph the population as a function of n and find when the population will have doubled.

20. If $f(x) = b^x$, prove $f(x_1 + x_2) = f(x_1) \cdot f(x_2)$ for all numbers x_1 and x_2.

6-2   Definition of a Logarithm

In § 4-3 the inverse of a function was defined. In the remainder of this chapter we consider the inverse of the exponential function. In this connection, note that in Figures 6.1 and 6.2, for a given positive value of y there is just one value of x, since a horizontal line above the x-axis intersects the graph just once. For $y \leq 0$, there is *no* corresponding value of x. Thus x is a function of y where $y = b^{kx}$; the domain (see § 4-1) of this function is $y > 0$.

The **logarithm** *of a positive number to a given positive base, other than* 1, *is the exponent of the power to which the base must be raised to equal the number.*

Thus, if a positive number N is expressed as a power of b, $b > 0$ and $b \neq 1$, by means of the equation

$$N = b^x, \tag{1}$$

the exponent x is called the logarithm of the number N to the base b. This relation is expressed in symbols by

$$x = \log_b N. \tag{2}$$

For emphasis, we repeat that a logarithm is an exponent, and that equations (1) and (2) state the same relation in two different ways: the former in **exponential form**, the latter in **logarithmic form**. The restrictions $b > 0$, $b \neq 1$ are discussed in § 6-1; the restriction $N > 0$ is explained at the beginning of the present section.

ILLUSTRATIONS.   In the following table we show the two different forms of several equivalent statements.

Exponential Form	Logarithmic Form	Exponential Form	Logarithmic Form
$4^3 = 64$	$\log_4 64 = 3$	$10^0 = 1$	$\log_{10} 1 = 0$
$10^3 = 1000$	$\log_{10} 1000 = 3$	$10^{-1} = 0.1$	$\log_{10} 0.1 = -1$
$10^2 = 100$	$\log_{10} 100 = 2$	$9^{\frac{3}{2}} = 27$	$\log_9 27 = \frac{3}{2}$
$10^1 = 10$	$\log_{10} 10 = 1$	$8^{-\frac{5}{3}} = \frac{1}{32}$	$\log_8 \frac{1}{32} = -\frac{5}{3}$

Historically, the importance of logarithms lay primarily in their usefulness in computation. With the growth of computing machines, the value of logarithms for computation has decreased, though it still remains substantial because of the cost and complexity of machines. On the other hand, logarithms continue to be important in theoretical work.

The following examples show how to find the logarithm in certain simple cases; later sections will treat cases where this simple procedure does not apply.

EXAMPLE 1.   Find the unknown number N if $\log_5 N = -2$.

Solution.   Write in exponential form:

$$N = 5^{-2}.$$

Evaluate the indicated power: $N = \dfrac{1}{5^2} = \dfrac{1}{25}$.

EXAMPLE 2.   Find the unknown base b if $\log_b 16 = \frac{2}{3}$.

Solution.   Write in exponential form:

$$b^{\frac{2}{3}} = 16.$$

Raise to the $\frac{3}{2}$ power: $(b^{\frac{2}{3}})^{\frac{3}{2}} = 16^{\frac{3}{2}}.$

Therefore $b = 64.$

EXAMPLE 3.   Find the value of $\log_{\frac{4}{9}} \frac{27}{8}$.

Solution.   Let $x = \log_{\frac{4}{9}} \frac{27}{8}.$

Write in exponential form: $(\frac{4}{9})^x = \frac{27}{8}.$

Express $\frac{4}{9}$ and $\frac{27}{8}$ as powers of $\frac{2}{3}$:

$$[(\tfrac{2}{3})^2]^x = (\tfrac{2}{3})^{-3}; \quad (\tfrac{2}{3})^{2x} = (\tfrac{2}{3})^{-3}.$$

Hence $2x = -3; \quad x = -\frac{3}{2}.$

Therefore $\log_{\frac{4}{9}} \frac{27}{8} = -\frac{3}{2}.$

EXERCISES

Express the following equalities in logarithmic form:

1. $10^4 = 10,000.$

2. $10^6 = 1,000,000.$

3. $10^{-2} = 0.01.$

4. $10^{-3} = 0.001.$

5. $2^3 = 8.$

6. $3^4 = 81.$

7. $16^{\frac{1}{4}} = 2.$

8. $243^{\frac{1}{5}} = 3.$

9. $27^{\frac{2}{3}} = 9.$

10. $32^{\frac{2}{5}} = 4.$

11. $(\frac{1}{8})^2 = \frac{1}{64}.$

12. $5^{-3} = \frac{1}{125}.$

13. $7^{-2} = \frac{1}{49}.$

14. $(\frac{1}{27})^{-\frac{2}{3}} = 9.$

15. $(\frac{25}{9})^{-\frac{3}{2}} = \frac{27}{125}.$

16. $7^0 = 1.$

17. $r^s = t.$

18. $a^c = b.$

Express the following equalities in exponential form:

19. $\log_7 49 = 2.$

20. $\log_2 64 = 6.$

21. $\log_8 16 = \frac{4}{3}.$

22. $\log_{27} 9 = \frac{2}{3}.$

23. $\log_{27} \frac{1}{9} = -\frac{2}{3}.$

24. $\log_{10} \frac{1}{100} = -2.$

25. $\log_{13} 1 = 0.$

26. $\log_{\frac{1}{32}} \frac{1}{16} = \frac{4}{5}.$

27. $\log_a c = b.$

Find the value of each of the following logarithms:

28. $\log_2 16.$

29. $\log_3 9.$

30. $\log_9 27.$

31. $\log_{16} 32.$

32. $\log_8 2.$

33. $\log_8 \frac{1}{2}.$

34. $\log_{10} 0.0001.$

35. $\log_9 1.$

36. $\log_5 0.04.$

37. $\log_b b^2.$

38. $\log_x x.$

39. $\log_c \sqrt{c}.$

Find the unknown b, x, or N in each of the following:

40. $\log_2 N = 5.$ **43.** $\log_b 2 = \frac{1}{7}.$ **46.** $\log_{10} 10^7 = x.$

41. $\log_{10} N = -5.$ **44.** $\log_6 36 = x.$ **47.** $\log_{\sqrt{2}} 8 = x.$

42. $\log_b 27 = 3.$ **45.** $\log_{36} 6 = x.$ **48.** $\log_{\sqrt{3}} x = -5.$

Evaluate each of the following by finding each logarithm and then performing the indicated arithmetical operations:

49. $\dfrac{\log_3 9 + \log_2 16}{\log_{10} 1000}.$

50. $\dfrac{\log_5 25 + \log_6 1}{\log_6 216 - \log_2 128}.$

51. $\dfrac{\log_4 \frac{1}{16} - \log_{10} 0.001}{\log_2 \frac{1}{32} + \log_8 8}.$

52. $\dfrac{\log_3 \frac{1}{27} + \log_{0.1} 100}{\log_2 64 \cdot \log_{\frac{1}{4}} 32}.$

53. $\dfrac{\log_{1.2} \frac{36}{25} \div \log_3 9\sqrt{3}}{\log_2 \frac{1}{2} - \log_4 \sqrt{2}}.$

54. $\dfrac{3 + \log_{10} (\log_{10} 10)}{\log_{10} 10{,}000 \cdot \log_{10} 0.01}.$

55. By changing from exponential to logarithmic form, or vice versa, show that **(a)** $b^{\log_b N} = N;$ **(b)** $\log_b 1 = 0;$ **(c)** $\log_b b = 1;$ **(d)** $\log_{1/b} x = \log_b (1/x).$

6-3   Logarithmic Functions and Graphs

The inverse of an exponential function is called a **logarithmic function**. To understand more specifically what this means, consider the general expression for an exponential function (§ 6-1), using different letters to avoid confusion. It can be written $z = cb^{kt}$ or $z/c = b^{kt}$. By (2), this is equivalent to

$$kt = \log_b \frac{z}{c} \quad \text{or} \quad t = \frac{1}{k} \log_b \frac{z}{c}.$$

But c and k are constants different from zero, and so we can let $C = 1/c$ and $K = 1/k$. Then $t = K \log_b Cz$. The variables are usually denoted by x and y, so we write

$$y = K \log_b Cx$$

as the general form of a logarithmic function.

Because of the relationship between a function and its inverse, the graph of $\log_2 x$ is obtained by interchanging the roles of x and y in Figure 6.1. Figure 6.3 shows the graph of $\log_{10} x$, for which coordinates can be obtained from graphing $y = 10^x$ or by the method to be discussed in § 6-5 and § 6-6. The vertical scale in Figure 6.3 is enlarged for convenience. The shape of this graph is typical of the graph of $\log_b x$ for $b > 1$. The case $b < 1$ is not ordinarily encountered in logarithms.

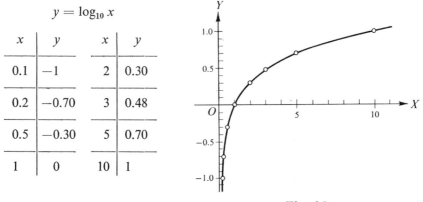

$y = \log_{10} x$

x	y	x	y
0.1	−1	2	0.30
0.2	−0.70	3	0.48
0.5	−0.30	5	0.70
1	0	10	1

Fig. 6.3

Note that (for $b > 1$) $\log_b x$ is positive when $x > 1$; $\log_b x$ is negative for $0 < x < 1$; $\log_b 1 = 0$; $\log_b x$ is not defined for $x \le 0$. All these can be seen from the definition. Likewise, if $c < d$ then $\log_b c < \log_b d$.

For any one given base the set of logarithms of all positive numbers constitute a **system of logarithms**. While any positive number except unity may be used as a base of a system of logarithms, two particular bases are most frequently used.

The **common**, or **Briggsian**, **system of logarithms**, named for Henry Briggs (1560–1631), employs the base 10. This system is the most convenient for computational purposes.

The **natural**, or **Napierian**, **system of logarithms**, named for John Napier (1550–1617), employs for its base the irrational number e (§ 6-1). This system is most convenient for theoretical purposes and will be met by the student who studies the calculus.

In this book, when the base is not expressed, the base 10 is to be understood. Thus, **log N** is understood to mean $\log_{10} N$, and the word *logarithm* is understood to mean common logarithm unless otherwise stated. The abbreviation **ln N** will be used for $\log_e N$.

EXERCISES

1. From Figure 6.3, estimate the logarithms of the following numbers to the base 10: **(a)** 8; **(b)** 2.5; **(c)** 1.3; **(d)** 0.7.

2. From Figure 6.1, estimate the logarithms of the following numbers to the base 2: **(a)** 7; **(b)** 2.5; **(c)** 1.3; **(d)** 0.7.

3. Graph $y = 3^x$ from $x = -3$ to $x = 4$, and from the graph estimate the value of **(a)** $3^{-0.5}$; **(b)** $\log_3 0.5$; **(c)** $\log_3 10$; **(d)** $\log_3 0.7$; **(e)** $\log_3 30$.

4. If the point $(64, 2)$ lies on the graph of $y = \log_b x$, what is the value of b?

5. Find **(a)** $\log 100$; **(b)** $\log 0.0001$; **(c)** $\ln e^2$; **(d)** $\ln e^{-1.2}$.

6. Find **(a)** $\log 10^{2.71828}$; **(b)** $\log 0.1$; **(c)** $\ln e^{3.1416}$; **(d)** $\ln 1$.

7. If 5 is used as the base of a system of logarithms, write the numbers whose logarithms are **(a)** 2; **(b)** -2; **(c)** 1; **(d)** -1; **(e)** 0; **(f)** 5.

8. What real numbers would have logarithms if **(a)** 1, **(b)** $\frac{1}{3}$; **(c)** 0, **(d)** π, **(e)** $\dfrac{1}{2\pi}$, were used as a base of a system of logarithms?

Simplify:

9. $4 \log 0.001$.

10. $3 + \log 100$.

11. $e^{\ln 3} + 10^{\log 0.1} + (\log \sqrt{3})^0$.

12. $e^{2 \ln 5} - 10^{3 \log 5} + 0^{\log 100}$.

13. On the same set of axes, sketch the graphs of $y = \log_2 x$ and $y = \log_4 x$.

Sketch the graphs of the following functions, showing the principal features but not plotting many points:

14. $\log (x + 3)$.   **16.** $3 \log x$.   **18.** $-e^x$.

15. $3 + \log x$.   **17.** $\log_3 x$.   **19.** e^{-x}.

6-4 Properties of Logarithms

Since logarithms are exponents, the laws which govern the operations with logarithms are, except for a difference in the manner of statement, the same as the laws which govern the operations with exponents. We repeat certain laws of exponents that have useful analogues in logarithms.

Law 1. $b^x \cdot b^y = b^{x+y}$.   (*Law for multiplication*)
Law 2. $b^x/b^y = b^{x-y}$.   (*Law for division*)
Law 3. $(b^x)^y = b^{xy}$.   (*Law for a power of a power*)

From the above three laws of exponents we derive the following properties of logarithms, which are used repeatedly in the application of logarithms to problems of computation. These properties are also useful in the many theoretical discussions in which logarithms appear.

They lie at the foundation of the simple calculating instrument called the "slide rule" (see § 6-10 and the appendix).

Property 1. *The logarithm of a product is equal to the sum of the logarithms of its factors, all logarithms being taken to the same base.*

We shall first prove this property for the case of a product of two factors; for example, we shall show that

$$\log_b MN = \log_b M + \log_b N. \tag{3}$$

Proof. Let $\qquad\qquad x = \log_b M \quad \text{and} \quad y = \log_b N.$

Write in exponential form: $\qquad M = b^x \quad \text{and} \quad N = b^y.$

Multiply M by N: $\qquad MN = b^x \cdot b^y = b^{x+y} \quad \text{(by Law 1).}$

Write in logarithmic form: $\qquad \log_b MN = x + y.$

Replace x and y by their values: $\qquad \log_b MN = \log_b M + \log_b N.$

We can prove Property 1 for any finite number of factors either by using the same method as in the proof of (3) or by using (3). For example, by use of (3) we may write

$$\log_b PQR = \log_b [(PQ)(R)] = \log_b PQ + \log_b R$$
$$= \log_b P + \log_b Q + \log_b R.$$

ILLUSTRATION 1. $\log_{10} 14 = \log_{10} (2 \cdot 7) = \log_{10} 2 + \log_{10} 7;$

$\qquad \log_6 210 = \log_6 (2 \cdot 3 \cdot 5 \cdot 7) = \log_6 2 + \log_6 3 + \log_6 5 + \log_6 7.$

Property 2. *The logarithm of a quotient is equal to the logarithm of the dividend minus the logarithm of the divisor, all logarithms being taken to the same base.*

For example, $\qquad \log_b \dfrac{M}{N} = \log_b M - \log_b N. \tag{4}$

The proof is similar to that for Property I.

ILLUSTRATION 2. $\log_9 \frac{47}{19} = \log_9 47 - \log_9 19;$

$\qquad \log_2 \frac{5}{21} = \log_2 5 - \log_2 (3 \cdot 7) = \log_2 5 - (\log_2 3 + \log_2 7)$
$\qquad\qquad = \log_2 5 - \log_2 3 - \log_2 7.$

Property 3. *The logarithm of a power of a number is equal to the exponent times the logarithm of the number, all logarithms being taken to the same base.*

For example, $\qquad \log_b M^p = p \log_b M. \tag{5}$

Proof.   Let $\qquad\qquad\qquad\qquad x = \log_b M.$

Write in exponential form: $\qquad M = b^x.$

Raise to the pth power: $\qquad M^p = (b^x)^p = b^{px} \qquad$ (by Law 3).

Write in logarithmic form: $\qquad\quad \log_b M^p = px.$

Replace x by its value: $\qquad\quad\; \log_b M^p = p \log_b M.$

The corresponding property for roots follows from the definition $\sqrt[q]{M} = M^{\frac{1}{q}}$. Setting $p = 1/q$ in (5),

$$\log_b \sqrt[q]{M} = \frac{1}{q} \log_b M. \qquad\qquad (6)$$

ILLUSTRATION 3. $\log_{10} 3^2 = 2 \log_{10} 3$; $\log_4 \sqrt[5]{31} = \frac{1}{5} \log_4 31$;

$$\log_{16} 8^{\frac{4}{5}} = \log_{16} (2^3)^{\frac{4}{5}} = \log_{16} 2^{\frac{12}{5}} = \tfrac{12}{5} \log_{16} 2 = \tfrac{12}{5} \cdot \tfrac{1}{4} = \tfrac{3}{5}.$$

Warnings.   The student should distinguish between

$$\log_b (M + N) \quad \text{and} \quad \log_b M + \log_b N;$$
$$\log_b (M - N) \quad \text{and} \quad \log_b M - \log_b N;$$
$$\log_b M \cdot \log_b N \quad \text{and} \quad \log_b M + \log_b N;$$
$$\log_b M/\log_b N \quad \text{and} \quad \log_b M - \log_b N.$$

In no one of the above pairs are the two expressions equivalent.

EXAMPLE 1.   Express $\log_4 2\pi\sqrt{l/g}$ as an algebraic sum of logarithms.

Solution.

$$\log_4 2\pi\sqrt{l/g} = \log_4 2 + \log_4 \pi + \log_4 (\sqrt{l}/\sqrt{g}) \qquad \text{(by Property 1)}$$
$$= \log_4 2 + \log_4 \pi + \log_4 \sqrt{l} - \log_4 \sqrt{g} \quad \text{(by Property 2)}$$
$$= \log_4 2 + \log_4 \pi + \tfrac{1}{2} \log_4 l - \tfrac{1}{2} \log_4 g \quad \text{(by Property 3)}.$$

EXAMPLE 2.   Express $\frac{1}{5} \log_5 3 - \log_5 7 + \log_5 19 - 2 \log_5 4$ as a single logarithm.

Solution.

$\frac{1}{5} \log_5 3 - \log_5 7 + \log_5 19 - 2 \log_5 4$

$= (\tfrac{1}{5} \log_5 3 + \log_5 19) - (\log_5 7 + 2 \log_5 4)$

$= (\log_5 3^{\frac{1}{5}} + \log_5 19) - (\log_5 7 + \log_5 4^2) \qquad \text{(by Property 3)}$

$= \log_5 (19 \cdot 3^{\frac{1}{5}}) - \log_5 (7 \cdot 4^2) \qquad\qquad \text{(by Property 1)}$

$= \log_5 \dfrac{19 \cdot 3^{\frac{1}{5}}}{7 \cdot 4^2} \qquad\qquad\qquad\qquad\quad \text{(by Property 2)}.$

EXAMPLE 3.   Having given

$$\log_{10} 2 = 0.3010, \quad \log_{10} 3 = 0.4771, \quad \text{and} \quad \log_{10} 5 = 0.6990,$$

find $\log_{10} 48/\sqrt{5}$.

Solution.

$$
\begin{aligned}
\log_{10} 48/\sqrt{5} &= \log_{10} 48 - \log_{10} \sqrt{5} && \text{(by Property 2)} \\
&= \log_{10} (3 \cdot 2^4) - \log_{10} 5^{\frac{1}{2}} \\
&= \log_{10} 3 + 4 \log_{10} 2 - \tfrac{1}{2} \log_{10} 5 && \text{(by Properties 1, 3)} \\
&= (0.4771) + 4(0.3010) - \tfrac{1}{2}(0.6990) \\
&= 0.4771 + 1.2040 - 0.3495 = 1.3316.
\end{aligned}
$$

EXERCISES

Express as a sum, difference, or multiple of logarithms of simpler quantities:

1. $\log_3 pq$.

2. $\log_2 (ab/c)$.

3. $\log 1000x$.

4. $\log_5 (5^3 \cdot 7^2)$.

5. $\log_7 \sqrt[5]{9}$.

6. $\log (3^5/2^4)$.

7. $\log_b (x^c y^d)$.

8. $\log (2^3 \cdot 3^4 \cdot 5)$.

9. $\ln \sqrt[6]{3^2 \cdot 7^5}$.

Express each of the following as a single logarithm:

10. $\log_a x + \log_a y$.

11. $\log_c a - \log_c b$.

12. $4 \log_x y + 3 \log_x z$.

13. $5 \log u - \tfrac{1}{5} \log v$.

14. $3 \log_b x + \log_b y - \tfrac{3}{2} \log_b z$.

15. $\tfrac{3}{4} \log_3 5 - \tfrac{1}{3} \log_3 4 - \tfrac{1}{2} \log_3 17$.

16. $\ln \pi + 2 \ln r + \ln h - \ln 3$.

★17. $\log_{100} 3 + \log_{10} 5$.

18. Prove in detail Property 2 of this section.

Prove each of the statements in Exercises 19 through 23 using **(a)** *Properties 1, 2, and 3 of this section;* **(b)** *only the definition of a logarithm and the laws of exponents:*

19. $\log_a PQR = \log_a P + \log_a Q + \log_a R$.

20. $\log_b [(PQ) \div R] = \log_b P + \log_b Q - \log_b R$.

21. $\log_c [P \div (QR)] = \log_c P - \log_c Q - \log_c R$.

22. $\log_a \dfrac{1}{P^m} = -m \log_a P$.

23. $\log_b \dfrac{1}{\sqrt[n]{u}} = -\dfrac{1}{n} \log_b u$.

Evaluate:

24. $\log_2 8^{10}$.

25. $\log_5 25^{\frac{1}{5}}$.

26. $\log \sqrt{1000}$.

27. $\log \sqrt[3]{0.01}$.

28. $\log_6 (\frac{1}{6})^{\frac{4}{3}}$.

29. $\ln e^{-10}$.

30. $\log_3 \sqrt[4]{27} + \log_3 \sqrt{3}$.

31. $\dfrac{\log 10^{3.6} \cdot \log_2 \sqrt[9]{2}}{\log_{100} 10^{\frac{3}{2}} - \log_{0.1} 100}$.

32. $\dfrac{(\log 10^{0.1} - \log 10^{-1})^2}{\log_5 (75 \sqrt[3]{5} \div \sqrt{45})}$.

33. $\log_2 \sqrt{32 \sqrt[3]{128 \sqrt[4]{2}}}$.

34. Show that **(a)** $10^{4 \log x} = x^4$; **(b)** $e^{\frac{1}{3} \ln y} = \sqrt[3]{y}$.

35. Given $\log 2 = 0.3010$ and $\log 3 = 0.4771$, find **(a)** $\log 6$; **(b)** $\log 8$; **(c)** $\log 5$.

36. If $\ln I = -kt + \ln I_0$, show that $I = I_0 e^{-kt}$.

37. If $\ln y = \frac{1}{3} \ln x + k$, show that $y = e^k \sqrt[3]{x}$.

38. **(a)** If y varies inversely as x, show that $\log y$ is a linear function of $\log x$. **(b)** Is the converse true? Why?

6-5   Logarithms to the Base Ten

We learned in § 1-8 that any positive number N can be written in scientific notation by using the equality $N = p \cdot 10^k$, where k is an integer and $1 \leq p < 10$. Taking the logarithm of each member of this equality, we obtain

$$\log N = \log p + k \log 10 = \log p + k = k + \log p.$$

Thus we see that the (common) logarithm of every positive number can be written in a form having two parts: an integer, or "whole number," k and a number $\log p$. The integer k is called the **characteristic** of the logarithm of N; the number $\log p$ is called the **mantissa** of the logarithm of N.

The characteristic k is a positive or negative integer or zero. When the characteristic is negative, it will be more convenient to use an equivalent form, writing the characteristic as the difference of two positive numbers of which the second is a multiple of 10. Thus, we replace -1 by $9 - 10$, -4 by $6 - 10$, -12 by $8 - 20$, and so on.

The mantissa is either zero or a positive number less than 1, as can be seen from Figure 6.3.

ILLUSTRATIONS.   The logarithm 0.4778 consists of characteristic 0 and mantissa .4778; the logarithm 4.8509 has characteristic 4 and mantissa .8509;

the logarithm 1.000 has characteristic 1 and mantissa .0000. The logarithm $(7.5237 - 10)$, which equals $(-3 + 0.5237)$, has characteristic -3, or $(7 - 10)$, and mantissa .5237. The logarithm $(-7.5237 + 10)$, which equals 2.4763, has characteristic 2 and mantissa .4763 since the mantissa cannot be negative. In the logarithm -1.6029, the decimal part is not the mantissa, for the same reason; the given logarithm should first be written in the form $(-2 + 0.3971)$ or $(8.3971 - 10)$, which identifies the characteristic as -2 or $(8 - 10)$ and the mantissa as .3971. The form $(8 - 10)$ of the characteristic is preferred for many purposes as will be seen in the following sections.

All numbers N which have the same sequence of digits have the same value of p in scientific notation and so the same value of $\log p$, regardless of the position of the decimal point among the digits. Hence the mantissas of all such numbers N are the same. It is this property of the mantissas, which is generally true only for *common* logarithms, that make these logarithms superior for computational purposes to logarithms with any other number as base.

The characteristic and mantissa of a common logarithm are found separately. First we consider the characteristic. Since the value of the characteristic of the logarithm of a number N is the value of k, in the scientific notation $p \cdot 10^k$ for N, the rule for finding the characteristic is that for finding k (§ 1-8). We restate the rule in terms of the characteristic instead of in terms of k.

Rule. *The characteristic of the logarithm of a positive number* N *is equal to the number of places the decimal point in* N *is removed from its position when* N *is written in scientific notation, and is positive or zero for numbers greater than* 1, *and negative for numbers less than* 1.

ILLUSTRATION. $N = p \cdot 10^k$.

N	$p \cdot 10^k$	Places decimal point is removed	N compared to 1	Characteristic of N
374	$3.74 \cdot 10^2$	2	$N > 1$	2
0.6287	$6.287 \cdot 10^{-1}$	1	$N < 1$	-1
4.0067	$4.0067 \cdot 10^0$	0	$N > 1$	0
0.0052390	$5.2390 \cdot 10^{-3}$	3	$N < 1$	-3

The mantissas of the logarithms of most numbers are nonrepeating, unending decimal fractions. By methods which are developed in advanced works, the mantissas can be computed to any required number of decimal places. Such computed values are given in **tables of logarithms,** also called tables of mantissas, which are known as four-place tables, five-place tables, etc., according to the number of decimal places in the tabulated values. In general, a table of logarithms contains the mantissas of the logarithms of numbers of a given number of significant digits, and is used to find the mantissas of the logarithms of given numbers and to find the sequences of digits corresponding to given mantissas. Since almost all the entries in a table of logarithms are approximate numbers, approximation is always assumed in dealing with numbers from such tables, and the symbol $\approx$ is not needed to emphasize that an approximation has been obtained.

We shall explain and illustrate the use of four-place tables of logarithms; the student can readily adapt these methods, when necessary, to the use of other tables.* Although mantissas are decimal fractions, they are sometimes given in tables without the decimal point, for convenience in printing. Likewise, some tables omit the first digit in all columns after the first, since it is repetitious. Such quirks are usually evident upon brief inspection of any new table.

Table II on pages 448 and 449 is a four-place table of logarithms. It gives directly to four decimal places the mantissa of the logarithm of any number which has no more than *three* significant digits. In the next section, interpolation will be applied to take care of a fourth digit.

The procedures discussed in this section may be summarized as follows:

Two operations are required to determine the **logarithm of a number:** (1) *the characteristic is determined by the use of the "Rule" stated in this section, and* (2) *the mantissa corresponding to the given sequence of digits is found from the table.*

EXAMPLE 1.   Find log 0.00378.

Solution.   By the "Rule" for characteristics, the characteristic is -3, or $(7 - 10)$.

To find the mantissa, we consider only the three-digit sequence of digits 378 of the given number. Separate the first two digits, 37, from the third digit, 8, and find on page 448 the entry which is in the row beginning with 37

---

* For five-place tables, see for instance J. B. Rosenbach, E. A. Whitman, and D. Moskovitz's *Mathematical Tables* (Ginn, Boston, 1943).

and in the column headed by 8. This entry is .5775, which is the required mantissa.

Therefore log 0.00378 = 7.5775 − 10.

The process of finding the number corresponding to a given logarithm is the inverse of this process; the number thus found is called the **antilogarithm** (abbreviated **antilog**) of the given logarithm.

Two operations are required to determine the **number corresponding to a given logarithm:** (1) *the sequence of digits which possesses the given mantissa is determined from the table, and* (2) *the proper position for the decimal point in this sequence of digits is determined by the given characteristic and the rule for characteristics.*

EXAMPLE 2.   Find N if log $N = 1.5079$.

Solution.   The mantissa, .5079, is found on page 448 in the row which begins with 32 and in the column headed by 2. Hence the three-figure sequence of digits the mantissa of whose logarithm is .5079 is 322 (also, .5079 is the mantissa of the logarithm of the four-figure sequence 3220).

The characteristic of log N is 1; hence N has two digits to the left of the decimal point.

Therefore, if log $N = 1.5079$, $N = 32.20$.*

Historical Note.   The first printed table of logarithms was a table of the logarithms of sines (§ 7-3), published by JOHN NAPIER in 1614.

EXERCISES

Write the characteristic and the mantissa of each of the following logarithms:

1. 2.5612.	**5.** 9.7843 − 10.	**9.** −1.6583.	**13.** −8.1623 + 10.
2. 1.8000.	**6.** 7.9124 − 10.	**10.** −0.8146.	**14.** −9.5810 + 10.
3. 0.32081.	**7.** 4.4444 − 10.	**11.** −4.0271.	**15.** −4.6803 + 6.
4. 14.07189.	**8.** 1.0000 − 10.	**12.** −7.4892.	**16.** −8.6615 + 12.

Write the characteristic of the logarithm of each of the following numbers:

17. 29.4.	**19.** 6870.	**21.** 0.062440.	**23.** 0.00002.
18. 2.94.	**20.** 68,700.	**22.** 0.0006244.	**24.** 0.090000.

---

* The difference between interpretations of 32.2 and 32.20 has been discussed in § 1-9. Both numbers have four-place logarithms 1.5079.

25. 1.   **27.** 0.1.   **29.** $3.764 \cdot 10^4$.   **31.** $7.346 \cdot 10^{-14}$.
26. 1000.   **28.** 10^{-6}.   **30.** $3.764 \cdot 10^{-4}$.   **32.** 19.32146.

Use Table II to find the logarithm of each of the following numbers:
33. 3.6.   **35.** 79.8.   **37.** 0.0987.   **39.** 80,000.   **41.** 0.00834.
34. 6.3.   **36.** 148.   **38.** 0.7890.   **40.** $2.14 \cdot 10^7$.   **42.** 0.00007.

43. For each of the following numbers, determine whether the mantissa of its logarithm will be the same as the mantissa of the logarithm of 4.312: **(a)** 43.12; **(b)** 2.134; **(c)** $4.312 \cdot 10^{-5}$; **(d)** 0.4312; **(e)** 14.312; **(f)** 431,200.

44. For each of the following numbers, determine whether the characteristic of its logarithm will be the same as the characteristic of the logarithm of $4.312 \cdot 10^3$: **(a)** 4.312; **(b)** $4.312 \cdot 10^{-3}$; **(c)** 2.1340; **(d)** 143.12; **(e)** $43.12 \cdot 10^4$; **(f)** $8.888 \cdot 10^3$.

If log N has a mantissa such that the significant digits in N are 5038, find N for each of the following characteristics:
45. 2.   **47.** 0.   **49.** 8 − 10.   **51.** 9 − 20.   **53.** −2.
46. 1.   **48.** 10.   **50.** 9 − 10.   **52.** 8 − 20.   **54.** −3.

Use Table II to find the antilogarithm of each of the following logarithms:
55. 1.4942.   **59.** 8.7482 − 10.   **63.** 9.9952.
56. 3.6776.   **60.** 9.1271 − 10.   **64.** 9.0170 − 10.
57. 0.9340.   **61.** 2.7007.   **65.** −2.3507.
58. 6.8129 − 10.   **62.** 0.4014.   **66.** −1.1232.

Find x if:
67. $10^x = 3$.   **69.** $x = 10^{0.8000}$.
68. $10^x = 5.41$.   **70.** $x = 10^{1.29}$.

71. Find in two ways: **(a)** $\log \frac{4}{5}$; **(b)** $\log \frac{3}{4}$. If the two answers do not agree, explain.

72. From Figure 6.3, estimate the logarithms of each of the following numbers to the base 10 and compare them with the values from Table II: **(a)** 6; **(b)** 3.5; **(c)** 1.3; **(d)** 0.6; **(e)** 0.3.

★73. Discuss what a logarithm table would be like if all numbers were expressed in binary notation (Exercise 57 of § 1-6) and logarithms were taken to the base 10_2.

6-6 Interpolation and Logarithms

For a number N with one more digit than appears for N in Table II, log N is found by the process of interpolation studied in § 3-8. As discussed in § 4-8, this is equivalent to assuming that a very short section of the curve in Figure 6.3 (for instance, the section between 4.04 and 4.05) is a straight line, which is indeed a good approximation. Interpolation is likewise used to find the antilogarithm if the mantissa is intermediate between entries in Table II; the principle of thus interpolating in an inverse function was discussed in § 4-8.

The following points need to be noted. Successive entries in Table II (for instance, log 4.04 = 0.6064 and log 4.05 = 0.6075) lie adjacent horizontally in a row—or at the end of one row and beginning of the next row—instead of adjacent vertically as in Table I. In general, linear interpolation is suitable when *one* additional digit in the independent variable is desired beyond those tabulated (§ 3-8). Numbers with more than four significant digits should be rounded off to four-digit accuracy before trying to use four-place tables. When interpolation gives an answer ending in 5 which must be rounded off to one less digit, it is rounded to an *even* digit (§ 1-9). A table of proportional parts, Table X, may be used to minimize arithmetic operations in interpolation, as discussed in § 3-8.

The examples show details of the work. With practice, much of this can be performed mentally, using obvious shortcuts. For instance, in Example 1 the values of c could be expressed in units of one ten-thousandth, thereby eliminating many of the decimals.

EXAMPLE 1.   Find log 40.46.

Solution.

Changes in Number		Number	Logarithm	Changes in Logarithm	
0.10	0.06	40.40	1.6064	c	0.0011
		40.46	y		
		40.50	1.6075		

$$\frac{c}{0.0011} = \frac{0.06}{0.10} = \frac{6}{10}$$

$$c = \frac{6}{10} \cdot 0.0011 = 0.0007$$

$$\log 40.46 = 1.6064 + 0.0007 = 1.6071$$

EXAMPLE 2.   Find antilog $(8.2814 - 10)$.

Solution.

Changes in Number		Number	Logarithm	Changes in Logarithm	
0.00010	c	0.01910	8.2810 − 10	0.0004	0.0023
		x	8.2814 − 10		
		0.01920	8.2833 − 10		

$$\frac{c}{0.00010} = \frac{0.0004}{0.0023} = \frac{4}{23}$$

$$c = 0.00002$$

$$\text{antilog } (8.2814 - 10) = 0.01910 + 0.00002$$

$$= 0.01912$$

EXERCISES

Verify the following, using Table II:

1. $\log 45.83 = 1.6612$.

2. $\log 8458 = 3.9273$.

3. $\log 0.2207 = 9.3438 - 10$.

4. $\log 0.008225 = 7.9152 - 10$.

5. antilog $2.8647 = 732.3$.

6. antilog $0.3818 = 2.409$.

7. antilog $(9.5558 - 10) = 0.3596$.

8. antilog $(8.2153 - 10) = 0.01642$.

Use Table II to find the logarithms of the following numbers:

9. 4.267.

10. 85.18.

11. 0.06582.

12. 0.3509.

13. 399.4.

14. 2793.

15. 0.1506.

16. 0.9617.

17. 0.7948.

18. 0.01836.

19. 11.39.

20. 12.71.

21. 0.000 684 51.

22. 7,802,000.

23. $7.008 \cdot 10^4$.

24. $2.173 \cdot 10^{-7}$.

Using Table II, find the antilogarithm of:

25. 1.6029.

26. 0.5501.

27. 2.9055.

28. 3.6689.

29. 0.5561.

30. 4.8191.

31. $9.9317 - 10$.

32. $9.7800 - 10$.

33. $7.4000 - 10$.

34. $8.1950 - 10$.

35. -1.4156.

36. -2.6690.

6-7 Simple Logarithmic Computations

By using the properties of logarithms (§ 6-4), the ordinary operation of multiplication or division of numbers can be reduced to the simpler operation of addition or subtraction of their respective logarithms. Likewise, the operation of raising to a power or extracting a root can be reduced to multiplying or dividing the logarithm of the base by the exponent of the power or index of the root.

EXAMPLE 1.   Compute $\dfrac{0.07177 \times 5.960 \times 0.1571}{99 \times 0.6305}$.

Solution.   Let F denote the value of the fraction. Then, by Properties 1 and 2 of § 6-4,

$$\log F = \log \text{numerator} - \log \text{denominator};$$
$$\log \text{numerator} = \log 0.07177 + \log 5.960 + \log 0.1571;$$
$$\log \text{denominator} = \log 99 + \log 0.6305.$$

The necessary operations and results are shown below.

$$\log 0.07177 = \ \ 8.8559 - 10$$
$$\log 5.960 = \ \ 0.7752$$
$$\log 0.1571 = \ \ 9.1962 - 10$$
$$\overline{} (+)$$
$$\log \text{numerator} = 18.8273 - 20 \qquad = 8.8273 - 10$$

$$\log 99 = \ \ 1.9956$$
$$\log 0.6305 = \ \ 9.7996 - 10$$
$$\overline{} (+)$$
$$\log \text{denominator} = 11.7952 - 10 \qquad = 1.7952$$
$$\log F = \qquad\qquad\qquad \overline{} (-)$$
$$ 7.0321 - 10$$
$$F = \text{antilog}\,(7.0321 - 10) = 0.001077$$

Therefore the value of the given fraction, computed to four significant digits, is 0.001077.

ILLUSTRATION.   To compute $(2.916)^4$ by logarithms, according to Property 3 we must find the logarithm of 2.916, multiply it by 4, and then find the antilogarithm of the resulting logarithm. To compute $\sqrt[4]{2.916}$, we proceed in the same manner except that we divide by 4.

EXAMPLE 2.   Compute: $(0.1545)^5$.

Solution.   Let $\qquad\qquad\qquad N = (0.1545)^5.$

Then $\qquad\qquad\qquad\qquad \log N = \ \ 5 \log 0.1545.$
$$\log 0.1545 = \ \ 9.1889 - 10$$
$$\log N = 5 \log 0.1545 = 45.9445 - 50$$
$$= \ \ 5.9445 - 10$$
$$N = \ \ 0.00008800.$$

Therefore $(0.1545)^5 = 0.000\,088\,00.$

Some details are worthy of comment, especially since they have a wider application than that in the present topic. A neat and systematic arrangement of the details of the computation diminishes the likelihood of error and often increases net speed. Before using the tables, the student should first analyze the problem to see what operations are involved, and then prepare a skeleton outline indicating the operations with spaces for the numbers.

Because of the effects of rounding off, the answer may differ by 1 or so in the last significant digit if the computation is done in two different ways; this is consistent with the idea of approximate numbers. As pointed out in § 1-9, if the given numbers have four-digit accuracy then the results of multiplication, division, raising to powers, and extracting roots will generally have this same accuracy. The rule for sums and differences is different (§ 1-9), but this question does not ordinarily arise in logarithmic computation since sums and differences must be found by actually adding or subtracting the terms themselves rather than their logarithms.

EXERCISES

Compute the following by use of a four-place table of logarithms:

1. 4.630×81.70.   **3.** 0.5823×86.47.   **5.** 0.001908×21.49.

2. 2980×0.7260.   **4.** 0.09528×4.315.   **6.** 76.81×0.042114.

7. $0.3600 \times 0.07192 \times 4595$.   **9.** $3.248 \times 85.64 \times 0.0003027$.

8. $974.6 \times 6.230 \times 0.001821$.   **10.** $0.0006892 \times 12790 \times 0.04326$.

11. $\dfrac{63.80}{2.910}$.   **13.** $\dfrac{1}{7261}$.   **15.** $\dfrac{0.001397}{0.03094}$.   **17.** $\dfrac{906.8}{0.07394}$.

12. $\dfrac{0.3670}{79.50}$.   **14.** $\dfrac{1}{0.04761}$.   **16.** $\dfrac{0.04308}{0.001316}$.   **18.** $\dfrac{0.00076482}{0.0056391}$.

19. $\dfrac{6.670 \times 8.390}{0.002750}$.   **20.** $\dfrac{0.1700 \times 27.40}{73.10}$.   **21.** $\dfrac{75800}{139.8 \times 7583}$.

22. $\dfrac{3.102 \times 68.27}{0.00007234 \times 176.3}$.   **23.** $\dfrac{57 \times 496 \times 1.732}{32.16 \times 0.9907}$.

24. $(482.0)^4$.   **28.** $(0.9162)^6$.   **32.** $\sqrt[4]{4685000}$.

25. $(25.80)^5$.   **29.** $(0.003281)^3$.   **33.** $\sqrt[3]{6.138 \cdot 10^7}$.

26. $(0.03879)^3$.   **30.** $(806.7)^{\frac{1}{4}}$.   **34.** $(719.6)^{\frac{3}{2}}$.

27. $(0.4725)^4$.   **31.** $(39.64)^{\frac{1}{5}}$.   **35.** $(8364)^{\frac{2}{3}}$.

36. $\left(\dfrac{6.294}{88.76}\right)^3$.   **37.** $\sqrt[3]{\dfrac{74.83}{4.020}}$.   **38.** $\sqrt[5]{\dfrac{(0.9278)^3}{0.06435}}$.   **39.** $\dfrac{(48.27)^{\frac{3}{4}}}{\sqrt{189.8}}$.

40. If $d = 0.02902\sqrt{DL}\sqrt{p}$, find d when $D = 38.96$, $L = 62.89$, and $p = 278.6$.

41. If $q = \frac{8}{15}cH^{\frac{5}{2}}\sqrt{2g}$, find q when $c = 0.4893$, $H = 1.760$, and $g = 32.16$.

42. The time T in seconds for one complete oscillation of a simple pendulum is given by the formula $T = 2\pi\sqrt{l/g}$, where l is the length of the pendulum in feet, and $g = 32.16$ feet per second per second. Find the time for a complete oscillation of a pendulum 3.726 feet long.

43. By using the formula of Exercise 42, find the length of a simple pendulum whose time of oscillation is $3\frac{1}{2}$ seconds.

44. An object weighing w pounds and moving at a speed of v feet per second has a kinetic energy of k foot-pounds which is given by the formula

$$k = \frac{wv^2}{2g} .$$

If the damage done by an automobile weighing 3600 pounds indicates that at its impact it had a kinetic energy of 300,000 foot-pounds, what must have been its speed? (Use $g = 32.16$ feet per second per second.)

45. If a curve in a road or railroad is banked so that there will be no tendency to skid or overturn at speed v miles per hour, the proper elevation h in feet of the outside edge above the inside edge is given by

$$\frac{h}{w} = \left(\frac{22v}{15}\right)^2 \cdot \frac{1}{gr} ,$$

where w is the width in feet, $g = 32.16$, and r is the radius of the curve in feet. Find h for $r = 5000$, $w = 26.0$, and **(a)** $v = 40$; **(b)** $v = 60$.

46. The maximum range R in nautical miles at which a radar can detect a target is given by

$$R = \frac{1}{6080}\sqrt[4]{\frac{P\sigma(Af)^2}{4\pi S\lambda^2}} ,$$

where P is the transmitter power in watts, S is the minimum detectable return signal in watts, A is the antenna area in square feet, f is a dimensionless efficiency factor, λ is the wave length in feet, and σ is the radar cross section of the target in square feet. Suppose that $P = 100,000$, $S = 3.0 \cdot 10^{-12}$, $\lambda = 0.15$, $A = 14$, and $f = 0.60$. At what range can it detect an aircraft with $\sigma = 160$? Give the answer to **(a)** four, **(b)** an appropriate number of, significant digits.

6-8   Further Logarithmic Computations

In some cases of computations of powers, it is well to change a logarithm involving a negative characteristic to such an equivalent form that the quotient will involve -10. For example, in finding a seventh root, if the radicand has logarithm $(7.9888 - 10)$ then we change this to the equivalent logarithm $(67.9888 - 70)$.

EXAMPLE.   Compute: $(0.7063)^{-\frac{1}{6}}$.

Solution.   Let $N = (0.7063)^{-\frac{1}{6}} = \dfrac{1}{(0.7063)^{\frac{1}{6}}}.$

Then $\log N = \log 1 - \log (0.7063)^{\frac{1}{6}}$

$= \log 1 - \tfrac{1}{6} \log 0.7063.$

$\log 1 = 0 \qquad\qquad\qquad = 10.0000 - 10$

$\log 0.7063 = \quad 9.8490 - 10$

$= 59.8490 - 60$

$\tfrac{1}{6} \log 0.7063 = \qquad\qquad\qquad \dfrac{9.9748 - 10}{0.0252}(-)$

$\log N = \qquad\qquad\qquad 0.0252$

$N = \qquad\qquad\qquad 1.060.$

Therefore $(0.7063)^{-\frac{1}{6}} = 1.060.$

We have defined only the logarithms of positive numbers. If some of the numbers involved are negative, the sign of the result of the operations can be determined by the laws of signs (§ 1-5 and § 2-7) independently of any calculation of values. Then the numerical value can be calculated by operations on positive numbers. Note that there is no connection between the sign of a logarithm and the sign to be attached to its antilogarithm.

ILLUSTRATION 1.

$$\frac{0.07177 \times (-5.960) \times (-0.1571)}{99 \times (-0.6305)} = -\frac{0.07177 \times 5.960 \times 0.1571}{99 \times 0.6305}$$

$$= -0.001077 \text{ by Example 1, § 6-7.}$$

Since the two expressions $\log (M + N)$ and $(\log M + \log N)$ are *not* identical, the logarithm of a sum is *not* found by taking the sum of the logarithms of the terms. All indicated additions and subtractions must be performed numerically.

ILLUSTRATION 2.   To compute $(0.07619)^{-0.6} + (1.012)^{1.2}$, each term must be computed separately as in the Example at the beginning of this section. The terms are found to be 4.687 and 1.014, so the answer is 5.701.

EXERCISES

Determine the sign of the result of each of the following:

1. $\sqrt[3]{-0.07213}$.   **3.** $(-4.078)^4$.   **5.** $(-0.0608)^{-\frac{5}{3}}$.

2. $(4.078)^{-3}$.   **4.** $(-0.9160)^{\frac{2}{3}}$.   **6.** $(-6.1)^2 \cdot (-0.83)^{-5}$.

Compute by use of a four-place table of logarithms:

7. $(-27.18)^3$.

8. $(-46.55)^{\frac{2}{5}}$.

9. $(-0.8164)^{-4}$.

10. $(-0.08164)^{-3}$.

11. $(0.07821)^{-5}$.

12. $(0.4489)^{-3}$.

13. $(0.04910)^{\frac{2}{3}}$.

14. $(0.8140)^{\frac{3}{2}}$.

15. $(284.7)^{-\frac{1}{6}}$.

16. $(67.36)^{-\frac{1}{2}}$.

17. $(0.6172)^{-\frac{1}{6}}$.

18. $(0.08294)^{-\frac{1}{3}}$.

19. $(0.03820)^{0.4}$.

20. $(0.0005182)^{-0.1}$.

21. $(365.7)^{-1.1}$.

22. $\sqrt[5]{\dfrac{(-76.23)^3}{(-0.3120)^2}}$.

23. $\dfrac{(-0.07164)^{\frac{2}{3}}}{\sqrt[7]{-2386}}$.

24. $\left(-\dfrac{4.306}{0.3949}\right)^{-4}$.

25. $4 - \sqrt[4]{161.8}$.

26. $(8165)^{\frac{1}{4}} + (0.8165)^{-\frac{1}{4}}$.

27. $\sqrt[3]{0.3681} - \sqrt[5]{(7.608)^2}$.

28. $13 + (6.403)^{0.2689}$.

29. $\dfrac{9^{\frac{3}{2}}}{8 + (-0.06837)^{\frac{3}{5}}}$.

30. $\dfrac{(48.93)^{\frac{3}{2}} - 100\sqrt{0.8614}}{892.5 \times (0.03296)^3}$.

31. $\log 4.060 + \log 8.990 - \log (4.060 + 8.990)$.

32. The number n of years since two independently-evolving languages split off from a common ancestral language is given approximately by $n = \dfrac{1000 \log r}{2 \log 0.864}$ where r is the proportion of words common to the two languages. Find n if $r = \frac{1}{2}$.

6-9 Logarithms to Bases Other than Ten

If the base b is different from 10, many of the convenient properties of common logarithms no longer hold. Thus the fact that the characteristic and the mantissa can be found separately depends on the fact that multiplication of a number by the base, 10, changes only the position of the decimal point and not the sequence of digits (§ 6-5); this is not true for most bases. Accordingly, for bases other than 10 there is no use trying to maintain the identity of the mantissa as a tabulated positive number, and it is usually better (especially in theoretical work) to write $\log_b N$, for $N < 1$, as a negative number. This is done in Table VII for natural logarithms.

ILLUSTRATION 1.   By the fourth column of Table VII, ln $0.34 = -1.0788$.

Antilogarithms for base e can also be found from Table VII, interpolating if necessary. Thus if $\ln x = 1.2809$ then $x = 3.6$. However, it is usually both more convenient and more illuminating to take advantage of the fact that the exponential and logarithmic functions are inverses of each other.

ILLUSTRATION 2.   If $\ln x = -1.7400$ then $e^{-1.7400} = x$ by definition; by the next to last column of Table VI, $e^{-1.7400} = 0.1755$.

The following example shows how logarithms to other bases can be computed, in the rare cases when they occur, from common logarithms.

EXAMPLE. Find $\log_7 12$.

Solution. Let	$x = \log_7 12.$
Change to exponential form:	$7^x = 12.$
Take logarithms to base 10:	$\log_{10} 7^x = \log_{10} 12.$
Apply Property 3 of § 6-4:	$x \log_{10} 7 = \log_{10} 12.$
Solve for x:	$x = \dfrac{\log_{10} 12}{\log_{10} 7}.$
From Table II:	$x = \dfrac{1.0792}{0.8451}.$

Hence, by use of Table II: $\log_7 12 = x = 1.276$.

Similar methods can be used to derive the following relations:

$$\log N = 0.4343 \ln N; \tag{7}$$

$$\ln N = 2.303 \log N. \tag{8}$$

EXERCISES

1. By the method of the example in this section (setting $x = \log_a N$, changing to exponential form, and taking logarithms to base b), prove

$$\log_a N = \frac{\log_b N}{\log_b a}.$$

2. From the formula in Exercise 1, prove

(a) $\log_a b = \dfrac{1}{\log_b a}$;   (b) $\ln N = \dfrac{\log N}{\log e}$.

Using Table VII, find:

3. $\ln 2.3$.   **5.** $\ln 0.61$.   **7.** $\ln 1$.   **9.** $\ln 6900$.

4. $\ln 0.3$.   **6.** $\ln \dfrac{1}{0.61}$.   **8.** $\ln 10$.   **10.** $\ln 0.0069$.

Using Table VI, find x:

11. $\ln x = -1.280$.   **13.** $\ln x = 0.847$.   **★15.** $\ln x = 2.500$.

12. $\ln x = 0.280$.   **14.** $\ln x = -1.847$.   **★16.** $\ln x = -4$.

Using Table II, find x:

17. $x = \log_3 5$.   **19.** $x = \log_{100} 37$.   **21.** $\log_2 x = 5.6380$.

18. $x = \log_5 10$.   **20.** $x = \log_{0.1} 37$.   **22.** $\log_{11} x = 0.5896$.

23. A certain radioactive element decomposes at such a rate that, if c is the fraction of the original number of atoms which remain after t hours, then $c = e^{-kt}$ where k is a constant. Given that after three hours half of the original atoms remain, **(a)** find k; **(b)** find when one-tenth of the original atoms remain.

24. Under favorable conditions, the number n of bacteria increases according to the law $n = ce^{kt}$ where t is the time in minutes. If there are $1 \cdot 10^6$ bacteria at time $t = 0$ and $2 \cdot 10^6$ bacteria at $t = 25$, find **(a)** the values of c and k; **(b)** the time when there will be $2 \cdot 10^7$ bacteria.

25. Reconcile the form of the law stated in Exercise 24 with the form developed in § 6-1.

26. The capacity C of an information-transmission channel (such as a telephone wire or radio transmission) is given by $C = W \log_2 \dfrac{P + N}{N}$ where W is the band width in cycles per second, P is the average power of the signal, N is the average power of the noise present, and C is measured in bits per second. (One "bit" is one binary digit; § 1-6, Exercise 57.) Find C if $W = 1000$ and **(a)** $P = 0.003$, $N = 0.001$; **(b)** $P = 0.003$, $N = 0.003$; **(c)** $P = 0.003$, $N = 0.030$.

6-10   Graphing on Logarithmic Scales

Certain functions behave in such a manner that it is convenient to graph the values of the logarithms of one or both variables instead of the values of the variables themselves. One way to do this is to look up the logarithms in a table or compute them.

Alternatively—and more conveniently if such work is to be done extensively—one may construct a **logarithmic scale,** on which the origin represents the value 1 of the variable and other convenient values of the variable are marked at distances from the origin proportional to their logarithms. Figure 6.4 illustrates this.

Fig. 6.4

A logarithmic scale is used on a *slide rule* (see the Appendix); with this mechanical device, multiplication is carried out by means of Property 1 of § 6-4, the sum of the logarithms of the factors being given by the sum of corresponding distances on the scale.

Just as for linear scales (§ 1-3 and § 4-4), there is available graph paper with the rulings already drawn to correspond to log x or log y or both; it is called **logarithmic graph paper** if both scales are logarithmic, and **semilogarithmic graph paper** if one scale is logarithmic, one linear.

The principal advantage of logarithmic or semilogarithmic plots is that certain equations have much simpler graphs (such as straight lines) when these scales are used than when linear scales are used.

ILLUSTRATION 1. To graph $x^2y^3 = 1$ on logarithmic scales, first form a table of corresponding values of the two variables. The pairs of corresponding

x	$\frac{1}{8} = 0.125$	1	8	27	64
y	4	1	$\frac{1}{4} = 0.25$	$\frac{1}{9} = 0.111$	$\frac{1}{16} = 0.0625$

values of x and y are plotted as coordinates of points on logarithmic scales in Figure 6.5.

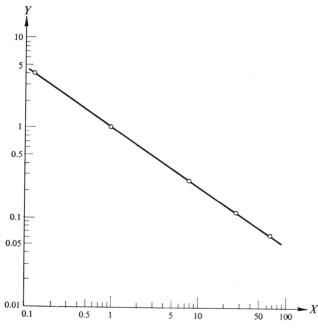

Fig. 6.5

Some further light is shed by taking the logarithms of both members of the given equation:

$$2 \log x + 3 \log y = \log 1 = 0.$$

This is a linear equation in $\log x$ and $\log y$.

ILLUSTRATION 2.   Suppose it is required to make a semilogarithmic graph of $y = 2^n$. Taking logarithms of both members of the given equation,

$$\log y = n \log 2.$$

Noting that $\log 2$ is a constant, it appears convenient to use a logarithmic scale for y and a linear scale for n. From the given equation we obtain a table of values. These are plotted in Figure 6.6.

n	-3	-2	-1	0	1	2	3
y	0.125	0.25	0.5	1	2	4	8

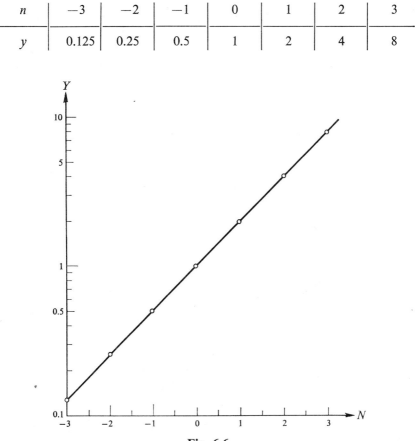

Fig. 6.6

EXERCISES

1. Using Table II construct a logarithmic scale for numbers from 0.1 to 100 with P_1 and P_{10}, the points marked 1 and 10, about two inches or five centimeters apart.

2. On a logarithmic scale compare the actual distances from P_1 to P_5, from P_{10} to P_{50}, and from $P_{0.1}$ to $P_{0.5}$. Give a reason for the result found.

3. Graph $xy = 3$ on logarithmic scales.

4. Graph $xy^2 = 9$ on logarithmic scales.

5. Graph $y = 10^x$ on semilogarithmic scales.

6. Graph $x = 2^{3y}$ on semilogarithmic scales.

7. The following table shows world production of petroleum in billions of barrels. Graph the production on a logarithmic scale against the year on a linear scale, and approximate the points by a straight line. Predict the production in 1970.

Year	1910	1920	1930	1940	1946	1949	1953	1960
Production	0.328	0.689	1.412	2.144	2.75	3.40	4.79	7.68

8. The table shows the world records in certain track events. Convert all data to yards and seconds, and graph the distance against time on logarithmic scales.

Distance	100 yards	220 yards	440 yards	880 yards	1 mile	2 miles	10 miles
Time (min.:sec.)	0:9.3	0:20.0	0:45.7	1:46.8	3:54.5	8:32.0	48:12.0

9. The mass of water vapor in saturated air (in grams per cubic meter) at various temperatures (in degrees centigrade) is given by the table. Graph on semilogarithmic scales.

Temperature	−20	−10	0	10	20	30
Mass	0.892	2.154	4.835	9.330	17.12	30.04

In Exercises 10 through 19, graph on scales chosen to give a straight-line graph, or as nearly so as practicable:

10. $x = \left(\dfrac{y}{3}\right)^4$.

11. $x = \left(\dfrac{4}{3}\right)^y$.

12. $4y = 3x$.

13. $y = x^3$.

14. $y = e^{3x}$.

15. $y = 100^{\frac{x}{10}}$.

16. $x = \dfrac{1}{y^4}$.

17. $\dfrac{y+1}{x} = 4$.

18. $y = \sqrt[3]{x}$.

19. Representative weights W in pounds and corresponding average basal metabolism M in calories per pound per day, as shown.

	Mouse	Guinea Pig	Hen	Cat	Dog	Man	Pig	Cow	Horse	Elephant
W	0.045	0.88	4.0	6.2	30	132	370	970	1000	7300
M	72	39	25	23	16	11.4	9.5	5.9	8.6	5.5

MISCELLANEOUS EXERCISES

Find, using tables only if necessary:

1. $\log_2 32$.

2. $\log_2 \frac{1}{16}$.

3. $\log_4 8$.

4. $\log_x x^{\frac{2}{3}}$.

5. $\log_9 \frac{1}{243}$.

6. $\log_{0.1} 1000$.

7. $\log_{1000} 1$.

8. $\ln e$.

9. $\ln e^{2.603}$.

10. $e^{\ln 4.19}$.

11. $10^{1.691}$.

12. $10^{-2.46}$.

13. $(\log 1000)^2$.

14. $\log (1000^2)$.

15. $(\log \sqrt{2})^0$.

16. $1/\log_3 10$.

Compute the following by use of four-place tables:

17. $\dfrac{246.8}{(0.2681)^{0.6} + (-89.76)^{-\frac{1}{3}}}$.

18. $\dfrac{(187.2)^3 + (-64.60)^4}{2.718\sqrt{0.06817}}$.

19. $\log \dfrac{7.390}{5.260}$.

20. $\dfrac{\log 7.390}{\log 5.260}$.

21. $\dfrac{\log 0.5823}{\log 87.29}$.

22. $\log \dfrac{0.003847}{0.07945}$.

23. If a sheet hung in the wind loses moisture at a rate proportional to the moisture remaining and loses one half its moisture in one hour, then the moisture M remaining after t hours is given approximately by $M = M_0 e^{-0.693t}$. Evaluate M for **(a)** $t = 3$, $M_0 = 10$; **(b)** $t = 10$, $M_0 = 40$.

24. It has been found that on the average the area A, in square miles, of a city in the United States is related to its population P by the relation $A = \frac{1}{357} P^{\frac{3}{4}}$. Find the expected area of a city of 200,000 population chosen at random.

25. The frequency f of the note sounded by a string of a musica instrument is given by

$$f = \frac{1}{2L} \sqrt{\frac{32.16\, TL}{m}},$$

where L is the length of the string in feet, T is the tension in pounds, and m is the mass of the string in pounds. If a harp string 4.82 feet long weighing 0.000215 pound is to sound the tone of A which has frequency 439 vibrations per second, what must be the tension on it?

26. The surface area A, in square inches, of an average adult person is given in terms of the weight W in pounds and height H in inches by $A = 30.7W^{0.425}H^{0.725}$. Find the area if $H = 72.0$ and $W = 180$.

Plot two or three points and sketch the graph of the following on linear scales:

27. $y = \frac{1}{3}e^{2x}$.   **30.** $y = \frac{1}{3}e^{2x+1}$.   **33.** $y = 2/e^x$.

28. $y = \frac{1}{3}e^{-2x}$.   **31.** $y = 3e^{2x-1}$.   **34.** $y = e^{x^2}$.

29. $x = \frac{1}{3}e^{2y}$.   **32.** $y = \frac{1}{3}e^{2x} + 1$.   **★35.** $y = xe^x$.

36. Identify the scales on which the graph of the following would be a straight line: **(a)** $y = x^3$; **(b)** $y = 3^x$; **(c)** $y = ax^3$; **(d)** $y = ax^b$; **(e)** $y = a^{bx}$; **(f)** $y = a^{bx+c}$.

37. If $\ln y = -at + b$ where a and b are constants, show that $y = ke^{-at}$ where k is some constant.

38. If $2.5 \ln y = \ln x + c$ where c is a constant, show that $y = e^a x^b$ for some constants a and b.

39. In the biological assay of drugs, it is often found that the dose d is related to A, the fraction of experimental subjects which react (in a specified way), by an equation of the form $d = d_{50} + f \log \dfrac{A}{1 - A}$, where d_{50} is the dose at which half of the subjects react and f reflects the sensitivity of the test. For digitalis injected into frogs, d_{50} is 4 units and $f \approx 1.2$. Graph this relationship and find the dosage at which not more than one frog in twenty would be expected to react.

CHAPTER 7

TRIGONOMETRIC FUNCTIONS

7-1 Angles

An **angle** is considered as generated by the rotation of a half-line (sometimes called a ray) about its endpoint. In Figure 7.1, suppose a half-line *VA*, starting from *V*, is rotated (as shown by the arrow) to a final position *VB*. Then the angle is called angle *AVB*. The point *V* about which the rotation takes place is called the **vertex** of the angle; the initial position, *VA*, of the half-line is called the **initial side** of the angle; and the final position, *VB*, is called the **terminal side.** If, as in Figure 7.1, the rotation is counterclockwise, the angle is called a **positive angle**; if clockwise, a **negative angle.** Angles are commonly denoted by Greek letters. Thus in Figure 7.1, the angle *AVB* is denoted by θ (read "theta"); the direction of the arrowhead shows that in this instance the angle is positive. A positive angle generated by a rotation of less than

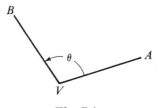

Fig. 7.1

one right angle (the angle between two perpendicular lines, frequently encountered in plane geometry) is called an **acute angle.**

This concept of angle is more general than the one usually used in elementary geometry. For instance, the usage developed in this section has no requirement as to the magnitude of the rotation, which may involve one or more complete revolutions. Thus in Figure 7.2, α (read "alpha") is an angle with initial side *VA* and terminal side *VB*, generated

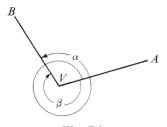

Fig. 7.2

by approximately $1\frac{1}{3}$ revolutions of VA in the positive direction; β (read "beta") is an angle generated by rotating VA approximately $\frac{2}{3}$ of a revolution in the negative direction.

Just as distances may be measured in inches or in centimeters or in other units, there are two common units of measurement for angles. One unit is the **degree.** An angle of $1°$ (read "one degree") is an angle of such size that 360 of them together make one complete revolution from the initial side. Thus an angle of $90°$ is a right angle. Subdivisions of a degree are a **minute** ($\frac{1}{60}$ of a degree) and a **second** ($\frac{1}{60}$ of a minute); these are respectively designated by $1' = \frac{1}{60}°$ and $1'' = \frac{1}{60}'$. Angles can also be expressed as a fraction—in particular, a decimal fraction—of a degree; thus $81.6°$, sometimes written $81°6$, means $81\frac{6}{10}$ degrees, which is $81° \ 36'$.

The other common unit of measure for angles is the **radian;** "one radian" is sometimes abbreviated "1 rad". An angle of one radian is such that on any circle with center at the vertex of the angle the minor arc on the circumference of this circle intercepted by the sides of the angle is equal in length to the radius of the circle. Thus in Figure 7.3 the angle AVB is 1 radian.

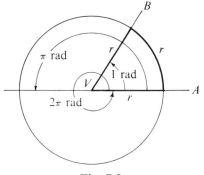

Fig. 7.3

One complete revolution is 360°. It is also 2π radians, since the circumference of a circle of radius r is $2\pi r$. The relationship between a degree and a radian follows from this: $360° = 2\pi$ radians, and

$$1° = \frac{1}{180}\pi \text{ radians} \approx 0.0174533 \text{ radian};\qquad (1)$$

$$1 \text{ radian} = 180°/\pi \approx 57.29578° \approx 57° \ 17.75'.\qquad (2)$$

For any other number n of degrees or radians, both members of the appropriate relationship may be multiplied by n. Alternatively, Table V (page 461) gives conversion tables between degrees and radians.

ILLUSTRATIONS.   An angle of $\frac{\pi}{2}$ radians is $\frac{\pi}{2} \cdot \frac{180°}{\pi}$, that is, 90°. An angle of 60° is $60 \cdot \frac{1}{180}\pi$ radians, that is, $\frac{1}{3}\pi$ radians. To convert 8.106 radians to degrees and minutes, either multiply the left and right members of (2) by 8.106 or—more conveniently—use Table V:

8	radians $\approx$	458° 21.97′
0.1	radian $\approx$	5° 43.77′
0.006	radian $\approx$	20.63′
8.106	radians $\approx$	464° 26.37′

If 8.106 is an approximate number, with 4 significant digits, then the answer should be rounded off. To decide how far to round off, note that 8.106 is presumably subject to uncertainty of about 1 in the last digit, that is, of 0.001 radian; converting to minutes, this is about 3′. Thus the answer is not quite reliable to the nearest minute, and must be rounded off at least to 464° 26′.

In describing the size of an angle, the word "radian" is often omitted. Thus an angle of $\pi/6$ is understood to be $\pi/6$ radians, which is 30°.

If a set of rectangular coordinate axes is given, an angle is said to be in **standard position** if its vertex is at the origin of the coordinate system and its initial side coincides with the positive part of the x-axis. An angle is said to **terminate** in (or to "be in") a certain quadrant if when the angle is placed in standard position its terminal side lies in that quadrant (§ 4-4). If the terminal side falls on one of the axes then the angle is not in any quadrant and is called a **quadrantal** angle; such angles are 0° or integral multiples of 90°. Two angles are called **coterminal** if their terminal sides coincide when the angles are placed in standard position.

ILLUSTRATIONS.   An angle of 30° is in the first quadrant, an angle of 120° is in the second quadrant, of 210° is in the third quadrant, of 300° is in the fourth quadrant, of 480° or of −240° is in the second quadrant. Angles of 120°, 480°, and −240° are coterminal (Figure 7.4).

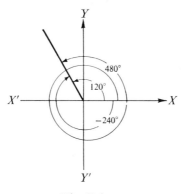

Fig. 7.4

EXERCISES

Express in degrees and minutes, treating the given number as exact:

1. 2 radians.   **4.** 1.6502 rad.   **7.** $\frac{5}{6}\pi$ rad.

2. 0.3 radian.   **5.** 0.699 rad.   **8.** 3π rad.

3. −3.1689 rad.   **6.** $\frac{1}{8}\pi$ radian.   **9.** $-\frac{3}{2}\pi$ rad.

Express in radians as a multiple of π:

10. 180°.   **12.** −720°.   **14.** 135°.   **16.** 300°.

11. 450°.   **13.** −90°.   **15.** 210°.   **17.** 45°.

Express in radians in decimal form, (**a**) *taking the given number as exact;* (**b**) *to the appropriate accuracy taking the given number as approximate:*

18. 27° 16.4′.   **20.** −5° 26.9′.   **22.** 230° 42′.

19. 69° 58.1′.   **21.** −81.7°.   **23.** 167° 28.0′.

Draw an angle of the specified size in standard position, and estimate from the graph the coordinates of one point, other than the vertex, on the terminal side:

24. 73°.   **25.** 136°.   **26.** 240°.   **27.** −120°.   **28.** −270°.

29. Draw an angle coterminal with 150° but lying between (**a**) 360° and 720°; (**b**) 0° and −360°.

30. A **mil** is 0.001 radian. Express in degrees and minutes (**a**) 1 mil; (**b**) 100 mils; (**c**) 50 mils; (**d**) 1000 mils.

7-2   Trigonometric Functions Defined

Let θ be an angle in standard position; $P: (x, y)$ a point, other than the origin, on its terminal side; and r the positive distance from the origin to P. Then the six **trigonometric functions** are defined as follows:

$$\textbf{sine } \boldsymbol{\theta} = \frac{y}{r} \qquad\qquad \text{abbreviated } \sin \theta$$

$$\textbf{cosine } \boldsymbol{\theta} = \frac{x}{r} \qquad\qquad \cos \theta$$

$$\textbf{tangent } \boldsymbol{\theta} = \frac{y}{x} \qquad\qquad \tan \theta$$

$$\textbf{cotangent } \boldsymbol{\theta} = \frac{x}{y} \qquad\qquad \text{ctn } \theta \text{ or cot } \theta$$

$$\textbf{secant } \boldsymbol{\theta} = \frac{r}{x} \qquad\qquad \sec \theta$$

$$\textbf{cosecant } \boldsymbol{\theta} = \frac{r}{y} \qquad\qquad \csc \theta$$

These ratios depend only on the angle θ, not on which point P on the terminal side is chosen, and hence they are functions of θ under the definition of function (§ 4-1). We shall prove this assertion for $\sin \theta$; the assertions about the other ratios can be proved in a similar manner. In Figure 7.5 let P_1 and P_2 be two possible choices of P, and construct lines P_1M_1 and P_2M_2 perpendicular to the x-axis. Then triangles OM_1P_1 and OM_2P_2 are similar; and by the properties of similar triangles in geometry, $M_1P_1/OP_1 = M_2P_2/OP_2$. Noting that r is always positive by definition and that y_2 necessarily has the same sign as y_1, we see that this proportion becomes $y_1/r_1 = y_2/r_2$. Hence $\sin \theta$ has the same value when computed from P_2 as when computed from P_1. In the special case of a

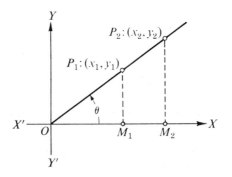

Fig. 7.5

quadrantal angle, OM_iP_i is no longer a proper triangle but the same proportion still holds.

EXAMPLE 1.   Find the values of the trigonometric functions of α if, when α is in standard position, one point on its terminal side is P: $(3, -4)$.

Solution.   Since $x = 3$ and $y = -4$, $r = \sqrt{3^2 + (-4)^2} = 5$ (Figure 7.6). Hence

$$\sin \alpha = \frac{y}{r} = \frac{-4}{5} = -\frac{4}{5};$$

$$\cos \alpha = \frac{x}{r} = \frac{3}{5};$$

$$\tan \alpha = \frac{y}{x} = \frac{-4}{3} = -\frac{4}{3};$$

$$\text{ctn } \alpha = \frac{x}{y} = -\frac{3}{4};$$

$$\sec \alpha = \frac{r}{x} = \frac{5}{3};$$

$$\csc \alpha = \frac{r}{y} = -\frac{5}{4}.$$

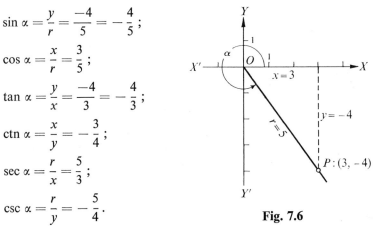

Fig. 7.6

EXAMPLE 2.   Find the values of the trigonometric functions of $\frac{1}{3}\pi$ radians.

Solution.   For an angle θ of $\frac{1}{3}\pi$ radians, which is 60°, it is known from elementary geometry (consider half of an equilateral triangle) that θ can be taken as the angle opposite the longer leg of a right triangle with sides of lengths 1, $\sqrt{3}$, and 2. Putting θ in standard position, then a point P: (x, y) on the terminal side has $r = 2$, $x = 1$, $y = \sqrt{3}$, as in Figure 7.7. Hence, as in Example 1,

$$\sin \frac{1}{3}\pi = \frac{\sqrt{3}}{2} = \frac{1}{2}\sqrt{3};$$

$$\cos \frac{1}{3}\pi = \frac{1}{2};$$

$$\tan \frac{1}{3}\pi = \frac{\sqrt{3}}{1} = \sqrt{3};$$

$$\text{ctn } \frac{1}{3}\pi = \frac{1}{\sqrt{3}} = \frac{1}{3}\sqrt{3};$$

$$\sec \frac{1}{3}\pi = \frac{2}{1} = 2;$$

$$\csc \frac{1}{3}\pi = \frac{2}{\sqrt{3}} = \frac{2}{3}\sqrt{3}.$$

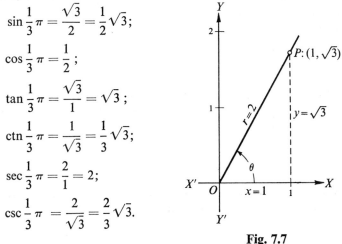

Fig. 7.7

EXAMPLE 3.   Find the values of the trigonometric functions of 225°.

Solution. $225° = 180° + 45°$. Hence 225° is in the third quadrant; x and y are numerically equal, and both are negative. One point on the terminal side is $P: (x, y)$ with $x = -1, y = -1, r = \sqrt{2}$. Hence

$$\sin 225° = \frac{-1}{\sqrt{2}} = -\frac{1}{2}\sqrt{2}; \qquad \csc 225° = \frac{\sqrt{2}}{-1} = -\sqrt{2};$$

$$\cos 225° = \frac{-1}{\sqrt{2}} = -\frac{1}{2}\sqrt{2}; \qquad \sec 225° = \frac{\sqrt{2}}{-1} = -\sqrt{2};$$

$$\tan 225° = \frac{-1}{-1} = 1; \qquad \operatorname{ctn} 225° = \frac{-1}{-1} = 1.$$

EXAMPLE 4.   Find the trigonometric functions of 270°.

Solution.   Put angle 270° in standard position; then one point on its terminal side is $(0, -1)$. Thus $x = 0, y = -1, r = 1$. By the definitions, $\sin 270° = -1/1 = -1$; $\cos 270° = 0/1 = 0$; $\operatorname{ctn} 270° = 0$; $\csc 270° = -1$. But $\tan 270°$ and $\sec 270°$ are not defined, since in their definitions the denominator would be zero.

This behavior is typical of quadrantal angles. It may also be noted that if θ is very near 270°, the *numerical* value of $\tan \theta$ and $\sec \theta$ will be very large, since their denominators will be near zero; however, the values may be either positive or negative, depending on the quadrant.

If the given angle is not such that coordinates of some point on its terminal side are readily determined numerically, the angle as specified can be laid off with a protractor (an angle-measuring device), a point on the terminal side selected and its coordinates measured; then the values of the trigonometric functions can be calculated as above. However, this is rarely done; instead, in this type of problem, use is made of tables (§ 7-3).

From the signs of x and y in the various quadrants (§ 4-4), it is evident that the values of the trigonometric functions have the following signs:

Quadrant of θ	sin θ	cos θ	tan θ	ctn θ	sec θ	csc θ
I	+	+	+	+	+	+
II	+	−	−	−	−	+
III	−	−	+	+	−	−
IV	−	+	−	−	+	−

EXAMPLE 5.   Given $\cos \theta = -\frac{5}{13}$, construct θ in standard position and find the values of the other trigonometric functions of θ.

Solution. By definition, $\cos\theta = x/r$. Consider a point P on the terminal side of θ with $r = 13$. To yield the specified value of $\cos\theta$, x must obviously be -5. Then by the Pythagorean theorem, $(-5)^2 + y^2 = 13^2$. Solving for y as in § 5-6, $y = \pm 12$. Therefore there are two possibilities for P; it may be P_1: $(-5, 12)$ or P_2: $(-5, -12)$. The two corresponding possibilities for θ, denoted as θ_1 and θ_2, are shown in Figure 7.8; any angle coterminal with these is likewise possible, but would have the same values for its trigonometric

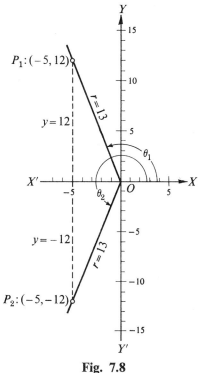

Fig. 7.8

functions. The values of the other trigonometric functions are found, as in Example 1, to be:

	$\sin\theta$	$\tan\theta$	$\text{ctn }\theta$	$\sec\theta$	$\csc\theta$
θ_1	$\frac{12}{13}$	$-\frac{12}{5}$	$-\frac{5}{12}$	$-\frac{13}{5}$	$\frac{13}{12}$
θ_2	$-\frac{12}{13}$	$\frac{12}{5}$	$\frac{5}{12}$	$-\frac{13}{5}$	$-\frac{13}{12}$

EXAMPLE 6. Angle θ is in standard position. Find the coordinates of the point on its terminal side at distance 1 from the origin.

Solution. In the definition of sine, we are here given that $r = 1$. Therefore $\sin\theta = y/1 = y$. Similarly $\cos\theta = x$. Thus the point is $(\cos\theta, \sin\theta)$.

In this book we speak of the six functions sine, cosine, tangent, cotangent, secant, and cosecant as "the trigonometric functions". The name is sometimes applied more widely, to any combination of these functions.

We have defined the trigonometric functions of an angle and seen how to find their values in some cases. Trigonometric functions can also be defined when the independent variable represents numbers instead of angles. If x represents a number, sine x is defined to be equal to the sine of x radians, and similarly for the other trigonometric functions.

As a result of this definition, the omission of "radians" from the description of an angle, as discussed in § 7-1, causes no confusion as to the value of the trigonometric functions. It is still convenient to speak of x as lying in a quadrant, just as though an angle of x radians were involved.

ILLUSTRATION 1.   Sin $\frac{1}{3}\pi$ is the same as sin ($\frac{1}{3}\pi$ radians), which is $\frac{1}{2}\sqrt{3}$ by Example 2.

It is of interest to note that, when the scales are of equal size on the two axes, the slope of a straight line (§ 4-7) is precisely the tangent of the angle that the line makes with the positive direction on the x-axis, where a line parallel to the x-axis is considered to make an angle of 0° with it. This can be seen by drawing a line through the origin parallel to the given line (Figure 7.9). Since the two lines are parallel they make equal angles θ with the x-axis, by geometry; they have equal slopes by § 4-7. The points (0, 0) and (x, y) are two points on the line through the origin; hence by definition the slope is y/x, which is also tan θ.

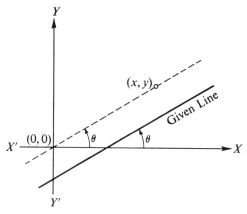

Fig. 7.9

ILLUSTRATION 2.   What angle ψ (read "psi") with the positive direction on the x-axis is made by the line whose equation is $x + y = 2$? Written in the form $y = ax + b$, this equation becomes $y = -x + 2$. Hence by § 4-7, the line has slope -1. Hence $\tan \psi = -1$. Such an angle is $135°$. One could also take ψ as $-45°$ or $495°$ or any other coterminal angle, but it is usual to take the smallest nonnegative angle meeting the requirements, in this case $135°$.

EXERCISES

Write the signs of the trigonometric functions of the following angles:

1. $387°$.   **3.** $290°$.   **5.** $-110°$.   **7.** $\frac{3}{4}\pi$.   **9.** $-\frac{1}{3}\pi$.

2. $130°$.   **4.** $722°$.   **6.** $230°$.   **8.** $\frac{7}{4}\pi$.   **10.** $\frac{7}{6}\pi$.

Find the values of the trigonometric functions of the following angles:

11. $\frac{1}{6}\pi$.   **15.** $\frac{5}{6}\pi$.   **19.** $\frac{7}{4}\pi$.   **23.** $-\frac{5}{4}\pi$.   **27.** 2π.

12. $\frac{1}{4}\pi$.   **16.** $\frac{7}{6}\pi$.   **20.** $\frac{11}{4}\pi$.   **24.** 0.   **28.** $\frac{3}{2}\pi$.

13. $\frac{3}{4}\pi$.   **17.** $\frac{5}{3}\pi$.   **21.** $\frac{8}{3}\pi$.   **25.** $\frac{1}{2}\pi$.   **29.** $-\pi$.

14. $\frac{2}{3}\pi$.   **18.** $\frac{11}{6}\pi$.   **22.** $-\frac{1}{4}\pi$.   **26.** π.   **30.** $-\frac{7}{2}\pi$.

Find all angles θ between $0°$ and $360°$ inclusive for which the specified relation holds:

31. $\sin \theta = \frac{1}{2}$.   **34.** $\cos \theta = \frac{1}{2}$.   **37.** $\operatorname{ctn} \theta = 1$.

32. $\sin \theta = -\frac{1}{2}\sqrt{2}$.   **35.** $\tan \theta = -1$.   **38.** $\sec \theta = 2$.

33. $\cos \theta = -\frac{1}{2}\sqrt{3}$.   **36.** $\tan \theta = \sqrt{3}$.   **39.** $\csc \theta = -\sqrt{2}$.

Find the angle which the line with the given equation makes with the positive direction on the x-axis:

40. $x - y = 3$.   **42.** $y + \sqrt{3}x = 0$.   **44.** $y = -2$.

41. $x - \sqrt{3}y = 4$.   **43.** $x + y = \sqrt{3}$.   **45.** $x = \sqrt{3}$.

Find the equation of a straight line through the specified point making the specified angle with the positive direction on the x-axis:

46. $(1, 2); 45°$.   **48.** $(-1, 5); 150°$.   **50.** $(4, -2); 90°$.

47. $(3, 4); 60°$.   **49.** $(2, -3); 135°$.   **51.** $(3, -1); 0°$.

52. Find the smallest positive angle which has its initial side along the positive direction of the y-axis and its terminal side along the line whose equation is **(a)** $2x + 2y = 1$; **(b)** $x - \sqrt{3}y + 5 = 0$.

53. Explain why **(a)** $\tan 90°$, **(b)** $\csc 0°$, is not defined.

54. Substitute their numerical values for the functions and simplify:

(a) $(\sin 150°)^2 + (\cos 150°)^2$;   **(b)** $1 + (\tan 120°)^2 - (\sec 120°)^2$;

(c) $\dfrac{\sin 240°}{\cos 240°} \cdot \operatorname{ctn} 240°$.

★55. In the discussion in the text about the relationship between the slope of a line and the tangent of the angle that the line makes with the positive direction of the x-axis, what difference would it make in this tangent if the angle were measured **(a)** in the negative direction? **(b)** in the positive direction but from the negative end of the x-axis? **(c)** from the positive direction on the x-axis around counterclockwise to the leftward direction on the line?

56. By measuring the coordinates of a point on a drawing of the angle, find approximately the values of the trigonometric functions of **(a)** $160°$; **(b)** $280°$; **(c)** $\frac{1}{8}\pi$; **(d)** $-\frac{2}{5}\pi$.

7-3 Tables of Trigonometric Functions

In the previous section we saw how to find the values of the trigonometric functions of an angle θ if the coordinates of a point on the terminal side of θ could be determined. If the coordinates cannot be determined exactly, they can be approximately measured from a drawing of the angle, but this method tends to be both inaccurate and inconvenient. Hence tables of the values of the trigonometric functions have been computed, analogously to tables of logarithms. Table IV (pages 456 through 460) presents such values for angles from 0° to 90° at intervals of 10′. For angles outside the domain 0° to 90° the values can be found by methods which will be discussed in § 7-6. In Table IV, for angles from 0° to 45° the angle appears at the left and the name of the function at the top of the column; for angles from 45° to 90° the angle appears at the right of the row and the name of the function at the bottom of the column.

ILLUSTRATION 1.   From Table IV,

$$\sin 10° \, 20' = 0.1794; \qquad \sin 79° \, 40' = 0.9838;$$
$$\cos 10° \, 20' = 0.9838; \qquad \cos 79° \, 40' = 0.1794;$$
$$\csc 10° \, 20' = 5.575; \qquad \csc 79° \, 40' = 1.016.$$

The interval of 10′ in the listing of angles corresponds roughly to three-digit accuracy (just as N in Table II is listed to three digits). Linear interpolation (§ 3-8) is applicable and yields approximate values of the trigonometric functions to four digits for angles given to the nearest minute. On the other hand, inspection of the tables indicates that knowledge of the angle to the nearest degree generally determines the values of the trigonometric functions to about two significant digits.

Warning. The cosine, cotangent, and cosecant functions in the first quadrant *decrease* as the angle increases. Hence their tabular differences (§ 3-8) are negative and the numerical value of the correction must be *subtracted*. This is similar to interpolation in a table of reciprocals.

ILLUSTRATION 2.   To find cos 10° 23', note from Table IV that:

Changes in angle		Angle	Cosine	Changes in cosine
10	3	10° 20' 10° 23' 10° 30'	0.9838 0.9838 + c 0.9833	c −0.0005

$$\frac{3}{10} \approx \frac{c}{-0.0005}$$

$$c \approx (-0.0005)\tfrac{3}{10} = -0.00015$$

$$\cos 10° 23' = 0.9838 - 0.00015$$

$$= 0.9836.$$

As discussed in § 3-8, most of this work can be performed mentally, especially with the aid of the table of proportional parts (Table X).

ILLUSTRATION 3.   To find θ if sin θ = 0.7116, note from Table IV that;

Changes in angle		Angle	Sine	Changes in sine
10'	c	45° 20' 45° 20' + c 45° 30'	0.7112 0.7116 0.7133	0.0004 0.0021

$$\frac{c}{10'} = \frac{0.0004}{0.0021} = \frac{4}{21}$$

$$c = \tfrac{4}{21} \cdot 10' \approx 0.2 \cdot 10' = 2'$$

$$\theta = 45° 20' + 2'$$

$$= 45° 22'.$$

Table VI lists values of the trigonometric functions of angles measured in radians, for angles from 0 to 2 radians, and hence also the values of trigonometric functions of pure numbers (§ 7-2). Interpolation can be used here also.

ILLUSTRATION 4.   From Table VI, sin 0.12 = 0.1197; cos 1.05 = 0.4976; by interpolation, sin 0.127 = 0.1266.

One other type of table deserves notice. Suppose, for instance, one desires to compute the value of $(432.0 \sin 10° 20')^3$. This could be done straightforwardly by logarithms (§ 6-7). Table II directly yields log 432.0. Illustration 1 shows that sin 10° 20′ = 0.1794, and log 0.1794 can be found from Table II in turn. However, as a shortcut, Table III lists the logarithms of the sine and of the other trigonometric functions; the intermediate step of looking up the value of the sine has been carried out in constructing the table and need not be repeated. (In general, this intermediate step was carried out to more significant digits before rounding off, so the answer may differ slightly in the last digit from the result of the two-step use of tables.)

ILLUSTRATION 5.   To evaluate $(432.0 \sin 10° 20')^3$, which we denote by x, use Table III and the laws of logarithms:

log 432.0	= 2.6355	by Table II
log sin 10° 20′	= 9.2538 − 10	by Table III
log of product	= 1.8893	adding
log x	= 5.6679	multiplying by 3
x	= 465,400	by Table II

Historical Note.   The first table related to sines of which we have record was computed by HIPPARCHUS (about 140 B.C.). He dealt with chords of a circle. Our definition gives | sin θ | as half the length of a chord of a circle of radius 1 and center at the origin.

EXERCISES

Find from either Table IV or Table VI:

1. sin 76° 13′. **5.** cos 56° 8′. **9.** sin 0.624.

2. cos 15° 28′. **6.** sin 8° 6′. **10.** cos 0.916.

3. ctn 28° 41′. **7.** sec 40° 56′. **11.** ctn $\frac{1}{5}$.

4. tan 69° 37′. **8.** csc 49° 38′. **12.** tan $\frac{1}{8}\pi$.

Find from Table IV and also from Table VI, converting the angle by Table V if necessary:

13. sin 37° 50′. **15.** ctn 4° 10′. **17.** cos 0.37.

14. cos 68° 40′. **★16.** csc 16° 0′. **18.** tan $\frac{3}{4}$.

Find θ, if it is in the first quadrant and:

19. $\sin \theta = 0.1822$. **25.** $\sin \theta = 0.7703$. **31.** $\sin \theta = \frac{1}{3}$.

20. $\cos \theta = 0.7528$. **26.** $\cos \theta = 0.5320$. **32.** $\cos \theta = \frac{2}{3}$.

21. $\tan \theta = 1.157$. **27.** $\mathrm{ctn}\ \theta = 2.591$. **33.** $\mathrm{ctn}\ \theta = \frac{1}{4}$.

22. $\mathrm{ctn}\ \theta = 0.3839$. **28.** $\tan \theta = 0.0603$. **34.** $\tan \theta = 2$.

23. $\cos \theta = 0.8246$. **29.** $\tan \theta = 3.639$. **35.** $\sec \theta = 3$.

24. $\sin \theta = 0.5500$. **30.** $\mathrm{ctn}\ \theta = 0.1311$. **36.** $\csc \theta = \pi$.

Compute without using logarithms:

37. $\sin 30° \tan 60° + \cos 0°$. **39.** $(\tan 45°/\sec 30°)^4$.

38. $\dfrac{\cos 45° \csc 60°}{\mathrm{ctn}\ 30°} - \sin 90°$. **40.** $\sqrt{\dfrac{\sin 60° \cos 0°}{(\tan 30°)^{-1}}}$.

Compute, using logarithms:

41. $\sqrt{31.20 \sin 62° 10'}$. **43.** $\left(\dfrac{\tan 51° 15'}{19 \cos 10° 18'}\right)^{2.600}$.

42. $\left(\dfrac{\cos 42° 40'}{0.04170}\right)^2$. **44.** $\sqrt{4.329 \cdot 10^4 \sin 26° 43' \mathrm{ctn}\ 40° 45'}$.

45. In Table VI, compare the magnitude of x, $\sin x$, and $\tan x$ for x in the first quadrant.

Explain why:

46. In Table VI, the value of $\cos x$ is the same for $x = 0.01$ as it is for $x = 0$.

47. In Table VI, $\cos 1.60$ is negative.

*48. In Table IV, linear interpolation is not accurate for $\mathrm{ctn}\ \theta$ and $\csc \theta$ if θ is near $0°$.

7-4 Identities

Many relationships exist among the trigonometric functions. The following are immediately obvious from the definitions of the functions (§ 7-2):

$$\csc \theta = \frac{1}{\sin \theta}\ ; \qquad \sec \theta = \frac{1}{\cos \theta}\ ; \qquad \mathrm{ctn}\ \theta = \frac{1}{\tan \theta}\ . \qquad (3)$$

$$\tan \theta = \frac{\sin \theta}{\cos \theta}\ ; \qquad \mathrm{ctn}\ \theta = \frac{\cos \theta}{\sin \theta}\ . \qquad (4)$$

Some matters of notation deserve comment here. In accordance with § 5-1 the above identities could well be written with the symbol "$\equiv$";

however, when no confusion will be caused, "=" is usually used. Secondly, *positive* powers of the trigonometric functions are often written in the form $\sin^2 x$, meaning $(\sin x)^2$. However, negative powers should be written only with the parentheses, to avoid confusion with the notation for the inverse of a function (§ 4-3). Thirdly, the expression to which a trigonometric function applies is terminated by a plus or minus sign, unless otherwise indicated by symbols of grouping; $\sin ab - c$ means $(\sin ab) - c$, not $\sin(ab - c)$ or $(\sin a)b - c$. It is also terminated by the beginning of another trigonometric function.

A somewhat more complicated identity than any in (3) and (4) is

$$\sin^2 \theta + \cos^2 \theta = 1. \tag{5}$$

The following proof is simple: By the definitions of the functions (§ 7-2) and the Pythagorean theorem (§ 4-5), if θ is in standard position and point (x, y) is on the terminal side of θ, then for any θ,

$$\sin^2 \theta + \cos^2 \theta = \left(\frac{y}{r}\right)^2 + \left(\frac{x}{r}\right)^2 = \frac{y^2 + x^2}{r^2} = \frac{r^2}{r^2} = 1.$$

Analogous identities are

$$1 + \tan^2 \theta = \sec^2 \theta; \tag{6}$$

$$1 + \text{ctn}^2 \theta = \csc^2 \theta. \tag{7}$$

These can be proved by an argument similar to that used for (5). Another method is both more convenient and more instructive, and will be shown for (6); with slight modification it applies to (7) also.

$$1 + \tan^2 \theta = 1 + \frac{\sin^2 \theta}{\cos^2 \theta} \qquad \text{by (4)}$$

$$= \frac{\cos^2 \theta + \sin^2 \theta}{\cos^2 \theta}$$

$$= \frac{1}{\cos^2 \theta} \qquad \text{by (5)}$$

$$= \sec^2 \theta \qquad \text{by (3).}$$

The identities (3) through (7) are called **fundamental** or **elementary trigonometric identities.** They can be used to change the form of expressions involving trigonometric functions (in particular to simplify such expressions) and to prove other identities. This is similar to the use of the identities for basic types of factoring of algebraic expressions (§ 2-5).

EXAMPLE.   Prove the identity $\tan^2 \alpha \sin^2 \alpha = \tan^2 \alpha - \sin^2 \alpha$.

Solution. $\tan^2 \alpha - \sin^2 \alpha = \dfrac{\sin^2 \alpha}{\cos^2 \alpha} - \sin^2 \alpha$ by (4)

$$= \sin^2 \alpha \left(\frac{1}{\cos^2 \alpha} - 1 \right)$$

$$= \sin^2 \alpha \, \frac{1 - \cos^2 \alpha}{\cos^2 \alpha}$$

$$= \sin^2 \alpha \, \frac{\sin^2 \alpha}{\cos^2 \alpha}$$ by (5)

$$= \sin^2 \alpha \tan^2 \alpha = \tan^2 \alpha \sin^2 \alpha$$ by (4).

No universal method for handling trigonometric identities can be stated, any more than for factoring, but it is often well to start with the more complicated member of the identity and make substitutions, using known identities, which make it look more like the other member in some respect. Thus, in the example we started with the right member since it had two terms, and made a substitution which shows $\sin^2 \alpha$ to be a factor of each term, resembling in this respect the left member. When no method of attack is obvious, it may help to express all functions in terms of sines and cosines.

Warning.   It is very desirable to follow this procedure of starting with one member and by changes of form obtaining the other member. A different process, which is sometimes used but should be avoided, is to start with the proposed identity, perform the same operations on *both* members, and come out with a known identity, concluding that this proves the original proposition. On its face this is logically fallacious; for instance, assuming $-\sin x = \sin x$ and squaring both sides we get $\sin^2 x = \sin^2 x$, which is true though the original assumption is not. The difficulties are analogous to those in producing equivalent equations (§ 5-4).

EXERCISES

1. Express $\sin x$ in terms of $\cos x$.

2. Express $\cos x$ in terms of $\sin x$.

3. Express $\operatorname{ctn} x$ in terms of $\cos x$.

4. Express $\tan x$ in terms of $\cos x$.

5. Obtain the other trigonometric functions of x, given that x is in Quadrant III and $\cos x = -\frac{5}{13}$, **(a)** using the identities of the present section; **(b)** by the methods of § 7-2.

Simplify:

6. $\sin \theta \operatorname{ctn} \theta$.

7. $\cos \theta \tan \theta$.

8. $\dfrac{\cos \alpha}{\sec \alpha}$.

9. $\dfrac{\operatorname{ctn} \beta}{\csc \beta}$.

10. $\tan t \operatorname{ctn} t$.

11. $(\sin^2 u - 1) \tan^3 u$.

12. $(1 - \cos^2 u) \csc u \operatorname{ctn} u$.

13. $\dfrac{1 + \operatorname{ctn}^2 \psi}{\sin^2 \psi}$.

14. $(2 \sec^2 z - 2) \operatorname{ctn}^5 z$.

15. $\dfrac{1 + \operatorname{ctn} \theta}{\csc \theta}$.

16. $\dfrac{\csc \theta - \sec \theta}{\sin \theta - \cos \theta}$.

17. $(1 + \cos s)(\operatorname{ctn} s - \csc s)$.

18. $\sqrt{4 \sin^2 x + 4/\sec^2 x}$.

Factor and simplify if possible:

19. $\cos^4 x - \sin^4 x$.

20. $1 - \tan^4 x$.

Prove the identities:

21. $\dfrac{1 + \sin^2 \theta \sec^2 \theta}{1 + \csc^2 \theta \cos^2 \theta} = \tan^2 \theta$.

22. $\operatorname{ctn}^2 x - \cos^2 x = \operatorname{ctn}^2 x \cos^2 x$.

23. $\dfrac{1}{\tan \phi + \operatorname{ctn} \phi} = \dfrac{\cos \phi}{\csc \phi}$.

24. $\dfrac{1}{\sec \gamma - \cos \gamma} = \csc \gamma \operatorname{ctn} \gamma$.

25. $\csc^2 x \sec^2 x = \csc^2 x + \sec^2 x$.

26. $(\tan y + \operatorname{ctn} y)^2 = \csc^2 y + \sec^2 y$.

27. $\dfrac{1}{1 + \sin t} + \dfrac{1}{1 - \sin t} = 2 \sec^2 t$.

28. $\dfrac{\sin \alpha}{1 + \cos \alpha} = \dfrac{1 - \cos \alpha}{\sin \alpha}$.

29. $\dfrac{\sin^2 x}{1 - \cos x} = 1 + \cos x$.

30. $\dfrac{\sin^2 3x}{\cos^2 3x} = \sec^2 3x - 1$.

31. $\sin^3 \tfrac{1}{2}x \cos^3 \tfrac{1}{2}x = \sin^6 \tfrac{1}{2}x \operatorname{ctn}^3 \tfrac{1}{2}x$.

Evaluate:

32. $x^2 + y^2$ when $x = a \cos \theta + b \sin \theta$, $y = a \sin \theta + b \cos \theta$.

33. $x^2 + y^2 + z^2$ when $x = r \sin \theta \cos \phi$, $y = r \sin \theta \sin \phi$, and $z = r \cos \theta$.

34. $\dfrac{x^2}{a^2} + \dfrac{y^2}{b^2}$ when $x = a \cos t$ and $y = b \sin t$.

35. $\dfrac{x^2}{a^2} - \dfrac{y^2}{b^2}$ when $x = a \sec \theta$ and $y = b \tan \theta$.

36. $x^{\frac{2}{3}} + y^{\frac{2}{3}}$ when $x = r^3 \cos^3 \phi$ and $y = r^3 \sin^3 \phi$.

7-5   Addition Formulas

The identities in the preceding section linked different trigonometric functions, or combinations of functions, of *one* angle. Now we consider some relationships involving *two* angles. The **sum of two angles** α and β is defined as the angle obtained by rotating the initial side first by the amount α and then by the further amount β, each in the proper direction. The **negative of an angle** simply means that the rotation is performed in the opposite direction.

First are listed some identities relating a trigonometric function of an angle and a function of the negative of the angle:

$$\begin{array}{lll}
\sin(-\theta) = -\sin\theta; & \csc(-\theta) = -\csc\theta; & \\
\cos(-\theta) = \cos\theta; & \sec(-\theta) = \sec\theta; & \quad(8) \\
\tan(-\theta) = -\tan\theta; & \operatorname{ctn}(-\theta) = -\operatorname{ctn}\theta. &
\end{array}$$

These are readily proved by using the definitions of the functions (§ 7-2): If (x, y) is a point on the terminal side of θ, taken in standard position, then $(x, -y)$ is a point on the terminal side of $-\theta$ as in Figure 7.10; hence $\sin\theta = y/r$, and

$$\sin(-\theta) = (-y)/r$$
$$= -(y/r) = -\sin\theta$$

as asserted in (8). For the other functions, proofs are similar.

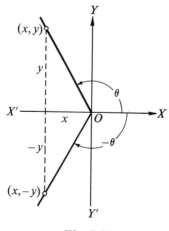

Fig. 7.10

Another identity asserts that if α and β are two angles then

$$\cos(\alpha - \beta) = \cos \alpha \cos \beta + \sin \alpha \sin \beta. \qquad (9)$$

Proof. Place angles α and β in standard positions, and let A and B be points on their respective terminal sides at distance 1 from the origin (Figure 7.11). Then by Example 6 of § 7-2, we have A: (cos α, sin α) and B: (cos β, sin β); angle BOA is ($\alpha - \beta$), though not in standard position, since adding angle BOA to β yields α as the sum. Figure 7.11 illustrates this in one case, but the relationships hold regardless of which quadrants α and β are in. In Figure 7.12 angle ($\alpha - \beta$), also denoted γ, is shown in standard position; triangles BOA and $B'OA'$ are congruent, since two

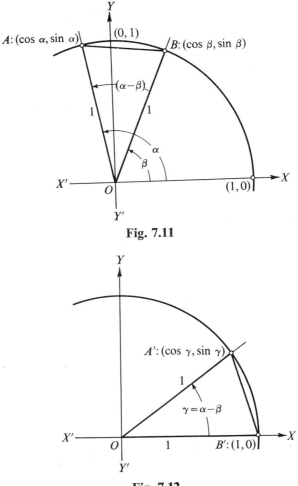

Fig. 7.11

Fig. 7.12

sides and the included angle of one triangle are respectively equal to the corresponding parts of the other triangle. Hence the distances AB and $A'B'$ are equal. Applying the distance formula from § 4-5, and simplifying by (5) of § 7-4,

$$\overline{AB}^2 = (\cos \alpha - \cos \beta)^2 + (\sin \alpha - \sin \beta)^2$$
$$= \cos^2 \alpha - 2 \cos \alpha \cos \beta + \cos^2 \beta + \sin^2 \alpha - 2 \sin \alpha \sin \beta + \sin^2 \beta$$
$$= 2 - 2 \cos \alpha \cos \beta - 2 \sin \alpha \sin \beta;$$
$$\overline{A'B'}^2 = (\cos \gamma - 1)^2 + (\sin \gamma - 0)^2$$
$$= \cos^2 \gamma - 2 \cos \gamma + 1 + \sin^2 \gamma$$
$$= 2 - 2 \cos \gamma$$
$$= 2 - 2 \cos (\alpha - \beta).$$

Equating $\overline{AB}^2$ to $\overline{A'B'}^2$,

$$2 - 2 \cos \alpha \cos \beta - 2 \sin \alpha \sin \beta = 2 - 2 \cos (\alpha - \beta),$$

whence (9) follows.

Warning. $\cos (\alpha - \beta) \neq \cos \alpha - \cos \beta.$

For instance, if $\alpha = 90°$ and $\beta = 30°$ then

$$\cos (\alpha - \beta) = \cos (90° - 30°) = \cos 60° = \tfrac{1}{2};$$
$$\cos \alpha - \cos \beta = \cos 90° - \cos 30° = 0 - \tfrac{1}{2}\sqrt{3} = -\tfrac{1}{2}\sqrt{3}.$$

EXAMPLE 1.   Find $\cos (-\tfrac{1}{12}\pi)$.

Solution. $\cos (-\tfrac{1}{12}\pi) = \cos \tfrac{1}{12}\pi$ by (8)

$$= \cos (\tfrac{1}{3}\pi - \tfrac{1}{4}\pi)$$
$$= \cos \tfrac{1}{3}\pi \cos \tfrac{1}{4}\pi + \sin \tfrac{1}{3}\pi \sin \tfrac{1}{4}\pi$$
$$= \tfrac{1}{2} \cdot \tfrac{1}{2}\sqrt{2} + \tfrac{1}{2}\sqrt{3} \cdot \tfrac{1}{2}\sqrt{2}$$
$$= \tfrac{1}{4}\sqrt{2}(1 + \sqrt{3}).$$

Various other identities can be derived from (9). For instance, using (8),

$$\cos (\alpha + \beta) = \cos [\alpha - (-\beta)]$$
$$= \cos \alpha \cos (-\beta) + \sin \alpha \sin (-\beta)$$
$$= \cos \alpha \cos \beta + \sin \alpha (-\sin \beta),$$

so

$$\cos (\alpha + \beta) = \cos \alpha \cos \beta - \sin \alpha \sin \beta. \tag{10}$$

Formulas (9) and (10), together with (14) and (15) later in this section, are called **addition formulas** since they relate to the algebraic sum of two angles.

To obtain another type of identity, in (9) set $\alpha = \tfrac{1}{2}\pi$ and $\beta = \theta$, and substitute $\cos \tfrac{1}{2}\pi = 0$, $\sin \tfrac{1}{2}\pi = 1$ as determined from the definitions (§ 7-2): $\cos\left(\tfrac{1}{2}\pi - \theta\right) = \cos \tfrac{1}{2}\pi \cos \theta + \sin \tfrac{1}{2}\pi \sin \theta$;

$$\cos\left(\tfrac{1}{2}\pi - \theta\right) = \sin \theta. \tag{11}$$

Likewise,

$$\sin\left(\tfrac{1}{2}\pi - \theta\right) = \cos \theta; \tag{12}$$

$$\tan\left(\tfrac{1}{2}\pi - \theta\right) = \operatorname{ctn} \theta. \tag{13}$$

The angle $\left(\tfrac{1}{2}\pi - \theta\right)$ is called the **complement** of θ; so (11), (12), and (13) are called the **complementary identities** and are sometimes stated "cofunctions of complementary angles are equal".

ILLUSTRATION. $\cos 57° 20' = \sin (90° - 57° 20') = \sin 32° 40'$.

This illustration shows why it is possible to condense Tables IV and III by having only one number in the table for both $\sin 32° 40'$ (top heading, and angle listed at the left side) and $\cos 57° 20'$ (bottom "heading", angle at right side of page).

Next are proved two more addition formulas:

$$\sin (\alpha + \beta) = \sin \alpha \cos \beta + \cos \alpha \sin \beta; \tag{14}$$

$$\sin (\alpha - \beta) = \sin \alpha \cos \beta - \cos \alpha \sin \beta. \tag{15}$$

These follow from (10) and (9) respectively; we show the proof only for (14):

$$\sin (\alpha + \beta) = \cos \left[\tfrac{1}{2}\pi - (\alpha + \beta)\right] \qquad \text{by (11)}$$
$$= \cos \left[\left(\tfrac{1}{2}\pi - \alpha\right) - \beta\right]$$
$$= \cos \left(\tfrac{1}{2}\pi - \alpha\right) \cos \beta + \sin \left(\tfrac{1}{2}\pi - \alpha\right) \sin \beta$$
$$= \sin \alpha \cos \beta + \cos \alpha \sin \beta.$$

EXAMPLE 2.   Express $\tan (\alpha - \beta)$ in terms of functions of α and β.

Solution. $\tan (\alpha - \beta) = \dfrac{\sin (\alpha - \beta)}{\cos (\alpha - \beta)}$

$$= \frac{\sin \alpha \cos \beta - \cos \alpha \sin \beta}{\cos \alpha \cos \beta + \sin \alpha \sin \beta}$$

$$= \frac{\dfrac{\sin \alpha \cos \beta}{\cos \alpha \cos \beta} - \dfrac{\cos \alpha \sin \beta}{\cos \alpha \cos \beta}}{\dfrac{\cos \alpha \cos \beta}{\cos \alpha \cos \beta} + \dfrac{\sin \alpha \sin \beta}{\cos \alpha \cos \beta}}.$$

Thus $$\tan (\alpha - \beta) = \frac{\tan \alpha - \tan \beta}{1 + \tan \alpha \tan \beta}. \tag{16}$$

Formula (16) has an interesting application to the slopes of straight lines (§ 4-7). If two lines make angles α and β respectively with the x-axis and have slopes m_1 and m_2 then $m_1 = \tan \alpha$ and $m_2 = \tan \beta$ by § 7-2. But from Figure 7.13 (and from similar diagrams for other

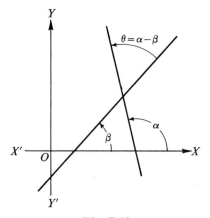

Fig. 7.13

quadrants and other relative sizes of α and β), the angle θ from the second line to the first line is $(\alpha - \beta)$. From Example 2, θ is given by

$$\tan \theta = \frac{m_1 - m_2}{1 + m_1 m_2} . \tag{17}$$

Historical Note. As a proposition about chords, the addition formula (14) was known to PTOLEMY (about 150 A.D.).

EXERCISES

1. Find a formula, similar to (16), for **(a)** $\tan (\alpha + \beta)$; **(b)** $\text{ctn} (\alpha - \beta)$; **(c)** $\text{ctn} (\alpha + \beta)$.

2. Find a formula, similar to (8) or (11)–(13), for **(a)** $\sin (180° - \theta)$; **(b)** $\cos (180° - \theta)$; **(c)** $\cos (\pi + \theta)$; **(d)** $\sin (2\pi - \theta)$; **(e)** $\tan (2\pi - \theta)$; **(f)** $\text{ctn} (\frac{3}{2}\pi + \theta)$.

3. Find without tables **(a)** $\sin 75°$; **(b)** $\cos 15°$; **(c)** $\tan (-\frac{1}{12}\pi)$; **(d)** $\sec (-105°)$.

4. Given $\sin \alpha = \frac{3}{5}$ with α in Quadrant II and $\tan \beta = -\frac{12}{5}$ with β in Quadrant IV, find **(a)** $\cos (\alpha + \beta)$; **(b)** $\sin (\beta - \alpha)$.

5. Given $\cos u = -\frac{4}{5}$ with u in Quadrant II and $\text{ctn} v = \frac{15}{8}$ with v in Quadrant III, find **(a)** $\cos (u - v)$; **(b)** $\sin (u + v)$.

Simplify:

6. $\sin 4\alpha \cos \alpha + \cos 4\alpha \sin \alpha$.

7. $\cos 2z \cos 5z + \sin 2z \sin 5z$.

8. $\sin (\theta + 30°) + \cos (\theta + 60°)$.

9. $\sin (60° + x) - \cos (30° + x)$.

10. $\dfrac{\cos (A + B) + \cos (A - B)}{\sin (A + B) + \sin (A - B)}$.

11. $\dfrac{\tan x + \tan y}{\tan x - \tan y}$.

12. $(\sin x \cos y + \cos x \sin y)^2 + (\cos x \cos y - \sin x \sin y)^2$.

Find a formula for:

13. $\sin (x + y + z)$.

14. $\sin x + \sin y$ where $x = \frac{1}{2}(A + B)$ and $y = \frac{1}{2}(A - B)$.

15. $\cos x + \cos y$ where $x = \frac{1}{2}(A + B)$ and $y = \frac{1}{2}(A - B)$.

16. A function $f(x)$ is called an **even function** if $f(-x) = f(x)$, and $f(x)$ is called an **odd function** if $f(-x) = -f(x)$, for all values of x in the domain of the function. For each of the following, tell whether it is an even function, odd function, both, or neither:

(a) x;	**(e)** $x^2 + x$;	**(i)** $\cos x$;	**(m)** $\sin^3 x$;
(b) x^2;	**(f)** $x^3 + x$;	**(j)** $\tan x$;	**(n)** $x \sin x$;
(c) x^{-4};	**(g)** $x + 1$;	**(k)** $\operatorname{ctn} x$;	**(o)** $x \cos x$;
(d) x^3;	**(h)** $\sin x$;	**(l)** $\sin^2 x$;	**(p)** $3/\sin x$.

17. Draw Figure 7.11 for a case with $\beta > \alpha$, and show in detail how the proof of identity (9) still holds.

7-6   Use of Tables for Angles in Other Quadrants

In § 7-3 we saw how to use tables (such as Tables IV and III) to find values of the trigonometric functions, or their logarithms, for angles in the first quadrant. This was useful for angles for which the exact values of the functions could not be readily calculated from the definitions (§ 7-2). The formulas in § 7-5 enable us to use a table covering first quadrant angles to find values of the trigonometric functions of angles in any quadrant.

We repeat from § 7-5 some useful formulas:

$$\sin (-\theta) = -\sin \theta; \qquad \csc (-\theta) = -\csc \theta;$$
$$\cos (-\theta) = \cos \theta; \qquad \sec (-\theta) = \sec \theta;$$
$$\tan (-\theta) = -\tan \theta; \qquad \operatorname{ctn} (-\theta) = -\operatorname{ctn} \theta.$$

Of particular importance are a few formulas which can be derived as special cases of (9), (10), (14), (15), with $\alpha = \pi$. They can also be derived in a manner analogous to the derivation of (8), by noting how the definitions of the functions apply to the given angle whose terminal side contains the point (x, y) and to a first quadrant angle whose terminal side contains $(|x|, |y|)$.

$$\sin (\pi - \theta) = \sin \theta; \qquad \sin (\pi + \theta) = -\sin \theta;$$
$$\cos (\pi - \theta) = -\cos \theta; \qquad \cos (\pi + \theta) = -\cos \theta;$$
$$\tan (\pi - \theta) = -\tan \theta; \qquad \tan (\pi + \theta) = \tan \theta;$$
$$\text{ctn} (\pi - \theta) = -\text{ctn} \theta; \qquad \text{ctn} (\pi + \theta) = \text{ctn} \theta;$$
$$\sec (\pi - \theta) = -\sec \theta; \qquad \sec (\pi + \theta) = -\sec \theta;$$
$$\csc (\pi - \theta) = \csc \theta; \qquad \csc (\pi + \theta) = -\csc \theta.$$

ILLUSTRATION. To find $\cos 117° 10'$, note that

$$\cos 117° 10' = \cos (180° - 62° 50')$$
$$= -\cos 62° 50'$$
$$= -0.4566.$$

Alternatively,

$$\cos 117° 10' = \cos (90° + 27° 10')$$
$$= \cos 90° \cos 27° 10' - \sin 90° \sin 27° 10'$$
$$= -\sin 27° 10' = -0.4566.$$

An incidental consequence of such formulas is the fact that in trigonometry the accuracy of an angle is to be measured by the precision with which the angle is stated (nearest degree, nearest minute, or the like) rather than by the number of digits in the measure of the angle. Thus $8° 0'$ and $368° 0'$ are coterminal and have the same accuracy; these angles are known to the nearest minute. Then their trigonometric functions are determined to about four significant digits (§ 7-3).

EXERCISES

Compare:

1. $\sin 227°$ and $\sin 47°$.
2. $\cos 170°$ and $\cos 10°$.
3. $\cos 280°$ and $\cos 80°$.
4. $\sin 100°$ and $\sin 80°$.
5. $\tan 145°$ and $\tan 35°$.
6. $\text{ctn } 350°$ and $\text{ctn } 10°$.
7. $\sec 253°$ and $\sec 73°$.
8. $\csc 190°$ and $\csc 10°$.
9. $\sin 110°$ and $\sin 20°$ or $\cos 20°$.
10. $\cos 110°$ and $\sin 20°$ or $\cos 20°$.
11. $\tan 115°$ and $\tan 25°$ or $\text{ctn } 25°$.

Find:

12. $\sin 126° 40'$.
13. $\cos 97° 50'$.
14. $\cos 254° 20'$.
15. $\sin 195° 10'$.
16. $\sin 342° 18'$.
17. $\cos 306° 43'$.

18. tan 126° 30′.   **22.** sec 124° 32′.   **26.** cos (−0.67 rad).

19. ctn 216° 20′.   **23.** csc 200° 19′.   **27.** sin (−1.04 rad).

20. ctn 312° 24′.   **24.** log sin 163° 42′.   **28.** sin 2.413.

21. tan 490° 57′.   **25.** log cos 298° 18′.   **29.** cos 3.920.

30. In Table III, **(a)** what is the relation between log tan θ and log ctn θ for any θ, and why? **(b)** why would there not be much advantage in listing log sec θ and log csc θ?

7-7 Periodicity of Functions

In § 4-6 we discussed the graph of a function in general, although the applications were mostly to algebraic functions; logarithmic and exponential functions were treated in § 6-1 and § 6-3. In preparation for discussing the graphs of trigonometric functions we define a general category of functions, a category which will shortly be seen to include trigonometric functions.

A function is called a **periodic function** if the graph repeats itself. Specifically, *a function* f(x) *is periodic if there is some number* p *different from zero such that* f(x + p) = f(x) *for all values of* x *in the domain of the function.* The smallest positive number *p*, if any, for which this holds is called **the period*** of $f(x)$, and any interval *p* units long in the domain of the independent variable is called **a period** or **a cycle** of the function.

ILLUSTRATION. Let $f(x)$ be the function whose graph is shown in Figure 7.14. Obviously $f(x + 2) = f(x)$ for all x, and such a relation holds for no smaller p. Hence this function is periodic with period 2.

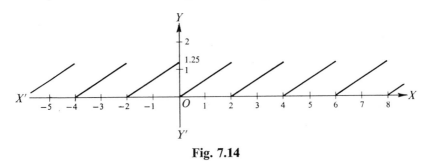

Fig. 7.14

---

* This is the terminology usual in mathematics. In physics, "period" is usually used only if the independent variable represents time; if it represents distance, the period is called the "wave length."

From (10) and (14), $\sin (\theta + 2\pi) = \sin \theta$ and $\cos (\theta + 2\pi) = \cos \theta$. Detailed inspection of values from tables, or of the graphs in the next section, shows that for any p less than 2π such a relation does not hold for all θ. For instance, try $p = \pi$: Then it is true for *some* values of θ that $\sin (\theta + \pi) = \sin \theta$; for instance $\sin (0 + \pi) = \sin \pi = 0 = \sin 0$. But this fails for some other values of θ; for instance, $\sin (\frac{1}{2}\pi + \pi) = -1$ but $\sin \frac{1}{2}\pi = 1 \neq -1$ so it fails for $\theta = \frac{1}{2}\pi$. Hence the sine and cosine are periodic functions with period 2π.

From (3) it follows that the secant and cosecant are likewise periodic functions with period 2π. The tangent and cotangent however have a smaller period, namely π.

The **amplitude** of a periodic function is defined as half the algebraic difference between the algebraically largest and smallest values, if any, of the function. Roughly speaking, this describes how far the curve swings above and below the middle. The function in Figure 7.14 has amplitude 0.625 since the values of the function range from 0 to 1.25, and $\frac{1}{2}(1.25 - 0)$ is 0.625.

The **frequency** of a periodic function is the reciprocal of the period. Thus, the frequency of $\cos x$ is $1/2\pi$, that is, about 0.16. The function in Figure 7.14 has frequency $\frac{1}{2}$. This is the number of periods or cycles in an interval of length one unit in the independent variable.

An analogous idea is that of symmetry. A function $f(x)$, or its graph, is called **symmetric about the line** $x = 0$, or about the y-axis, if for all values of x in the domain, $f(-x) = f(x)$; that is, if when the graph is folded along the y-axis its left and right halves coincide. A graph is called **symmetric about the origin** if whenever the point (x, y) is on the graph so is $(-x, -y)$; that is, if each line through the origin intersects the graph at equal distances in the two directions.

ILLUSTRATION.   The function x^2 is symmetric about $x = 0$ since it is true that $(-x)^2 = x^2$ for all x.

EXERCISES

Determine (a) *whether the specified function, denoted* f(x), *is periodic, and if so what its period, frequency, and amplitude are;* (b) *whether* f(x) *is symmetric about* x $= 0$; (c) *whether the graph of* y $=$ f(x) *is symmetric about the origin:*

1. x.

2. x^2.

3. x^3.

4. $\sin^2 x$.

5. $\cos^3 x$.

6. $\sin (-x)$.

7. π.

8. $x \sin x$.

*9. $\sin x + \cos x$.

In Exercises 10 and 11, sketch the graph of a function f(x) *which is periodic and:*

10. Has period 6 and is given by $f(x) = |\, 2x \,|$ if $-3 \leq x \leq 3$.

11. Has period 3 and is given by $f(x) = 2$ if $0 \leq x \leq 1.5$ and is given by $f(x) = -1$ if $-1.5 < x < 0$.

★12. Compare the ideas of symmetry about $x = 0$ and about the origin with the idea of odd and even functions (Exercise 16 of § 7-5).

7-8   Graphs of Trigonometric Functions

Given a particular trigonometric function, a table of values can be computed and the graph drawn accordingly, just as for an algebraic function. In this context, the independent variable is usually taken as a number instead of an angle; see § 7-2. The graphs of the six trigonometric functions are shown in Figures 7.15 through 7.20. Tables of values are not shown since they involve only selections from Table VI for angles in the first quadrant and application of § 7-6 for other quadrants.

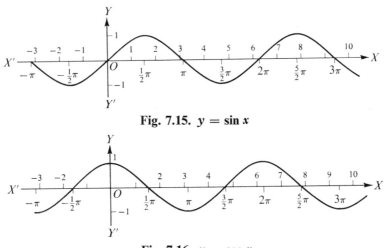

Fig. 7.15. $y = \sin x$

Fig. 7.16. $y = \cos x$

Since $\sin x$ and $\cos x$ are periodic with period 2π (§ 7-7), it follows that the part of the graph between $x = 0$ and $x = 2\pi$ (or any other interval of length 2π) determines the rest of the graph. In fact, if the graph is duplicated on transparent paper and this transparency is shifted 2π units, or any integral multiple thereof, to the right or left, then the shifted curve will fall on top of the original one.

The wave-shaped curve obtained as the graph of sin x is called a
sine curve or **sinusoid**. More generally, the name is applied to any curve
obtainable from the graph of sin x by shifting, stretching, or compress-
ing it uniformly. From (14), $\sin (\theta + \tfrac{1}{2}\pi) = \cos \theta$; hence the graph of
cos x is simply the graph of sin x shifted $\tfrac{1}{2}\pi$ units to the left, and is also
a sinusoid. We see that sin x has amplitude 1, since its values range from
-1 to $+1$, and $\tfrac{1}{2}[1 - (-1)]$ is 1.

Unlike the graphs of sin x and cos x, the graph of tan x is not continu-
ous. Rather, tan x is not defined when x is $\pm\tfrac{1}{2}\pi$, $\pm\tfrac{3}{2}\pi$, etc.; and when

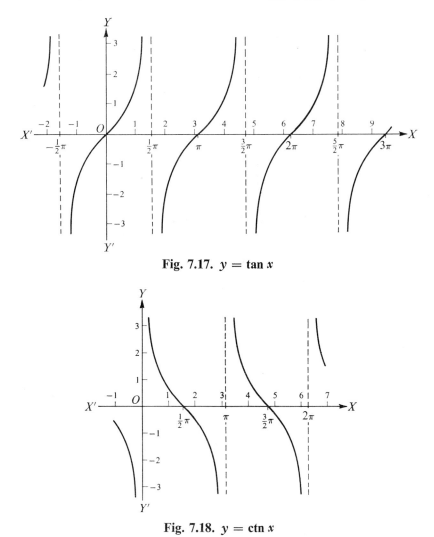

Fig. 7.17. $y = \tan x$

Fig. 7.18. $y = \text{ctn } x$

x comes nearer and nearer to such a value, $|\tan x|$ increases indefinitely and the curve extends farther and farther out while approaching more and more closely the lines $x = \frac{1}{2}\pi$, $x = -\frac{1}{2}\pi$, $x = \frac{3}{2}\pi$, etc. A line with this relationship to the graph is called an **asymptote**. The tangent function does not have an amplitude since it has no greatest or least value.

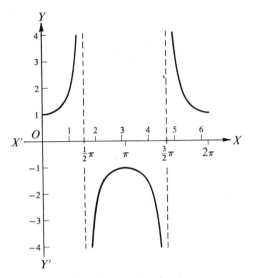

Fig. 7.19. One cycle of $y = \sec x$

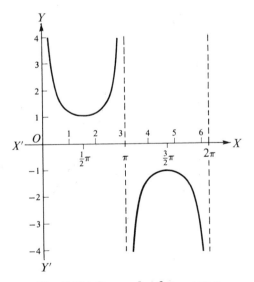

Fig. 7.20. One cycle of $y = \csc x$

EXAMPLE.   Graph the function 1.5 sin 4x.

Solution.   Significant points are shown in the table of values. The period of this function is $\frac{1}{2}\pi$ (which is about 1.57), since when x increases by $\frac{1}{2}\pi$, $4x$ increases by $4 \cdot \frac{1}{2}\pi$ or 2π so that sin 4x has completed a cycle. In such a case it is convenient to start by choosing significant values for $4x$ and finding the corresponding values for x and y.

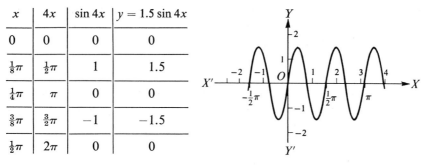

x	$4x$	$\sin 4x$	$y = 1.5 \sin 4x$
0	0	0	0
$\frac{1}{8}\pi$	$\frac{1}{2}\pi$	1	1.5
$\frac{1}{4}\pi$	π	0	0
$\frac{3}{8}\pi$	$\frac{3}{2}\pi$	-1	-1.5
$\frac{1}{2}\pi$	2π	0	0

Fig. 7.21. $y = 1.5 \sin 4x$

Note that the resulting graph, Figure 7.21, of 1.5 sin 4x differs from the graph of sin x in two respects: abscissas have been compressed by a factor $\frac{1}{4}$, and ordinates have been stretched by a factor 1.5. The amplitude of 1.5 sin 4x is 1.5. The frequency of 1.5 sin 4x is $1/(\frac{1}{2}\pi)$, that is, $2/\pi$ or about 0.64.

EXERCISES

For each of the following functions, find the (a) *period,* (b) *amplitude,* (c) *frequency; or else show that the function is not periodic:*

1. 2 sin 3x.

2. 2 cos 3x.

3. 3 cos $\frac{1}{2}x$.

4. 5 sin $\frac{1}{2}x$.

5. $-\cos x$.

6. cos $(-x)$.

7. 2 sin $(x + \frac{1}{3}\pi)$.

8. 3 cos $(x - \frac{1}{3}\pi)$.

9. $-\frac{1}{2}$ tan 2x.

10. $\frac{1}{4}$ ctn 6x.

11. 2 tan $(3x - 1)$.

12. 3 ctn $(2x + 1)$.

13. 1 + 3 cos² x.

14. 2 - $\frac{1}{3}$ cos⁵ x.

15. cos (x^2).

16. sin $(1/x)$.

17. 1 + 2 sec $\frac{1}{2}x$.

18. 2 - $\frac{1}{3}$ csc 3x.

In Exercises 19 and 20, find (a) *the period,* (b) *the frequency, of:*

19. *a* sin 436,000,000*t*, which represents the carrier wave for television channel 4 with *t* in seconds.

20. *a* sin 3,200,000π*t*, which represents the carrier wave for a radio broadcast at the upper end of the standard broadcast band with *t* in seconds.

21—38. Graph the functions in the corresponding Exercises 1 through 18.

7-9 Simple Harmonic Motion

If a weight is suspended on a spring, it will hang motionless in some equilibrium position. If thereafter it is pulled down a units and then released, it will oscillate up and down. If friction and air resistance can be neglected, then its position is given by

$$y = -a \cos ct = a \sin (ct - \tfrac{1}{2}\pi),$$

where y is the distance up or down from the equilibrium position (taken as positive if upward), t is the time after release, and c is a constant which reflects the properties of the particular spring.

More generally, if t were measured from an arbitrary time instead of the time of release, the equation would have the form

$$y = a \sin (ct + b). \tag{18}$$

The derivation of these equations requires more advanced mathematics and the application of physical principles; it will not be attempted in this book. However, this type of equation occurs frequently and deserves a name. Motion which can be characterized by an equation of the form (18) is called **simple harmonic motion**.

Similar equations apply to the motion of a point on a vibrating string (such as on a musical instrument) and to alternating currents in electricity.

ILLUSTRATION. Consider ordinary home electrical current, and denote its voltage by E. Such current is nominally called "110 volts" but actually the amplitude is 155 volts (110 is an *average* value instead of amplitude). The current is "60 cycle"; that is, it has 60 cycles per second. Thus if t is in seconds, the frequency of the function is 60 so the period is $\frac{1}{60}$. Hence in (18), $a = 155$ and $c \cdot \frac{1}{60} = 2\pi$ or $c = 120\pi$, and so $E = 155 \sin (120\pi t + b)$.

In (18), $y = 0$ when $t = -b/c$. Thus if the graph of $y = a \sin ct$ is shifted to the left by the amount b/c units, it coincides with the graph of $y = a \sin (ct + b)$. In the case of a weight on a spring, discussed at the beginning of this section, this shift is $-\frac{1}{2}\pi/c$ (or $\frac{3}{2}\pi/c$) units of time. The quantity b/c is called the **phase shift** of the motion or current $y = a \sin (ct + b)$ and describes its relationship to the basic sine wave $y = a \sin ct$.

EXERCISES

For those of the following functions which represent simple harmonic motion, state (**a**) *the period,* (**b**) *the amplitude, and* (**c**) *the phase shift;* (**d**) *graph the given function,* (**e**) *graph a sine wave with the same frequency but amplitude* 1 *and phase shift* 0, *and* (**f**) *graph a sine wave with the same frequency and phase but amplitude* 1:

1. $3 \sin 24\pi t$.	**5.** $2 \cos 3\pi t$.	**9.** $4 \sin (t + 1)$.
2. $2 \sin 6\pi t$.	**6.** $5 \cos \frac{1}{2}t$.	**10.** $\frac{1}{3} \sin (t - \frac{1}{2})$.
3. $2 \sin (6t + 1)\pi$.	**7.** $\frac{1}{8} \sin \frac{1}{3}t$.	**11.** $\tan t$.
4. $3 \sin (\frac{1}{2}t - \frac{1}{3})\pi$.	**8.** $-2 \sin t$.	**12.** $4 \cdot 10^3 \sin (3 \cdot 10^6 t + k)$.

Discuss the relationship of the following to simple harmonic motion:

13. $4 + \sin \pi t$.   **14.** $\sin (\pi/t)$.   **15.** $t \sin t$.

Prove:

16. $x = r \sin \theta$ and $y = r \cos \theta$ is a parametric representation (§ 4-10) for a circle, and if θ varies directly as time then x undergoes simple harmonic motion and so does y.

17. $\sin (at + b) + \sin (at + c)$ represents a simple harmonic motion; that is, the sum of two simple harmonic motions of the same amplitude and frequency is again a simple harmonic motion. *Hint:* Use Exercise 14 of § 7-5 to change the given expression into the form (18).

7-10   Multiple Angle Formulas

In connection with periodic functions we have seen that it is often of interest to consider trigonometric functions of multiples of an angle— for instance, $\sin k\theta$ instead of $\sin \theta$. A commonly occurring value of k is 2. It is easy to give relationships between functions of 2θ and functions of θ, and vice versa.

In (14), set $\alpha = \beta = \theta$:

$$\sin 2\theta = \sin (\theta + \theta) = \sin \theta \cos \theta + \cos \theta \sin \theta$$

or

$$\sin 2\theta = 2 \sin \theta \cos \theta. \tag{19}$$

Similarly, from (10),

$$\begin{aligned}
\cos 2\theta &= \cos \theta \cos \theta - \sin \theta \sin \theta \\
&= \cos^2 \theta - \sin^2 \theta \\
&= \cos^2 \theta - (1 - \cos^2 \theta) \\
&= 2 \cos^2 \theta - 1.
\end{aligned}$$

Thus

$$\cos 2\theta = \cos^2 \theta - \sin^2 \theta;$$
$$\cos 2\theta = 2 \cos^2 \theta - 1;$$
$$\cos 2\theta = 1 - 2 \sin^2 \theta.$$ (20)

The identities (19)–(20), and similar ones which can be derived for other functions, are called **double angle formulas**.

Solving the last two equations for $\cos^2 \theta$ and for $\sin^2 \theta$ respectively, we obtain relations which are sometimes useful in converting a term involving a square of a trigonometric function to a linear term:

$$\cos^2 \theta = \tfrac{1}{2}(1 + \cos 2\theta);$$ (21)

$$\sin^2 \theta = \tfrac{1}{2}(1 - \cos 2\theta).$$ (22)

Identities such as (21) and (22) are often written in the form

$$\cos^2 \tfrac{1}{2}x = \tfrac{1}{2}(1 + \cos x) \quad \text{or} \quad \cos \tfrac{1}{2}x = \pm\sqrt{\tfrac{1}{2}(1 + \cos x)}$$ (23)

and so are called **half-angle formulas**.

EXAMPLE 1.   Express $\tan \tfrac{1}{2}x$ in terms of functions of x.

Solution. $\tan \tfrac{1}{2}x = \dfrac{\sin \tfrac{1}{2}x}{\cos \tfrac{1}{2}x} = \dfrac{2 \sin \tfrac{1}{2}x \cos \tfrac{1}{2}x}{2 \cos \tfrac{1}{2}x \cos \tfrac{1}{2}x} = \dfrac{\sin x}{2 \cos^2 \tfrac{1}{2}x}$

$$= \dfrac{\sin x}{1 + \cos x}.$$ (24a)

Changing to a form which is sometimes more convenient,

$$\tan \tfrac{1}{2}x = \dfrac{\sin x (1 - \cos x)}{1 - \cos^2 x} = \dfrac{\sin x (1 - \cos x)}{\sin^2 x}$$

$$= \dfrac{1 - \cos x}{\sin x}.$$ (24b)

Note that, unlike $\sin \tfrac{1}{2}x$ and $\cos \tfrac{1}{2}x$, $\tan \tfrac{1}{2}x$ can be expressed without radicals.

EXAMPLE 2.   Find the exact value of $\cos \tfrac{3}{8}\pi$.

Solution.   Since $\tfrac{3}{8}\pi$ is in the first quadrant, $\cos \tfrac{3}{8}\pi$ is positive and the plus sign must be used before the radical in (23):

$$\cos \tfrac{3}{8}\pi = \cos \tfrac{1}{2}(\tfrac{3}{4}\pi) = \sqrt{\tfrac{1}{2}(1 + \cos \tfrac{3}{4}\pi)}$$

$$= \sqrt{\tfrac{1}{2}(1 - \tfrac{1}{2}\sqrt{2})} = \tfrac{1}{2}\sqrt{2 - \sqrt{2}}.$$

EXAMPLE 3. Express $\sin 3\theta$ in terms of $\sin \theta$.

Solution. $\sin 3\theta = \sin (\theta + 2\theta)$

$$= \sin \theta \cos 2\theta + \cos \theta \sin 2\theta$$
$$= \sin \theta \, (1 - 2 \sin^2 \theta) + \cos \theta \cdot 2 \sin \theta \cos \theta$$
$$= \sin \theta - 2 \sin^3 \theta + 2 \sin \theta \cos^2 \theta$$
$$= \sin \theta - 2 \sin^3 \theta + 2 \sin \theta \, (1 - \sin^2 \theta)$$
$$= 3 \sin \theta - 4 \sin^3 \theta.$$

Historical Note. VIETA (1540–1603) was familiar with the expression of $\cos 3\theta$ in terms of functions of θ, and used it in solving cubic equations.

EXERCISES

Find the following, both by a half-angle formula and by Table IV:

1. $\sin 15°$.　　　　**3.** $\cos 105°$.　　　　**5.** $\cos 135°$.

2. $\cos 45°$.　　　　**4.** $\sin 112\frac{1}{2}°$.　　　　**6.** $\tan 75°$.

Express the specified function in terms of functions of the second variable:

7. $\cos 3\alpha$; α.　　　　**10.** $\cos \frac{1}{6}x$; $\frac{2}{3}x$.　　　　**13.** $\sin 6\theta$; θ.

8. $\cos 4\alpha$; α.　　　　**11.** $\sec \alpha$; 2α.　　　　**14.** $\cos 4A$; $\frac{1}{2}A$.

9. $\sin x$; $4x$.　　　　**12.** $\text{ctn } 2t$; $4t$.　　　　**15.** $\tan 16B$; $64B$.

Find the values of the specified functions, given that $\sec A = -\frac{5}{4}$, $\frac{1}{2}\pi < A < \pi$, *and* $\tan B = \frac{12}{5}$, $\pi < B < \frac{3}{2}\pi$:

16. $\sin 2A$.　　　　**20.** $\sin \frac{1}{2}A$.　　　　**24.** $\tan \frac{1}{4}A$.

17. $\sin 2B$.　　　　**21.** $\sin \frac{1}{2}B$.　　　　**25.** $\tan \frac{1}{2}B$.

18. $\cos 2A$.　　　　**22.** $\cos \frac{1}{4}A$.　　　　**26.** $\sin (-2A)$.

19. $\cos 2B$.　　　　**23.** $\cos \frac{1}{2}B$.　　　　**27.** $\cos (-\frac{1}{2}B)$.

Simplify:

28. $\cos^4 x - \sin^4 x$.

29. $2 \cos \theta \csc 2\theta$.

30. $\dfrac{\sin 6x}{\sin 2x} - \dfrac{\cos 6x}{\cos 2x}$.

31. $\tan y + \text{ctn } y$.

32. $\csc 8t + \text{ctn } 8t$.

33. $\dfrac{1 - \tan^2 x}{1 + \tan^2 x}$.

34. $\sin x \cos^3 x - \cos x \sin^3 x$.

35. $\sin^2 \frac{1}{2}x \cos^2 \frac{1}{2}x$.

7-11   Summary of Trigonometric Identities

Collected here for reference are the more commonly used identities developed in this chapter.

The reciprocal identities:

$$\csc \theta = \frac{1}{\sin \theta}; \qquad \sec \theta = \frac{1}{\cos \theta}; \qquad \text{ctn } \theta = \frac{1}{\tan \theta}. \qquad (3)$$

The quotient identities:

$$\tan \theta = \frac{\sin \theta}{\cos \theta}; \qquad \text{ctn } \theta = \frac{\cos \theta}{\sin \theta}. \qquad (4)$$

The Pythagorean relationships:

$$\sin^2 \theta + \cos^2 \theta = 1; \qquad (5)$$

$$1 + \tan^2 \theta = \sec^2 \theta; \qquad (6)$$

$$1 + \text{ctn}^2 \theta = \csc^2 \theta. \qquad (7)$$

The negative angle formulas:

$$\sin (-\theta) = -\sin \theta; \quad \cos (-\theta) = \cos \theta; \quad \tan (-\theta) = -\tan \theta. \qquad (8)$$

The addition formulas:

$$\sin (\alpha + \beta) = \sin \alpha \cos \beta + \cos \alpha \sin \beta; \qquad (14)$$

$$\sin (\alpha - \beta) = \sin \alpha \cos \beta - \cos \alpha \sin \beta; \qquad (15)$$

$$\cos (\alpha + \beta) = \cos \alpha \cos \beta - \sin \alpha \sin \beta; \qquad (10)$$

$$\cos (\alpha - \beta) = \cos \alpha \cos \beta + \sin \alpha \sin \beta; \qquad (9)$$

$$\tan (\alpha - \beta) = \frac{\tan \alpha - \tan \beta}{1 + \tan \alpha \tan \beta}. \qquad (16)$$

The double angle formulas:

$$\sin 2\theta = 2 \sin \theta \cos \theta; \qquad (19)$$

$$\cos 2\theta = \cos^2 \theta - \sin^2 \theta = 2 \cos^2 \theta - 1 = 1 - 2 \sin^2 \theta. \qquad (20)$$

The half-angle formulas:

$$\sin^2 \tfrac{1}{2}\theta = \tfrac{1}{2}(1 - \cos \theta); \qquad (22)$$

$$\cos^2 \tfrac{1}{2}\theta = \tfrac{1}{2}(1 + \cos \theta); \qquad (21)$$

$$\tan \tfrac{1}{2}\theta = \frac{\sin \theta}{1 + \cos \theta} = \frac{1 - \cos \theta}{\sin \theta}. \qquad (24)$$

MISCELLANEOUS EXERCISES

Given $\cos \alpha = -\frac{7}{25}$ *with* α *in Quadrant II and* $\tan \beta = -\frac{3}{4}$ *with* β *in Quadrant IV, find:*

1. $\sin^2 \alpha$.	**5.** $\sqrt{\sin \alpha}$.	**9.** $\sin \alpha - \sin \beta$.
2. $\sin 2\alpha$.	**6.** $\sin (\alpha + \frac{1}{2}\pi)$.	**10.** $\cos \alpha + \cos \beta$.
3. $\sin \frac{1}{2}\alpha$.	**7.** $\sin (\alpha - \beta)$.	**11.** $\sin 2(\alpha - \beta)$.
4. $\frac{1}{2} \sin \alpha$.	**8.** $\cos (\alpha + \beta)$.	**12.** $\sin \frac{1}{2}(\alpha - \beta)$.

Derive a formula, in terms of functions of α *and of* β, *for:*

13. $\tan (\alpha + \beta)$, using **(a)** the same method as in Example 2 of § 7-5; **(b)** identities (16) and (8).

14. $\operatorname{ctn} (\alpha - \beta)$, using **(a)** the same method as in Example 2 of § 7-5; **(b)** identities (16) and (3).

15. $\tan 2\theta$, using **(a)** identities (4), (19), and (20); **(b)** identities (8) and (16).

Simplify:

16. $(\cos^2 \theta - \sin^2 \theta)^2 + 4 \sin^2 \theta \cos^2 \theta$.

17. $\cos^2 4x + 2 \sin 4x \cos 4x - \sin^2 4x$.

18. $\dfrac{\csc A \csc B}{\operatorname{ctn} A - \operatorname{ctn} B}$.

19. $\dfrac{1}{1 + \sin x} + \dfrac{1}{1 - \sin x}$.

Prove the identities:

20. $\sin A + \sin B = 2 \sin \frac{1}{2}(A + B) \cos \frac{1}{2}(A - B)$.

21. $\cos A + \cos B = 2 \cos \frac{1}{2}(A + B) \cos \frac{1}{2}(A - B)$.

22. $\dfrac{\sin^3 x}{\tan x - \sin x} = \dfrac{1 + \cos x}{\sec x}$.

23. $\dfrac{1 + \sin 4x - \cos 4x}{1 + \sin 4x + \cos 4x} = \tan 2x$.

24. If a circuit consists of a coil with inductance L henrys, a condenser with capacitance C farads, and negligible resistance, and if the initial charge on the condenser is Q_0 coulombs, then t seconds after the circuit is closed the charge Q on the condenser is given by

$$Q = Q_0 \sin \left(\frac{t}{\sqrt{LC}} + \frac{1}{2} \right) \pi.$$

What is the frequency of oscillation if $L = 0.20$ and $C = 500 \cdot 10^{-6}$?

Sketch the graph of:

25. $\sin 2x$.

26. $\cos 2x$.

27. $\sin \frac{1}{2}x$.

28. $2 \sin x$.

29. $\sin (x + 2)$.

30. $\sin (2 - x)$.

31. $\sin^2 x$.

32. $\sqrt{\sin x}$.

33. $\frac{1}{2} \cos \frac{1}{2}x$.

34. $\frac{1}{2} \cos \frac{1}{2}\pi x$.

35. $\frac{1}{2} \cos (\frac{1}{2}\pi + x)$.

36. $\frac{1}{2}\pi \cos x$.

If x *and* y *are sinusoidal functions of a parameter* t *then the graph of* y *against* x *is called a* **Lissajous curve.** *Graph this curve for:*

37. $x = 4 \sin t, \ y = 4 \cos t$.

38. $x = 4 \sin t, \ y = 3 \cos t$.

39. $x = \sin 2t, \ y = \cos t$.

40. $x = \sin 3t, \ y = \cos t$.

41. $x = \cos 3t, \ y = \cos t$.

42. $x = \sin 3t, \ y = \cos 2t$.

Substitute in a trigonometric identity such as (5) *to obtain an equation in* x *and* y *without* t *from the equations given in:*

*43. Exercise 37.

*44. Exercise 38.

CHAPTER 8

COMPLEX NUMBERS

8-1 Imaginary and Complex Numbers

This chapter continues the study of imaginary and complex numbers and thus serves as a review and an extension of § 3-9.

In solving the equation $x^2 + 1 = 0$ by the usual laws of algebra, we would write the solution in the form $\pm\sqrt{-1}$. Since the square of either a positive or a negative real number is always positive, $\sqrt{-1}$ cannot belong to the real number system. Accordingly, the symbol $\sqrt{-1}$, called the **imaginary unit** and usually designated by i, represents a new kind of number with the property that

$$i^2 = (\sqrt{-1})^2 = -1.$$

If we now assume that we may operate with i as if it were a literal number symbol subject to the rules of algebra as they apply to real numbers, we have, for any positive real number N,

$$\sqrt{-N} = \sqrt{i^2 N} = i\sqrt{N};$$

that is, the square root of any negative number can be expressed as the product of a real number and the number i.

A number which may be expressed in the form $(a + bi)$ where a and b represent real numbers is called a **complex number.** In referring to such numbers we shall, as a matter of convenience, often use phrases such as "the complex number $(a + bi)$." The number a is called the **real part** and bi is called the **imaginary part** of the complex number. Whenever $b \neq 0$, the complex number $(a + bi)$ is called an **imaginary number.** When $a = 0$ but $b \neq 0$, the complex number $(a + bi)$ may be expressed in the form bi and is called a **pure imaginary number.** When $b = 0$, the complex number $(a + bi)$ represents the real number $a + 0i$, or a. Thus real numbers, pure imaginary numbers, and imaginary numbers are particular kinds of complex numbers and are numbers in the complex number system.

ILLUSTRATION. $(3 - 5i)$, $(-\sqrt{3} + 2i)$, and $(-\sqrt{5} - i\sqrt{2})$ represent imaginary numbers; $-3i$ and $2i\sqrt{7}$ represent pure imaginary numbers; and 5, $\sqrt[3]{-3}$, and $-\sqrt{2}$ represent real numbers. All these represent complex numbers.

Two complex numbers that differ only in the signs of their imaginary parts are called **conjugate complex numbers,** and either is called the conjugate of the other. Thus $(a + bi)$ and $(a - bi)$ represent conjugate complex numbers, as do also bi and $-bi$. A real number is its own conjugate.

With the property of the symbol i that $i^2 = -1$ and the assumption that we may operate with i as if it were a literal number subject to the rules of algebra as they apply to real numbers, we can develop a consistent algebra of complex numbers* which includes the algebra of real numbers as a particular case.

Two complex numbers are defined to be equal if and only if their real parts are equal and their imaginary parts are equal; that is,

$$a + bi = c + di \quad \text{if and only if} \quad a = c \quad \text{and} \quad b = d.$$

As an immediate consequence of this definition, we have

If the complex number $a + bi = 0$, *then* $a = 0$ *and* $b = 0$.

The above definition of equality of complex numbers is not an arbitrarily chosen definition, but is the only possible definition that is consistent with the definition of equality of real numbers. Thus if $a + bi = c + di$, then $a - c = (d - b)i$, whence $(a - c)^2 = -(d - b)^2$, which is possible only when $a - c = 0$ and $d - b = 0$. The desirability of the above definition can also be seen from the graphical representation of complex numbers discussed in § 8-3.

If i is raised to successive positive integral powers, we obtain

$$i = \sqrt{-1};$$
$$i^2 = -1;$$
$$i^3 = i^2(i) = (-1)i = -i;$$
$$i^4 = (i^2)(i^2) = (-1)^2 = 1;$$

$$i^5 = i^4(i) = 1(i) = i;$$
$$i^6 = i^4(i^2) = 1(-1) = -1;$$
$$i^7 = i^4(i^3) = 1(-i) = -i;$$
$$i^8 = i^4(i^4) = (1)^2 = 1;$$

$$i^9 = (i^4)^2(i) = i; \quad \text{and so forth.}$$

* For a more thorough discussion of the algebra of complex numbers, see B. E. Meserve's *Fundamental Concepts of Algebra* (Addison-Wesley, Reading, Massachusetts, 1953), pp. 1–57.

Similarly, $i^{-1} = 1/i = i^4/i = i^3 = -i;$

$i^{-2} = 1/i^2 = i^4/i^2 = i^2 = -1;$

$i^{-3} = 1/i^3 = i^4/i^3 = i;$ and so forth.

Thus the integral powers of i have only four different values: i, -1, $-i$, and 1, which are taken on in a regular order.

EXERCISES

Write each of the following in the form (a + bi) *where* a *and* b *repre-sent real numbers and* x, y, *and* z *represent positive numbers:*

1. $\sqrt{-4}$.

2. $-2\sqrt{-9}$.

3. $-\sqrt{-25x^4}$.

4. $\sqrt{-18y^2}$.

5. $\sqrt{5x^2/(-10y^4)}$.

6. i^{10}.

7. i^{11}.

8. i^{12}.

9. i^{27}.

10. i^{205}.

11. $4 - \sqrt{-4x^2y^4z^6}$.

12. $\sqrt{-24} + \sqrt{24}$.

13. $\frac{1}{2}(2 + \sqrt{-225})$.

14. $\frac{1}{3}(-6 - \sqrt{-729})$.

15. $\frac{1}{8}(-4 - 2\sqrt{784})$.

Find the real values of x *and* y *for which each of the following equations is satisfied:*

16. $x + yi = 4 - 3i$.

17. $4x + 7yi = 12 - 35i$.

18. $x^2 + y^2i = 4$.

19. $(x + 2x) + (2y - y)i = 3 + 4i$.

20. $(x + 2) + (-3y + 12)i = -x + yi$.

21. $x^2 + y^2i = 2x + 3 + i$.

8-2   The Four Fundamental Operations on Complex Numbers

We now define the four fundamental operations of addition, subtrac-tion, multiplication, and division of complex numbers so that these operations include, as special cases, the corresponding operations with real numbers.

To **add** (*or* **subtract**) *two complex numbers, such as* (a + bi) *and* (c + di), *add (or subtract) the real and imaginary parts separately:*

$$(a + bi) + (c + di) = (a + c) + (b + d)i;$$
$$(a + bi) - (c + di) = (a - c) + (b - d)i.$$

ILLUSTRATION 1.

$$(3 - 5i) + (4 + 3i) = (3 + 4) + (-5 + 3)i = 7 - 2i;$$
$$(3 - 5i) - (4 + 3i) = (3 - 4) + (-5 - 3)i = -1 - 8i.$$

To form the **product** *of two complex numbers, such as* (a + bi) *and* (c + di), *multiply them according to the laws for real numbers and substitute* $i^2 = -1$:

$$(a + bi)(c + di) = ac + adi + bci + bdi^2,$$

and, since $i^2 = -1$,

$$(a + bi)(c + di) = (ac - bd) + (ad + bc)i.$$

ILLUSTRATION 2.

$$(-2 + 5i)(-1 - 2i) = 2 + 4i - 5i - 10i^2 = 12 - i.$$

To express as a single complex number the **quotient** *of one complex number, such as* (a + bi), *by another complex number, such as* (c + di), *where* (c + di) $\neq 0$, *multiply both numerator and denominator of the indicated quotient* (a + bi)/(c + di) *by* (c − di), *the conjugate of the denominator:*

$$\frac{a + bi}{c + di} = \frac{a + bi}{c + di} \cdot \frac{c - di}{c - di}$$

$$= \frac{ac - adi + bci - bdi^2}{c^2 - d^2 i^2}$$

$$= \frac{(ac + bd) + (bc - ad)i}{c^2 + d^2}.$$

Therefore

$$\frac{a + bi}{c + di} = \frac{ac + bd}{c^2 + d^2} + \frac{bc - ad}{c^2 + d^2} i, \quad \text{if} \quad (c + di) \neq 0.$$

The multiplication by $(c - di)$ is analogous to the use of a rationalizing factor (§ 3-5).

ILLUSTRATION 3.

$$\frac{2 - 3i}{1 - 2i} = \frac{2 - 3i}{1 - 2i} \cdot \frac{1 + 2i}{1 + 2i} = \frac{2 + 4i - 3i - 6i^2}{1 - 4i^2} = \frac{8 + i}{5} = \frac{8}{5} + \frac{1}{5}i.$$

Warning. In all problems involving complex numbers each complex number should first be expressed in the form $(a + bi)$. Then proceed according to the usual rules of algebra and substitute $i^2 = -1$. For example, if a and b are positive real numbers,

$$\sqrt{-a}\sqrt{-b} = i\sqrt{a} \cdot i\sqrt{b} = i^2 \cdot \sqrt{ab} = -\sqrt{ab},$$

but
$$\sqrt{-a}\sqrt{-b} \neq \sqrt{(-a)(-b)}, \quad \text{or} \quad \sqrt{ab}.$$

EXERCISES

Simplify to the form (a + bi):

1. $(3 + 4i) + (5 - 7i)$.

2. $(2 + 3i) + (-6 + i)$.

3. $(-2 - 5i) - (2 - 3i)$.

4. $(5 - 8i) - (-1 + i)$.

5. $\sqrt{-9} + 2\sqrt{-25} - 3\sqrt{-16}$.

6. $\sqrt{-3} - 7\sqrt{-12} + 2\sqrt{-27}$.

7. $(3 - \sqrt{-36}) - (1 + \sqrt{-9})$.

8. $(7 + \sqrt{-8}) - (\sqrt{-50} + 1)$.

9. $(5i)(2i)$.

10. $(3i)(-4i)$.

11. $\sqrt{-20}\sqrt{-50}\sqrt{-15}$.

12. $\sqrt{-64}\sqrt{-72}\sqrt{-108}$.

13. $(2 + 3i)(-6 + i)$.

14. $(3 + 4i)(5 - 7i)$.

15. $(4 - 3i)^2$.

16. $(-1 + 2i)^2$.

17. $(1 + \sqrt{-3})(2 - \sqrt{-12})$.

18. $(\sqrt{8} - \sqrt{-6})(-\sqrt{-24} - \sqrt{2})$.

19. $(-3\sqrt{-2})^2$.

20. $6i(2 - 3i)$.

21. $(\frac{1}{2} - 3\sqrt{-\frac{3}{4}})^2$.

22. $(-\frac{2}{3} + \sqrt{-\frac{2}{3}})^2$.

23. $(5i^5 - 3i^3)(6i^6 - 4i^4)$.

24. $(2i^5 - 3i^4 + i^3 + 5i^2)^3$.

25. $(2 + 3i) \div (1 - 4i)$.

26. $(4 - i) \div (3 + 2i)$.

27. $(4 - \sqrt{-5}) \div (2 + 3\sqrt{-5})$.

28. $(9 - \sqrt{-8}) \div (\sqrt{-2} + 3)$.

Indicate which statements are true, which are false, and justify your answers:

29. The sum of two conjugate complex numbers is real.

30. If the sum of two imaginary numbers is real, the numbers are conjugates.

31. If the difference of two complex numbers is real, their imaginary parts are equal.

32. The product of two conjugate complex numbers is real and nonnegative.

33. The sum of the conjugates of two complex numbers is equal to the conjugate of their sum.

34. The product of the conjugates of two complex numbers is equal to the conjugate of their product.

If, instead of denoting a complex number by (a + bi), *it is written as a pair* (a, b) *then* (a, b) + (c, d) = (a + c, b + d). *In this notation, write the rule for:*

35. Subtraction.   **36.** Multiplication.   **37.** Division.

8-3   Graphical Representation of Complex Numbers

We have seen in § 1-3 that each real number may be represented by a
point on a straight line. To represent a complex number graphically,
take a coordinate plane (§ 4-4) and represent $(a + bi)$ by the point with
coordinates (a, b). Thus in Figure 8.1, the point P_1 represents $(a + bi)$.
A coordinate plane used in this manner is called a **complex plane;**
$X'X$ is called the axis of real numbers or **axis of reals,** and $Y'Y$ the
axis of pure imaginary numbers or **axis of imaginaries.** A point $(0, b)$
on the axis of imaginaries represents the pure imaginary number bi; a
point $(a, 0)$ on the axis of reals represents the real number $(a + 0i)$ or
a, just as in § 1-3. Two complex numbers are equal if and only if their
representative points coincide.

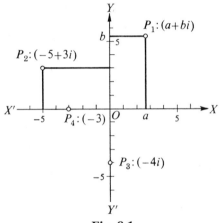

Fig. 8.1

ILLUSTRATIONS.   In Figure 8.1, the point P_2 represents $(-5 + 3i)$, the
point P_3 represents the pure imaginary number $-4i$, and the point P_4 represents the real number -3.

The location of the point $P: (a + bi)$ representing the complex number $(a + bi)$ can also be described in another way, providing the same
unit of length is used on the two axes. As in Figure 8.2, let r be the
distance OP from the origin to P, and let θ be the angle from the positive
axis of reals to the line OP. By the Pythagorean theorem, $r = \sqrt{a^2 + b^2}$.
The length r is called the **absolute value** or **modulus** of the complex
number $(a + bi)$ and is denoted $|a + bi|$; the angle θ is called the
argument of the complex number.* As in Example 5 of § 7-2, θ may

---

* Another name sometimes applied to θ is "the amplitude of $(a + bi)$", but this
will be avoided here because of the different usage of "amplitude" in § 7-7.

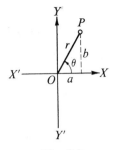

Fig. 8.2

be replaced by any angle coterminal with it; that is, by $(\theta + k \cdot 360°)$ where k may represent any integer (positive, negative, or zero). Unless otherwise indicated, we shall select the smallest nonnegative value of the argument.

From the definition of sine and cosine (§ 7-2) it follows that

$$a = r \cos \theta \quad \text{and} \quad b = r \sin \theta, \tag{1}$$

so

$$a + bi = r(\cos \theta + i \sin \theta), \tag{2}$$

where the right member of (2) is called the **polar** or **trigonometric form** of the complex number. It is sometimes abbreviated by r cis θ or by $r \angle \theta$. The same number is also given by

$$r[\cos (\theta + k \cdot 360°) + i \sin (\theta + k \cdot 360°)]$$

where k may represent any integer (positive, negative, or zero).

In contrast, $(a + bi)$ is called the **rectangular** or **algebraic form** of the complex number.

EXAMPLE 1. Represent graphically the complex number $(-2 + 2i)$. Write the number in polar form, using the smallest nonnegative value of its argument.

Solution. The point P (Figure 8.3), representing $(-2 + 2i)$, is in the second quadrant. From Figure 8.3 we find

$$r = \sqrt{(-2)^2 + (2)^2} = 2\sqrt{2};$$

and $\tan \theta = -1,$

from which we obtain $\theta = 135°$. This can also be written $\theta = \frac{3}{4}\pi$ radians.

Therefore the polar form of $(-2 + 2i)$ is $2\sqrt{2} (\cos 135° + i \sin 135°)$.

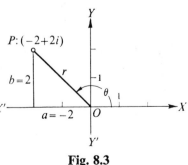

Fig. 8.3

EXAMPLE 2.   Represent

$$4(\cos 300° + i \sin 300°)$$

graphically, and write the complex number in its rectangular form.

Solution.   First, lay off the angle
$\theta = 300°$. On its terminal side locate
the point P which is 4 units from the
origin. The point P represents the given
complex number. From Figure 8.4 we
obtain

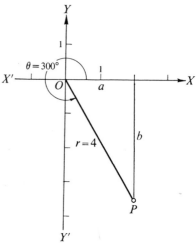

$$a = 4 \cos 300° = 4(\tfrac{1}{2}) = 2,$$

and $b = 4 \sin 300° = 4(-\tfrac{1}{2}\sqrt{3})$

$$= -2\sqrt{3}.$$

Therefore the rectangular form of
$4(\cos 300° + i \sin 300°)$ is

$$2 - 2i\sqrt{3}.$$

Fig. 8.4

Historical Note.   The graphical representation of complex numbers was
discovered independently by the Norwegian CASPAR WESSEL in 1797, by the
Frenchman JEAN R. ARGAND in 1806, and by the German CARL F. GAUSS in
1831. The Englishman JOHN WALLIS gave a geometric treatment of imaginary
numbers in his *Algebra* (1685).

EXERCISES

Represent graphically (**a**) *the following complex numbers;* (**b**) *their
conjugates; and* (**c**) *their negatives:*

1. $2 + 5i$.   **3.** $1 - 3i$.   **5.** $-2i$.   **7.** $\frac{1}{3}(2 - i\sqrt{3})$.

2. $-3 + 4i$.   **4.** $-\frac{1}{2} - \frac{5}{2}i$.   **6.** -2.   **8.** $-i + 3\sqrt{2}$.

*Represent graphically each of the following numbers, and write each
number in polar form using the smallest nonnegative value of its argument:*

9. $1 + i$.   **13.** $i - \sqrt{3}$.   **17.** -1.

10. $\sqrt{3} + i$.   **14.** $-5i$.   **18.** $\frac{3}{2}(-1 + i\sqrt{3})$.

11. $4 - 4i\sqrt{3}$.   **15.** $\frac{3}{2}i$.   **19.** $\frac{1}{6}(-\sqrt{3} - i)$.

12. $-3 - 3i$.   **16.** 8.   **20.** $-3(1 - i)$.

Represent graphically, and write each number in rectangular form:

21. $6(\cos 60° + i \sin 60°)$.   **26.** $\frac{3}{2}(\cos 0° + i \sin 0°)$.

22. $4(\cos 150° + i \sin 150°)$.   **27.** $\cos \pi + i \sin \pi$.

23. $2(\cos 300° + i \sin 300°)$.   **28.** $\frac{3}{4}(\cos \frac{3}{2}\pi + i \sin \frac{3}{2}\pi)$.

24. $3\sqrt{2}(\cos 225° + i \sin 225°)$.   **29.** $2(\cos 134° + i \sin 134°)$.

25. $5(\cos 90° + i \sin 90°)$.   **30.** $10(\cos 248° + i \sin 248°)$.

Represent the specified numbers **(a)** *algebraically or trigonometrically in a general form;* **(b)** *graphically for a typical case:*

31. Two distinct complex numbers with equal real parts.

32. Two distinct complex numbers with equal imaginary parts.

33. A complex number in polar form, and its conjugate.

34. A complex number which is its own conjugate.

35. A complex number which is its own negative.

36. A positive number and its argument.

37. A negative number and its argument.

38. A number in rectangular form with argument 270°.

8-4   Graphical Representation of Addition and Subtraction of Complex Numbers

To add two complex numbers, $(a + bi)$ and $(c + di)$, graphically, first draw the lines OP_1 and OP_2 (Figure 8.5), which join the origin to the points that represent these numbers in the complex plane. Then complete the parallelogram $OP_1P_3P_2$ having OP_1 and OP_2 as adjacent sides. The complex number corresponding to the vertex P_3 is the sum of the two given complex numbers.

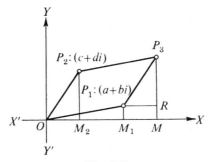

Fig. 8.5

The above construction for P_3 may be verified as follows: In Figure 8.5 the right triangles P_1RP_3 and OM_2P_2 are congruent, since the hypotenuse and an acute angle of the one are equal respectively to the hypotenuse and an acute angle of the other; hence $P_1R = OM_2$, and $RP_3 = M_2P_2$. Therefore we have

$$OM = OM_1 + M_1M = OM_1 + P_1R = OM_1 + OM_2 = a + c,$$

and

$$MP_3 = MR + RP_3 = M_1P_1 + M_2P_2 = b + d.$$

These statements hold regardless of the signs of a, b, c, and d; the distances are to be interpreted as directed line segments (§ 1-3).

To subtract one complex number $(c + di)$ from another complex number $(a + bi)$ graphically, we merely add $(a + bi)$ and $(-c - di)$.

The graphical addition of complex numbers follows the same law as that which governs the addition of vectors as, for example, in the study of forces, velocities, and accelerations in physics. For this reason complex numbers are often used to represent vectors. See also § 9-2.

EXERCISES

Perform the indicated addition or subtraction graphically, and check the results algebraically:

1. $(2 + 3i) + (3 + i)$.
2. $(1 + 4i) + (2 - i)$.
3. $(-1 + 2i) - (3 + \frac{1}{2}i)$.
4. $(-2 - 2i) - (-2 - 3i)$.
5. $(-3) - (-1 + 2i)$.
6. $(-3i) - (1 - i)$.
7. $2i + (1 + i) + (\frac{5}{2} - i)$.
8. $5 + (2 - 2i) + (4i - 1)$.

9. Let $(a + bi)$ correspond to the force with horizontal component a and vertical component b. (a) Find the sum of the complex numbers corresponding to a force with components 60 pounds upward and 50 pounds to the left and a force of 80 pounds directly downward. (b) The sum corresponds to the resultant of the forces. Find the absolute value and the argument of each of the original forces and of the resultant.

10. Repeat Exercise 9 if the first of the given forces has components 5 pounds upward and 10 pounds to the left, and the second force has components 30 pounds to the right and 20 pounds downward.

8-5 Multiplication and Division of Complex Numbers in the Polar Form

Let $r_1(\cos \theta_1 + i \sin \theta_1)$ and $r_2(\cos \theta_2 + i \sin \theta_2)$ be two complex numbers in the polar form. By multiplication

$$r_1(\cos \theta_1 + i \sin \theta_1) \cdot r_2(\cos \theta_2 + i \sin \theta_2)$$
$$= r_1 r_2[\cos \theta_1 \cos \theta_2 + i \cos \theta_1 \sin \theta_2 + i \sin \theta_1 \cos \theta_2$$
$$+ i^2 \sin \theta_1 \sin \theta_2]$$
$$= r_1 r_2[(\cos \theta_1 \cos \theta_2 - \sin \theta_1 \sin \theta_2)$$
$$+ i(\sin \theta_1 \cos \theta_2 + \cos \theta_1 \sin \theta_2)].$$

Applying the addition formulas from § 7-5,

$$r_1(\cos \theta_1 + i \sin \theta_1) \cdot r_2(\cos \theta_2 + i \sin \theta_2)$$
$$= r_1 r_2[\cos (\theta_1 + \theta_2) + i \sin (\theta_1 + \theta_2)]. \quad (3)$$

This method can be extended to find the product of more than two complex numbers by first multiplying two of the numbers, then multiplying their product by the third, and so on. Thus

$$r_1(\cos \theta_1 + i \sin \theta_1) \cdot r_2(\cos \theta_2 + i \sin \theta_2) \cdots r_n(\cos \theta_n + i \sin \theta_n)$$
$$= r_1 r_2 \cdots r_n[\cos (\theta_1 + \theta_2 + \cdots + \theta_n) + i \sin (\theta_1 + \theta_2 + \cdots + \theta_n)].$$
$$\textbf{(4)}$$

Hence we have the following theorem.

Theorem 1. *The absolute value of the product of two or more complex numbers is the product of their absolute values, and the argument of the product is the sum of their arguments.*

Similarly,

$$\frac{r_1(\cos \theta_1 + i \sin \theta_1)}{r_2(\cos \theta_2 + i \sin \theta_2)} = \frac{r_1}{r_2}[\cos (\theta_1 - \theta_2) + i \sin (\theta_1 - \theta_2)]. \quad (5)$$

This may be stated in words as follows:

Theorem 2. *The absolute value of the quotient of two complex numbers is the quotient of their absolute values, and the argument of the quotient is the argument of the dividend minus the argument of the divisor.*

EXAMPLE 1.   Find $2(\cos 48° + i \sin 48°) \cdot 3(\cos 72° + i \sin 72°)$.

Solution. $2(\cos 48° + i \sin 48°) \cdot 3(\cos 72° + i \sin 72°)$

$$= [2 \cdot 3][\cos (48° + 72°) + i \sin (48° + 72°)]$$
$$= 6(\cos 120° + i \sin 120°)$$
$$= 6[(-\tfrac{1}{2}) + i(\tfrac{1}{2}\sqrt{3})]$$
$$= -3 + 3i\sqrt{3}.$$

EXAMPLE 2.   Find the quotient: $\dfrac{4(\cos 153° + i \sin 153°)}{2(\cos 288° + i \sin 288°)}$.

Solution.

$$\frac{4(\cos 153° + i \sin 153°)}{2(\cos 288° + i \sin 288°)} = \frac{4}{2} [\cos (153° - 288°) + i \sin (153° - 288°)]$$
$$= 2[\cos (-135°) + i \sin (-135°)]$$
$$= 2[(-\tfrac{1}{2}\sqrt{2}) + i(-\tfrac{1}{2}\sqrt{2})]$$
$$= -\sqrt{2} - i\sqrt{2}.$$

EXERCISES

Perform the indicated operations; then express the results in rectangular form:

1. $[5(\cos 72° + i \sin 72°)][4(\cos 48° + i \sin 48°)]$.

2. $[2(\cos 130° + i \sin 130°)][3(\cos 200° + i \sin 200°)]$.

3. $\dfrac{28(\cos 240° + i \sin 240°)}{7(\cos 30° + i \sin 30°)}$.

4. $\dfrac{5\sqrt{2}(\cos \tfrac{5}{3}\pi + i \sin \tfrac{5}{3}\pi)}{6(\cos \tfrac{1}{3}\pi + i \sin \tfrac{1}{3}\pi)}$.

5. $(\sqrt{2} \operatorname{cis} \tfrac{3}{2}\pi)(3\sqrt{2} \operatorname{cis} \tfrac{2}{3}\pi)$.

6. $(\sqrt{7} \operatorname{cis} \tfrac{1}{8}\pi)(2 \operatorname{cis} \tfrac{7}{8}\pi)$.

7. $(3 \operatorname{cis} \tfrac{1}{4}\pi) \div (\sqrt{2} \operatorname{cis} \tfrac{3}{4}\pi)$.

8. $1 \div (\sqrt{2} \operatorname{cis} 315°)$.

Change the following complex numbers to polar form and perform the indicated operations on their polar forms; then express the result in rectangular form. Check by performing the indicated operations on the rectangular forms:

9. $(4\sqrt{3} + 4i)(1 - i\sqrt{3})$.

10. $(1 - i\sqrt{3})(\sqrt{3} + i)$.

11. $(-2 - 2i)(-5i)$.

12. $(\tfrac{1}{2} + \tfrac{1}{2}i\sqrt{3}) \div (2 - 2i\sqrt{3})$.

13. $1 \div (-\sqrt{2} + i\sqrt{2})$.

14. $(2i) \div [4\sqrt{2}(1 - i)]$.

15. $(1 + i\sqrt{3})(1 - i)(2 + 2i)$.

16. $(2\sqrt{3} + 2i)(\sqrt{3} - i) \div (6i)$.

17. Prove Theorem 2; that is, prove the relationship (5).

8-6   Powers of Complex Numbers

The formula
$$(\cos \theta + i \sin \theta)^n = \cos n\theta + i \sin n\theta \tag{6}$$
holds for every positive integer n and is known as **De Moivre's theorem.** It can be verified for any given positive integer n, using formula (4) of § 8-5 with $\theta_1 = \theta_2 = \cdots = \theta_n$. De Moivre's theorem holds for all real values of n and, indeed, for all complex values of n, although the interpretation of the latter assertion will not be undertaken in this book.

De Moivre's theorem is useful in expressing powers of complex numbers. If
$$z = a + bi = r(\cos \theta + i \sin \theta),$$
then
$$z^n = (a + bi)^n = r^n(\cos n\theta + i \sin n\theta). \tag{7}$$

Thus,

the absolute value of the n*th power of a complex number is equal to the* n*th power of the absolute value of the number, and an argument of the* n*th power of the complex number is equal to* n *times the argument of the number.*

EXAMPLE.   Find $(-2 + 2i)^5$.

Solution. By Example 1 of § 8-3, the polar form of $(-2 + 2i)$ is $2\sqrt{2}(\cos 135° + i \sin 135°)$. Hence, by (7), we obtain

$$
\begin{aligned}
(-2 + 2i)^5 &= [2\sqrt{2}(\cos 135° + i \sin 135°)]^5 \\
&= (2\sqrt{2})^5(\cos 675° + i \sin 675°) \\
&= 128\sqrt{2}(\cos 315° + i \sin 315°) \\
&= 128\sqrt{2}[(\tfrac{1}{2}\sqrt{2}) + i(-\tfrac{1}{2}\sqrt{2})] = 128 - 128i.
\end{aligned}
$$

Historical Note. De Moivre's theorem is named for ABRAHAM DE MOIVRE (1667–1754), who was born in France but spent most of his life in London. He was a friend of Newton and a fellow of the Royal Society.

EXERCISES

Find the indicated powers, giving the results **(a)** *in polar form;* **(b)** *in rectangular form:*

1. $[3(\cos 45° + i \sin 45°)]^2$.

2. $[2(\cos 120° + i \sin 120°)]^5$.

3. $[\sqrt{3}(\cos \tfrac{7}{6}\pi + i \sin \tfrac{7}{6}\pi)]^4$.

4. $[\sqrt[3]{2}(\cos \tfrac{4}{3}\pi + i \sin \tfrac{4}{3}\pi)]^3$.

5. $(\sqrt{3} - i)^5$.

6. $(-\sqrt{2} - i\sqrt{2})^7$.

7. $(-\tfrac{1}{2}\sqrt{3} + \tfrac{1}{2}i)^{10}$.

8. $(1 - i)^{13}$.

9. If $A = 2(\cos \frac{2}{3}\pi + i \sin \frac{2}{3}\pi)$ and $B = \cos \frac{1}{6}\pi + i \sin \frac{1}{6}\pi$, find in rectangular form the values of **(a)** A^7; **(b)** B^9; **(c)** A^7B^9; **(d)** $1/A$; **(e)** A^5/B^{10}.

10. If $u = 2 - 2i\sqrt{3}$ and $v = i - \sqrt{3}$, find in rectangular form the values of **(a)** u^4; **(b)** v^6; **(c)** $1/u$; **(d)** u^4v^6; **(e)** u^4/v^6; **(f)** $u^4 + v^6$.

8-7   Roots of Complex Numbers

Theorem. *Every complex number* r($\cos \theta + i \sin \theta$), *except zero, has exactly* n *distinct* nth *roots given by the formula*

$$\sqrt[n]{r}\left[\cos \frac{\theta + k \cdot 360°}{n} + i \sin \frac{\theta + k \cdot 360°}{n}\right], \tag{8}$$

where k *takes the values* 0, 1, 2, $\cdots$, (n − 1).

Proof. A complex number $c + di$ is by definition an nth root of a given complex number $a + bi$ if and only if $(c + di)^n = a + bi$. But

$$a + bi = r[\cos (\theta + k \cdot 360°) + i \sin (\theta + k \cdot 360°)]$$

where k may represent any integer (positive, negative, or zero). Then by (7) the complex numbers of the form (8) are the nth roots of $(a + bi)$. The radical $\sqrt[n]{r}$ means the positive nth root of the positive number r. If we now assign to k the values 0, 1, 2, $\cdots$, (n − 1), we obtain the following n distinct nth roots of $(a + bi)$:

$$\sqrt[n]{r}\left[\cos \frac{\theta}{n} + i \sin \frac{\theta}{n}\right], \quad \sqrt[n]{r}\left[\cos \frac{\theta + 360°}{n} + i \sin \frac{\theta + 360°}{n}\right],$$

$$\sqrt[n]{r}\left[\cos \frac{\theta + 2 \cdot 360°}{n} + i \sin \frac{\theta + 2 \cdot 360°}{n}\right],$$

$$\cdot \quad \cdot \quad \cdot \quad \cdot \quad \cdot \quad \cdot \quad \cdot \quad \cdot \quad \cdot \quad \cdot \quad \cdot \quad \cdot \quad \cdot \quad \cdot$$

$$\sqrt[n]{r}\left[\cos \frac{\theta + (n - 1)360°}{n} + i \sin \frac{\theta + (n - 1)360°}{n}\right].$$

Moreover, if k is assigned any integral value other than 0, 1, 2, $\cdots$, (n − 1), we merely obtain expressions which are equivalent to those already found.

EXAMPLE. Find the fourth roots of $(2 - 2i\sqrt{3})$ and represent them graphically.

Solution. The point P representing the complex number $(2 - 2i\sqrt{3})$ is in the fourth quadrant. From Figure 8.6 we find

$$r = \sqrt{(2)^2 + (-2\sqrt{3})^2} = 4;$$

and $$\tan \theta = -\sqrt{3},$$

from which we obtain $\theta = 300°$.

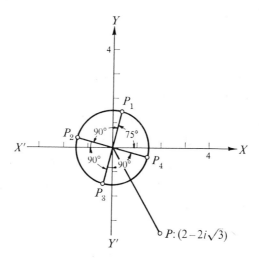

Fig. 8.6

Hence we have in polar form

$$2 - 2i\sqrt{3} = 4(\cos 300° + i \sin 300°)$$

$$= 4[\cos (300° + k \cdot 360°) + i \sin (300° + k \cdot 360°)],$$

where k is zero or any integer, positive or negative. It follows from formula (8) that the four fourth roots of $(2 - 2i\sqrt{3})$ are given by

$$4^{\frac{1}{4}}\left[\cos \frac{300° + k \cdot 360°}{4} + i \sin \frac{300° + k \cdot 360°}{4}\right],$$

or $$\sqrt{2}[\cos (75° + k \cdot 90°) + i \sin (75° + k \cdot 90°)],$$

where k takes the values 0, 1, 2, and 3.

By assigning to k the successive values 0, 1, 2, and 3, we obtain the following four fourth roots of $(2 - 2i\sqrt{3})$ in polar form:

$$\sqrt{2}(\cos 75° + i \sin 75°), \qquad \sqrt{2}(\cos 255° + i \sin 255°),$$

$$\sqrt{2}(\cos 165° + i \sin 165°), \qquad \sqrt{2}(\cos 345° + i \sin 345°).$$

These results may also be written in the following compact form:

$$\sqrt{2}(\cos\theta + i\sin\theta), \quad \text{where} \quad \theta = 75°, 165°, 255°, 345°.$$

They can be changed, at least approximately, to rectangular form by using a table of trigonometric functions (Table IV).

These four fourth roots are represented graphically in Figure 8.6 by the four points P_1, P_2, P_3, and P_4, which lie at equal intervals on the circumference of a circle of radius $\sqrt{2}$ and with center at the origin.

EXERCISES

Find the following roots and represent the results (a) *in polar form;* (b) *in rectangular form;* (c) *graphically:*

1. Square roots of $64(\cos 240° + i\sin 240°)$.

2. Cube roots of $64(\cos 180° + i\sin 180°)$.

3. Sixth roots of $32\sqrt{2}(1 + i)$.   **7.** Square roots of -1.

4. Fourth roots of $8 - 8i\sqrt{3}$.   **8.** Fourth roots of 1.

5. Square roots of $1 - i$.   **9.** Sixth roots of 1.

6. Square roots of $-1 + i\sqrt{3}$.   **10.** Cube roots of $-8i$.

Any polynomial of degree n *with complex numbers as coefficients has exactly* n *complex zeros. Find all the roots of each of the following equations:*

11. $x^5 - 1 = 0$.   **13.** $x^3 - 64 = 0$.   **15.** $x^4 = i\sqrt{3} - 1$.

12. $x^8 - 1 = 0$.   **14.** $x^3 - 64i = 0$.   **16.** $x^6 + 64i = 0$.

Find all complex numbers which are zeros of the function:

17. $x^2 + 4 - 4i$.   **18.** $x^3 - 4 + 4i\sqrt{3}$.

19. If n is a positive integer, show that the nth roots of any complex number $(a + bi)$ are equally spaced on the circumference of a circle of radius $\sqrt[2n]{a^2 + b^2}$ in the complex plane.

★20. Show that $(x + y)(x + \omega y)(x + \omega^2 y) = x^3 + y^3$, where ω and ω^2 are the two imaginary cube roots of unity.

★21. Show that

$$(x + y + z)(x + \omega y + \omega^2 z)(x + \omega^2 y + \omega z) = x^3 + y^3 + z^3 - 3xyz,$$

where ω and ω^2 are the two imaginary cube roots of unity.

MISCELLANEOUS EXERCISES

Write in the form (a + bi)*:*

1. $(2 + 2i) + (4 - 4i\sqrt{3})$.

2. $(2 + 2i) - (4 - 4i\sqrt{3})$.

3. $(2 + 2i)(4 - 4i\sqrt{3})$.

4. $(2 + 2i)/(4 - 4i\sqrt{3})$.

5. $(2 + 2i)^3$.

6. $(2 + 2i)^{-3}$.

7. $(2 + 2i)^{\frac{1}{3}}$.

8. $|\, 2 + 2i\, |$.

9. $|\, (2 + 2i) + (4 - 4i\sqrt{3})\, |$.

10. $|\, 2 + 2i\, | + |\, 4 - 4i\sqrt{3}\, |$.

11. $|\, (2 + 2i)(4 - 4i\sqrt{3})\, |$.

12. $|\, 2 + 2i\, | \cdot |\, 4 - 4i\sqrt{3}\, |$.

Suppose z *denotes a complex number* (a + bi), *and* $\bar{z}$ *denotes its conjugate. For each of the following statements, tell whether it is true or false, and why:*

13. $z + \bar{z}$ is real.

14. $z - \bar{z}$ is real.

15. $z\bar{z}$ is real.

16. z^2 is real.

17. $|\, z\, |^2 = |\, z^2\, |$.

18. $|\, z\, | = |\, \bar{z}\, |$.

19. $\overline{(\bar{z})} = z$.

20. $|\, z\, | = |\, iz\, |$.

21. $\sqrt{|\, z\, |} = |\, \sqrt{z}\, |$.

22. $|\, z_1 + z_2\, | = |\, z_1\, | + |\, z_2\, |$.

23. A real number a can be considered as the complex number $(a + 0i)$. Prove that $|\, a\, |$ as defined in § 8-3 then equals $|\, a\, |$ as defined in § 1-3.

★24. If $z = r(\cos \theta + i \sin \theta)$ and $\theta = 4\pi t$, show that (**a**) the imaginary part of z, (**b**) the real part of z, undergoes simple harmonic motion.

CHAPTER 9

TRIGONOMETRY

9-1 Right Triangles

Let ABC be a right triangle with right angle at C and with sides of length a, b, c opposite the respective vertices (Figure 9.1). It is usual to denote the angles, as well as the vertices, by A, B, and C, since there is seldom any danger of confusion. The angles are considered positive and less than 180°. By placing angle A in standard position, it is evident from the definitions of the trigonometric functions that

$$\sin A = \frac{a}{c}; \quad \cos A = \frac{b}{c}; \quad \tan A = \frac{a}{b}. \tag{1a}$$

Similar formulas hold for B:

$$\sin B = \frac{b}{c}; \quad \cos B = \frac{a}{c}; \quad \tan B = \frac{b}{a}. \tag{1b}$$

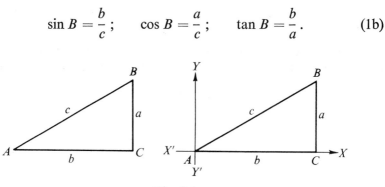

Fig. 9.1

This can be argued by symmetry. Alternatively, recall from geometry that in any triangle the sum of the angles is 180°; hence, in a right triangle the sum of the two acute angles (here A and B) is 90°, and by (11)–(13) of § 7-5 the cosine of one equals the sine of the other and the tangent of one equals the cotangent of the other.

232

These relationships can be summarized by saying that in a right triangle, the *sine* of an acute angle is the ratio of the *side opposite* that angle to the *hypotenuse*; the *cosine* is the ratio of the *adjacent side* to the *hypotenuse*; and the *tangent* is the ratio of the *opposite side* to the *adjacent side*. Historically, these relationships were originally used to define the trigonometric functions, with applications to nonacute angles coming later, but in this book it is convenient to develop (1a) and (1b) as a consequence of the more general definition. Another useful form of (1a) and (1b) is $a = c \sin A$, $b = c \cos A$, and so on.

These properties of a right triangle can be applied to solve various practical problems.

EXAMPLE. A post is located on the north bank of a river which flows due east. A man stands on the other bank, directly opposite the post. He walks 100 feet along the bank, and then finds that he must look 28° east of north to see the post. How wide is the river?

Solution. In Figure 9.2, ACP is a right angle; angle PAN is 28°. Angles PAN and CAP are complementary, so $\alpha = 90° - 28° = 62°$. Then

$$\tan \alpha = \frac{x}{100} \; ;$$

$$x = 100 \tan \alpha$$

$$= 100 \cdot 1.881.$$

$$x \approx 190 \text{ feet.}$$

The answer is stated to only two significant digits since the given angle is only of this degree of accuracy (§ 7-3).

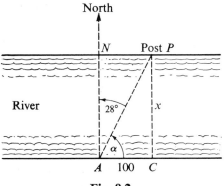

Fig. 9.2

Other, general, triangles can often be handled by subdividing them into right triangles.

The **angle of elevation** of an object is the angle above the horizontal at which the object appears; the **angle of depression** is a similar angle below the horizontal.

The distinction between exact and approximate numbers (§ 1-9) is particularly important in trigonometry. Any quantities which are measured are necessarily approximate. The accuracy of the approximation may be indicated verbally ("to the nearest foot"), by scientific notation, or by the appearance of decimal expressions such as 0.300. If the accuracy is not specified, it must be inferred from the context or from the accuracy of measurement which would be realistic for the type of quantity in question. Each of these alternatives appears in exercises in this chapter. Thus in the preceding example, the given angle is stated to the nearest degree; hence the answer is rounded to two significant digits, which is the corresponding accuracy (§ 7-3 and § 7-6).

Quantities which are not measured may be either exact or approximate. Accuracy of approximation may be indicated in the same general ways as for measured quantities. On the other hand, if the given data are small whole numbers, they are usually intended as exact. Thus in speaking of a right triangle with sides 3, 4, and 5, one means a theoretically specified triangle with exact sides.

EXERCISES

Find the other angles and sides of a right triangle ABC (C = 90°) *in which:*

1. $a = 3.0, c = 5.0$.
2. $a = 15.0, b = 8.0$.
3. $b = 4, c = 6$.
4. $b = 16, c = 20$.
5. $a = 3.347, b = 5.120$.
6. $a = 16.80, c = 25.79$.
7. $b = 0.02672, c = 0.1078$.
8. $b = 0.1823, a = 0.1982$.
9. $A = 29° 0', c = 5$.
10. $B = 56° 0', c = 8$.
11. $B = 11° 26', c = 0.2300$.
12. $A = 72° 49', c = 0.01600$.
13. $A = 35° 0', a = 7$.
14. $B = 70° 0', b = 21$.
15. $B = 32° 18', a = 31.2$.
16. $A = 80° 24', b = 0.0515$.

17. A ladder 20.0 feet long is leaning against a vertical wall and makes an angle of 20° 0' with the wall. Find how far the ladder's foot and top are from the bottom of the wall if the ground is level.

18. A guy wire 40.0 feet long is attached to a pole 30.0 feet above the level ground. **(a)** How far from the foot of the pole will the wire reach the ground? **(b)** What angle does the wire make with the pole?

19. An airplane is 8000 feet above level country, and its shadow is 6000 feet from the point directly underneath. Find the angle of elevation of the sun.

20. A swimming pool is 100.0 feet long, 4.0 feet deep at one end, 12.0 feet deep at the other end, with a uniformly sloping bottom. Find the length as measured along the bottom, and the angle to the horizontal at which the bottom slopes.

21. The shadow of a vertical pole on level ground is 43 feet long when the sun is 42° above the horizon. How tall is the pole?

22. A man on top of a mountain 3000 feet above a level plain looks 22° 16' below the horizontal to see a landmark on the plain. Neglecting curvature of the earth, find the distance between the man and the landmark.

23. Find the angle between a diagonal of a cube and an edge of the cube.

24. In a circle of radius 15 inches, what is the length of a chord subtending a central angle of 36° 28'?

25. Treating the earth as a sphere of radius 3960 miles, **(a)** how far from the earth's axis is a point on the surface at latitude 42° 18'? **(b)** how far above the earth's surface is a satellite which is directly overhead at a point at latitude 42° 18', if the satellite and a point on the earth's equator are at equal distances from the earth's axis?

26. At a point 310 feet away from the base on level ground (measured to the nearest foot), the angle of elevation of the top of a building is 17° 0' and the angle of elevation of the top of a sign on the front of the building is 22° 37'. Find how far the sign extends above the building.

9-2   Vectors

A quantity which has both magnitude and direction is called a **vector.** Such quantities occur frequently in physics and its various applications. Examples are forces, velocities, and accelerations. A vector is represented graphically by a directed line segment, whose length represents the magnitude of the vector and whose direction represents the direction of the vector. No initial point is specified for a vector.

For example, a force of 40 pounds upward is represented by a line segment of length 40 (to whatever scale is chosen), with direction upward, regardless of the point at which the force is applied. An airplane velocity of 400 miles per hour northeast is represented by a line of length 400, directed 45° east of north. In this connection one distinguishes between **speed** and **velocity:** speed is the magnitude of the velocity vector. Different directions mean different velocities even if the speeds are the same.

The **vector sum** (for short, **sum**), or **resultant,** of two vectors $\overrightarrow{OA}$ and $\overrightarrow{OB}$ is defined as the diagonal $\overrightarrow{OC}$ of the parallelogram $OACB$ (Figure 9.3). Experience with velocities, accelerations, and so on shows that if two effects of the same character are represented by vectors then their combined effect is represented by the resultant of the two vectors.

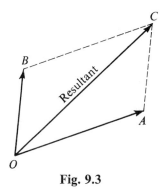

Fig. 9.3

EXAMPLE 1.   A ship is headed west at 20.0 knots (nautical miles per hour) crossing a current which carries the ship due north at 4.0 knots. What is the actual course and speed of the ship's motion?

Solution.   The ship's velocity through the water is represented by vector $\overrightarrow{OA}$ in Figure 9.4 and the current by vector $\overrightarrow{OB}$. The actual ship's motion is

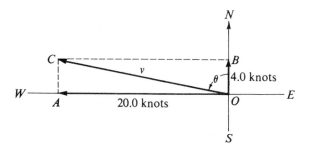

Fig. 9.4

the resultant $\overrightarrow{OC}$. Here the two vectors are perpendicular, so the speed, which is the magnitude v of their resultant, can be found by the Pythagorean theorem:

$$v = \sqrt{(20.0)^2 + (4.0)^2} \approx 20.4, \text{ in knots.}$$

The direction or "course" is conveniently measured by the angle θ west of north. As in the previous section,

$$\tan \theta = \frac{20.0}{4.0} = 5.0; \qquad \theta \approx 79°.$$

The ship is therefore making good 20.4 knots on course 79° west of north ("N 79° W" or "W 11° N").

In the case of an airplane, the magnitude and direction of the motion through the air are called the "air speed" and "heading"; the magnitude and direction of the resultant of this motion and the wind are called the "ground speed" and "course." In the case of a ship, the magnitude and direction of the resultant of the current and the ship's motion through the water are called the "speed made good" and the "course made good."

It should be noted that the parallelogram law for addition of vectors is the same as the law for the graphic addition of complex numbers (§ 8-4). Hence vectors are often represented by complex numbers, especially complex numbers in polar form (§ 8-3).

The inverse process to the addition of vectors is the decomposition or **resolution** of a vector into two vectors whose sum is the given vector. These vectors are then called **components** of the given vector. The components are not unique unless something further is specified, such as their directions. If, as is common, one seeks components parallel to the x-axis and the y-axis, they are called the **x-component** and **y-component** respectively. Another commonly sought result is the horizontal component and the vertical component of a vector which lies in a vertical plane. The preceding statements are phrased for vectors lying in a plane; if we were concerned with unique decompositions of vectors in three-dimensional space, there would be three components for each vector.

EXAMPLE 2.   An automobile weighing 3100 pounds stands on a road which makes an angle of 8° with the horizontal. Disregarding friction, what force f parallel to the road is required to hold the automobile stationary?

Solution.   The automobile's weight is a vector directed toward the center of the earth, that is, directly downward ($\overrightarrow{OW}$ in Figure 9.5). This can be resolved into components $\overrightarrow{OA}$ and $\overrightarrow{OB}$ respectively parallel and perpendicular

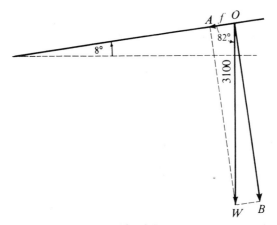

Fig. 9.5

to the road surface. But the component $\overrightarrow{OB}$ perpendicular to the road does not tend to move the automobile either uphill or downhill; only $\overrightarrow{OA}$ does that. In triangle OAW,

$$\frac{f}{3100} = \cos 82°;$$

$$f = 3100 \cos 82° = 431.5^+.$$

If the given data are assumed accurate to two significant digits, corresponding to the nearest degree of angle, then the required force is approximately 430 pounds.

If components in mutually perpendicular directions (such as x- and y-components) are found for two or more vectors, they may be added to obtain the components of the resultant, just as the real and imaginary parts of complex numbers are added.

EXERCISES

1. An aircraft heads due south at 400 miles per hour. Wind is blowing from the west at 80 miles per hour. In what direction and at what speed does the aircraft move relative to the ground?

2. A swimmer heads straight across a river at $1\frac{1}{2}$ miles per hour. The current is 1 mile per hour downstream. **(a)** Find the speed and direction of his motion. **(b)** How far is he carried downstream before reaching the other bank if the river is 300 feet wide?

3. A ship is traveling at 12.0 knots on a course 30° 0′ east of north. Find the north-south and east-west components of its velocity.

4. An automobile is accelerated 4.0 feet per second per second forward at a sharp dip in an otherwise level road. The acceleration of gravity, 32.0 feet per second per second, acts downward on the driver. Find the magnitude and direction of the resultant acceleration on the driver.

5. An aircraft can fly at 450 knots through the air. Wind is blowing from the north at 30 knots. **(a)** In what direction should the aircraft be headed in order that its course over the ground will be due west? **(b)** What then will be its ground speed?

6. A swimmer can swim $1\frac{1}{2}$ miles per hour. If the river current flows **(a)** 1 mile per hour, **(b)** 2 miles per hour, in what direction should he head in order to reach the other bank directly opposite his starting place?

7. A train weighing 2000 tons is on a grade which rises 4.00 feet in every 100.00 feet of horizontal distance. Neglecting friction, how much force is needed to keep the train from rolling downhill?

*8. Find the vector sum of the three following forces, all of which are in the same plane: one of 30 pounds directly downward, one of 40 pounds acting upward to the left at 45° above the horizontal, and one of 20 pounds acting downward to the right at 15° below the horizontal.

*9. One force is 4.24 pounds directly upward. Another is 2.86 pounds downward to the left at 30° 0′ from the vertical. Find a third force such that the vector sum of the three is zero (that is, the forces are in equilibrium).

*10. Find the magnitude and direction of the resultant of vectors which are represented by the two complex numbers **(a)** $(2 + 3i)$ and $(-5 + i)$; **(b)** $2(\cos 270° + i \sin 270°)$ and $3(\cos 180° + i \sin 180°)$.

9-3   The Law of Sines

The procedures of § 9-1, although suitable for right triangles, do not apply directly to oblique triangles (that is, triangles without a right angle). The following relation is often useful in such cases.

Law of Sines.   *In any triangle, the sines of the angles are proportional to the lengths of the sides opposite them.*

In symbols, denoting the angles by A, B, C, and the sides opposite them by a, b, c respectively,

$$\frac{\sin A}{a} = \frac{\sin B}{b} = \frac{\sin C}{c}. \tag{2}$$

Proof. We shall prove the first of the equalities in (2); the others follow in similar manner. Two cases must be considered, according as (i) both of the angles A and B are acute or (ii) one is obtuse (that is, between 90° and 180°), say A; not more than one angle can be obtuse since the sum of the angles of any triangle is 180°.

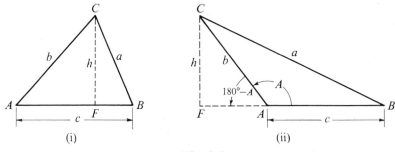

Fig. 9.6

As in Figure 9.6, let h denote the length of the perpendicular CF from C to the side AB (extended if necessary). In case (i), AFC and BFC are right triangles and the methods of § 9-1 show that $h = b \sin A$ and $h = a \sin B$. Equating these,

$$b \sin A = a \sin B.$$

Then the first part of (2) follows by dividing both members by ab.

In case (ii), again $h = a \sin B$, while from triangle AFC we get

$$h = b \sin (180° - A)$$
$$= b \sin A \qquad \text{by § 7-6.}$$

The rest of the proof proceeds as in case (i).

The sides and angles of a triangle are called **parts** of the triangle. If two angles of a triangle are known, the third angle can immediately be found since the sum of the angles of a triangle is always 180°. Notice that the three angles determine the shape but not the size of a triangle. If any three parts, not all of which are angles, of a triangle are given, then the remaining parts can be found (provided there *is* any triangle with these parts); finding them is called **solving the triangle.**

EXAMPLE 1.   Solve the triangle in which $a = 6$, $B = 15°$, $C = 120°$.

Solution. $A = 180° - (B + C) = 45°.$

$$\frac{\sin A}{a} = \frac{\sin C}{c}; \quad c = \frac{a \sin C}{\sin A} = \frac{6 \cdot \frac{1}{2}\sqrt{3}}{\frac{1}{2}\sqrt{2}} = 3\sqrt{6} \approx 7.347.$$

$$\frac{\sin A}{a} = \frac{\sin B}{b}; \quad b = \frac{a \sin B}{\sin A} = \frac{6 \sin 15°}{\frac{1}{2}\sqrt{2}} = 6\sqrt{2} \sin 15°.$$

The value of b can be calculated either by finding the exact value of $\sin 15°$ as in (15) of § 7-5 or by using Table IV; it would also be possible to write $b = a \sin B \csc A$. By the first method,

$$b = 6\sqrt{2} \cdot \tfrac{1}{4}(\sqrt{6} - \sqrt{2}) = 3(\sqrt{3} - 1) \approx 2.20.$$

Thus the answer is $A = 45°$, $b \approx 2.20$, $c \approx 7.347$.

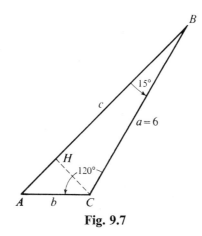

Fig. 9.7

One cannot check by substitution, as in equations. Instead a computation should be made which will tie together the answers obtained, yet repeat the previous computation as little as possible, if at all, so as to minimize the danger of repeating a mistake. A good check in this example is obtained by noting that in Figure 9.7,

$$7.347 \approx c = AH + HB$$
$$= b \cos A + a \cos B$$
$$= 2.20 \cos 45° + 6 \cos 15°$$
$$\approx 1.56^- + 5.795$$
$$= 7.35.$$

The agreement is within the accuracy expected from rounding off.

The particular method of checking in this example is less important than the general principle involved: Since the check calculation involves all the parts of the answer and uses different functions than the solution, it would be highly likely to detect any error.

EXAMPLE 2.   Solve the triangle in which $A = 45°$, $a = 4$, $c = 5$.

Solution. $\dfrac{\sin A}{a} = \dfrac{\sin C}{c}$; $\sin C = \dfrac{c \sin A}{a} = \dfrac{5 \cdot \frac{1}{2}\sqrt{2}}{4} \approx 0.8839.$

$$C = 62° \, 7' \quad \text{or} \quad 117° \, 53'$$

$$A + C = 107° \, 7' \quad \text{or} \quad 162° \, 53'$$

$$B = 180° - (A + C) = 72° \, 53' \quad \text{or} \quad 17° \, 7'$$

$$b = \frac{a \sin B}{\sin A} \approx 5.405 \quad \text{or} \quad 1.665$$

The answers may be checked as in Example 1. Evidently there are *two* triangles, ABC_1 and ABC_2 in Figure 9.8, which satisfy the given conditions.

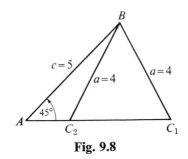

Fig. 9.8

If two sides and the angle opposite one of them are given, as in Example 2, there may be two, one, or no triangles satisfying these conditions. This depends on the size of the angle and the relative sizes of the two sides, as can be seen by the geometrical construction illustrated in Figure 9.9.

If the angles are ones for which the exact values of the trigonometric

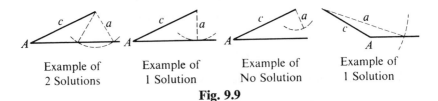

Example of   Example of   Example of   Example of
2 Solutions   1 Solution   No Solution   1 Solution

Fig. 9.9

functions cannot be easily found, it may be convenient to use Table III (logarithms of trigonometric functions) in the computation.

Historical Note. The Law of Sines was known in substance to PTOLEMY (about 150 B.C.).

EXERCISES

Solve the triangles, given:

1. $a = 20$, $B = 45°$, $C = 30°$.

2. $b = \frac{1}{2}$, $A = 75°$, $C = 60°$.

3. $c = 12$, $A = 30°$, $C = 135°$.

4. $b = 100$, $B = 120°$, $A = 45°$.

5. $a = 18.60$, $A = 19° \, 20'$, $B = 63° \, 50'$.

6. $a = 428.0$, $B = 69° \, 0'$, $C = 34° \, 30'$.

7. $b = 0.04672$, $A = 81° \, 47'$, $B = 40° \, 4'$.

8. $c = 0.9027$, $B = 39° \, 26'$, $A = 41° \, 34'$.

9. $b = 5$, $c = 3$, $C = 30°$.

10. $a = 7\frac{1}{2}$, $b = 8$, $A = 60°$.

11. $b = 5$, $a = 2$, $A = 30°$.

12. $b = 8$, $c = 5$, $C = 60°$.

13. $b = 1$, $a = 2$, $B = 30°$.

14. $b = 3000$, $c = 2000$, $B = 120° \, 0'$.

15. $a = 0.075$, $c = 0.100$, $A = 135°$.

16. $a = 19.6$, $b = 9.9$, $B = 150°$.

17. Discuss what happens to the Law of Sines in the special case of a right triangle.

18. Discuss whether the Law of Sines could be applied if all the three given parts of a triangle were sides.

19. If one side and two angles are given, what difference does it make whether or not one of the angles is opposite the given side?

20. Give a numerical example, and illustrate the corresponding geometrical construction, of a triangle with one side and two angles given such that **(a)** the angle opposite the given side is acute and there is just one solution; **(b)** the angle opposite the given side is acute and there is no solution; **(c)** the angle opposite the given side is obtuse and there is just one solution.

21. If two sides and one angle are given, can there ever be **(a)** two solutions? **(b)** no solution?

22. A tree stands upright on a slope which is inclined 12° to the horizontal. The tree casts a shadow 32 feet long directly up the slope when the angle of elevation of the sun is 60°. How tall is the tree?

23. An east-west line 2000 feet long is measured on one bank of a river. From the western end of this line a post on the other bank bears 56° 18′ east of north. From the other end of the line, the post bears 7° 0′ east of north. Find (**a**) the angle between the two lines of sight to the post; (**b**) the width of the river.

24. A horizontal roadbed is cut into the side of a mountain. The roadbed is 40 feet wide and the outer edge is at the original surface. The mountainside slopes at 30° to the horizontal and the side of the cut slopes at 45°. (**a**) How wide is the whole cut, measured along the original surface? (**b**) What is the greatest vertical depth of the cut below the original surface?

25. An airplane navigator sights one landmark as being directly ahead 30° below the horizontal, and another landmark as being directly ahead 60° below the horizontal. The two landmarks are 10,000 yards apart. (**a**) How far is the airplane from the further landmark? (**b**) What is the altitude of the airplane?

26. A pole on level ground leans 7° 22′ away from the vertical and directly away from the sun. The sun's elevation is 42° 17′ and the pole's shadow is 38.60 feet long. Find the length of the pole.

27. A pole 60 feet high leans directly toward or away from the sun. Its shadow on level ground is 45 feet long when the sun's elevation is 45°. Find the amount and direction of inclination of the pole.

28. A pole 60 feet high leans directly toward or away from the sun. Its shadow on level ground is 210 feet long when the sun's elevation is 15°. Find the amount and direction of inclination of the pole.

29. A television transmitter tower 230 feet high subtends an angle of 30° 0′ at a point 300 feet down hill from the base of the tower. Find the angle at which the hill slopes.

30. From an airplane, two ships are sighted to the north directly abeam of the airplane, at angles of depression of 30° and 75° respectively. If the airplane is at 20,000 feet altitude, how far apart are the ships?

31. An airplane heads due west at 400 knots air speed. A wind of 25 knots is expected to blow from variable directions. (**a**) Can it ever blow the airplane off course by exactly 8°? If so, what is the resulting ground speed? (**b**) What is the most it can blow the airplane off course?

32. One boy can pull with a force of 50 pounds and another boy with a force of 25 pounds. **(a)** Can they produce a resultant force whose direction differs from that of the 50-pound force by exactly 20°? If so, what is the magnitude of the resultant? **(b)** What is the greatest possible difference in angle between the resultant and the 50-pound force?

9-4 The Law of Cosines

In a triangle with angles A, B, C, and sides a, b, c opposite them respectively,

$$a^2 = b^2 + c^2 - 2bc \cos A. \tag{3a}$$

This is called the **Law of Cosines.** Similarly,

$$b^2 = a^2 + c^2 - 2ac \cos B, \tag{3b}$$

$$c^2 = a^2 + b^2 - 2ab \cos C. \tag{3c}$$

Proof of (3a). Place the triangle so that the angle A is in standard position (§ 7-1), as in Figure 9.10. The coordinates of B are obviously $(c, 0)$. By § 7-2, the coordinates of C are $(b \cos A, b \sin A)$. Applying the formula for the distance between two points (§ 4-5), the square of the distance between points B and C is given by

$$\begin{aligned}
a^2 &= (b \cos A - c)^2 + (b \sin A - 0)^2 \\
&= b^2 \cos^2 A - 2bc \cos A + c^2 + b^2 \sin^2 A \\
&= b^2 (\cos^2 A + \sin^2 A) + c^2 - 2bc \cos A \\
&= b^2 + c^2 - 2bc \cos A \qquad \text{by (3) of § 7-4.}
\end{aligned}$$

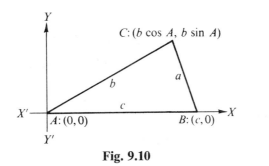

Fig. 9.10

The Law of Cosines involves three sides and an angle. It can therefore be applied if the known parts of a triangle are the *three* sides or are two sides and the angle *included* between them. Notice that the Law of Sines cannot be applied in such cases since there would be more than one unknown quantity. If two sides and the angle *opposite* one of them are given, then either the Law of Sines or the Law of Cosines can be applied, but the Law of Sines is usually more convenient unless the only part required to be found is the third side. If one side and two angles are given, then the Law of Sines can be applied, but the Law of Cosines cannot since it would involve too many unknowns at once.

The Law of Cosines, unlike the Law of Sines, has a form inconvenient for logarithmic calculations. Other formulas, convenient for this purpose, have been developed* but are now relatively little used. Instead, computing machines are normally employed if the amount of computation is burdensome.

EXAMPLE. Solve the triangle in which $A = 60°$, $b = 10$, $c = 3$.

Solution.   By (3a), $a^2 = 10^2 + 3^2 - 2 \cdot 10 \cdot 3 \cdot \cos 60°$

$$= 100 + 9 - 60 \cdot \tfrac{1}{2}$$

$$= 79.$$

$$a = \sqrt{79} \approx 8.888.$$

Then another angle can be found either by the Law of Cosines or by the Law of Sines.

$$b^2 = a^2 + c^2 - 2ac \cos B;$$

$$\cos B = \frac{a^2 + c^2 - b^2}{2ac} = \frac{79 + 9 - 100}{6\sqrt{79}} = -\frac{2\sqrt{79}}{79} \approx -0.2250.$$

As an angle of a triangle, B must be between $0°$ and $180°$. In this example, $\cos B$ is negative, so B is in the second quadrant:

$$B = 103° \, 0'.$$

$$C = 180° - (A + B) = 17° \, 0'.$$

As a check, C can be computed by the Law of Sines or Law of Cosines.

EXERCISES

In a triangle:

  1. Find a if $b = c = 4$ and $A = 30°$.

  2. Find b if $a = \tfrac{1}{2}$, $c = \tfrac{1}{4}$, $B = 60°$.

  3. Find A if $a = 100\sqrt{2}$, $b = 100$, $c = 200$.

* For a treatment of such formulas, see for instance J. B. Rosenbach, E. A. Whitman, and D. Moskovitz's *Essentials of Trigonometry*, second edition (Ginn, Boston, 1961).

4. Find C if $a = 2$, $b = 5$, $c = 6$.

5. Find c if $a = 5$, $b = 7$, $B = 60°$.

Solve the triangles, given:

6. $a = 2$, $b = 3$, $C = 60°$.

7. $A = 120°$, $b = 3$, $c = 4$.

8. $B = 45° \, 0'$, $a = 10.00$, $c = 8.00$.

9. $a = 0.0200$, $c = 0.0300$, $B = 30° \, 0'$.

10. $a = 4$, $b = 5$, $c = 7$.

11. $a = 20$, $b = 30$, $c = 40$.

12. $a = 0.200$, $b = 0.300$, $c = 0.250$.

13. $a = 34$, $b = 30$, $c = 16$.

★**14.** $a = 17.68$, $b = 29.03$, $C = 27° \, 34'$.

★**15.** $a = 34.71$, $b = 19.43$, $c = 24.86$.

16. Find the form to which the formulas (3a), (3b), (3c) reduce in a right triangle where $C = 90°$.

17. Find the resultant of the vectors represented by the complex numbers $6(\cos 17° + i \sin 17°)$ and $5(\cos 152° + i \sin 152°)$.

18. Find the resultant of a force of 100 pounds directed straight upward and a force of 60 pounds directed downward at 60° to the vertical.

19. If the lengths of the sides of an isosceles triangle are a, a, and b, prove $b^2 = 2a^2(1 - \cos B)$.

20. Express the length of a chord of a circle as a function of the radius r and the central angle θ.

21. Points A and B are separated by a hill. From a point C on the same level as A and B, the angle between the lines of sight to A and to B are 45° apart. The distance CA is 6.0 miles and the distance CB is 9.0 miles. Find the straight line distance AB.

22. An airplane heads due west at 300 knots air speed. The wind blows from 20° east of north at 20 knots. Find the actual course and ground speed of the airplane.

23. An airplane is to be flown on course due west at 300 knots ground speed. The wind blows from 20° east of north at 20 knots. Find the necessary heading and air speed.

24. Two ships depart from a rendevous at the same time; one makes 20 knots on course 260° (measured clockwise from north) and the other makes 12 knots on course 150° (measured in the same way). Find **(a)** their distance apart, **(b)** the direction from the second to the first, after 2 hours.

25. A pilot is flying from airport X to airport Y, which are 200 miles apart. After traveling 80 miles he finds he has been blown 10° off course. Find **(a)** how much he should change course then; **(b)** how much farther than a straight line path he will have flown by the time he reaches Y.

26. Prove that in any triangle, $\cos \frac{1}{2}A = \frac{1}{2}\sqrt{\dfrac{(b+c)^2 - a^2}{bc}}$.

27. Prove that $b \sin C/\sin (C + \frac{1}{2}A)$ is the length of the internal bisector of angle A in a triangle.

9-5   Arcs and Areas

A radian was defined in § 7-1 to be an angle of such size that when it is placed at the center of a circle of radius r, it subtends an arc of length r. It follows by proportions that an angle of θ radians, similarly located, subtends an arc of length s given by

$$s = r\theta. \tag{4}$$

ILLUSTRATION 1.   To find the length of an arc of a circle of radius 100.0 centimeters which is subtended by a central angle of 32° 17′, first convert this angle to radians. By Table V, the angle is 0.563450 radian, which rounds off to 0.5634 radian if the angle is to the nearest minute. Setting $r = 100$ in (4), we have $s = 56.34$ centimeters.

Consider a point moving around a circle of radius r. The distance traveled per unit time is the speed v; the change in angle, in radians, per unit time is called the **angular speed** and is usually denoted by ω (read "omega"). From (4) it follows that

$$v = r\omega. \tag{5}$$

ILLUSTRATION 2.   Suppose a wheel is 3 feet in diameter and makes 100 revolutions per minute. Each revolution is 2π radians, so ω is 200π (radians) per minute, and r is $\frac{3}{2}$ feet. Hence the linear speed of a point on the periphery is given in feet per minute by

$$v = \tfrac{3}{2} \cdot 200\pi = 300\pi \approx 942.$$

Let us turn our attention now to areas. One learns early in mathematics that the area of a triangle is half the product of the base and the altitude. Given sufficient parts of the triangle, the previous sections show how to compute a base and altitude, so the area can be found. Special formulas, in convenient form to eliminate some of the intermediate steps, have been derived for various combinations of given parts. We shall develop only a sample one.*

In Figure 9.6 (page 240), the area K of the triangle is given by $K = \frac{1}{2}ch$. But, as remarked in connection with that figure, $h = b \sin A$. Hence

$$K = \tfrac{1}{2}bc \sin A. \tag{6}$$

Similar formulas may be written in terms of $\sin B$ and of $\sin C$.

Considering now areas in circles, the configuration (Figure 9.11) bounded by an arc of a circle and the radii to the ends of this arc is called a **sector** of the circle. The area of a sector is proportional to the angle between the radii. For the whole circle the area is πr^2 and the angle is 2π radians. Hence, if arc AB is subtended by angle θ and K_θ denotes the area of the sector AOB then $K_\theta : \theta = \pi r^2 : 2\pi$, or

$$K_\theta = \tfrac{1}{2}r^2\theta, \tag{7}$$

where the angle must be measured in radians.

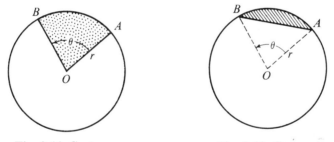

Fig. 9.11. Sector   Fig. 9.12. Segment

A **segment** of a circle is the figure bounded by an arc of the circle and the chord of this arc (that is, the straight line segment joining the two ends of the arc; see Figure 9.12). Just as was done for a sector, suppose arc AB is subtended by angle θ. Then the area K_s of the segment AB is given by the difference of the areas in (7) and (6):

$$K_s = \tfrac{1}{2}r^2\theta - \tfrac{1}{2}r^2 \sin \theta$$

or

$$K_s = \tfrac{1}{2}r^2(\theta - \sin \theta). \tag{8}$$

* For others, see J. B. Rosenbach, E. A. Whitman, and D. Moskovitz's *Essentials of Trigonometry*, second edition (Ginn, Boston, 1961), pp. 100 through 102.

ILLUSTRATION 3.   In a circle of radius 10 inches, consider a central angle θ of 32° 17′. By Illustration 1, this is 0.5634 radian. Hence by (7) the sector with this angle has area 28.17 square inches. By (8) and Table IV, the area of the segment with this angle is given in square inches by

$$K_s \approx \tfrac{1}{2} \cdot 100(0.5634 - 0.5341) = 1.46.$$

EXERCISES

1. Find the length of the arc, the area of the sector, and the area of the segment, if the central angle subtending them and the radius of the circle are respectively:

(a) $\tfrac{1}{12}\pi$, 6 inches;

(b) $\tfrac{1}{8}\pi$, 2 meters;

(c) $\tfrac{3}{4}\pi$, 4 miles;

(d) 75°, 5 feet;

(e) 29° 0′, 1.64 centimeters;

(f) 65° 19′, 0.04270 mile;

(g) 95° 4′, 0.200 yard;

(h) 217° 0′, 40.00 centimeters;

(i) 300°, 100 meters;

(j) 1°, 10 kilometers.

2. Find the central angle, both in radians and in degrees and minutes, which subtends an arc of the given length in a circle of the given radius:

(a) arc 30π inches, radius 300 inches;

(b) arc 0.01π foot, radius 0.02 foot;

(c) arc 16 yards, radius 64 yards;

(d) arc 150 centimeters, radius 40 centimeters.

3. Find the length of arc subtended at 1000 yards by an angle of (a) 1 radian; (b) 0.01 radian; (c) 1°; (d) 1′; (e) 1″.

4. Assuming the earth is a sphere of radius 3960 miles and rotates on its axis once every 24 hours, find (a) the number of miles in an arc of 1° on the equator of the earth; (b) the number of miles in an arc of 1′ on the equator of the earth; (c) the angular speed of rotation of the earth; (d) the linear speed, produced by the rotation, of a point on the earth's equator.

5. Find the area of a triangle, given: (a) $a = 2$, $b = 3$, $C = 70°$; (b) $b = 0.4$, $c = 0.5$, $A = 120°$.

6. The blades of an electric fan are 12 inches in diameter and make 1700 revolutions per minute. Find the linear speed, in feet per second, of the tips of the blades.

7. Find in radians per second the angular speed of the wheels of an automobile traveling 60 miles per hour if the tires have outside diameter 32 inches.

8. Find **(a)** the angular speed, in radians per minute, of the minute hand of a clock, and **(b)** the distance the tip of this hand travels in two hours if the hand is four inches long.

9. Find the angular speed, in radians per second, and the linear speed, in miles per hour, of the earth in its orbit around the sun, assuming the orbit is a circle of radius 93,000,000 miles and is traversed in 365 days.

10. The length of a highway curve, in the shape of an arc of a circle, is 0.1 mile and the direction of the highway changes 30°. Find the radius of the curve in feet.

11. A highway curve 400 feet long is in the shape of an arc of a circle of radius 2000 feet. Find, in degrees, the change of direction of the highway produced by this curve.

12. An electric motor which makes 3000 revolutions per minute has on its shaft a gear wheel of radius $\frac{1}{2}$ inch, which meshes with another gear wheel of radius 4 inches. Find the angular speed, in radians per second and in revolutions per minute, of the second gear wheel.

13. Find the area of the smaller segment of a circle cut off by a chord 8 centimeters long and 3 centimeters from the center.

14. A cylindrical tank has its axis horizontal, is 15 feet long, and has a diameter of 6 feet. It contains gasoline to a depth of 2 feet. How many cubic feet of gasoline does it contain? How many gallons? (1 cubic foot is 7.481 U.S. gallons.)

MISCELLANEOUS EXERCISES

Solve the triangles, given:

1. $A = 120°, B = 15°, c = 5$.
2. $A = 120°, b = 20, c = 50$.
3. $A = 120°, a = 3, c = 4$.
4. $B = 135°, C = 30°, c = 0.1000$.
5. $a = \frac{1}{2}, b = \frac{1}{4}, c = \frac{3}{8}$.
6. $b = 2.00 \cdot 10^4, a = 6.00 \cdot 10^4, c = 5.00 \cdot 10^4$.
7. $B = 30° \, 0', a = 20.0, c = 5.00$.
8. $B = 30°, b = 20, c = 5$.
9. $B = 30°, b = 20, c = 25$.
10. $C = 60°, a = 10, c = 9$.

11. Outline a method for finding the area of the triangle in **(a)** Exercise 1; **(b)** Exercise 2; **(c)** Exercise 5; **(d)** Exercise 8.

12. Find the resultant of the vectors represented by the complex numbers 4(cos 121° + i sin 121°) and 3(cos 181° + i sin 181°).

13. One force, of 100 pounds, acts vertically downward; another force, of 80 pounds, acts downward at 30° to the vertical. Find their resultant **(a)** by trigonometric solution of a triangle; **(b)** by finding the x-component and y-component of each and combining the components as in addition of complex numbers.

14. An airplane heads 58° west of north at 300 knots, but actually travels 67° west of north. The wind is blowing from 45° east of north. Find the wind speed and the ground speed of the airplane.

15. An airplane can fly at 400 knots air speed. The wind is 50 knots from the northeast. Find the proper heading to make good a course of due east, and find what the ground speed would then be.

16. An airplane is to be flown on a triangular search pattern with legs of 500 miles, 200 miles, and 450 miles. Neglecting curvature of the earth, find the direction of the third leg if the first leg is due north and the general direction of the second is easterly.

17. From an airplane on a straight course over a known point, a beacon 30 miles away is observed 70° to one side of the course. After traveling 50 miles, in what direction should the beacon be seen?

18. The centrifugal force f, tending to throw outward an object on the rim of a rotating circle, is given in pounds by $f = m\omega^2 r/g$, where ω is the angular speed in radians per second, m is the mass of the object in pounds, r is the radius in feet, and g is the acceleration of gravity, about 32 feet per second per second. **(a)** Express f as a function of m, r, and the linear speed v. **(b)** Find the centrifugal force if a 3000-pound automobile turns at 30 miles per hour (44 feet per second) a curve of radius 550 feet. **(c)** Find the angular velocity required so that on a circle of radius 10 feet a man with mass M pounds will be subject to a centrifugal force equal to M ("one g").

19. A circle of radius 3 has its center on the periphery of another circle of radius 3. Find the area common to the two circles.

*20. An airplane, which can fly at 700 knots, is 100 nautical miles due west of an unidentified object which is at the same altitude and is traveling 500 knots in direction 39° east of north. Find the course and length of time required for the airplane to intercept the object.

CHAPTER 10

LINEAR AND QUADRATIC SYSTEMS
OF EQUATIONS

10-1 Equations in Two Unknowns

The graph of a function was defined in § 4-6. Closely related is the **graph of an equation** in two unknowns such as x and y:

If a graph (or locus) in the xy *coordinate plane and an equation in two unknowns,* x *and* y, *are so related that*
  1. *the coordinates* (x, y) *of every point that lies on the graph satisfy the equation, and*
  2. *every solution of the equation corresponds to a point* (x, y) *on the graph,*

then the equation is said to represent the graph and the graph to represent the equation.

We shall consider first linear equations, and then quadratic equations, in two unknowns, following the pattern for equations in one unknown in Chapter 5.

An equation of the form

$$ax + by + c = 0, \tag{1}$$

where a, b, and c are arbitrary constants and a and b are not both zero, is called a **general equation of the first degree in x and y,** or a **general linear equation in x and y.** When b is zero, equation (1) reduces to a general linear equation in x as defined in § 5-2.

Any equation of the first degree in x and y—that is, any linear equation in x and y—can be put in the form (1) where a, b, and c are constants. The graph of any linear equation in x and y is a straight line. If $b \neq 0$ then (1) can be written $y = -\dfrac{a}{b}x - \dfrac{c}{b}$, which was shown in § 4-7 to have as its graph a straight line with slope $-a/b$. If $b = 0$ then

(1) reduces to $ax + c = 0$ or $x = -c/a$, which has for its graph the line parallel to the y-axis with x-intercept $-c/a$. Thus in either case the graph is a straight line as asserted.

It follows that any two distinct points are sufficient to determine the graph of a linear equation in x and y. In practice it is easier to draw the line accurately when the plotted points are not too close together. The coordinates of the points where the line crosses the coordinate axes (that is, the intercepts as in § 4-6) are usually easy to obtain. Let $x = 0$ and find y; then let $y = 0$ and find x. A third point should be used as a check.

EXAMPLE 1.   Draw the graph of the equation $2x + 3y + 6 = 0$.

Solution.   When $x = 0$, $y = -2$; when $y = 0$, $x = -3$. The third point used as a check is $x = 3$, $y = -4$. These corresponding values of x and y are shown in the following table:

$2x + 3y + 6 = 0$

x	y
0	-2
-3	0
3	-4

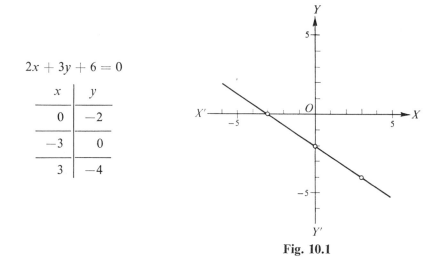

Fig. 10.1

A linear equation has an unlimited number of solutions; namely, the pairs of coordinates of the points on the line which is its graph are solutions of the equation. The same thing can be seen algebraically: if $b \neq 0$ in (1), choose values of x and obtain corresponding values of y; if $b = 0$, choose any value of y and obtain the value of x, which is constant.

An equation of the form

$$ax^2 + bxy + cy^2 + dx + ey + f = 0,$$

where a, b, c, d, e, and f are arbitrary constants, and where a, b, and c

are not all zero, is called a **general equation of the second degree in *x* and *y*** or a **general quadratic equation in *x* and *y*.**

An equation which can be put in the form displayed above with *a*, *b*, and *c* *not all zero* is called a **quadratic equation in *x* and *y*.** A quadratic equation of this form in which *d* and *e* are both zero is called a **pure quadratic equation.** As in the case of quadratic equations in one unknown, we shall limit our discussions and exercises to quadratic equations whose coefficients are real numbers.

ILLUSTRATIONS.   The following are quadratic equations in *x* and *y*:

$$x^2 + y^2 = 9; \qquad 4x^2 + 9y^2 = 36;$$

$$y^2 - 4x^2 = 9; \qquad y = 2x^2 + 3x - 4;$$

$$xy = 6; \qquad ax^2 + bxy + y^2 = 5;$$

$$2x^2 - 4xy - 3y^2 + x - 5 = 9.$$

In analytic geometry it is proved that *the graph of any quadratic equation in* x *and* y *which has real solutions is a* **parabola,** *a* **circle,** *an* **ellipse,** *a* **hyperbola,** *a* **pair of straight lines** *(which may coincide), or a* **point.** All these curves are grouped under the general name of **conic sections,** or simply **conics**—so called because they may be obtained as plane sections of a right circular cone (Figure 10.2).

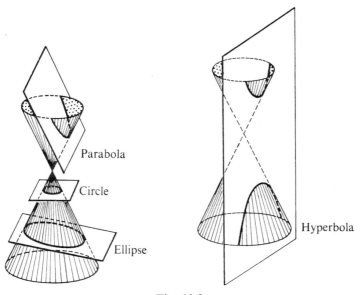

Parabola

Circle

Ellipse

Hyperbola

Fig. 10.2

The graph of $y = ax^2 + bx + c$ is a parabola; an example is shown in Figure 4.5 on page 96. The graphs of the other two curves, an ellipse and a hyperbola, are shown in the following examples.

EXAMPLE 2.   Plot the graph of the equation $25x^2 + 9y^2 = 225$.

Solution. First find the intercepts directly from the original equation. Thus, when $x = 0$, $y = \pm 5$; when $y = 0$, $x = \pm 3$.

Then solve for y in terms of x: $y = \pm \frac{5}{3}\sqrt{9 - x^2}$.

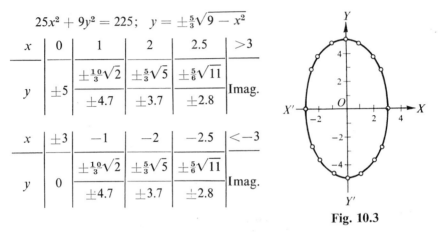

$$25x^2 + 9y^2 = 225; \quad y = \pm\tfrac{5}{3}\sqrt{9 - x^2}$$

x	0	1	2	2.5	>3
y	± 5	$\pm\frac{10}{3}\sqrt{2}$ / ± 4.7	$\pm\frac{5}{3}\sqrt{5}$ / ± 3.7	$\pm\frac{5}{6}\sqrt{11}$ / ± 2.8	Imag.

x	± 3	-1	-2	-2.5	<-3
y	0	$\pm\frac{10}{3}\sqrt{2}$ / ± 4.7	$\pm\frac{5}{3}\sqrt{5}$ / ± 3.7	$\pm\frac{5}{6}\sqrt{11}$ / ± 2.8	Imag.

Fig. 10.3

The graph is a closed curve and is called an **ellipse.**

EXAMPLE 3.   Plot the graph of the equation $xy = 6$.

Solution. Solve for y in terms of x: $y = 6/x$. There is no value of y for which $x = 0$ and no value of x for which $y = 0$. A set of corresponding values of x and y are shown in the accompanying table.

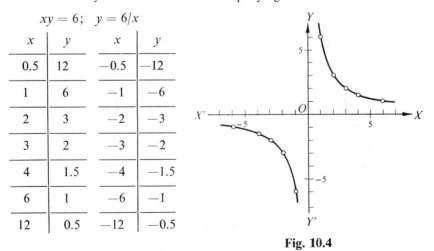

$$xy = 6; \quad y = 6/x$$

x	y	x	y
0.5	12	-0.5	-12
1	6	-1	-6
2	3	-2	-3
3	2	-3	-2
4	1.5	-4	-1.5
6	1	-6	-1
12	0.5	-12	-0.5

Fig. 10.4

The graph in Example 3 is an open curve and is called a **hyperbola**. It has two separate parts, called **branches**.

Historical Note. Early writers on conic sections include MENAECHMUS (about 350 B.C.), EUCLID (about 300 B.C.), and APOLLONIUS (about 220 B.C.). The latter wrote a systematic treatise of some four hundred theorems on this subject. KEPLER (about 1610) stated that the planets move in elliptical orbits. The projective geometry of DESARGUES (about 1640) and PASCAL (about 1650) gave us new theorems in which conics are involved. The analytical treatment of conics is due to such men as FERMAT (about 1635) and PASCAL (about 1637).

EXERCISES

Write in the standard form $ax + by + c = 0$, *if possible, and give a set of values for* a, b, *and* c*:*

1. $y = 3x - 2$.

2. $y - 2 = x + 2$.

3. $y - k = m(x - h)$.

4. $Ay + (Bx - C) = (Ay + Bx) + C$.

5. $3y - 4x + 1 = 3(y - 4x + 1)$.

6. $(y - p)(y - q) = y^2 + x$.

Express in the form of a polynomial equated to zero, and describe as a linear equation, a quadratic equation, a pure quadratic equation, or an impossible equation:

7. $y^2 - x^2 = 2y$.

8. $y^2 - x^2 = (y - x)^2$.

9. $\dfrac{y}{x - y} + \dfrac{x}{x + y} = 0$.

10. $\dfrac{2y + 1}{y + 1} = \dfrac{6y + 5}{3y - 2}$.

11. $(y - x)^2 = (y + x)^2$.

12. $(x + y)^2 + 1 = (x - y)^2 + 4xy$.

Without graphing, find **(a)** *the* x-*intercept,* **(b)** *the* y-*intercept, of the graph of:*

13. $x - 2y + 3 = 0$.

14. $3x + 2y + 5 = 0$.

15. $3y - 2x = 6$.

16. $\frac{2}{3}y + \frac{3}{2}x = 12$.

17. $ax + by + c = 0$.

18. $x/a + y/b = 1$.

Graph, and name the type of graph:

19. $2x - 3y = 6$.

20. $5y - 2x = 20$.

21. $3x + 4y = 12$.

22. $3x + 4y = 0$.

23. $x^2 + y^2 = 4$.

24. $x^2 + 4y^2 = 36$.

25. $x^2 - 4y^2 = 36$.

26. $x^2 - 4y^2 = 0$.

27. $x^2 - 4y = 0$.

28. $x + 4y^2 = 9$.

29. $2y - 1 = 0$.

30. $3x + 5 = 0$.

31. $x^2 + (y - 2)^2 = 25$.

32. $(x - 2)^2 + (y + 1)^2 = 9$.

In each of the following exercises, graph the two equations on the same coordinate plane:

33. $x + 3y = 6,$ $x - 3y + 6 = 0.$

34. $2x - 5y = 10,$ $4x = 10y + 1.$

35. $2xy = 1,$ $2x + y = 1.$

10-2   Graphic Solution of Linear Systems

Now let us consider two or more linear equations in two unknowns, for instance,

$$\begin{cases} a_1x + b_1y + c_1 = 0, & (2) \\ a_2x + b_2y + c_2 = 0. & (3) \end{cases}$$

Two or more equations which are linear in x and y are said to form a **system of simultaneous linear equations** when each unknown represents the same number in all the equations. A **solution** of a system of simultaneous equations in two unknowns, x and y, is a pair of corresponding values of x and y which satisfy all of these equations at the same time. To **solve** such a system is to find all of its solutions.

We saw in the previous section that any equation of the form (2) has an unlimited number of solutions. Each solution of equation (2) corresponds to a point on a straight line which is the graph of the given equation. Similarly, each solution of equation (3) corresponds to a point on a second straight line, the graph of equation (3). Thus to find graphically the solution of a system of linear equations in two unknowns, plot the graphs of the equations on the same axes and to the same scale, and estimate the coordinates of the point of intersection. It can be seen that use of a different scale on the y-axis than on the x-axis does not change the coordinates of the points of intersection, nor does it change the fact that a linear equation represents a straight line graph. The graphic method will, in general, give the solution only approximately.

The equations of a system are called **consistent** if the system has a solution, **inconsistent** if the system has no solution. If the equations are consistent, they are called **dependent** if the set of solutions is not changed when some one of the equations is omitted; if none of the equations can be omitted without changing the set of solutions, the equations are called **independent.** The same adjective is applied to the system as a whole as it is to the equations.

For instance, if the lines that correspond to the equations of a linear system meet at only *one* point, the system has only *one* solution (Example 1). If there are just two equations, then omitting either equation leaves a single equation, which has an unlimited number of solutions; so, the set of solutions is changed. Thus, the system is consistent and independent.

If the lines coincide (Example 2), they have an unlimited number of solutions, and the solutions are not changed if one equation is omitted; thus the equations are consistent and dependent. If the lines are parallel (Example 3), then they have no point in common and the system is inconsistent.

If there are only two equations in a system of simultaneous linear equations, the alternatives just discussed exhaust the possibilities. However, if there are three or more equations then there is another way in which the equations can be inconsistent: even though *pairs* of the equations have a solution, the solution may be different for different pairs so that there is *no* set of values of the unknowns which satisfies *all* of the equations simultaneously. This is the case, for instance, if the system consists of three linear equations and their graphs form a triangle instead of intersecting in a single point (as, for instance, in the case of the equations $x = 1$, $y = 0$, $x + y = 5$).

EXAMPLE 1.   Solve graphically:
$$\begin{cases} x - 2y - 4 = 0, \\ 3x + 2y - 4 = 0. \end{cases}$$

Solution.

L_1: $x - 2y - 4 = 0$

x	0	4	-2
y	-2	0	-3

L_2: $3x + 2y - 4 = 0$

x	0	$1\frac{1}{3}$	-2
y	2	0	5

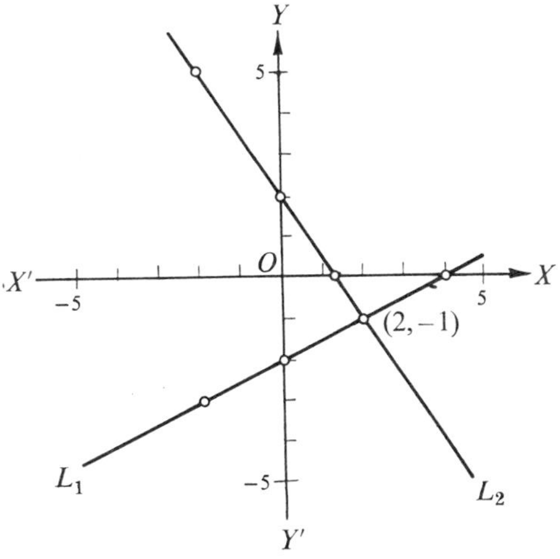

Fig. 10.5

The two lines appear to intersect at the point $(2, -1)$. Since the pair of values, 2 for x and -1 for y, satisfies both equations, it is the solution of the system.

EXAMPLE 2.   Solve graphically:

$$\begin{cases} 3x - y + 3 = 0, \\ 6x - 2y + 6 = 0. \end{cases}$$

Solution.

L_1: $3x - y + 3 = 0$

x	0	−1	1
y	3	0	6

L_2: $6x - 2y + 6 = 0$

x	0	−1	1
y	3	0	6

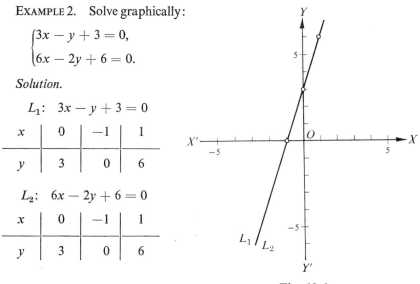

Fig. 10.6

The two lines are coincident; hence they have an unlimited number of points in common. Therefore the equations are consistent and dependent. These two equations are in fact equivalent (§ 5-4).

EXAMPLE 3.   Solve graphically:

$$\begin{cases} 2x + 3y + 6 = 0, \\ 2x + 3y - 4 = 0. \end{cases}$$

Solution.

L_1: $2x + 3y + 6 = 0$

x	0	−3	3
y	−2	0	−4

L_2: $2x + 3y - 4 = 0$

x	0	2	−4
y	$1\frac{1}{3}$	0	4

Fig. 10.7

The two lines appear parallel and in this particular case can be proved to be parallel by the use of similar triangles, by an algebraic test for the consistency of two linear equations, or by finding their slopes (§ 4-7). Therefore there is no solution, and the equations are inconsistent.

EXERCISES

Solve the following systems of linear equations graphically. Classify as consistent and dependent, consistent and independent, or inconsistent:

1. $\begin{cases} x + 2y = 0, \\ 3x - y = 7. \end{cases}$

2. $\begin{cases} 2x - y + 7 = 0, \\ y + x - 1 = 0. \end{cases}$

3. $\begin{cases} 2x - 3y - 1 = 0, \\ 4y - 3x + 3 = 0. \end{cases}$

4. $\begin{cases} y - 2x = -4, \\ 2y - x = -5. \end{cases}$

5. $\begin{cases} 3x + 2y + 1 = 0, \\ y - x = 6. \end{cases}$

6. $\begin{cases} 3y + 2x + 4 = 0, \\ y = 5x + 1. \end{cases}$

7. $\begin{cases} 2y - 3x + 2 = 0, \\ 5y - 2x + 15 = 0. \end{cases}$

8. $\begin{cases} r = 5s + 3, \\ s = 5r + 3. \end{cases}$

9. $\begin{cases} 2x - 3y = 4, \\ 6y = 4x + 1. \end{cases}$

10. $\begin{cases} 2x - 3y = 4, \\ 6y = 4x - 8. \end{cases}$

11. $\begin{cases} x = 2y + 3, \\ y = \frac{1}{2}x - \frac{3}{2}. \end{cases}$

12. $\begin{cases} x = 2y + 3, \\ 4y - 2x = 7. \end{cases}$

13. $\begin{cases} 0.1u - 3v = 8, \\ 0.2u - 4v = 24. \end{cases}$

14. $\begin{cases} x + y = 4, \\ \frac{1}{6}x - \frac{1}{2}y = \frac{2}{5}. \end{cases}$

15. $\begin{cases} x + 2y = 0, \\ 3x - y = 7, \\ 2x - 3y = 7. \end{cases}$

16. $\begin{cases} 2x - y + 7 = 0, \\ y + x - 1 = 0, \\ x + 2 = 0. \end{cases}$

17. $\begin{cases} x + 2y = 0, \\ 3x - y = 7, \\ 2x - 3y = 4. \end{cases}$

18. $\begin{cases} 2x - y + 7 = 0, \\ y + x - 1 = 0, \\ x - 2y = 6. \end{cases}$

10-3 Algebraic Solution of Linear Systems in Two Unknowns

As seen in the previous section, the results obtained by the graphic solution of a system of equations are, in general, only approximate. Precise solutions may be obtained algebraically. This is done by replacing the given system by another system derived from it so that the two systems are equivalent. By analogy with single equations in one unknown (§ 5-4), two systems of equations are called **equivalent** if the two systems have exactly the same solutions, no more and no less. The aim is to obtain an equivalent system in which one of the equations contains only one unknown. The values of this solitary unknown can then be found as in Chapter 5; the other unknowns are said to have been **eliminated.** The value found for the one unknown can then be substituted wherever that unknown appears. If there were only two unknowns originally, then only one remains and its value can be found as in Chapter 5. If there were more than two unknowns originally, the process can be repeated until all the unknowns have been determined one by one.

This raises the question: What changes in a system produce another system equivalent to it? From the definitions, it is evident that one such operation is (i) *replacing one of the equations of the system by another equation equivalent to it.* For instance, the equation $x + 3y = 5$ is equivalent to the equation $2x + 6y = 10$; so the following two systems are equivalent:

$$\begin{cases} 4x + 6y = 3, \\ x + 3y = 5; \end{cases} \qquad \begin{cases} 4x + 6y = 3, \\ 2x + 6y = 10. \end{cases}$$

Another operation which yields an equivalent system is (ii) *replacing one equation by a new equation which is obtained by adding a constant multiple of the members of another equation to the respective members of the specified equation.* For example, if we start with the system

$$\begin{cases} 4x + 6y = 3, \\ x + 3y = 5, \end{cases}$$

and add -2 times the members of the second equation to those of the first equation, we get the equivalent system

$$\begin{cases} 2x = -7, \\ x + 3y = 5. \end{cases}$$

This operation (ii) is sometimes described as "adding a multiple of another equation to the specified equation."

The operations (i) and (ii) can be combined into a single operation: (ii') *An equivalent system of equations is obtained when any equation of the system is replaced by the sum of a constant nonzero multiple of itself and a constant multiple of another equation of the system.* These operations provide the basis for the second of the following two methods of solution.

We shall show, by an example, how to solve a system of two linear equations in two unknowns by two **methods of elimination:**

      I. Elimination by substitution;

     II. Elimination by addition or subtraction.

In the method of elimination by substitution we first use one of the given equations to express one unknown (say, y) explicitly as an expression in the other (say, x). The unknown y may then be eliminated by using this expression in place of y (that is, by substituting for y) in the other given equation.

In the method of elimination by addition or subtraction we first choose multipliers for each equation such that in the new equations the coefficients of one of the unknowns will have the same numerical value. This unknown may then be eliminated by addition of the new equations if its coefficients are of opposite sign, or by subtraction if its coefficients are of the same sign. Subtraction can of course be expressed as an algebraic addition. Elimination by addition or subtraction is generally more convenient than by substitution, though substitution is logically more direct.

EXAMPLE.   Solve algebraically:
$$\begin{cases} 4x - 8y - 17 = 0, & (4) \\ 12x + 16y + 9 = 0. & (5) \end{cases}$$

Solution.

I.   *Elimination by substitution.*

Solve (4) for x in terms of y: $x = \frac{1}{4}(8y + 17)$.   (6)

Substitute (6) in (5): $12 \cdot \frac{1}{4}(8y + 17) + 16y + 9 = 0$.   (7)

Solve (7) for y: $24y + 51 + 16y + 9 = 0$; $y = -\frac{3}{2}$.

Substitute $y = -\frac{3}{2}$ in (4): $4x - 8(-\frac{3}{2}) - 17 = 0$.   (8)

Solve (8) for x: $x = \frac{5}{4}$.

Hence the solution of the given system is $x = \frac{5}{4}$, $y = -\frac{3}{2}$; also written in the form $(\frac{5}{4}, -\frac{3}{2})$.

Check.   Substitute $x = \frac{5}{4}$, $y = -\frac{3}{2}$ in (4) and (5):
$$4(\tfrac{5}{4}) - 8(-\tfrac{3}{2}) - 17 = 5 + 12 - 17 = 0;$$
$$12(\tfrac{5}{4}) + 16(-\tfrac{3}{2}) + 9 = 15 - 24 + 9 = 0.$$

II.   *Elimination by addition or subtraction.*

Multiply (4) by 3: $12x - 24y - 51 = 0$.   (9)

Rewrite (5): $12x + 16y + 9 = 0$.   (10)

Subtract (10) from (9): $-40y - 60 = 0$.   (11)

Solve (11) for y: $y = -\frac{3}{2}$.

Substitute $y = -\frac{3}{2}$ in (4): $4x - 8(-\frac{3}{2}) - 17 = 0$.   (12)

Solve (12) for x: $x = \frac{5}{4}$.

Hence the solution of the given system is $x = \frac{5}{4}$, $y = -\frac{3}{2}$; also written in the form $(\frac{5}{4}, -\frac{3}{2})$.

Check.   As in part I of this example.

The equation obtained after eliminating all but one unknown may be an identity, a conditional equation satisfied by just one number, or a conditional equation that cannot be satisfied. The corresponding systems of equations are respectively consistent with an unlimited number of solutions, consistent with a single pair of values as its solution (that is, consistent with a unique solution), and inconsistent with no solution.

EXERCISES

1–14. Solve algebraically the systems in Exercises 1 through 14 of § 10-2.

Solve each of the following systems of linear equations algebraically and check the results:

15. $\begin{cases} 4x - 7y = 5, \\ 2x + 5y = 3. \end{cases}$

16. $\begin{cases} 2x + 3y = 0, \\ 6x - 7y + 8 = 0. \end{cases}$

17. $\begin{cases} 3x + 4y = 7, \\ 4x + 3y = 5. \end{cases}$

18. $\begin{cases} 2x - 5y = 6, \\ 4x + 3y = 12. \end{cases}$

19. $\begin{cases} y = ax + b, \\ y = x + c. \end{cases}$

20. $\begin{cases} ax + by + c = 0, \\ dx + ey + f = 0. \end{cases}$

21. $\begin{cases} y - b = m_1(x - a), \\ y - d = m_2(x - c). \end{cases}$

22. $\begin{cases} 2x + 3y - 18 = 0, \\ 2(2x + 1) - 3(7 - y) = 5. \end{cases}$

23. $\begin{cases} \frac{1}{2}(r - s) + \frac{1}{3}(2s + 3) = -\frac{7}{6}, \\ \frac{1}{5}(r - 1) + \frac{1}{4}(7 - s) = 1. \end{cases}$

24. $\begin{cases} \frac{1}{3}(2a + 3) - \frac{1}{4}(2a + 3b) = 1, \\ \frac{1}{5}(3b - 8) - \frac{3}{2}(2a - 3b) = 4. \end{cases}$

25. $\begin{cases} \dfrac{u}{v - 5} - \dfrac{u + 2}{v - 7} = 0, \\ \dfrac{2v - u}{u - v} + \dfrac{5}{v - u} + 4 = 0. \end{cases}$

Solve the systems of equations in Exercises 26 through 28 as linear equations in $\dfrac{1}{x}$ and $\dfrac{1}{y}$ (the use of $u = \dfrac{1}{x}$ and $v = \dfrac{1}{y}$ is optional) algebraically and check the results:

26. $\begin{cases} \dfrac{2}{x} - \dfrac{3}{y} = \dfrac{1}{2}, \\ \dfrac{1}{x} + \dfrac{2}{y} + \dfrac{11}{12} = 0. \end{cases}$

27. $\begin{cases} \dfrac{1}{x} - \dfrac{4}{y} = 2, \\ \dfrac{2}{x} - \dfrac{6}{y} = 5. \end{cases}$

28. $\begin{cases} \dfrac{2a}{x} - \dfrac{b}{y} = 3, \\ \dfrac{4a}{3x} - \dfrac{3b}{2y} = \dfrac{17}{6}. \end{cases}$

29. Systems of equations may also be written in the form

$$\frac{y + 2x}{2} = \frac{x - 5}{3} = \frac{y - 3}{1}.$$

Solve this system and check the result.

30. Solve the system for x and y and check the result:

$$3x + 4y + 8 = x + y - 6 = 4x - 5y + 8.$$

Find the real values of x *and* y *for which:*

31. $(x - 4) + (3x + 2y - 1)i = 2y + 3i.$

32. $(x + 2y) + (2x - y)i = 7 + 9i.$

33. $(3x + 2y) + (6x + 4y)i = 5 + 5i.$

34. $(x - yi) + (2y + 3xi) = 7i.$

35. **(a)** Show algebraically that the following equations are consistent: $x - 2y = 5$, $3x + y = 1$, and $2x - y = 4$. **(b)** Discuss the result of (*a*) in the light of § 10-2.

36. **(a)** Determine whether the following equations define two numbers: $x - 2y = 5$, $3x + y = 1$, $2x - y = -4$. **(b)** Discuss this in the light of § 10-2.

37. Given the equations $3x - 2y = 5$ and $6x - 4y = c$, find a value for c such that their graphs **(a)** coincide; **(b)** do not coincide.

38. Given the equations $3x + 4y = 2$ and $kx + 12y = 5$, find a value for k such that their graphs **(a)** are parallel; **(b)** intersect.

39. Find values of r and s such that the graphs of $2x - 5y = 7$ and $rx + 10y = s$ **(a)** coincide; **(b)** are distinct parallel lines; **(c)** are distinct intersecting lines.

Solve each of the following exercises by introducing two unknowns:

40. The sum of two numbers is 43; their difference is 13. Find the numbers.

41. The sum of two numbers is 17; if three times the first number is added to the second number the result is 31. Find the numbers.

42. If two-thirds of one number plus one-third of another number is 40, and if three-fourths of the first number is 3 more than half the second number, what are the numbers?

43. The sum of the acute angles of any right triangle is 90°. If, for a particular right triangle, the difference of the acute angles is 26°, what are the angles?

44. If one acute angle of a right triangle were increased by 12° and the other decreased by 12°, then the first would be twice the second. Find the angles.

45. A jar of pennies and nickels contains 124 coins. The coins are worth a total of $2.60. How many nickels are there in the jar? How many pennies?

46. A bomber is sent toward a target 3200 miles away flying 600 miles per hour. Four hours later a fighter plane is sent out from the target area flying 1200 miles per hour to intercept the bomber. How far from the target will they meet, and when?

47. The charges for sending a telegram from a certain city to another consist of a flat rate for the first 15 words and a uniform charge for each additional word. If a telegram of 21 words costs $1.50 and a telegram of 25 words costs $1.70, find the flat rate and the rate for additional words.

48. At a certain movie theater, admission tickets are 80 cents for adults and 30 cents for children. If the receipts from 740 tickets were $240, how many tickets of each kind were sold?

49. The line with equation $y = mx + b$ passes through a point (x, y) if and only if the coordinates of the point satisfy the equation. Find values of m and b so that the line will contain the points $(2, 3)$ and $(5, -1)$.

50. As in Exercise 49, find values for m and b, and write an equation for the line through **(a)** $(4, 3)$ and $(10, 12)$; **(b)** $(3, 5)$ and $(-1, 17)$.

51. A certain wire has a resistance of 0.42 ohm at a temperature of 20° centigrade and a resistance of 0.48 ohm at 70° centigrade. If the resistance R is a linear function of the temperature T, find this function.

52. The receipts from a concert were $1700. First-floor seats sold for $4.00 and balcony seats for $2.50. If the numbers of those buying each kind of seat had been reversed, the receipts would have been $1550. How many of each kind were sold?

53. Find two numbers such that **(a)** their sum is 12 and their difference is 3; **(b)** the sum of their reciprocals is 24 and the difference of their reciprocals is 4.

54. If either 25 pounds of flour and 10 pounds of sugar or 16 pounds of flour and 16 pounds of sugar can be purchased for $3.20, find the price of each per pound.

55. A chemist has two bottles of the same acid, one containing a 10% acid solution and the other a 4% acid solution. How many cubic centimeters of each solution are needed to make 120 cubic centimeters of a solution that is 6% acid?

56. One ton of an alloy that is 80% copper is to be obtained by fusing some alloy that is 68% copper and some that is 83% copper. How many pounds of each alloy must be used?

57. Solve the system for x and y:

$$\begin{cases} x \sin \alpha + y \cos \alpha = c, \\ x \cos \alpha - y \sin \alpha = d. \end{cases}$$

10-4   Algebraic Solution of Linear Systems in More Unknowns

As remarked in the previous section, if there are more than two unknowns then the procedure is to eliminate one unknown after another. In the following example, we first eliminate z and then y.

$$\begin{cases} x + 2y - z = 6, & \text{(13)} \\ 2x - y + 3z = -13, & \text{(14)} \\ 3x - 2y + 3z = -16. & \text{(15)} \end{cases}$$

EXAMPLE. Solve:

Solution.

Multiply (13) by 3:	$3x + 6y - 3z = 18.$	(16)
Rewrite (14):	$2x - y + 3z = -13.$	(17)
Add (16) and (17) and divide by 5:	$x + y = 1.$	(18)
Subtract (14) from (15):	$x - y = -3.$	(19)
Add (18) and (19):	$2x = -2.$	(20)
Solve (20) for x:	$x = -1.$	
Substitute $x = -1$ in (18):	$y = 2.$	
Substitute $x = -1, y = 2$ in (13):	$z = -3.$	

Hence the solution of the given system is $x = -1, y = 2, z = -3$; also written in the form $(-1, 2, -3)$.

Check. Substitute these values in (13), (14), and (15):

$$(-1) + 2(2) - (-3) = -1 + 4 + 3 = 6;$$
$$2(-1) - (2) + 3(-3) = -2 - 2 - 9 = -13;$$
$$3(-1) - 2(2) + 3(-3) = -3 - 4 - 9 = -16.$$

EXERCISES

Solve and check:

1. $\begin{cases} x - y + z = 6, \\ x - z = 1, \\ y + z = 4. \end{cases}$

2. $\begin{cases} 2x + y + z = 0, \\ x + y = -2, \\ x - z = 4. \end{cases}$

3. $\begin{cases} 5u - v + w + 9 = 0, \\ u + v - 2w = 3, \\ u - 2v - w = -9. \end{cases}$

4. $\begin{cases} 2a - 2b + c = 5, \\ 4a + 3b - c = 1, \\ 8a + b + c = 5. \end{cases}$

5. $\begin{cases} 6x + 2y = 3, \\ 4x + 3y + 5z = 2, \\ 3x + 2z = 4. \end{cases}$

6. $\begin{cases} x - y - 2z = 2, \\ x + 2y - 2z = 1, \\ 3x + 6y + 4z = -5. \end{cases}$

7. $\begin{cases} 2(x - y) + 3z = 5, \\ 2(x - z) + y = -1, \\ 4x - y - 3z = 0. \end{cases}$

8. $\begin{cases} 2z - y + 1 = 0, \\ 3x + 2y + 3 = 0, \\ 4x - 3y + 4z + 3 = 0. \end{cases}$

9. $\begin{cases} \frac{3}{4}x + \frac{1}{2}y + \frac{2}{3}z = 8, \\ \frac{1}{8}x - \frac{1}{4}y - \frac{1}{2}z = 1, \\ \frac{1}{4}x - \frac{3}{2}y - \frac{5}{6}z + 3 = 0. \end{cases}$

10. $\begin{cases} \frac{1}{3}x - \frac{3}{2}y + \frac{5}{6}z = \frac{5}{2}, \\ \frac{1}{4}x - \frac{1}{3}y + \frac{1}{6}z = \frac{3}{4}, \\ \frac{1}{7}x - \frac{5}{6}y + \frac{1}{7}z = \frac{5}{3}. \end{cases}$

11. $\begin{cases} x - y + z - w = -1, \\ x - 2y + 3z - 2w = 0, \\ 2x + y - 2z + w = -3, \\ 3x - 4y - 5z + w = 3. \end{cases}$

12. $\begin{cases} 5r + s - t = 1, \\ s + 2t + u = -7, \\ 2r - 3s + 3t - u = 3, \\ 2r + 3s + u = -3. \end{cases}$

Solve each of the following exercises by introducing two or more unknowns:

13. The sum of the angles of any plane triangle is 180°. If one angle is twice another and the third angle is equal to one-fourth of the sum of the first two, find the angles.

14. The largest angle of a triangle is equal to the sum of the other two. The smallest angle is equal to one-fourth of the largest. Find the angles.

15. A bag of nickels, dimes, and quarters contains 555 coins worth $48.75. There are three times as many dimes as quarters. How many of each type of coin are in the bag?

16. The parabola with equation $y = ax^2 + bx + c$ passes through a point (x, y) if and only if the coordinates of the point satisfy the equation of the parabola. Find values of a, b, and c, and state an equation for the parabola passing through the points $(1, 4)$, $(3, 10)$, and $(-1; 14)$.

17. As in Exercise 16, find equations for parabolas passing through the points **(a)** $(1, 2)$, $(2, -4)$, and $(4, -22)$; **(b)** $(1, 0)$, $(4, 21)$, and $(-2, 15)$.

18. A and B can do a certain task if both work together 3 days and B then works alone one day; A and C can do the task if they work together 4 days and A then works alone 2 days. It would take C twice as long as it would B to do it alone. **(a)** How long would it take each working alone? **(b)** If B can be hired at \$2.40 an hour, what would be an equivalent rate for each of the others?

10-5   Graphic Solution of Quadratic Systems

The principles of graphic solution of a system of equations in two unknowns, presented in § 10-2, apply even if the equations are not linear as they were in the examples in that section. A system of equations is called quadratic if each equation is either linear or quadratic and at least one is quadratic. Such a system may have as many as four solutions.

EXAMPLE.   Solve graphically:
$$\begin{cases} y^2 = 2x + 5, \\ 3x^2 - 2y^2 = 1. \end{cases}$$

Solution.

$$C_1: \quad y^2 = 2x + 5; \quad y = \pm\sqrt{2x + 5}$$

x	0	1	2	3	4	-2.5	-1	-2	< -2.5
y	$\pm\sqrt{5}$	$\pm\sqrt{7}$	$\pm\sqrt{9}$	$\pm\sqrt{11}$	$\pm\sqrt{13}$	0	$\pm\sqrt{3}$	$\pm\sqrt{1}$	Imag.
	± 2.2	± 2.6	± 3	± 3.3	± 3.6		± 1.7	± 1	

$$C_2: \quad 3x^2 - 2y^2 = 1; \quad y = \pm\sqrt{\tfrac{1}{2}(3x^2 - 1)}$$

x	0	1	2	3	4	± 0.6	-1	-2	-3	-4
y	Imag.	$\pm\sqrt{1}$	$\pm\sqrt{\frac{11}{2}}$	$\pm\sqrt{13}$	$\pm\sqrt{\frac{47}{2}}$	0	$\pm\sqrt{1}$	$\pm\sqrt{\frac{11}{2}}$	$\pm\sqrt{13}$	$\pm\sqrt{\frac{47}{2}}$
		± 1	± 2.3	± 3.6	± 4.8		± 1	± 2.3	± 3.6	± 4.8

The coordinates of the four points of intersection, namely, $x = 2.7$,

$y = 3.2$; $x = -1.4$, $y = 1.5$; $x = -1.4$, $y = -1.5$; $x = 2.7$, $y = -3.2$, are the approximate real solutions of the system.

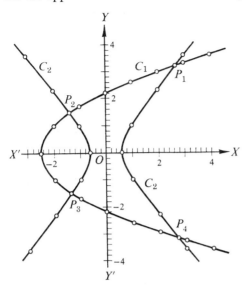

Approximate Real Solutions

Point	x	y
P_1	2.7	3.2
P_2	-1.4	1.5
P_3	-1.4	-1.5
P_4	2.7	-3.2

Fig. 10.8

Note. If the two curves of a system have a point of tangency, the system is considered to have two identical solutions for this point.

EXERCISES

Solve graphically:

1. $\begin{cases} xy = -6, \\ 3x + 2y = 5. \end{cases}$

5. $\begin{cases} y^2 = 4 + x, \\ x^2 = 4 - y. \end{cases}$

9. $\begin{cases} x^2 + y^2 = 36, \\ x + y = 9. \end{cases}$

2. $\begin{cases} x = 3y - 3, \\ 2x^2 + y = 2. \end{cases}$

6. $\begin{cases} 4x^2 + y^2 = 36, \\ x^2 + y^2 = 25. \end{cases}$

10. $\begin{cases} 9x^2 + 4y^2 = 144, \\ 2x + y = 10. \end{cases}$

3. $\begin{cases} x^2 + y^2 = 25, \\ x - 2y = 3. \end{cases}$

7. $\begin{cases} x^2 + 2y = 8, \\ x^2 + y^2 = 16. \end{cases}$

11. $\begin{cases} x^2 + y^2 = 25, \\ xy + 7 = 0. \end{cases}$

4. $\begin{cases} 2x^2 + y^2 = 8, \\ 2x + y = 1. \end{cases}$

8. $\begin{cases} y^2 - x^2 = 4, \\ 3x^2 = 4y + 8. \end{cases}$

12. $\begin{cases} y^2 = 3(2 + x), \\ 4x^2 + 5y^2 = 20. \end{cases}$

10-6 Algebraic Solution of Quadratic Systems

The algebraic solution of a system of two quadratic equations in two unknowns, in general, leads to a fourth-degree equation in one of the unknowns. We shall confine our attention to the solution of certain special systems of equations which lead to a quadratic equation, or to an equation in quadratic form, in one of the unknowns.

In general, an attempt should first be made to solve for one unknown in terms of the other, then substitute in one of the equations (the other equation if only one has been used previously), and finally solve, if possible, the resulting equation in one unknown. Each value of one unknown, together with a corresponding value of the other unknown, will be a solution of the given system. The methods and details of solution, for the principal types of quadratic systems which are manageable, will be shown in examples.

If one of the given equations is linear, the system can always be solved by the method of elimination by substitution. Solve the linear equation for one of the unknowns in terms of the other, substitute in the given quadratic equation, and solve the resulting quadratic equation in one unknown. The corresponding values for the other unknown are best found by substituting in the *linear* equation. Finally *pair off* the corresponding values of the unknowns, each such pair giving one solution.

EXAMPLE 1. Solve algebraically:
$$\begin{cases} 4x^2 - 6xy + 9y^2 = 63, & (21) \\ 2x - 3y + 3 = 0. & (22) \end{cases}$$

Solution.

Solve (22) for y:	$y = \frac{1}{3}(2x + 3)$.	(23)
Substitute (23) in (21):	$4x^2 - 6x[\frac{1}{3}(2x + 3)] + 9[\frac{1}{3}(2x + 3)]^2 = 63$.	(24)
Expand (24):	$4x^2 - 4x^2 - 6x + 4x^2 + 12x + 9 = 63$.	(25)
Combine in (25):	$4x^2 + 6x - 54 = 0$.	(26)
Divide (26) by 2:	$2x^2 + 3x - 27 = 0$.	(27)
Factor (27):	$(2x + 9)(x - 3) = 0$.	

$2x + 9 = 0$.	$x - 3 = 0$.
$x = -\frac{9}{2}$.	$x = 3$.
Substitute in (23): $y = \frac{1}{3}[2(-\frac{9}{2}) + 3]$.	$y = \frac{1}{3}[2(3) + 3]$.
$y = -2$.	$y = 3$.

Hence the solutions of the given system are $x = -\frac{9}{2}$, $y = -2$, and $x = 3$, $y = 3$; also written in the form $(-\frac{9}{2}, -2)$ and $(3, 3)$.

The answers can be checked by substitution in the original equations (21) and (22).

The method of elimination by substitution may also be used for systems of equations in which one of the equations involves only one unknown, and for systems in which one of the equations is of the form $bxy + f = 0$ and the other is of the form $ax^2 + cy^2 + f = 0$.

If each of the given equations is of the form $ax^2 + cy^2 + f = 0$, then both equations are linear in x^2 and y^2, and the system can always be solved by the method of elimination by addition or subtraction. Eliminate either x^2 or y^2, and solve for the unknown remaining. The corresponding values of the unknown which was eliminated may then be found by substituting the values of the unknown obtained in either of the given equations, the simpler preferred. Finally, pair off the corresponding values of x and y, each such pair giving one solution. For each of the two values for the unknown first found, there will be two values for the other unknown, making four solutions for the system.

EXAMPLE 2.   Solve algebraically:
$$\begin{cases} 4x^2 + 7y^2 = 32, & (28) \\ 11y^2 - 3x^2 = 41. & (29) \end{cases}$$

Solution.

Multiply (28) by 3:	$12x^2 + 21y^2 = 96.$	(30)
Multiply (29) by 4:	$-12x^2 + 44y^2 = 164.$	(31)
Add (30) and (31):	$65y^2 = 260.$	(32)
Divide (32) by 65:	$y^2 = 4.$	
Extract square roots:	$y = \pm 2.$	

$y = 2.$	$y = -2.$
Substitute in (28): $4x^2 + 7(2)^2 = 32.$	$4x^2 + 7(-2)^2 = 32.$
$x^2 = 1.$	$x^2 = 1.$
$x = \pm 1.$	$x = \pm 1.$

$x = 1,$	$x = -1,$	$x = 1,$	$x = -1,$
$y = 2.$	$y = 2.$	$y = -2.$	$y = -2.$

Hence the solutions of the given system are $x = 1$, $y = 2$; $x = -1$, $y = 2$; $x = 1$, $y = -2$; and $x = -1$, $y = -2$; also written in the form $(1, 2)$, $(-1, 2)$, $(1, -2)$, and $(-1, -2)$.

The method of elimination by addition and subtraction may also be used for other types of systems of equations, such as those in Exercises 7 and 8 of this section.

In a system of pure quadratic equations each of the given equations is of the form $ax^2 + bxy + cy^2 + f = 0$, that is, the linear terms are missing. If $b = 0$ in both equations, the method of Example 2 applies. Otherwise the following method is often useful.

If $f \neq 0$ in each of the given equations, first eliminate the constant term between the two equations. Solve the resulting equation for one unknown in terms of the other, which gives two equations linear in x and y, at least one of which must hold for any solution of the given system. Our problem now becomes one of solving *two* systems of the type considered in Example 1 where the quadratic may be either of the given equations, the simpler preferred, and the linear equation is one of those mentioned above. Each solution of either of these two new systems will be a solution of the given system. See Example 3.

If $f = 0$ in at least one given equation, this equation is used in place of the one to be obtained above by eliminating the constant terms. See Example 4.

The above method is particularly adaptable to systems where the resulting equation can be expressed as the product of two linear factors equated to zero.

EXAMPLE 3. Solve algebraically:
$$\begin{cases} 2x^2 - 3xy = 2, & (33) \\ 4x^2 + 9y^2 = 10. & (34) \end{cases}$$

Solution.

Multiply (33) by 5:	$10x^2 - 15xy \qquad = 10.$	(35)
Rewrite (34):	$4x^2 \qquad\quad + 9y^2 = 10.$	(36)
Subtract (36) from (35):	$6x^2 - 15xy - 9y^2 = 0.$	(37)
Divide (37) by 3:	$2x^2 - 5xy - 3y^2 = 0.$	(38)
Factor (38):	$(2x + y)(x - 3y) = 0.$	

	$2x + y = 0.$	$x - 3y = 0.$	
	$y = -2x. \quad (39)$	$x = 3y. \quad (39)$	
Substitute (39) in (33)	$2x^2 - 3x(-2x) = 2.$	$2(3y)^2 - 3(3y)y = 2.$	
	$8x^2 = 2.$	$9y^2 = 2.$	
	$x^2 = \frac{1}{4}.$	$y^2 = \frac{2}{9}.$	
	$x = \pm\frac{1}{2}.$	$y = \pm\frac{1}{3}\sqrt{2}.$	

	$x = \frac{1}{2}.$	$x = -\frac{1}{2}.$	$y = \frac{1}{3}\sqrt{2}.$	$y = -\frac{1}{3}\sqrt{2}.$
Using (39):	$y = -2(\frac{1}{2}).$	$y = -2(-\frac{1}{2}).$	$x = 3(\frac{1}{3}\sqrt{2}).$	$x = 3(-\frac{1}{3}\sqrt{2}).$
	$y = -1.$	$y = 1.$	$x = \sqrt{2}.$	$x = -\sqrt{2}.$

Hence the solutions of the given system are $x = \frac{1}{2}$, $y = -1$; $x = -\frac{1}{2}$, $y = 1$; $x = \sqrt{2}$, $y = \frac{1}{3}\sqrt{2}$; and $x = -\sqrt{2}$, $y = -\frac{1}{3}\sqrt{2}$; also written $(\frac{1}{2}, -1)$, $(-\frac{1}{2}, 1)$, $(\sqrt{2}, \frac{1}{3}\sqrt{2})$, and $(-\sqrt{2}, -\frac{1}{3}\sqrt{2})$.

EXAMPLE 4.   Solve algebraically:
$$\begin{cases} 2x^2 - xy = 28, & (40) \\ 4x^2 - 9xy - 28y^2 = 0. & (41) \end{cases}$$

Solution.   Factor (41): $(4x + 7y)(x - 4y) = 0.$

Substitute (42) in (40) $\Bigg\}$:	$\begin{aligned} 4x + 7y &= 0. \\ x &= -\tfrac{7}{4}y. \quad (42) \\ 2(-\tfrac{7}{4}y)^2 - y(-\tfrac{7}{4}y) &= 28. \\ 63y^2 &= 224. \\ y^2 &= \tfrac{32}{9}. \\ y &= \pm\tfrac{4}{3}\sqrt{2}. \end{aligned}$	$\begin{aligned} x - 4y &= 0. \\ x &= 4y. \quad (42) \\ 2(4y)^2 - y(4y) &= 28. \\ 28y^2 &= 28. \\ y^2 &= 1. \\ y &= \pm 1. \end{aligned}$

	$y = \tfrac{4}{3}\sqrt{2}.$	$y = -\tfrac{4}{3}\sqrt{2}.$	$y = 1.$	$y = -1.$
Using (42):	$x = -\tfrac{7}{4}(\tfrac{4}{3}\sqrt{2}).$	$x = -\tfrac{7}{4}(-\tfrac{4}{3}\sqrt{2}).$	$x = 4(1).$	$x = 4(-1).$
	$x = -\tfrac{7}{3}\sqrt{2}.$	$x = \tfrac{7}{3}\sqrt{2}.$	$x = 4.$	$x = -4.$

Hence the solutions of the given system are $x = -\frac{7}{3}\sqrt{2}$, $y = \frac{4}{3}\sqrt{2}$; $x = \frac{7}{3}\sqrt{2}$, $y = -\frac{4}{3}\sqrt{2}$; $x = 4$, $y = 1$; and $x = -4$, $y = -1$; also written $(-\frac{7}{3}\sqrt{2}, \frac{4}{3}\sqrt{2})$, $(\frac{7}{3}\sqrt{2}, -\frac{4}{3}\sqrt{2})$, $(4, 1)$, and $(-4, -1)$.

EXERCISES

Solve algebraically. Express each irrational solution in simplified radical form, and in decimal form accurate to two decimal places. If directed by the instructor, also solve graphically the systems marked by a dagger (†).

†1. $\begin{cases} x^2 + y^2 = 20, \\ x + y = 2. \end{cases}$

†2. $\begin{cases} x^2 - y^2 = 16, \\ x + y = 2. \end{cases}$

†3. $\begin{cases} y^2 - 4x^2 = 16, \\ 2x - y = 2. \end{cases}$

4. $\begin{cases} xy = 10, \\ 3x + 2y = 12. \end{cases}$

†5. $\begin{cases} y^2 - 2x^2 = 1, \\ y^2 + x^2 = 49. \end{cases}$

†6. $\begin{cases} x^2 + 3y^2 = 7, \\ 3x^2 - 2y^2 = 10. \end{cases}$

7. $\begin{cases} x^2 + y^2 = 6, \\ x^2 + 5y = 10. \end{cases}$

8. $\begin{cases} x^2 - 2xy = 10, \\ 3x^2 + xy = 2. \end{cases}$

9. $\begin{cases} 2x^2 + 3xy + y^2 = 0, \\ xy - y^2 + 6 = 0. \end{cases}$

16. $\begin{cases} 4x^2 + 3xy + 9y^2 = 15, \\ 2x - 3y = 5. \end{cases}$

10. $\begin{cases} 2x^2 + xy - y^2 = 0, \\ xy + y + 6 = 0. \end{cases}$

†17. $\begin{cases} 2x^2 + y^2 = 18, \\ xy = 4. \end{cases}$

11. $\begin{cases} x^2 - 3xy + y^2 = 1, \\ 2x^2 - 7xy + 2y^2 = -1. \end{cases}$

18. $\begin{cases} 2x^2 - 3xy = 2y^2, \\ 10x^2 - xy + 4y^2 = 28. \end{cases}$

12. $\begin{cases} 4x^2 + 3xy + 2 = 0, \\ y^2 + xy = 3. \end{cases}$

19. $\begin{cases} 2x^2 - 5y^2 + 8 = 0, \\ x^2 - 7y^2 + 4 = 0. \end{cases}$

13. $\begin{cases} x^2 + y^2 + x - 6y = 7, \\ x + y = 1. \end{cases}$

20. $\begin{cases} x^2 + xy + 2y^2 = 8; \\ xy + 4 = 0. \end{cases}$

†14. $\begin{cases} y^2 = 6(x + 2), \\ y^2 = -4(x - 1). \end{cases}$

21. $\begin{cases} 2x^2 - 2xy - 3y^2 = -6, \\ 2x^2 - xy = 4. \end{cases}$

15. $\begin{cases} 13x^2 + 5xy + 36 = 0, \\ 7x^2 + xy = 6. \end{cases}$

22. $\begin{cases} 4x^2 - 5xy + 3y^2 = 6, \\ 2x^2 - 3xy + 2y^2 = 4. \end{cases}$

Find the real values of x *and* y *for which:*

23. $(x + iy)^2 = x^2 + 2xyi - y^2 = 5 - 12i.$

24. $(x + iy)^2 = -3 + 4i.$

Solve each of the following problems by introducing two unknowns:

25. Find two positive numbers such that the sum of their squares is equal to 250 and the difference of their squares is equal to 88.

26. The sum of two positive numbers is 26. Their squares differ by 104. What are the numbers?

27. The sum of the circumferences of two circles is 28π inches, and their combined area is 106π square inches. What are the radii of the two circles?

28. A group of neighbors plan to pay equal amounts toward a power mower to cost \$240. If by adding 2 more neighbors to the group the cost to each is reduced by \$4, find the number in the original group and the amount each was to pay.

29. A rectangular garden is surrounded by a walk 5 feet wide. The area of the garden is 1000 square feet and the area of the walk is 750 square feet. Find the dimensions of the garden.

30. A rectangular piece of tin has an area of 192 square inches. An open box containing 192 cubic inches can be made from it by cutting a 2-inch square from each corner and turning up the ends and sides. What are the dimensions of the piece of tin?

31. Find two numbers such that their difference is equal to their product and the sum of their reciprocals is 5.

32. Find two numbers such that the difference of their reciprocals is $\frac{1}{3}$ and the product of the numbers is $4\frac{1}{2}$.

MISCELLANEOUS EXERCISES

Solve algebraically:

1. $\begin{cases} y^2 = 4x, \\ 2x + y = 4. \end{cases}$

2. $\begin{cases} y^2 + x = 2y, \\ x + y = 2. \end{cases}$

3. $\begin{cases} 2x^2 + 3y^2 = 6, \\ 3x^2 + 4y^2 = 12. \end{cases}$

4. $\begin{cases} 4x^2 - 25y^2 = 11, \\ 2x - 5y = 11. \end{cases}$

Hint. Divide the respective members of the first equation by those of the second.

5. $\begin{cases} x^4 - y^4 = 27, \\ x^2 + y^2 = 3. \end{cases}$

6. $\begin{cases} x^2 - 5xy + 4y^2 = 74, \\ x - 4y = 37. \end{cases}$

7. $\begin{cases} x - y = 21, \\ \sqrt{x} + \sqrt{y} = 7. \end{cases}$

Hint. Let $u = \sqrt{x}$, $v = \sqrt{y}$.

8. $\begin{cases} 2\sqrt{x} - \sqrt{y} = 5, \\ 3\sqrt{x} + 2\sqrt{y} = 18. \end{cases}$

9. $\begin{cases} \dfrac{2}{x^2} - \dfrac{5}{y^2} = 3, \\ \dfrac{1}{x^2} + \dfrac{3}{y^2} = 7. \end{cases}$

10. $\begin{cases} \dfrac{3}{y^2} - \dfrac{2}{x^2} = 1, \\ \dfrac{6}{y^2} - \dfrac{7}{x^2} = 2. \end{cases}$

11. $\begin{cases} 3x^2 - 16xy + 5y^2 = 32, \\ x^2 - 3xy + 2y^2 = 8. \end{cases}$

Eliminate the parameter t *to obtain an equation in* x *and* y, *first obtaining if possible a simpler equation by subtracting or dividing corresponding members of the given equations:*

12. $\begin{cases} x = t^2 - t + 1, \\ y = 3t^2 - 4. \end{cases}$

13. $\begin{cases} x = (1 - t)^2(1 + t), \\ y = (1 - t)(1 + t)^2. \end{cases}$

Solve each of the following problems by introducing two or more unknowns:

14. Find two positive numbers such that the square of the first is equal to twice the second and the negative of the first is twelve less than the second.

15. Any three-digit number may be written in the form

$$100h + 10t + u$$

in terms of its hundreds' digit h, its tens' digit t, and its units' digit u. Find a three-digit number such that the sum of its digits is 10, the units' digit is equal to the sum of the tens' digit and the hundreds' digit, and the tens' digit is four times the hundreds' digit.

16. Find a two-digit number such that the sum of the digits is 15 and the number is increased by 9 when the order of the digits is reversed.

17. The formula $s = s_0 + v_0 t - 16t^2$ is often used for falling bodies where s is the height of the body at any time t, s_0 is the height when $t = 0$, v_0 is the velocity when $t = 0$, and the coefficient 16 is used for one half of the acceleration of gravity, all units being in feet and seconds. If $s = 10,000$ when $t = 5$, and $s = 8550$ when $t = 10$, find s_0 and v_0.

18. Find the dimensions of a rectangular window having a diagonal of 68 inches and a perimeter of 184 inches.

19. Find a quadratic function $f(x)$ such that $f(1) = 2$, $f(2) = 5$, $f(-2) = 21$.

20. A farmer is plowing a rectangular field which contains 3600 square rods. When he has plowed a strip 5 rods wide around the field, he has plowed 600 square rods more than half the field. Find the length and breadth of the field.

21. One formula that gives the relation between the height h in feet above sea level and the temperature t in degrees centigrade at which water boils is $h = a + bt + ct^2$. Using $h = 0$ for $t = 100$, $h = 1500$ for $t = 99$, and $h = 2990$ for $t = 98$, find a, b, and c.

22. In analytic geometry it is shown that the general equation of the circle is $x^2 + y^2 + Dx + Ey + F = 0$. Find, if possible, the equation of the circle passing through each of the following sets of points: **(a)** $(-4, -2)$, $(0, 2)$, $(-4, 6)$; **(b)** $(-3, 0)$, $(2, 5)$, $(5, 4)$; **(c)** $(-1, -1)$, $(2, 2)$, $(4, 4)$.

23. The small wheels of a certain steam locomotive make as many revolutions in going 200 feet as the drive wheels do in going 450 feet. If the difference in the circumference of the wheels is 110 inches, find the circumference of each.

24. From a boat the angle of elevation of the top of a lighthouse is 15° 0'. After the boat is sailed 300 feet directly toward the lighthouse, the angle of elevation is 24° 0'. **(a)** Express the right-triangle relationships between these facts, the height h of the lighthouse above the observer, and the initial distance x of the boat from the base of the lighthouse. **(b)** Solve for h.

25. From the top of a 75-foot fire tower, a helicopter is seen at an angle of elevation of 30°. From the base of the tower, the angle of elevation of the helicopter is 45°. Using right-triangle relationships and simultaneous equations, find the height of the helicopter above the top of the tower.

26. A weight of 500 pounds is supported by two cables, one at an angle 30° to the horizontal and carrying a tension of t pounds, the other at an angle 60° to the horizontal and carrying a tension of s pounds. **(a)** Express the horizontal and vertical components of these tensions in terms of t and s. **(b)** Set the algebraic sum of the horizontal components equal to zero and the algebraic sum of the vertical components of the two tensions equal to 500 pounds, and solve for t and s.

Note. The authors feel that a few exercises should reflect the ambiguity, the absence of essential information, the excessive information, and even the impossible situations that are frequently met in practical problems. Recognition of such situations may be an important part of any of the following exercises.

27. Find a quadratic function $f(x)$ such that $f(0) = 5$, $f(1) = 4$, $f(2) = 7$, and $f(3) = 14$.

★28. Find the equation of the line through the given set of points: **(a)** $(-2, 2)$, $(6, -2)$, and $(12, -5)$; **(b)** $(-3, 4)$, $(0, 1)$, and $(4, -4)$; **(c)** $(3, 4)$ and the point of intersection of $x + y = 7$ and $y = x + 1$.

★29. A man rowing upstream drops his hat at point A. Thirty minutes later at B, he notices its loss and rows back at the same rate (with respect to still water), picking up the hat at C, $\frac{1}{4}$ of a mile below A. Find **(a)** how long the hat is in the water; **(b)** the rate of the current; **(c)** his rate of rowing; **(d)** the distance AB.

★30. A quadrilateral $ABCD$ circumscribes a circle; the sides are tangent at E, F, G, and H respectively, and are 10, 8, 7, and 9 inches in length. Designate AE by x, BF by y, CG by z, and DH by w. **(a)** Write four equations involving x, y, z, and w. **(b)** Solve for x if possible; if it is not possible, explain why. **(c)** If the condition is added that AE is

2 inches longer than *EB*, determine whether it is now possible to find values for *x*, *y*, *z*, and *w*. If so, find these values.

⋆**31.** A manufacturer has available three scarce raw materials: 2400 pounds of *A*, 310 pounds of *B*, and 28 pounds of *C*. He is equipped to make three different products: P, of which each unit requires 20 pounds of *A*, 2 pounds of *B*, and 1 pound of *C*; Q, of which each unit requires 25 pounds of *A*, 5 pounds of *B*, and 0 pounds of *C*; and R, of which each unit requires 150 pounds of *A*, 10 pounds of *B*, and $\frac{1}{2}$ pound of *C*. Can the manufacturer use up all of his supply of raw materials by making an appropriate number of units of each product? If so, how many of each should he make?

10-7 Triangular Form of a Linear System*

In § 10-3 and § 10-4 we saw that one method of solving a system of linear equations is elimination by addition and subtraction. The multipliers in that process were chosen as they were found convenient in the particular problem. A more systematic approach, which is preferable for some purposes though less efficient in many particular cases, will now be considered.

First write the equations with the constant terms in the right members and with the unknowns, in some chosen order, in the left members. Thus if the given system is

$$x + 2y = z + 6, \tag{43}$$
$$3z + 2x - y + 13 = 0, \tag{44}$$
$$3x - 2y + 3z + 16 = 0, \tag{45}$$

and the chosen order for the unknowns is the alphabetical order, the system would be rewritten as in the Example of § 10-4:

$$x + 2y - z = 6, \tag{13}$$
$$2x - y + 3z = -13, \tag{14}$$
$$3x - 2y + 3z = -16. \tag{15}$$

Next, proceed with systematic elimination, using the following operations (compare § 10-3):

(i) Replacing one equation of the system by any equation equivalent to it;

---

* The material from here to the end of the chapter can be omitted without disturbing the following chapters, but the present material serves as a useful background to the study of determinants.

(ii') Replacing one equation of the system by the sum of a constant nonzero multiple of itself and a constant multiple of another equation of the system;

(iii) Interchanging two equations of the system.

With these operations we aim to obtain an equivalent system which is in **triangular form,** that is, in which the first equation involves the first unknown but no other unknowns; the second equation involves the second unknown and possibly the first unknown but no other unknowns; the third equation involves the third unknown and possibly the first two unknowns but no others; and so on.

Let us do this with the system consisting of the equations (13), (14), (15). To eliminate the last unknown, z, from all except the last equation, we can first apply the operation (ii') to replace the second equation by the difference of itself and the third equation, that is, by the algebraic sum of itself and -1 times the third equation.

$$\left\{ \begin{array}{l} x + 2y - z = 6, \\ -x + y \quad\quad = 3, \\ 3x - 2y + 3z = -16. \end{array} \right.$$

Next we apply (ii') and replace the first equation by 3 times itself plus 1 times the third equation (this and the preceding step could be done in either order):

$$\left\{ \begin{array}{l} 6x + 4y \quad\quad = 2, \\ -x + y \quad\quad = 3, \\ 3x - 2y + 3z = -16. \end{array} \right.$$

The first of these equations can then be simplified by multiplying it by $\frac{1}{2}$, as permitted by (i):

$$\left\{ \begin{array}{l} 3x + 2y \quad\quad = 1, \\ -x + y \quad\quad = 3, \\ 3x - 2y + 3z = -16. \end{array} \right.$$

Thus the system has been reduced to the required form as far as the last variable, z, is concerned. To eliminate the next variable, y, from all but the last two equations, apply (ii') to replace the first equation by itself minus twice the second equation:

$$\left\{ \begin{array}{l} 5x \quad\quad\quad = -5, \\ -x + y \quad\quad = 3, \\ 3x - 2y + 3z = -16. \end{array} \right.$$

Multiplying the first equation by $\frac{1}{5}$,

$$\left\{ \begin{array}{ll} x & = -1, \qquad (46) \\ -x + y & = 3, \qquad (47) \\ 3x - 2y + 3z = -16. \qquad (48) \end{array} \right.$$

Thus the given equations have been reduced to triangular form. From (46), $x = -1$. Substituting this fact in (47), $1 + y = 3$, so that $y = 2$. Substituting in (48), $3z = -9$ so that $z = -3$.

Hence the solution of the system is $x = -1$, $y = 2$, $z = -3$. This can be checked by substituting in the original equations (43), (44), and (45).

Actually the process hardly takes as long to carry out as to describe. Some of the steps can be carried out mentally, though it is unwise to try to do too many steps without writing down intermediate results, since this is a frequent cause of errors.

Obviously the operations just used can be applied to any system; if an unknown is missing where desired, equations can be interchanged by (iii). In some cases it will prove impossible to carry the process to completion, but this itself is significant as will be seen in § 10-10. The process is tedious if there are many equations and unknowns. Much effort has been devoted to finding efficient procedures for solving large systems. However, a system with, say, 20 equations and 20 unknowns taxes the capacity even of a large electronic computing machine, yet such systems often arise in applications.

EXERCISES

If possible, reduce to triangular form and solve:

   1—12. The systems in Exercises 1 through 12 of § 10-4.

   13—14. The systems in Exercises 13 and 14 of § 10-2.

   ★15—18. The systems in Exercises 15 through 18 of § 10-2.

10-8   Matrices

In this section we shall consider arrays of numbers in which each array consists of rows and columns, each row having an entry for each column and vice versa. Such an array is called a **rectangular array,** or **matrix,** and is usually enclosed in brackets. If the array has m rows and n columns, it is called an $m \times n$ **matrix** (read "m by n matrix").

If $m = n$, it is called a **square matrix.** The numbers appearing in the array are called the **elements** of the matrix. It is to be noted that a matrix is simply an array of elements; there is no single number or "value" attached to it. In § 11-4 we shall associate a number (the value of the determinant of the matrix) with each square matrix.

In a square matrix the **principal diagonal** is the set of elements which lie on a line from the upper left element to the bottom right element.

ILLUSTRATION.

$$\begin{bmatrix} 1 & -2 \\ 4 & 0 \\ -\frac{3}{8} & 6 \end{bmatrix}, \quad \begin{bmatrix} a_1 & b_1 & c_1 \\ a_2 & b_2 & c_2 \\ a_3 & b_3 & c_3 \end{bmatrix}, \quad \text{and} \quad [\pi \quad \sqrt{2} \quad -3 \quad 1]$$

are respectively a 3×2 matrix, a 3×3 matrix (and hence a square matrix), and a 1×4 matrix. The second of these has for its principal diagonal the elements a_1, b_2, c_3.

Matrices are used to display information, such as coefficients in systems of equations, and to systematize computation. In mathematical economics, matrices with very large numbers of rows and columns are used in expressing input and output data for processes involving many materials. In advanced mathematics and mathematical physics, matrices are used to represent sets of vectors; in advanced geometry, they are used to represent transformations. There is also an algebra of matrices.

EXERCISES

Tell the number of (**a**) *rows,* (**b**) *columns, of the given matrix;* (**c**) *tell whether the matrix is square;* (**d**) *if the matrix has a principal diagonal, tell what elements lie on it:*

1. $\begin{bmatrix} 1 \\ \frac{1}{2} \\ 3 \end{bmatrix}$. **2.** $\begin{bmatrix} a & b & c \\ d & e & f \end{bmatrix}$. **3.** $\begin{bmatrix} 2 & \frac{2}{3} & -1 \\ 1 & 16 & 0 \\ 0 & 0 & 0 \end{bmatrix}$. **4.** $\begin{bmatrix} a_{11} & a_{12} & a_{13} \\ a_{21} & a_{22} & a_{23} \\ a_{31} & a_{32} & a_{33} \end{bmatrix}$.

Write a matrix with the specified properties:

5. 2×3, with each element a positive even integer.

6. 3×4, with each element of the second row twice the corresponding element of the first row.

7. 3×3, with each element on the principal diagonal equal to 1 and each element which lies above the principal diagonal equal to zero.

10-9   Use of Matrices in Solving Linear Systems

One use of matrices is to provide an abbreviated notation for the process of solving a system of simultaneous linear equations by elimination (§ 10-3, § 10-4, § 10-7).

If a system of simultaneous linear equations is given, we first write the system with the constant terms in the right members and the unknowns, in a chosen order, in the left members, just as we did in reducing the system to triangular form (§ 10-7). Then the **matrix of coefficients** of the system is the matrix whose first column consists of the coefficients of the first unknown (say, x), whose second column consists of the coefficients of the second unknown (say, y), and so on for each unknown, taking the rows in the same order as the equations and supplying a zero in place of any missing term. The **augmented matrix** of coefficients of the system is the matrix which consists of the matrix of coefficients with one additional column at the right, consisting of the constant terms of the equations. This last column is sometimes marked off, for instance by a dashed line, to emphasize its special role.

ILLUSTRATION.   For the system

$$x + 2y - z = 6, \tag{13}$$
$$2x - y + 3z = -13, \tag{14}$$
$$3x - 2y + 3z = -16, \tag{15}$$

the matrix M of coefficients and the augmented matrix M' are given by

$$M = \begin{bmatrix} 1 & 2 & -1 \\ 2 & -1 & 3 \\ 3 & -2 & 3 \end{bmatrix}, \quad M' = \begin{bmatrix} 1 & 2 & -1 & 6 \\ 2 & -1 & 3 & -13 \\ 3 & -2 & 3 & -16 \end{bmatrix}.$$

A matrix is said to be in **triangular form** if it is square and all elements on the principal diagonal are different from zero and all elements which lie above the principal diagonal are equal to zero.

The following operations on a matrix are permitted for present purposes:

(i) Multiplying each element in a row by any constant different from zero;

(ii') Replacing each element of any specified row by the sum of a nonzero multiple of that element (the same multiple for each element in the row) and another multiple (the same multiple for each element in the row) of the corresponding elements of another chosen row;

(iii) Interchanging any two rows.

It is immediately seen that these operations on matrices precisely correspond to the operations on equations used in § 10-7; moreover, if a linear system is reduced to triangular form then the corresponding operations reduce its matrix of coefficients to triangular form, and vice versa. We consider again the system discussed in § 10-7.

EXAMPLE. Solve:
$$\begin{cases} x + 2y = z + 6, & (43) \\ 3z + 2x - y + 13 = 0, & (44) \\ 3x - 2y + 3z + 16 = 0. & (45) \end{cases}$$

Solution. First rewrite the system in standard form:
$$\begin{cases} x + 2y - z = 6, \\ 2x - y + 3z = -13, \\ 3x - 2y + 3z = -16. \end{cases}$$

Then the augmented matrix is:
$$\left[\begin{array}{ccc|c} 1 & 2 & -1 & 6 \\ 2 & -1 & 3 & -13 \\ 3 & -2 & 3 & -16 \end{array} \right].$$

Replace the second row by 1 times itself plus -1 times the third row, obtaining the matrix shown at the right:
$$\left[\begin{array}{ccc|c} 1 & 2 & -1 & 6 \\ -1 & 1 & 0 & 3 \\ 3 & -2 & 3 & -16 \end{array} \right].$$

Replace the first row by 3 times itself plus 1 times the third row, obtaining zeros above the diagonal of the matrix of coefficients in the third column (corresponding to the elimination of z from the first two equations):
$$\left[\begin{array}{ccc|c} 6 & 4 & 0 & 2 \\ -1 & 1 & 0 & 3 \\ 3 & -2 & 3 & -16 \end{array} \right].$$

Multiply the first row by $\frac{1}{2}$:
$$\left[\begin{array}{ccc|c} 3 & 2 & 0 & 1 \\ -1 & 1 & 0 & 3 \\ 3 & -2 & 3 & -16 \end{array} \right].$$

Replace the first row by itself plus -2 times the second row, obtaining zero in the only place above the diagonal in the second column:
$$\left[\begin{array}{ccc|c} 5 & 0 & 0 & -5 \\ -1 & 1 & 0 & 3 \\ 3 & -2 & 3 & -16 \end{array} \right].$$

Then the part of the augmented matrix which corresponds to the matrix of coefficients has been reduced to triangular form. However, for convenience we multiply the first row by $\frac{1}{5}$:
$$\left[\begin{array}{ccc|c} 1 & 0 & 0 & -1 \\ -1 & 1 & 0 & 3 \\ 3 & -2 & 3 & -16 \end{array} \right].$$

The rows of the last matrix correspond to the equations

$$\begin{cases} x & = -1, & (46) \\ -x + y & = 3, & (47) \\ 3x - 2y + 3z = -16. & (48) \end{cases}$$

Hence $x = -1$ by (46); substituting in (47), $y = 2$; from (48), $z = -3$. As in § 10-7, these answers can be checked by substitution in the original equations.

In using matrices in solving systems of linear equations, as in reducing a system of equations to triangular form (§ 10-7), the work can be done more quickly than it can be explained. The student is cautioned that the successive matrices, as found in the example, are *not equal* one to another. Rather, one *leads to* another, as may be indicated by an arrow.

EXERCISES

Solve the given system of equations by use of matrices, and check:

1—2. The systems in Exercises 1 and 2 of § 10-2.

3—12. The systems in Exercises 3 through 12 of § 10-4.

13. $\begin{cases} 2x - 3y = -11, \\ 5x + 2y = 4. \end{cases}$

14. $\begin{cases} 6x + 3y = 5, \\ 3x - 2y = -\frac{4}{3}. \end{cases}$

15. $\begin{cases} 2y + z + x - 1 = 0, \\ z - 2x = 1, \\ 2z + 6y + \frac{1}{2} = 0. \end{cases}$

16. $\begin{cases} 3x + 5z + 4y = 1, \\ x - y = 3 + z, \\ y + 2z + 2 = 0. \end{cases}$

17. $\begin{cases} y + 3z + 4w = 5, \\ x - y - 2z - 3w = -2, \\ 4x + y + z + 5w = 5, \\ x + y + z + w = 2. \end{cases}$

18. $\begin{cases} 3x = 1 + 2(z + w), \\ 2(x + y) + 3(z - w) = 4, \\ x + 3(y - 2z) = 0, \\ 4y - 3z - w = 2. \end{cases}$

19. $\begin{cases} 4x + 2y - 3u - 2v = 0, \\ 3x - y + 5z - u = 2, \\ 5x + 4z + 3v = 8, \\ 2x + 3y - 4z + v = 3, \\ y - 3z - 2u - v = 0. \end{cases}$

20. With reference to the warning that successive matrices used in solving a given system of equations are not "equal" one to another, what is the effect on the solution of the system if the following operations are performed on the augmented matrix: **(a)** two rows are interchanged? **(b)** two columns are interchanged? **(c)** the elements in one row are multiplied by a number different from 0? (d) the elements of a column, other than the last column, are multiplied by 4? (e) the elements of the last column are multiplied by 4?

10-10 Linear Systems Not Leading to Matrices in Triangular Form

In some cases it is impossible to reduce the matrix of coefficients to triangular form. The following cases arise:

(A) Whenever a matrix, derived from the augmented matrix of coefficients by the allowed operations, has a row in which each element is zero except the element in the last column, then the system has no solution. (This row makes the impossible statement that a sum of a number of zeros is different from zero.)

(B) If a row of such a derived matrix consists *entirely* of zeros, it can be disregarded for purposes of solving the system. (This row corresponds to the trivial equation in which each coefficient is zero and the constant term is zero.)

(C) If it is impossible to obtain either a matrix of type (A) or a matrix in which the part corresponding to the matrix of coefficients, disregarding any rows which are entirely zeros, is triangular, then some of the unknowns are not determined by the equations.

EXAMPLE 1.   Solve $\begin{cases} x + y = 5, \\ x + y = 7. \end{cases}$

Solution. $\begin{bmatrix} 1 & 1 & | & 5 \\ 1 & 1 & | & 7 \end{bmatrix} \rightarrow \begin{bmatrix} 0 & 0 & | & -2 \\ 1 & 1 & | & 7 \end{bmatrix}$. Hence there is no solution.

EXAMPLE 2.   Solve $\begin{cases} x + y = 2, \\ x - y = 4, \\ x + 2y = 1. \end{cases}$

Solution.   Write the augmented matrix:
$\begin{bmatrix} 1 & 1 & | & 2 \\ 1 & -1 & | & 4 \\ 1 & 2 & | & 1 \end{bmatrix}$.

Add the third row to twice the second row, and then multiply the new second row by $\frac{1}{3}$, obtaining successively:
$\begin{bmatrix} 1 & 1 & | & 2 \\ 3 & 0 & | & 9 \\ 1 & 2 & | & 1 \end{bmatrix} \rightarrow \begin{bmatrix} 1 & 1 & | & 2 \\ 1 & 0 & | & 3 \\ 1 & 2 & | & 1 \end{bmatrix}$.

Subtract the third row from twice the first row, and then subtract the second row from the new first row:

$$\begin{bmatrix} 1 & 0 & | & 3 \\ 1 & 0 & | & 3 \\ 1 & 2 & | & 1 \end{bmatrix} \rightarrow \begin{bmatrix} 0 & 0 & | & 0 \\ 1 & 0 & | & 3 \\ 1 & 2 & | & 1 \end{bmatrix}.$$

Thus $x = 3$, and then $y = -1$. The first equation has become the trivial statement $0x + 0y = 0$. Accordingly, although there are three equations in only two unknowns, this system has a solution.

Check. Substituting in the given system,

$$3 - 1 = 2, \quad 3 + 1 = 4, \quad 3 - 2 = 1.$$

EXAMPLE 3. Solve $\begin{cases} x + y + z = 6, \\ x + y + 2z = 9. \end{cases}$

Solution.
$$\begin{bmatrix} 1 & 1 & 1 & | & 6 \\ 1 & 1 & 2 & | & 9 \end{bmatrix} \rightarrow \begin{bmatrix} 2 & 2 & 2 & | & 12 \\ 1 & 1 & 2 & | & 9 \end{bmatrix} \rightarrow \begin{bmatrix} 1 & 1 & 0 & | & 3 \\ 1 & 1 & 2 & | & 9 \end{bmatrix}$$
$$\rightarrow \begin{bmatrix} 1 & 1 & 0 & | & 3 \\ 0 & 0 & 2 & | & 6 \end{bmatrix}.$$

Evidently there is no way to eliminate another coefficient of an unknown in the first row. Thus $z = 3$, but x and y are undetermined though subject to the relation obtained by rewriting the first row: $x + y = 3$. Such a result is not surprising, since there are fewer equations than unknowns.

We recall from § 10-2 that a system of equations which has one or more solutions is called consistent, and that a system which has no solution is called inconsistent.

EXERCISES

Solve the given system of equations as far as possible, by use of matrices, and check:

1. $\begin{cases} 2r + s = 4, \\ 7r - 3s = 1, \\ 3r - 2s + 1 = 0. \end{cases}$

2. $\begin{cases} 3x + 4y = 1, \\ x - 2y = 7, \\ 5x + 9y = -5. \end{cases}$

3. $\begin{cases} 4x + 2y = -1, \\ x + y = -1, \\ x + \frac{1}{3}y = 0, \\ x + 3y = -4. \end{cases}$

4. $\begin{cases} 3x + 6y + 3 = 0, \\ x + 2y + 1 = 0, \\ 2x + 4y + 2 = 0. \end{cases}$

5. $\begin{cases} u - 5v + 2 = 0, \\ 3v + 2u = 9, \\ v + u = 4. \end{cases}$

8. $\begin{cases} x + y - 3z = 8, \\ 3x + 2y + 6z = 6, \\ 2x - 3y + z + 6 = 0, \\ x - 3y - 11z - 4 = 0. \end{cases}$

6. $\begin{cases} x + 2y - 3z = 6, \\ x - y + z = 1, \\ 2x - 3y - 4z = 5, \\ 3x + y + z = 3. \end{cases}$

9. $\begin{cases} 3x - 2y + 4z = 3, \\ x + 4y - 2z = 1, \\ x - 2y = 1, \\ y + z = 0. \end{cases}$

7. $\begin{cases} x - y + z + 2 = 0, \\ 5y - 3x = 7, \\ 2z + 5x + 1 = 0, \\ 3y + 4z + 6 = 0. \end{cases}$

10. $\begin{cases} x + 2y - 7z + 1 = 0, \\ 2x - y + z = 3. \end{cases}$

11. Graph the equations in Example 1 in the text.

12. Graph the equations in Example 2 in the text.

CHAPTER 11

DETERMINANTS

11-1   Introduction

In the preceding chapter we considered rectangular arrays, called matrices; a matrix was considered an entity but no single "value" was attached to it. In the present chapter, a value—called the determinant of the matrix—will be assigned to each *square* matrix, and we shall study properties of determinants and their use in connection with systems of equations. To render this chapter as self-contained as possible, necessary definitions concerning matrices are repeated from the previous chapter.

A **matrix** is an array of numbers, or symbols representing numbers, consisting of rows and columns, each row having an entry for each column and vice versa. The array is enclosed in brackets. If there are m rows and n columns, the array is called an $m \times n$ **matrix** (read "m by n matrix"). If $m = n$, it is called a **square matrix** and n is called the **order** of the matrix. This chapter is primarily concerned with square matrices. The numbers appearing in the array are called the **elements** of the matrix.

If M is a matrix, and N is a matrix obtained by deleting some columns, or some rows, or both, from M without disturbing the relative positions of the remaining elements, then N is called a **submatrix** of M. For completeness, M is also called a submatrix of itself.

ILLUSTRATION. $\begin{bmatrix} 2 & 3 & 1 \\ 4 & 0 & -1 \end{bmatrix}$ is a 2×3 matrix. Its submatrices are

$$\begin{bmatrix} 2 & 3 & 1 \\ 4 & 0 & -1 \end{bmatrix}, \quad \begin{bmatrix} 2 & 3 \\ 4 & 0 \end{bmatrix}, \quad \begin{bmatrix} 2 & 1 \\ 4 & -1 \end{bmatrix}, \quad \begin{bmatrix} 3 & 1 \\ 0 & -1 \end{bmatrix}, \quad \begin{bmatrix} 2 \\ 4 \end{bmatrix}, \quad \begin{bmatrix} 3 \\ 0 \end{bmatrix}, \quad \begin{bmatrix} 1 \\ -1 \end{bmatrix},$$

[2 3 1],   [4 0 −1],   [2 3],   [2 1],   [3 1],   [4 0],

[4 −1],   [0 −1],   [2],   [3],   [1],   [4],   [0],   [−1].

The first of these is the matrix itself. Each of the 2×2 submatrices, listed next, is obtained by deleting one column; each of the 2×1 submatrices, by deleting two columns; each of the 1×3 submatrices, by deleting a row; and so on.

In the case of a square matrix, the elements which lie on the line from the upper left corner to the bottom right corner constitute the **principal diagonal,** or **the diagonal,** of the matrix. The elements on a line from the upper right to lower left corners constitute the **secondary diagonal.**

EXERCISES

Find **(a)** *all the* 2×2 *submatrices,* **(b)** *all the* 2×1 *submatrices, of the given matrix;* **(c)** *if the matrix is square, state its order and list the elements on the principal diagonal:*

1. $\begin{bmatrix} 3 & 1 \\ -2 & 0 \\ \frac{1}{2} & 2 \end{bmatrix}$.   **2.** $\begin{bmatrix} a & b \\ c & d \\ e & f \end{bmatrix}$.   **3.** $\begin{bmatrix} a_{11} & a_{12} & a_{13} \\ a_{21} & a_{22} & a_{23} \\ a_{31} & a_{32} & a_{33} \end{bmatrix}$.   **4.** $\begin{bmatrix} a_1 & b_1 \\ a_2 & b_2 \end{bmatrix}$.

11-2   Determinants of Order Two

Applying either of the methods of elimination of § 10-3 to the system of two linear equations in two unknowns,

$$\left. \begin{array}{l} a_1 x + b_1 y = c_1, \\ a_2 x + b_2 y = c_2, \end{array} \right\} \tag{1}$$

we obtain $$x = \frac{c_1 b_2 - c_2 b_1}{a_1 b_2 - a_2 b_1}, \qquad y = \frac{a_1 c_2 - a_2 c_1}{a_1 b_2 - a_2 b_1}, \tag{2}$$

provided $a_1 b_2 - a_2 b_1 \neq 0$.

Since any system of two linear equations in two unknowns can be arranged in the form of (1), the equations in (2) may be used as formulas for the solutions of such systems provided $a_1 b_2 - a_2 b_1 \neq 0$.

We observe that the values of x and y given by (2) appear as fractions with a common denominator which is a combination of the coefficients of the equations in the system—that is, a combination of the elements of the matrix of coefficients of the system. This motivates the definition of the **determinant of a matrix of order two,** which is also called a **determinant of order two** or a **determinant of the second order.**

The **determinant** *of the* 2×2 *square matrix* $\begin{bmatrix} a_1 & b_1 \\ a_2 & b_2 \end{bmatrix}$ *is defined to be* $(a_1 b_2 - a_2 b_1)$ *and is denoted by* $\begin{vmatrix} a_1 & b_1 \\ a_2 & b_2 \end{vmatrix}$.

Thus
$$\begin{vmatrix} a_1 & b_1 \\ a_2 & b_2 \end{vmatrix} = a_1 b_2 - a_2 b_1. \tag{3}$$

In words this becomes, "The determinant of a second order matrix is the product of the elements on the principal diagonal minus the product of the elements on the secondary diagonal."

The process of writing down the right member of (3) is called **expanding the determinant,** and the right member of (3) may be called the **expansion** of the determinant if it is desired to refer specifically to this algebraic sum instead of referring either to the determinant notation or to a simplified form of the algebraic sum.

ILLUSTRATIONS. $\begin{vmatrix} p & q \\ r & s \end{vmatrix} = ps - qr;$ $\begin{vmatrix} 3 & a \\ -b & 2 \end{vmatrix} = 6 - a(-b) = 6 + ab;$

$$\begin{vmatrix} 2 & -1 \\ 5 & -4 \end{vmatrix} = 2(-4) - 5(-1) = -3.$$

Using the definition of a determinant, we now observe that the numerators of the values of x and y in (2) may also be written as determinants of the second order, namely:

$$c_1 b_2 - c_2 b_1 = \begin{vmatrix} c_1 & b_1 \\ c_2 & b_2 \end{vmatrix}, \quad \text{and} \quad a_1 c_2 - a_2 c_1 = \begin{vmatrix} a_1 & c_1 \\ a_2 & c_2 \end{vmatrix}.$$

We may therefore write the solution of the linear system (1) in the form

$$x = \frac{\begin{vmatrix} c_1 & b_1 \\ c_2 & b_2 \end{vmatrix}}{\begin{vmatrix} a_1 & b_1 \\ a_2 & b_2 \end{vmatrix}}, \quad y = \frac{\begin{vmatrix} a_1 & c_1 \\ a_2 & c_2 \end{vmatrix}}{\begin{vmatrix} a_1 & b_1 \\ a_2 & b_2 \end{vmatrix}}, \tag{4}$$

provided that the determinant in the denominator, called the **determinant of the system,** *is not equal to zero.*

For ease in recalling the determinants involved in (4), the following relationship between them may be noted: The denominator is the determinant of the matrix of coefficients of the unknowns in the equations as written in the standard form (1). The numerator in the value of an unknown is the determinant of the matrix which is obtained from the matrix of coefficients by replacing the coefficients of that unknown by the corresponding constant terms, where each constant term appears in the member of the equation opposite the unknowns.

EXAMPLE.   Solve by determinants: $\begin{cases} 4x - 8y = 17, \\ 12x + 16y = -9. \end{cases}$

Solution.   Since the given system is in the form of (1) and

$$\begin{vmatrix} 4 & -8 \\ 12 & 16 \end{vmatrix} = 64 + 96 = 160,$$

the determinant of the system is not zero, and we have by (4):

$$x = \frac{\begin{vmatrix} 17 & -8 \\ -9 & 16 \end{vmatrix}}{160} = \frac{272 - 72}{160} = \frac{200}{160} = \frac{5}{4},$$

$$y = \frac{\begin{vmatrix} 4 & 17 \\ 12 & -9 \end{vmatrix}}{160} = \frac{-36 - 204}{160} = \frac{-240}{160} = -\frac{3}{2}.$$

This solution, $x = \frac{5}{4}$, $y = -\frac{3}{2}$, may be checked by substituting in the given equations.

Historical Note. Although the invention of determinants is usually credited to the German mathematician GOTTFRIED WILHELM LEIBNIZ (1646–1716), the Japanese mathematician SEKI KŌWA (1642–1708) considered determinants somewhat earlier than Leibniz.

EXERCISES

1–8.   Use determinants to solve the systems of equations in Exercises 1 through 8 of § 10-2.

Expand the determinants of the following matrices, and simplify:

9. $\begin{bmatrix} 3 & 2 \\ \frac{1}{4} & -\frac{1}{2} \end{bmatrix}$.

10. $\begin{bmatrix} 5 & 1 \\ 3 & 0 \end{bmatrix}$.

11. $\begin{bmatrix} a & b \\ 3 & 4 \end{bmatrix}$.

12. $\begin{bmatrix} \frac{1}{2} & -2 \\ x & y \end{bmatrix}$.

13. $\begin{bmatrix} x^2 & y^2 \\ x & y \end{bmatrix}$.

14. $\begin{bmatrix} e^3 & e^{-3} \\ e^5 & e^{-1} \end{bmatrix}$.

15. $\begin{bmatrix} \log 8 & 3 \\ \log 16 & 5 \end{bmatrix}$.

16. $\begin{bmatrix} \sin \theta & \cos \theta \\ -\cos \theta & \sin \theta \end{bmatrix}$.

17. $\begin{bmatrix} \tan \theta & \sec \theta \\ \operatorname{ctn} \theta & \csc \theta \end{bmatrix}$.

18–25.   Use determinants to solve the systems of equations in Exercises 18 through 25 of § 10-3.

Solve for x:

26. $\begin{vmatrix} 6 & 2 \\ x & 1 \end{vmatrix} = 0.$

27. $\begin{vmatrix} 6 & 5 + x \\ x & 1 \end{vmatrix} = 0.$

Expand the determinants and thence prove the equalities:

28. $\begin{vmatrix} a_1 & b_1 \\ a_2 & b_2 \end{vmatrix} = \begin{vmatrix} a_1 & a_2 \\ b_1 & b_2 \end{vmatrix}.$

30. $\begin{vmatrix} a_1 & b_1 \\ a_2 & b_2 \end{vmatrix} = \begin{vmatrix} a_1 & b_1 + ka_1 \\ a_2 & b_2 + ka_2 \end{vmatrix}.$

29. $\begin{vmatrix} a_1 & b_1 \\ a_2 & b_2 \end{vmatrix} = - \begin{vmatrix} a_2 & b_2 \\ a_1 & b_1 \end{vmatrix}.$

31. $\begin{vmatrix} ka_1 & b_1 \\ ka_2 & b_2 \end{vmatrix} = k \begin{vmatrix} a_1 & b_1 \\ a_2 & b_2 \end{vmatrix}.$

11-3   Determinants of Order Three

Applying the methods of Chapter 10 to the system of three linear equations in three unknowns,

$$\left. \begin{array}{l} a_1 x + b_1 y + c_1 z = d_1, \\ a_2 x + b_2 y + c_2 z = d_2, \\ a_3 x + b_3 y + c_3 z = d_3, \end{array} \right\} \tag{5}$$

we obtain

$$x = \frac{d_1 b_2 c_3 + d_3 b_1 c_2 + d_2 b_3 c_1 - d_3 b_2 c_1 - d_1 b_3 c_2 - d_2 b_1 c_3}{a_1 b_2 c_3 + a_3 b_1 c_2 + a_2 b_3 c_1 - a_3 b_2 c_1 - a_1 b_3 c_2 - a_2 b_1 c_3},$$

$$y = \frac{a_1 d_2 c_3 + a_3 d_1 c_2 + a_2 d_3 c_1 - a_3 d_2 c_1 - a_1 d_3 c_2 - a_2 d_1 c_3}{a_1 b_2 c_3 + a_3 b_1 c_2 + a_2 b_3 c_1 - a_3 b_2 c_1 - a_1 b_3 c_2 - a_2 b_1 c_3},$$

$$z = \frac{a_1 b_2 d_3 + a_3 b_1 d_2 + a_2 b_3 d_1 - a_3 b_2 d_1 - a_1 b_3 d_2 - a_2 b_1 d_3}{a_1 b_2 c_3 + a_3 b_1 c_2 + a_2 b_3 c_1 - a_3 b_2 c_1 - a_1 b_3 c_2 - a_2 b_1 c_3},$$

provided that the common denominator is not zero. This motivates the definition of the **determinant of a matrix of order three,** also called a **determinant of order three** or a **determinant of the third order.**

*The **determinant** of the 3×3 square matrix* $\begin{bmatrix} a_1 & b_1 & c_1 \\ a_2 & b_2 & c_2 \\ a_3 & b_3 & c_3 \end{bmatrix}$ *is denoted by replacing the brackets by vertical bars, and is defined by the relation*

$$\begin{vmatrix} a_1 & b_1 & c_1 \\ a_2 & b_2 & c_2 \\ a_3 & b_3 & c_3 \end{vmatrix} = a_1 b_2 c_3 + a_3 b_1 c_2 + a_2 b_3 c_1 - a_3 b_2 c_1 - a_1 b_3 c_2 - a_2 b_1 c_3. \tag{6}$$

There are several schemes for writing down the six terms in the expansion of a determinant of the third order. The following simple scheme is convenient for determinants of the third order but is artificial in that it can *not* be used for determinants of higher order. General methods of expanding determinants will be given in later sections.

Any determinant of the third order may be expanded as follows:

1. Rewrite the first and second columns to the right of the determinant, as in Figure 11.1.

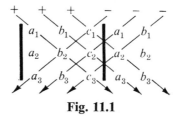

Fig. 11.1

2. The products of the elements in each of the three diagonals running down from left to right are added, and the products of the elements in each of the three diagonals running down from right to left are subtracted.

3. The algebraic sum of the six products thus formed is the expansion of the determinant.

ILLUSTRATION.

$$\begin{vmatrix} 1 & 2 & -1 \\ 2 & -1 & 3 \\ -3 & -4 & 5 \end{vmatrix} = (-5) + (-18) + 8 - (-3) - (-12) - 20 = -20.$$

Using the definition of a determinant of the third order, we may write the solution of the linear system (5) in the form

$$x = \frac{\begin{vmatrix} d_1 & b_1 & c_1 \\ d_2 & b_2 & c_2 \\ d_3 & b_3 & c_3 \end{vmatrix}}{\begin{vmatrix} a_1 & b_1 & c_1 \\ a_2 & b_2 & c_2 \\ a_3 & b_3 & c_3 \end{vmatrix}}, \quad y = \frac{\begin{vmatrix} a_1 & d_1 & c_1 \\ a_2 & d_2 & c_2 \\ a_3 & d_3 & c_3 \end{vmatrix}}{\begin{vmatrix} a_1 & b_1 & c_1 \\ a_2 & b_2 & c_2 \\ a_3 & b_3 & c_3 \end{vmatrix}}, \quad z = \frac{\begin{vmatrix} a_1 & b_1 & d_1 \\ a_2 & b_2 & d_2 \\ a_3 & b_3 & d_3 \end{vmatrix}}{\begin{vmatrix} a_1 & b_1 & c_1 \\ a_2 & b_2 & c_2 \\ a_3 & b_3 & c_3 \end{vmatrix}}, \quad (7)$$

provided that the determinant in the denominator, called the **determinant of the system,** *is not equal to zero.*

Just as with linear systems in two unknowns, each of the fractions in the answers (7) has for its denominator the determinant of the matrix of the coefficients in the system of equations (5). Also the numerator in the value of an unknown is the determinant of the matrix obtained from the matrix of coefficients by replacing the coefficients of that unknown by the constant terms.

EXAMPLE.   Solve by determinants: $\begin{cases} x + 2y - z = 6, \\ 2x - y + 3z = -13, \\ 3x - 2y + 3z = -16. \end{cases}$

Solution.

$$x = \frac{\begin{vmatrix} 6 & 2 & -1 \\ -13 & -1 & 3 \\ -16 & -2 & 3 \end{vmatrix}}{\begin{vmatrix} 1 & 2 & -1 \\ 2 & -1 & 3 \\ 3 & -2 & 3 \end{vmatrix}} = \frac{-18 + (-96) + (-26) - (-16) - (-36) - (-78)}{-3 + 18 + 4 - 3 - (-6) - 12}$$

$$= \frac{-10}{10} = -1;$$

$$y = \frac{\begin{vmatrix} 1 & 6 & -1 \\ 2 & -13 & 3 \\ 3 & -16 & 3 \end{vmatrix}}{10} = \frac{20}{10} = 2; \qquad z = \frac{\begin{vmatrix} 1 & 2 & 6 \\ 2 & -1 & -13 \\ 3 & -2 & -16 \end{vmatrix}}{10} = \frac{-30}{10} = -3.$$

This solution, $x = -1$, $y = 2$, $z = -3$, may be checked by substituting in the given equations.

EXERCISES

1–10. Solve Exercises 1 through 10 of § 10-4 by the use of determinants.

11. Use determinants to solve the system of equations $x - 2y = z$, $2x + 3y = 7z$, $5x + 29z = 19y$.

11-4   Determinants of Any Order

As a preliminary to defining determinants of any order and developing some of their more important properties, we introduce the notion of **inversion.** Consider the various possible arrangements of a set of elements, such as letters or numbers. If some particular order of these elements is regarded as the natural order, then any other order is said to have as many inversions as it presents occurrences in which one element is followed somewhere by a second element which precedes it somewhere in the natural order.

ILLUSTRATION.   Assuming that $a, b, c, d, \cdots$ is the natural order of letters, the arrangement *cbad* has three inversions: *c* before *b*, *c* before *a*, and *b* before *a*. Likewise, assuming that 1, 2, 3, 4, $\cdots$ is the natural order of positive integers, the arrangement 4321 has six inversions: 4 before 3, 4 before 2, 4 before 1, 3 before 2, 3 before 1, and 2 before 1.

We now define the **determinant of an $n \times n$ matrix,** also called an **nth order determinant,** where n is any positive integer. Determinants are not defined for matrices which are not square. For convenient exposition we shall denote the elements of the matrix by letters with subscripts, the elements in the same column having the same letter, and the elements in the same row having the same subscript. The symbol for the determinant is the array of elements of the matrix, with the brackets replaced by vertical lines:

$$\begin{vmatrix} a_1 & b_1 & \cdot & \cdot & \cdot & r_1 \\ a_2 & b_2 & \cdot & \cdot & \cdot & r_2 \\ a_3 & b_3 & \cdot & \cdot & \cdot & r_3 \\ \cdot & \cdot & \cdot & \cdot & \cdot & \cdot \\ a_n & b_n & \cdot & \cdot & \cdot & r_n \end{vmatrix}$$

The determinant of an n $\times$ n *matrix is defined to be the algebraic sum of all the possible products of* n *factors each, where*

(1) *each product has as factors one element, and only one, from each row and each column, and*

(2) *to each product there is prefixed a plus or a minus sign, according as the number of inversions of the rows in which successive factors lie is even* (*which includes zero*) *or odd, after the factors are arranged in the natural order of the columns.* In the notation of the above array, this number of inversions is the number of inversions of the subscripts when the letters are arranged in the order in which they appear in the array.

Each of the above-mentioned products with its proper sign is a term of the determinant, and their algebraic sum is called the **expansion** or the **value** of the determinant. The element in the upper left corner of the matrix is called the **leading element,** and the place which it occupies is called the **leading position.**

Comparing this definition with those in § 11-2 and § 11-3, it is seen that our definitions of determinants of orders two and three are special cases of the general definition of determinant. As in § 11-2, the phrase "expansion of the determinant" is used to emphasize that one is considering the algebraic sum specified in the definition of the determinant.

Warning. The diagrammatic method of writing the expansion of a third-order determinant given in § 11-3 does *not* apply to fourth and higher order determinants.

EXERCISES

Determine the number of inversions of integers in each of the following arrangements if 1, 2, 3, $\cdots$ *is the natural order:*

1. 213.   **2.** 321.   **3.** 123.   **4.** 3214.   **5.** 15243.   **6.** 54321.

Determine the number of inversions of letters in each of the following arrangements if a, b, c, $\cdots$ *is the natural order:*

7. *adbc.*   **8.** *bdac.*   **9.** *dcba.*   **10.** *acedb.*   **11.** *abhcgfde.*

Determine the number of inversions **(a)** *of subscripts in each of the following arrangements when the letters are in natural order;* **(b)** *of letters when the subscripts are in natural order:*

12. $a_2b_3c_1.$ **13.** $a_2b_3d_4c_1.$ **14.** $d_3c_1b_2a_4.$ **15.** $a_2d_1e_3c_4b_5.$

16. Determine the signs of the following terms in the expansion of the adjoining determinant of the fourth order:

(a) $a_1b_2c_3d_4;$ **(d)** $a_3b_4c_2d_1;$

(b) $a_1b_2c_4d_3;$ **(e)** $c_1a_2d_3b_4;$

(c) $a_4b_3c_2d_1;$ **(f)** $d_1a_2c_3b_4.$

$$\begin{vmatrix} a_1 & b_1 & c_1 & d_1 \\ a_2 & b_2 & c_2 & d_2 \\ a_3 & b_3 & c_3 & d_3 \\ a_4 & b_4 & c_4 & d_4 \end{vmatrix}$$

17. Write out the expansions of the two determinants in definition (3) of § 11-2 and definition (6) of § 11-3 by use of the definition in the present section.

Write out the expansion of the following determinants by the definition:

18. $\begin{vmatrix} 3 & -2 & 1 \\ 1 & 2 & -1 \\ 1 & 0 & 2 \end{vmatrix}.$ **19.** $\begin{vmatrix} -1 & \frac{1}{2} & 2 \\ 2 & 1 & 0 \\ 3 & 2 & 1 \end{vmatrix}.$ **20.** $\begin{vmatrix} 2 & e^x & e^{-x} \\ 3 & e^{3x} & e^{-3x} \\ 0 & e^{5x} & e^{-5x} \end{vmatrix}.$

11-5   Properties of Determinants

From the definition in the previous section we can deduce some properties of determinants. These properties are important not only for their own sake but also as examples of how conclusions can be derived from an unfamiliar basis where intuition is of little help—in contrast to the case in plane and solid geometry. In most cases our discussions are expressed in terms of determinants of the third order, but this is merely for brevity in writing as similar proofs can be given for determinants of any order.

Property 1.   *If the corresponding rows and columns of a matrix are interchanged, the determinant of the matrix is not changed.*

Proof.   We wish to show that $D = D'$, where (for $n = 3$)

$$M = \begin{bmatrix} a_1 & b_1 & c_1 \\ a_2 & b_2 & c_2 \\ a_3 & b_3 & c_3 \end{bmatrix} \quad \text{and} \quad M' = \begin{bmatrix} a_1 & a_2 & a_3 \\ b_1 & b_2 & b_3 \\ c_1 & c_2 & c_3 \end{bmatrix}.$$

Let D be the determinant of M, and D' be the determinant of M'. By the definition of a determinant, both D and D' have exactly the same terms in their expansions, except possibly for sign, since these terms are respectively formed by taking one element, and only one, from each row and each column in M and from each column and each row in M', thus always obtaining the same elements as factors. We shall now show that the corresponding terms of D and D' will have the same signs prefixed to them by showing that the number of inversions in the subscripts in any term of D when the letters are in natural order is equal to the number of inversions of the letters of the corresponding term of D' when the subscripts are in natural order. Assuming that the letters are in their natural order, the inversions in the subscripts can be removed, one by one, by interchanging two adjacent subscripts in turn, leaving the other subscripts in their respective positions. Now each such interchange in subscripts introduces one inversion in the letters. Hence to place the subscripts in their natural order introduces the *same* number of inversions in the letters as there were originally inversions in the subscripts.

It follows directly from Property 1 that *for every theorem concerning the effect which something about the columns of a matrix has on the determinant of the matrix, there is a corresponding theorem concerning the rows, and conversely.* Furthermore, the proof of either theorem establishes the other theorem also.

Property 2.   *If each of the elements of a column (or row) of a matrix is zero, the value of the determinant of the matrix is zero.*

Proof.   Each term of the expansion of the determinant will contain as one of its factors an element from the column (or row) of zeros. Hence each term of the expansion will equal zero.

Property 3. *If two columns (or two rows) of a matrix are interchanged, the sign of the determinant of the matrix is changed.*

Proof. First consider the effect of interchanging any two adjacent rows. This corresponds to an interchange of two adjacent subscripts in each term of the expansion and hence increases or decreases the number of inversions in the subscripts of each term by one. Therefore the sign of each term of the expansion will be changed, and hence the sign of the determinant will be changed.

Next consider the effect of interchanging any two nonadjacent rows; suppose they are separated by k intermediate rows. This is equivalent to $(2k + 1)$ interchanges of adjacent rows: k interchanges to bring the lower row just below the upper row, one to interchange them, and k more to take the upper row into the original position of the lower row. But $(2k + 1)$ is always an odd number. Therefore, since each interchange of two adjacent rows changes the sign of the determinant, the interchange of any two rows brings about an odd number of changes of sign, and the sign of the determinant will be changed.

ILLUSTRATION 1.
$$\begin{vmatrix} a_1 & b_1 & c_1 \\ a_2 & b_2 & c_2 \\ a_3 & b_3 & c_3 \end{vmatrix} = - \begin{vmatrix} a_3 & b_3 & c_3 \\ a_2 & b_2 & c_2 \\ a_1 & b_1 & c_1 \end{vmatrix}.$$

Property 4. *If two columns (or two rows) of a matrix are identical, the value of the determinant of the matrix is zero.*

Proof. Denote the value of the determinant by D. If we interchange the two identical columns, the value of the determinant is unchanged. But, by Property 3, such an interchange changes D into $-D$. Hence $D = -D$; that is, $2D = 0$, or $D = 0$.

Property 5. *If each of the elements of a column (or row) of a matrix is multiplied by the same number* m, *the value of the determinant of the matrix is multiplied by* m.

Proof. Each term of the expansion of the new determinant will contain as one of its factors one element from the column (or row) of the given matrix multiplied by m. Hence each term of this expansion is m times the corresponding term of the expansion of the determinant of the given matrix.

ILLUSTRATION 2.
$$\begin{vmatrix} ma_1 & b_1 & c_1 \\ ma_2 & b_2 & c_2 \\ ma_3 & b_3 & c_3 \end{vmatrix} = m \begin{vmatrix} a_1 & b_1 & c_1 \\ a_2 & b_2 & c_2 \\ a_3 & b_3 & c_3 \end{vmatrix}.$$

Property 6.   *If each element of any column (or row) of a matrix is expressed as the sum of two, or more, terms, then the determinant of the matrix may be expressed as the sum of two, or more, determinants.*

For example,

$$\begin{vmatrix} (a_1 + a_1') & b_1 & c_1 \\ (a_2 + a_2') & b_2 & c_2 \\ (a_3 + a_3') & b_3 & c_3 \end{vmatrix} = \begin{vmatrix} a_1 & b_1 & c_1 \\ a_2 & b_2 & c_2 \\ a_3 & b_3 & c_3 \end{vmatrix} + \begin{vmatrix} a_1' & b_1 & c_1 \\ a_2' & b_2 & c_2 \\ a_3' & b_3 & c_3 \end{vmatrix}.$$

Proof.   In this special case, as in the general case, each term of the expansion of the determinant on the left is equal to the sum of the corresponding terms of the expansion of the determinants on the right. For example,

$$(a_1 + a_1')b_2c_3 = a_1b_2c_3 + a_1'b_2c_3.$$

Property 7.   *The value of the determinant of a matrix is not changed if to the elements of any column (or row) of the matrix are added m times the corresponding elements of any other column (or row), respectively.*

For example,

$$\begin{vmatrix} a_1 & b_1 & c_1 \\ a_2 & b_2 & c_2 \\ a_3 & b_3 & c_3 \end{vmatrix} = \begin{vmatrix} a_1 & (b_1 + mc_1) & c_1 \\ a_2 & (b_2 + mc_2) & c_2 \\ a_3 & (b_3 + mc_3) & c_3 \end{vmatrix}.$$

Proof.   The proof follows directly from Properties 6, 5, and 4, in the order named:

$$\begin{vmatrix} a_1 & (b_1 + mc_1) & c_1 \\ a_2 & (b_2 + mc_2) & c_2 \\ a_3 & (b_3 + mc_3) & c_3 \end{vmatrix} = \begin{vmatrix} a_1 & b_1 & c_1 \\ a_2 & b_2 & c_2 \\ a_3 & b_3 & c_3 \end{vmatrix} + \begin{vmatrix} a_1 & mc_1 & c_1 \\ a_2 & mc_2 & c_2 \\ a_3 & mc_3 & c_3 \end{vmatrix}$$

$$= \begin{vmatrix} a_1 & b_1 & c_1 \\ a_2 & b_2 & c_2 \\ a_3 & b_3 & c_3 \end{vmatrix} + m\begin{vmatrix} a_1 & c_1 & c_1 \\ a_2 & c_2 & c_2 \\ a_3 & c_3 & c_3 \end{vmatrix}$$

$$= \begin{vmatrix} a_1 & b_1 & c_1 \\ a_2 & b_2 & c_2 \\ a_3 & b_3 & c_3 \end{vmatrix}.$$

Note that when Property 7 is applied, the column (or row) whose elements are each multiplied by m is *left intact*, and only the elements in the recipient column (or row) are replaced by the corresponding algebraic sums.

Warning.

$$\begin{vmatrix} (a_1 + mb_1) & b_1 & c_1 \\ (a_2 + mb_2) & b_2 & c_2 \\ (a_3 + mb_3) & b_3 & c_3 \end{vmatrix} = \begin{vmatrix} a_1 & b_1 & c_1 \\ a_2 & b_2 & c_2 \\ a_3 & b_3 & c_3 \end{vmatrix},$$

but

$$\begin{vmatrix} (ma_1 + b_1) & b_1 & c_1 \\ (ma_2 + b_2) & b_2 & c_2 \\ (ma_3 + b_3) & b_3 & c_3 \end{vmatrix} = m \begin{vmatrix} a_1 & b_1 & c_1 \\ a_2 & b_2 & c_2 \\ a_3 & b_3 & c_3 \end{vmatrix}.$$

EXERCISES

Show, without expanding the determinants, that:

1. $$\begin{vmatrix} 6 & 1 & -4 \\ 0 & 3 & 1 \\ \frac{1}{2} & -2 & 5 \end{vmatrix} = \begin{vmatrix} 6 & 0 & \frac{1}{2} \\ 1 & 3 & -2 \\ -4 & 1 & 5 \end{vmatrix} = - \begin{vmatrix} -4 & 1 & 5 \\ 1 & 3 & -2 \\ 6 & 0 & \frac{1}{2} \end{vmatrix}.$$

2. $$\begin{vmatrix} 3 & -1 & 1 \\ 2 & 8 & 7 \\ -4 & 1 & 5 \end{vmatrix} = \begin{vmatrix} -1 & 1 & 3 \\ 8 & 7 & 2 \\ 1 & 5 & -4 \end{vmatrix} = - \begin{vmatrix} 1 & -1 & -3 \\ 8 & 7 & 2 \\ 1 & 5 & -4 \end{vmatrix}.$$

3. $$\begin{vmatrix} 3 & 0 & 1 \\ -6 & -4 & -2 \\ 9 & 2 & -1 \end{vmatrix} = 3 \begin{vmatrix} 1 & 0 & 1 \\ -2 & -4 & -2 \\ 3 & 2 & -1 \end{vmatrix} = -6 \begin{vmatrix} 1 & 0 & 1 \\ 1 & 2 & 1 \\ 3 & 2 & -1 \end{vmatrix}.$$

4. $$\begin{vmatrix} 8 & 1 & -4 \\ -6 & 0 & 3 \\ 2 & 3 & -1 \end{vmatrix} = 0.$$

6. $$\begin{vmatrix} 5 & 4 & 1 \\ -2 & -2 & 0 \\ 1 & -3 & 4 \end{vmatrix} = 0.$$

5. $$\begin{vmatrix} 2 & 1 & a & (a+1) \\ 3 & 1 & b & (b+1) \\ 4 & 1 & c & (c+1) \\ 5 & 1 & d & (d+1) \end{vmatrix} = 0.$$

7. $$\begin{vmatrix} v & w & z & (x+y) \\ v & x & y & (w+z) \\ v & y & w & (x+z) \\ v & z & x & (w+y) \end{vmatrix} = 0.$$

8. Prove the following corollary to Property 4: *If the corresponding elements of two columns (or two rows) of a matrix are proportional, the value of the determinant of the matrix is zero.*

Find a matrix whose determinant equals the given determinant and in which each element, except one, in **(a)** *a column is zero;* **(b)** *a row is zero.*

9. $\begin{vmatrix} 1 & 4 & -2 \\ 5 & 0 & 2 \\ -1 & 1 & 3 \end{vmatrix}$.

10. $\begin{vmatrix} 1 & 2 & -2 \\ 3 & -5 & 4 \\ -1 & 1 & 3 \end{vmatrix}$.

11. $\begin{vmatrix} 0 & 5 & 4 & 2 \\ 3 & 0 & -1 & -2 \\ 1 & 4 & -2 & -5 \\ -2 & -3 & 1 & 3 \end{vmatrix}$.

12. $\begin{vmatrix} 4 & -1 & 3 & 2 \\ 2 & 3 & 2 & -1 \\ 1 & 2 & 1 & -4 \\ 1 & 2 & -5 & 7 \end{vmatrix}$.

13. Why is it not always possible to equate a given determinant to the determinant of a matrix in which all the elements in a column or row are zero?

Express each of the following determinants as the algebraic sum of two determinants, and simplify if possible:

14. $\begin{vmatrix} a_1 & (b_1 + c_1) & d_1 \\ a_2 & (b_2 + c_2) & d_2 \\ a_3 & (b_3 + c_3) & d_3 \end{vmatrix}$.

15. $\begin{vmatrix} x & y & z \\ 2x & 4y & 5z \\ (x + 3a) & (y + 3b) & (z + 3c) \end{vmatrix}$.

16. If ω is an imaginary cube root of unity, show that

$$\begin{vmatrix} 1 & \omega & \omega^2 \\ \omega & \omega^2 & 1 \\ \omega^2 & 1 & \omega \end{vmatrix} = 0.$$

17. Prove $\begin{vmatrix} 0 & -a_1 & -a_2 \\ a_1 & 0 & -a_3 \\ a_2 & a_3 & 0 \end{vmatrix} = 0.$

★18. State and prove a general theorem, for determinants of various orders, based upon the result stated in Exercise 17.

11-6   Expansion of Determinants by Minors

Suppose b_i is an element of a square matrix M, and M' is the sub-matrix obtained by deleting the row and the column of M in which b_i lies. Then the determinant of M' is called the **minor** of b_i. We shall denote this minor by B_i.

ILLUSTRATION 1.   In the matrix

$$\begin{bmatrix} a_1 & b_1 & c_1 \\ a_2 & b_2 & c_2 \\ a_3 & b_3 & c_3 \end{bmatrix},$$

the minor C_2 of the element c_2 is given by $C_2 = \begin{vmatrix} a_1 & b_1 \\ a_3 & b_3 \end{vmatrix}$.

Theorem.   *The determinant* D *of a matrix* M *of order* n *may be expressed as the sum of the* n *products formed by multiplying each element of any column (or row) by its minor, assigning to each product a plus or a minus sign according as the sum of the number of the column and the number of the row in which that element lies is even or odd.*

Before undertaking the proof of this theorem, its meaning will be illustrated by an application to a particular case.

ILLUSTRATION 2.

$$\begin{vmatrix} a_1 & b_1 & c_1 \\ a_2 & b_2 & c_2 \\ a_3 & b_3 & c_3 \end{vmatrix} = a_1 \begin{vmatrix} b_2 & c_2 \\ b_3 & c_3 \end{vmatrix} - a_2 \begin{vmatrix} b_1 & c_1 \\ b_3 & c_3 \end{vmatrix} + a_3 \begin{vmatrix} b_1 & c_1 \\ b_2 & c_2 \end{vmatrix}$$

$$= a_1 A_1 - a_2 A_2 + a_3 A_3.$$

Proof of Theorem.   First we show that in the expansion of the given determinant D, the sum of all the terms of D which involve the leading element a_1 is equal to $a_1 A_1$. This follows almost directly from the definition of a determinant, since, except possibly for sign, each term of D which involves a_1 is formed by multiplying a_1 by one element, and only one, from each of the remaining rows and columns of M, that is, by a term of the minor A_1. Moreover, the sign of each term of D which involves a_1 is the same as the sign of the corresponding term formed by multiplying a_1 by the required term of A_1, since writing a_1 before any term of A_1 will not change the number of inversions of its letters or subscripts.

Next we show that in the expansion of the given determinant D, the sum of all the terms of D which involve the element k_i in the ith row and the kth column is equal to $(-1)^{i+k}k_iK_i$. The element k_i can be brought into the position of the leading element by interchanging the ith row with each preceding row in turn and then interchanging the kth column with each preceding column in turn without disturbing the relative positions of the elements which lie outside of the ith row and the kth column, thus leaving unchanged the minor K_i of the element k_i. In making these changes, the sign of the value of the determinant will have been changed $(i-1) + (k-1)$, or $(i+k-2)$, times (Property 3). Hence, if we let D' denote the value of the determinant of this final matrix with k_i in the position of the leading element, then

$$D' = (-1)^{i+k-2}D = (-1)^{i+k}D.$$

By the first part of our proof, the sum of all the terms in the expansion of D' which involve k_i is equal to k_i times its minor in D'. But the minor of k_i in D' is the same as its minor in D. Hence the sum of all the terms in the expansion of the given determinant D which involve k_i is equal to $(-1)^{i+k}k_iK_i$.

Finally, using the results of the above two parts of our proof, we may write out the expansion of the determinant D in terms of the elements of any column or row and their minors. This follows from the fact that each term in the expansion of D contains one, and only one, of the elements of that column or row. Take, for instance, the first column. Then the sum of all the terms which involve a_1 is a_1A_1, the sum of all the terms which involve a_2 is $-a_2A_2$, and so on. In like manner, we may expand in terms of the elements of any column or row and their minors.

ILLUSTRATION 3.   For the determinant

$$D = \begin{vmatrix} a_1 & b_1 & c_1 & d_1 \\ a_2 & b_2 & c_2 & d_2 \\ a_3 & b_3 & c_3 & d_3 \\ a_4 & b_4 & c_4 & d_4 \end{vmatrix},$$

we have $D = a_1A_1 - a_2A_2 + a_3A_3 - a_4A_4$

$\qquad = -a_2A_2 + b_2B_2 - c_2C_2 + d_2D_2$, and so on.

Corollary. *If, in the expansion of a determinant by minors of the elements of any column (or row), the elements of this column (or row) are replaced by the corresponding elements of any other column (or row), the resulting expression equals zero.*

Proof. By the Theorem of this section, we may write

$$D = \begin{vmatrix} a_1 & b_1 & c_1 & d_1 \\ a_2 & b_2 & c_2 & d_2 \\ a_3 & b_3 & c_3 & d_3 \\ a_4 & b_4 & c_4 & d_4 \end{vmatrix} = a_1A_1 - a_2A_2 + a_3A_3 - a_4A_4.$$

We wish to prove that any sum such as

$$c_1A_1 - c_2A_2 + c_3A_3 - c_4A_4$$

is zero. This expression is identical with the expansion, by minors of the elements of the first column, of the determinant of the matrix

$$\begin{vmatrix} c_1 & b_1 & c_1 & d_1 \\ c_2 & b_2 & c_2 & d_2 \\ c_3 & b_3 & c_3 & d_3 \\ c_4 & b_4 & c_4 & d_4 \end{vmatrix}$$

obtained by replacing the column of a's by the column of c's with corresponding subscripts. By Property 4 this determinant equals zero. The same proof applies to a determinant of any order n.

EXERCISES

Expand the determinant in the specified manner and evaluate the result:

$$. \; D_1 = \begin{vmatrix} -2 & 3 & 0 & 1 \\ 0 & 0 & 2 & 0 \\ 4 & 0 & 1 & 3 \\ -1 & 5 & 0 & 9 \end{vmatrix}. \qquad D_2 = \begin{vmatrix} \frac{1}{2} & 0 & 6 & 1 \\ 0 & 0 & -4 & 2 \\ \frac{1}{4} & 0 & 8 & -1 \\ 1 & 3 & 0 & 0 \end{vmatrix}.$$

1. Expand D_1 **(a)** by minors of the elements of the first row; **(b)** by minors of the elements of the second row; **(c)** by minors of the elements of the fourth row; **(d)** by the definition in § 11-4.

2. Expand D_1 by minors of the elements **(a)** of the first column; **(b)** of the third column; **(c)** of the fourth column.

3. Expand D_2 by minors of the elements **(a)** of the first column; **(b)** of the second column; **(c)** of the fourth column.

4. Expand D_2 **(a)** by minors of the elements of the first row; **(b)** by minors of the elements of the second row; **(c)** by minors of the elements of the fourth row; **(d)** by the definition in § 11-4.

11-7 Evaluation of Determinants

The expansion of a determinant by minors according to the elements of any column or row enables us to evaluate a determinant of any order. This process, however, may be considerably shortened by first making use of the properties in § 11-5.

EXAMPLE 1. Evaluate the determinant D of the matrix

$$\begin{bmatrix} 4 & 1 & 0 & 3 \\ -2 & -2 & 7 & -6 \\ 6 & 4 & -9 & 12 \\ 10 & -3 & 2 & -9 \end{bmatrix}.$$

Solution. Removing the factors 2 and 3 from the first and fourth columns respectively, we have

$$D = (2)(3) \begin{vmatrix} 2 & 1 & 0 & 1 \\ -1 & -2 & 7 & -2 \\ 3 & 4 & -9 & 4 \\ 5 & -3 & 2 & -3 \end{vmatrix} = 6 \cdot 0 = 0,$$

since the resulting second and fourth columns are identical.

Usually the given matrix is best transformed into a matrix in which all of the elements, except one, in some particular column or row are zeros; then the resulting determinant is expanded by minors of the elements of the row or column containing the zeros. Thus the given determinant is expressed in terms of a determinant of lower order. The process may then be repeated until the resulting determinants are of the second or third order and can readily be expanded.

EXAMPLE 2. Evaluate the determinant D of the matrix M given by

$$M = \begin{bmatrix} 2 & -1 & 2 & -1 \\ 1 & 1 & -1 & 2 \\ 1 & 2 & 1 & -3 \\ 1 & 3 & 4 & 7 \end{bmatrix}.$$

Solution with Explanations. We select the first element in the second row of the given matrix as a convenient one to use in reducing all the other elements in the same row to zero. This is not the only possible choice, but it has the advantage that at least one of the elements of the row is 1 and the others are numerically small.

To obtain a matrix with the desired zeros in its second row, and whose determinant has a known relationship to D, we first add -1 times the elements in the first column to the corresponding elements in the second column. In the resulting matrix, we then add the elements in its first column to the corresponding elements in its third column. Finally, we add -2 times the elements in the first column to the corresponding elements in the fourth column. These steps in the reduction process are shown below.

$$D = \begin{vmatrix} 2 & -1 & 2 & -1 \\ 1 & 1 & -1 & 2 \\ 1 & 2 & 1 & -3 \\ 1 & 3 & 4 & 7 \end{vmatrix} = \begin{vmatrix} 2 & (-1-2) & 2 & -1 \\ 1 & (1-1) & -1 & 2 \\ 1 & (2-1) & 1 & -3 \\ 1 & (3-1) & 4 & 7 \end{vmatrix}$$

$$= \begin{vmatrix} 2 & -3 & (2+2) & -1 \\ 1 & 0 & (-1+1) & 2 \\ 1 & 1 & (1+1) & -3 \\ 1 & 2 & (4+1) & 7 \end{vmatrix}$$

$$= \begin{vmatrix} 2 & -3 & 4 & (-1-2\cdot2) \\ 1 & 0 & 0 & (2-2\cdot1) \\ 1 & 1 & 2 & (-3-2\cdot1) \\ 1 & 2 & 5 & (7-2\cdot1) \end{vmatrix} = \begin{vmatrix} 2 & -3 & 4 & -5 \\ 1 & 0 & 0 & 0 \\ 1 & 1 & 2 & -5 \\ 1 & 2 & 5 & 5 \end{vmatrix}.$$

The writing of the above reduction process is often condensed as follows:

$$D = \begin{vmatrix} 2 & (-1-2) & (2+2) & (-1-2\cdot2) \\ 1 & (1-1) & (-1+1) & (2-2\cdot1) \\ 1 & (2-1) & (1+1) & (-3-2\cdot1) \\ 1 & (3-1) & (4+1) & (7-2\cdot1) \end{vmatrix} = \begin{vmatrix} 2 & -3 & 4 & -5 \\ 1 & 0 & 0 & 0 \\ 1 & 1 & 2 & -5 \\ 1 & 2 & 5 & 5 \end{vmatrix}.$$

The various intermediate matrices need not be written down. However, to avoid possible confusion in condensing several reductions, it is a good working rule to leave one column or row intact, and to use the same two columns or rows only once in combination.

Now, if in the above display the last determinant is expanded by minors of the elements of the second row, all of which are zero except the first, we obtain only one third-order determinant in the expansion. This minor is preceded by a minus sign, since the element 1 in the second row and first column has an odd number ($2 + 1$, or 3) as the sum of the numbers of its row and column. If we then remove the factor 5 from the third column, we have

$$D = -(1) \begin{vmatrix} -3 & 4 & -5 \\ 1 & 2 & -5 \\ 2 & 5 & 5 \end{vmatrix} = -5 \begin{vmatrix} -3 & 4 & -1 \\ 1 & 2 & -1 \\ 2 & 5 & 1 \end{vmatrix}.$$

Although the last determinant may now be evaluated by the special methods given for determinants of the third order, we proceed as before to find an equal determinant of a matrix with each element, except one, of some particular column or row equal to zero. Thus if we add the elements of the third row to the elements of the first and second rows, we obtain

$$D = -5 \begin{vmatrix} (-3+2) & (4+5) & (-1+1) \\ (1+2) & (2+5) & (-1+1) \\ 2 & 5 & 1 \end{vmatrix} = -5 \begin{vmatrix} -1 & 9 & 0 \\ 3 & 7 & 0 \\ 2 & 5 & 1 \end{vmatrix};$$

whence

$$D = (-5)(1) \begin{vmatrix} -1 & 9 \\ 3 & 7 \end{vmatrix} = -5[(-7) - (27)] = 170.$$

EXERCISES

Evaluate:

1. $\begin{vmatrix} 2 & 4 \\ 3 & -5 \end{vmatrix}$.

2. $\begin{vmatrix} 2 \sin x & \sin 2x \\ -2 \cos x & \cos 2x \end{vmatrix}$.

3. $\begin{vmatrix} 0 & 3 & 0 \\ 1 & 8 & -2 \\ 4 & -1 & 6 \end{vmatrix}$.

4. $\begin{vmatrix} 3 & 2 & 0 \\ 6 & -\frac{1}{2} & 5 \\ 9 & -1 & 0 \end{vmatrix}$.

5. $\begin{vmatrix} 5 & 15 & 10 \\ -2 & 3 & 3 \\ 1 & -2 & 1 \end{vmatrix}$.

6. $\begin{vmatrix} 1 & 4 & 1 \\ 2 & 16 & 8 \\ 1 & 6 & 1 \end{vmatrix}$.

7. $\begin{vmatrix} 0 & 2 & 3 & 1 \\ 1 & -2 & 2 & -2 \\ 0 & 0 & -3 & 0 \\ 2 & 1 & 4 & -5 \end{vmatrix}$.

8. $\begin{vmatrix} -1 & 0 & 1 & 3 \\ 4 & 12 & 3 & -3 \\ 2 & 3 & -2 & -1 \\ -2 & 0 & -3 & 5 \end{vmatrix}$.

9. $\begin{vmatrix} 0 & 1 & -1 & 3 \\ 2 & 0 & 2 & -1 \\ 3 & 4 & 3 & 0 \\ -4 & 2 & 2 & 5 \end{vmatrix}$.

10. $\begin{vmatrix} -4 & 3 & -9 & -6 \\ 1 & -1 & 2 & 3 \\ -2 & -1 & -4 & 1 \\ 4 & -5 & -8 & 8 \end{vmatrix}$.

11. $\begin{vmatrix} 2 & 5 & -1 & 5 & -4 \\ 0 & 0 & 1 & -2 & 3 \\ 0 & 4 & -2 & 0 & 1 \\ 1 & 2 & 0 & 4 & -3 \\ -2 & 1 & 3 & -7 & -4 \end{vmatrix}$.

12. $\begin{vmatrix} 2 & -2 & 0 & 1 & 1 \\ 1 & 0 & 0 & 0 & 4 \\ 0 & 2 & 1 & -1 & 4 \\ -1 & 0 & -3 & 0 & 1 \\ -1 & -1 & 0 & 2 & -1 \end{vmatrix}$.

13. $\begin{vmatrix} b & a & a & 1 \\ a & b & a & 1 \\ a & a & b & 1 \\ a & a & a & 1 \end{vmatrix}.$

14. $\begin{vmatrix} 1 & 1 & 1 & 1 \\ g & -g & h & h \\ g & g & g & -h \\ h & -h & -h & g \end{vmatrix}.$

15. $\begin{vmatrix} (x+1) & 2 & 3 & 4 \\ 1 & (x+2) & 3 & 4 \\ 1 & 2 & (x+3) & 4 \\ 1 & 2 & 3 & (x+4) \end{vmatrix}.$

16. $\begin{vmatrix} (a+b) & c & c \\ a & (b+c) & a \\ b & b & (a+c) \end{vmatrix}.$

17. Solve $\begin{vmatrix} x & 1 & 2 \\ -1 & x & -2 \\ -3 & 1 & -1 \end{vmatrix} = 0.$

18. Solve $\begin{vmatrix} 3 & 4 & -x \\ x & 5 & 3 \\ 2 & 1 & -1 \end{vmatrix} = 0.$

The **area of the triangle** *whose vertices in rectangular coordinates are* (x_1, y_1), (x_2, y_2), *and* (x_3, y_3) *is given by the absolute value of*

$$\tfrac{1}{2} \begin{vmatrix} 1 & x_1 & y_1 \\ 1 & x_2 & y_2 \\ 1 & x_3 & y_3 \end{vmatrix}.$$

Find, by determinants, the area of the triangle having the following vertices:

19. $(2, -3)$, $(-1, 2)$, $(5, 4)$.   **20.** $(2, 4)$, $(-7, -2)$, $(4, 0)$.

Show by determinants that the following sets of points are collinear:

21. $(0, -24)$, $(4, 12)$, $(2, -6)$.   **22.** $(-2, 1)$, $(-4, 3)$, $(2, -3)$.

★ *Find, by determinants, an equation of the straight line passing through the following pairs of points:*

23. $(0, 4)$, $(3, 6)$.   **24.** $(-2, 3)$, $(-5, -1)$.   **25.** $(0, 0)$, $(6, -8)$.

11-8   Systems of n Linear Equations in n Unknowns

Suppose it is required to solve a system of n linear equations in n unknowns by means of determinants. For brevity in writing, let us take $n = 4$ (although the method used is applicable to the general case), and consider the following system:

$$
\begin{cases}
a_1x + b_1y + c_1z + d_1w = k_1, & (8) \\
a_2x + b_2y + c_2z + d_2w = k_2, & (9) \\
a_3x + b_3y + c_3z + d_3w = k_3, & (10) \\
a_4x + b_4y + c_4z + d_4w = k_4, & (11)
\end{cases}
$$

which is to be solved for the unknowns x, y, z, and w, *if a solution exists.* Let us denote by Δ (read "delta") the determinant

$$
\Delta = \begin{vmatrix}
a_1 & b_1 & c_1 & d_1 \\
a_2 & b_2 & c_2 & d_2 \\
a_3 & b_3 & c_3 & d_3 \\
a_4 & b_4 & c_4 & d_4
\end{vmatrix}
\tag{12}
$$

of the matrix of coefficients of the unknowns in equations (8), (9), (10), and (11) given above.

To solve for x, we multiply both members of (8), (9), (10), and (11) by $A_1, -A_2, A_3$, and $-A_4$ respectively, and add, thus obtaining

$$
(a_1A_1 - a_2A_2 + a_3A_3 - a_4A_4)x + (b_1A_1 - b_2A_2 + b_3A_3 - b_4A_4)y
$$

$$
+ (c_1A_1 - c_2A_2 + c_3A_3 - c_4A_4)z
$$

$$
+ (d_1A_1 - d_2A_2 + d_3A_3 - d_4A_4)w
$$

$$
= k_1A_1 - k_2A_2 + k_3A_3 - k_4A_4.
\tag{13}
$$

The coefficient of x in (13) is equal to Δ by the Theorem of § 11-6, and the coefficients of y, z, and w are each equal to zero by the Corollary in § 11-6. Hence (13) becomes

$$
\Delta \cdot x = k_1A_1 - k_2A_2 + k_3A_3 - k_4A_4.
\tag{14}
$$

But the right member of equation (14) is equal to the determinant of a matrix of the fourth order obtained from the matrix of coefficients by replacing the column consisting of the coefficients of x in the given system of equations, namely a_1, a_2, a_3, a_4, by the constant terms k_1, k_2, k_3, k_4 respectively. Equation (14) may then be written in the form

$$\Delta \cdot x = \begin{vmatrix} k_1 & b_1 & c_1 & d_1 \\ k_2 & b_2 & c_2 & d_2 \\ k_3 & b_3 & c_3 & d_3 \\ k_4 & b_4 & c_4 & d_4 \end{vmatrix}. \tag{15}$$

Similarly, by multiplying both members of (8), (9), (10), and (11) by $-B_1$, B_2, $-B_3$, B_4, then by C_1, $-C_2$, C_3, $-C_4$, and finally by $-D_1$, D_2, $-D_3$, D_4 respectively, and adding in each case, we obtain

$$\Delta \cdot y = \begin{vmatrix} a_1 & k_1 & c_1 & d_1 \\ a_2 & k_2 & c_2 & d_2 \\ a_3 & k_3 & c_3 & d_3 \\ a_4 & k_4 & c_4 & d_4 \end{vmatrix}, \qquad \Delta \cdot z = \begin{vmatrix} a_1 & b_1 & k_1 & d_1 \\ a_2 & b_2 & k_2 & d_2 \\ a_3 & b_3 & k_3 & d_3 \\ a_4 & b_4 & k_4 & d_4 \end{vmatrix},$$

$$\Delta \cdot w = \begin{vmatrix} a_1 & b_1 & c_1 & k_1 \\ a_2 & b_2 & c_2 & k_2 \\ a_3 & b_3 & c_3 & k_3 \\ a_4 & b_4 & c_4 & k_4 \end{vmatrix}. \tag{16}$$

If $\Delta \neq 0$, then from the equations in (15) and (16) we obtain

$$x = \frac{\begin{vmatrix} k_1 & b_1 & c_1 & d_1 \\ k_2 & b_2 & c_2 & d_2 \\ k_3 & b_3 & c_3 & d_3 \\ k_4 & b_4 & c_4 & d_4 \end{vmatrix}}{\Delta}, \qquad y = \frac{\begin{vmatrix} a_1 & k_1 & c_1 & d_1 \\ a_2 & k_2 & c_2 & d_2 \\ a_3 & k_3 & c_3 & d_3 \\ a_4 & k_4 & c_4 & d_4 \end{vmatrix}}{\Delta},$$

$$z = \frac{\begin{vmatrix} a_1 & b_1 & k_1 & d_1 \\ a_2 & b_2 & k_2 & d_2 \\ a_3 & b_3 & k_3 & d_3 \\ a_4 & b_4 & k_4 & d_4 \end{vmatrix}}{\Delta}, \qquad w = \frac{\begin{vmatrix} a_1 & b_1 & c_1 & k_1 \\ a_2 & b_2 & c_2 & k_2 \\ a_3 & b_3 & c_3 & k_3 \\ a_4 & b_4 & c_4 & k_4 \end{vmatrix}}{\Delta}. \tag{17}$$

That the values of x, y, z, and w given by formulas (17) actually satisfy equations (8), (9), (10), and (11) can be easily established by direct substitution in these equations. Hence, if the determinant Δ of the matrix of coefficients of the given equations is *not zero*, the equations have *one and only one solution*, namely the values of x, y, z, and w given by formulas (17).

The above method is applicable to the solution of a system of n linear equations in n unknowns. By virtue of § 11-7, this method is sometimes more efficient than the procedure developed in § 10-9. We summarize our results in the following rule, sometimes referred to as **Cramer's Rule.**

Rule. A system of n *linear equations in* n *unknowns has a single solution provided that the determinant of the matrix of coefficients of the unknowns is not equal to zero. Each unknown is equal to a fraction whose denominator is the determinant of the matrix of the coefficients of the unknowns and whose numerator is the determinant of the matrix obtained from the matrix of the coefficients of the unknowns by replacing the column of coefficients of this unknown by the corresponding column of constant terms, when these constant terms are on the side of the equations opposite the unknowns.*

EXAMPLE.   Solve:
$$\begin{cases} 2x + 2y - z + w = -2, \\ 3x - y + 3z = 0, \\ 3y - 2z - w = 9, \\ x + z - 2w = 9. \end{cases}$$

Solution.   We have

$$x = \begin{vmatrix} -2 & 2 & -1 & 1 \\ 0 & -1 & 3 & 0 \\ 9 & 3 & -2 & -1 \\ 9 & 0 & 1 & -2 \end{vmatrix} \div \begin{vmatrix} 2 & 2 & -1 & 1 \\ 3 & -1 & 3 & 0 \\ 0 & 3 & -2 & -1 \\ 1 & 0 & 1 & -2 \end{vmatrix} = \frac{-17}{17} = -1.$$

Similarly we find $y = 3$, $z = 2$, and $w = -4$.

Historical Note.   Cramer's Rule is named for GABRIEL CRAMER (1704–1752) of Geneva.

EXERCISES*

Solve the following systems of equations by use of determinants and check by substitution:

1. $\begin{cases} 3x - 4y = 6, \\ 2x + 5y + 1 = 0. \end{cases}$

3. $\begin{cases} 3r = 2s + 5, \\ 6r + 6s + 5 = 0. \end{cases}$

2. $\begin{cases} 3x - 4y = -5, \\ 2x + 5y = 15. \end{cases}$

4. $\begin{cases} 2y + 5x + 1 = 3z, \\ 2x = y + z - 4, \\ 3y - 2z = 6. \end{cases}$

* For other exercises on systems with two or three unknowns, see §10-2 and §10-4.

5. $\begin{cases} 5B - A + 2C + 6 = 0, \\ 6C - B - 2A + 4 = 0, \\ A + B - 2C = 0. \end{cases}$

6. $\begin{cases} 2u + v + 9 = 3w, \\ u + 3v + 2w = 0, \\ 3u = 6v + w + 1. \end{cases}$

7. $\begin{cases} ax + 2by + 2cz = 4, \\ 3ax - by + 4cz = 2, \\ 2cz + 2ax - by = 0. \end{cases}$

8. $\begin{cases} 4v - 3t + 2s + 5 = 0, \\ 5u - 2t - 4v = 1, \\ 4t + 3v - 2u = 0, \\ t - u + v + s = 3. \end{cases}$

9. $\begin{cases} 4z - 3w - 2x = 3, \\ 3y - 4z + 2w = 1, \\ 2x + 4y - 3z + 6 = 0, \\ x - y - z + w + 2 = 0. \end{cases}$

10. $\begin{cases} x + y + z - w - t = 1, \\ x + 4y - 3w = -3, \\ 2x - 3y + z + 2w = 0, \\ 3x - w - 2t + 1 = 0, \\ 3x - 3z + w - 2t = 0. \end{cases}$

11—12. The systems in Exercises 11 and 12 of § 10-4.

13—15. The systems in Exercises 17 through 19 of § 10-9.

16. In an electrical network, the algebraic sum of the currents at any junction is zero and the algebraic sum of the voltage changes in any circuit is zero. The voltage drop E, in volts, across a resistance R ohms is given by $E = IR$, where I is the current in amperes. In the circuit shown in Figure 11.2, with two batteries and three resistances, it is given that E_1 is 6 volts, E_2 is 12 volts, R_1 is 5 ohms, R_2 is 10 ohms, and R_3 is 2 ohms. Hence

$\begin{cases} I_1 + I_2 - I_3 = 0, \\ 6 - 5I_1 - 2I_3 = 0, \\ 12 - 10I_2 - 2I_3 = 0. \end{cases}$

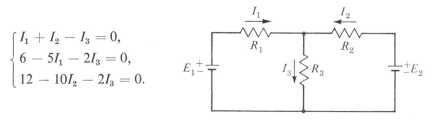

Fig. 11.2. A Simple Electrical Network

Solve these equations; that is, find the currents across the three resistances.

11-9   Rank of a Matrix

In connection with Cramer's Rule we observed that an exceptional case arises if the determinant of the matrix of coefficients of the unknowns is zero. Before examining this case in more detail, we define a useful tool.

The **rank** of a matrix M is the order of the largest square submatrix of M which has determinant different from zero. The rank of M is often denoted $r(M)$.

ILLUSTRATIONS. $\begin{bmatrix} 3 & 1 \\ 0 & 2 \end{bmatrix}$ has rank 2, since $\begin{vmatrix} 3 & 1 \\ 0 & 2 \end{vmatrix} = 6 \neq 0.$

$\begin{bmatrix} 3 & 1 & 2 & -1 \\ 6 & 2 & 4 & -2 \\ -9 & -3 & -6 & 3 \end{bmatrix}$ has rank 1, since (as can easily be verified using

Properties 5 and 4 of § 11-5) all square 3×3 and 2×2 submatrices have determinant 0, while there is at least one 1×1 submatrix (in fact, several) with nonzero determinant, such as [3]. We note that the given matrix is not square and hence has no determinant.

EXERCISES

Find the rank of each of the following matrices:

1. $\begin{bmatrix} 3 & 1 \\ 5 & 1 \end{bmatrix}.$

2. $\begin{bmatrix} 2 & -1 \\ 1 & 2 \end{bmatrix}.$

3. $\begin{bmatrix} 2 & 7 \\ 2 & 7 \end{bmatrix}.$

4. $\begin{bmatrix} 4 & -9 \\ 8 & -18 \end{bmatrix}.$

5. $\begin{bmatrix} 1 & 0 \\ 16 & 0 \end{bmatrix}.$

6. $\begin{bmatrix} 1 & 2 & 3 \\ 0 & 4 & -1 \\ 0 & 6 & 2 \end{bmatrix}.$

7. $\begin{bmatrix} 3 & 1 & 0 \\ 2 & -2 & 6 \\ 0 & 4 & 3 \end{bmatrix}.$

8. $\begin{bmatrix} 2 & 1 & -1 \\ 3 & 0 & 4 \\ -1 & -2 & 6 \end{bmatrix}.$

9. $\begin{bmatrix} 3 & 1 & 0 \\ 5 & 1 & 0 \end{bmatrix}.$

10. $\begin{bmatrix} 1 & 2 & 3 & 4 \\ 1 & 2 & 3 & 5 \end{bmatrix}.$

11. $\begin{bmatrix} 1 & 2 & -5 \\ 2 & 4 & -10 \\ -3 & -6 & 15 \end{bmatrix}.$

12. $\begin{bmatrix} 3 & 0 & 3 & -6 \\ 1 & 0 & 1 & -2 \\ 2 & 0 & 2 & -4 \end{bmatrix}.$

13. $\begin{bmatrix} 2 & 0 & -4 & 4 \\ 3 & 1 & -5 & 3 \\ 6 & 4 & -8 & 0 \\ 1 & 2 & 0 & -2 \end{bmatrix}.$

14. What is the effect on the rank of a matrix, and why, if **(a)** two columns are interchanged? (b) each element of a row is multiplied by 3? (c) some multiple of each element of one column is added to the corresponding element of another column?

★**15.** Prove that if M is a 4×4 matrix and every 3×3 submatrix of M has determinant 0 then $r(M) < 3$.

11-10   Systems of m Linear Equations in n Unknowns

In § 11-8 we considered systems of linear equations in which the number of unknowns equals the number of equations. Let us now consider the more general case of m linear equations in n unknowns.

A few general principles can easily be deduced. First suppose the number of equations exceeds the number of unknowns: $m > n$. Now if we consider the first n equations, then (as in § 11-8) they usually have exactly one solution. But this solution generally will not satisfy the remaining equations, which have not yet entered into the process of finding the solution (though in rare cases they might be satisfied, "by accident"). Hence if $m > n$ the system is usually inconsistent (§ 10-2). On the other hand, if $m < n$ then even if further equations, $(n - m)$ in number, were included to give a total of n equations, there would usually still be a solution. The given system is less restrictive than the extended system, so the given system would be expected to be consistent, and indeed to have many solutions.

A more exact result will now be stated. Consider the system

$$
\left.
\begin{aligned}
a_{11}x_1 + a_{12}x_2 + \cdots + a_{1n}x_n &= b_1, \\
a_{21}x_1 + a_{22}x_2 + \cdots + a_{2n}x_n &= b_2, \\
\cdot \;\; \cdot \;\; \cdot \;\; \cdot \;\; \cdot \;\; \cdot \;\; \cdot \;\; \cdot \;\; \cdot \;\; \cdot \;\; \cdot & \\
a_{m1}x_1 + a_{m2}x_2 + \cdots + a_{mn}x_n &= b_m,
\end{aligned}
\right\}
\tag{18}
$$

and the matrices

$$
M = \begin{bmatrix} a_{11} & a_{12} & \cdots & a_{1n} \\ a_{21} & a_{22} & \cdots & a_{2n} \\ \cdot & \cdot & \cdot & \cdot \\ a_{m1} & a_{m2} & \cdots & a_{mn} \end{bmatrix},
\qquad
N = \begin{bmatrix} a_{11} & a_{12} & \cdots & a_{1n} & b_1 \\ a_{21} & a_{22} & \cdots & a_{2n} & b_2 \\ \cdot & \cdot & \cdot & \cdot & \cdot \\ a_{m1} & a_{m2} & \cdots & a_{mn} & b_m \end{bmatrix}.
$$

Thus M is the matrix of coefficients of the unknowns $x_1, x_2, \cdots, x_n$; N, called the **augmented matrix** (§ 10-9), consists of M and an additional column whose elements are the constant terms.

Theorem.   *The system* (18) *is consistent if and only if the rank of* N *is the same as the rank of* M. *If these ranks are equal and* M′ *is one of the largest submatrices of* M *with determinant different from zero, then the unknowns whose coefficients appear in* M′ *can be determined, but usually only in terms of the remaining unknowns* (*if any*) *and the constants.*

The proof of this theorem is beyond the scope of this book*; we content ourselves with some illustrations, partly taken from § 10-10. The first of these is so simple that the answer could be found by inspection, but the method is general.

ILLUSTRATION 1.   Consider the system

$$\begin{cases} x + y = 5, \\ x + y = 7, \end{cases} \quad \text{where} \quad M = \begin{bmatrix} 1 & 1 \\ 1 & 1 \end{bmatrix}, \quad N = \begin{bmatrix} 1 & 1 & 5 \\ 1 & 1 & 7 \end{bmatrix}.$$

By the methods of the previous section, M has rank 1 and N has rank 2. By the theorem, the system is inconsistent.

If we had not applied the theorem, but rather had immediately tried to find a solution by Cramer's rule, the difficulty would have become apparent since $\Delta = 0$ in the equations (17).

ILLUSTRATION 2.   Consider the system $\begin{cases} x + y = 2, \\ x - y = 4, \\ x + 2y = 1. \end{cases}$

Since the number of equations exceeds the number of unknowns ($m = 3$, $n = 2$), it does not seem likely that there will be a solution. However, to determine the facts, apply the theorem. By the methods of the previous section, we find that both M and N have rank 2. By the theorem, the equations are consistent. Proceeding as indicated in the second sentence of the theorem, take two of the equations for which the submatrix of coefficients is of maximum rank; for instance,

$$\begin{cases} x + y = 2, \\ x - y = 4. \end{cases}$$

These are readily found to have the solution $x = 3$, $y = -1$. Since the system is consistent, this must satisfy the third equation also. The solution can be checked by substituting in the three given equations.

Instead of applying the theorem directly to the given system, we may first replace the given system by an equivalent system (§ 10-3) for which the ranks are easier to find. This process is somewhat analogous to the

---

* For further discussion of linear systems, see for instance Chapter IX of J. V. Uspensky's *Theory of Equations* (McGraw-Hill, New York, 1948). It may be said that in essence the proof consists of observing the effect on the various determinants when the operations specified in § 10–9 are performed.

transformation of a matrix so as to simplify finding the value of its determinant (§ 11-7), except that in the present connection operations are permitted only on rows, not on columns.

ILLUSTRATION 3.   Consider the system
$$\begin{cases} x + y - z + w = 1, \\ 2x + 2y - 2z + 2w = 2, \\ x \qquad\qquad - w = 3, \\ x \qquad\qquad + w = 1. \end{cases}$$

Adding -2 times the members of the first equation to those of the second equation, and adding the members of the third equation to those of the fourth, we get

$$\left. \begin{array}{l} x + y - z + w = 1, \\ 0x + 0y + 0z + 0w = 0, \\ x \qquad\quad - w = 3, \\ 2x \qquad\qquad = 4. \end{array} \right\} \tag{19}$$

It is now easily seen that both M and N have rank 3, so the equations are consistent. Selecting from (19) three equations involved in a largest possible submatrix with nonzero determinant,

$$\begin{cases} x + y - z + w = 1, \\ x \qquad\quad - w = 3, \\ 2x \qquad\qquad = 4. \end{cases}$$

Then $2x = 4$ so $x = 2$, whence $w = -1$. The first equation then reduces to $y - z = 0$, so $y = z$ where z may have any value. To check, substitute in the original equations:

$$2 + z - z + (-1) \equiv 1; \qquad\qquad 4 + 2z - 2z + (-2) \equiv 2;$$
$$2 - (-1) \equiv 3; \qquad\qquad\qquad 2 + (-1) \equiv 1.$$

In Illustration 3, explicit values were determined for x and w. In another example it might, for instance, be found that x, y, and w are determined in terms of z, instead of some of them being explicit numbers.

ILLUSTRATION 4.   Consider the system

$$\left. \begin{array}{l} x + y - z = 0, \\ 2x - y - 8z = 0, \\ 3x + 5y + z = 0. \end{array} \right\} \tag{20}$$

Obviously there is at least one solution: $x = 0$, $y = 0$, $z = 0$. Since the number of equations equals the number of unknowns, there might be expected to be just one solution. However, in starting to apply Cramer's Rule, the difficulty quickly arises that $\Delta = 0$. It is found that both M and N have rank 2. By the theorem, we can solve for two unknowns whose coefficients are involved in a 2×2 submatrix of M with nonzero determinant, such as x and y in

$$\begin{cases} x + y - z = 0, \\ 2x - y - 8z = 0. \end{cases}$$

We may treat z as though it were a constant and solve for x and y, or alternatively treat x/z and y/z as unknowns; in either method, there are two equations in two unknowns. We obtain $x = 3z$, $y = -2z$, where z may have any value. This solution may be checked by substitution in the original equations:

$$3z - 2z - z \equiv 0, \quad 6z - (-2z) - 8z \equiv 0, \quad 9z + (-10z) + z \equiv 0.$$

A linear equation, such as those in (20), in which the constant term is zero, is called a linear **homogeneous** equation.

EXERCISES

Solve the following systems of equations in so far as it is possible:

1—10. Exercises 1 through 10 of § 10-10.

11—18. Exercises 11 through 18 of § 10-2.

19. $\begin{cases} x + 3y = 0, \\ 3x - 2y = 0. \end{cases}$

20. $\begin{cases} x + 4y = 0, \\ 2x + 8y = 0. \end{cases}$

21. $\begin{cases} 2x + y = 3, \\ x - 2y = 4, \\ 3x + 4y = 2. \end{cases}$

22. $\begin{cases} 2x + y = 3, \\ x - 2y = 4, \\ 3x + 4y = 5. \end{cases}$

23. $\begin{cases} x + 3y - 2z = 4, \\ 3x - 2y + z = 1, \\ 3x - 13y + 8z = 10. \end{cases}$

24. $\begin{cases} x + 3y - 2z = 4, \\ 3x - 2y + z = 1, \\ 3x - 13y + 8z = -10. \end{cases}$

25. $\begin{cases} x + 3y - 2z = 0, \\ 3x - 2y + z = 0, \\ 3x - 13y + 8z = 0. \end{cases}$

26. $\begin{cases} x + 3y - 2z = 4, \\ 3x - 2y + z = 1, \\ 3x - 13y = -10. \end{cases}$

27. $\begin{cases} 2x - y + z = 0, \\ x - 3y - z = 0, \\ y - 2z = 0. \end{cases}$

28. $\begin{cases} x - 2y + z - 1 = 0, \\ 2x = y - z, \\ y - x - z = 4, \\ 4x - 3y - 2z = 3. \end{cases}$

29. $\begin{cases} x + 3y + 2z - w = 0, \\ 2x - y + z + 4w = 0, \\ x + 10y + 5z - 7w = 0. \end{cases}$

Prove, with reference to the notation of this section and § 11-8:

30. If $m = n$ and $\Delta \neq 0$, then $r(M) = r(N)$ and the system is consistent.

31. If $m = n$, $\Delta = 0$, and at least one of the numerators in equation (17) is not zero, then the system is inconsistent.

32. If a system of n homogeneous linear equations in n unknowns has a solution other than the trivial one in which each unknown is zero, then $\Delta = 0$.

CHAPTER 12

THEORY OF EQUATIONS AND INEQUALITIES

12-1 Character of the Roots of a Quadratic Equation

In Chapter 5 we studied how to solve linear and quadratic equations. In the present chapter, we consider properties of a more theoretical nature for such equations and for equations of higher degree. Inequalities, which were touched on briefly in § 1-4, are also studied further.

It is often helpful to obtain certain information about the roots of a quadratic equation, such as whether they are real or imaginary, equal or unequal, rational or irrational, without actually finding the roots.

If r_1 and r_2 denote the roots of the general quadratic equation $ax^2 + bx + c = 0$, then, by the quadratic formula (§ 5-8), we may take

$$r_1 = \frac{-b + \sqrt{b^2 - 4ac}}{2a} \quad \text{and} \quad r_2 = \frac{-b - \sqrt{b^2 - 4ac}}{2a}.$$

The expression $(b^2 - 4ac)$, which appears under the radical sign, is called the **discriminant** of the quadratic function $(ax^2 + bx + c)$. In considering the numerical character of the roots, we shall need to know whether this expression is positive, zero, or negative, a perfect square or not. The use of the discriminant is shown below.

If the coefficients a, b, *and* c *are* **real** *numbers, then*

The roots of $ax^2 + bx + c = 0$ are	when
real and unequal	$b^2 - 4ac > 0$
real and equal	$b^2 - 4ac = 0$
imaginary	$b^2 - 4ac < 0$

If the roots are real and the coefficients a, b, *and* c *are* **rational** *numbers, then*

The roots of $ax^2 + bx + c = 0$ are	when
rational	$(b^2 - 4ac)$ is a perfect square
irrational	$(b^2 - 4ac)$ is not a perfect square

We observe that when the coefficients of a quadratic equation are real and one root is real, the other root must be real also. Similarly, when the coefficients are real and one root is imaginary, say $c + di$ where $d \neq 0$, the other root must be imaginary and will have the form $c - di$. Even when one or more of the coefficients are imaginary, the two roots are equal when and only when the discriminant is zero, that is, $b^2 - 4ac = 0$.

EXAMPLE 1.   Determine the character of the roots of

(a) $15x^2 - 11x - 14 = 0$;   (b) $15x^2 - 11x + 14 = 0$.

Solution.   **a.** Here $a = 15$, $b = -11$, and $c = -14$; hence

$$b^2 - 4ac = (-11)^2 - 4(15)(-14) = 121 + 840$$
$$= 961 = (31)^2.$$

Since a, b, and c are rational and the discriminant $(b^2 - 4ac)$ is positive and a perfect square, the roots are real, unequal, and rational.

b. Here $a = 15$, $b = -11$, and $c = 14$; hence

$$b^2 - 4ac = (-11)^2 - 4(15)(14) = 121 - 840$$
$$= -719.$$

Since a, b, and c are real and the discriminant is negative, the roots are imaginary.

EXAMPLE 2.   Determine the values of the constant m for which the equation $5x^2 - 4x + 2 + m(4x^2 - 2x - 1) = 0$ will have equal roots.

Solution.   Arrange the given equation in the standard form:

$$(5 + 4m)x^2 + (-4 - 2m)x + (2 - m) = 0.$$

Here $a = 5 + 4m$, $b = -4 - 2m$,   and $c = 2 - m$.

If the roots are to be equal, the discriminant $(b^2 - 4ac)$ must be equal to zero. Hence

$$[-(4 + 2m)]^2 - 4(5 + 4m)(2 - m) = 0.$$

Expand: $16 + 16m + 4m^2 - 4(10 + 3m - 4m^2) = 0.$
Combine: $20m^2 + 4m - 24 = 0.$
Divide by 4: $5m^2 + m - 6 = 0.$
Factor: $(5m + 6)(m - 1) = 0.$

$5m + 6 = 0.$	$m - 1 = 0.$
$m = -\frac{6}{5}.$	$m = 1.$

In § 5-3 we saw how the *real* roots of an equation in the form $f(x) = 0$ can be found by locating graphically the zeros of the function $f(x)$. This graph naturally reflects the character of the roots, since only real values are graphed.

Suppose in particular the equation is quadratic:

$$f(x) = ax^2 + bx + c = 0.$$

Then there are three possibilities. If the graph of $f(x)$ crosses the x-axis in two distinct points, the roots of $f(x) = 0$ are real and unequal; if the graph of $f(x)$ touches but does not cross the x-axis, the roots of $f(x) = 0$ are real and equal; and if the graph of $f(x)$ does not cross or touch the x-axis, the roots of $f(x) = 0$ are imaginary. These three cases are illustrated in Figure 12.1.

$C_1: f_1(x) = x^2 - 4x - 1$

x	-1	0	1	2	3	4	5
$f_1(x)$	4	-1	-4	-5	-4	-1	4

$C_2: f_2(x) = x^2 - 4x + 4$

x	-1	0	1	2	3	4	5
$f_2(x)$	9	4	1	0	1	4	9

$C_3: f_3(x) = x^2 - 4x + 8$

x	-1	0	1	2	3	4	5
$f_3(x)$	13	8	5	4	5	8	13

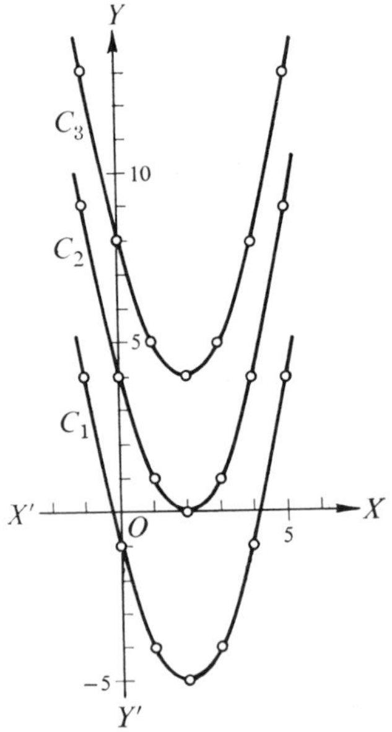

Fig. 12.1

The graphs in Figure 12.1 represent the left members of the equations

$$x^2 - 4x - 1 = 0, \quad x^2 - 4x + 4 = 0, \quad x^2 - 4x + 8 = 0.$$

The values of the roots of these equations and also the character of their roots as determined graphically and algebraically are compared in the following table:

CURVE and EQUATION	VALUES OF ROOTS		CHARACTER OF ROOTS FROM	
	Graphically	Algebraically	Graph	Discriminant
C_1 $f_1(x) = 0$	approximately $-0.2, 4.2$	$2 \pm \sqrt{5}$ or, to two decimals, 4.24, -0.24	real and unequal	$b^2 - 4ac = 20$; real, unequal, and irrational
C_2 $f_2(x) = 0$	2, 2	2, 2	real, equal, and rational	$b^2 - 4ac = 0$; real, equal, and rational
C_3 $f_3(x) = 0$	not shown; imaginary	$2 \pm 2i$	imaginary	$b^2 - 4ac = -16$; imaginary

In analytic geometry it is proved that *the graph of any quadratic function* f(x) $= ax^2 + bx + c$ *with real coefficients is a* **parabola** (§ 10-1) *which opens upward if* a *is positive and opens downward if* a *is negative.* If the parabola opens upward, it is said to be concave upward and has a lowest point, at which the function has its minimum value (§ 4-9); if the parabola opens downward, it is said to be concave downward and has a highest point, at which the function has its maximum value. In either case, this point is called the **vertex** of the parabola, its abscissa x is $-b/2a$, and its ordinate y is $(4ac - b^2)/4a$. These values can be found by completing the square and expressing the function in the form

$$f(x) = a\left(x + \frac{b}{2a}\right)^2 + \frac{4ac - b^2}{4a}. \tag{1}$$

Historical Note. The first recognition of imaginary roots for a quadratic equation seems to have been made by CARDAN (1545). He gives $5 + \sqrt{-15}$ and $5 - \sqrt{-15}$ as the two numbers whose sum is 10 and whose product is 40, and his method of finding them is that of solving the quadratic equation $x^2 - 10x = -40$.

EXERCISES

State whether the discriminant is positive, negative, or zero, and describe the character of the roots of each of the following equations:*

1. $3x^2 - 5x - 2 = 0.$

2. $16y^2 + 24y + 9 = 0.$

3. $z^2 - 0.3z + 0.3 = 0.$

4. $\frac{1}{4}r^2 + \frac{1}{3}r - \frac{1}{2} = 0.$

5. $2y^2 + 4y - 2 = 3y + 6.$

6. $x^2 - 6x + 4 = 4 - 6x.$

7. $w^2 + 4 = 5w - w^2 + 4.$

8. $4z^2 + 0.5z + 0.01 = 0.$

9. $y^2 + 2\sqrt{2}y = 2.$

10. $5u^2 + \sqrt{20}\,u + 1 = 0.$

★11. $9x^2 + 6ix - 1 = 0.$

★12. $iy^2 - 3y + 6i = 0.$

Determine the character of the roots of the quadratic equations in Exercises 13 through 18 by means of a graph, and check by use of the discriminant:

13. $3 + x = x^2.$

14. $3 + 2x = x^2.$

15. $x^2 = 3x + 5.$

16. $4x^2 + 2 = x - x^2.$

17. $25x^2 - 30x + 9 = 0.$

18. $16x^2 - 20x + 20 = 30x - 9x^2 - 4.$

Determine the value or values of the constant k or m for which the following equations have equal roots:

19. $2 - mx = x^2 + 3.$

20. $mx^2 + 3x = m - 3.$

21. $m(y^2 - 1) = 4y + 5.$

22. $m(z^2 + z + 1) = z + 1.$

23. $y^2 - 16 = k(y + 4).$

24. $x^2 - 2(k + 4)x + 16k = 0.$

Determine the value or values of the constant c or k for which each of the following expressions will be a perfect trinomial square:

25. $y^2 + 12y + c.$

26. $z^2 + kz + 196.$

27. $kx^2 - kx + 4.$

28. $y^2 + cy + (5 - 2c).$

Substitute b for y and determine the value or values of b for which the line y = b and the curve having the given equation (a) are tangent (the resulting equation in x has real and equal roots); (b) intersect in distinct points (real and unequal roots); (c) do not intersect (imaginary roots):

29. $y = x^2 + 2x - 4.$

30. $y = 3 - 6x - x^2.$

31. $x^2 + y^2 = 16.$

32. $x^2 + y^2 + 2x + 2y = 2.$

---

* If additional introductory exercises are desired, the Exercises for § 5-7 and § 5-8 may be used.

Form the quadratic equation of the form $ax^2 + bx + c = 0$ *whose left member may be expressed as the given product. Find the discriminant of each equation and discuss its significance.*

33. $x(x - \sqrt{3})$.

35. $(x - 3 + 2i)(x - 3 + 2i)$.

34. $(x - 5i)(x + 4i)$.

36. $(3x + 4i - \sqrt{5})(2x - \sqrt{5})$.

For each of the functions in Exercises 37 through 42 **(a)** *sketch its graph;* **(b)** *complete the square;* **(c)** *find the coordinates of the highest or lowest point;* **(d)** *find the maximum or minimum value:*

37. $x^2 + 6x$.

39. $x^2 + 5x + 6$.

41. $3 + 4x - x^2$.

38. $x^2 + 6x + 5$.

40. $5x + 6 - x^2$.

42. $5 - x^2$.

43. Explain why the rewriting of $f(x)$ as in the equation (1) shows that the maximum or minimum is at the point stated.

44. Assume that the height of a projectile is given by $s = v_0 t - 16t^2$ and find the time required for it to reach its maximum height when **(a)** $v_0 = 480$ feet per second; **(b)** $v_0 = 3200$ feet per second.

45. As in Exercise 44, consider a ball thrown upward with an initial velocity of 48 feet per second, and find **(a)** the time required for the ball to reach its maximum height; **(b)** the maximum height.

Compare **(a)** *the roots of the two equations,* **(b)** *the discriminants of the two left members:*

46. $x^2 + 4x + 5 = 0$, $2x^2 + 8x + 10 = 0$.

47. $x^2 + \frac{1}{2}x - \frac{1}{3} = 0$, $6x^2 + 3x - 2 = 0$.

12-2   Roots and Factors of Quadratics

We find upon adding the two roots, r_1 and r_2, of the general quadratic equation, $ax^2 + bx + c = 0$, that

$$r_1 + r_2 = \frac{-b + \sqrt{b^2 - 4ac}}{2a} + \frac{-b - \sqrt{b^2 - 4ac}}{2a} = \frac{-2b}{2a} = -\frac{b}{a}.$$

Upon multiplying the two roots, we obtain

$$r_1 r_2 = \frac{-b + \sqrt{b^2 - 4ac}}{2a} \cdot \frac{-b - \sqrt{b^2 - 4ac}}{2a}$$

$$= \frac{(-b)^2 - (b^2 - 4ac)}{4a^2} = \frac{4ac}{4a^2} = \frac{c}{a}.$$

We may state these formulas in words as follows:

The **sum of the roots** *of any quadratic equation in the standard form is equal to the quotient obtained when the coefficient of the first-degree term with its sign changed is divided by the coefficient of the second-degree term.*

The **product of the roots** *of any quadratic equation in the standard form is equal to the quotient obtained when the constant term is divided by the coefficient of the second-degree term.*

ILLUSTRATION.   In the equation $5x^2 - 2x - 3 = 0$, the sum of the roots is $\frac{2}{5}$ and the product of the roots is $-\frac{3}{5}$.

The formulas for the sum and the product of the roots are useful in checking the roots of a quadratic equation and also in forming a quadratic equation when its roots are given.

These formulas are also useful in deriving the factored form of any quadratic expression $(ax^2 + bx + c)$. If r_1 and r_2 are the roots of the quadratic equation $ax^2 + bx + c = 0$, we may write

$$ax^2 + bx + c = a\left(x^2 + \frac{b}{a}x + \frac{c}{a}\right)$$
$$= a[x^2 - (r_1 + r_2)x + r_1 r_2]$$
$$= a(x - r_1)(x - r_2).$$

This identity can be used to factor expressions of the form $(ax^2 + bx + c)$ by first solving the corresponding quadratic equation. With the aid of the previous section, we see that these linear factors of the quadratic expression $(ax^2 + bx + c)$ will be *real* linear factors with *rational* coefficients when the coefficients a, b, and c are rational and the discriminant $(b^2 - 4ac)$ is a perfect square.

EXAMPLE 1.   Form a quadratic equation, with integral coefficients, whose roots are $\frac{1}{3}(2 \pm \sqrt{5})$.

Solution.   Let $r_1 = \frac{1}{3}(2 + \sqrt{5})$ and $r_2 = \frac{1}{3}(2 - \sqrt{5})$.
Add r_1 and r_2: $r_1 + r_2 = \frac{4}{3}$.
Multiply r_1 by r_2: $r_1 r_2 = \frac{1}{9}(4 - 5) = -\frac{1}{9}$.
Therefore one equation with these roots is

$$x^2 + (-\tfrac{4}{3})x + (-\tfrac{1}{9}) = 0,$$

or $9x^2 - 12x - 1 = 0$.

EXAMPLE 2.   Factor $(12x^2 - 7x - 10)$ by first solving the equation $12x^2 - 7x - 10 = 0$.

Solution. Solving $12x^2 - 7x - 10 = 0$ by the quadratic formula, we obtain

$$x = \frac{7 \pm \sqrt{529}}{24} = \frac{7 \pm 23}{24} \, ; \quad x = \tfrac{5}{4} \text{ and } x = -\tfrac{2}{3}.$$

Therefore, we have

$$12x^2 - 7x - 10 = 12(x - \tfrac{5}{4})(x + \tfrac{2}{3}) = (4x - 5)(3x + 2).$$

EXAMPLE 3. Find the roots of the equation $3x^2 - 2kx + 4 = 0$, having given that one root is three times the other.

Solution. Let r and $3r$ be the two roots of the given equation. Then, using the formula for the product of the roots, we have

$$r \cdot 3r = \tfrac{4}{3}; \quad 3r^2 = \tfrac{4}{3}; \quad r^2 = \tfrac{4}{9}; \quad r = \pm \tfrac{2}{3}.$$

Therefore, the two roots are $\tfrac{2}{3}$ and 2, or $-\tfrac{2}{3}$ and -2.

Note that we can now determine k. The sum of the roots is $\tfrac{8}{3}$ or $-\tfrac{8}{3}$, and so $\tfrac{2}{3}k = \pm\tfrac{8}{3}$ and $k = \pm 4$.

EXERCISES

Find, without solving, the sum and the product of the roots of the equations:

1. $t^2 - 3t = 6.$ **3.** $3y = y^2.$ **5.** $x^2 + 3 = k(x + 4).$

2. $6x^2 + x = 9.$ **4.** $4w^2 - 9 = 0.$ **6.** $a(u^2 + 2) = 3u - 2.$

In each case form a quadratic equation, with integral coefficients, having the given numbers as roots:

7. 3, 4.   **11.** $\tfrac{1}{3}, \tfrac{1}{3}.$ **15.** $\pm 3i.$ **19.** $c, -c.$

8. 2, 5.   **12.** $-\tfrac{1}{4}, -\tfrac{5}{4}.$ **16.** $2 \pm i.$ **20.** $r, -2r.$

9. $-1, 2.$ **13.** $-2, 0.$ **17.** $2 \pm \sqrt{3}.$ **21.** $\tfrac{1}{4}(1 \pm i\sqrt{7}).$

10. $2, -5.$ **14.** $\pm 3\sqrt{2}.$ **18.** $3 \pm i\sqrt{2}.$ **22.** $\tfrac{2}{5}(3 \pm i\sqrt{15}).$

23. $\tfrac{2}{3}(-2 \pm i\sqrt{3}).$ **24.** $\tfrac{1}{2}(-3 \pm \sqrt{5}).$

Factor the given quadratic expressions by first solving a quadratic equation:

25. $18x^2 + 9x - 20.$ **27.** $3x^2 - 4x - 5.$

26. $84 - 145x - 75x^2.$ **28.** $6x^2 + 3x - 1.$

In each of the following equations determine the value or values of the constant k *or* m *for which* **(a)** *one root is* 3; **(b)** *one root is* -1; **(c)** *the sum of the roots is* 4; **(d)** *the roots are equal:*

29. $x^2 + mx + 2 = 0.$ **31.** $4 = 6x + kx^2.$

30. $3x^2 - kx + 6 = 0.$ **32.** $mx^2 - 16x - m = 0.$

In Exercises 33 through 37 determine the value or values of k *and* m *satisfying the given conditions:*

33. $x^2 - 12x + m = 0$: one root is **(a)** equal to the other; **(b)** twice the other.

34. $v^2 - mv + m - 1 = 0$: one root is **(a)** equal to the other; **(b)** twice the other.

35. $3z^2 + 4kz - 2 = 0$: the sum of the roots is equal to **(a)** 2; **(b)** the product of the roots; **(c)** twice their product; **(d)** the negative of their product.

36. $k^2(z^2 + 1) - k(z + 1) = 3z$: the product of the roots is equal to **(a)** their sum; **(b)** six times their sum; **(c)** one-sixth their sum.

37. $(kx)^2 + 6x + 4 = 0$: one root is **(a)** the reciprocal of the other; **(b)** the negative reciprocal of the other.

38. If one root of the equation $3x^2 - 6x + c = 0$ is **(a)** $\frac{1}{2}(2 + \sqrt{5})$, **(b)** $\frac{1}{2}(2 - i\sqrt{3})$, find the other root.

39. Form a quadratic equation whose roots are **(a)** the sum and the product of the roots of $5x^2 + 3 = 2x$; **(b)** the negative reciprocals of the sum and the product of the roots of $3x - 5 = 2x^2$; **(c)** numerically equal but opposite in sign to the roots of $7x^2 + 5x = 8$.

40. Find the roots of a quadratic equation if **(a)** the sum of its roots is $\frac{5}{3}$, and their product is $\frac{2}{3}$; **(b)** the sum of its roots is -5, and their product is $-\frac{3}{2}$.

41. Show that the roots of $ax^2 + bx + c = 0$ are the negatives of the roots of $ax^2 - bx + c = 0$.

42. Show that the roots of $ax^2 + bx + c = 0$ are the reciprocals of the roots of $cx^2 + bx + a = 0$.

43. Show that when the coefficients are real numbers the roots of $ax^2 + bx + c = 0$ are real and unequal if a and c are of opposite sign. Is the converse true?

12-3   Inequalities

An **inequality** is a statement that one expression represents a number which *is greater than* or *is less than* (§ 1-4) the number represented by another expression. Each of the expressions is called a **member** of the inequality, and each member must represent a *real* number, since the order relations (greater than and less than) have been defined only for real numbers. Even though not explicitly stated with each inequality, this restriction on the character of its members is always assumed.

From this definition of an inequality, we see that the statement "*a* is greater than *b*" (written symbolically $a > b$) is an inequality. Also the statement "$(ax + b)$ is less than *c*" (written symbolically $ax + b < c$) is an inequality. If $a > b$, then $(a - b)$ represents a positive number and $a - b = k$ where *k* represents a positive number. Hence we have three equivalent ways of expressing the statement that *a* is greater than *b*. In similar manner, "$c < d$," "$(c - d)$ represents a negative number," and "$c - d = -k$ where *k* represents a positive number" are merely three ways of expressing the statement that *c* is less than *d*.

If **a** *is greater than or equal to* **b**, that is, *a* is not less than *b*, the relation between *a* and *b* is written symbolically $a \geq b$. Likewise, $c \leq d$ means that *c* is less than or equal to *d*. Relations such as $a \geq b$ and $c \leq d$ are also sometimes called inequalities.

In the symbol for inequality the point is toward the smaller member. Two inequalities are said to be of the **same sense**, or **alike in sense**, if their symbols for inequality point in the same direction, and to be **unlike**, or **opposite**, **in sense** if their symbols for inequality point in opposite directions. Thus, $a > b$ and $c > d$ are alike in sense, as are also $b < a$ and $d < c$; $a > b$ and $d < c$ are opposite in sense.

In dealing with inequalities we find certain analogies between them and equalities. For example, the operations upon inequalities depend on certain properties (to be presented in the next section) which are analogous to the axioms of equalities. Also, inequalities are divided into two classes which are defined as follows:

If an inequality is valid for all values of the symbols for which both its members are defined, the inequality is called an **absolute** *or* **unconditional inequality**.

ILLUSTRATIONS OF ABSOLUTE INEQUALITIES.

$9 > 6$; $\pi < \frac{22}{7}$; $-3 < 2$; $-3 < -2$;
$a^2 + b^2 > 0$ for real numbers *a* and *b* if either $a \neq 0$ or $b \neq 0$.

If an inequality is false for at least one set of values of the symbols involved for which both members are defined, the inequality is called a **conditional inequality**.

ILLUSTRATIONS OF CONDITIONAL INEQUALITIES.

$x + 2 < 5$,　true only when　$x < 3$;
$x^2 + 4 > 5x$,　true only when　$x < 1$　or　$x > 4$.

EXERCISES

For each inequality, state whether it is absolute or conditional; if conditional, give if possible one set of values of the literal number symbols for which it is valid and one for which it is false:

1. $3 < 5$.	**10.** $x^2 < 9$.	**19.** $\sin x \leq 1$.
2. $5 < 3$.	**11.** $x^2 > 9$.	**20.** $|\sin x| \leq 1$.
3. $-3 < -5$.	**12.** $x + 3 < 9$.	**21.** $|\cos x| \leq \frac{1}{2}$.
4. $-5 < -3$.	**13.** $x + 3 < -9$.	**22.** $\sin^2 x \leq 1$.
5. $x < 3$.	**14.** $3 - x < -9$.	**23.** $|\cos 2x| \leq 1$.
6. $3 < x$.	**15.** $(3 - x)^2 < 9$.	**24.** $|\sin \frac{1}{2}x| \leq \frac{1}{2}$.
7. $3 > y$.	**16.** $(3 - x)^2 < -9$.	**25.** $|\tan x| \leq 1$.
8. $x > y$.	**17.** $(3 - x)^2 > -9$.	**26.** $\sec x \geq 1$.
9. $x > 2y$.	**18.** $(3 - x)^2 > 0$.	**27.** $|\sec x| \geq 1$.

The point P: (x, y) *is in the coordinate plane (§ 4-4). State the following conditions upon the location of* P *as inequalities involving* x *or* y *or both:*

28. Below the x-axis.   **30.** Below the line $y = 3$.

29. Within the second quadrant. **31.** To the right of the line $x = -2$.

   32. Between the lines $x = 2$ and $x = 6$.

   33. Between the lines $y = -1$ and $y = 4$.

   34. Not between the lines $x = -2$ and $x = -1$.

   35. Above the line $y = 3$ and to the left of the line $x = 5$.

   36. More than 4 units from the point $(1, -2)$.

37. State what is shown by each of the following conditions or sets of conditions as to whether the inequality $f(x) > 0$ is absolute or conditional: **(a)** $f(0) = 0$; **(b)** $f(0) > 0$; **(c)** $f(-3) > 0$, $f(1) > 0$, $f(10) > 0$; **(d)** $f(-5) < 0$, $f(4) < 0$, $f(9) > 0$; **(e)** $f(a) > 0$, $f(b) > 0$, $f(c) < 0$; **(f)** $f(a) > 0$ for all a.

12-4 Properties of Inequalities

The following properties are useful in transforming inequalities. The proofs are simple, following almost immediately from the properties of real numbers and the definition of an inequality. However, to give students an idea as to the nature of the proofs, the proof of the first of these properties is given. The proofs of the remaining five properties are left as exercises for the student.*

---

* For a thorough discussion of these properties, see B. E. Meserve's *Fundamental Concepts of Algebra* (Addison-Wesley, Reading, Massachusetts, 1953).

Property I. *If both members of an inequality are increased or diminished by the same number, the resulting inequality is of the same sense as the given inequality; that is,*

$$\text{if } a > b, \text{ then } a + c > b + c \text{ and } a - c > b - c.$$

Proof.   By hypothesis: $a > b.$

Change the form: $a - b = k, \quad \text{where} \quad k > 0.$

Add and subtract c: $a + c - b - c = k.$

Combine terms: $(a + c) - (b + c) = k.$

Change the form: $a + c > b + c.$

  In like manner we can prove $a - c > b - c.$

Property II. *If both members of an inequality are multiplied or divided by the same positive number, the resulting inequality is of the same sense as the given inequality; that is,*

$$\text{if } a > b, \text{ then } ac > bc \text{ and } (a \div c) > (b \div c) \text{ when } c > 0.$$

Property III. *If both members of an inequality are multiplied or divided by the same negative number, the sense of the resulting inequality is opposite to that of the given inequality; that is,*

$$\text{if } a > b \text{ and } c < 0, \text{ then } ac < bc \text{ and } (a \div c) < (b \div c).$$

By virtue of Property III, the inequality resulting from changing the sign of each member of an inequality is opposite in sense to that of the given inequality.

Property IV. *If both members of an inequality are positive numbers, the inequality formed by taking like positive powers, or roots, of both members is of the same sense as the given inequality; that is, for any positive number* m,

$$\text{if } a > b > 0, \text{ then } a^m > b^m \text{ and } \sqrt[m]{a} > \sqrt[m]{b}.$$

While it is possible to broaden the scope of Property IV so as to include negative values for a and b, the above statement is sufficient for our purpose.

Property V. *If the members of an equality are positive, and are divided by the members of an inequality which are of like sign, the resulting inequality is of the opposite sense; that is,*

$$\text{if } a > b, \text{ then } (c \div a) < (c \div b) \text{ when } a \text{ and } b \text{ have like signs and } c > 0.$$

By virtue of Property V, if two numbers of like sign are unequal, their reciprocals are unequal in the opposite sense; that is,

$$\text{if } ab > 0 \text{ and } a < b, \text{ then } \frac{1}{a} > \frac{1}{b}.$$

Property VI. *If* a < b < c *then* a < c.

This is called the **transitivity** property of inequalities.

These properties enable us to derive new inequalities from known ones, somewhat as equivalent equations are derived from given equations (§ 5-4 and § 10-3) or new trigonometric identities are derived from known ones (§ 7-4).

In proving absolute inequalities involving literal expressions for numbers or quantities, we are proving theorems that describe numbers or relations between them. Thus by proving that $b + \frac{1}{b} > 2$ for $b > 0$ and $b \neq 1$, we shall prove the theorem: The sum of any positive number other than 1 and its reciprocal is always larger than 2.

EXAMPLE.   Prove that $a^2 + \frac{1}{a^2} > 2$ if $a > 0$ and $a \neq 1$.

Proof.   Either $a - \frac{1}{a} > 0$ or $\frac{1}{a} - a > 0$, since $a \neq 1$.

Square both members: $a^2 - 2 + \frac{1}{a^2} > 0$ or $\frac{1}{a^2} - 2 + a^2 > 0.$

Add 2 to both members: $a^2 + \frac{1}{a^2} > 2$ or $\frac{1}{a^2} + a^2 > 2.$

Since any positive number b may be represented by a^2 where $a > 0$, this also proves $b + (1/b) > 2$ if $b > 0$ and $b \neq 1$.

EXERCISES

Prove or disprove that if a < b *and* 0 < c < d *then:*

1. $3a < 3b.$	**9.** $-3a < 3b.$	**17.** $3ac < 3bc.$
2. $5x < 5d.$	**10.** $3a < 5b.$	**18.** $5ac < 5ad.$
3. $-3a < -3b.$	**11.** $5a < 3b.$	**19.** $c + a < b + c.$
4. $-5c < -5d.$	**12.** $3b < 3d.$	**20.** $a + c < b + d.$
5. $-3a > -3b.$	**13.** $3a < 3c.$	**21.** $a - d < b - d.$
6. $-5c > -5d.$	**14.** $c^2 < d^2.$	**22.** $a + 3 < b + 3.$
7. $\frac{1}{3}a < \frac{1}{3}b.$	**15.** $a^2 < b^2.$	**23.** $a + 3 < b + 5.$
8. $0 \cdot a < 0 \cdot b.$	**16.** $c + (1/c) > c.$	**24.** $a + 5 < b + 3.$

25. Prove the following properties as stated in this section:
(a) Property II; **(b)** Property III; **(c)** Property IV; **(d)** Property V; **(e)** Property VI.

Prove each of the following, assuming that the letters represent unequal positive numbers:

26. $a^2 + b^2 < (a + b)^2$.   **28.** $\frac{1}{2}(x + y) > \sqrt{xy}$.

27. $a^2 + b^2 + c^2 < (a + b + c)^2$.   **29.** $4x(x + y) < 8x^2 + y^2$.

Given that $0 < a < b$ and $0 < c < d$, classify each of the following inequalities as absolute or conditional:

30. $a + 3c < b + 3d$.   **35.** $ad < bc$.

31. $a + 5d < b + 5c$.   **36.** $c^2 > c$.

32. $a - 5d < b - 5c$.   **37.** $3d + 5 > 0$.

33. $ac < bd$.   **38.** $c^2 - 5c + 4 > 0$.

34. $a/d < b/c$.   **39.** $c^2 - 5c + 6 > 0$.

Prove each of the following, assuming that each of the letters may represent any real number:

40. $a^2 + b^2 \geq 2ab$.   **43.** $|x + y| \leq |x| + |y|$.

41. $\sin x \cos 2x \leq 1$.   **44.** $|x - 2| \geq |x| - 2$.

42. $\sin x + \cos 2x \leq 2$.   **45.** $|x - y| \geq |x| - |y|$.

46. Suppose $1 < f(x) < g(x)$ for each value of x. What can be said about **(a)** $f(x) - g(x)$? **(b)** $2f(x)$? **(c)** $f(x) \cdot g(x)$?

47. In Figure 12.2 it is given that O is the center of the circle and the radius is 1, PR and QS are perpendicular to OQ, and $0 < \theta < \frac{1}{2}\pi$. Evidently the area of triangle OPR is less than the area of the sector OQR which in turn is less than the area of the triangle OQS. **(a)** Express each of these three areas in terms of θ or trigonometric functions of θ.

(b) Thence prove: $\cos \theta < \dfrac{\sin \theta}{\theta} < \dfrac{1}{\cos \theta}$ for any acute angle θ.

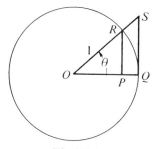

Fig. 12.2

12-5 Algebraic Solutions of Conditional Inequalities

The conditional inequalities most commonly met are those in one unknown, to which type our present discussion will be limited. When this unknown is x, the inequality can be rewritten in one of the two forms $f(x) > 0$ or $f(x) < 0$. If various values are assigned to x and the corresponding values computed for a particular $f(x)$, we expect that $f(x)$ will be positive for some of these values of x while for others $f(x)$ will be negative, or zero, or possibly undefined.

In solving inequalities, we first need to find those values of x at which the function $f(x)$ will change sign as x assumes values taken in algebraic order. In this connection, the following facts are significant, though the last one can be rigorously proved only in more advanced studies.

Any rational function $f(x)$ with real coefficients is **single-valued,** has a **real** number as its value for each real value of x (except for values of x for which the denominator of the function is zero), and is **continuous.** *First,* it is single-valued, since to each assumed value of x there corresponds *one and only one* value of $f(x)$, except that $f(x)$ is not defined for any value of x for which the denominator of $f(x)$ is zero. *Second,* its value is real, since it is assumed that only real numbers are used as coefficients and as values of x. *Third,* it is continuous except for values of x which make the denominator zero, since to small changes in x there correspond small changes in $f(x)$. Graphically, these statements mean that except for cases of values of x for which a denominator is zero, any line parallel to the y-axis will cut the graph once and only once and the graph of $f(x)$ is a curve without breaks.

It follows that when $f(x)$ is a rational function, a change in sign of $f(x)$ can occur only at those values of x at which a factor in either the numerator or the denominator of $f(x)$ becomes zero. Thus, by equating both the numerator and the denominator of $f(x)$ to zero, and solving the resulting equations, we have all the values of x, called **critical values** of x, at which $f(x)$ can change sign. The critical values of x, arranged in algebraic order, divide the values of x into intervals, *within each of which* f(x) *must always have the same sign.* If this sign is the one required to satisfy the inequality, then all values of x on the given interval satisfy the inequality.

The **solution of an inequality** is the set of values of the unknown for which the inequality is satisfied. Thus the solution of an inequality ordinarily consists of many (indeed, infinitely many) values of the unknown.

This is in contrast to the solution of an equation which ordinarily includes only one or a few values of the unknown. For both equations and inequalities in one unknown a particular value of the unknown is sometimes called **a solution** if it satisfies the equation or inequality.

ILLUSTRATION. The critical values for the inequality $(x - 2)/(x + 3) > 0$ are given by the equations $x - 2 = 0$ and $x + 3 = 0$, and are 2 and -3. The corresponding *possible* ranges of values for which the inequality *may*, or *may not*, hold are $x < -3$, $-3 < x < 2$, and $x > 2$.

A linear inequality in x, that is, an inequality in which each member is linear in x, can be solved algebraically in a manner similar to that employed in the solution of a linear equation.

EXAMPLE 1.   For what values of x is $\frac{7}{6} + \frac{1}{2}x < x - \frac{1}{3}$?

Solution. Multiply by 6: $7 + 3x < 6x - 2.$
Subtract $(7 + 6x)$ from both members: $3x - 6x < -2 - 7.$
Combine like terms: $-3x < -9.$
Divide by -3 and reverse inequality sign: **$x > 3.$**
   Hence the given inequality is satisfied when $x > 3$.

EXAMPLE 2.   For what values of x is $(x^2 - 4x)/(x - 2) > 0$?

Solution. Let $f(x) = (x^2 - 4x)/(x - 2).$
Equate numerator of $f(x)$ to zero: $x(x - 4) = 0.$
Equate denominator of $f(x)$ to zero: $x - 2 = 0.$
Solve for critical values of x: $x = 0, 4, 2.$

Now write the possible ranges of x for which $f(x)$ must always have the same sign, and test one value of x in each of these intervals. These steps are shown in the following table:

$x < 0$	$x = 0$ $0 < x < 2$	$x = 2$ $2 < x < 4$	$x = 4$ $x > 4$
Try $x = -1$. $f(-1) = -\frac{5}{3}$. $\therefore f(x) < 0$ for $x < 0$.	Try $x = 1$. $f(1) = 3$. $\therefore$ **$f(x) > 0$ for** **$0 < x < 2$.**	Try $x = 3$. $f(3) = -3$. $\therefore f(x) < 0$ for $2 < x < 4$.	Try $x = 5$. $f(5) = \frac{5}{3}$. $\therefore$ **$f(x) > 0$ for** **$x > 4$.**

Hence the inequality is satisfied when $0 < x < 2$ and when $x > 4$. Note that in effect we have also solved the related inequality $(x^2 - 4x)/(x - 2) < 0$, which is satisfied when $x < 0$ and when $2 < x < 4$.

EXERCISES

Find the values of the variables for which the inequalities are satisfied:

1. $3x - 12 > 0$.   **8.** $w^2 + 9 < 0$.   **15.** $x^2 + 5x - 3 > 0$.

2. $4x + 20 > 0$.   **9.** $t^2 + 16 > 0$.   **16.** $x^2 + 4x < 0$.

3. $x + 6 < 3x$.   **10.** $x^2 - 4x + 3 > 0$.   **17.** $x^2(x - 3) > 0$.

4. $6 - x > 2x - 3$.   **11.** $x^2 + 6x + 5 < 0$.   **18.** $x^2(x - 5) < 0$.

5. $2z < z - 3$.   **12.** $4x - 4 - x^2 < 0$.   **19.** $x^3(x + 1) > 0$.

6. $x^2 - 4 < 0$.   **13.** $10x - x^2 > 25$.   **20.** $x(x + 1)^2 < 0$.

7. $y^2 - 1 > 0$.   **14.** $x^2 - x + 4 > 0$.   **21.** $x^3(x + 1)^2 < 0$.

22. $\frac{1}{2}x - 2 < \frac{1}{3}x - 3$.   **24.** $x(x - 1)(x + 2) > 0$.

23. $\frac{2}{3}y + \frac{3}{4} > \frac{1}{3}(2y - 5)$.   **25.** $x(x - 1)^2(x - 3)(x + 2)^3 < 0$.

26. $\dfrac{x + 2}{x - 1} < 0$.   **28.** $\dfrac{3x + 6}{3 - 4x} > 0$.   **30.** $\dfrac{2}{1 + 2x - 3x^2} < 0$.

27. $\dfrac{x - 3}{x + 4} > 0$.   **29.** $\dfrac{3x}{x^2 - 4} < 0$.   **31.** $\dfrac{x^2 + 2x - 3}{x + 2} > 0$.

Find the values of x *for which each of the following radicals represents a real number:*

32. $\sqrt{3x - 2}$.   **34.** $\sqrt{3x^2 + 8x + 4}$.

33. $\sqrt{5 - 2x}$.   **35.** $\sqrt{-x - x^2}$.   **36.** $\sqrt{\dfrac{-x + 4}{x + 2}}$.

12-6 Graphic Solutions of Inequalities

An inequality, like an equation, can be solved either algebraically or graphically. Algebraic solutions were considered in the previous section; graphical methods will be considered in the present section. While the methods of solution are independent, the student should compare the two methods, as each may help him understand the other.

If the inequality has the form $f(x) > 0$, then it is satisfied for those values of x for which the graph of $f(x)$ lies above the x-axis. If the inequality has the form $f(x) < 0$, then it is satisfied for those values of x for which the graph of $f(x)$ lies below the x-axis.

EXAMPLE 1.   Find the values of x for which $2x^2 + x < 6$.

Solution.   We first subtract 6 from both members and write the given inequality in the form $2x^2 + x - 6 < 0$. Let $f(x) = 2x^2 + x - 6$. Then the given inequality is satisfied by all values of x for which the graph of $f(x)$ lies *below* the x-axis. Hence we graph $f(x)$, noting that the points where the graph crosses the x-axis are especially important.

$$f(x) = 2x^2 + x - 6$$

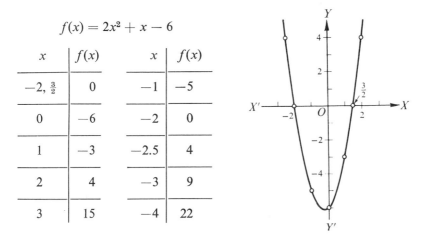

x	$f(x)$	x	$f(x)$
$-2, \frac{3}{2}$	0	-1	-5
0	-6	-2	0
1	-3	-2.5	4
2	4	-3	9
3	15	-4	22

Fig. 12.3

From the graph we see that the given inequality is satisfied when $-2 < x < \frac{3}{2}$.

The same result can be obtained algebraically by the method used in § 12-5.

We may also solve graphically inequalities involving two unknowns such as x and y. For example, it may be desired to find the pairs of values of x and y for which $y - x + 2 > 0$, as in Example 2 below.

If $f(x, y)$ is a polynomial, it can change sign only after becoming zero. Thus the graph of $f(x, y) = 0$ divides the coordinate plane into regions, within any one of which $f(x, y)$ must always have the same sign. If this sign is the one required to satisfy the inequality, then the inequality is satisfied at all points (x, y) in this region. Either all the points in the region have coordinates which satisfy the inequality, or none do. Accordingly, it suffices to test the inequality for one point in the region. Then we may indicate the solution of the inequality by shading the appropriate regions on the coordinate plane.

EXAMPLE 2. Solve the inequality $y - x + 2 > 0$.

Solution. The real zeros of the function $(y - x + 2)$ are the coordinates of the points on the graph of $y - x + 2 = 0$ (Figure 12.4). This line divides the coordinate plane into two regions, one above and to the left of the line and one below the line. By testing one point such as $(-1, 2)$ from the upper region, and another such as $(3, -1)$ from the region below the line, we find that all points above the line satisfy $y - x + 2 > 0$ and that all points below the line fail to satisfy the given inequality. The region above the line is the graph of the solution of the given inequality and is shaded in Figure 12.4. The solution of the given inequality may also be indicated algebraically as the set of pairs $(x, x - 2 + k)$ where x may be replaced by any real number and k may be replaced by any positive number.

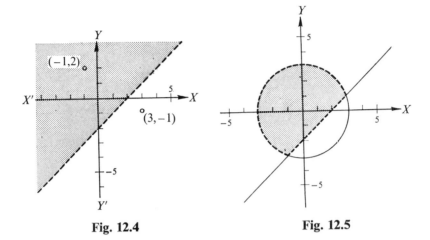

Fig. 12.4   Fig. 12.5

EXAMPLE 3.   Solve graphically the system of inequalities

$$\begin{cases} y - x + 2 > 0, \\ x^2 + y^2 < 9. \end{cases}$$

Solution.   The graph of the solution of $y - x + 2 > 0$ is the set of points above the line in Figure 12.4. The graph of the solution of $x^2 + y^2 < 9$ is the set of points inside the circle of radius 3 with center at the origin. The graph of the solution of the given system of inequalities is the set of points which are above the line and inside the circle. This region is shaded in Figure 12.5.

EXERCISES

Solve graphically:

1—31. The inequalities in Exercises 1 through 31 of § 12-5.

32. $\sin x < 0$.

33. $\cos x > 0$.

34. $\cos x > \frac{1}{2}$.

35. $\sin x < \frac{1}{2}$.

36. $\sin 2x < -0.3$.

37. $\cos \frac{1}{2}x > -0.2$.

Graph the corresponding equalities on a coordinate plane and shade the regions on which the inequalities are satisfied:

38. $y - x > 0.$ **40.** $3x - 2y > 12.$ **42.** $x^2 + y^2 - 1 < 0.$

39. $x + y - 4 < 0.$ **41.** $x^2 + y^2 > 16.$ **43.** $xy < 0.$

For each of the following sets of inequalities, show graphically the regions in which the inequalities hold simultaneously:

44. $\begin{cases} x < y, \\ x + y > 0. \end{cases}$ **47.** $\begin{cases} x^2 + y^2 < 25, \\ x^2 + y^2 > 9. \end{cases}$ **50.** $\begin{cases} 4x^2 + 9y^2 < 144, \\ x^2 - y^2 < 9. \end{cases}$

45. $\begin{cases} 2x - y < 3, \\ 3x + 6y > 12. \end{cases}$ **48.** $\begin{cases} x^2 + y^2 > 25, \\ x^2 + y^2 < 9. \end{cases}$ **51.** $\begin{cases} x - 4 < 0, \\ x - 1 > 0, \\ y + 1 > 0. \end{cases}$

46. $\begin{cases} x + 2y > 1, \\ y - x > 2, \\ x < 3. \end{cases}$ **49.** $\begin{cases} x^2 - y^2 > 1, \\ x^2 + 4y > 0. \end{cases}$ **52.** $\begin{cases} x^2 > 0, \\ y^3 < 0. \end{cases}$

Graph on a coordinate plane:

53. $|x| < 3.$ **55.** $y^2 < 9.$ **57.** $|x| + |y| < 4.$

54. $y \leq |x|.$ **56.** $|xy| > xy.$ **58.** $|x| - |y| > 4.$

(a) *Solve algebraically for* x. *Show* **(b)** *on a number scale,* **(c)** *on a co-ordinate plane, all the points whose coordinates satisfy the conditions.*

59. $x + 2 < 5x.$ **62.** $\dfrac{x + 3}{x - 5} > 2.$ **64.** $\begin{cases} x + 1 < 0, \\ x - 3 > 0. \end{cases}$

60. $4x - 5 < x.$

61. $6x^2 - 8x < 8.$ **63.** $|x| \geq 2.$ **65.** $\begin{cases} 4 - x^2 > 0, \\ 4 + x < 0. \end{cases}$

Find algebraically the intervals on which each of the following functions is positive and the intervals on which it is negative. Using these facts, make a rough sketch of the graph of the function.

66. $(x - 2)(x - 3).$ **70.** $(x - 2)/(x - 3)^2.$

67. $(x - 2)^2(x - 3).$ **71.** $(x - 2)(x - 5)(x - 3).$

68. $(x - 2)^3(x - 3).$ **72.** $(x - 2)^2(x - 5)^3(x - 3).$

69. $(x - 2)^2/(x - 3).$ **73.** $x(x + 2)^2(x - 3)(x + 5)^4.$

74. $\dfrac{(x - 1)(x + 3)^2}{x(x + 1)^5}.$

75. In Exercise 21 of § 4-9, find algebraically and graphically the speeds which permit at least 900 cars per hour to pass.

76. A manufacturer makes two products, the first in lots of x units and the second in lots of y units. To avoid wasting too much time in changing from one product to the other, the lots are required to be large enough that

$$\frac{4000}{x} + \frac{8000}{y} \leq 7.$$

(a) To keep the inventory within available storage space, it is required that $7x + y \leq 11{,}000$. Show graphically the combinations, if any, of lot sizes which satisfy both of these requirements. **(b)** Do the same if the second condition is replaced by $7x + y \leq 5000$.

77. To use the full light-gathering ability of an optical telescope, the minimum useful magnification M is $3a$, where a is the diameter of the telescope lens in inches. The maximum useful magnification is $40a$, because of the limited resolving power of the eye. **(a)** Show graphically the useful combinations of a and M. **(b)** What is the smallest telescope for which hundred-fold magnification is justified?

78. A girl is considering buying some records at $1.50 each and some trinkets at 50 cents each. Express each of the following conditions algebraically and graphically: **(a)** the numbers x of records and y of trinkets cannot be negative; **(b)** she can spend no more than $12; **(c)** there are only five records she wishes to buy; **(d)** all the preceding conditions apply simultaneously.

79. An explorer needs to take along 18 and 75 milligrams respectively of the vitamins niacin and ascorbic acid for each day. No vitamin preparations are available, so he is to get these by eating liver, containing 67 and 141 milligrams per pound respectively of niacin and ascorbic acid, and oranges, for which the corresponding figures are 1 and 222. Show graphically the weights of liver and oranges which will supply enough **(a)** niacin; **(b)** ascorbic acid; **(c)** of both.

*80. On a thirty-minute television show the entertainment costs $3000 per minute and runs x minutes; the commercials fill the rest of the time and cost $500 per minute. It is estimated that the audience will number 80,000 times the number of minutes of entertainment, minus 1000 times the number of minutes of commercials. There must be between three and ten minutes, inclusive, of commercials. Show algebraically and graphically the possible values of A, the size of the audience, as a function of C, the total cost in dollars.

12-7   Factors and Remainders of Polynomials

In § 12-1 and § 12-2 we considered quadratic polynomials and equations. We turn now to polynomials and polynomial equations in general. Functional notation (§ 4-2) is convenient here.

Remainder Theorem.   *When a polynomial* $f(x)$ *is divided by* $(x - r)$, *the remainder is equal to* $f(r)$.

Proof.   Divide the polynomial $f(x)$ by $(x - r)$; denote the quotient thus obtained by $Q(x)$ and the remainder by R. Since, by the definition of division, *the dividend is equal to the quotient times the divisor plus the remainder*, we have

$$f(x) = (x - r)Q(x) + R,$$

where $Q(x)$ is of degree $(n - 1)$ in x if $f(x)$ is of degree n, and R (being of lower degree than the divisor) is a constant. Moreover, since this equality is an identity in x, it is true for all values of x, including $x = r$; hence

$$f(r) = (r - r)Q(r) + R.$$

Since $Q(x)$ is a polynomial in x, $Q(r)$ is a finite number, and

$$(r - r)Q(r) = 0.$$
$$\therefore \quad R = f(r).$$

EXAMPLE 1.   Find the remainder when $(x^4 - 2x^2 + 3x - 5)$ is divided by $(x + 2)$.

Solution.   Here $f(x) = x^4 - 2x^2 + 3x - 5$;

$$x - r = x + 2, \quad \text{whence} \quad r = -2.$$
But $\qquad f(r) = f(-2) = (-2)^4 - 2(-2)^2 + 3(-2) - 5 = -3.$

Therefore, by the remainder theorem, $R = -3$. This can be verified by long division.

EXAMPLE 2.   Find the values of m for which $(x - 3)$ will divide into $(x^3 - m^2x^2 - mx - 6)$ with a remainder equal to 15.

Solution.   Here $f(x) = x^3 - m^2x^2 - mx - 6$;

$$x - r = x - 3, \quad \text{whence} \quad r = 3; \quad \text{and} \quad R = 15.$$
But $\qquad f(r) = f(3) = (3)^3 - m^2(3)^2 - m(3) - 6.$

Therefore, by the remainder theorem,

$$R = 27 - 9m^2 - 3m - 6 = 15;$$
from which $\qquad 3m^2 + m - 2 = 0;$
$$(m + 1)(3m - 2) = 0;$$
$$m = -1 \text{ or } \tfrac{2}{3}.$$

Factor Theorem. If r *is a zero of a polynomial* f(x), *then* (x − r) *is a factor of* f(x). *Equivalently, if* r *is a root of a polynomial equation* f(x) = 0, *then* (x − r) *is a factor of* f(x).

Proof. By the remainder theorem,

$$f(x) = (x - r)Q(x) + f(r).$$

By hypothesis, r is a zero of $f(x)$; that is, r is a root of $f(x) = 0$ (§ 4-9). Hence $f(r) = 0$.

$$\therefore \quad f(x) = (x - r)Q(x),$$

and $(x - r)$ is a factor of $f(x)$.

EXAMPLE. Determine whether $(x + 2)$ is a factor of the polynomial $(x^4 - 2x^2 + 3x - 2)$.

Solution. Here $f(x) = x^4 - 2x^2 + 3x - 2$;

$$x - r = x + 2, \quad \text{whence} \quad r = -2.$$

But $\qquad f(r) = f(-2) = (-2)^4 - 2(-2)^2 + 3(-2) - 2 = 0.$

Hence, by the factor theorem, $(x + 2)$ is a factor of $f(x)$.

The **converse of the factor theorem** also holds: *If* (x − r) *is a factor of* f(x), *then* r *is a root of* f(x) = 0.

Proof. Since $(x - r)$ is a factor, $f(x) = (x - r)Q(x)$. Setting $x = r$, the factor $(x - r)$ is zero, and so the product $f(x)$ is zero as asserted.

We may observe also that if r is a root of a polynomial equation $f(x) = 0$ and $Q(x)$ is the quotient of $f(x)$ by $(x - r)$, then the other roots of $f(x) = 0$ must be solutions of $Q(x) = 0$, which is called the **depressed equation.** This follows from the fact, established in the proof of the factor theorem, that $f(x) = (x - r)Q(x)$; $f(x)$ can be zero only if one of its factors is zero.

EXERCISES

1. Find by long division the remainder when

$$x^4 + 2x^3 - 4x^2 + 3x + 2$$

is divided by (**a**) $(x - 1)$; (**b**) $(x + 1)$; (**c**) $(x + 2)$; (**d**) $(x - 3)$. Also in each case find the remainder by use of the remainder theorem.

In Exercises 2 through 5, by use of the remainder theorem, find the remainder when:

2. $(5x^3 - 6x^2 + x + 3)$ is divided by $(x - 2)$.

3. $(x^4 - x^3 + 3x - 7)$ is divided by $(x + 1)$.

4. $(2x^4 - 3x^3 - 3x^2 + x)$ is divided by **(a)** $(x - 3)$; **(b)** $(x + 2)$.

5. $(3x^5 - 6x^3 - x^2 + 4)$ is divided by **(a)** $(x + 1)$; **(b)** $(x - \frac{1}{3})$.

6. Show that $(x - 1)$ is a factor of $19x^{85} - 47x^{74} + 28$.

7. Is $(x + 4)$ a factor of $(x^3 - 7x - 36)$? Why?

8. Given $f(x) = 2x^2 + 3x + 1$. **(a)** Show that $(2x + 1)$ is a factor of $f(x)$. **(b)** Is $f(-1) = 0$? **(c)** If so, is the result obtained in (b) a consequence of that in (a)?

Show that the given number is a root of the given equation, and by long division or otherwise, find the depressed equation when this root is removed:

9. $x^2 + 3x + 2 = 0$; $x = -1$.   **11.** $x^4 - 2x^3 + 1 = 0$; $x = 1$.

10. $x^3 - 27 = 0$; $x = 3$.   **12.** $x^4 - 4x^3 + 3x^2 = 0$; $x = 0$.

Find the values of k, *or of* m, *or both, so that:*

13. $(2x^3 - 9x^2 - kx + 39)$ is divisible by $(x - 3)$.

14. $(3x^2 - mx - m^2 - 9)$ is divisible by $(x + 2)$.

15. $(x^3 + kx^2 - 3x - 15)$ divided by $(x - 2)$ has remainder 3.

16. $(6y^2 - y - 2)$ is divisible by **(a)** $(y - k)$; **(b)** $(y + 2m)$.

17. $(x^3 - kx^2 + mx + 6)$ is divisible by $(x + 2)(x + 3)$.

Show that if n *is a positive integer, then:*

18. $(x - a)$ is a factor of $(x^n - a^n)$.

19. $(x + a)$ is a factor of $(x^n - a^n)$ if n is even.

20. $(x + a)$ is a factor of $(x^n + a^n)$ if n is odd.

12-8   The Number of Roots of a Polynomial Equation

Fundamental Theorem of Algebra.   *Every polynomial equation in a single variable* x *has at least one root.*

We shall assume this theorem without proof and prove four related theorems.* It is to be remembered that we are admitting complex numbers (both real and imaginary) as coefficients and as roots.

Theorem I.   *Every polynomial in* x *of degree* n *in* x *can be decomposed into* n *linear factors.*

Proof.   Let $f(x) = a_0x^n + a_1x^{n-1} + \cdots + a_{n-1}x + a_n$, $a_0 \neq 0$. By the fundamental theorem, $f(x) = 0$ has as least one root. Let r_1 denote

* For a proof of the Fundamental Theorem of Algebra and further discussion of other topics in this chapter, see L. E. Dickson's *New First Course in the Theory of Equations* (Wiley, New York, 1939) or J. V. Uspensky's *Theory of Equations* (McGraw-Hill, New York, 1948).

this root. Then, by the factor theorem, $(x - r_1)$ is a factor of $f(x)$; so that

$$f(x) = (x - r_1)Q_1(x), \qquad (2)$$

where $Q_1(x)$ is a polynomial of degree $(n - 1)$ and a_0x^{n-1} is its term of highest degree.

Again, by the fundamental theorem, there is at least one root of the depressed equation $Q_1(x) = 0$. Denote it by r_2. Then $(x - r_2)$ is a factor of $Q_1(x)$; so that $Q_1(x) = (x - r_2)Q_2(x)$, and, from (2),

$$f(x) = (x - r_1)(x - r_2)Q_2(x),$$

where $Q_2(x)$ is a polynomial of degree $(n - 2)$ and a_0x^{n-2} is its term of highest degree.

Continuing this process n times, thus obtaining n linear factors (not necessarily distinct), we have as a final result:

$$f(x) = (x - r_1)(x - r_2) \cdots (x - r_n)Q_n(x),$$

where $Q_n(x)$ is the final quotient and consists only of the term a_0x^{n-n}, or a_0. Therefore we have

$$f(x) = a_0(x - r_1)(x - r_2) \cdots (x - r_n), \quad a_0 \neq 0, \qquad (3)$$

where $r_1, r_2, \cdots, r_n$ are n roots of $f(x) = 0$. The numbers $r_1, r_2, \cdots, r_n$ need not be distinct, they need not be rational, and some or all of them may be imaginary. We shall refer to the right member of (3) as the **factored form** of $f(x)$. However, to make this statement we must admit irrational and imaginary coefficients of the terms in the factors, contrary to the practice in § 2-5.

Theorem II.   *A polynomial equation,* $f(x) = 0$, *of degree* n *in* x *can have no more than* n *distinct roots.*

Proof.   Let r be any number. Then, from (3),

$$f(r) = a_0(r - r_1)(r - r_2) \cdots (r - r_n).$$

Now, if r is *not* equal to any one of the n numbers $r_1, r_2, \cdots, r_n$, then each of the factors $(r - r_1)$, $(r - r_2)$, $\cdots$, $(r - r_n)$ is different from zero. Also $a_0 \neq 0$ by definition (§ 5-1); hence $f(r) \neq 0$. Therefore the number r is *not* a root of $f(x) = 0$, and $f(x) = 0$ has *no* roots other than the numbers $r_1, r_2, \cdots, r_n$. Thus the theorem is proved.

The roots $r_1, r_2, \cdots, r_n$ need not all be distinct, and some or all of them may be imaginary. If a number r' is equal to two or more of the roots $r_1, r_2, \cdots, r_n$, then r' is said to be a **multiple root**. If r' is equal to exactly two of the roots, r' is a **double root**; if equal to exactly three of the roots, r' is a **triple root**; or if equal to exactly m of the roots, r' is a **root of multiplicity** m. A root which is not a multiple root is called a **simple root.**

ILLUSTRATIONS.

2 is a double root of $(x - 3)(x - 2)(x - 2) = 0$.
1 is a triple root of $(x - 1)^3(x - 2)^2 = 0$.

Theorem III. *Every polynomial equation of degree* n *in* x *has exactly* n *roots, where a root of multiplicity* m *is counted as* m *roots.*

Proof. The existence of n roots follows directly from Theorem I. The absence of more roots follows from Theorem II.

This theorem only asserts the existence of the roots; it does not tell how to find them. On the other hand, by use of the factored form (3), we can always write an equation when its roots are given:

To form a polynomial equation in x **whose roots are** r_1, r_2, $\cdots$, r_n, *equate to zero the product of the corresponding factors* $(x - r_1)$, $(x - r_2)$, $\cdots$, $(x - r_n)$.

EXAMPLE 1. Form an equation with integral coefficients which has the following roots and no others: $-\frac{1}{2}$, 1 as a double root, $(1 + i)$, and $(1 - i)$.

Solution. Any equation of the form

$$a_0(x + \tfrac{1}{2})(x - 1)(x - 1)[x - (1 + i)][x - (1 - i)] = 0, \quad a_0 \neq 0,$$

has the given roots and no others. Taking $a_0 = 2$, this equation may be written in the desired form:

$$2(x + \tfrac{1}{2})(x - 1)^2[(x - 1) - i][(x - 1) + i] = 0,$$
$$(2x + 1)(x^2 - 2x + 1)[(x - 1)^2 - i^2] = 0,$$
$$(2x + 1)(x^2 - 2x + 1)(x^2 - 2x + 2) = 0,$$

or

$$2x^5 - 7x^4 + 10x^3 - 5x^2 - 2x + 2 = 0.$$

Theorem IV. *If two polynomials in the same variable of degree not greater than* n *are equal for more than* n *distinct values of the variable, the coefficients of like powers of the variable are equal and the equality is an identity.*

Proof. Let $f(x)$ and $g(x)$ be the two polynomials, where

$$f(x) = a_0x^n + a_1x^{n-1} + \cdots + a_n,$$

and

$$g(x) = b_0x^n + b_1x^{n-1} + \cdots + b_n.$$

Then, by hypothesis,

$$a_0x^n + a_1x^{n-1} + \cdots + a_n = b_0x^n + b_1x^{n-1} + \cdots + b_n, \qquad (4)$$

or $\qquad (a_0 - b_0)x^n + (a_1 - b_1)x^{n-1} + \cdots + (a_n - b_n) = 0, \qquad (5)$

is satisfied by more than n distinct values of x. But if one or more of the coefficients $(a_0 - b_0), (a_1 - b_1), \cdots, (a_n - b_n)$ in equation (5) were not zero, we should have an equation of degree n, or less, with more than n distinct roots. This is impossible, by Theorem III. Therefore each of the coefficients in equation (5) must be zero, and we have

$$a_0 - b_0 = 0, \quad a_1 - b_1 = 0, \quad \cdots, \quad a_n - b_n = 0,$$

whence $\qquad a_0 = b_0, \quad a_1 = b_1, \quad \cdots, \quad a_n = b_n, \qquad (6)$

and so the two polynomials are identically equal.

EXAMPLE 2.   Find the values of the constants A and B in the identity

$$7 - x \equiv A(x - 1) + B(x + 2).$$

Solution.   Rearranging the given identity, we have

$$7 - x \equiv (A + B)x + (2B - A).$$

Equating coefficients of like powers of x as in Theorem IV, we obtain

$$\begin{cases} A + B = -1, \\ -A + 2B = 7. \end{cases}$$

Solving this system of equations, we find $A = -3$ and $B = 2$.

Historical Note.   The first satisfactory proof of the fundamental theorem was given by the German mathematician CARL FRIEDRICH GAUSS (1777–1855). Previously proofs had been given by D'ALEMBERT (1746), EULER (1749), and LAGRANGE (1772). Gauss gave four proofs for this theorem. The first, published in 1799, was his dissertation for the doctorate.

EXERCISES

Form equations with integral coefficients having the following roots and no others:

1. $3, 2, -1$.

2. $-3, -2, 1$.

3. $-5, 2$.

4. $4, 1, -2, 0$.

5. $3, 1, 1, -2$.

6. $\frac{1}{2}, 1, -2$.

7. $\frac{1}{2}, \frac{1}{2}, -2$.

8. $\frac{2}{3}, -\frac{3}{2}, -\frac{3}{2}, -1$.

9. $2, (1 \pm \sqrt{3})$.

10. $\pm\sqrt{2}, \pm 3i$.

11. $\frac{2}{5}, (3 \pm i\sqrt{5})$.

12. $\frac{1}{2}(-2 \pm \sqrt{3}), \pm i\sqrt{2}$.

13. $2, \frac{4}{5}, 0, \pm 2i\sqrt{3}$.

14. $\pm 3, \pm\sqrt{3}, \pm\frac{1}{3}i$.

15. $\frac{1}{4}(1 \pm i\sqrt{5}), \pm\sqrt{3}$.

16. -3 as a triple root.

17. $\frac{1}{2}$ as a root of multiplicity 4.

18. $(-2 + \sqrt{3})$ and $(-2 - \sqrt{3})$ as double roots.

19. $(4 + i\sqrt{2})$ and $(4 - i\sqrt{2})$ as double roots.

20. 2 as a double root and -1 as a triple root.

21. 1 as a triple root and i and $-i$ as double roots.

Find the values of the constants A, B, *and* C *in the following identities:*

22. $5x + 2 \equiv A(x - 2) + B(x + 2)$.

23. $2x - 5 \equiv A(x + 1) + B(x - 3)$.

24. $x + 28 \equiv A(2x + 1) - B(x - 3)$.

25. $27 + 8x \equiv A(x + 4) + B(2x + 3)$.

26. $13 - 2x - x^2 \equiv A(x^2 + 1) + Bx(x + 3) + C(x - 1)(x + 3)$.

27. $11x - 18 - 3x^2 \equiv A(x - 4)^2 + B(x + 2)(x - 2) + C(3x - 10)$.

28. $x^2 - 3x - 1 \equiv A(x^2 - x - 3) + (Bx + C)(x - 3)$.

Write as the product of polynomials of first or second degree with real coefficients:

★29. $x^3 + 1$.   **★30.** $x^4 + 1$.

12-9 Imaginary and Quadratic Surd Roots

We shall now consider two theorems concerning imaginary numbers and quadratic surds as roots of a polynomial equation. These theorems generalize a result which in the case of a quadratic equation is evident from the quadratic formula (§ 5-8).

Theorem V. *If an imaginary number* (a + bi) *is a root of a polynomial equation with* **real** *coefficients, then the conjugate imaginary number* (a − bi) *is also a root; that is, imaginary roots occur in conjugate pairs.*

Proof. Let the equation be $f(x) = 0$. By hypothesis, $(a + bi)$ is a root of $f(x) = 0$, so that $f(a + bi) = 0$ and $[x - (a + bi)]$ is a factor of $f(x)$. We shall show that $D(x)$ is a factor of $f(x)$, where

$$D(x) = [x - (a + bi)][x - (a - bi)],$$

and therefore that $[x - (a - bi)]$ is a factor of $f(x)$, and so

$$f(a - bi) = 0.$$

From the definition of $D(x)$ we have

$$D(x) = [(x - a) - bi][(x - a) + bi] = (x - a)^2 + b^2$$
$$= x^2 - 2ax + (a^2 + b^2).$$

We see that the coefficients of $D(x)$ are real numbers. Now divide $f(x)$ by $D(x)$ until a remainder $(Rx + S)$ is obtained. Denote the quotient by $Q(x)$; R and S are real since the coefficients of $D(x)$ are real. Then we may write

$$f(x) = D(x)Q(x) + Rx + S. \qquad (7)$$

Since $D(x)$ has the factor $[x - (a + bi)]$, $D(a + bi) = 0$. Also, by hypothesis, $f(a + bi) = 0$. Substituting $(a + bi)$ for x in (7), we obtain

$$0 = 0 \cdot Q(a + bi) + R \cdot (a + bi) + S,$$

or $\qquad\qquad (Ra + S) + (Rb)i = 0. \qquad (8)$

Since a complex number cannot be zero unless both its real and imaginary parts are zero (§ 8-1), we must have

$$Ra + S = 0 \quad \text{and} \quad Rb = 0.$$

But, by hypothesis, $(a + bi)$ is imaginary; that is, $b \neq 0$. Hence $R = 0$, so $0 \cdot a + S = 0$, and $S = 0$. That is, the remainder is zero when $f(x)$ is divided by $D(x)$. Therefore $[x - (a - bi)]$ is a factor of $f(x)$, and $(a - bi)$ is a root of $f(x) = 0$.

As an immediate consequence of Theorems V and I, we have the following:

Corollary.   *Every polynomial of degree at least 1 with real coefficients can be expressed as a product of real factors each of which is either linear or quadratic.*

The linear factors correspond to the real roots, and the quadratic factors to *pairs* of conjugate imaginary roots.

Theorem VI.   *If a quadratic surd* $(a + \sqrt{b})$, *where* a *and* b *are rational but* $\sqrt{b}$ *is irrational, is a root of a polynomial equation with* **rational** *coefficients, then the conjugate surd* $(a - \sqrt{b})$ *is also a root.*

The proof is similar to that for Theorem V.

EXERCISES

If f(x) = 0, *a polynomial equation with real coefficients, has the given
number as a root, find if possible another root:*

1. $3i$. **3.** $1 + 4i$. **5.** $i\sqrt{5}$. **7.** $\frac{1}{2}(1 - i)$. **9.** 6.

2. $-5i$. **4.** $4 - 3i$. **6.** $-i\sqrt{7}$. **8.** $\frac{1}{5}(-3 + 2i)$. **10.** $-\frac{1}{2}$.

*If a polynomial equation with rational coefficients has the given number
as a root, find if possible another root:*

11. $\sqrt{3}$. **13.** $\frac{4}{3}\sqrt{15}$. **15.** $\dfrac{1 - 3\sqrt{2}}{5}$. **16.** 1.

12. $-3\sqrt{5}$. **14.** $-3 + 8\sqrt{2}$. **17.** 0.

*Form polynomial equations of the lowest possible degree and with
integral coefficients having the following numbers as roots:*

18. $3, (-1 + 2i)$. **20.** $\frac{1}{2}, \frac{1}{3}(1 - i\sqrt{6})$. **22.** $-\sqrt{3}, 2i$.

19. $-1, (3 - \sqrt{2})$. **21.** $\frac{1}{3}\sqrt{3}, \frac{1}{2}(1 + i\sqrt{2})$. **23.** $(3i\sqrt{2} \pm 1)$.

Solve the following equations, having the roots indicated:

24. $2x^3 - 3x^2 - 8x + 12 = 0; \frac{3}{2}$. **27.** $2x^4 + x^3 - 2x = 1; -\frac{1}{2}, 1$.

25. $2x^3 + 3x^2 + 4x + 6 = 0; -\frac{3}{2}$. **28.** $x^4 + 8x + 8 = 10x^2; 2, 2$.

26. $x^4 - 4x^3 - 4x = 1; 2 - \sqrt{5}$. **29.** $x^4 = 2x^3 - 4x + 4; 1 + i$.

30. Show that $(-1 + 2i)$ and $(-1 - 2i)$ are double roots of

$$x^4 + 4x^3 + 14x^2 + 20x + 25 = 0.$$

31. Show that the equation $x^2 - 2x + 1 + 2i = 0$ has the root
$(2 - i)$, but that the conjugate $(2 + i)$ is not a root. Does this contradict
Theorem V?

32. Show that the equation $x^2 + (1 - 2\sqrt{2})x + 2 - \sqrt{2} = 0$ has
the root $(-1 + \sqrt{2})$, but that the conjugate $(-1 - \sqrt{2})$ is not a root.
Does this contradict Theorem VI?

33. Prove that a polynomial equation of odd degree with real coefficients has at least one real root.

12-10 Synthetic Division

The division of a polynomial $f(x)$ by a binomial of the form $(x - r)$
may be considerably shortened by the process known as **synthetic
division.** This process will be shown by means of the following illustration.

ILLUSTRATION. Consider the division of $(3x^3 - 2x^2 + 4x - 27)$ by $(x - 2)$, the ordinary process by long division being shown below:

$$\begin{array}{l}
\textbf{(dividend) } 3x^3 - 2x^2 + 4x - 27 \underline{\,|\, x - 2 \textbf{ (divisor)}} \\
\quad\quad\underline{3x^3 - 6x^2} \qquad\qquad \underline{|\, 3x^2 + 4x + 12 \textbf{ (quotient)}} \\
\quad\quad\quad\quad 4x^2 + 4x \\
\quad\quad\quad\quad \underline{4x^2 - 8x} \\
\quad\quad\quad\quad\quad\quad 12x - 27 \\
\quad\quad\quad\quad\quad\quad \underline{12x - 24} \\
\quad\quad\quad\quad\quad\quad\quad\quad -3 \textbf{ (remainder)}
\end{array}$$

We first abbreviate the process by writing only the coefficients, and refraining from writing those terms that are merely repetitions. For example, we omit the $3x^3$ under the $3x^3$ at the left, the -27 under the -27, the x in the divisor, and the whole quotient (whose coefficients are shown in bold face below):

$$\begin{array}{l}
3 - 2 + 4 - 27 \underline{\,|\, -2} \\
\underline{\;-6} \\
\mathbf{+\,4} \\
\quad\quad \underline{-8} \\
\quad\quad \mathbf{+\,12} \\
\quad\quad\quad\quad \underline{-24} \\
\quad\quad\quad\quad -3
\end{array}$$

We next replace -2 by 2 (this makes our divisor appear as r, not $-r$) so that we can find the successive coefficients of the quotient and the remainder by addition instead of subtraction. By making this change and condensing the process still further by writing the coefficients of the quotient and the remainder on the same line, we have

$$\begin{array}{l}
3 - 2 + \;\;4 - 27 \underline{\,|\, +2} \\
\underline{\;+6 + \;\;8 + 24} \\
3 + 4 + 12 - \;\;3
\end{array}$$

The first three numbers in the third line are the *coefficients* of the *quotient* $(3x^2 + 4x + 12)$, and the last number is the *remainder*, -3.

This process is summarized in the following rule:

To divide a polynomial $f(x)$ **by** $(x - r)$ **by synthetic division,** *arrange* f(x) *in descending powers of* x, *as, for example,*

$$f(x) = a_0 x^n + a_1 x^{n-1} + \cdots + a_{n-1} x + a_n. \tag{9}$$

Arrange the detached coefficients $a_0, a_1, \cdots, a_{n-1}, a_n$ *in order in the first line, supplying any missing power of* x *with a zero coefficient, and write* r *at the right.*

Bring down a_0 *in the first place in the third line. Multiply* a_0 *by* r, *writing the product in the second line under* a_1, *and their sum in the third line; multiply this sum by* r, *add the product to* a_2, *and write the sum in the third line, and so on; until finally a product is added to the last coefficient of* f(x).

The last sum in the third line is the remainder. The preceding sums are the coefficients of the powers of x *in the quotient, beginning with* x^{n-1} *and arranged in descending order.*

EXAMPLE 1.   Divide $(2x^4 - x^2 + 3x - 5)$ by $(x + 3)$ by synthetic division.

Solution.   Here the divisor $(x - r)$ is $(x + 3)$, so $r = -3$.

$$\begin{array}{r} 2 + 0 - 1 + 3 - 5 \,\underline{|-3} \\ -6 + 18 - 51 + 144 \\ \hline 2 - 6 + 17 - 48 + 139 \end{array}$$

The *quotient* is $(2x^3 - 6x^2 + 17x - 48)$, and the *remainder* is 139.

By the remainder theorem, we may find the value of a polynomial $f(x)$ when $x = r$ by dividing $f(x)$ by $(x - r)$ by synthetic division; the remainder thus obtained is $f(r)$. Thus in Example 1, when $x = -3$ the value of $(2x^4 - x^2 + 3x - 5)$ is 139.

EXAMPLE 2.   Given that $5x^4 - 6x^3 - 15x - 2 = 0$ has the root 2, find the depressed equation.

Solution.   Divide the left member of the equation by $(x - 2)$ by synthetic division.

$$\begin{array}{r} 5 - 6 + 0 - 15 - 2 \,\underline{|2} \\ + 10 + 8 + 16 + 2 \\ \hline 5 + 4 + 8 + 1 + 0 \end{array}$$

The quotient is $(5x^3 + 4x^2 + 8x + 1)$, so the depressed equation is

$$5x^3 + 4x^2 + 8x + 1 = 0.$$

EXERCISES

By long division and by synthetic division, find the quotient and remainder in:

1. $(3x^5 - 5x^3 + 4) \div (x - 2)$.

2. $(x^4 + x^3 - 3) \div (x + 2)$.

By synthetic division, find the quotient and remainder in:

3. $(2x^2 - 5x - 1) \div (x + 4)$.   **5.** $(2 + z - 6z^2 + z^3) \div (z - 3)$.

4. $(2x^3 - 7x^2 + 8) \div (x - 5)$.   **6.** $(a^3 - 4a^2 - 3a) \div (a + 1)$.

7. $(3x^5 + 2x^2 + 5x) \div (x - 1)$.

8. $(2x^3 - x^2 + 4) \div (x - \frac{1}{2})$.

9. $(-x^3 + 3x + 1) \div (x + 2)$.

10. $(\frac{40}{3}x^2 - x^5 + \frac{7}{3}) \div (x - 3)$.

11. $(9x^4 - 15x^3 + 11x^2 + 3x + 1) \div (x - \frac{1}{3})$.

12. $(x^3 - ax^2 + 2a^2x + 3a^3) \div (x + 2a)$.

13. $(2x^3 + 0.3x^2 - 0.65x - 1.617) \div (x - 0.2)$.

★14. $(x^4 + 2x^3 - 7x^2 - 8x + 10) \div [(x + 3)(x - 1)]$.

★15. $(2x^5 - 3x^4 - 11x^3 + 5x^2 + 2x + 6) \div [(x - 3)(x + 2)]$.

★16. $(2x^4 - 12x^3 + 27x^2 - 54x + 81) \div (x - 3)^2$.

Solve by use of synthetic division:

17. Given $f(x) = 2x^3 - 3x^2 + 5$, find **(a)** $f(2)$; **(b)** $f(-1)$.

18. Given $f(x) = -3x^3 - 2x^2 - x - 4$, find **(a)** $f(1)$; **(b)** $f(-3)$.

19. Given $f(x) = 6x^3 - x^2 - 4x + 5$, find **(a)** $f(\frac{1}{3})$; **(b)** $f(-\frac{3}{2})$.

20. Given $f(y) = y^4 + 3y^3 - 5y^2 + 9$, find $f(-2)$.

21. Given $g(u) = 2u^3 - 3u^2 - 5u + 3$, find $g(-0.6)$.

Given that the specified number is a root of the equation, find the depressed equation by synthetic division:

22. $x^3 - 6x^2 + 9x - 2 = 0$; root 2.

23. $2x^4 + 7x^3 + 4x^2 - 17x - 60 = 0$; root -3.

24. $y^6 - y^5 - 27y + 27 = 0$; root 1.

25. $2y^3 + y^2 + 13y = 7$; root $\frac{1}{2}$.

★26. (a) Show that any polynomial of the form (9) in this section can also be written in **nested form:**

$$f(x) = (\cdots (((a_0x + a_1)x + a_2)x + a_3)x + \cdots + a_{n-1})x + a_n.$$

(b) Compare the successive steps in evaluating the nested form for $x = r$ with the successive steps in the rule for synthetic division.

★27. Suppose a certain computing machine must find powers by multiplication (for instance, $x^3 = x \cdot x \cdot x$) and that each multiplication of two numbers requires 200 microseconds, whereas each addition or subtraction of two numbers requires 10 microseconds (one microsecond is 10^{-6} second). If all other times are neglected, how long will it require to find the value of $(23x^3 - 71x^2 + 36x - 7)$ for $x = 3.916$ by substituting in (a) the polynomial in the form given? (b) the nested form of the polynomial?

*28. Under the conditions of Exercise 27, how long would it take by methods (a) and (b) to evaluate $(ax^3 + bx^2 + cx + d)$ for 10,000 values of x for each of 1000 sets of coefficients?

12-11   Rational Roots

If a polynomial equation with integral coefficients has any rational roots, they can be readily determined by testing each number which the following theorem indicates to be a possible root.

Theorem VII. *If a rational number* b/c, *where* b/c *is in its lowest terms, is a root of a polynomial equation*

$$a_0 x^n + a_1 x^{n-1} + \cdots + a_{n-1} x + a_n = 0, \tag{10}$$

with integral coefficients, then b *is a factor of* a_n *and* c *is a factor of* a_0.

Proof. Since b/c is a root of equation (10), we have

$$a_0 \left(\frac{b}{c}\right)^n + a_1 \left(\frac{b}{c}\right)^{n-1} + \cdots + a_{n-1} \left(\frac{b}{c}\right) + a_n = 0, \tag{11}$$

which, on multiplying each member of (11) by c^n, becomes

$$a_0 b^n + a_1 b^{n-1} c + \cdots + a_{n-1} b c^{n-1} + a_n c^n = 0. \tag{12}$$

Adding $-a_n c^n$ to both members of (12) and factoring b from the resulting left member, we obtain

$$b(a_0 b^{n-1} + a_1 b^{n-2} c + \cdots + a_{n-1} c^{n-1}) = -a_n c^n. \tag{13}$$

Therefore, since the coefficients $a_0, a_1, \cdots, a_{n-1}, a_n$ are integers by hypothesis, the left member of (13) is an integer having b as a factor. Hence b must also be a factor of the right member, $-a_n c^n$. But b has no factor except ± 1 in common with c, since b/c is given to be in lowest terms. Hence b must be a factor of a_n.

Similarly, from (12) we obtain

$$a_0 b^n = -c(a_1 b^{n-1} + \cdots + a_{n-1} b c^{n-2} + a_n c^{n-1}). \tag{14}$$

Since the right member of (14) is an integer having c as a factor, c must also be a factor of the left member, $a_0 b^n$. But c has no factor except ± 1 in common with b. Hence c must be a factor of a_0.

Therefore, the question of whether a polynomial equation with integral coefficients has *any rational roots* may be settled by testing each fraction whose numerator is a factor of the constant term, and whose denominator is a factor of the coefficient of the highest power of x, to see whether the fraction satisfies the equation.

If the coefficient of the highest power of x is unity, c must be $+1$ or -1, and the rational root b/c must be an integer. Hence:

Corollary. *Any rational root of a polynomial equation*

$$x^n + p_1 x^{n-1} + \cdots + p_{n-1}x + p_n = 0,$$

which has integral coefficients and in which the coefficient of x^n *is unity, is an integer and an exact divisor of the constant term* p_n.

EXAMPLE 1.   Solve $x^4 - x^3 + 2x^2 - 4x - 8 = 0$.

Solution.   By the above Corollary, all possible rational roots are found among the numbers ± 1, ± 2, ± 4, and ± 8, the exact divisors of the constant term -8.

Let $f(x) = x^4 - x^3 + 2x^2 - 4x - 8$.

Testing 1 by synthetic division (or by substitution), we find $f(1) = -10$; hence 1 is not a root of $f(x) = 0$.

$$
\begin{array}{r}
1 - 1 + 2 - 4 - 8\ \lfloor 1 \\
+1 + 0 + 2 - 2\ \quad \\
\hline
1 + 0 + 2 - 2 - 10
\end{array}
$$

Testing -1, we find $f(-1) = 0$; hence -1 is a root of $f(x) = 0$ and $(x + 1)$ is a factor of $f(x)$. The quotient of $f(x)$ by $(x + 1)$, as is shown by the synthetic division, is $(x^3 - 2x^2 + 4x - 8)$.

$$
\begin{array}{r}
1 - 1 + 2 - 4 - 8\ \lfloor -1 \\
-1 + 2 - 4 + 8\ \quad \\
\hline
1 - 2 + 4 - 8 + 0
\end{array}
$$

We now have

$$f(x) = (x + 1)(x^3 - 2x^2 + 4x - 8),$$

where the first factor corresponds to the root -1. The remaining roots of $f(x) = 0$ are the roots of the first depressed equation $x^3 - 2x^2 + 4x - 8 = 0$. Let $Q_1(x) = x^3 - 2x^2 + 4x - 8$.

Since 1 is not a root of $f(x) = 0$, it cannot be a root of the depressed equation. There are no further negative roots, since for $x < 0$ each term of $Q_1(x)$ is negative; otherwise we should have to test -1 again since it might be a *multiple* root.

Testing 2, we find $Q_1(2) = 0$; hence 2 is a root of $Q_1(x) = 0$ and of $f(x) = 0$, and $(x - 2)$ is a factor of $Q_1(x)$. The quotient of $Q_1(x)$ by $(x - 2)$, as is shown by the synthetic division, is $(x^2 + 4)$.

$$
\begin{array}{r}
1 - 2 + 4 - 8\ \lfloor 2 \\
+2 + 0 + 8\ \quad \\
\hline
1 + 0 + 4 + 0
\end{array}
$$

The remaining roots of $f(x) = 0$ are the roots of the second depressed equation $x^2 + 4 = 0$; namely, $\pm 2i$.

Therefore the roots of the given equation are -1, 2, $\pm 2i$.

EXAMPLE 2.   Factor $(3x^3 + 4x^2 - 7x + 2)$ into linear factors.

Solution.   Denote the given polynomial by $f(x)$. By the factor theorem and its converse (§ 12-7), the linear factors of $f(x)$ correspond to the roots of $f(x) = 0$. By Theorem VII, all possible rational roots of $f(x) = 0$ are found among the numbers ± 1, ± 2, $\pm\frac{1}{3}$, and $\pm\frac{2}{3}$.

Testing ± 1, ± 2, and $\pm\frac{1}{3}$, we find that none of these is a root of $f(x) = 0$.

Testing $\frac{2}{3}$, we find $f(\frac{2}{3}) = 0$; hence $\frac{2}{3}$ is a root of $f(x) = 0$ and $(x - \frac{2}{3})$ is a factor of $f(x)$.

The remaining roots of $f(x) = 0$ are the roots of the depressed equation $3x^2 + 6x - 3 = 0$, which can be written $x^2 + 2x - 1 = 0$; namely, $(-1 \pm \sqrt{2})$.

$$\begin{array}{r} 3 + 4 - 7 + 2 \,\lfloor\tfrac{2}{3} \\ +2 + 4 - 2 \\ \hline 3 + 6 - 3 + 0 \end{array}$$

Therefore the roots of the equation $3x^3 + 4x^2 - 7x + 2 = 0$ are $\frac{2}{3}$ and $(-1 \pm \sqrt{2})$, and the three factors of $(3x^3 + 4x^2 - 7x + 2)$ are $(3x - 2)$, $(x + 1 - \sqrt{2})$, and $(x + 1 + \sqrt{2})$.

Factors involving irrational numbers are admitted here in accordance with § 12-8, in contrast to Chapter 2. It may be noted that the first factor could also be taken as $(x - \frac{2}{3})$, but then another factor, 3, would be required.

EXERCISES

Using Theorem VII, write the set of numbers among which all possible rational roots must be found:

1. $x^3 + 3x^2 - 2x - 18 = 0$.   4. $9x^6 - x^4 + 5x + 1 = 0$.

2. $x^4 + 2x^3 + 3x^2 - 27 = 0$.   5. $6x^5 - 3x^3 + 5x + \frac{5}{2} = 0$.

3. $3x^4 + 2x^2 - x + 5 = 0$.   6. $5y^6 - 8y^4 + \frac{1}{2}y^3 + 3 = 0$.

Solve each of the following equations by trial until the equation is depressed to a quadratic; then solve the quadratic. Express all irrational roots correct to two decimal places:

7. $x^3 + 8x^2 + 17x + 6 = 0$.

8. $2x^3 - 3x^2 + 2x - 3 = 0$.

9. $2y^3 + 9y^2 + 3y - 4 = 0$.

10. $3z^3 - 5z^2 + 14z = 8$.

11. $x^4 + 4x^3 + 2x^2 - x + 6 = 0$.

12. $8x^4 + 26x^3 - 15x^2 - 26x + 7 = 0$.

13. $2u^4 + 7u^3 + u^2 - 10u = 0$.

14. $9r^2 - 6r^3 + 10r^2 - 6r - 1 = 0$.

15. $x^5 + 3x^4 + 6x^3 + 10x^2 + 9x + 3 = 0$.

Factor each of the following polynomials (**a**) *as far as possible with rational coefficients;* (**b**) *into linear factors:*

16. $x^3 - 5x^2 - 2x + 24$.

17. $3x^4 - 4x^3 + 4x^2 - 4x + 1$.

18. $8y^3 + 22y^2 + 8y - 3$.

19. $3v^3 - 5v^2 - 2v + 4$.

20. $2a^4 + 4a^3 + a^2 - 2a - 1$.

21. $x^3 - \frac{2}{3}x^2 + \frac{8}{3}x + 1$.

Find the rational values of c *such that* (x − c) *will:*

22. Divide into $(x^3 - x^2 - 4x + 4)$ with remainder 0.

23. Divide into $(x^3 - 13x + 3)$ with remainder -9.

24. Divide into $(2x^3 - x^2 + 2x + 4)$ with remainder 5.

25. The trisection of an angle θ with $\cos \theta = a$ has its algebraic equivalent in the solution of the following equation: $4x^3 - 3x = a$, where $x = \cos \frac{1}{3}\theta$. (**a**) Derive this formula (*Hint:* See Exercise 7 of § 7-10). (**b**) Solve for x when $a = -1$.

26. What must be the edge of a cube if its volume could be doubled by an increase of 3 inches in one dimension and of 6 inches in another and a decrease of 2 inches in the third?

27. How long is the edge of a cube if, after a slice 1 inch thick is cut off from one side, the volume of the remaining figure is 294 cubic inches?

28. A rectangular box with a capacity of 64 cubic inches is to be made from a 12-inch square of tin by cutting a small square from each of the four corners and bending the projecting sides through 90°. Find the side of the square to be cut out. How many solutions are possible?

12-12   Approximating Real Roots

The preceding sections present some properties of roots of equations and tell how to find certain special roots such as rational ones, but they do not provide any general method for finding *all* roots. In the case of equations of the first and second degrees, Chapter 5 shows how to find the roots algebraically; that is, the roots are expressed in terms of the coefficients by formulas which involve only a finite number of such operations as additions, subtractions, multiplications, divisions, and extractions of roots. Equations of the third and fourth degrees can also be solved algebraically, though in general only tediously.* *Polynomial equations of degree higher than the fourth cannot, in general, be solved algebraically.* This was first proved in 1824 by the brilliant Norwegian

---

* See the authors' *College Algebra*, fourth edition (Ginn, Boston, 1958), pp. 361–368.

mathematician Niels Henrick Abel (1802–1829); the proof is beyond the scope of this book.

In view of these difficulties in solving algebraically equations of degree higher than two, one naturally turns to graphic solutions. The ordinary graphical method of solution (§ 5-3) has the disadvantage that the answer is obtained with very limited accuracy—typically, to the nearest tenth. By successively enlarging the graph in the neighborhood of the desired root, one can attain a better approximation. Usually, however, it is more convenient to use a corresponding algebraic method of approximation. This is a method of trial using the following location principle, either alone or in connection with linear interpolation. Both this method and the graphical method apply only to *real* roots.

Location Principle*. *If* f(x) *is a polynomial with real coefficients, and if, for the real numbers* a *and* b, f(a) *and* f(b) *have opposite signs, the equation* f(x) = 0 *has at least one root between* a *and* b, *and has an odd number of such roots if a root of multiplicity* m *is counted as* m *roots; if* f(a) *and* f(b) *have like signs, either the equation* f(x) = 0 *has no roots between* a *and* b *or it has an even number of roots between those numbers.*

This principle applies to all single-valued continuous functions (see § 12-5). Graphically this principle asserts that if at $x = a$ the curve is on one side of the x-axis and at $x = b$ the curve is on the opposite side, the curve must cross the x-axis an odd number of times between a and b. If at $x = a$ and at $x = b$ the curve is on the same side of the x-axis, the curve must cross the x-axis an even number of times between a and b if it crosses at all. Since zero is an even number, the last clause of the theorem actually covers the case of no roots as well, but the alternatives are stated separately for emphasis.

In choosing values of x for a table of corresponding values of x and $f(x)$, it is desirable to have some method of determining an interval within which the real roots (if there are any) must lie. The following facts, stated without proof, provide a means of finding such an interval. The algebraically larger end of the interval is called an **upper bound** to the roots; the other end, a **lower bound.**

Let $f(x)$ be a polynomial with *real* coefficients among which the coefficient of the highest power of x is *positive*. If $r \geq 0$, and if all the numbers in the third row of the synthetic division of $f(x)$ by $(x - r)$ are

---

* A proof is given in almost any text on the theory of functions of a real variable, and in some of the more rigorous texts on advanced calculus. See, for instance, R. Courant's *Differential and Integral Calculus*, second edition (Interscience, New York, 1937), Vol. 1, p. 66.

positive or zero, then no real root of $f(x) = 0$ is greater than r, and r is an *upper bound* to the real roots of $f(x) = 0$; if $s \leq 0$, and if the numbers in the third row of the synthetic division of $f(x)$ by $(x - s)$ are alternately positive (or zero) and negative (or zero), then no real root of $f(x) = 0$ is less than s, and s is a *lower bound* to the real roots of $f(x) = 0$.

ILLUSTRATIONS.   The following synthetic divisions show that 6 is an upper bound and -2 is a lower bound to the roots of $x^3 - 6x^2 + 15 = 0$, whereas 5 and -1 cannot be relied on to be such bounds.

$$
\begin{array}{l}
1 - 6 + 0 + 15 \,\underline{|\,5} \\
 + 5 - 5 - 25 \\
\hline
1 - 1 - 5 - 10
\end{array}
\qquad
\begin{array}{l}
1 - 6 + 0 + 15 \,\underline{|\,\mathbf{6}} \\
 + 6 + 0 + 0 \\
\hline
1 + 0 + 0 + 15
\end{array}
$$

$$
\begin{array}{l}
1 - 6 + 0 + 15 \,\underline{|\,-1} \\
 - 1 + 7 - 7 \\
\hline
1 - 7 + 7 + 8
\end{array}
\qquad
\begin{array}{l}
1 - 6 + 0 + 15 \,\underline{|\,\mathbf{-2}} \\
 - 2 + 16 - 32 \\
\hline
1 - 8 + 16 - 17
\end{array}
$$

EXAMPLE.   Find the real roots of the equation

$$f(x) = x^3 - 3x^2 + 4x - 5 = 0 \tag{15}$$

(a) to one decimal place by trial and to the second decimal place by linear interpolation; (b) correct to two decimal places by trial; and (c) to the third decimal place by linear interpolation.

Solution.   If equation (15) has any rational roots, it should first be depressed to one having no rational roots by removing the corresponding linear rational factors. Testing the only possible rational roots, ± 1 and ± 5, the exact divisors of the constant term -5, we find that no one of these values satisfies (15). Hence (15) has no rational roots.

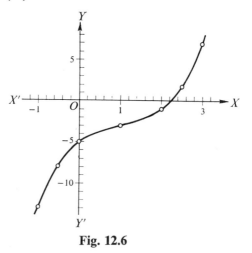

Fig. 12.6

From the graph of $y = f(x) = x^3 - 3x^2 + 4x - 5$ (Figure 12.6) we note that there is only one real root, that between 2 and 3, which is approximately 2.2. The remaining two roots must be imaginary.

a. In order to determine between what tenths this root actually lies, we compute $f(x)$ for successive tenths near the approximation 2.2 until a change in sign of $f(x)$ is obtained. Since $f(2.2) = -0.072$ and $f(2.3) = 0.497$, (15) has a root between 2.2 and 2.3.

x	2.2	2.3
$f(x)$	−0.072	0.497

In order to determine the digit in the hundredths' place, we use the method of linear interpolation (§ 4-8) summarized below.

The correction c_1 for the hundredths' digit can be found from the proportion $\dfrac{c_1}{0.1} = \dfrac{0.072}{0.569}$, from which is obtained $c_1 \approx 0.013$, or 0.01 to the nearest hundredth. Hence the real root of (15) is

x	$f(x)$
$0.1\left[c_1\begin{bmatrix}2.2\\2.2+c_1\\2.3\end{bmatrix}\right.$	$\left.\begin{bmatrix}-0.072\\0\\0.497\end{bmatrix}0.072\right]0.569$

approximately **2.21.** The last digit may not be accurate.

b. By the above method we see that the real root of (15) is between 2.2 and 2.3 but apparently closer to 2.2. We next compute $f(x)$ at intervals of 0.01 in x between 2.2 and 2.3 until a change in sign of $f(x)$ locates the root between successive hundredths. If we were going to stop with two decimal places, and wished to be *certain* of the second decimal place instead of closely approximating it, we should also need to compute $f(x)$ at the midpoint of this interval. The re-

x	2.21	2.215	2.22
$f(x)$	−0.0184	0.0086	0.0358

sults, exhibited in the adjoining table, show that the only real root of (15), *correct* to two decimal places, is **2.21.**

The decision to try *small* values for the hundredths' digit first was influenced by Figure 12.6.

c. In order to determine the digit in the thousandths' place, we continue with the method of linear interpolation, using the results obtained in (*b*), but not computing $f(2.215)$ because the extra information it gives is not needed if we are going on.

The correction c_2 for the thousandths' digit can be found similarly from the proportion $\dfrac{c_2}{0.01} = \dfrac{0.0184}{0.0542}$, from which $c_2 \approx 0.0034$, or 0.003 to the nearest thousandth. Hence the real root of (15) is approximately **2.213.**

x	$f(x)$
$0.01\left[c_2\begin{bmatrix}2.21\\2.21+c_2\\2.22\end{bmatrix}\right.$	$\left.\begin{bmatrix}-0.0184\\0\\0.0358\end{bmatrix}0.0184\right]0.0542$

The method of linear interpolation is applicable not only to polynomial equations but also to irrational equations and to transcendental equations, provided the coefficients are real. Location by linear interpolation (or slightly more elaborate methods studied in more advanced courses) is generally preferred to successive trials without interpolation if one does occasional calculations by hand, since interpolation usually yields a given accuracy with less work than does the trial method. For slide rule or simple computing machines, a more complicated method of Graeffe* is more efficient.

For some modern electronic computing machines, the "trial" method is preferred; the greater rapidity with which such machines can do very simple calculations offsets the greater number of trials required. In this case, once it is known that there exists a root of $f(x) = 0$ between $x = a$ and $x = b$, the machine may be instructed to find the sign of $f([a + b]/2)$ and thus locate the root in one half of the interval; the process may be repeated as often as necessary.

EXERCISES†

Apply the statement just preceding the Illustrations in this section to determine an upper bound and a lower bound to the real roots of each of the following equations:

1. $x^3 - 5x + 13 = 0$.   **3.** $x^4 - 2x^3 - 8x^2 - 48x - 64 = 0$.

2. $x^3 + x^2 - 10x + 10 = 0$.   **4.** $x^4 + x^3 - x^2 - 5x - 3 = 0$.

By use of the location principle show that:

5. The equation $x^3 - 5x + 1 = 0$ has at least one root between **(a)** 0.2 and 0.3; **(b)** 0.20 and 0.21; **(c)** 2.1 and 2.2; **(d)** 2.12 and 2.13; **(e)** −2.3 and −2.4; **(f)** −2.33 and −2.34.

6. The equation $x^3 - 2x + 5 = 0$ has at least one root between **(a)** −2.0 and −2.1; **(b)** −2.09 and −2.10; **(c)** −2.094 and −2.095. **(d)** The given equation has either no roots or an even number of roots between −1 and −2.

7. The equation $x^3 + 3x^2 - 4x - 11 = 0$ **(a)** has at least one root between −1.78 and −1.79; **(b)** cannot have an odd number of roots between −2 and −3.

---

* See, for instance, J. B. Scarborough's *Numerical Mathematical Analysis*, fourth edition (Johns Hopkins Press, Baltimore, 1958).

† A table of squares and cubes of three-digit numbers will be helpful, though not essential, in many of these problems; see for instance J. B. Rosenbach, E. A. Whitman, and D. Moskovitz's *Mathematical Tables* (Ginn, Boston, 1943).

8. The equation $x^3 - 3x^2 - 6x + 2 = 0$ **(a)** has at least one root between 0.29 and 0.30; **(b)** has either no roots or an even number of roots between 1.11 and 1.12.

In Exercises 9 through 16, locate the indicated roots of each of the following equations between two successive tenths, and then find the roots to two decimal places by linear interpolation; if so directed, check to determine if the roots are correct to two decimal places:

9. $x^3 + 4x - 3 = 0$: the real root.

10. $x^3 - 3x - 1 = 0$: **(a)** the positive root; **(b)** the numerically larger negative root; **(c)** the numerically smaller negative root.

11. $x^3 - 9x + 6 = 0$: **(a)** the root between -3 and -4; **(b)** the smaller positive root; **(c)** the larger positive root.

12. $2x^3 - 6x^2 + 3 = 0$: **(a)** the root between 0 and 1; **(b)** the root between 0 and -1; **(c)** the root between 2 and 3.

13. $2x^4 - x^2 - 3x - 4 = 0$: the root between 1 and 2.

14. $x^3 + 6x^2 + 6x - 6 = 0$: **(a)** the positive root; **(b)** the root between -2 and -3; **(c)** the root between -4 and -5.

15. $x^4 - x^3 + x - 2 = 0$: **(a)** the positive root; **(b)** the negative root.

16. $x^5 + x^3 + x - 1 = 0$: the real root.

17. Prove **(a)** the first part, **(b)** the second part, of the statement preceding the Illustrations in this section.

Find to three significant digits by solving an equation of the form $x^n - k = 0$ *without using tables:*

18. $\sqrt{65}$.   **19.** $\sqrt{0.79}$.   **20.** $\sqrt[3]{7}$.   **21.** $\sqrt[3]{60}$.

Find to one decimal place, and interpolate for a second decimal place in, the solution of the following equations:

★22. $\cos^3 x - 2 \sin x = 0.800$, $0 < x < \frac{1}{2}\pi$.

★23. $e^x + \ln x = 1$.

MISCELLANEOUS EXERCISES

(a) *Graph* f(x). **(b)** *Solve the inequality* f(x) > 0. **(c)** *Find the discriminant of* f(x). **(d)** *Discuss the relationship, if any, between the answers to the preceding parts:*

1. $f(x) = x^2 + 3x - 4$.   **3.** $f(x) = x^2 + 4x + 4$.

2. $f(x) = x^2 + 3x + 4$.   **4.** $f(x) = 4x^2 + 4x + 1$.

In each of the following equations, does f(x) *have a zero between* x = 1 *and* x = 2? *Why?*

5. $f(x) = 3x^3 - 2x^2 - 18x + 18$.

6. $f(x) = 9x^4 - 12x^3 - 50x^2 + 72x - 24$.

(**a**) *Find the rational roots, if any, of* f(x) = 0. (**b**) *Sketch the graph of* f(x). (**c**) *Solve the inequality* f(x) < 0.

7. $f(x) = 2x^3 - 15x^2 + 37x - 30$.

8. $f(x) = 64x^4 + 128x^3 + 92x^2 + 28x + 3$.

(**a**) *Express* f(x) *as a polynomial.* (**b**) *State the relationship between the coefficients of this polynomial and the roots of* f(x) = 0.

9. $f(x) = (x - r_1)(x - r_2)(x - r_3)$.

10. $f(x) = (x - r_1)(x - r_2)(x - r_3)(x - r_4)$.

★11. $f(x) = (x - r_1)(x - r_2)(x - r_3) \cdots (x - r_n)$.

Describe as many as possible different methods of doing the following, and carry out one of the methods:

12. Show that $(x + 2a^2)$ is a factor of $(x^7 + 128a^{14})$.

13. Determine k so that $(x - 3)$ is a factor of $(x^3 + k^2x^2 + 2kx - 26)$.

Discuss the applicability of the fundamental theorem of algebra to the following:

14. $(\log x) + 4 = 0$.   **15.** $\sin^2 x - 6 = 0$.

CHAPTER 13

TRIGONOMETRIC AND LOGARITHMIC EQUATIONS

13-1 Logarithmic and Exponential Equations

Equations were defined in Chapter 5. The analysis and examples in Chapters 5, 10, and 12 dealt almost exclusively with algebraic equations— not because the principles were restricted to that type of equation, but because use of the relatively familiar algebraic expressions made it possible to learn about equations without being distracted by certain peculiarities of other types of functions. Now, however, there is a good foundation for dealing with logarithmic, exponential, and trigonometric functions occurring in equations.

An equation in which the unknown occurs in an exponent is called an **exponential equation.**

ILLUSTRATION 1. $3^x = 25$ and $3^{x^2+2} = 81$ are exponential equations.

An equation in which there occurs the logarithm of an expression involving the unknown is called a **logarithmic equation.**

ILLUSTRATION 2. $\log (x^2 + 4x) = 5$ and $\log x + \log (x + 2) = 12$ are logarithmic equations.

Although some exponential equations may be solved by inspection, such equations may more generally be solved by taking the logarithm of each member, applying the fundamental properties of logarithms, and using a table of logarithms.

Many logarithmic equations in one unknown may be transformed into polynomial equations in that unknown by using the fundamental properties of logarithms and the definition of a logarithm.

EXAMPLE 1.   Solve $5^{x+2} = 625$ for x.

Solution.   Since 625 is a power of 5, we change it to the form 5^4. This gives us the equation

$$5^{x+2} = 5^4. \tag{1}$$

Equation (1) is equivalent to $x + 2 = 4$; hence we have $x = 2$.

EXAMPLE 2.   Solve: $5^x = 3^{x+2}$.

Solution.   Take the logarithm of each member:

$$\log 5^x = \log 3^{x+2}.$$

Apply Property 3 of § 6-4: $x \log 5 = (x + 2) \log 3$.

Solve for x: $x(\log 5 - \log 3) = 2 \log 3$,

$$x = \frac{\log 9}{\log 5 - \log 3}.$$

Evaluate, using Table II: $x = \dfrac{0.9542}{0.6990 - 0.4771} = \dfrac{0.9542}{0.2219}$

$$= 4.299, \text{ to four significant digits.}$$

EXAMPLE 3.   Solve $e^{2x} - 2e^x + 1 = 0$.

Solution.   Factor: $(e^x - 1)^2 = 0$,

$$e^x = 1,$$
$$x = 0.$$

EXERCISES

1. Solve $y = cx^n$ for n.

2. Solve $y = ae^{bx}$ for x.

3. Solve $r = ce^{-kt}$ for t.

4. Solve $l = ar^{n-1}$ for n.

Solve:

5. $2^{x+8} = 32$.

6. $27^{6x-5} = 9^{2x}$.

7. $2^{x^2+5x} = \frac{1}{16}$.

8. $5^{12-x^2} = 25^{2x}$.

9. $8^{x^2} = 2^{4x} \cdot 16$.

10. $2^x \cdot 5 = 10^x$.

11. $10^{2x-3} = 43$.

12. $10^{2-3x} = 34$.

13. $e^{5x} = 20$.

14. $3^{5x} = 13$.

15. $2^{3x} = 3^{2x+1}$.

16. $5^{x+2} = 7^{x-2}$.

17. $\log \log x = -0.4685$.

18. $(1.04)^x = 3.500$.

19. $e^{2x} - 4e^x + 4 = 0$.

20. $e^{-2x} - 4e^{-x} + 3 = 0$.

21. $\log_3 (x + 1) + \log_3 (x + 3) = 1$.

22. $\log_4 (x + 3) - \log_4 x = 3$.

23. Solve $y = \ln (-x \pm \sqrt{1 + x^2})$ for x.

24. Solve $y = \ln (x \pm \sqrt{x^2 - 1})$ for x, given that $x \geq 1$.

25. Solve $I = \dfrac{E}{R} (1 - e^{-Rt/L})$ for t.

26. The difference in intensities I_1 and I_2 of two sounds (or of power in two electrical signals) is expressed as a number n of decibels, where $n = 10 \log (I_1/I_2)$. What is the ratio of two intensities which differ by one decibel?

27. A certain radioactive element decomposes at such a rate that, if c is the fraction of the original number of atoms which remain after t hours, then $c = e^{-kt}$ where k is a constant. Given that after three hours half of the original atoms remain, **(a)** find k; **(b)** find when one-tenth of the original atoms remain.

28. In the Illustration in § 6-1, after how many hours will $N = 20,000$?

29. Find b and c if the points $(2, 10)$ and $(6, 40)$ lie on the graph of $y = cb^{\frac{1}{2}x}$.

30. Find k and n if the points $(0.1, 2)$ and $(10, -4)$ lie on the graph of $= k \log nx$.

13-2   Algebraic Solution of Trigonometric Equations

An equation in which occurs a trigonometric function of the unknown is called a **trigonometric equation.** Because of the periodicity of trigonometric functions (§ 7-7), a trigonometric equation usually has an unlimited number of solutions, whereas an algebraic equation of the nth degree has only n solutions (§ 12-8). In connection with trigonometric equations, the unknown is often considered as representing a pure number rather than an angle (§ 7-2); if it represents an angle, the angle is normally measured in radians.

ILLUSTRATION 1.   If x is considered as an angle, then $\sin x = \frac{1}{2}$ has the solutions $30°$, $150°$, $390°$, $510°$, $-210°$, $-330°$, and all angles coterminal with these. In radians, the solutions are $(\frac{1}{6}\pi + 2k\pi)$ and $(\frac{5}{6}\pi + 2k\pi)$ where k is any integer (positive, zero, or negative); coterminal angles, by definition, differ by a multiple of 2π. If x represents a pure number, the solutions are still of the form $(\frac{1}{6}\pi + 2k\pi)$ and $(\frac{5}{6}\pi + 2k\pi)$ for k an integer, though we can no longer speak of angles, coterminal or otherwise.

Because of this proliferation of solutions, it is convenient to adopt a brief notation, which can be extended to sets in general. The set of all numbers that can be expressed in a specified form will be denoted by enclosing the form in brackets: $\{\frac{1}{6}\pi + 2k\pi\}$ means the set of all numbers expressible in the form $(\frac{1}{6}\pi + 2k\pi)$. If nothing is specified about the parameter, k in this instance, it may have any integer as its value. Otherwise the permissible values are specified at the end of the bracket; for example, $\{i^n; n = 0, 1, 2\}$ means the set consisting of i^0, i^1, and i^2. Thus the answers to Illustration 1 can be written $\{\frac{1}{6}\pi + 2k\pi, \frac{5}{6}\pi + 2k\pi\}$.

Just as in proving trigonometric identities, no universal routine procedure for solving trigonometric equations can be specified. The following hints are often helpful:

(1) If the equation involves only one trigonometric function and the variable is the same in each occurrence of the function, try treating this function as a new variable (compare this with "equations in quadratic form," § 5-9) and solving for its value. From this, the values of the original variable can then be found.

(2) Write the equation with one member zero and try to factor the other member. Then at least one factor must be zero.

(3) If the equation involves more than one function, or a function of different multiples of a variable, use trigonometric identities, and try to change the equation into one of the forms just discussed.

The remarks in § 5-4 about equivalent equations, and in particular extraneous roots, apply to trigonometric equations as well.

EXAMPLE.   Solve $5 \tan 3x + 2 = 0$.

Solution. Set $y = \tan 3x$; then $5y + 2 = 0$ so $y = -\frac{2}{5}$. Thus
$$\tan 3x = -\tfrac{2}{5} = -0.4000.$$
By Table VI, $\tan 0.381 = +0.4000$, so by § 7-6,
$$\tan (\pi - 0.381) = \tan 2.761 = -0.4000,$$
and $\qquad\qquad \tan (2\pi - 0.381) = \tan 5.902 = -0.4000.$

Thus the equation is satisfied by the members of the set
$$\{2.761 + 2k\pi,\ 5.902 + 2k\pi\},$$
as values of $3x$. These can be combined as
$$3x = 2.761 + k\pi.$$
Hence $\qquad\qquad x = 0.920 + \tfrac{1}{3}k\pi.$

ILLUSTRATION 2.   To solve the equation $2 \sin^2 x + 3 \sin x - 2 = 0$, factor:
$$(2 \sin x - 1)(\sin x + 2) = 0.$$
Hence $2 \sin x - 1 = 0$ or $\sin x = -2$. Since $|\sin x| \leq 1$ for all x by definition (§ 7-2), the condition $\sin x = -2$ can never be satisfied. Hence the only solutions are those of $2 \sin x - 1 = 0$. These have already been found in Illustration 1 to be $\{\tfrac{1}{6}\pi + 2k\pi,\ \tfrac{5}{6}\pi + 2k\pi\}$.

ILLUSTRATION 3.   To solve the equation $3 \sin x - \cos 2x = 1$, note that two different multiples of x are involved. This diversity can be removed by applying a multiple-angle formula, (20), from § 7-10:
$$3 \sin x - (1 - 2 \sin^2 x) - 1 = 0;$$
$$2 \sin^2 x + 3 \sin x - 2 = 0,$$
which is the equation already solved in Illustration 2.

EXERCISES

Solve:

1. $2 \sin x + \sqrt{3} = 0.$

2. $\sqrt{2} \cos x + 1 = 0.$

3. $\tan x - 1 = 0.$

4. $\operatorname{ctn} x = 0.$

5. $\sec z = 2.$

6. $\csc y + 2 = 0.$

7. $5 \cos x + 3 = 0.$

8. $6 \sin x + 5 = 0.$

9. $4 \sin^2 x = 1.$

10. $3 \tan^2 x = 1.$

11. $\sin 2x = 1.$

12. $\cos 2x + \frac{1}{2} = 0.$

13. $\sin 3t = 0.$

14. $\tan \frac{1}{4}\theta = 1.$

15. $(2 \sin x + 1)(\operatorname{ctn}^2 3x - 1) = 0.$

16. $\sin 5x \cos 3x + \sin 5x = 0.$

17. $4 \cos^3 4x = 3 \cos 4x.$

18. $\sin \frac{1}{4}x - 4 \sin^3 \frac{1}{4}x = 0.$

19. $\sin 2x = \cos x.$

20. $\cos 6x = \sin 3x.$

21. $4 \sin x \cos x = 1.$

22. $2 \cos^2 x = \sin x + 1.$

23. $\cos 2y + 2 \cos y = 0.$

24. $\cos 8z + 2 \sin 4z = 0.$

25. $\tan 2x = 2 \cos x.$

26. $2 \tan 2x - \sec^2 2x = 2.$

27. $\tan^2 x - \sec x = 5.$

28. $2 \sin x = 3 \cos x.$

29. $\begin{cases} y = 3 \cos x, \\ y = 3(1 - \cos x). \end{cases}$

30. $\begin{cases} y = a \sin x, \\ y = a \sin 2x. \end{cases}$

31. $\begin{cases} r = 2 \cos \theta, \\ r = \sin 2\theta. \end{cases}$

32. $\begin{cases} r \cos \theta \cos \phi = 1, \\ r \cos \theta \sin \phi = 1, \\ r \sin \theta = \sqrt{7}; \\ -\frac{1}{2}\pi \le \phi \le \frac{1}{2}\pi, 0 \le \theta < 2\pi, r \ge 0. \end{cases}$

33. $\cos x \sin 4x - \cos 4x \sin x = 1.$

34. $\cos 2x \cos 7x + \sin 2x \sin 7x = -\frac{1}{2}.$

13-3 Graphic Solution of Trigonometric Equations

Graphic solution of trigonometric equations follows the same principles as for algebraic equations (§ 5-3). The unlimited number of solutions of most trigonometric equations, already discussed in the previous section, is reflected in the periodicity of the graphs of the trigonometric functions (§ 7-7).

In the case of complicated equations, it is frequently helpful not to require that one member of the equation be zero (as was usually done in § 4-9 and § 5-3) but rather to graph the two members of the equation on the same set of coordinate axes. Where the graphs intersect, the two members are equal and the equation is satisfied.

EXAMPLE.   Solve $x \cos x = 1$.

Solution.   Write the given equation in the form $\cos x = 1/x$. Graph $y = \cos x$ and $y = 1/x$; it is convenient to use different scales on the two axes. We see from Figure 13.1 that there is an unlimited number of solutions;

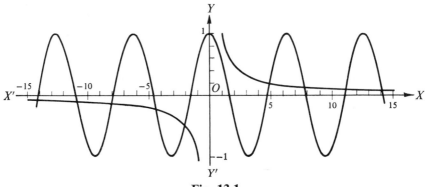

Fig. 13.1

eight of them are approximately $-14.2, -10.9, -8.0, -4.5, -2.1, 4.9, 7.7,$ 11.1, 14.0. We may note that if $|x|$ is large then $1/x$ is near zero and the equation reduces to $\cos x \approx 0$, and so the solutions are nearly $\{\frac{1}{2}\pi + k\pi\}$ when $|x|$ is large.

EXERCISES

Solve graphically:

1. $x \sin x = 1,\ 0 \leq x \leq 8.$

2. $x \cos x = -\frac{1}{2},\ -\frac{1}{2}\pi \leq x \leq \frac{3}{2}\pi.$

3. $x + \sin x = 1,\ -10 \leq x \leq 10.$

4. $x - \sin x = 1,\ -10 \leq x \leq 10.$

5. $\sin x = x^2,\ -5 \leq x \leq 5.$

6. $\tan x = \frac{1}{2}x,\ 0 \leq x \leq 2\pi.$

7. $\sec x = x,\ -6 \leq x \leq 6.$

8. $\sin 2x = \frac{1}{4}x + 1,\ -4 \leq x \leq 4.$

9. $2 \cos \frac{1}{3}x = x + 3,\ -3 \leq x \leq 3.$

10. $\log x = \sin \pi x,\ 0 \leq x \leq 2.5.$

11. A tank is in the form of a right circular cylinder 10 feet long and 6 feet in diameter with axis horizontal. It contains 25 cubic feet of liquid. Find the depth of the liquid to the nearest tenth of a foot.

13-4   Graphic Combination of Functions

In graphing a function, it is usually desirable that some of the plotted points fall near significant parts of the graph such as zeros of the function or maximum or minimum points. In simple cases, systematic plotting of successive values (such as integral values) of the independent variable, say x, will usually show the trend of the curve and indicate whether additional points need to be plotted to determine the graph better in the vicinity of points of interest.

However in complicated cases, trends may be difficult to discern by this method. The following procedure is often helpful if the function is expressed as a sum of terms: Plot the terms individually, note where they have significant behavior either individually (such as a maximum point) or in relation to each other (for instance, approximately equal numerically but opposite in sign, thus adding nearly to zero). Then in such a vicinity, choose a further value of x and find y either by computation or by scaling and adding the values of y from the graph.

EXAMPLE 1.   Graph the function $(x + \cos \pi x)$.

Solution.   In Figure 13.2, the dashed curves are the graphs of $y = x$ and $y = \cos \pi x$. The solid curve shows their sum, that is, the given function.

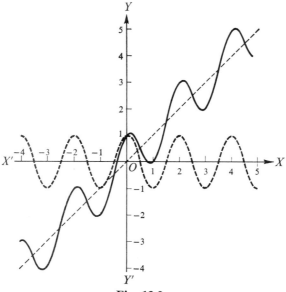

Fig. 13.2

An analogous procedure is sometimes helpful for *products*. One use is in visualizing the zeros of the respective factors, which together constitute the zeros of the product. Another application is in graphing a product in which the numerical value of one factor is limited.

EXAMPLE 2.   Graph the function $e^{-\frac{1}{2}x} \cos \pi x$.

Solution.   The factor $\cos \pi x$ varies from $+1$ through 0 to -1 and back. Hence the product varies from $e^{-\frac{1}{2}x}$ through 0 to $-e^{-\frac{1}{2}x}$ and back. In Figure 13.3, the graphs of $e^{-\frac{1}{2}x}$ and $-e^{-\frac{1}{2}x}$ are shown dashed; the graph of the product is the solid curve.

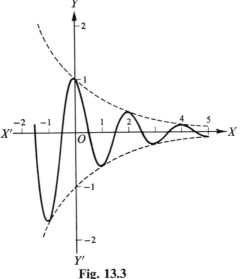

Fig. 13.3

EXERCISES

Graph:

1. $x + \cos 2\pi x$.

2. $x - \sin 2\pi x$.

3. $x \cos 2\pi x$.

4. $-x \sin 2\pi x$.

5. $\sin x + \sin 2x$.

6. $\cos x + \cos 2x$.

7. $\sin x \sin 2x$.

8. $\cos x \cos 2x$.

9. $e^{-x} \sin 2\pi x$.

10. $e^x \cos 3\pi x$.

11. $x \sin^2 4\pi x$.

12. $x^2 \sin 4\pi x$.

13. (a) Graph $(3 \sin x + 2 \cos x)$; (b) prove that $(A \sin kx + B \cos kx)$ can always be written in the form $C \cos (kx + p)$.

14. In an "amplitude modulated" radio transmission, the electromagnetic field is a function of time t of the form $F = A \sin (ct + b)$ where $c/2\pi$ is the frequency of the "carrier wave" and $A = k \sin (Ct + B)$ where $C/2\pi$ is the frequency of the audio tone being conveyed. If t is in seconds, $b = 0$, $B = 0$, $k = 1$, $c = 3,200,000\pi$ (that is, 1600 kilocycles), and $C = 512\pi$ ("middle C"), sketch the graph of the function F for a large enough interval of t to show the general behavior.

13-5 Principal Values of the Independent Variable in a Trigonometric Function

The inverse of a function $f(x)$ was defined in § 4-3. The definition applies to trigonometric functions as well as others. However, the periodicity of trigonometric functions poses the difficulty that, for a given value of $f(x)$, there are usually many possible values of x (as was seen in § 13-2). Hence before we can speak of the inverse function, the domain of x must be restricted. The values of x so restricted are sometimes called the **principal values,** by analogy with principal roots (§ 3-2).

For positive values of $f(x)$, it is natural to choose the principal value of x in the first quadrant (using that phrase even though x represents a number instead of an angle; see § 7-2), specifically $0 \le x \le \frac{1}{2}\pi$. For negative values of $f(x)$, a natural choice of the principal value of x exists for the sine, cosine, tangent, and cotangent, as seen in Figures 13.4 through 13.7 where the part of the curve corresponding to principal

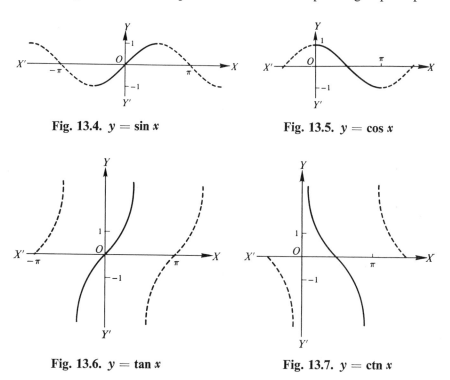

Fig. 13.4. $y = \sin x$ **Fig. 13.5.** $y = \cos x$

Fig. 13.6. $y = \tan x$ **Fig. 13.7.** $y = \operatorname{ctn} x$

values is drawn solidly and the rest is dashed. For the secant and cosecant, it is impossible to make a choice which uses only a single continuous section of the curve; for reasons which only become clear

in studying the calculus, the preferred choice is that shown in Figures
13.8 and 13.9.

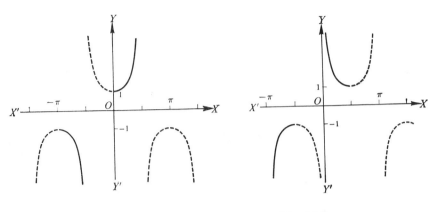

Fig. 13.8. $y = \sec x$ **Fig. 13.9.** $y = \csc x$

These choices of principal values may be summarized as follows:

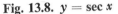

$$\sin x: \quad -\tfrac{1}{2}\pi \leq x \leq \tfrac{1}{2}\pi;$$
$$\cos x: \quad 0 \leq x \leq \pi;$$
$$\tan x: \quad -\tfrac{1}{2}\pi < x < \tfrac{1}{2}\pi;$$
$$\operatorname{ctn} x: \quad 0 < x < \pi;$$
$$\sec x: \quad -\pi \leq x < -\tfrac{1}{2}\pi \quad \text{or} \quad 0 \leq x < \tfrac{1}{2}\pi;$$
$$\csc x: \quad -\pi < x \leq -\tfrac{1}{2}\pi \quad \text{or} \quad 0 < x \leq \tfrac{1}{2}\pi.$$

ILLUSTRATION.   For cos $4x$, the principal values of $4x$ are on the interval
$0 \leq 4x \leq \pi$. Hence the principal values of x are on the interval $0 \leq x \leq \tfrac{1}{4}\pi$.

EXERCISES

Describe and graph the principal values of t *in:*

1. sin $2t$.   **4.** sin πt.   **7.** sec $3t$.

2. cos $2t$.   **5.** tan $2\pi t$.   **8.** csc $\tfrac{1}{3}t$.

3. cos $3t$.   **6.** ctn $4t$.   **9.** 3 sin $\tfrac{1}{2}t$.

Find the principal values which are solutions of the following equations:

10. sin $x = \tfrac{1}{2}$.   **12.** tan $3x = -1$.   **14.** sec $\pi x = 2$.

11. cos $x = -\tfrac{1}{2}$.   **13.** ctn $\tfrac{1}{2}x = -\sqrt{3}$.   **15.** csc $100x = -\sqrt{2}$.

13-6   Inverse Trigonometric Functions

When the independent variable is restricted to principal values, each value of an elementary trigonometric function corresponds to a single value of the independent variable, as described in the previous section. Accordingly, the definition of inverse function (§ 4-3) applies. However, it is preferred in the case of trigonometric functions to use the prefix **Arc** to denote the inverse instead of using the notation $f^{-1}(y)$ to denote the inverse of $y = f(x)$. This use of "Arc" avoids confusing the notation for inverse with the use of -1 as an exponent; we recall from § 7-4 that $\sin^2 x$ is used to denote $(\sin x)^2$. Thus if $y = \sin x$ then $x = \text{Arc} \sin y$. The graphs of some of the inverse trigonometric functions are shown in Figures 13.10 through 13.12.

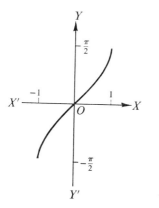

Fig. 13.10. $y = \text{Arc} \sin x$

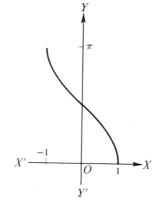

Fig. 13.11. $y = \text{Arc} \cos x$

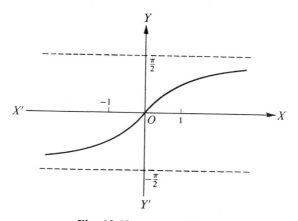

Fig. 13.12. $y = \text{Arc} \tan x$

Since $|\sin t| \le 1$ and $|\cos t| \le 1$ for all t, it follows that Arc sin x and Arc cos x are defined only for $-1 \le x \le 1$. This is reflected by the fact that the graphs in Figures 13.10 and 13.11 do not extend to the left of $x = -1$ nor to the right of $x = 1$. The tangent and cotangent functions, however, take on all values, and so x is not restricted in Arc tan x and Arc ctn x. For Arc sec x and Arc csc x we must have $x \le -1$ or $x \ge 1$; see graphs of the secant and cosecant functions (Figures 13.8 and 13.9).

ILLUSTRATION 1.   If $x = $ Arc cos $(-\frac{1}{2})$ then, by definition, $\cos x = -\frac{1}{2}$. The solution is taken as the appropriate principal value, namely $x = \frac{2}{3}\pi$.

ILLUSTRATION 2.   If $y = 2 \cos 3x$ then $\frac{1}{2}y = \cos 3x$, $3x = $ Arc cos $\frac{1}{2}y$, and so $x = \frac{1}{3}$ Arc cos $\frac{1}{2}y$.

Note that sin (Arc sin y) $= y$ from the definition of Arc sin. Corresponding results hold for the other inverse trigonometric functions. The reverse statement, about Arc sin (sin x), is not accurate unless the independent variable is restricted to principal values.

ILLUSTRATION 3.   By definition, $\theta = $ Arc tan $\frac{1}{3}$ requires that tan $\theta = \frac{1}{3}$. Hence tan (Arc tan $\frac{1}{3}$) $= \tan \theta = \frac{1}{3}$. On the other hand,

$$\text{Arc tan } (\tan \tfrac{1}{4}\pi) = \text{Arc tan } 1 = \tfrac{1}{4}\pi,$$
$$\text{Arc tan } (\tan \tfrac{5}{4}\pi) = \text{Arc tan } 1 = \tfrac{1}{4}\pi.$$

ILLUSTRATION 4.   If $x = $ Arc tan $\frac{1}{2} - $ Arc tan $\frac{1}{3}$, let $A = $ Arc tan $\frac{1}{2}$ and $B = $ Arc tan $\frac{1}{3}$. Then $x = A - B$. By the subtraction formula (16) of Chapter 7,

$$\tan x = \tan (A - B) = \frac{\tan A - \tan B}{1 + \tan A \tan B}$$

$$= \frac{\dfrac{1}{2} - \dfrac{1}{3}}{1 + \dfrac{1}{2} \cdot \dfrac{1}{3}} = \frac{3 - 2}{6 + 1} = \frac{1}{7}.$$

But from the original data, clearly $0 < x < \frac{1}{2}\pi$. Hence $x = $ Arc tan $\frac{1}{7}$.

EXERCISES

Find:

1. Arc sin $\frac{1}{2}$.

2. Arc cos $\frac{1}{2}$.

3. Arc sin $(-\frac{1}{2})$.

4. Arc sin $(-\frac{1}{2}\sqrt{3})$.

5. Arc cos (-1).

6. Arc cos 0.

7. Arc tan (-1).

8. Arc sec (-1).

9. Arc ctn 0.

10. Arc sin 0.6518.

11. Arc cos (-0.3515).

12. Arc tan 4.

Simplify:

13. cos (Arc cos x).   **17.** cos (Arc sin x).   **21.** sin (Arc tan x).

14. sin (Arc sin 2x).   **18.** sin (Arc cos x).   **22.** cos (Arc ctn x).

15. tan (Arc ctn y).   **★19.** Arc cos (cos x).   **23.** sin (Arc cos $\frac{12}{13}$).

16. sec (Arc cos x).   **★20.** Arc sin (sin x).   **24.** cos (Arc sin $\frac{4}{5}$).

   25. cos [Arc sin $(-\frac{3}{5})$].   **27.** Arc cos $\frac{4}{5}$ + Arc sin $\frac{4}{5}$.

   26. sin [Arc cos $(-\frac{24}{25})$].   **28.** Arc ctn $\frac{1}{3}$ + Arc ctn $\frac{1}{2}$.

Graph:

29. $y = $ Arc ctn x.   **31.** $y = $ Arc csc x.   **33.** $y = \frac{1}{3}$ Arc cos 4x.

30. $y = $ Arc sec x.   **32.** $y = 2$ Arc sin 3x.   **34.** $y = $ Arc tan $(x - 2)$.

   35. $y = $ Arc ctn $(x + \pi)$.   **36.** $y = \pi$ Arc sec πx.

If superscript -1 denotes inverse function, prove:

37. $\sin^{-1}(-1) = -\frac{1}{2}\pi$.   **39.** $\sin^{-1} 3x \neq 3 \sin^{-1} x$.

38. $\sin^{-1}x \neq \dfrac{1}{\sin x}$.   **40.** $\cos^{-1} t + \cos^{-1} u \neq \cos^{-1} (t + u)$.

MISCELLANEOUS EXERCISES

Find, exactly, all the values of x *such that* $0 \leq x \leq 2\pi$ *and the equation is satisfied:*

1. $\sin 3x = \frac{1}{2}$.   **3.** $\sin 3x = 1$.   **5.** $\cos \frac{1}{2}x = \frac{1}{2}$.

2. $\sin 3x = -\frac{1}{2}$.   **4.** $\sin \frac{1}{3}x = \frac{1}{2}$.   **6.** $\cos 4x = 0$.

   7. $\cos 4x = -1$.   **9.** $2 \sin x \cos x = \cos 2x$.

   8. $2 \sin x \cos 2x = \cos 2x$.   **10.** $\tan 6x = 2 \cos 3x$.

Find the solutions of the equations (exactly if possible, otherwise by tables or graphs); in the case of periodic members, find all solutions within one period:

11. $e^x + e^{-x} = 2$.   **17.** $\sin 3x + \sin x = 2$.

12. $e^{2x} + e^x = 6$.   **18.** $x + \sin x = 4$.

13. $\ln 2 + \ln x = 3$.   **19.** $x \sin x + 3 = 0$.

14. $\log 2x + \log x = 3$.   **20.** $\cos x + \sin x = 1$.

15. $\log 2x - \log x = 3$.   **21.** $\cos x + \sin x = 0$.

16. $\sin 2 + \sin x = 3$.   **22.** $\cos x + \sin x = 3$.

Sketch the graph of:

23. $3 \ln x$.   **25.** $e^{-x} \cos 3\pi x$.   **27.** Arc sin $3\pi x$.

24. $\sin 3\pi x \ln x$.   **26.** $\sin 3\pi x + \ln x$.   **28.** $\sin (1/x)$.

CHAPTER 14

SEQUENCES

14-1 Summation Notation

A **sequence** of numbers is a set of numbers so arranged that there is a first, a second, a third, etc., number in the set. The successive numbers are called **terms** or **members** of the sequence. This differs from the usage of "term" in algebraic expressions (§ 2-1); in a sequence the terms are not necessarily to be added or subtracted. We shall consider only sequences of real numbers or literal number symbols standing for real numbers, although the definitions obviously could be generalized to cover other numbers.

A sequence can also be described as a function whose domain (§ 4-1) is a specified set of integers, usually the set of positive integers. Then the independent variable is usually denoted by n and the values of the function for $n = 1$, $n = 2$, and so on, are the first term, second term, and so on. However, instead of functional notation, the members of the sequence are commonly denoted in some fashion such as $a_1, a_2, a_3, \cdots$, where a_1 is the first term, a_2 is the second term, and in general a_n denotes the nth term, n being any positive integer.

A sequence may consist of randomly chosen numbers. But in many cases there is some regularity of the terms. If so, one may be able to determine useful properties of the sequence, such as the sum of its terms, without enumerating explicitly each term. The arithmetic and geometric progressions considered in this chapter are two common types of such sequences.

In many places, particularly in considering sums of terms of a sequence, it is convenient to employ a special notation, called the **summation notation.** We write

$$\sum_{k=1}^{n} a_k \equiv a_1 + a_2 + a_3 + \cdots + a_n, \tag{1}$$

which is read "the sum of a_k from $k = 1$ to n." In the left member of this identity, the symbol Σ (which is the Greek capital letter sigma, corresponding to S) denotes that a sum is to be taken, and the a_k indicates that the terms to be summed are denoted by a with various subscripts. The symbols above and below the Σ indicate that k is an integer running from 1 to n inclusive; k is called the **index**. Often other letters, such as i or j, are used for the index; this use of i is not to be confused with $\sqrt{-1}$. To conserve space, the left member of (1) is sometimes printed $\sum_{k=1}^{n} a_k$. The index need not start at 1; for example, we can equally well write

$$\sum_{k=0}^{r} b_k = b_0 + b_1 + b_2 + \cdots + b_r.$$

ILLUSTRATIONS.

$$\sum_{k=1}^{5} x_k = x_1 + x_2 + x_3 + x_4 + x_5.$$

$$\sum_{j=0}^{15} (j + 1) = 1 + 2 + 3 + 4 + \cdots + 16 = 136.$$

$$\sum_{i=1}^{4} (-1)^i i^3 = -1 + 8 - 27 + 64 = 44.$$

$$\sum_{n=2}^{6} 3^n = 3^2 + 3^3 + \cdots + 3^6 = 1089.$$

The additions in the last two illustrations can be performed by brute force, but easier methods for finding the sums will be studied in § 14-3 and § 14-5.

EXERCISES

Write out (a) *the first five terms,* (b) *the fifteenth term,* (c) *the kth term,* (d) *the* (n + 1)*th term, of the sequence in which the nth term is:*

1. $\dfrac{1}{n}$.   **3.** $(n + 1)^2$.   **5.** $\dfrac{n^2}{n + 1}$.   **7.** $\dfrac{(-1)^{n+1}}{\log (n + \frac{1}{2})}$.

2. $n^2 + 1$.   **4.** 2^{n-1}.   **6.** $(-1)^n n(n + 1)$.   **8.** $\sin \frac{1}{2} n \pi$.

Write out the sum indicated (it is not required to carry out the addition):

9. $\sum_{k=1}^{5} (2k + 1)$.   **11.** $\sum_{n=1}^{4} \sqrt{n}$.   **13.** $\sum_{k=2}^{3} y^{-5k}$.

10. $\sum_{i=3}^{7} \dfrac{1}{i}$.   **12.** $\sum_{j=1}^{4} \dfrac{x^j}{j(j + 1)}$.   **14.** $\sum_{n=-4}^{4} (n^3 + 1)$.

Write out the first three terms and the last term of the indicated sum:

15. $\displaystyle\sum_{k=1}^{n} \frac{k}{k+1}$.   **16.** $\displaystyle\sum_{i=3}^{n} 2^i$.   **17.** $\displaystyle\sum_{n=0}^{k} x^n$.   **18.** $\displaystyle\sum_{n=-1}^{N} (a^n - 1)$.

Try to guess a simple formula for the nth term of a sequence whose first five terms are as specified, and verify that the formula does produce these terms:

19. 1, 3, 9, 27, 81.   **21.** $-e^{-x}, e^{-2x}, -e^{-3x}, e^{-4x}, -e^{-5x}$.

20. 1, $\frac{1}{4}$, $\frac{1}{9}$, $\frac{1}{16}$, $\frac{1}{25}$.   **22.** 3, $-\frac{5}{2}$, $\frac{7}{4}$, $-\frac{9}{8}$, $\frac{11}{16}$.

Write out each summation and thereby prove the following equalities:

23. $\displaystyle\sum_{k=1}^{9} 2^k = \sum_{k=0}^{8} 2^{k+1} = \sum_{k=2}^{10} 2^{k-1}$.

24. $\displaystyle\sum_{k=1}^{5} (2k+7) = \sum_{j=1}^{5} (2j+7) = \sum_{i=4}^{8} (2i+1) = \sum_{n=0}^{4} (2n+9)$.

Find the first five terms in the sequence in which each term after the first term is determined by the specified relationship to the preceding term:

25. $a_n = 2a_{n-1}$, $n > 1$; $a_1 = 3$.

26. $a_n = (a_{n-1})^2$, $n > 1$; $a_1 = \frac{2}{3}$.

27. $x_n = -(2x_{n-1} + 3)$, $n > 1$; $a_1 = 4$.

28. $b_n = -b_{n-1}/(b_{n-1} + 1)$, $n > 1$; $b_1 = 1$.

Let $\displaystyle\prod_{k=1}^{n} a_k = a_1 a_2 a_3 \cdots a_n$. *Write out the following expressions (it is not required to carry out the multiplications):*

29. $\displaystyle\prod_{k=1}^{6} (2k-1)$.   **30.** $\displaystyle\prod_{j=2}^{5} j^2$.   **31.** $\displaystyle\prod_{n=0}^{6} \frac{2n+1}{2(n+1)}$.

14-2   Arithmetic Progressions

An **arithmetic progression** *is a sequence of numbers in which each term, after the first, can be obtained from the preceding one by adding to it a fixed number called the* **common difference.** We shall use **A. P.** as an abbreviation for *arithmetic progression*.

ILLUSTRATIONS.   The sequence of numbers $\frac{1}{2}$, 2, $\frac{7}{2}$, 5, $\cdots$ is an A. P. with the common difference $\frac{3}{2}$; similarly the sequence of numbers 8, 3, -2, -7, $\cdots$ is an A. P. with the common difference -5.

Any particular term of an A. P. can be found by listing the successive terms until the desired one is reached. However, this process may be quite tedious. Furthermore, this process is so specific that it may not give a full understanding of the general behavior. Accordingly, one often wishes to express a general term of the sequence in terms of some properties characterizing the sequence, without writing all the preceding terms. Thus we shall find a formula for the nth term of any A. P. as a function of n and the values of the first term and common difference.

Let us denote the first term of an A. P. by a_1, the common difference by d, the number of terms by n, and the nth term by a_n. Then, by the definition of an A. P.,

$$\text{the second term is } a_1 + d,$$
$$\text{the third term is } a_1 + 2d,$$
$$\text{the fourth term is } a_1 + 3d,$$

. . . .

$$\text{the tenth term is } a_1 + 9d,$$

. . . .

$$\text{the } n\text{th term is } a_1 + (n - 1)d.$$

Hence the nth term a_n of an A. P. is given by the formula

$$a_n = a_1 + (n - 1)d. \tag{2}$$

EXAMPLE 1.   Find the fifteenth term of the A. P. $10, 8\frac{2}{3}, 7\frac{1}{3}, 6, \cdots$.

Solution.   Here $a_1 = 10$, $d = -\frac{4}{3}$, and $n = 15$. From formula (2) we obtain

$$a_{15} = 10 + (15 - 1)(-\tfrac{4}{3}) = -8\tfrac{2}{3}.$$

EXAMPLE 2.   How many integers are there between 50 and 350 which are divisible by 13?

Solution.   The smallest and largest integers between 50 and 350 which are divisible by 13 are found by trial to be 52 and 338 respectively. Hence $a_1 = 52$, $d = 13$, and $a_n = 338$. From formula (2) we obtain

$$338 = 52 + (n - 1)(13).$$

Therefore $n = 23.$

EXAMPLE 3.   If the seventh term of an A. P. is 6 and the twelfth term is -9, find the first term.

Solution.   Here $a_1 + (7 - 1)d = 6$ and $a_1 + (12 - 1)d = -9$.

To solve these two simultaneous equations in a_1 and d, subtract each member of the second equation from the corresponding member of the first. We have

$$-5d = 15, \quad \text{or} \quad d = -3.$$

Hence $a_1 + 6(-3) = 6, \quad \text{or} \quad a_1 = 24.$

The terms of an A. P. between any two given terms of the sequence are called **arithmetic means** between those two terms. If only one arithmetic mean is inserted between any two given terms, this term is called **the arithmetic mean** of the other two.

To insert a given number of arithmetic means, say k, between two given numbers, first find d by the use of formula (2) where the given terms are taken as a_1 and a_n and where $n = k + 2$. Then write down the required intermediate terms.

EXAMPLE 4.   Insert seven arithmetic means between -2 and 4.

Solution.   Here $a_1 = -2$, $a_n = 4$, and $n = 7 + 2 = 9$. From formula (2) we have $4 = (-2) + (9 - 1)d$, and $d = \frac{3}{4}$. Hence the required arithmetic means are

$$-1\tfrac{1}{4}, \; -\tfrac{1}{2}, \; \tfrac{1}{4}, \; 1, \; 1\tfrac{3}{4}, \; 2\tfrac{1}{2}, \text{ and } 3\tfrac{1}{4}.$$

Historical Note.   The earliest mathematical documents, the tablets in Babylonia (about 1800 B.C.) and the Rhind papyrus (about 1650 B.C.), contain examples of progressions.

EXERCISES

Write the first five terms of the A. P. whose first term and common difference are, respectively:

1. 15, 4.   **2.** 10, -3.   **3.** $-3, -5$.   **4.** $-\frac{5}{4}, \frac{1}{2}$.

Continue, to two additional terms, such of the following sequences as are arithmetic progressions:

5. 4, 9, 14, 19, $\cdots$.   **8.** 1, 0.1, 0.01, 0.001, $\cdots$.

6. 4, 2, 0, -2, $\cdots$.   **9.** $a, (2a + b), (3a + 2b), \cdots$.

7. $\frac{1}{2}, \frac{1}{3}, \frac{1}{4}, \frac{1}{5}, \cdots$.   **10.** $x, y, (2y - x), (3y - 2x), \cdots$.

Find the value of x *for which the sequence forms an A. P.:*

11. x, 8, 10.   **12.** $\frac{2}{3}, -\frac{3}{4}, x$.   **13.** $-10, x, 5$.

In an A. P.:

14. If the first term is 5 and the common difference is 3, write the seventh term without writing intermediate terms.

15. If the first term is $-\frac{1}{3}$ and the common difference is -2, write the eighth term without writing intermediate terms.

16. If the first term is -4 and the common difference is $\frac{1}{3}$, what is the tenth term? the nth term?

17. If the first term is 6 and the common difference is $-2\frac{1}{2}$, what is the sixteenth term? the nth term?

18. If the first term is 8 and the tenth term is -10, what is the common difference?

19. If the fourth term is -6 and the ninth term is 12, find **(a)** the common difference; **(b)** the first term.

20. Which term is -54 if the A. P. starts 6, 2, -2, -6, $\cdots$?

21. If the fifth term is t and the sixth term is u, write the first three terms.

22. (a) Can any two numbers, chosen at random, be the first two terms if nothing else is specified? **(b)** How about three numbers?

Insert:

23. Four arithmetic means between 4 and 7.

24. Three arithmetic means between -1 and 9.

25. The arithmetic mean between **(a)** x and y; **(b)** $6\frac{1}{2}$ and $7\frac{1}{4}$; **(c)** $(4 - 3\sqrt{2})$ and $(7 + 9\sqrt{2})$.

In each of the following exercises an affirmative proof should be based on some general form of an A. P., such as a, (a + d), (a + 2d), $\cdots$, *or a disproof should be based on a numerical instance where the proposition fails:*

26. If a sequence of numbers forms an A. P., prove that the products obtained by multiplying each member in the sequence by a constant c also form an A. P.

27. Determine whether the reciprocals of the terms of an A. P. with $d \neq 0$ also form an A. P.

28. Determine whether the squares of the terms of an A. P. with $d \neq 0$ also form an A. P.

29. If a given sequence of numbers is an A. P., show whether the sequence obtained by taking every third number is an A. P.

If amount A_0 *of money is placed at* **simple** *interest of* r *percent per year then each year the amount is increased by* $\frac{1}{100}rA_0$.

30. Show that the amount A_n after n years is given by

$$A_n = A_0 + \tfrac{1}{100}nrA_0.$$

31. What will $1000 at simple interest of 3% amount to after 10 years?

14-3 The Sum of the First n Terms of an A. P.

Let us denote by s_n the sum of the first n terms of an A. P. For example, in the A. P. 2, 5, 8, 11, $\cdots$, the sum of the first three terms is given by

$$s_3 = 2 + 5 + 8 = 15.$$

To derive a general formula for s_n, we first write the indicated sum in both direct and reverse order:

$$s_n = a_1 + (a_1 + d) + (a_1 + 2d) + \cdots + (a_n - d) + a_n,$$

and $s_n = a_n + (a_n - d) + (a_n - 2d) + \cdots + (a_1 + d) + a_1.$

Adding the corresponding members of these two equations, we obtain

$$2s_n = (a_1 + a_n) + (a_1 + a_n) + (a_1 + a_n) + \cdots + (a_1 + a_n) + (a_1 + a_n)$$

where the right member has n terms, so that

$$2s_n = n(a_1 + a_n).$$

Hence the sum s_n of the first n terms of an A. P. is given by the formula

$$s_n = \tfrac{1}{2}n(a_1 + a_n). \tag{3}$$

In the notation of § 14-1,

$$\sum_{i=1}^{n} a_i = \tfrac{1}{2}n(a_1 + a_n).$$

Substituting in formula (3) the value of a_n given in formula (2), we obtain another formula for the sum s of the first n terms of an A. P.,

$$s_n = \tfrac{1}{2}n[2a_1 + (n - 1)d]. \tag{4}$$

EXAMPLE 1.   Find the sum of the first fifteen terms of the arithmetic progression 10, $8\frac{2}{3}$, $7\frac{1}{3}$, 6, $\cdots$.

Solution.   As in Example 1 of § 14-2, $a_1 = 10$, $d = -\frac{4}{3}$, $n = 15$. From (4),

$$s_{15} = \tfrac{15}{2}[20 + 14(-\tfrac{4}{3})] = 10.$$

EXAMPLE 2.   Find the sum of the integers between 50 and 350 which are divisible by 13.

Solution.   As in Example 2, § 14-2, $a_1 = 52$, $d = 13$, and $a_n = 338$. We are to find s; n is also unknown.

$a_n = a_1 + (n - 1)d.$	$s = \tfrac{1}{2}n(a_1 + a_n).$
$338 = 52 + (n - 1)(13).$	$s = \tfrac{23}{2}(52 + 338).$
$n = 23.$	$s = \mathbf{4485.}$

The five quantities a_1, d, n, a_n, and s_n are called the **elements** of an A. P. which consists of n terms. If any three are given for a particular A. P., the other two may be found from formulas (2) and (3) or from formulas (2) and (4), with the obvious restriction that values of n other than positive integers are to be rejected.

EXAMPLE 3.   Given $d = 4$, $a_n = 43$, and $s_n = 252$; find the missing elements of the A. P.

Solution.

$a_n = a_1 + (n - 1)d.$	$s_n = \frac{1}{2}n(a_1 + a_n).$
$43 = a_1 + (n - 1)(4).$	$252 = \frac{1}{2}n(a_1 + 43).$
$a_1 = 47 - 4n. \rightarrow$	$252 = \frac{1}{2}n[(47 - 4n) + 43].$
	$252 = 45n - 2n^2.$
	$2n^2 - 45n + 252 = 0.$
	$(n - 12)(2n - 21) = 0.$

$n - 12 = 0.$	$2n - 21 = 0.$
$n = 12.$	$n = \frac{21}{2}.$
$a_1 = 47 - 4(12).$	Impossible.
$a_1 = -1.$	

EXERCISES

Find a_n *and* s_n *for each of the following A. P.'s:*

1. $5, 7, 9, \cdots ; n = 8.$

3. $-2, -6, -10, \cdots ; n = 14.$

2. $6, 3, 0, \cdots ; n = 9.$

4. $\frac{1}{4}, \frac{5}{12}, \frac{7}{12}, \cdots ; n = 13.$

5. $0, 1/a, 2/a, \cdots ; n = 23.$

6. $x, (2x - 4y), (3x - 8y), \cdots ; n = k.$

Find the other elements of the A. P. for which:

7. $a_1 = 6$, $n = 8$, $a_n = 41.$

8. $d = -5$, $n = 14$, $s_n = -\frac{49}{2}.$

9. $n = 16$, $a_n = \frac{15}{4}$, $s_n = 30.$

10. $a_1 = 1$, $d = -3$, $s_n = -186.$

11. $a_1 = x$, $a_n = y$, $s_n = 10(x + y).$

12. $d = u$, $a_n = 3u$, $s_n = 0.$

13. The eighth term of an A. P. is 21 and the common difference is 4. Find **(a)** the fifteenth term; **(b)** the sum of the first twenty-five terms.

14. Find the sum of the first n positive **(a)** odd integers; **(b)** even integers; **(c)** integers ending in 7.

15. Find the sum of all positive integers less than 300 which **(a)** are multiples of 6; **(b)** end in 6.

16. The tenth term of an A. P. is 20 and the fifth term is 0. Find the sum of the terms from the eighth to the eighteenth, inclusive.

17. The sum of the first and fifth terms of an A. P. is 7, and the sum of the twelfth and sixteenth terms is 18. Find the sum of the first twelve terms.

18. A new employee is paid $5000 the first year, with an increase of $200 per year each subsequent year. **(a)** What is his pay during the tenth year? **(b)** What is his total pay during the first ten years?

19. A person saves 1 cent the first week, 3 cents the second week, 5 cents the third week, and so on for fifty weeks. What weekly saving for the same period would have yielded the same total savings for this period?

20. Find formulas for d and s_n when a_1, n, and a_n are given.

21. Find formulas for a_1 and s_n when d, n, and a_n are given.

22. Find three numbers in A. P. such that their sum equals 18 and the sum of their squares equals 116.

Find:

23. $\sum\limits_{j=1}^{16} 3j$.   **24.** $\sum\limits_{k=1}^{49} (3k + 1)$.   **25.** $\sum\limits_{i=4}^{60} (3 - 2i)$.

14-4   Geometric Progressions

We consider now another type of systematic sequence.

A **geometric progression** *is a sequence of numbers in which each term, after the first, can be obtained from the preceding one by multiplying it by a fixed number called the* **common ratio.** We shall use **G. P.** as an abbreviation for *geometric progression.*

ILLUSTRATIONS.   The sequence of numbers 2, 8, 32, 128, $\cdots$ is a G. P. with the common ratio 4; and similarly the sequence 6, -4, $\frac{8}{3}$, $-\frac{16}{9}$, $\cdots$ is a G. P. with the common ratio $-\frac{2}{3}$.

Let us denote the first term of a G. P. by a_1, the common ratio by r, the number of terms by n, and the nth term by a_n. Then, by the definition of a G. P.,

the second term is $a_1 r$,
the third term is $a_1 r^2$,
the fourth term is $a_1 r^3$,

. . . .

the tenth term is $a_1 r^9$,

. . . .

the nth term is $a_1 r^{n-1}$.

Hence the nth term a_n of a G. P. is given by the formula

$$a_n = a_1 r^{n-1}. \tag{5}$$

EXAMPLE 1.　Find the tenth term of the G. P. $-4, 2, -1, \frac{1}{2}, \cdots$.

Solution.　Here $a_1 = -4$, $r = -\frac{1}{2}$, and $n = 10$. From formula (5) we obtain

$$a_{10} = (-4)(-\tfrac{1}{2})^{10-1} = \tfrac{1}{128}.$$

EXAMPLE 2.　If the sixth term of a G. P. is 3 and the ninth term is -81, find the first term.

Solution.　Here $a_1 r^{6-1} = 3$ and $a_1 r^{9-1} = -81$.

Dividing each member of the second equation by the corresponding member of the first, we obtain

$$r^3 = -27. \tag{6}$$

The roots of equation (6) are -3 and $\frac{3}{2}(1 \pm i\sqrt{3})$. We limit our solutions to real values, in accordance with § 14-1. Hence

$$r = -3,$$

so　　　　　　　$a_1(-3)^5 = 3$,　or　$a_1 = -\tfrac{1}{81}$.

The terms of a G. P. between any two given terms of the sequence are called **geometric means** between those two terms. If only one geometric mean is inserted between any two given terms, this single term is called **a geometric mean** of the other two. It is not proper to speak of *the* geometric mean, since either ar or $-ar$ may be taken as a geometric mean of a and ar^2.

To insert a given number of geometric means, say k, between two given numbers, find r by use of formula (5) where the given terms are taken as a_1 and a_n while $n = k + 2$. Then write down the required intermediate terms.

EXAMPLE 3.   Insert five geometric means between 3 and 192.

Solution. Here $a_1 = 3$, $a_n = 192$, and $n = 5 + 2 = 7$. From formula (5) we have

$$192 = 3r^{7-1}, \quad r^6 = 64, \quad \text{and} \quad r = \pm 2.$$

There are two possible sets of real-valued geometric means.

For $r = 2$:	For $r = -2$:
6, 12, 24, 48, and **96.**	-6, **12**, -24, **48**, and -96.

EXERCISES

Write the first five terms of the G. P. whose first term and common ratio, respectively, are:

1. 5, 2.   **2.** $-8, \frac{1}{2}$.   **3.** 81, $-\frac{1}{3}$.   **4.** $-\frac{8}{9}, -\frac{3}{2}$.

Continue, to two additional terms, such of the following sequences as are geometric progressions or arithmetic progressions:

5. 1, 2, 4, 8, $\cdots$.

6. 8, 4, 2, 1, $\cdots$.

7. 3, -6, 12, -24, $\cdots$.

8. 3, 6, 9, 12, $\cdots$.

9. $\frac{1}{3}, \frac{1}{9}, \frac{1}{27}, \frac{1}{81}, \cdots$.

10. $-4, -6, -8, -10, \cdots$.

11. $\frac{1}{2}, \frac{1}{3}, \frac{1}{4}, \frac{1}{5}, \cdots$.

12. $x^3, x^4, x^5, x^6, \cdots$.

13. $10^{-3}, 10^{-5}, 10^{-7}, 10^{-9}, \cdots$.

14. $\sin \theta, \sin 2\theta, \sin 3\theta, \cdots$.

Find without writing intermediate terms:

15. The seventh term of the G. P. $\frac{1}{3}, -1, 3, -9, \cdots$.

16. The eleventh term of the G. P. $-\frac{1}{48}, \frac{1}{24}, -\frac{1}{12}, \cdots$.

17. The fifteenth term of the G. P. 1, $1/a$, $1/a^2$, $\cdots$.

18. The sixtieth term of the G. P. $10^{100}, 10^{98}, 10^{96}, \cdots$.

19. Which term is $\frac{1}{64}$ in the G. P. 64, 32, 16, $\cdots$.

For what values of x *are the given numbers real and in geometric progression?*

20. x, 20, -10.

21. 8, 2, x.

22. $-\frac{3}{8}, x, -\frac{2}{27}$.

23. 1, x, 1.

24. $\sqrt{2x + 5}, -6, 4\sqrt{x + 7}$.

25. $\sqrt{1 - x}, \sqrt{-6x}, \sqrt{14 - 4x}$.

26. Under what conditions is the sequence a, b, c an **(a)** A. P.? **(b)** G. P.? **(c)** A. P. and a G. P. at the same time?

27. Write the first four terms of the G. P. whose fifth term is 6 and whose common ratio is (a) $\frac{2}{3}$; (b) $-\frac{3}{2}$; (c) $-\frac{1}{3}$.

28. Write the first five terms (a) of an A. P. and (b) of a G. P. whose first two terms are p and q respectively.

29. Insert three geometric means between 1 and $\frac{1}{256}$.

30. Insert two geometric means between $\frac{1}{3}$ and -243.

31. Insert a geometric mean between (a) p and q; (b) $9p^2$ and q^4.

32. Insert a geometric mean between $\sin \theta$ and $\operatorname{ctn} \theta$.

33. Show that there is no real number which is a geometric mean between 4 and -16.

34. The third term of a G. P. is 54 and the sixth term is -2. Find (a) the common ratio; (b) the first term.

35. Find, if possible, the first and second terms of a G. P. whose third term is 6, whose fifth term is 9, and whose seventh term is 12.

36. Find all possible sets of three real numbers in G. P. such that the product of the numbers is -64 and the sum of their squares is 84.

37. Can we assign values at random to (a) a_1, r, and a_n, (b) a_1, n, and a_n, (c) a_1, r, and n, of a G. P.?

38. If each term of a G. P. is multiplied by a constant c, do the products form a G. P.? Prove.

39. If each term of a G. P. is increased by c, do the sums (a) always, (b) ever, form a G. P.? Prove.

40. A chemist has a precipitate which consists of 1 gram of the compound he is seeking and 1 gram of impurities. Each time he washes the precipitate, he removes half of the impurities. How many times must he wash it before there remains less than 0.0001 gram of impurities?

41. A certain person claims that one of his ancestors of the sixth generation before him was of royal blood. Assuming no duplications, find how many ancestors he has of that generation.

If an amount A_0 of money is placed at **compound** *interest of* r *percent per year compounded annually then each year the amount is multiplied by* $(1 + \frac{1}{100}r)$.

42. Show that the amount A_n after n years is given by

$$A_n = (1 + \tfrac{1}{100}r)^n A_0.$$

★43. What will $1000 at compound interest of 3% compounded annually amount to after 10 years?

14-5 The Sum of the First n Terms of a G. P.

Let us denote by s_n the sum of the first n terms of a G. P. To derive the formula for s_n we first write the indicated sum and then the indicated sum multiplied by r:

$$s_n = a_1 + a_1 r + a_1 r^2 + \cdots + a_1 r^{n-2} + a_1 r^{n-1},$$

and $$r s_n = \qquad a_1 r + a_1 r^2 + \cdots + a_1 r^{n-2} + a_1 r^{n-1} + a_1 r^n.$$

Subtracting the corresponding members of these two equations, we obtain

$$s_n - r s_n = a_1 - a_1 r^n.$$

Hence the sum s_n of the first n terms of a G. P. is given by the formula

$$s_n = a_1 \frac{1 - r^n}{1 - r}, \quad \text{if } r \neq 1. \tag{7}$$

Since $a_n = a_1 r^{n-1}$ and hence $r a_n = a_1 r^n$, formula (7) can be written in the form

$$s_n = \frac{a_1 - r a_n}{1 - r}, \quad \text{if } r \neq 1. \tag{8}$$

The five quantities a_1, r, n, a_n, and s_n are called the **elements** of a G. P. with n terms.

EXAMPLE.   Given $r = 2$, $n = 5$, and $a_n = -48$; find the other elements of the G. P.

Solution.

$$a_n = a_1 r^{n-1}. \qquad\qquad s_n = a_1 \frac{1 - r^n}{1 - r}.$$

$$-48 = a_1 (2)^{5-1}. \qquad\qquad s_n = (-3)\frac{1 - 2^5}{1 - 2}.$$

$$a_1 = -3. \qquad\qquad s_n = -93.$$

EXERCISES

Find a_n and s_n for the G. P.:

1. $5, 10, 20, \cdots; n = 6$.
2. $32, -16, 8, \cdots; n = 8$.
3. $\frac{1}{32}, \frac{1}{16}, \frac{1}{8}, \cdots; n = 9$.
4. $1, x, x^2, \cdots; n = 20$.
5. $-0.02, -0.002, -0.0002, \cdots; n = 7$.
6. $e^{-x}, e^{-2x}, e^{-3x}, \cdots; n = 8$.

Find the other elements of the G. P. for which:

7. $n = 6$, $r = \frac{1}{2}$, $s_n = 504$.

8. $r = 2$, $a_n = -960$, $s_n = -1890$.

9. $a_1 = \frac{1}{3}$, $a_n = 72$, $s_n = \frac{259}{3}$.

10. $a_1 = 1$, $n = 6$, $a_n = 32$.

11. $a_1 = \frac{1}{16}$, $r = 2$, $a_n = 64$.

12. $a_1 = 2$, $n = 3$, $s_n = 26$.

For a G. P.:

13. Derive a formula for s_n in terms of r, n, and a_n.

14. Find a formula for s_n if $r = 1$.

14-6   Geometric Progressions with Infinitely Many Terms

Let us consider the indicated sum of a geometric progression

$$a_1 + a_1 r + a_1 r^2 + \cdots + a_1 r^{n-1} + \cdots,$$

where the common ratio is numerically less than 1 and the sequence continues indefinitely; that is, where $|r| < 1$ and the number of terms is infinite. This is called a geometric progression with infinitely many terms or, for short, an **infinite geometric progression.**

From formula (7), the sum of the first n terms of this geometric progression is given by

$$s_n = a_1 \frac{1 - r^n}{1 - r} = \frac{a_1}{1 - r} - \frac{a_1 r^n}{1 - r}.$$

Since $|r| < 1$, $|r^n|$ decreases as n increases, and by increasing n sufficiently we can make $|r^n|$, and with it $|a_1 r^n/(1 - r)|$, differ from zero by as small an amount as we please. But $a_1/(1 - r)$ remains unchanged, since it does not depend on n. Hence s_n can be made to differ from $a_1/(1 - r)$ by as small an amount as we please by making n sufficiently large. This latter statement is expressed symbolically by

$$\lim_{n \to \infty} s_n = \frac{a_1}{1 - r}, \tag{9}$$

which is read "the limit of s_n as n increases without bound is $a_1/(1 - r)$." This limit, $a_1/(1 - r)$, is called the **sum** of the infinite geometric progression. It is also written

$$\sum_{k=1}^{\infty} ar^{k-1} = \frac{a_1}{1 - r}.$$

EXAMPLE 1.   Find the sum of the following G. P. with infinitely many terms: $2, \frac{4}{3}, \frac{8}{9}, \cdots$.

Solution.   Here $a_1 = 2$, $|r| = |\frac{2}{3}| < 1$, and the number of terms is infinite. From formula (9) we obtain

$$\lim_{n \to \infty} s_n = \frac{2}{1 - \frac{2}{3}} = 6.$$

EXAMPLE 2.   Convert the repeating decimal $0.3272727 \cdots$ into an equivalent common fraction.

Solution.   The given repeating decimal may be written in the form

$$0.3272727 \cdots = 0.3 + 0.027 + 0.00027 + 0.0000027 + \cdots.$$

The terms of the right member, after the first term, form a geometric progression with infinitely many terms in which $a_1 = 0.027$ and in which $|r| = |0.01| < 1$. From formula (9) we have

$$\lim_{n \to \infty} s_n = \frac{0.027}{1 - 0.01} = \frac{3}{110},$$

and therefore $0.3272727 \cdots = \frac{3}{10} + \frac{3}{110} = \frac{36}{110} = \frac{18}{55}$.

It can be shown that any repeating decimal can be converted into an equivalent common fraction.

EXERCISES

Find the sum of the infinite G. P.:

1. $3, 1, \frac{1}{3}, \cdots$.

2. $16, 4, 1, \cdots$.

3. $2, -\frac{1}{4}, \frac{1}{32}, \cdots$.

4. $-\frac{4}{3}, \frac{2}{9}, -\frac{1}{27}, \cdots$.

5. $1, (1.04)^{-1}, (1.04)^{-2}, \cdots$.

6. $1/n, 1/n^2, 1/n^3, \cdots; n > 1$.

7. $\sin^2 0.1, \sin^4 0.1, \sin^6 0.1, \cdots$.

8. $(2 + \sqrt{3}), 1, (2 - \sqrt{3}), \cdots$.

9. In Example 1 in the text, **(a)** graph s_n as a function of n; **(b)** plot the successive values of s_n on a number scale (Figure 1.1, page 5).

Convert the following repeating decimals into equivalent common fractions:

10. $0.4444 \cdots$.

11. $0.6666 \cdots$.

12. $0.06363 \cdots$.

13. $3.297297 \cdots$.

14. $0.867272 \cdots$.

15. $2.39999 \cdots$.

16. Convert $2.949494\cdots$ into an equivalent fraction, considering

(a) $2.949494\cdots = 2 + 0.94 + 0.0094 + \cdots$;

(b) $2.949494\cdots = 2.9 + 0.049 + 0.00049 + \cdots$.

17. What distance will a tennis ball travel before coming to rest if it is dropped from a height of 63 inches and if after each fall it rebounds $\frac{11}{20}$ of the distance it fell?

*18. In pursuing a tortoise, Achilles in the first minute reduces the distance between them to half what it was, in the next half-minute reduces the remaining distance by half of itself, in the next quarter-minute reduces the still remaining distance by half, and so on. How long does it take him to overtake the tortoise?

*19. If in Exercise 18 Achilles halves the distance in one minute, halves the remaining distance in the next minute, halves the distance still remaining in the next minute, and so on, how long does it take him to overtake the tortoise?

MISCELLANEOUS EXERCISES

1. On a ship, time is marked by striking one bell at the end of the first half hour, two bells after the first hour, three bells after the first hour and a half; and so on up to a maximum of eight bells. How many bells are struck during a cycle?

2. An article is originally sold for $50, and then resold four times. What is the price at the final sale if at each resale the price is (a) 40% higher than the price at the previous sale? (b) the price at the previous sale plus 40% of the original price?

3. Suppose an automobile costing $3000 depreciates in value each year by 20% of its value at the beginning of the year. What is it worth at the end of four years?

4. Find the sum of the first hundred positive (a) integers; (b) odd integers.

5. Find the sum of all positive integers, of not more than three digits, that are (a) exactly divisible by 3; (b) integral powers of 3.

6. If a city with 10,000 population in 1930 increased 20% in population each decade, what would be its population in 1970?

7. Find the tenth term of the A. P. whose first term is 2 and whose first, fourth, and thirteenth terms form a G. P.

8. Find two numbers whose difference is 8 and whose (a) arithmetic mean is 8; (b) positive geometric mean is $8\sqrt{2}$.

9. The three digits of a positive three-digit integer form an A. P., and their sum is 21. If the digits are reversed, the new number is 396 more than the original number. Find the original number.

10. Suppose that in a certain radioactive material, each atom which fissions emits two neutrons, and each neutron is absorbed in causing another atom to fission. If one neutron is introduced into the material, how many neutrons are there ten generations later?

11. A contractor charges as follows for drilling a well: $30 for moving his tools, plus $1.50 for the first foot of depth, $1.55 for the second foot, $1.60 for the third foot, and so on. (a) Express the cost C in dollars as a function of the depth d in feet. (b) Find the depth of a well costing $336.

12. A man borrows $120 and agrees to pay each month $10 on the principal and 4% interest on the amount of the unpaid principal as of the beginning of the month. Find (a) the length of time before the loan will thus be paid off; (b) the total of principal and interest to be paid.

13. A ball is dropped from a height of 18 feet. On each rebound it rises to a height two-thirds of that from which it fell. (a) How far will it rise on the fifth rebound? (b) How far has it traveled when at the top of the fifth rebound? (c) How far will it travel before coming to rest?

14. If nine-tenths of the air in a container is removed by each stroke of an air pump, what fractional part of the air remains after (a) three strokes? (b) ten strokes?

15. The inventor of the game of chess is said to have suggested that his reward be as follows: one grain of wheat for the first square of the chessboard, two for the second, four for the third, eight for the fourth, and so on through the sixty-four squares of the board. If it takes ten thousand grains of wheat to weigh a pound, find the weight of the wheat required to provide this reward.

16. Bode's Law for the approximate distance between the Sun and other objects in the solar system, in units of the distance between the Sun and the Earth, is $d_1 = 0.4$, $d_n = 0.4 + 0.3(2^{n-2})$ for $n > 1$, where $n = 1, 2, \cdots, 10$, respectively indicate Mercury, Venus, Earth, Mars, the asteroids, Jupiter, Saturn, Uranus, Neptune, and Pluto. Do the d_j form an A. P.? G. P.?

A sequence of numbers whose reciprocals form an arithmetic progression is called a **harmonic progression (H. P.).** *If three numbers are an H. P. then the second is called a* **harmonic mean** *between the other two.*

*17. Continue, to two additional terms, such of the following sequences as are harmonic progressions:

(a) $\frac{1}{6}, \frac{1}{8}, \frac{1}{10}, \frac{1}{12}, \cdots$; (c) $\frac{3}{2}, \frac{4}{3}, \frac{5}{4}, \frac{6}{5}, \cdots$;

(b) $1, \frac{1}{2}, \frac{1}{4}, \frac{1}{8}, \cdots$; (d) $\csc t, \csc 2t, \csc 3t, \cdots$.

*18. Find the sixth term of an H. P. whose first and second terms are a and b respectively.

*19. An automobile travels a certain distance at the speed of a miles per hour and returns at b miles per hour. Show that the average speed for the round trip is the harmonic mean of a and b.

*20. A set of musical strings, of identical characteristics except for length, have vibration frequencies 400, 800, 1200, 1600, and 2000 vibrations per second, respectively. Prove that the lengths of these strings form an H. P., using the facts stated in Exercise 11 of § 4-11.

14-7 The Axiom of Mathematical Induction

We consider in the remainder of this chapter a method for dealing with some assertions which are true for all numbers in a certain category. Unlike such identities as $(x + 1)(x - 1) = x^2 - 1$, the problems to be studied are of such a nature that one cannot consider all the numbers simultaneously but rather must proceed from one number to another.

The method is based on the following, called the **axiom of mathematical induction,** which is a basic part of logic.

If a proposition involving the positive integer n *has the properties that*
(I) *the proposition is true for* n $= 1$, *and*
(II) *whenever the proposition is true for* n $=$ k *it is also true for* n $=$ k $+ 1$,
then *the proposition is true for all positive integral values of* n.

By definition, an axiom is a basic assumption, not susceptible of proof. However, the axiom of mathematical induction is very plausible. To see this, suppose (I) and (II) hold. By (I), the proposition holds for $n = 1$. Then by (II) it also holds for $n = 1 + 1 = 2$. Applying (II) again, the proposition holds for $n = 2 + 1 = 3$. Applying (II) still another time, the proposition holds for $n = 3 + 1 = 4$, and so on without end.

Here is a way to visualize the axiom: Consider an infinitely long row of sticks or dominoes, standing on end (Figure 14.1a), which may be knocked over starting with the first one. If they are spaced close together and the first one is toppled in the proper direction, the rest will all fall in succession (Figure 14.1b); this corresponds to both parts (I) and (II) holding in the axiom. But if the first one is never toppled, nothing

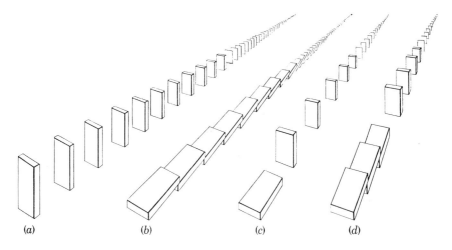

(a)   (b)   (c)   (d)

Fig. 14.1. Analogy between Mathematical Induction and a Row of Dominoes

happens and the row still stands (Figure 14.1a again), illustrating the necessity of part (I) of the axiom. On the other hand, if the dominoes are spaced too far apart then toppling one need not cause the others to fall (Figure 14.1c), illustrating the need for part (II) of the axiom. And if they are in most cases close enough together but one space is left empty, the successive toppling comes to an end (Figure 14.1d); this shows that (II) is required for *all* values of *n*. Figure 14.1b also illustrates the remark at the beginning of this section that in this type of problem one cannot consider all numbers (here, dominoes) simultaneously, but must proceed from one to another. On the other hand, we cannot consider every single domino one-at-a-time, for the process would never be finished. It is the virtue of part (II) of the axiom that it gives a method for proceeding from one to the next without considering each one successively.

In algebra and other branches of mathematics, many theorems which can be easily verified for a few special cases are proved for the general case by mathematical induction. Although part (I) of the axiom is required only for $n = 1$, it is often advisable to try also several other easy values of n as a precaution against trying to prove an erroneous proposition, as well as possibly to find a guide to a procedure for proving part (II).

Our first example is one which can also be handled as an arithmetic progression, but the present procedure avoids the special device used in § 14-3 to find the formula for the sum of an A. P. and hence is more generally applicable. On the other hand, mathematical induction is only applicable to the investigation of a proposition which has already been formulated; it gives no procedure for deducing what formulation would be the right one to consider.

EXAMPLE 1.   Prove by mathematical induction that

$$1 + 3 + 5 + \cdots + (2n - 1) = n^2. \tag{10}$$

This may be stated in words: the sum of the first n positive odd integers is equal to n^2.

Proof.   **(I)** If $n = 1$ then $2n - 1 = 1$, and the left member of (10) consists of a single term. We have:

If $n = 1$, $1 = 1^2$.

Thus the proposition expressed by equation (10) is verified for $n = 1$. This is sufficient for part (I), but let us go farther:

If $n = 2$, $1 + 3 = 4 = 2^2$.

If $n = 3$, $1 + 3 + 5 = 9 = 3^2$.

(II) Let k represent a particular value of n for which (10) is true.   Then

$$1 + 3 + 5 + \cdots + (2k - 1) = k^2. \tag{11}$$

Now suppose $n = k + 1$. Then the left member of (10) becomes the sum of the first $(k + 1)$ positive odd integers, namely

$$1 + 3 + 5 + \cdots + (2k - 1) + (2k + 1).$$

Adding $(2k + 1)$ to both members of (11), and factoring,

$$1 + 3 + 5 + \cdots + (2k - 1) + (2k + 1) = k^2 + (2k + 1)$$
$$= (k + 1)^2.$$

Thus we have shown that *if* the sum of the first k positive odd integers is equal to k^2 *then* the sum of the first $(k + 1)$ positive odd integers is equal to $(k + 1)^2$. In other words, *if* the proposition (10) is true for $n = k$ *then* it is also true for $n = k + 1$; that is, *if* the proposition is true for one positive integral value of n *then* it is true also for the next greater integer.

Conclusion.   We have shown that the proposition is true for $n = 1$, and that if it is true for $n = k$ then it is true for $n = k + 1$. Hence, by mathematical induction, it is true for *all* positive integral values of n.

EXAMPLE 2.   Prove by mathematical induction that $(x^n - y^n)$ is divisible by $(x - y)$ for all positive integral values of n.

Proof.   **(I)** If $n = 1$, then $(x^n - y^n)$ is $(x - y)$, which is obviously divisible by $(x - y)$.

(II) Let k be a positive integer such that $(x^k - y^k)$ is divisible by $(x - y)$. If $n = k + 1$, $(x^n - y^n)$ becomes $(x^{k+1} - y^{k+1})$. Upon subtracting and adding xy^k, we obtain

$$x^{k+1} - y^{k+1} = x^{k+1} - xy^k + xy^k - y^{k+1}$$
$$= x(x^k - y^k) + y^k(x - y).$$

Each of the two terms of the right member of this identity is divisible by $(x - y)$, the first term by the assumption stated above and the second term by inspection. Therefore the complete right member—and accordingly also the left member, $(x^{k+1} - y^{k+1})$—is also divisible by $(x - y)$. Hence *if* the proposition is true for $n = k$ *then* it is also true for $n = k + 1$.

Conclusion.   Hence by mathematical induction the proposition is true for all positive integral values of n.

Mathematical induction is sometimes called **complete induction.** This contrasts with ordinary, or **incomplete,** induction as employed in the natural sciences, where a generalization is often made on the basis of a large number of experiments or observations.

The following alternative version of the axiom of mathematical induction is more general in form. However, it is logically equivalent to the version already stated, since in both cases one simply deals with a set of index numbers which could be used for counting.

If a proposition involving the integer n *has the properties that* **(I)** *it is true for a certain value of* n, *say for* $n = n_0$, *and* **(II)** *whenever it is true for* $n = k \geq n_0$ *it is also true for* $n = k + 1$, *then the proposition is true for all integral values of* n *such that* $n \geq n_0$.

EXERCISES

Prove the statements in Exercises 1 through 19 by use of mathematical induction, n *being a positive integer.*

1. $4 + 5 + 6 + \cdots + (n + 3) = \frac{1}{2}n(n + 7)$.

2. $4 + 7 + 10 + \cdots + (3n + 1) = \frac{1}{2}n(3n + 5)$.

3. $5 + 4 + 3 + \cdots + (6 - n) = \frac{1}{2}n(11 - n)$.

4. $5 + 5^2 + 5^3 + \cdots + 5^n = \frac{5}{4}(5^n - 1)$.

5. $\dfrac{1}{1 \cdot 2} + \dfrac{1}{2 \cdot 3} + \dfrac{1}{3 \cdot 4} + \cdots + \dfrac{1}{n(n + 1)} = \dfrac{n}{n + 1}$.

6. $\dfrac{1}{1 \cdot 3} + \dfrac{1}{3 \cdot 5} + \dfrac{1}{5 \cdot 7} + \cdots + \dfrac{1}{(2n - 1)(2n + 1)} = \dfrac{n}{2n + 1}$.

7. $1 + 2 + 4 + \cdots + 2^{n-1} = 2^n - 1$.

8. $a + ar + ar^2 + \cdots + ar^{n-1} = a(1 - r^n)/(1 - r)$.

9. $a + (a + d) + (a + 2d) + \cdots + [a + (n - 1)d] = \frac{1}{2}n[2a + (n - 1)d]$.

10. $1^3 + 3^3 + 5^3 + \cdots + (2n - 1)^3 = n^2(2n^2 - 1)$.

11. $6 \cdot 1^2 + 6 \cdot 2^2 + 6 \cdot 3^2 + \cdots + 6n^2 = n(n + 1)(2n + 1)$.

12. $4^2 + 7^2 + 10^2 \cdots + (3n + 1)^2 = \frac{1}{2}(n + 1)(6n^2 + 9n + 2) - 1$.

13. $\displaystyle\sum_{j=1}^{n} (3j + 2) = \frac{1}{2}n(3n + 7)$.   **14.** $\displaystyle\sum_{j=1}^{n} j(j + 2) = \frac{1}{6}n(n + 1)(2n + 7)$.

15. The number of lines formed by joining n distinct points, no three of which are collinear, is $\frac{1}{2}n(n - 1)$.

16. The sum of the interior angles of a convex polygon of n sides is equal to $(n - 2) \cdot 180°$, $n \geq 3$.

17. The number of diagonals in a convex polygon of n sides is $\frac{1}{2}n(n - 3)$.

18. $(x^{2n} - y^{2n})$ is divisible by $(x + y)$.

19. $(x^{2n-1} + y^{2n-1})$ is divisible by $(x + y)$.

20. It is given that $u_n = 3u_{n-1} + 1$ for each positive integer n greater than 1, and that $u_1 = 1$. Prove that for every positive integer n,

$$u_n = 3^0 + 3^1 + 3^2 + 3^3 + \cdots + 3^{n-1}.$$

★21. It is given that $u_{n+1} = u_{n-1} + u_n$ for each positive integer n, and that $u_0 = 1$ and $u_1 = 1$. Prove that for every positive integer n,

$$(u_{n+1})^2 - u_n u_{n+2} = (-1)^{n+1}.$$

14-8   Fallacies in Applying Mathematical Induction

In the analogy with a row of dominoes in the previous section, it was observed that both (I) and (II) in the axiom of mathematical induction are necessary. It is instructive to consider some illustrations of a more mathematical nature, again showing that neither part by itself is sufficient. These examples, and the exercises following them, are not particularly important in themselves but rather are intended to emphasize the importance of correct and careful reasoning and to show how paradoxes can arise in the absence of such reasoning.

ILLUSTRATION 1.   Consider this proposition: the expression $(n^2 - n + 41)$ represents a prime number for *all* positive integral values of n. By substitution, the expression is found to represent a prime number for $n = 1$ (and, indeed, for each of the values $n = 1, 2, 3, \cdots, 40$). Thus (I) holds. However, for $n = 41$, $(n^2 - n + 41)$ becomes $(41^2 - 41 + 41)$, or 41^2, which is not a prime number. Thus (I) is not sufficient by itself to prove a proposition true for all integral values of n.

ILLUSTRATION 2.   If we should assume that the *erroneous* formula

$$2 + 4 + 6 + \cdots + 2n = n^2 + n + 2,$$

where n is any positive integer, were true for $n = k$, in accordance with the hypothesis of (II), then we could prove the formula also true for $n = k + 1$, as follows.

If we assume that

$$2 + 4 + 6 + \cdots + 2k = k^2 + k + 2$$

then we should have

$$2 + 4 + 6 + \cdots + 2k + (2k + 2) = k^2 + k + 2 + (2k + 2)$$
$$= (k^2 + 2k + 1) + (k + 1) + 2$$
$$= (k + 1)^2 + (k + 1) + 2.$$

Thus *if* the formula is true for $n = k$ then it is also true for $n = k + 1$, and (II) holds. However, the formula is not true for $n = 1$ (in fact, not for *any* value of n). Thus (II) by itself does not ensure the validity of a proposition; (I) is also needed.

EXERCISES

Criticize the following outlines of alleged proofs. That is, if the proposition and outline are correct, complete the details of the outline; if the proposition is correct but the proposed proof is incorrect, point out the error and give a correct proof; if the proposition is wrong, prove that it is wrong and point out the error in the alleged proof.

1. Proposition:

$$1 + 3 + 6 + \cdots + \tfrac{1}{2}n(n + 1) = \tfrac{1}{6}(n^3 + 3n^2 + 2n + 18)$$

for all positive integers n. Proposed proof: By mathematical induction.

2. Proposition: $4 + 8 + 12 + \cdots + 4(n + 1) = 3n^2 - n + 10$ for all positive integers n. Proposed proof: By mathematical induction.

3. Proposition: $2 + 2^2 + 2^3 + \cdots + 2^n = 2(2^n - 1)$ for all positive integers n. Proposed proof: If this proposition is true for $n = k$, then

$$2 + 2^2 + 2^3 + \cdots + 2^{k+1} = 2(2^k - 1) + 2^{k+1} = 2(2^{k+1} - 1),$$

so the proposition also holds for $n = k + 1$. Hence by mathematical induction it holds for all positive integers n.

4. Proposition: $(x^n - y^n)$ is divisible by $(x + y)$ for all positive integers n. Proposed proof: For $n = 1$, $(x^n - y^n)$ becomes $(x - y)$, which is obviously divisible by $(x + y)$. Hence, by mathematical induction, the proposition holds.

5. Given: There are 15 boys sitting in the 15 chairs around a round table. Proposition: There are 225 boys sitting around this table. Proposed proof: We shall prove by mathematical induction that there are at least n boys around the table, counting counterclockwise beginning with any chosen boy, for all positive integers n. (I) If $n = 1$, this is certainly true; just pick the one boy. (II) Suppose it is true for $n = k$. Then consider the last of these k boys; count in the boy to his left, and the statement holds for $n = k + 1$. Hence the proposition about n boys holds for all positive integers n, and in particular for $n = 225$ as asserted.

6. Proposition: Every group containing n students is composed of students all of the same age. Proposed proof: (I) If $n = 1$, the group contains only one student and there is no other to differ in age, so the proposition holds. (II) Suppose the proposition holds for $n = k$, and that we have a group with $(k + 1)$ students. Leave out the first student for the moment; there are k others, so by the hypothesis of (II), these others are of the same age. Now include the first student but leave out the $(k + 1)$th student; again there are k students, who by hypothesis must all be of the same age. Thus both the first and the last students are of the same age as the others. Hence all of the students are of the same age. By mathematical induction, this holds for all n.

CHAPTER 15

PERMUTATIONS, COMBINATIONS, AND PROBABILITY

15-1 Permutations and Combinations Defined

As an introduction to this subject, suppose the president of an organization is to select a committee of two from among a certain five persons. How many possible choices are there?

If we call the persons A, B, C, D, and E, then one possible choice for a committee would consist of A and B, which choice we shall designate AB. In fact, any one of the following committees is possible: AB, AC, AD, AE, BC, BD, BE, CD, CE, or DE. Thus we see that there are ten choices.

But if, in addition, the first appointee acts as chairman, then each of the ten possible pairs will give two possible committees, depending on the order of making the appointments. Thus, while AB and BA would be identical committees physically, still, if the order of selection is of importance, then these two pairs must be regarded as "distinct choices," and the answer is twenty.

The student should consider also other situations, such as three members to a committee or four persons to choose from. He will see that from any given set of objects (such as numbers, letters, persons, or tools) a group can be chosen in various ways depending on the number of objects given, on the number to be taken, on whether the order of selection is taken into account, and on the restrictions, if any, concerning the types of selections permitted. For example, it might be required that the two members of a committee should not belong to the same political party.

A selection in a definite order, or an arrangement in a definite order, is called a **permutation.**

A selection without regard to order is called a **combination.**

ILLUSTRATION 1.   The permutations of the three letters a, b, and c, taken *two* at a time, are

$$ab, ba, ac, ca, bc, \text{ and } cb,$$

each of which is a distinct *ordered arrangement* of two letters.

The combinations of these same letters, likewise two at a time, are

$$ab, ac, \text{ and } bc,$$

each representing a different *selection* of two letters made without regard to order. While ab and ba are distinct permutations, they are the same combination.

ILLUSTRATION 2.   The three letters a, b, and c can be arranged, *three* at a time, in the six permutations

$$abc, acb, bac, bca, cab, \text{ and } cba.$$

However, all six of these permutations represent one and the same combination.

15-2   Fundamental Principle

We begin the study of permutations and combinations by considering the principle upon which the entire subject is based.

Fundamental Principle.   *If one thing can be done in* p *different ways, and if after it has been done in any one of these ways a second thing can be done in any one of* q *different ways, then the two things can be done together, in the order stated, in* pq *different ways.*

Proof.   Denote the p ways of doing the first thing by $f_1, f_2, f_3, \cdots, f_p$, and the q ways of doing the second thing by $s_1, s_2, s_3, \cdots, s_q$. As in the previous section, list the ways of doing, in the stated order, the two things:

$$f_1 s_1, \quad f_1 s_2, \quad \cdots, \quad f_1 s_q, \quad f_2 s_1, \quad f_2 s_2, \quad \cdots, \quad f_2 s_q, \quad f_3 s_1, \quad \cdots, \quad f_p s_q.$$

But there are p possible subscripts for f; with each of these there are q possibilities for s—altogether, pq entries in the list.

EXAMPLE 1.   There are six candidates for president of a club and four for vice-president. In how many ways can the two offices together be filled?

Solution.   With each of the *six* different ways of filling the office of president there is a choice of *four* different ways of filling the office of vice-president. Hence these two offices can together be filled in $6 \cdot 4$, or 24, different ways.

Employing the same reasoning as in the proof and solution above, the fundamental principle may at once be extended to the following generalized form.

If one thing can be done in p *different ways, a second thing in* q *different ways, a third in* r *different ways, and so on until a last thing can be done in* z *different ways, then the number of different ways in which all the things can be done in the order stated is* p · q · r · · · z.

EXAMPLE 2.   How many three-digit positive integers can be formed from the digits 1, 5, 6, 7, and 8, if repetition of digits is allowed?

Solution.   The first digit can be chosen as any one of the *five* given digits; then the second digit can also be chosen as any one of *five*, and likewise for the third digit. Altogether we can choose in 5 · 5 · 5, or 125, ways.

Note.   Here and elsewhere, "digits" are in the ordinary decimal system unless otherwise specified. Somewhat similar examples could be given with "binary" digits (§ 1-6, Exercise 57).

EXAMPLE 3.   How many three-digit positive integers can be formed from the digits 1, 5, 6, 7, and 8, with no digit repeated?

Solution.   As in Example 2, the first digit can be chosen in any one of *five* ways; but then the second digit must be one of the other *four* given digits and the third digit must be one of the remaining *three* digits. Thus there are 5 · 4 · 3, or 60, choices.

EXAMPLE 4.   How many three-digit positive even integers can be formed from the digits 1, 5, 6, 7, and 8, with no digit repeated?

Solution.   In Examples 2 and 3 it made no difference whether we chose first the hundreds' digit, then the tens' digit and then the units' digit, or first the units' digit, then the tens' digit and then the hundreds' digit. In the present example, it is preferable to consider the units' digit first, since it is subject to a direct condition by the requirement of evenness, whereas the tens' digit and the hundreds' digit are subject only to the indirect requirement that digits not be repeated. For the number to be even, the units' digit must be even; hence there are *two* choices, either 6 or 8. For the tens' digit, we may use any one of the *four* digits not used in the units' place, leaving *three* digits to choose among for the hundreds' place. Thus there are 2 · 4 · 3, or 24, possible numbers of the kind specified.

EXERCISES

1. List the personnel of the distinct committees of two members which can be selected from among the six persons *A*, *B*, *C*, *D*, *E*, and *F*.

2. In how many ways can a judge award first, second, and third places in a contest with twelve entries?

3. In a certain manufacturing plant, the first operation can be done on any one of four machines, the second on only one machine, the third on any one of six machines, and the fourth on either of two machines. Over how many routes can the raw material be processed?

4. An automobile designer is considering two body designs, three hood designs, and six fender designs. How many models would be required to show all possible ways of combining the designs?

5. A chemistry student is trying to identify an unknown substance. He knows that it is a compound of a metal and a basic radical, and that the metal is one of eleven possibilities, and that the base is one of six, any one of which can combine with any one of the metals. Among how many possible compounds must he choose?

6. A lunch cart offers five kinds of sandwiches, three kinds of beverage, and six kinds of dessert. Find the number of possible choices of a lunch consisting of one of each of these types of items.

7. A clothing store stocks socks made of either nylon or wool, each in five colors and seven sizes. How many pairs are needed for a complete assortment?

8. A man tries to choose the winner of each of twenty football games. Excluding ties, how many different predictions are possible?

9. In assembling some electrical equipment, six wires enter a box which has six terminals. In how many ways can the wires be connected to the terminals, one wire to each terminal?

10. A person driving from New York to Minneapolis with a stopover in Chicago has a choice of five highways to Chicago and three from there on. **(a)** How many different routes are possible? **(b)** If he is to return by a route neither half of which was traveled on the outward trip, how many nonidentical round-trip routes are there?

11. From the digits 1, 3, 4, 7, 8, and 9, find how many positive **(a)** integers, each consisting of three digits, **(b)** integers, each of three different digits, **(c)** odd integers of three digits, **(d)** integers consisting of three odd digits, can be formed.

12. From the digits 1, 2, and 4, how many positive integers can be formed which **(a)** consist of five digits? **(b)** are less than 100,000?

13. In choosing an ace, king, queen, and jack from a deck of 52 cards, how many different selections are possible if **(a)** they must all be in a specified suit, spades? **(b)** they must all be in the same suit? **(c)** they may be in any suit? **(d)** they must be of different suits?

14. In the Hawaiian language each syllable consists either of a vowel or of a consonant followed by a vowel. The vowels are a, e, i, o, u; the consonants are h, k, l, m, n, p, w. How many distinct **(a)** syllables, **(b)** words of not more than three syllables, are possible, repetitions of syllables being permitted?

*15. There are estimated to be at least 10,000 genetic loci in a human being; each locus controls some hereditary characteristic, though possibly only a very minor one. If at each locus there are at least two alternatives possible, **(a)** at least how large is the number of possible persons with distinct heredities? **(b)** Find to the nearest integral power of ten the ratio of this number to the population of the world, which is approximately 3,000,000,000.

16. How many binary numbers (§ 1-6, Exercise 57) are there with **(a)** 6 digits? **(b)** not more than 6 digits? **(c)** not more than 32 digits?

15-3   The Factorial Symbol

We digress briefly to define a special notation which is convenient in calculating numbers of permutations and combinations, and for other purposes.

The product of all the positive integers from 1 to n *inclusive is denoted by the symbol* **n**!, read **n factorial** or **factorial n**. Thus we may write

$$n! = 1 \cdot 2 \cdot 3 \cdots (n-1)n \quad \text{or} \quad n! = n(n-1)(n-2) \cdots 2 \cdot 1,$$

where n is a positive integer. The symbol $\lfloor n$ is sometimes used instead of $n!$

ILLUSTRATIONS. $6! = 1 \cdot 2 \cdot 3 \cdot 4 \cdot 5 \cdot 6 = 720.$

Whenever r is an integer sufficiently large that each indicated factor is a positive integer,

$$(r-1)! = 1 \cdot 2 \cdot 3 \cdots (r-2)(r-1);$$
$$(r+2)! = (r+2)(r+1)r \cdots 2 \cdot 1;$$
$$50! = 1 \cdot 2 \cdot 3 \cdots 49 \cdot 50$$
$$\approx 3.041 \times 10^{64} \text{ by Table VIII on page 467.}$$

We have defined $n!$ only for positive integers n. It will prove convenient also to define $0!$, and to do so in such a way as to satisfy the relation $n! = n \cdot (n-1)!$ which clearly holds for all positive integers $n > 1$. Setting $n = 1$ in this relation, we find that we must then have **0! = 1**, and we so define it. This will permit setting $r = 1$ in the rth term of the binomial expansion (§ 15-7).

EXERCISES

Simplify:

1. $\dfrac{8!}{6!}$.

2. $\dfrac{3!}{7!}$.

3. $\dfrac{4!\,9!}{6!\,7!}$.

4. $\dfrac{8!}{3!\,5!}$.

5. $\dfrac{4!\,5!}{6!+8!}$.

6. $\dfrac{8!-7!}{4!\,7!}$.

7. $\dfrac{3!-5!}{4!+6!}$.

8. $\dfrac{1}{6!}+\dfrac{1}{4!}$.

9. $\dfrac{(n+2)!}{(n+1)!}$.

10. $\dfrac{(n-1)!}{(n+1)!}$.

11. $\dfrac{(3r)!}{3r!}$.

12. $\dfrac{n!}{(n-k)!}$.

13. $\dfrac{0!}{5!}$.

14. $\dfrac{(n+r)!}{(n+r-3)!}$.

15. $\dfrac{[(2m)!]^3}{(2m-1)!\,(2m)!\,(2m+1)!}$.

16. From Table VIII, write the following to three significant digits in scientific notation: **(a)** 12!; **(b)** 20!; **(c)** 6!.

17. Show that $2\cdot4\cdot6\cdots(2n)=2^n n!$.

18. Show that **(a)** $n!$ is even for $n>1$; **(b)** $n!$ ends in a zero for $n>4$.

19. Show that

$$n(n-1)(n-2)\cdots(n-r+2)(n-r+1)=n!/(n-r)!.$$

15-4   Permutations of n Different Things Taken r at a Time

Combining the ideas in the preceding sections, let us now study one particular category of permutations, namely, where a set of things is given and we are to choose a certain number of them.

By "*the permutations of* n *different things taken* r *at a time,*" r ≤ n, *is meant all the possible distinct ordered arrangements consisting of* r *things chosen from* n *different things.* The total number of such different arrangements is represented by the symbol $P(n, r)$ and is read "the number of permutations of n different things taken r at a time." The symbols $_nP_r$ and P_r^n are also employed.

The number $P(n, r)$ is equal to the number of ways of filling r different places by choosing from n different things. The first place can be filled by any one of the n given things, the second place by any one of the $(n - 1)$ things remaining after the first place has been filled, the third place by any one of the $(n - 2)$ things remaining after the second place has been filled, and so on, until finally the rth place is filled by any one of the $[n - (r - 1)]$ things remaining after the $(r - 1)$th place has been filled. Hence the total number is given by the formula

$$P(n, r) = n(n - 1)(n - 2)\cdots(n - r + 1). \tag{1}$$

Stated in words, *the number of permutations of* n *different things taken* r *at a time is the product of all integers from* n *to* (n − r + 1) *inclusive.* There are *r* factors in all.

ILLUSTRATIONS. $P(9, 4) = 9 \cdot 8 \cdot 7 \cdot 6 = 3024;$

$P(k, 3) = k(k − 1)(k − 2),$ *k* an integer greater than or equal to 3.

In the special case when *r* = *n*, the factor (*n* − *r* + 1) is (*n* − *n* + 1), or 1, and we have

$$P(n, n) = n(n − 1)(n − 2) \cdots 3 \cdot 2 \cdot 1 = n!. \tag{2}$$

Stated in words, *the number of permutations of* n *different things taken* n *at a time is factorial* n.

EXAMPLE.   Four persons enter a bus in which eight seats are vacant. In how many ways can they be seated?

First Solution.   The first person to enter has a choice of any one of *eight* seats. The second person can then be seated in any one of *seven* seats, the third person in any one of *six* seats, and the fourth person in any one of *five* seats. Hence the persons can be seated in

$8 \cdot 7 \cdot 6 \cdot 5$, or 1680, ways.

Second Solution.   Each seating arrangement represents a different arrangement of four seats out of a group of eight seats; hence the number of seating arrangements is given by

$P(8, 4) = 8 \cdot 7 \cdot 6 \cdot 5 = 1680.$

EXERCISES *

1. Find the value of **(a)** $P(6, 2)$; **(b)** $P(32, 3)$; **(c)** $P(6, 6)$; **(d)** $P(14, 4)$; **(e)** $P(7, 5)$.

2. Find the value of **(a)** $P(20, 3)$; **(b)** $P(8, 6)$; **(c)** $P(9, 9)$; **(d)** $P(200, 2)$; **(e)** $P(729, 1)$.

3. A farmer has five fields to plow. In how many different orders can he do his plowing?

4. A biologist has seven culture tubes to examine. In how many orders can he do this?

5. A stock broker receives simultaneously eight instructions to sell stock. In how many ways can he select the first three instructions to be executed?

* Each exercise in this chapter should be solved from the basic ideas and principles of the subject rather than from the formulas developed. Although the formulas are often convenient as a check or as a simpler way of expressing results, they should not be used as a substitute for thinking through the conditions of the exercise.

6. A baseball manager is preparing a batting order. How many batting orders are possible **(a)** after he has decided on the nine players? **(b)** when he still has to choose his team from among thirteen players?

7. How many integers greater than **(a)** 300,000, **(b)** 600,000, can be formed from the digits 1, 2, 3, 4, 5, and 9, no digit being repeated in any one integer?

8. Show that $P(n, r) = n \cdot P(n - 1, r - 1)$.

15-5 Permutations of n Things Not All Different

In the example of the preceding section the solution would be the same if four automobiles were to be placed in eight vacant parking spaces. The nature of the objects considered is immaterial provided they can be distinguished from one another and provided the number of objects available and the number of objects to be chosen remain unchanged. But if some of the objects are indistinguishable, then further consideration is needed.

EXAMPLE 1.   Find the number of permutations of the eight letters of the word *repealed*, taken eight at a time.

Solution.   Denote the required number of permutations by P. Now suppose that the three e's in the word *repealed* are temporarily replaced by e_1, e_2, and e_3, three distinct letters. Any rearrangement of e_1, e_2, and e_3 is an artificial permutation; it cannot be detected in the word *repealed*, where the e's are identical. Corresponding to each of the P permutations of the letters r, e, p, e, a, l, e, d, we can arrange e_1, e_2, and e_3 in 3! ways, giving $P \cdot 3!$ permutations of r, e_1, p, e_2, a, l, e_3, d. But these eight distinct letters, taken eight at a time, have 8! permutations; hence we have

$$P \cdot 3! = 8!, \quad \text{and} \quad P = 8!/3! = 6720.$$

The method used to solve Example 1 can be employed to prove the following general theorem:

If P *represents the number of distinct permutations of* n *things taken all at a time, and if exactly* p *of these things are alike, then* $P = n!/p!$; *if* p *are alike and* q *others are alike (but are unlike the previous ones) then* $P = n!/(p! \cdot q!)$; *if* p *are alike,* q *others are alike, and* r *others are alike, then*

$$P = \frac{n!}{p! \cdot q! \cdot r!} ;$$

and so on.

Proof.   We shall assume, for convenience, that the n given things are letters. Let P represent the number of permutations—each being distinct, as is required by the definition of a permutation. If we replace the p letters which are alike by p letters distinct from one another and from the others of the n given letters (for instance, by using subscripts, as in Example 1), then for each of the P permutations we can get $p!$ permutations by rearranging the p new letters while keeping the position of the other letters fixed. Hence if this change is made in all the P permutations, there would then be $P \cdot p!$ permutations. If all the other letters are distinct, then $n! = P \cdot p!$, so $P = n!/p!$.

If q other letters are alike, then by replacing each of them by new and distinct letters, we shall similarly have $P \cdot p! \cdot q!$ permutations. By continuing in this manner until all the like letters have been replaced (say the last step involves z like letters), we have $P \cdot p! \cdot q! \cdot r! \cdots z!$ permutations. But we now have n different letters taken n at a time, which gives $n!$ permutations; hence

$$P \cdot p! \cdot q! \cdot r! \cdots z! = n!,$$

and

$$P = \frac{n!}{p! \cdot q! \cdot r! \cdots z!}. \qquad (3)$$

EXAMPLE 2.   In how many distinct ways can four nickels, five dimes, two quarters, and one half dollar be distributed among twelve boys if each boy is to receive one coin?

Solution.   If the twelve coins were all different, they could be distributed among twelve boys in $P(12, 12)$, or $12!$, ways. But four of the coins are of one kind, five of another kind, and two of a third kind. Hence the required number is

$$\frac{12!}{4! \cdot 5! \cdot 2!}, \quad \text{or} \quad 83{,}160.$$

In such formulas it is usually best to write out the products which the factorial symbols represent, since the result can often be greatly simplified. Alternatively, one can use a table of factorials (Table VIII).

EXERCISES

1. Nine students are lined up in a row for a group photograph. How many visually distinguishable arrangements are possible if the club includes one set of identical triplets, wearing matching clothes?

2. An electronics exhibitor carries with him five identical amplifiers, four identical rectifiers, two identical condensers, and one relay. In how many distinct ways can these be arranged in a row?

3. A ship makes a signal by hoisting three flags in a vertical array. How many distinguishable such signals can be made from (**a**) five different flags? (**b**) twenty-six different flags?

4. How many distinct signals can be made with eight flags by displaying them all at a time in a vertical array, if three are white, two are red, one is checkered, and the rest are yellow?

5. How many permutations can be made of the letters of the word (**a**) *dean*, (**b**) *lawyer*, when taken four at a time?

6. How many permutations can be made of the letters of the word (**a**) *ear*, (**b**) *eye*, (**c**) *light*, (**d**) *radar*, (**e**) *proposition*, when taken all at a time?

7. A student has two small books, five medium-sized books, and three large ones; all the books are different. In how many ways can they be arranged on a shelf so that all books of the same size are together?

8. In how many ways can two different mathematics books, five different English books, and four different history books be arranged on a shelf so that all books on each subject are together?

9. A grocer wishes to put a row of cans all the way across the front of a display window. There is room for twenty cans, to include peaches, pears, grapefruit, cherries, and apricots in equal numbers, one brand and style of each. (**a**) How many displays are possible? (**b**) How many of these will have a can of peaches at the left end? (**c**) How many will have a can of pears at both ends? (**d**) How many will have the same fruit at the right end as at the left end?

10. In how many ways can six persons (**a**) take seats in a row of six chairs? (**b**) form a circle?

Suggestion. In (*b*), consider the position of any one of the persons as fixed; in other words, use the position of one person as a reference point. Then arrange the other five persons in the remaining positions.

11. In how many ways can eleven diplomats be seated at a round table?

12. In how many ways can five boys and five girls be seated at a round table so that the boys and girls are seated alternately? Find also the number if there are one boy and one girl who are not to occupy adjacent seats.

13. Each of the four quadrants of one face of a revolvable circular disk is to be colored a different color. If six colors are available, in how many ways may the colors be assigned?

15-6   Combinations of n Different Things Taken r at a Time

By "*the combinations of* n *different things taken* r *at a time*," $r \leq n$, *is meant all the possible selections consisting of* r *different things chosen from the* n *given things, without regard to the order of arrangement or selection.* The total number of such different selections is represented by the symbol $C(n, r)$ and is read "the number of combinations of n things taken r at a time." The symbols $\binom{n}{r}$, $_nC_r$, and C_r^n are also employed.

The fundamental difference between permutations and combinations is that the order, or arrangement, is not considered for combinations. To illustrate this, consider the letters a, b, c, d, taken two at a time. They have twelve permutations (ab, ac, ad, ba, bc, bd, ca, cb, cd, da, db, dc) and six combinations (ab, ac, ad, bc, bd, cd). Note that the letters in each combination, such as ab, can be used to form two permutations, ab and ba.

In general, consider any one of the $C(n, r)$ possible combinations, or selections, consisting of r different things chosen from the n given things. From each of these combinations we can form $r!$ permutations by merely rearranging the order of the r elements. Thus from all the possible combinations we can form $C(n, r) \cdot r!$ different permutations, and these are all the possible permutations of n given things taken r at a time. Hence $C(n, r) \cdot r! = P(n, r)$, and

$$C(n, r) = \frac{P(n, r)}{r!}. \tag{4}$$

Stated in words, *the number of combinations of* n *different things taken* r *at a time is equal to the number of permutations of* n *different things taken* r *at a time divided by factorial* r.

Let us write out (4), substituting from (1):

$$C(n, r) = \frac{n(n-1)(n-2)\cdots(n-r+1)}{r!}. \tag{5}$$

It may be noted that there are r factors in the denominator and also in the numerator.

If we multiply both numerator and denominator of the right member of formula (5) by $(n-r)!$, we obtain

$$C(n, r) = \frac{n(n-1)(n-2)\cdots(n-r+1)(n-r)!}{r!\,(n-r)!} = \frac{n!}{r!\,(n-r)!}. \tag{6}$$

By replacing r by $(n - r)$ throughout, we have

$$C(n, n - r) = \frac{n!}{(n - r)! [n - (n - r)]!} = \frac{n!}{(n - r)! \, r!},$$

whence $C(n, r) = C(n, \, n - r).$ (7)

Stated in words, *the number of combinations of* n *different things taken* r *at a time is the same as the number of combinations of* n *different things taken* (n − r) *at a time.*

This is also easily seen by noting that whenever r of the n things form one combination, the $(n - r)$ remaining also form a combination. Hence there are just as many combinations of n things taken $(n - r)$ at a time as of n things taken r at a time, and $C(n, n - r) = C(n, r)$.

EXAMPLE 1. A track coach has a group of seven men from which to pick a squad of three men to enter a certain event. How many different squads can he select?

First Solution. Let T represent the required number of squads. Now if the order of arrangement is taken into consideration, there are $7 \cdot 6 \cdot 5$, or 210, possible arrangements of three men from the group of seven. Since we can form 3! arrangements with each of the required squads, the T squads can be arranged in $T \cdot 3!$ ways, and these are all the possible arrangements of three men from the given group. Therefore we have

$$T \cdot 3! = 210, \quad \text{and} \quad T = \frac{210}{3!} = 35.$$

Second Solution. The required number of squads represents a selection of three out of seven men. Hence we have

$$T = C(7, 3) = 35.$$

EXAMPLE 2. In how many ways can an unordered pile of forty-eight cards be dealt from a deck of fifty-two cards?

Solution. The number is

$$C(52, 48) = C(52, 4) = 270{,}725.$$

EXERCISES

1. Find the value of **(a)** $C(6, 2)$; **(b)** $C(32, 3)$; **(c)** $C(14, 14)$; **(d)** $C(14, 4)$; **(e)** $C(16, 14)$.

2. Find the value of **(a)** $C(20, 3)$; **(b)** $C(8, 6)$; **(c)** $C(10, 10)$; **(d)** $C(200, 2)$; **(e)** $C(729, 728)$.

3. An assembler has at hand sixteen of a certain type of transistor. The equipment he is assembling requires four such transistors. How many selections can he make without regard to order?

4. How many subcommittees of three senators each can be chosen from a committee of thirteen senators?

5. An instructor decides to assign three problems from a set of ten. From among how many assignments can he choose?

6. An inspector in a manufacturing plant tests four parts out of one hundred parts produced. In how many ways can he choose the ones to be tested?

7. A young man has thirty pictures of movie stars, but has space to pin up only five. In how many ways can he choose the five?

8. A research scientist is testing whether there is interaction between drugs, of which two might be given simultaneously. If he is concerned with ten drugs, how many pairs must be considered?

9. The tennis squad of University A consists of eleven players and that of University B of eight players. Find the number of doubles matches that can be arranged between the two squads.

10. In how many ways can the ten baseball teams of the American League be paired, **(a)** without regard, **(b)** with regard, to which team is at home?

11. A farmer buys three cows, one pig, and ten sheep from a seller who has seven cows, four pigs, and ten sheep. How many choices has he?

12. For dinner there is a choice of two out of five appetizers, one out of four entrees, three out of seven side dishes, one out of three beverages, and one out of six desserts. How many nonidentical dinners are possible?

13. In how many ways can a party of twelve persons be divided into **(a)** two equal groups? **(b)** three equal groups?

14. From a committee consisting of seven men and four women, a subcommittee is formed consisting of four men and three women. How many different subcommittees are possible?

15. On an examination there are ten questions, of which eight are to be answered, and these must include at least four out of the first five. How many choices are possible?

16. Prove that $C(n + 1, r) = C(n, r - 1) + C(n, r)$.

15-7 The Binomial Theorem

The theorem which enables us to write any power of a binomial as a sequence of terms is known as the **binomial theorem.** We proceed with its development.

By actual multiplication, we obtain the following:

$$(a + x)^1 = a + x,$$
$$(a + x)^2 = a^2 + 2ax + x^2,$$
$$(a + x)^3 = a^3 + 3a^2x + 3ax^2 + x^3,$$
$$(a + x)^4 = a^4 + 4a^3x + 6a^2x^2 + 4ax^3 + x^4,$$
$$(a + x)^5 = a^5 + 5a^4x + 10a^3x^2 + 10a^2x^3 + 5ax^4 + x^5.$$

To see a pattern which may help in writing a general formula, let us look more closely at, for instance, the case of $(a + x)^3$.

$$
\begin{aligned}
(a + x)^3 &= (a + x)(a + x)(a + x) \\
&= (aa + ax + xa + xx)(a + x) \\
&= aaa + aax + axa + axx + xaa + xax + xxa + xxx \quad (8) \\
&= a^3 + 3a^2x + 3ax^2 + x^3. \quad (9)
\end{aligned}
$$

Thus each of the eight terms in the detailed expansion (8) involves one of the letters, either a or x, from the first factor $(a + x)$, one of the letters —again either a or x—from the second $(a + x)$, and one from the third. For instance, the second term in (8) has a's from the first two factors $(a + x)$ and x from the third. In collecting like terms, equation (9), this second term will be combined with the other terms which also have exactly one x (and hence two a's).

More generally, in expanding $(a + x)^n$, each term will contain n factors; each of the factors is either a or x. In collecting like terms, the terms involving x^r will involve x from r of the factors $(a + x)$ and necessarily a from the other factors, $(n - r)$ in number; thus each term involving x^r will have the form $a^{n-r}x^r$. The number of such terms will be the number of ways in which we can select the r factors which are to be x, out of the n factors in each term. By § 15-6, this number is $C(n, r)$. For instance, the number of terms a^2x in the expansion of $(a + x)^3$ is $C(3, 1)$, which is 3; compare equation (9). The number of terms a^4x^2 in the expansion of $(a + x)^6$ is $C(6, 2)$, which is 15.

Hence

$$(a + x)^n = C(n, 0)a^nx^0 + C(n, 1)a^{n-1}x^1 + C(n, 2)a^{n-2}x^2$$
$$+ \cdots + C(n, r)a^{n-r}x^r + \cdots + C(n, n)a^0x^n. \quad (10)$$

Simplifying, we get the **binomial formula** or **binomial theorem:**

$$(a + x)^n = a^n + C(n, 1)a^{n-1}x + C(n, 2)a^{n-2}x^2$$
$$+ \cdots + C(n, r)a^{n-r}x^r + \cdots + C(n, n)x^n. \qquad (11)$$

In summation notation (§ 14-1),

$$(a + x)^n = \sum_{r=0}^{n} C(n, r)a^{n-r}x^r.$$

EXAMPLE 1.   Expand $(a + 2b^2)^5$ by the binomial theorem and simplify each term.

Solution.   By (11) and (5),

$$(a + 2b^2)^5 = [a + (2b^2)]^5$$

$$= a^5 + 5a^4(2b^2) + \frac{5 \cdot 4}{2!} a^3(2b^2)^2 + \frac{5 \cdot 4 \cdot 3}{3!} a^2(2b^2)^3$$

$$+ \frac{5 \cdot 4 \cdot 3 \cdot 2}{4!} a(2b^2)^4 + \frac{5 \cdot 4 \cdot 3 \cdot 2 \cdot 1}{5!} (2b^2)^5$$

$$= a^5 + 10a^4b^2 + 40a^3b^4 + 80a^2b^6 + 80ab^8 + 32b^{10}.$$

Combining formulas (10), (5), and (6), we can write explicitly the coefficients of the rth term u_r and the $(r + 1)$th term u_{r+1} of the binomial expansion of $(a + x)^n$:

$$u_r = C(n, r - 1)a^{n-r+1}x^{r-1} = \frac{n(n - 1) \cdots (n - r + 2)}{(r - 1)!} a^{n-r+1}x^{r-1}$$

$$= \frac{n!}{(r - 1)! \, (n - r + 1)!} a^{n-r+1}x^{r-1}; \qquad (12)$$

$$u_{r+1} = C(n, r)a^{n-r}x^r = \frac{n(n - 1) \cdots (n - r + 1)}{r!} a^{n-r}x^r$$

$$= \frac{n!}{r! \, (n - r)!} a^{n-r}x^r . \qquad (13)$$

EXAMPLE 2.   In the expansion of $(a^2 + 2x)^{12}$, find and simplify **(a)** the sixth term; **(b)** the term involving x^4.

Solution. $(a^2 + 2x)^{12} = [(a^2) + (2x)]^{12}.$

(a) The exponent of $(2x)$ is $6 - 1$ or **5**, that of (a^2) is $12 - $ **5** or 7.

The denominator of the coefficient is **5**! and the numerator has the **5** factors 12, 11, 10, 9, and 8.

Hence the sixth term is $\dfrac{12 \cdot 11 \cdot 10 \cdot 9 \cdot 8}{5!} (a^2)^7 (2x)^5$

or $792 a^{14}(32x^5)$ or $25{,}344 a^{14} x^5$.

(b) The exponent of $(2x)$ is **4**; that of (a^2) is $12 - $ **4** or 8.
The denominator of the coefficient is **4!** and the numerator has the **4** factors 12, 11, 10, and 9.

Hence the required term is $\dfrac{12 \cdot 11 \cdot 10 \cdot 9}{4!} (a^2)^8 (2x)^4$ or $7920 a^{16} x^4$.

Using the binomial theorem, we can express the total number of combinations of n things taken any number at a time. Namely, if we let $a = x = 1$ in equation (11), we obtain

$$(1 + 1)^n = 1 + C(n, 1) + C(n, 2) + \cdots + C(n, r) + \cdots + C(n, n),$$

or $\boldsymbol{C(n, 1) + C(n, 2) + \cdots + C(n, r) + \cdots + C(n, n) = 2^n - 1.}$

Stated in words, *the total number of combinations of* n *things taken successively* 1, 2, 3, $\cdots$, n *at a time is* $(2^n - 1)$.

EXAMPLE 3.   In how many ways can a person invite one or more of four friends to the theater?

Solution.   The number is

$$C(4, 1) + C(4, 2) + C(4, 3) + C(4, 4) = 2^4 - 1 = 15.$$

Historical Note.   The binomial theorem, for positive integral powers, was known to the Persian poet and mathematician OMAR KHAYYÁM (about 1100). ISAAC NEWTON (1642–1727) in 1664 or 1665 extended the use of the binomial theorem to fractional and negative values of n as an aid to his calculus. NIELS HENRIK ABEL (1802–1829) of Norway showed that the theorem holds for all values of n, including imaginary numbers.

EXERCISES

Find and simplify the specified terms in the expansions of the expressions:

1. Term involving x^4 in the expansion of $(a + x)^{10}$.

2. Term involving y^7 in the expansion of $(b + y)^{11}$.

3. Term involving b^6 in the expansion of $(b - z)^{15}$.

4. Term involving a^6 in the expansion of $(a + x)^9$.

5. Term involving a^{10} in the expansion of $(x^2 + a^2)^{16}$.

6. Term involving u^3 in the expansion of $(u^{\frac{1}{2}} - a^{\frac{1}{2}})^{18}$.

7. 6th term of $(a + b)^{10}$.

8. 4th term of $(x + 2y)^{12}$.

9. 7th term of $(3a - x)^{11}$.

10. 8th term of $(c - d)^{13}$.

11. 6th term of $(e^{-x} - e^{x})^{9}$.

12. 11th term of $(2x + x^{-1})^{13}$.

13. Middle term of $(x + 2)^{14}$.

14. Middle terms of $(\frac{1}{2}x - \sqrt{x})^{7}$.

Expand by the binomial theorem and simplify each term:

15. $(x + y)^4$.   **17.** $(a - c)^6$.   **19.** $(2x + 3y)^7$.

16. $(x + y)^5$.   **18.** $(2a - t)^6$.   **20.** $(x^3 - x^{-1})^5$.

21. Of seven men in a squad, one or more are to be selected for a special duty. How many selections are possible?

22. A girl has ten pieces of candy. How many choices can she make of one or more to eat, if the candies are **(a)** all different? **(b)** identical?

23. **(a)** How many different sums of money, consisting of four coins each, can be formed from a cent, a nickel, a dime, a quarter, and a half-dollar? **(b)** How many different sums of money can be formed if the above coins are all available?

24. Form a triangular array (called **Pascal's triangle**) as follows. On the first line is one number, 1. On the nth line are n numbers, of which the first and last are 1 and each of the other numbers is the sum of the two numbers in the next line above it, one number just to the left and one just to the right. For instance, in the fifth line of the following display, $4 = 1 + 3$, $6 = 3 + 3$, and $4 = 3 + 1$.

$$
\begin{array}{ccccccccc}
(a + x)^0 & & & & 1 & & & & \\
(a + x)^1 & & & 1 & & 1 & & & \\
(a + x)^2 & & 1 & & 2 & & 1 & & \\
(a + x)^3 & 1 & & 3 & & 3 & & 1 & \\
(a + x)^4 & 1 & 4 & & 6 & & 4 & & 1 \\
\end{array}
$$

(a) Construct the sixth row and compare the numbers in it with the coefficients of the expansion of $(a + x)^5$ by formula (11). *(b)** Using mathematical induction and Exercise 16 of § 15-6, prove that the numbers in the nth row are the coefficients in the expansion of $(a + x)^{n-1}$.

15-8   Relationship between the Terms of a Binomial Expansion

A useful relationship between successive terms of the binomial expansion of $(a + x)^n$ can be seen by taking the ratio of successive terms in (10). For this purpose, the forms (12) and (13) are convenient:

$$\frac{u_{r+1}}{u_r} = \frac{C(n, r)}{C(n, r - 1)} \cdot \frac{x}{a} = \frac{(n - r + 1)x}{ra}.$$

This, together with (5), provides the following description of *the binomial expansion of* $(a + x)^n$:

1. *The number of terms in the expansion is* $(n + 1)$.
2. *The first term is* a^n; *the second is* $na^{n-1}x$.
3. *The exponents of* a *decrease by* 1 *and those of* x *increase by* 1 *from term to term, their sum in each term being* n.
4. *If in any term the coefficient is multiplied by the exponent of* a, *and this product is divided by the exponent of* x *increased by* 1, *the result is the coefficient of the next term.*
5. *The coefficients of terms equidistant from the ends of the expansion are the same.*

EXAMPLE 1.   Find the first four terms in the expansion of $(a^{\frac{1}{2}} - 3b^2)^{11}$ and simplify each term.

Solution.

$$\begin{aligned}
(a^{\frac{1}{2}} - 3b^2)^{11} &= [(a^{\frac{1}{2}}) + (-3b^2)]^{11} \\
&= (a^{\frac{1}{2}})^{11} + 11(a^{\frac{1}{2}})^{10}(-3b^2) + \frac{11 \cdot 10}{2!}(a^{\frac{1}{2}})^9(-3b^2)^2 \\
&\quad + \frac{11 \cdot 10 \cdot 9}{3!}(a^{\frac{1}{2}})^8(-3b^2)^3 + \cdots \\
&= a^{\frac{11}{2}} - 33a^5b^2 + 495a^{\frac{9}{2}}b^4 - 4455a^4b^6 + \cdots.
\end{aligned}$$

EXAMPLE 2.   Find the value of $(1.01)^8$ to five significant digits by expanding a binomial whose terms have the sum 1.01.

Solution.

$$\begin{aligned}
(1.01)^8 &= (1 + 0.01)^8 \\
&= 1^8 + 8 \cdot 1^7 \cdot (0.01)^1 + \frac{8 \cdot 7}{2!} \cdot 1^6 \cdot (0.01)^2 + \frac{8 \cdot 7 \cdot 6}{3!} \cdot 1^5 \cdot (0.01)^3 \\
&\quad + \frac{8 \cdot 7 \cdot 6 \cdot 5}{4!} \cdot 1^4 \cdot (0.01)^4 + \cdots \\
&= 1 + 0.08 + 0.0028 + 0.000056 + 0.0000007 + \cdots \\
&= 1.082856 \cdots, \text{ or } 1.0829, \text{ to the required accuracy.}
\end{aligned}$$

This value of $(1.01)^8$ can also be found in tables of compound interest.

If we apply the laws governing the formation of the successive terms of the binomial formula to the expansion of $(a + x)^n$ where n is any real number *not* a positive integer or zero, we obtain the succession of terms known as the **binomial series**. This binomial series, instead of having a final term, is an unending, or infinite, series, since no zero factor ever arises.

We are interested here only in learning how to form the series and in some simple applications such as using the binomial series to find powers of certain numbers. Justification of this work with series is beyond the scope of this book.

EXAMPLE 3.   Find the first four terms in the expansion of $1/\sqrt[3]{a^3 - x^3}$ and simplify each term.

Solution.

$$\frac{1}{\sqrt[3]{a^3 - x^3}} = [a^3 + (-x^3)]^{-\frac{1}{3}}$$

$$= (a^3)^{-\frac{1}{3}} + (-\tfrac{1}{3})(a^3)^{-\frac{4}{3}}(-x^3) + \frac{(-\frac{1}{3})(-\frac{4}{3})}{2!}(a^3)^{-\frac{7}{3}}(-x^3)^2$$

$$+ \frac{(-\frac{1}{3})(-\frac{4}{3})(-\frac{7}{3})}{3!}(a^3)^{-\frac{10}{3}}(-x^3)^3 + \cdots$$

$$= a^{-1} + \tfrac{1}{3}a^{-4}x^3 + \tfrac{2}{9}a^{-7}x^6 + \tfrac{14}{81}a^{-10}x^9 + \cdots.$$

In some cases, to change the form of the expression before expanding makes little difference in the effort required. In other cases—notably in finding numerical values of roots—the work can be shortened by removing a factor so that one term in the binomial is 1.

ILLUSTRATION. $\sqrt[3]{210} = \sqrt[3]{216 - 6} = 6(1 - \tfrac{1}{36})^{\frac{1}{3}}$. If the binomial is expanded, all terms after the first few are found to be of negligible magnitude.

EXERCISES

Expand by the binomial theorem and simplify each term:

1. $(x + y)^7$.   **4.** $(3x - c)^7$.

2. $(a + b)^8$.   **6.** $\left(\tfrac{2}{3}a + \tfrac{3}{2a}\right)^9$.

5. $\left(2 + \tfrac{x}{a}\right)^6$.

3. $(2a - x)^9$.   **7.** $(ab^{-1} - a^{-1}b)^8$.

Find the first four terms in the expansion and simplify each term:

8. $(x + z)^{16}$.   **10.** $(p - \tfrac{1}{2}q)^{15}$.   **12.** $(3x + 2)^{22}$.

9. $(x^2 + a^2)^{13}$.   **11.** $(x^{\frac{1}{3}} + y^{\frac{1}{3}})^{12}$.   **13.** $(x - 2)^{103}$.

Use the binomial theorem to find the value of each of the following to five significant digits:

14. $(1.01)^6$.   **16.** $(98)^5$.   **18.** $(1002)^4$.

15. $(1.002)^{11}$.   **17.** $(5.1)^4$.   **19.** $(0.999)^5$.

By grouping terms, express as binomials; expand by the binomial theorem, and simplify:

20. $(x + y + z)^3$.   **21.** $(a + b - c)^4$.   **22.** $(1 - x + x^2 - x^3)^3$.

Find:

23. The last four terms of $(e^{\frac{1}{3}x} - e^{-\frac{1}{3}x})^{16}$.

24. The last five terms of $(2 - x)^{20}$.

25. The value of n if the coefficients of the eighth and seventeenth terms in the expansion of $(a + x)^n$ are equal.

Find the first four terms in the binomial series and simplify each term:

26. $(a^2 + x^2)^{\frac{1}{2}}$.   **28.** $(a^{\frac{1}{2}} + 4x^{\frac{1}{2}})^{-1}$.   **30.** $(x + 2)^k$.

27. $(a - 3x^6)^{\frac{1}{3}}$.   **29.** $\sqrt{a^{2n} - y^{2n}}$.   **31.** $(1 + h)^{\frac{1}{h}}$.

Use the binomial series to find the numerical value of each of the following to five significant digits:

32. $\sqrt{1.002}$.   **34.** $\sqrt[4]{1.01}$.   **36.** $(1.01)^{-6}$.   **38.** $80^{\frac{3}{4}}$.

33. $\sqrt{0.99}$.   **35.** $\sqrt{26}$.   **37.** $(0.9)^{-7}$.   **39.** $\sqrt[3]{63.99}$.

Show that if x *is very small, then:*

40. $\dfrac{1}{(1 + x)^n}$ is approximately equal to $(1 - nx)$.

41. $\sqrt{1 + x}$ is approximately equal to $(1 + \frac{1}{2}x)$.

*42. Prove the binomial formula for positive integral exponents by mathematical induction, collecting the terms involving x^r in $(a + x)^{k+1}$.

MISCELLANEOUS EXERCISES ON PERMUTATIONS AND COMBINATIONS

1. A railroad company orders one-way tickets printed for trips between the twenty principal stations on its lines. How many items must the printer make up if the tickets are **(a)** good only in the specified direction? **(b)** good in either direction?

2. In an intercommunication system there are to be twelve outlets, and each is connected to each other by a direct private wire. How many wires are needed?

3. A stamp dealer displays sixty sets of postage stamps. A boy is allowed a choice of four of these for his birthday. How many choices has he?

4. A student is required to memorize and recite three out of ten specified passages from Shakespeare. In how many ways can he **(a)** select three passages for simultaneous study? **(b)** present three of the ten passages?

5. A manufacturer makes shirts in nine different patterns, each in ten neck sizes and three sleeve lengths. How many items must a store carry to have a complete stock?

6. A telephone dial has holes numbered 0 to 9 inclusive and eight of these are also lettered. How many different telephone numbers, distinguishable as dialed, are possible with this dial, if each "number" consists of two letters followed by five numbers where the first number is not zero?

7. A doctor wishes to test each of twelve patients for possible allergy to each of ten agents. How many tests must he make?

8. A psychologist wishes to test the reaction of twelve persons to a certain sound. If there are sixteen volunteers, how many possible groups of subjects does he have?

9. An astronomer wishes to measure on a photograph the distance between the image of a certain star and each of three other star images nearby. If there are seven images nearby, how many choices of the three stars does he have?

10. A physics student is supplied with eight wires having resistances of 1, 2, 5, 25, 50, 100, 500, and 1000 ohms, respectively. When wires are connected one after another in series, the total resistance is the sum of the resistances of the individual wires used. How many different resistances are available, the type of connection mentioned above being permitted?

11. A commission of nine members is to be appointed, consisting of three American, three British, and three French representatives. There are five American candidates, three British candidates, and ten French candidates. In how many ways can the commission be made up?

12. **(a)** Find the total number of combinations of nine different things. **(b)** A man finds nine different records by his favorite pianist available in a music store. Among how many choices of what records to buy, if any, must he decide?

13. A state makes automobile license plates which have two letters from our alphabet (excluding *I*, *O*, and *Q*) followed by four digits of which the first is not zero. How many different plates are possible?

14. Two political parties each present one candidate for each of six offices. In how many ways can a voter vote **(a)** if he votes a straight ticket? **(b)** if he is willing to split his ticket? **(c)** if two of the offices must be voted for on a single ticket but the others may be split?

15. Switches controlling six lights, three machines, and a timer are to be placed in a horizontal line on a control board. All the light switches are to be kept together; likewise the machine switches; and each switch is labeled as to which unit it controls. In how many ways can the board be arranged?

16. In how many ways can four mathematics books, two physics books, five English books, and a history book, all different from one another, be arranged on a shelf so that all books on each subject are together?

17. A student has three different explanations for his failure in English, five different explanations for his failure in physics, and only two different explanations for his failure in mathematics. How often can he explain the whole situation to the dean **(a)** without using identically the same story twice? **(b)** without repeating any one explanation?

18. To open a certain type of lock requires three successive settings of a pointer on a number. The dial has 100 numbers. Find how many locks are possible if no two have the same "combination" and no "combination" is to involve two consecutive settings on the same number.

19. What is the smallest value of x such that $C(x, 4) \geq P(8, 3)$?

20. At a certain college there are ten subjects open to freshmen. Each freshman must take English and either physics or mathematics or both, and a total of five subjects. In how many ways can his choice of studies be made?

21. With an ordinary 52-card deck, **(a)** how many different bridge hands of 13 cards are possible? **(b)** How many of these contain the ace, king, queen, jack, and ten of spades? **(c)** How many contain 13 spades?

22. In multiplying out $(a + b + c + d)^5$, how many terms will there be before collecting like terms?

★23. Five chemical compounds are dissolved in water. Each separates into a positive ion and a negative ion. A reaction will occur if, among other things, any compound consisting of one of the positive ions and one of the negative ions is insoluble. How many such compounds must be considered?

15-9   Meaning of Probability

The study of probability developed mainly from two types of problems: those connected with games of chance and those connected with mortality and insurance. Among the former are problems concerning the tossing of coins, throwing of dice, drawing of lottery tickets, and so on. Growing out of the latter are problems connected with insurance, annuities, and statistical studies of physical, biological, and social phenomena. As any general treatment is beyond the scope of this book, our discussion must necessarily be limited to the simplest of applications.* However, the methods developed in these simple cases can be extended to a large variety of problems and are basic in the theory of probability.

One fundamental idea is that of events which are "**equally likely to occur**." This we consider as an essentially undefined, intuitive idea, playing in probability a role somewhat analogous to the idea of "point" in geometry. It may shed some light on this idea to say that when there is no more reason for one thing to happen than another, it is presumed that the two are equally likely to happen. Thus an ordinary coin, tossed at random, has no more reason to land heads than tails; so we say that these results—that is, ways of landing—are equally likely. This statement is borne out by the fact that if a coin is tossed many times, it comes down heads about as often as tails†; of course, in such a discussion we suppose that all coins, dice, etc., are "true"—that is, not loaded—and that there is no control of any toss or throw nor any possibility of standing on edge.

The idea of probability in cases where the obvious alternatives are *not* "equally likely" may be approached by first rephrasing the statement that the alternatives of a coin landing heads and landing tails are equally likely. We may restate this in several ways: "A tossed coin comes down heads about half the time," or "The probability that a tossed coin will come down heads is one half," or "The probability that a tossed coin will come down heads is one out of two." Consider similarly the throw of a

* For a fuller discussion see, among others, F. Mosteller, R. E. K. Rourke, and G. B. Thomas, Jr.'s *Probability and Statistics* (Addison-Wesley, Reading, Mass., 1961); W. W. R. Ball's *Mathematical Recreations and Essays*, revised by H. S. M. Coxeter (Macmillan, New York, 1955); and W. Feller's *An Introduction to Probability Theory and its Applications*, Vol. 1, second edition (Wiley, New York, 1957).

† For a description of experiments on actual coin-tossing, see J. V. Uspensky's *Introduction to Mathematical Probability* (McGraw-Hill, New York, 1937).

single die, and suppose that we wish to throw a "four." Any one of the six faces may equally well turn up. Thus the chances—that is, the probability—of throwing a "four" are said to be one out of six, or $\frac{1}{6}$, since only one of the six possible and equally likely results is successful in producing a "four." The other five of the six cases fail to produce a "four."

Definition of Probability. *If an event must result in some one of* n *equally likely ways, and if* s *of these ways are considered successes and the others failures, then the* **probability** p *of a successful result is the ratio of the number of successful ways to the total number of ways, or*

$$p = \frac{s}{n}. \tag{14}$$

ILLUSTRATIONS. The probability of getting 5 or more with one throw of a die is two out of six, or $\frac{2}{6}$, or $\frac{1}{3}$, since there are two successful ways, either a 5 or a 6, and there are six possible results.

The probability of drawing an odd number in a random draw from slips numbered 1, 2, 3, 4, 5, 6, 7, 8, and 9 is $\frac{5}{9}$, as the draw must result in one of nine equally likely ways of which five (namely, 1, 3, 5, 7, and 9) are successes.

In the notation of the above definition of probability, if s ways are successes, then the other $(n - s)$ must be failures. Hence the probability q of failure is given by

$$q = \frac{n - s}{n}.$$

In case of an event which is certain to happen, it must be that all the ways are successes, that is, $s = n$ and $p = 1$; for an event certain to fail, $s = 0$ and $p = 0$. But, in any case,

$$p + q = \frac{s}{n} + \frac{n - s}{n} = 1.$$

That is, *in any event, the probability of success plus the probability of failure is 1 (certainty)*, which simply reflects the fact that the event must either succeed or fail. This assumes, as is stated in the definition of probability, that "failure" is synonymous with lack of success. If a third category, say "indecisive," were allowed, then modifications of these statements would be necessary.

Probabilities are often phrased in terms of odds. If $p > q$, then the odds are p to q in favor of the event; if $p < q$, then the odds are q to p against the event. Numbers proportional to p and q may also be used instead. For example, the odds against rolling a "four" with a single die are $\frac{5}{6}$ to $\frac{1}{6}$, or 5 to 1.

EXAMPLE 1.   From a group consisting of five men and seven women, a committee of four is to be chosen by lot. Find the probability that the committee will consist of two men and two women.

Solution.   A committee of four can be selected from the twelve persons in $C(12, 4)$, or 495, ways, all equally likely. The number of ways which are successes is obtained as follows: the two men can be chosen in $C(5, 2)$, or 10, ways, and the women in $C(7, 2)$, or 21, ways. Thus a committee of two men and two women can be chosen in $10 \cdot 21$, or 210, ways, and the required probability is $\frac{210}{495} = \frac{14}{33} = 0.424^+$.

EXAMPLE 2.   Six married couples are to be seated by lot at a circular table. Find the probability that one particular couple will draw adjacent chairs.

Solution.   Consider the woman of this particular couple as seated. There are left for her husband eleven chairs, two of which are adjacent to hers. Hence the required probability is $\frac{2}{11}$.

EXAMPLE 3.   Find the odds for or against getting 5 or more with one throw of a die.

Solution.   By the first of the illustrations above, $p = \frac{1}{3}$. But $p + q = 1$; hence $q = \frac{2}{3}$. The odds *against* getting 5 or more are $\frac{2}{3}$ to $\frac{1}{3}$, or 2 to 1.

EXAMPLE 4.   If the odds against an event are 3 to 2, what is the probability of its happening?

Solution.   Here q and p must be proportional to 3 and 2, or $q/p = \frac{3}{2}$. But $p + q = 1$; hence $q = 1 - p$. Therefore, we have

$$\frac{1-p}{p} = \frac{3}{2}, \quad 2 - 2p = 3p, \quad \text{and} \quad p = \frac{2}{5}.$$

Warning.   In Example 4, q and p are in the ratio of 3 to 2; but they *cannot equal* 3 and 2, since neither can be greater than 1.

EXAMPLE 5.   Fifty lottery tickets are sold at one dollar each; the winner is to get forty dollars. What is the financial prospect of the buyer of one ticket?

Solution.   Of the fifty choices of a winner, *one* of the choices is worth $40.00 to this man; the other forty-nine are worth nothing.

The average value to him of the various equally likely possibilities is thus ($40 + 0 + 0 + 0 + \cdots + 0)/50$, or $0.80, a net loss of 20 cents.

In the solution of Example 5 observe that $0.80 = $40 \times \frac{1}{50}$, which is a special case of the following definition:

If a person is to receive m *units in case a certain event results successfully, and the probability of success of that event is* p, *then his* **expectation** *is said to be* mp *units.*

A related definition is the one following:

If p *is the probability of success in one trial of an event, then* kp *is the* **probable number** *of successes in* k *trials.* When *kp* is not an integer, we use the integer nearest to *kp*.

Historical Note. The theory of probability is commonly considered to have started with the correspondence between BLAISE PASCAL (1623–1662) and PIERRE DE FERMAT (1608–1665) over the proper division of the stakes in an interrupted game of chance.

EXERCISES

1. (**a**) List the various possible equally likely outcomes in choosing at random a letter from $col_1l_2e_1ge_2$. (**b**) How many of these outcomes are an *e*? (**c**) What is the probability that the choice will be an *e*? (**d**) What is the probability that the choice will not be an *e*?

2. (**a**) List by initial the various possible equally likely outcomes in choosing successively two different girls from Mary, Joan, Elizabeth, Susan, and Katherine. (**b**) How many of these include Mary as first choice? (**c**) If a pair is chosen as stated, what is the probability that it will include Mary as first choice? (**d**) That it will not include Mary as first choice?

3. From an assortment containing six blue light bulbs, three red ones, and three white ones, a bulb is chosen at random. What is the probability that it will (**a**) be red? (**b**) not be white?

4. A man is to choose one of a set of eight sealed envelopes. What is the probability of drawing an envelope containing money (**a**) from the set when two of the envelopes contain dollar bills and the rest contain blank paper? (**b**) from a set of empty envelopes?

5. A man has in his pocket a fifty-cent piece, two dimes, and two pennies. He draws one coin out at random. What are the odds that it is worth at least a dime?

6. Five runners of equal ability run a race. (**a**) What are the odds for or against one particular man winning? **(b)** If the winner is to receive $100, what is the value of the expectation of one particular man?

7. From an ordinary deck of 52 playing cards, one is selected at random. What is the probability that **(a)** it is a spade? **(b)** it is an ace or a king?

8. Out of a group of ten girls, three have blue eyes. If two of the girls are selected at random, what is the probability that both will have blue eyes?

9. From a panel of twelve arbitrators, three are chosen by lot. What is the probability that a certain individual of the panel will be one of those chosen?

10. Four bolts and four nuts are mixed together. If two parts are chosen at random, what is the probability that **(a)** one will be a nut and one a bolt? **(b)** either both will be nuts or both will be bolts?

11. A junk dealer prices an article at $4, and figures that he has one chance in eight of selling it. **(a)** What is his expectation of income? **(b)** If he paid 20 cents for it, what is his expectation of profit? **(c)** What would be his expected profit on the 20-cent article if he priced it at $0.80 with three chances out of four of selling it?

12. A person awakened by a storm which has left the house dark selects two socks at random from among ten different pairs which have been mixed together in a drawer. What is the probability that he will select a pair?

13. From a dozen apples, three of which have a worm inside, seven apples are chosen at random. What is the probability that none of them contains a worm?

14. Eight light bulbs are to be chosen from eleven which are on hand, and are to be connected in series; that is, none will light unless all do. If two of the eleven bulbs are burned out, what is the probability that those chosen will not light?

15. The tickets in a box are numbered 1 to 50 inclusive, and two tickets are drawn. Is the sum of their numbers more likely to be odd or even, and what are the odds?

16. Of five castings, two are tested and one is found to be bad. For each possible proportion of bad castings in the original batch of five, calculate the probability of this occurrence.

17. From a jar containing six cookies, three are drawn, two of which are chocolate and one is molasses. For all possible proportions of chocolate and molasses cookies in the jar, calculate the probability of this occurrence.

15-10   Compound Probabilities

We have considered problems on the probability of success or failure in a *single* event, and now we shall proceed to consider more complicated situations.

EXAMPLE 1.   From a bag containing four white and three black balls, one ball is drawn and then replaced. The balls are thoroughly mixed, and another is drawn. Find the probability that both balls will be white.

Solution.   By the fundamental principle of § 15-2, there are $7 \cdot 7$, or 49, ways in which the two draws can be made. Since a white ball can be drawn in any one of *four* ways on the first draw and in any one of *four* ways on the second draw, there are $4 \cdot 4$, or 16, ways in which a white ball can be drawn on both trials. Hence the required probability is $\frac{16}{49}$.

EXAMPLE 2.   In Example 1, what is the probability that both balls will be white if the first ball drawn is not returned to the bag?

Solution.   The two draws can be made in $7 \cdot 6$, or 42, ways; two white balls can be drawn in $4 \cdot 3$, or 12, ways. The probability of drawing two white balls is $\frac{12}{42}$, or $\frac{2}{7}$, which is $\frac{7}{8}$ of the answer for Example 1.

In Example 1, the first ball drawn *is returned* to the bag before the second drawing; hence the second draw *is not affected* by the first draw and is said to be **independent** of it. In Example 2, the first ball drawn *is not returned* to the bag; hence the second draw *is affected* by the first draw and is said to be **dependent** on it.

Now observe that in Example 1 the answer ($\frac{16}{49}$) is the product of the probability ($\frac{4}{7}$) of success on the first draw times the probability (also $\frac{4}{7}$) of success on the second draw. In Example 2, the answer ($\frac{12}{42}$) is the product of the probability ($\frac{4}{7}$) of success on the first draw and the probability ($\frac{3}{6}$) of success on the second draw after the first has succeeded. The methods used in solving these two examples can be used to prove the following theorem:

Theorem I.   *If the probability of success of a first event is* p_1, *and if, after this event has resulted in success, the probability of success of a second event (which may or may not be dependent on the first event) is* p_2, *then the probability of success in both events in the order stated is* p_1p_2.

Proof.   Let n_1 be the number of (equally likely) ways in which the first event can result, and s_1 the number of successes. Let n_2 be the number of ways in which the second event can result after the first has resulted successfully, and s_2 the number of successes. But the second event may depend on the first; what about the number of results and successes in the second if the first fails? It does not matter! If the first fails, both cannot succeed; the probability of success in *both* does not depend upon the probability of success in the second after failure in the first. So we may take the number of results and successes of the second event in all cases to be n_2 and s_2. Then the total number of ways in which the two events can result is $n_1 n_2$; the number of successful ways is $s_1 s_2$. Hence the desired probability is

$$p = \frac{s_1 s_2}{n_1 n_2} = \frac{s_1}{n_1} \cdot \frac{s_2}{n_2} = p_1 p_2.$$

This theorem and proof, as well as Theorem II which follows, can readily be extended to more than two events.

EXAMPLE 3. From a bag containing six white balls, three black balls, and thirteen red balls, one ball is drawn at random. What is the probability that it is either white or black?

Solution. Of the twenty-two ways in which the draw can be made, the six which yield a white ball and the three which yield a black ball, a total of nine, are successes. The required probability is $\frac{9}{22}$.

Since the drawing of a white ball in Example 3 *excludes* the drawing of a black ball, and vice versa, these two events are said to be **mutually exclusive.**

Now observe that in Example 3 the probability $(\frac{9}{22})$ that one or the other of these two mutually exclusive events will succeed is the sum of their individual probabilities $(\frac{6}{22}$ and $\frac{3}{22})$ of success. The solution in this example suggests the following theorem, the proof of which is left to the student.

Theorem II. *If an event can result in* n *ways, each equally likely, of which* s_1 *are of one kind and* s_2 *are of another kind, the two kinds being mutually exclusive, then the probability that the event will result in one or the other of these* s_1 *and* s_2 *ways is the sum of their respective probabilities.*

EXAMPLE 4. Apply Theorem II if a coin is tossed m times and comes down heads h times and tails t times.

Solution. The probability that the coin comes down heads is $\frac{1}{2}$; the probability that it comes down tails is also $\frac{1}{2}$. The probability that it comes down either heads or tails is $\frac{1}{2} + \frac{1}{2}$ or 1. Note that $n = 2$, $s_1 = 1$, $s_2 = 1$, regardless of m, h, and t.

EXAMPLE 5.   According to Mendel's theory of heredity, among pea plants the color of a certain part of the seed is determined as follows: In the one cell which develops into this part of the seed are two genes which determine color (as well as other genes which determine other things but are outside our problem). These genes may be either of two kinds which we shall call *A* and *a*. If both are of kind *a*, the color will be green; otherwise it will be yellow. When a plant is fertilized by pollination, this cell gets one of its genes from the plant on which it grows and the other from the plant which produces the pollen. Assuming that the cell for a particular seed is equally likely to get genes *A* and *a* from each source, what is the probability that the seed will be yellow?

First Solution.   The probability of getting a gene of kind *a* from one plant is $\frac{1}{2}$, and from the other plant also $\frac{1}{2}$; hence, by Theorem I, the probability of getting a gene of kind *a* from *both* plants is $\frac{1}{4}$. Thus the probability that the color will be green is $\frac{1}{4}$; that it will be yellow, $1 - \frac{1}{4}$, or $\frac{3}{4}$.

Second Solution.   The following pairs of genes are equally likely: *AA*, *Aa*, *aA*, and *aa*. The first three show yellow; hence, by definition, the probability is $\frac{3}{4}$.

EXAMPLE 6.   If a die is thrown seven times, what is the probability that it will come up 3 exactly twice?

Solution.   For the two times it is to come up 3, there are $C(7, 2)$, or 21, mutually exclusive choices (for instance, the first two times, the first and third times, etc.). But the probability of coming up 3 on both of two specified trials is $\frac{1}{6} \cdot \frac{1}{6}$, or $(\frac{1}{6})^2$; of not coming up 3 on the other five trials, $\frac{5}{6} \cdot \frac{5}{6} \cdot \frac{5}{6} \cdot \frac{5}{6} \cdot \frac{5}{6}$, or $(\frac{5}{6})^5$. Hence the probability of coming up 3 on the specified trials and not on the others is $(\frac{1}{6})^2 \cdot (\frac{5}{6})^5$. The desired probability is, by Theorem II, the product $21 \cdot (\frac{1}{6})^2 \cdot (\frac{5}{6})^5$.

By analogy with Theorem II and the reasoning of Example 5 of § 15-9, we may extend the definition of expectation as follows:

If an event can result in certain mutually exclusive ways, the **expectation** *(that is, the* **total expectation***) is the sum of the expectations of these mutually exclusive results.*

EXAMPLE 7.   Fifty lottery tickets are sold; one number is to get forty dollars and another five dollars. What is the expectation of the holder of one ticket?

Solution.   As to the $40 prize, his expectation is $\frac{1}{50} \cdot \$40$, or $0.80; as to the $5 prize, his expectation is $\frac{1}{50} \cdot \$5$, or $0.10. His total expectation is thus $0.90—a loss if the ticket cost him $1.

EXERCISES

1. (**a**) List the various possible equally likely outcomes, including repetitions, if one chooses at random an integer between 1 and 4 inclusive, and chooses at random an integer between 3 and 7 inclusive, and multiplies them together. (**b**) How many of the products are odd numbers? (**c**) What is the probability that the product will be an odd number?

2. A box contains eleven capsules, with the names of six seniors, three juniors, and two sophomores. Two names are drawn and placed on the table. What is the probability that (**a**) the first name drawn is that of a senior? (**b**) the first is not a sophomore? (**c**) the first is a senior and the second is a junior? (**d**) both are seniors?

3. A job applicant estimates that his chance of passing a qualifying examination is $\frac{2}{3}$ and his chance of being appointed if he does pass is $\frac{3}{4}$. What is the probability that he will receive the job?

4. In a certain place there is one chance in two that it will rain on April 1, one chance in five that it will rain on July 1, and two chances in three that it will rain on November 1. What is the probability that it will rain on (**a**) all, (**b**) none, of these three days?

5. At the time of a certain marriage, the probabilities that the man and the woman will live fifty more years are 0.352 and 0.500, respectively. (**a**) What is the probability that both will be alive fifty years later? (**b**) If the probability that the marriage will not be dissolved by divorce or separation is 0.846, what is the probability that they will have a fiftieth wedding anniversary?

6. A floor lamp has three sockets, independent of each other. Of eight available bulbs, four are no good. If three bulbs are selected at random, what is the chance that there will be light?

7. Of one hundred envelopes in a box, one contains a $50 bill, five others each a $1 bill, while the rest are empty. Find (**a**) the probability that the first envelope drawn contains the $50 bill; (**b**) the expectation of the first draw; (**c**) the probability that the fifth draw will yield a bill if the preceding draws have yielded three $1 bills; (**d**) the expectation of the draw described in (*c*).

8. One bag contains three white and five black balls, and a second bag contains four white and six black balls. A man draws one ball from each bag. Find (**a**) the probability that both balls are black; (**b**) the probability that both balls are of the same color; (**c**) whether the probability that he draws first a black and then a white ball depends on which bag he draws from first.

9. Teams A, B, and C are tied for the leadership of a league. It is decided that B is to play C, and the winner is to play A for the championship. If the teams are of equal ability, what probability has each of becoming champion?

10. A boy's father offers to let his son choose in advance whether to receive \$60 if he makes all A grades, or to receive \$10 for each A. The boy believes his probabilities of making A's in his three courses are respectively $\frac{2}{3}$, $\frac{1}{2}$, and $\frac{3}{4}$. Which should he choose?

11. It is estimated that at a busy street corner a jaywalker will be hit once in a hundred times. What is his probability of remaining unhit if he makes **(a)** one round trip? **(b)** a round trip daily for thirty days?

12. A haystack contains 10,000 cubic feet of hay and two needles. **(a)** What is the probability that at least one of the needles is in a certain cubic foot of the stack? **(b)** How nearly is this twice the probability for a similar stack with only one needle?

13. On each problem a student has an 80% probability of doing it correctly. In an assignment of five problems **(a)** what is the number he can expect to get correct? **(b)** What is the probability that he will get at least four correct?

14. An event with probability p of success is tried N times. Find the probability that it succeeds exactly n times.

15. If five throws of a die are made in succession, find the probability that **(a)** the first two throws will each result in a six but the other three will not; **(b)** exactly two sixes will appear; **(c)** two consecutive sixes, and no other sixes, will appear.

16. Solve Example 5 of § 15-10 if the plants crossed are of types **(a)** Aa and aa; **(b)** AA and Aa.

★17. In Example 5 of § 15-10, what is the probability that a plant from this seed could have only yellow seeds?

15-11   Empirical Probabilities

So far we have considered problems in which probabilities could be deduced by analyzing the situation in terms of equally likely results. Some problems are too complicated for such an analysis. For instance, a man aged thirty will live to be eighty or else will die before reaching that age, but the alternatives do not seem equally likely, and there are so many factors involved that the previous type of analysis seems hopeless.

In such cases we can only estimate probabilities from experience and observation, that is, empirically. First, then, we define a term by which to express the results of experience.

If N *trials of an event have been made, of which* S *are successes, then the* **relative frequency** P *of success is given by*

$$P = \frac{S}{N}.$$

ILLUSTRATION.   If it has been found that, out of 1000 healthy men of age thirty, 452 lived to be seventy years old, then in this group the relative frequency of attaining age seventy was $\frac{452}{1000}$, or 0.452.

Experience shows that in situations where the probability can be deduced (such as the tossing of a coin as mentioned in § 15-9) and the relative frequency *in a large number of trials* is also found, then *probability and relative frequency are approximately equal.* Hence it is reasonable to suppose that this equality holds also in cases where we are unable to calculate the probability. By a "large number" we mean enough so that accidental runs of "good luck" and "bad luck" cancel out, and the relative frequency is not substantially affected by increasing the number of trials.

EXAMPLE 1.   What is the probability that a man like those described in the above illustration will live to age seventy?

Solution.   The relative frequency was 0.452; in the absence of any better basis for judgment, the probability is also taken to be 0.452.

EXAMPLE 2.   How many times would a die be expected to turn up 5 or more if thrown a dozen times?

Solution.   In the first illustration in § 15-9 it was found that the probability of turning up 5 or more in a single throw is $\frac{1}{3}$. Approximately, the relative frequency is also $\frac{1}{3}$. If S is the number of successes, then, as above $P = S/N$, or in this case $\frac{1}{3} = S/12$ and $S = \frac{12}{3}$, or 4. Thus the answer is 4.

In this case the number of trials is *not* large, and the number observed in an experiment may differ considerably from that predicted. The result found by this type of reasoning might not be an integer, in which case we take the nearest integer.

EXAMPLE 3.   If the probability of success in one trial of an event is p, and it is tried N times, what is the expected number S of successes?

Solution.   As in Example 2, $p = P$ approximately and $P = S/N$; so $S = NP$ and approximately $S = Np$.

EXERCISES

1. In a herd of cattle 26 male calves and 24 female calves were born. Find the relative frequency of male calves among the births.

2. The population of various regions of the United States in 1960 was: Northeast 44,678,000; North Central 51,619,000; South 54,973,000; West, 28,053,000. Find the relative frequency of residents of the four regions.

3. On farms in the United States in 1960 there were 101,520,000 cattle, 29,481,000 sheep, 58,464,000 hogs, and 3,089,000 horses and mules. In 1890 the corresponding numbers were 60,014,000; 44,518,000; 48,130,000; and 18,054,000. For each year find, to three significant digits, the relative frequency of each kind of livestock.

4. In 1959 there were 71,502,394 automobiles, buses, and trucks registered in the United States, and 288,300 were reported stolen. On this basis, find the number that may be expected to be stolen from among the 50,000 insured by a certain insurance company.

5. In a certain year, there were approximately the following numbers of persons employed in the general types of occupation stated: professional and technical, 7,042,000; farm, 6,528,000; managerial, 6,940,000; clerical and sales, 14,312,000; craftsmen and machine operators, 21,128,000; service and labor, 12,743,000. Find, to three significant digits, the relative frequency of (**a**) professional and technical personnel; (**b**) farm workers. In a group of one hundred employed persons chosen at random, what is the expected number of (**c**) professional and technical personnel? (**d**) farm workers?

6. The number of deaths in the United States in a certain year was 1,659,000, of which infectious and parasitic diseases caused 22,860, cancer 259,090, heart disease 645,390, other circulatory and related troubles 270,220, influenza and pneumonia 57,320, motor vehicle accidents 35,320, other accidents 54,030, suicide 18,330, and homicide 8,330. Find, to three decimal places, the relative frequency of each of these causes and of all other causes.

7. In English language text, on the average, 1000 letters include the following numbers of particular letters: E, 131; T, 105; A, 82; O, 80; N, 71; R, 68; I, 63; S, 61. (**a**) Write these as relative frequencies. (**b**) Count 500 consecutive letters in a newspaper article or nontechnical book, and compare the relative frequencies with the answers to (*a*). (**c**) How are the answers to (*a*) and (*b*) likely to compare with the combined results for 500 words from each of ten different articles?

MISCELLANEOUS EXERCISES ON PROBABILITY

1. From a bag containing two red and eight white balls, one ball is drawn at random and replaced, the balls being thoroughly mixed after each draw. **(a)** What is the probability that the first ball drawn is red? **(b)** Out of fifty draws, what is the expected number of draws giving a red ball?

2. If an integer between 1 and 100 inclusive is chosen at random, what is the probability that it will **(a)** end in a 3? **(b)** end in an odd number? **(c)** have a repeated digit? **(d)** be a positive integral power of 3?

3. If an integer between 1 and 500 inclusive is chosen at random, what is the probability that it is the square of an integer?

4. A machine has three parts; if any one of them fails, the machine fails. Suppose that the probability of failure during a certain period of time is 0.1 for the first part, 0.3 for the second part, and 0.01 for the third part. Find to three significant digits the probability that the machine will fail during this period.

5. Two distinct integers between 1 and 10 inclusive are chosen at random. What is the probability that both are odd?

6. A mail-order house sends advertisements to 10% of the population of a city of 400,000. It is estimated that the probability that a recipient will buy is $\frac{1}{80}$. **(a)** What is the expected number of purchasers resulting from the campaign? **(b)** If the advertising costs $300 to prepare and $20 per thousand for printing, mailing, etc., while the profit on the sale to each customer is $3, what are the expected profits?

7. What is the probability of obtaining **(a)** exactly five points, **(b)** at most five points, if two dice are thrown?

8. There are five sections of a certain course at 11 o'clock, three sections at 10 o'clock, and two at 9 o'clock. Four students are assigned to sections at random. Find the probability that **(a)** all will be assigned at 10 o'clock; **(b)** all will be assigned to the same section.

9. Suppose an important message about a disaster is sent in triplicate. The copy sent by one channel has three chances in five of arriving; by another channel, four chances in five of arriving; by a third channel, one chance in three of arriving. What is the probability that **(a)** at least one arrives? **(b)** all three arrive?

10. In a year, a machine made 30,000 parts, of which 150 were defective. If the defects occur at random, **(a)** what is the expected number of defective parts among the first 800 made the next year? What is the probability that the first three parts made in the next year will all be (**b**) defective? (**c**) good?

11. A certain door can be opened by one of a set of twelve keys. A man picks up two of these keys at random, and goes to the door. If there is one chance in three that the door is unlocked, what is the probability that he will be able to open the door without breaking it or returning for another key?

12. A company manufacturing a piece of hardware finds that in the long run 2% of its product is defective, and that these defective pieces occur at random and not in runs. What is the probability that, of six pieces, at least one will be defective?

13. Three coins are tossed simultaneously. What is the probability that (**a**) exactly two, (**b**) at least two, of them fall heads up? (**c**) If the three are tossed simultaneously two hundred times, how many times may it be expected that exactly two heads will appear?

14. Of twenty castings, three are defective. If five of the castings are inspected, what is the probability that (**a**) at least one of the defective castings, (**b**) all three defective ones, will be inspected?

15. On a true-false test containing ten questions, one student knew none of the answers and guessed on each question. What was the probability that he scored at least 60%?

★16. Suppose that each electronic tube which is in working condition at the beginning of an hour has probability 0.0002 of failing during that hour. Find the probability that (**a**) a radio with five tubes will not suffer a tube failure in one hour of operation; (**b**) a television set with 25 tubes will not suffer a tube failure in 100 hours of operation; (**c**) a radar set with 2500 tubes will not suffer a failure in 10 hours of operation. It is suggested that answers be evaluated by the binomial theorem, to three decimal places in (a) and two places in (b), and by evaluating a power of the answer to (b) to two places for (c).

★17. It is known that if untreated mice are exposed to a certain disease, 60% of them contract it. (**a**) Three mice are treated with a certain vaccine and then exposed to the disease, but only one contracts it. What is the probability that at least two mice will fail to get the disease if this particular vaccine has no effect? (**b**) Find the corresponding probability if twelve mice are treated and four contract the disease.

THE SLIDE RULE

A-1 Basic Idea of the Slide Rule; Multiplication

A slide rule is essentially a device for performing mechanically some of the operations with logarithms which were studied in Chapter 6.

Let us consider multiplication. By Property 1 of § 6-4,

$$\log MN = \log M + \log N. \tag{1}$$

The indicated addition can be performed graphically as follows. On a logarithmic scale (Figure 6.4 in § 6-10), the origin is marked "1" and other numbers are plotted at distances from the origin representing the logarithms of the numbers. The sum of two such distances therefore represents the sum of the logarithms, which by (1) is the logarithm of the product. Figure A.1 illustrates this graphical addition in the case $M = 2$, $N = 3$, $MN = 6$.

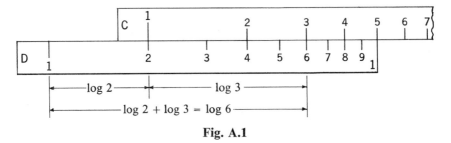

Fig. A.1

The essential part of a **slide rule** is a pair of logarithmic scales, one fixed and one movable parallel to it; on most slide rules the two are labeled **D** and **C** respectively. To multiply M by N, slide the movable scale so that 1 on it lies opposite M on the fixed scale. Then locate N on the movable scale; opposite it on the fixed scale is the value of MN. To help locate the opposite value, a slide rule has a movable hair line, usually on a glass or plastic slider, which may be set over N.

To assist in locating a number such as M on one of the scales, the interval between successive integers is divided to show tenths, and each tenth in turn is subdivided to show several equal parts, the number of such parts depending on the space available in that section of the scale. Thus a number of about three significant digits can be located on the

436

scale or read off from a given location on the scale. This is one digit less than in the case of a four-place table of logarithms.

Reading from the scale gives only the succession of digits in the answer, corresponding to the information supplied by the mantissa of a logarithm. The decimal point is best located by rounding off the factors and then computing an approximate answer.

EXAMPLE 1.   Find by slide rule 0.0342×28.1.

Solution.   Locate 342 on the fixed scale (D scale in Figure A.2). Opposite 342 on the D scale, set 1 on the movable scale (C in Figure A.2). Locate 281 on the movable, C, scale; opposite it on the fixed, D, scale, read off the value, 961. This is the sequence of digits in the answer. To locate the decimal point, note that the product is approximately 0.03×30, or 0.9. Hence the answer is 0.961, approximately correct to three significant digits.

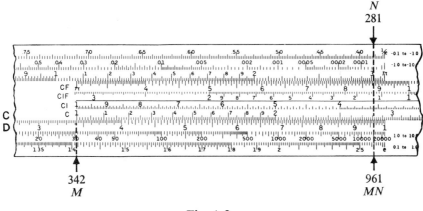

Fig. A.2

If the location of N on the movable scale falls beyond the end of the fixed scale so there is no value opposite N, simply set opposite M on the fixed scale the 1 on the *other end* of the movable scale. This corresponds to carrying a digit into the characteristic when adding the mantissas of logarithms. In terms of logarithmic scales, it may be thought of as follows. A logarithmic scale (Figure 6.4 in § 6-10) has many "cycles," in each of which the first digit runs from 1 to 10; successive cycles differ only in the location of the decimal point. Thus if the decimal point is handled separately, as in Example 1, then all that matters is the position within a cycle relative to its ends. A slide rule shows only one cycle; using the 1 at the other end of the movable scale is equivalent to moving to the corresponding position in the adjacent cycle of a logarithmic scale.

EXAMPLE 2.   Find by slide rule 0.0657×872.

Solution.   Locate 657 on the fixed, D, scale (Figure A.3). Opposite 657 on the D scale, set 1 at the right end of the movable, C, scale. Locate 872 on the movable, C, scale. Opposite it on the fixed, D, scale is 573, the succession of digits in the answer. The decimal point is located by approximating the factors: $0.07 \times 900 \approx 60$. Thus the answer is 57.3.

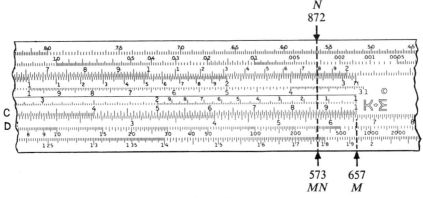

Fig. A.3

Some slide rules are made in circular form, so that the two 1's coincide and the readings progress in endless succession.

EXERCISES

Compute by slide rule:

1. 16×4.   **3.** 16×8.   **5.** 4.92×1.230.

2. 3×24.   **4.** 3×42.   **6.** 1.680×4.29.

7. 96.3×72.0.   **9.** 0.607×0.0482.

8. 839×0.0614.   **10.** 0.398×0.865.

11—16. Exercises 1 through 6 of § 6-7.

17. $16,820 \times 4.62$.   **18.** $581,000 \times 0.0326$.

19. Discuss what a slide rule would be like if it were designed in terms of natural logarithms instead of common logarithms.

20. Discuss whether addition and subtraction can be performed on a slide rule.

21. Suppose several different distances, each given in inches, must be converted to centimeters. One inch equals 2.54 centimeters. Describe how to so this by slide rule without repeatedly moving the movable scale.

A-2 Division; Successive Operations

To multiply more than two factors, multiply the first two factors as in the preceding section. This result is then multiplied in the same way by the next factor, and so on. Note that the intermediate result need not be read off; if the hair line is set at this location, it serves to locate the position to which 1 on the movable scale is to be set to start the next multiplication.

For division, reverse the operations in multiplication. Thus, to find M where $M = P/N$, note that then $MN = P$. Locate P on the fixed scale (corresponding to the answer MN in multiplication). Set opposite it N on the movable scale. Then opposite 1 on the movable scale, read the sequence of digits in the answer M off the fixed scale. The 1 on either end of the movable scale may be used. The decimal point is located by approximate computation; often scientific notation is convenient.

EXAMPLE 1.   Find by slide rule $0.961 \div 28.1$.

Solution.   Locate 961 on the fixed, D, scale (Figure A.2). Slide the movable, C, scale so that 281 on the movable scale lies opposite this 961. Then opposite 1 on the movable scale is 342, the sequence of digits in the answer. The decimal point may be located by approximation: $0.9 \div 30 = 0.03$. Thus the answer is 0.0342.

Combinations of multiplication and division can be done in successive steps. The answer to one step, as represented by the location of the hair line, is the beginning of the next step. The work involved is usually minimized by alternating multiplications and divisions as far as possible.

EXAMPLE 2.   Find by slide rule $\dfrac{0.07177 \times 5.960 \times 0.1571}{99}$.

Solution.   Locate 7177 on the fixed, D, scale; this section of the scale cannot be read to four digits on an ordinary slide rule, so in effect we round off to 718. Set opposite this the right hand 1 on the movable, C, scale. Set the hair line at 596 on the movable scale. The corresponding sequence of digits on the fixed scale is 428 (for the product 7177×596) but need not be read. Instead, keep the hair line in this position and slide the movable scale so 99 is set at the hair line. Then move the hair line until it is over the right hand 1 on the movable scale. This corresponds to 432 on the fixed scale, which is the sequence of digits for $7177 \times 596 \div 99$, but again this need not be read off. To multiply this result by 1571, keep the hair line in this position, and move the movable scale so the 1 at the left end is at the hair line. Then set the hair line at 1571 on the movable scale. Opposite this on the fixed scale is the sequence of digits in the answer, 679. The decimal point is located by approximate computation:

$$\frac{0.07 \times 6 \times \frac{1}{6}}{100} \approx 0.0007.$$

Thus the answer is 0.000679.

Sometimes it is more efficient to perform the operations in a different order. Thus in Example 2, fewer settings of the movable scale are required if the operations are grouped as follows:

$$[(0.07177 \div 99) \times 5.960] \times 0.1571.$$

Negative numbers as such do not appear on a slide rule. Operations with them are handled by treating the sign separately by the laws of signs and using the slide rule to compute the numerical value—just as in the case of logarithms, § 6-8.

EXERCISES

Compute by slide rule:

1. $18.73 \times 48.5 \times 219.$

2. $0.813 \times 281.6 \times 0.048.$

3. $0.00692 \times 32.16 \times 2.718.$

4. $91 \times 561 \times 8.10 \times 403.$

5. $256 \div 8.$

6. $60 \div 90.$

7. $43.2 \div 168.3.$

8. $704 \div 0.615.$

9. $0.321 \div 0.069.$

10. $0.0817 \div 94.3.$

11. $(-69) \div 880.$

12. $432 \div (-518).$

13. $1 \div 74.6.$

14. $\dfrac{148.6 \times 45.9}{68.3}.$

15. $\dfrac{807 \times 0.0316}{492}.$

16. $\dfrac{236 \times 8.41 \times 0.349}{28.4 \times 184.0}.$

17—33. Exercises 7 through 23 of § 6-7.

A-3   Other Scales

The C and D scales discussed in § A-1 are basic. Most slide rules also have some other scales, useful for special purposes.

Simplest to explain are the **folded** scales **CF** and **DF**. They differ from C and D only in that C and D consist of a cycle running from 1 to 10 as discussed in connection with Example 2 of § A-1, whereas CF and DF have a cycle running in effect from π to 10π. Whenever number M on the C scale is opposite a number N on the D scale, then M on the CF scale is also opposite N on the DF scale. Note that in multiplication, it is 1 on the movable scale, rather than the end of the scale (that is, π, in the case of a folded scale) which must be set opposite the first factor.

ILLUSTRATION 1.   In Example 2 of § A-2, after the next-to-last step of the solution the C scale is in position extending to the left of the fixed, D, scale. To use the C scale for the next multiplication requires that it be moved so that 1 at the left end is set where 1 at the right end now lies. Instead of moving the C scale in this manner, leave it in position as at the end of the previous step and locate the factor, 1571, on the folded scale CF. The value opposite this on the DF scale, 679, is the sequence of digits in the answer, just as in § A-2, and is obtained by one fewer motions of the movable scale.

The folded scales are particularly convenient if one factor is π.

Many slide rules also have a **reciprocal** scale, marked **CI**. The numbers marked on it are the sequences of digits in the reciprocals of the numbers aligned with them on the C scale. Thus the CI scale may be used in multiplication to replace division with the C scale. There is sometimes a similar reciprocal scale, **CIF**, with the folded scale CF.

Often included is a scale, marked **L**, which is simply a linear scale such as on page 5 or on an ordinary ruler. Since D is a logarithmic scale, any number on the D scale aligns with the mantissa of its logarithm on the L scale.

ILLUSTRATION 2.   Aligned with 2 on the D scale is 301 on the L scale, reflecting the fact that $\log 2 = 0.3010$.

Nearly all slide rules include scales, marked **A** and **B**, which are logarithmic scales with cycles half as long as on the C and D scales. Since $2 \log N = \log N^2$, this means that aligned with any number N on the D scale is N^2 on the A scale. (If, as on many slide rules, these two scales are on opposite sides then the hair line may be used to correlate them.) Aligned with any number M on the A scale is $\sqrt{M}$ on the D scale. However, here one must be careful to choose the proper half, left or right, of the A scale, just as in choosing the proper column, $\sqrt{N}$ or $\sqrt{10N}$, in a table of square roots (Table I). This may be done easily by rounding off M and computing approximate square roots.

ILLUSTRATION 3.   Opposite 4 on the left half of the A scale is 2 on the D scale; $\sqrt{4} = 2$. Opposite 4 on the right half of the A scale is 632 on the D scale; $\sqrt{40} = 6.32$ and $\sqrt{0.4} = 0.632$.

Sometimes there is also a **K** scale, which can be used with the D scale to find cubes and cube roots just as the A scale is used to find squares and square roots.

Some slide rules include scales, usually marked **LL**, which are useful in finding other powers and roots, based on the relationship

$$\log M^p = p \log M; \qquad \qquad (2)$$
$$\log (\log M^p) = \log p + \log (\log M). \qquad (3)$$

The multiplication indicated in (2) is performed by slide rule; thus (3) replaces formula (1) of § A-1. In most cases these log log scales are referenced to the C scales, but the student should test some known powers to be sure. To use these LL scales, locate M on the LL scale, set opposite it 1 on the C scale, and locate p on the C scale. Opposite it on the LL scale is the sequence of digits in M^p.

Similarly,

$$\log \sqrt[p]{M} = \log M^{\frac{1}{p}} = \frac{\log M}{p}.$$

Locate M on the LL scale and set opposite it p on the C scale. Then opposite 1 on the C scale, find on the LL scale the sequence of digits in $\sqrt[p]{M}$.

Appropriate positive or negative powers of 10 may be factored out before using the slide rule, as was done in § 3-2 for tables.

EXERCISES

Compute by slide rule, to the accuracy possible on a slide rule except where otherwise instructed:

1. $(260)^2$.   **4.** $(0.681)^2$.   **7.** $\sqrt{4720}$.   **10.** $\sqrt[3]{936}$.

2. $(2.6)^2$.   **5.** $\sqrt{4.72}$.   **8.** $\sqrt{0.396}$.   **11.** $1/4380$.

3. $(0.0438)^2$.   **6.** $\sqrt{3.96}$.   **9.** $\sqrt[3]{93.6}$.   **12.** $1/0.0784$.

13—26. Exercises 13 through 26 of § 3-2.

27—47. Exercises 7 through 27 of § 3-8.

48—53. Exercises 38 through 43 of § 1-9.

54—76. Exercises 24 through 46 of § 6-7.

77—98. Exercises 7 through 28 of § 6-8.

99—102. Exercises 35 through 38 of § 3-2.

103—106. Miscellaneous Exercises 23 through 26 of § 6-10.

107—108. Exercises 23 and 24 of § 6-9.

109. Find $\log (\log 3)$.

110. Exercise 26 of § 6-9.

A-4 Trigonometry by Slide Rule

Most slide rules include scales plotted according to the logarithms of the trigonometric functions. These are usually located on the back side of the slide, which can be pulled out and reversed if necessary. The arrangement varies from one slide rule to another. The following description is typical; whether it applies to a particular slide rule can be checked by testing some known values such as $\sin 90° = 1$, $\sin 30° = 0.5$, $\tan 45° = 1$, $\tan 30° = 0.577$.

On the scale labeled **S** are marked values of angles, at distances proportional to the logarithms of the sines of the angles. Associated with this is one of the ordinary scales—D on most slide rules, A on some others. In a particular case, the scale to be used can be determined by testing as discussed in the previous paragraph.

Two uses of the S scale are evident. Firstly, by comparing the S scale and the ordinary scale, related so that $\sin 90° = 1$, values of the sine can be read off just as from a table (though usually to fewer digits). For instance, $\sin 45° = 0.707$. Secondly, multiplications and divisions involving sines can be performed just as with numbers (§ A-1 and § A-2) except that the operations must be so arranged that the sines are always located on the movable scale if that is where the S scale lies. If necessary set the ends on the fixed and movable scales opposite each other to shift from the fixed scale onto the movable scale or vice versa.

EXAMPLE.   Find $6.80 \sin 21° 36'$.

Solution.   Locate 68 on the appropriate fixed scale (Figure A.4). Opposite this location set 1 on the movable scale; that is, 90° on the S scale. Note* that

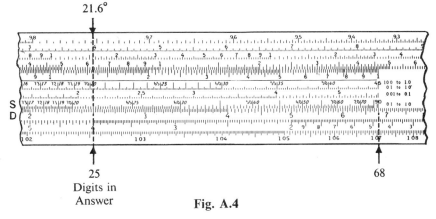

Fig. A.4

* On some slide rules, trigonometric scales are marked in 10′ (that is, $\frac{1}{6}°$) intervals instead of 6′ (0.1°) intervals as assumed in this statement.

$21° 36' = 21.6°$; set the hair line at $21.6°$ on the S scale. Opposite this on the fixed scale is the sequence of digits in the answer, 25. The decimal point is located by approximate computation: $\sin 21.6°$ is a little less than $\frac{1}{2}$, so the answer is 2.50.

One cycle of a logarithmic scale only handles sines from 1 to 0.1, that is, for angles from 90° to about 6°. Smaller angles involve going to another cycle. In another cycle the sequence of digits in the *function* $\sin \theta$ is the same as in this cycle, with the decimal point moved, but the *angles* do not bear such a simple relationship in successive cycles and so are usually marked on another scale labeled **ST**. It may also be con- venient to keep in mind the approximation for angles near 0 (see Exercise 45 of § 7-3):

$$\sin \theta \approx \theta \approx \tan \theta \quad \text{when } \theta \text{ is in radians and near 0.} \quad (4)$$

Cosines are replaced by sines through the relationship

$$\cos \theta = \sin (90° - \theta).$$

Sometimes these complementary angles are shown in red or in italics on the sine, S, scale.

Tangents are provided by another scale, labeled **T**, and used (like sines) with the appropriate ordinary scale. For very small angles, (4) shows that the ST scale may be used for tangents as well as sines. For angles larger than 45°, and for cotangents, use the relationship

$$\tan \theta = \operatorname{ctn} (90° - \theta) = \frac{1}{\tan (90° - \theta)}.$$

EXERCISES

Read from a slide rule:

1. $\sin 41°$.

2. $\sin 68°$.

3. $\sin 3.8°$.

4. $\sin 2.5°$.

5. (a) $\tan 25°$; (b) $\tan 62° 20'$.

6. (a) $\tan 17° 8'$; (b) $\tan 59°$.

7. (a) $\cos 28°$; (b) $\cos 68°$.

8. (a) $\operatorname{ctn} 32°$; (b) $\operatorname{ctn} 71°$.

By slide rule, find θ if it satisfies the relationship in:

9—26. Exercises 19 through 36 of § 7-3.

Compute by slide rule:*

27—30. Exercises 41 through 44 of § 7-3.

31—56. Exercises 1 through 26 of § 9-1.

57—63. Exercises 1 through 7 of § 9-2.

* For additional exercises, those in later sections of Chapter 9 can be used.

TABLES

N	N^2	$\sqrt{N}$	$\sqrt{10N}$	N^3	$\sqrt[3]{N}$	$\sqrt[3]{10N}$	$\sqrt[3]{100N}$	$1/N$
1	1	1.0 00	3.1 62	1	1.0 00	2.1 54	4.6 42	1.00 00
2	4	1.4 14	4.4 72	8	1.2 60	2.7 14	5.8 48	.500 00
3	9	1.7 32	5.4 77	27	1.4 42	3.1 07	6.6 94	.333 33
4	16	2.0 00	6.3 25	64	1.5 87	3.4 20	7.3 68	.250 00
5	25	2.2 36	7.0 71	125	1.7 10	3.6 84	7.9 37	.200 00
6	36	2.4 49	7.7 46	216	1.8 17	3.9 15	8.4 34	.166 67
7	49	2.6 46	8.3 67	343	1.9 13	4.1 21	8.8 79	.142 86
8	64	2.8 28	8.9 44	512	2.0 00	4.3 09	9.2 83	.125 00
9	81	3.0 00	9.4 87	729	2.0 80	4.4 81	9.6 55	.111 11
10	100	3.1 62	10.0 00	1 000	2.1 54	4.6 42	10.0 00	.100 00
11	121	3.3 17	10.4 88	1 331	2.2 24	4.7 91	10.3 23	.090 91
12	144	3.4 64	10.9 54	1 728	2.2 89	4.9 32	10.6 27	.083 33
13	169	3.6 06	11.4 02	2 197	2.3 51	5.0 66	10.9 14	.076 92
14	196	3.7 42	11.8 32	2 744	2.4 10	5.1 92	11.1 87	.071 43
15	225	3.8 73	12.2 47	3 375	2.4 66	5.3 13	11.4 47	.066 67
16	256	4.0 00	12.6 49	4 096	2.5 20	5.4 29	11.6 96	.062 50
17	289	4.1 23	13.0 38	4 913	2.5 71	5.5 40	11.9 35	.058 82
18	324	4.2 43	13.4 16	5 832	2.6 21	5.6 46	12.1 64	.055 56
19	361	4.3 59	13.7 84	6 859	2.6 68	5.7 49	12.3 86	.052 63
20	400	4.4 72	14.1 42	8 000	2.7 14	5.8 48	12.5 99	.050 00
21	441	4.5 83	14.4 91	9 261	2.7 59	5.9 44	12.8 06	.047 62
22	484	4.6 90	14.8 32	10 648	2.8 02	6.0 37	13.0 06	.045 45
23	529	4.7 96	15.1 66	12 167	2.8 44	6.1 27	13.2 00	.043 48
24	576	4.8 99	15.4 92	13 824	2.8 84	6.2 14	13.3 89	.041 67
25	625	5.0 00	15.8 11	15 625	2.9 24	6.3 00	13.5 72	.040 00
26	676	5.0 99	16.1 25	17 576	2.9 62	6.3 83	13.7 51	.038 46
27	729	5.1 96	16.4 32	19 683	3.0 00	6.4 63	13.9 25	.037 04
28	784	5.2 92	16.7 33	21 952	3.0 37	6.5 42	14.0 95	.035 71
29	841	5.3 85	17.0 29	24 389	3.0 72	6.6 19	14.2 60	.034 48
30	900	5.4 77	17.3 21	27 000	3.1 07	6.6 94	14.4 22	.033 33
31	961	5.5 68	17.6 07	29 791	3.1 41	6.7 68	14.5 81	.032 26
32	1 024	5.6 57	17.8 89	32 768	3.1 75	6.8 40	14.7 36	.031 25
33	1 089	5.7 45	18.1 66	35 937	3.2 08	6.9 10	14.8 88	.030 30
34	1 156	5.8 31	18.4 39	39 304	3.2 40	6.9 80	15.0 37	.029 41
35	1 225	5.9 16	18.7 08	42 875	3.2 71	7.0 47	15.1 83	.028 57
36	1 296	6.0 00	18.9 74	46 656	3.3 02	7.1 14	15.3 26	.027 78
37	1 369	6.0 83	19.2 35	50 653	3.3 32	7.1 79	15.4 67	.027 03
38	1 444	6.1 64	19.4 94	54 872	3.3 62	7.2 43	15.6 05	.026 32
39	1 521	6.2 45	19.7 48	59 319	3.3 91	7.3 06	15.7 41	.025 64
40	1 600	6.3 25	20.0 00	64 000	3.4 20	7.3 68	15.8 74	.025 00
41	1 681	6.4 03	20.2 48	68 921	3.4 48	7.4 29	16.0 05	.024 39
42	1 764	6.4 81	20.4 94	74 088	3.4 76	7.4 89	16.1 34	.023 81
43	1 849	6.5 57	20.7 36	79 507	3.5 03	7.5 48	16.2 61	.023 26
44	1 936	6.6 33	20.9 76	85 184	3.5 30	7.6 06	16.3 86	.022 73
45	2 025	6.7 08	21.2 13	91 125	3.5 57	7.6 63	16.5 10	.022 22
46	2 116	6.7 82	21.4 48	97 336	3.5 83	7.7 19	16.6 31	.021 74
47	2 209	6.8 56	21.6 79	103 823	3.6 09	7.7 75	16.7 51	.021 28
48	2 304	6.9 28	21.9 09	110 592	3.6 34	7.8 30	16.8 69	.020 83
49	2 401	7.0 00	22.1 36	117 649	3.6 59	7.8 84	16.9 85	.020 41
50	2 500	7.0 71	22.3 61	125 000	3.6 84	7.9 37	17.1 00	.020 00
N	N^2	$\sqrt{N}$	$\sqrt{10N}$	N^3	$\sqrt[3]{N}$	$\sqrt[3]{10N}$	$\sqrt[3]{100N}$	$1/N$

N	N^2	$\sqrt{N}$	$\sqrt{10N}$	N^3	$\sqrt[3]{N}$	$\sqrt[3]{10N}$	$\sqrt[3]{100N}$	$1/N$
51	2 601	7.1 41	22.5 83	132 651	3.7 08	7.9 90	17.2 13	.019 61
52	2 704	7.2 11	22.8 04	140 608	3.7 33	8.0 41	17.3 25	.019 23
53	2 809	7.2 80	23.0 22	148 877	3.7 56	8.0 93	17.4 35	.018 87
54	2 916	7.3 48	23.2 38	157 464	3.7 80	8.1 43	17.5 44	.018 52
55	3 025	7.4 16	23.4 52	166 375	3.8 03	8.1 93	17.6 52	.018 18
56	3 136	7.4 83	23.6 64	175 616	3.8 26	8.2 43	17.7 58	.017 86
57	3 249	7.5 50	23.8 75	185 193	3.8 49	8.2 91	17.8 63	.017 54
58	3 364	7.6 16	24.0 83	195 112	3.8 71	8.3 40	17.9 67	.017 24
59	3 481	7.6 81	24.2 90	205 379	3.8 93	8.3 87	18.0 70	.016 95
60	3 600	7.7 46	24.4 95	216 000	3.9 15	8.4 34	18.1 71	.016 67
61	3 721	7.8 10	24.6 98	226 981	3.9 36	8.4 81	18.2 72	.016 39
62	3 844	7.8 74	24.9 00	238 328	3.9 58	8.5 27	18.3 71	.016 13
63	3 969	7.9 37	25.1 00	250 047	3.9 79	8.5 73	18.4 69	.015 87
64	4 096	8.0 00	25.2 98	262 144	4.0 00	8.6 18	18.5 66	.015 62
65	4 225	8.0 62	25.4 95	274 625	4.0 21	8.6 62	18.6 63	.015 38
66	4 356	8.1 24	25.6 90	287 496	4.0 41	8.7 07	18.7 58	.015 15
67	4 489	8.1 85	25.8 84	300 763	4.0 62	8.7 50	18.8 52	.014 93
68	4 624	8.2 46	26.0 77	314 432	4.0 82	8.7 94	18.9 45	.014 71
69	4 761	8.3 07	26.2 68	328 509	4.1 02	8.8 37	19.0 38	.014 49
70	4 900	8.3 67	26.4 58	343 000	4.1 21	8.8 79	19.1 29	.014 29
71	5 041	8.4 26	26.6 46	357 911	4.1 41	8.9 21	19.2 20	.014 08
72	5 184	8.4 85	26.8 33	373 248	4.1 60	8.9 63	19.3 10	.013 89
73	5 329	8.5 44	27.0 19	389 017	4.1 79	9.0 04	19.3 99	.013 70
74	5 476	8.6 02	27.2 03	405 224	4.1 98	9.0 45	19.4 87	.013 51
75	5 625	8.6 60	27.3 86	421 875	4.2 17	9.0 86	19.5 74	.013 33
76	5 776	8.7 18	27.5 68	438 976	4.2 36	9.1 26	19.6 61	.013 16
77	5 929	8.7 75	27.7 49	456 533	4.2 54	9.1 66	19.7 47	.012 99
78	6 084	8.8 32	27.9 28	474 552	4.2 73	9.2 05	19.8 32	.012 82
79	6 241	8.8 88	28 1 07	493 039	4.2 91	9.2 44	19.9 16	.012 66
80	6 400	8.9 44	28.2 84	512 000	4.3 09	9.2 83	20.0 00	.012 50
81	6 561	9.0 00	28.4 60	531 441	4.3 27	9.3 22	20.0 83	.012 35
82	6 724	9.0 55	28.6 36	551 368	4.3 44	9.3 60	20.1 65	.012 20
83	6 889	9.1 10	28.8 10	571 787	4.3 62	9.3 98	20.2 47	.012 05
84	7 056	9.1 65	28.9 83	592 704	4.3 80	9.4 35	20.3 28	.011 90
85	7 225	9.2 20	29.1 55	614 125	4.3 97	9.4 73	20.4 08	.011 76
86	7 396	9.2 74	29.3 26	636 056	4.4 14	9.5 10	20.4 88	.011 63
87	7 569	9.3 27	29.4 96	658 503	4.4 31	9.5 46	20.5 67	.011 49
88	7 744	9.3 81	29.6 65	681 472	4.4 48	9.5 83	20.6 46	.011 36
89	7 921	9.4 34	29.8 33	704 969	4.4 65	9.6 19	20.7 24	.011 24
90	8 100	9.4 87	30.0 00	729 000	4.4 81	9.6 55	20.8 01	.011 11
91	8 281	9.5 39	30.1 66	753 571	4.4 98	9.6 91	20.8 78	.010 99
92	8 464	9.5 92	30.3 32	778 688	4.5 14	9.7 26	20.9 54	.010 87
93	8 649	9.6 44	30.4 96	804 357	4.5 31	9.7 61	21.0 29	.010 75
94	8 836	9.6 95	30.6 59	830 584	4.5 47	9.7 96	21.1 05	.010 64
95	9 025	9.7 47	30.8 22	857 375	4.5 63	9.8 30	21.1 79	.010 53
96	9 216	9.7 98	30.9 84	884 736	4.5 79	9.8 65	21.2 53	.010 42
97	9 409	9.8 49	31.1 45	912 673	4.5 95	9.8 99	21.3 27	.010 31
98	9 604	9.8 99	31.3 05	941 192	4.6 10	9.9 33	21.4 00	.010 20
99	9 801	9.9 50	31.4 64	970 299	4.6 26	9.9 67	21.4 72	.010 10
100	10 000	10.0 00	31.6 23	1 000 000	4.6 42	10.0 00	21.5 44	.010 00
N	N^2	$\sqrt{N}$	$\sqrt{10N}$	N^3	$\sqrt[3]{N}$	$\sqrt[3]{10N}$	$\sqrt[3]{100N}$	$1/N$

N	0	1	2	3	4	5	6	7	8	9
10	.0000	.0043	.0086	.0128	.0170	.0212	.0253	.0294	.0334	.0374
11	.0414	.0453	.0492	.0531	.0569	.0607	.0645	.0682	.0719	.0755
12	.0792	.0828	.0864	.0899	.0934	.0969	.1004	.1038	.1072	.1106
13	.1139	.1173	.1206	.1239	.1271	.1303	.1335	.1367	.1399	.1430
14	.1461	.1492	.1523	.1553	.1584	.1614	.1644	.1673	.1703	.1732
15	.1761	.1790	.1818	.1847	.1875	.1903	.1931	.1959	.1987	.2014
16	.2041	.2068	.2095	.2122	.2148	.2175	.2201	.2227	.2253	.2279
17	.2304	.2330	.2355	.2380	.2405	.2430	.2455	.2480	.2504	.2529
18	.2553	.2577	.2601	.2625	.2648	.2672	.2695	.2718	.2742	.2765
19	.2788	.2810	.2833	.2856	.2878	.2900	.2923	.2945	.2967	.2989
20	.3010	.3032	.3054	.3075	.3096	.3118	.3139	.3160	.3181	.3201
21	.3222	.3243	.3263	.3284	.3304	.3324	.3345	.3365	.3385	.3404
22	.3424	.3444	.3464	.3483	.3502	.3522	.3541	.3560	.3579	.3598
23	.3617	.3636	.3655	.3674	.3692	.3711	.3729	.3747	.3766	.3784
24	.3802	.3820	.3838	.3856	.3874	.3892	.3909	.3927	.3945	.3962
25	.3979	.3997	.4014	.4031	.4048	.4065	.4082	.4099	.4116	.4133
26	.4150	.4166	.4183	.4200	.4216	.4232	.4249	.4265	.4281	.4298
27	.4314	.4330	.4346	.4362	.4378	.4393	.4409	.4425	.4440	.4456
28	.4472	.4487	.4502	.4518	.4533	.4548	.4564	.4579	.4594	.4609
29	.4624	.4639	.4654	.4669	.4683	.4698	.4713	.4728	.4742	.4757
30	.4771	.4786	.4800	.4814	.4829	.4843	.4857	.4871	.4886	.4900
31	.4914	.4928	.4942	.4955	.4969	.4983	.4997	.5011	.5024	.5038
32	.5051	.5065	.5079	.5092	.5105	.5119	.5132	.5145	.5159	.5172
33	.5185	.5198	.5211	.5224	.5237	.5250	.5263	.5276	.5289	.5302
34	.5315	.5328	.5340	.5353	.5366	.5378	.5391	.5403	.5416	.5428
35	.5441	.5453	.5465	.5478	.5490	.5502	.5514	.5527	.5539	.5551
36	.5563	.5575	.5587	.5599	.5611	.5623	.5635	.5647	.5658	.5670
37	.5682	.5694	.5705	.5717	.5729	.5740	.5752	.5763	.5775	.5786
38	.5798	.5809	.5821	.5832	.5843	.5855	.5866	.5877	.5888	.5899
39	.5911	.5922	.5933	.5944	.5955	.5966	.5977	.5988	.5999	.6010
40	.6021	.6031	.6042	.6053	.6064	.6075	.6085	.6096	.6107	.6117
41	.6128	.6138	.6149	.6160	.6170	.6180	.6191	.6201	.6212	.6222
42	.6232	.6243	.6253	.6263	.6274	.6284	.6294	.6304	.6314	.6325
43	.6335	.6345	.6355	.6365	.6375	.6385	.6395	.6405	.6415	.6425
44	.6435	.6444	.6454	.6464	.6474	.6484	.6493	.6503	.6513	.6522
45	.6532	.6542	.6551	.6561	.6571	.6580	.6590	.6599	.6609	.6618
46	.6628	.6637	.6646	.6656	.6665	.6675	.6684	.6693	.6702	.6712
47	.6721	.6730	.6739	.6749	.6758	.6767	.6776	.6785	.6794	.6803
48	.6812	.6821	.6830	.6839	.6848	.6857	.6866	.6875	.6884	.6893
49	.6902	.6911	.6920	.6928	.6937	.6946	.6955	.6964	.6972	.6981
50	.6990	.6998	.7007	.7016	.7024	.7033	.7042	.7050	.7059	.7067
51	.7076	.7084	.7093	.7101	.7110	.7118	.7126	.7135	.7143	.7152
52	.7160	.7168	.7177	.7185	.7193	.7202	.7210	.7218	.7226	.7235
53	.7243	.7251	.7259	.7267	.7275	.7284	.7292	.7300	.7308	.7316
54	.7324	.7332	.7340	.7348	.7356	.7364	.7372	.7380	.7388	.7396
N	0	1	2	3	4	5	6	7	8	9

N	0	1	2	3	4	5	6	7	8	9
55	.7404	.7412	.7419	.7427	.7435	.7443	.7451	.7459	.7466	.7474
56	.7482	.7490	.7497	.7505	.7513	.7520	.7528	.7536	.7543	.7551
57	.7559	.7566	.7574	.7582	.7589	.7597	.7604	.7612	.7619	.7627
58	.7634	.7642	.7649	.7657	.7664	.7672	.7679	.7686	.7694	.7701
59	.7709	.7716	.7723	.7731	.7738	.7745	.7752	.7760	.7767	.7774
60	.7782	.7789	.7796	.7803	.7810	.7818	.7825	.7832	.7839	.7846
61	.7853	.7860	.7868	.7875	.7882	.7889	.7896	.7903	.7910	.7917
62	.7924	.7931	.7938	.7945	.7952	.7959	.7966	.7973	.7980	.7987
63	.7993	.8000	.8007	.8014	.8021	.8028	.8035	.8041	.8048	.8055
64	.8062	.8069	.8075	.8082	.8089	.8096	.8102	.8109	.8116	.8122
65	.8129	.8136	.8142	.8149	.8156	.8162	.8169	.8176	.8182	.8189
66	.8195	.8202	.8209	.8215	.8222	.8228	.8235	.8241	.8248	.8254
67	.8261	.8267	.8274	.8280	.8287	.8293	.8299	.8306	.8312	.8319
68	.8325	.8331	.8338	.8344	.8351	.8357	.8363	.8370	.8376	.8382
69	.8388	.8395	.8401	.8407	.8414	.8420	.8426	.8432	.8439	.8445
70	.8451	.8457	.8463	.8470	.8476	.8482	.8488	.8494	.8500	.8506
71	.8513	.8519	.8525	.8531	.8537	.8543	.8549	.8555	.8561	.8567
72	.8573	.8579	.8585	.8591	.8597	.8603	.8609	.8615	.8621	.8627
73	.8633	.8639	.8645	.8651	.8657	.8663	.8669	.8675	.8681	.8686
74	.8692	.8698	.8704	.8710	.8716	.8722	.8727	.8733	.8739	.8745
75	.8751	.8756	.8762	.8768	.8774	.8779	.8785	.8791	.8797	.8802
76	.8808	.8814	.8820	.8825	.8831	.8837	.8842	.8848	.8854	.8859
77	.8865	.8871	.8876	.8882	.8887	.8893	.8899	.8904	.8910	.8915
78	.8921	.8927	.8932	.8938	.8943	.8949	.8954	.8960	.8965	.8971
79	.8976	.8982	.8987	.8993	.8998	.9004	.9009	.9015	.9020	.9025
80	.9031	.9036	.9042	.9047	.9053	.9058	.9063	.9069	.9074	.9079
81	.9085	.9090	.9096	.9101	.9106	.9112	.9117	.9122	.9128	.9133
82	.9138	.9143	.9149	.9154	.9159	.9165	.9170	.9175	.9180	.9186
83	.9191	.9196	.9201	.9206	.9212	.9217	.9222	.9227	.9232	.9238
84	.9243	.9248	.9253	.9258	.9263	.9269	.9274	.9279	.9284	.9289
85	.9294	.9299	.9304	.9309	.9315	.9320	.9325	.9330	.9335	.9340
86	.9345	.9350	.9355	.9360	.9365	.9370	.9375	.9380	.9385	.9390
87	.9395	.9400	.9405	.9410	.9415	.9420	.9425	.9430	.9435	.9440
88	.9445	.9450	.9455	.9460	.9465	.9469	.9474	.9479	.9484	.9489
89	.9494	.9499	.9504	.9509	.9513	.9518	.9523	.9528	.9533	.9538
90	.9542	.9547	.9552	.9557	.9562	.9566	.9571	.9576	.9581	.9586
91	.9590	.9595	.9600	.9605	.9609	.9614	.9619	.9624	.9628	.9633
92	.9638	.9643	.9647	.9652	.9657	.9661	.9666	.9671	.9675	.9680
93	.9685	.9689	.9694	.9699	.9703	.9708	.9713	.9717	.9722	.9727
94	.9731	.9736	.9741	.9745	.9750	.9754	.9759	.9763	.9768	.9773
95	.9777	.9782	.9786	.9791	.9795	.9800	.9805	.9809	.9814	.9818
96	.9823	.9827	.9832	.9836	.9841	.9845	.9850	.9854	.9859	.9863
97	.9868	.9872	.9877	.9881	.9886	.9890	.9894	.9899	.9903	.9908
98	.9912	.9917	.9921	.9926	.9930	.9934	.9939	.9943	.9948	.9952
99	.9956	.9961	.9965	.9969	.9974	.9978	.9983	.9987	.9991	.9996
N	0	1	2	3	4	5	6	7	8	9

The characteristic of each logarithm on this page ends with −10.

′	0° log sin	0° log tan	1° log sin	1° log tan	2° log sin	2° log tan	3° log sin	3° log tan	
0	—	—	8.2419	8.2419	8.5428	8.5431	8.7188	8.7194	60
1	6.4637	6.4637	8.2490	8.2491	8.5464	8.5467	8.7212	8.7218	59
2	6.7648	6.7648	8.2561	8.2562	8.5500	8.5503	8.7236	8.7242	58
3	6.9408	6.9408	8.2630	8.2631	8.5535	8.5538	8.7260	8.7266	57
4	7.0658	7.0658	8.2699	8.2700	8.5571	8.5573	8.7283	8.7290	56
5	7.1627	7.1627	8.2766	8.2767	8.5605	8.5608	8.7307	8.7313	55
6	7.2419	7.2419	8.2832	8.2833	8.5640	8.5643	8.7330	8.7337	54
7	7.3088	7.3088	8.2898	8.2899	8.5674	8.5677	8.7354	8.7360	53
8	7.3668	7.3668	8.2962	8.2963	8.5708	8.5711	8.7377	8.7383	52
9	7.4180	7.4180	8.3025	8.3026	8.5742	8.5745	8.7400	8.7406	51
10	7.4637	7.4637	8.3088	8.3089	8.5776	8.5779	8.7423	8.7429	50
11	7.5051	7.5051	8.3150	8.3150	8.5809	8.5812	8.7445	8.7452	49
12	7.5429	7.5429	8.3210	8.3211	8.5842	8.5845	8.7468	8.7475	48
13	7.5777	7.5777	8.3270	8.3271	8.5875	8.5878	8.7491	8.7497	47
14	7.6099	7.6099	8.3329	8.3330	8.5907	8.5911	8.7513	8.7520	46
15	7.6398	7.6398	8.3388	8.3389	8.5939	8.5943	8.7535	8.7542	45
16	7.6678	7.6678	8.3445	8.3446	8.5972	8.5975	8.7557	8.7565	44
17	7.6942	7.6942	8.3502	8.3503	8.6003	8.6007	8.7580	8.7587	43
18	7.7190	7.7190	8.3558	8.3559	8.6035	8.6038	8.7602	8.7609	42
19	7.7425	7.7425	8.3613	8.3614	8.6066	8.6070	8.7623	8.7631	41
20	7.7648	7.7648	8.3668	8.3669	8.6097	8.6101	8.7645	8.7652	40
21	7.7859	7.7860	8.3722	8.3723	8.6128	8.6132	8.7667	8.7674	39
22	7.8061	7.8062	8.3775	8.3776	8.6159	8.6163	8.7688	8.7696	38
23	7.8255	7.8255	8.3828	8.3829	8.6189	8.6193	8.7710	8.7717	37
24	7.8439	7.8439	8.3880	8.3881	8.6220	8.6223	8.7731	8.7739	36
25	7.8617	7.8617	8.3931	8.3932	8.6250	8.6254	8.7752	8.7760	35
26	7.8787	7.8787	8.3982	8.3983	8.6279	8.6283	8.7773	8.7781	34
27	7.8951	7.8951	8.4032	8.4033	8.6309	8.6313	8.7794	8.7802	33
28	7.9109	7.9109	8.4082	8.4083	8.6339	8.6343	8.7815	8.7823	32
29	7.9261	7.9261	8.4131	8.4132	8.6368	8.6372	8.7836	8.7844	31
30	7.9408	7.9409	8.4179	8.4181	8.6397	8.6401	8.7857	8.7865	30
31	7.9551	7.9551	8.4227	8.4229	8.6426	8.6430	8.7877	8.7886	29
32	7.9689	7.9689	8.4275	8.4276	8.6454	8.6459	8.7898	8.7906	28
33	7.9822	7.9823	8.4322	8.4323	8.6483	8.6487	8.7918	8.7927	27
34	7.9952	7.9952	8.4368	8.4370	8.6511	8.6515	8.7939	8.7947	26
35	8.0078	8.0078	8.4414	8.4416	8.6539	8.6544	8.7959	8.7967	25
36	8.0200	8.0200	8.4459	8.4461	8.6567	8.6571	8.7979	8.7988	24
37	8.0319	8.0319	8.4504	8.4506	8.6595	8.6599	8.7999	8.8008	23
38	8.0435	8.0435	8.4549	8.4551	8.6622	8.6627	8.8019	8.8028	22
39	8.0548	8.0548	8.4593	8.4595	8.6650	8.6654	8.8039	8.8048	21
40	8.0658	8.0658	8.4637	8.4638	8.6677	8.6682	8.8059	8.8067	20
41	8.0765	8.0765	8.4680	8.4682	8.6704	8.6709	8.8078	8.8087	19
42	8.0870	8.0870	8.4723	8.4725	8.6731	8.6736	8.8098	8.8107	18
43	8.0972	8.0972	8.4765	8.4767	8.6758	8.6762	8.8117	8.8126	17
44	8.1072	8.1072	8.4807	8.4809	8.6784	8.6789	8.8137	8.8146	16
45	8.1169	8.1170	8.4848	8.4851	8.6810	8.6815	8.8156	8.8165	15
46	8.1265	8.1265	8.4890	8.4892	8.6837	8.6842	8.8175	8.8185	14
47	8.1358	8.1359	8.4930	8.4933	8.6863	8.6868	8.8194	8.8204	13
48	8.1450	8.1450	8.4971	8.4973	8.6889	8.6894	8.8213	8.8223	12
49	8.1539	8.1540	8.5011	8.5013	8.6914	8.6920	8.8232	8.8242	11
50	8.1627	8.1627	8.5050	8.5053	8.6940	8.6945	8.8251	8.8261	10
51	8.1713	8.1713	8.5090	8.5092	8.6965	8.6971	8.8270	8.8280	9
52	8.1797	8.1798	8.5129	8.5131	8.6991	8.6996	8.8289	8.8299	8
53	8.1880	8.1880	8.5167	8.5170	8.7016	8.7021	8.8307	8.8317	7
54	8.1961	8.1962	8.5206	8.5208	8.7041	8.7046	8.8326	8.8336	6
55	8.2041	8.2041	8.5243	8.5246	8.7066	8.7071	8.8345	8.8355	5
56	8.2119	8.2120	8.5281	8.5283	8.7090	8.7096	8.8363	8.8373	4
57	8.2196	8.2196	8.5318	8.5321	8.7115	8.7121	8.8381	8.8392	3
58	8.2271	8.2272	8.5355	8.5358	8.7140	8.7145	8.8400	8.8410	2
59	8.2346	8.2346	8.5392	8.5394	8.7164	8.7170	8.8418	8.8428	1
60	8.2419	8.2419	8.5428	8.5431	8.7188	8.7194	8.8436	8.8446	0
	log cos	log ctn	log cos	log ctn	log cos	log ctn	log cos	log ctn	
	89°		88°		87°		86°		′

Angle	log sin	log cos	log tan	log ctn	
0° 0′	—	0.0000	—	—	90° 0′
0° 10′	7.4637–10	0.0000	7.4637–10	2.5363	89° 50′
0° 20′	7.7648–10	0.0000	7.7648–10	2.2352	89° 40′
0° 30′	7.9408–10	0.0000	7.9409–10	2.0591	89° 30′
0° 40′	8.0658–10	0.0000	8.0658–10	1.9342	89° 20′
0° 50′	8.1627–10	0.0000	8.1627–10	1.8373	89° 10′
1° 0′	8.2419–10	9.9999–10	8.2419–10	1.7581	89° 0′
1° 10′	8.3088–10	9.9999–10	8.3089–10	1.6911	88° 50′
1° 20′	8.3668–10	9.9999–10	8.3669–10	1.6331	88° 40′
1° 30′	8.4179–10	9.9999–10	8.4181–10	1.5819	88° 30′
1° 40′	8.4637–10	9.9998–10	8.4638–10	1.5362	88° 20′
1° 50′	8.5050–10	9.9998–10	8.5053–10	1.4947	88° 10′
2° 0′	8.5428–10	9.9997–10	8.5431–10	1.4569	88° 0′
2° 10′	8.5776–10	9.9997–10	8.5779–10	1.4221	87° 50′
2° 20′	8.6097–10	9.9996–10	8.6101–10	1.3899	87° 40′
2° 30′	8.6397–10	9.9996–10	8.6401–10	1.3599	87° 30′
2° 40′	8.6677–10	9.9995–10	8.6682–10	1.3318	87° 20′
2° 50′	8.6940–10	9.9995–10	8.6945–10	1.3055	87° 10′
3° 0′	8.7188–10	9.9994–10	8.7194–10	1.2806	87° 0′
3° 10′	8.7423–10	9.9993–10	8.7429–10	1.2571	86° 50′
3° 20′	8.7645–10	9.9993–10	8.7652–10	1.2348	86° 40′
3° 30′	8.7857–10	9.9992–10	8.7865–10	1.2135	86° 30′
3° 40′	8.8059–10	9.9991–10	8.8067–10	1.1933	86° 20′
3° 50′	8.8251–10	9.9990–10	8.8261–10	1.1739	86° 10′
4° 0′	8.8436–10	9.9989–10	8.8446–10	1.1554	86° 0′
4° 10′	8.8613–10	9.9989–10	8.8624–10	1.1376	85° 50′
4° 20′	8.8783–10	9.9988–10	8.8795–10	1.1205	85° 40′
4° 30′	8.8946–10	9.9987–10	8.8960–10	1.1040	85° 30′
4° 40′	8.9104–10	9.9986–10	8.9118–10	1.0882	85° 20′
4° 50′	8.9256–10	9.9985–10	8.9272–10	1.0728	85° 10′
5° 0′	8.9403–10	9.9983–10	8.9420–10	1.0580	85° 0′
5° 10′	8.9545–10	9.9982–10	8.9563–10	1.0437	84° 50′
5° 20′	8.9682–10	9.9981–10	8.9701–10	1.0299	84° 40′
5° 30′	8.9816–10	9.9980–10	8.9836–10	1.0164	84° 30′
5° 40′	8.9945–10	9.9979–10	8.9966–10	1.0034	84° 20′
5° 50′	9.0070–10	9.9977–10	9.0093–10	0.9907	84° 10′
6° 0′	9.0192–10	9.9976–10	9.0216–10	0.9784	84° 0′
6° 10′	9.0311–10	9.9975–10	9.0336–10	0.9664	83° 50′
6° 20′	9.0426–10	9.9973–10	9.0453–10	0.9547	83° 40′
6° 30′	9.0539–10	9.9972–10	9.0567–10	0.9433	83° 30′
6° 40′	9.0648–10	9.9971–10	9.0678–10	0.9322	83° 20′
6° 50′	9.0755–10	9.9969–10	9.0786–10	0.9214	83° 10′
7° 0′	9.0859–10	9.9968–10	9.0891–10	0.9109	83° 0′
7° 10′	9.0961–10	9.9966–10	9.0995–10	0.9005	82° 50′
7° 20′	9.1060–10	9.9964–10	9.1096–10	0.8904	82° 40′
7° 30′	9.1157–10	9.9963–10	9.1194–10	0.8806	82° 30′
7° 40′	9.1252–10	9.9961–10	9.1291–10	0.8709	82° 20′
5° 50′	9.1345–10	9.9959–10	9.1385–10	0.8615	82° 10′
8° 0′	9.1436–10	9.9958–10	9.1478–10	0.8522	82° 0′
8° 10′	9.1525–10	9.9956–10	9.1569–10	0.8431	81° 50′
8° 20′	9.1612–10	9.9954–10	9.1658–10	0.8342	81° 40′
8° 30′	9.1697–10	9.9952–10	9.1745–10	0.8255	81° 30′
8° 40′	9.1781–10	9.9950–10	9.1831–10	0.8169	81° 20′
8° 50′	9.1863–10	9.9948–10	9.1915–10	0.8085	81° 10′
9° 0′	9.1943–10	9.9946–10	9.1997–10	0.8003	81° 0′
	log cos	log sin	log ctn	log tan	Angle

Angle	log sin	log cos	log tan	log ctn	
9° 0′	9.1943–10	9.9946–10	9.1997–10	0.8003	81° 0′
9° 10′	9.2022–10	9.9944–10	9.2078–10	0.7922	80° 50′
9° 20′	9.2100–10	9.9942–10	9.2158–10	0.7842	80° 40′
9° 30′	9.2176–10	9.9940–10	9.2236–10	0.7764	80° 30′
9° 40′	9.2251–10	9.9938–10	9.2313–10	0.7687	80° 20′
9° 50′	9.2324–10	9.9936–10	9.2389–10	0.7611	80° 10′
10° 0′	9.2397–10	9.9934–10	9.2463–10	0.7537	80° 0′
10° 10′	9.2468–10	9.9931–10	9.2536–10	0.7464	79° 50′
10° 20′	9.2538–10	9.9929–10	9.2609–10	0.7391	79° 40′
10° 30′	9.2606–10	9.9927–10	9.2680–10	0.7320	79° 30′
10° 40′	9.2674–10	9.9924–10	9.2750–10	0.7250	79° 20′
10° 50′	9.2740–10	9.9922–10	9.2819–10	0.7181	79° 10′
11° 0′	9.2806–10	9.9919–10	9.2887–10	0.7113	79° 0′
11° 10′	9.2870–10	9.9917–10	9.2953–10	0.7047	78° 50′
11° 20′	9.2934–10	9.9914–10	9.3020–10	0.6980	78° 40′
11° 30′	9.2997–10	9.9912–10	9.3085–10	0.6915	78° 30′
11° 40′	9.3058–10	9.9909–10	9.3149–10	0.6851	78° 20′
11° 50′	9.3119–10	9.9907–10	9.3212–10	0.6788	78° 10′
12° 0′	9.3179–10	9.9904–10	9.3275–10	0.6725	78° 0′
12° 10′	9.3238–10	9.9901–10	9.3336–10	0.6664	77° 50′
12° 20′	9.3296–10	9.9899–10	9.3397–10	0.6603	77° 40′
12° 30′	9.3353–10	9.9896–10	9.3458–10	0.6542	77° 30′
12° 40′	9.3410–10	9.9893–10	9.3517–10	0.6483	77° 20′
12° 50′	9.3466–10	9.9890–10	9.3576–10	0.6424	77° 10′
13° 0′	9.3521–10	9.9887–10	9.3634–10	0.6366	77° 0′
13° 10′	9.3575–10	9.9884–10	9.3691–10	0.6309	76° 50′
13° 20′	9.3629–10	9.9881–10	9.3748–10	0.6252	76° 40′
13° 30′	9.3682–10	9.9878–10	9.3804–10	0.6196	76° 30′
13° 40′	9.3734–10	9.9875–10	9.3859–10	0.6141	76° 20′
13° 50′	9.3786–10	9.9872–10	9.3914–10	0.6086	76° 10′
14° 0′	9.3837–10	9.9869–10	9.3968–10	0.6032	76° 0′
14° 10′	9.3887–10	9.9866–10	9.4021–10	0.5979	75° 50′
14° 20′	9.3937–10	9.9863–10	9.4074–10	0.5926	75° 40′
14° 30′	9.3986–10	9.9859–10	9.4127–10	0.5873	75° 30′
14° 40′	9.4035–10	9.9856–10	9.4178–10	0.5822	75° 20′
14° 50′	9.4083–10	9.9853–10	9.4230–10	0.5770	75° 10′
15° 0′	9.4130–10	9.9849–10	9.4281–10	0.5719	75° 0′
15° 10′	9.4177–10	9.9846–10	9.4331–10	0.5669	74° 50′
15° 20′	9.4223–10	9.9843–10	9.4381–10	0.5619	74° 40′
15° 30′	9.4269–10	9.9839–10	9.4430–10	0.5570	74° 30′
15° 40′	9.4314–10	9.9836–10	9.4479–10	0.5521	74° 20′
15° 50′	9.4359–10	9.9832–10	9.4527–10	0.5473	74° 10′
16° 0′	9.4403–10	9.9828–10	9.4575–10	0.5425	74° 0′
16° 10′	9.4447–10	9.9825–10	9.4622–10	0.5378	73° 50′
16° 20′	9.4491–10	9.9821–10	9.4669–10	0.5331	73° 40′
16° 30′	9.4533–10	9.9817–10	9.4716–10	0.5284	73° 30′
16° 40′	9.4576–10	9.9814–10	9.4762–10	0.5238	73° 20′
16° 50′	9.4618–10	9.9810–10	9.4808–10	0.5192	73° 10′
17° 0′	9.4659–10	9.9806–10	9.4853–10	0.5147	73° 0′
17° 10′	9.4700–10	9.9802–10	9.4898–10	0.5102	72° 50′
17° 20′	9.4741–10	9.9798–10	9.4943–10	0.5057	72° 40′
17° 30′	9.4781–10	9.9794–10	9.4987–10	0.5013	72° 30′
17° 40′	9.4821–10	9.9790–10	9.5031–10	0.4969	72° 20′
17° 50′	9.4861–10	9.9786–10	9.5075–10	0.4925	72° 10′
18° 0′	9.4900–10	9.9782–10	9.5118–10	0.4882	72° 0′
	log cos	log sin	log ctn	log tan	Angle

Angle	log sin	log cos	log tan	log ctn	
18° 0′	9.4900–10	9.9782–10	9.5118–10	0.4882	**72° 0′**
18° 10′	9.4939–10	9.9778–10	9.5161–10	0.4839	71° 50′
18° 20′	9.4977–10	9.9774–10	9.5203–10	0.4797	71° 40′
18° 30′	9.5015–10	9.9770–10	9.5245–10	0.4755	71° 30′
18° 40′	9.5052–10	9.9765–10	9.5287–10	0.4713	71° 20′
18° 50′	9.5090–10	9.9761–10	9.5329–10	0.4671	71° 10′
19° 0′	9.5126–10	9.9757–10	9.5370–10	0.4630	**71° 0′**
19° 10′	9.5163–10	9.9752–10	9.5411–10	0.4589	70° 50′
19° 20′	9.5199–10	9.9748–10	9.5451–10	0.4549	70° 40′
19° 30′	9.5235–10	9.9743–10	9.5491–10	0.4509	70° 30′
19° 40′	9.5270–10	9.9739–10	9.5531–10	0.4469	70° 20′
19° 50′	9.5306–10	9.9734–10	9.5571–10	0.4429	70° 10′
20° 0′	9.5341–10	9.9730–10	9.5611–10	0.4389	**70° 0′**
20° 10′	9.5375–10	9.9725–10	9.5650–10	0.4350	69° 50′
20° 20′	9.5409–10	9.9721–10	9.5689–10	0.4311	69° 40′
20° 30′	9.5443–10	9.9716–10	9.5727–10	0.4273	69° 30′
20° 40′	9.5477–10	9.9711–10	9.5766–10	0.4234	69° 20′
20° 50′	9.5510–10	9.9706–10	9.5804–10	0.4196	69° 10′
21° 0′	9.5543–10	9.9702–10	9.5842–10	0.4158	**69° 0′**
21° 10′	9.5576–10	9.9697–10	9.5879–10	0.4121	68° 50′
21° 20′	9.5609–10	9.9692–10	9.5917–10	0.4083	68° 40′
21° 30′	9.5641–10	9.9687–10	9.5954–10	0.4046	68° 30′
21° 40′	9.5673–10	9.9682–10	9.5991–10	0.4009	68° 20′
21° 50′	9.5704–10	9.9677–10	9.6028–10	0.3972	68° 10′
22° 0′	9.5736–10	9.9672–10	9.6064–10	0.3936	**68° 0′**
22° 10′	9.5767–10	9.9667–10	9.6100–10	0.3900	67° 50′
22° 20′	9.5798–10	9.9661–10	9.6136–10	0.3864	67° 40′
22° 30′	9.5828–10	9.9656–10	9.6172–10	0.3828	67° 30′
22° 40′	9.5859–10	9.9651–10	9.6208–10	0.3792	67° 20′
22° 50′	9.5889–10	9.9646–10	9.6243–10	0.3757	67° 10′
23° 0′	9.5919–10	9.9640–10	9.6279–10	0.3721	**67° 0′**
23° 10′	9.5948–10	9.9635–10	9.6314–10	0.3686	66° 50′
23° 20′	9.5978–10	9.9629–10	9.6348–10	0.3652	66° 40′
23° 30′	9.6007–10	9.9624–10	9.6383–10	0.3617	66° 30′
23° 40′	9.6036–10	9.9618–10	9.6417–10	0.3583	66° 20′
23° 50′	9.6065–10	9.9613–10	9.6452–10	0.3548	66° 10′
24° 0′	9.6093–10	9.9607–10	9.6486–10	0.3514	**66° 0′**
24° 10′	9.6121–10	9.9602–10	9.6520–10	0.3480	65° 50′
24° 20′	9.6149–10	9.9596–10	9.6553–10	0.3447	65° 40′
24° 30′	9.6177–10	9.9590–10	9.6587–10	0.3413	65° 30′
24° 40′	9.6205–10	9.9584–10	9.6620–10	0.3380	65° 20′
24° 50′	9.6232–10	9.9579–10	9.6654–10	0.3346	65° 10′
25° 0′	9.6259–10	9.9573–10	9.6687–10	0.3313	**65° 0′**
25° 10′	9.6286–10	9.9567–10	9.6720–10	0.3280	64° 50′
25° 20′	9.6313–10	9.9561–10	9.6752–10	0.3248	64° 40′
25° 30′	9.6340–10	9.9555–10	9.6785–10	0.3215	64° 30′
25° 40′	9.6366–10	9.9549–10	9.6817–10	0.3183	64° 20′
25° 50′	9.6392–10	9.9543–10	9.6850–10	0.3150	64° 10′
26° 0′	9.6418–10	9.9537–10	9.6882–10	0.3118	**64° 0′**
26° 10′	9.6444–10	9.9530–10	9.6914–10	0.3086	63° 50′
26° 20′	9.6470–10	9.9524–10	9.6946–10	0.3054	63° 40′
26° 30′	9.6495–10	9.9518–10	9.6977–10	0.3023	63° 30′
26° 40′	9.6521–10	9.9512–10	9.7009–10	0.2991	63° 20′
26° 50′	9.6546–10	9.9505–10	9.7040–10	0.2960	63° 10′
27° 0′	9.6570–10	9.9499–10	9.7072–10	0.2928	**63° 0′**
	log cos	log sin	log ctn	log tan	Angle

Angle	log sin	log cos	log tan	log ctn	
27° 0′	9.6570–10	9.9499–10	9.7072–10	0.2928	63° 0′
27° 10′	9.6595–10	9.9492–10	9.7103–10	0.2897	62° 50′
27° 20′	9.6620–10	9.9486–10	9.7134–10	0.2866	62° 40′
27° 30′	9.6644–10	9.9479–10	9.7165–10	0.2835	62° 30′
27° 40′	9.6668–10	9.9473–10	9.7196–10	0.2804	62° 20′
27° 50′	9.6692–10	9.9466–10	9.7226–10	0.2774	62° 10′
28° 0′	9.6716–10	9.9459–10	9.7257–10	0.2743	62° 0′
28° 10′	9.6740–10	9.9453–10	9.7287–10	0.2713	61° 50′
28° 20′	9.6763–10	9.9446–10	9.7317–10	0.2683	61° 40′
28° 30′	9.6787–10	9.9439–10	9.7348–10	0.2652	61° 30′
28° 40′	9.6810–10	9.9432 -10	9.7378–10	0.2622	61° 20′
28° 50′	9.6833–10	9.9425–10	9.7408–10	0.2592	61° 10′
29° 0′	9.6856–10	9.9418–10	9.7438–10	0.2562	61° 0′
29° 10′	9.6878–10	9.9411–10	9.7467–10	0.2533	60° 50′
29° 20′	9.6901–10	9.9404–10	9.7497–10	0.2503	60° 40′
29° 30′	9.6923–10	9.9397–10	9.7526–10	0.2474	60° 30′
29° 40′	9.6946–10	9.9390–10	9.7556–10	0.2444	60° 20′
29° 50′	9.6968–10	9.9383–10	9.7585–10	0.2415	60° 10′
30° 0′	9.6990–10	9.9375–10	9.7614–10	0.2386	60° 0′
30° 10′	9.7012–10	9.9368–10	9.7644–10	0.2356	59° 50′
30° 20′	9.7033–10	9.9361–10	9.7673–10	0.2327	59° 40′
30° 30′	9.7055 -10	9.9353–10	9.7701–10	0.2299	59° 30′
30° 40′	9.7076–10	9.9346–10	9.7730–10	0.2270	59° 20′
30° 50′	9.7097–10	9.9338–10	9.7759–10	0.2241	59° 10′
31° 0′	9.7118–10	9.9331–10	9.7788–10	0.2212	59° 0′
31° 10′	9.7139–10	9.9323–10	9.7816–10	0.2184	58° 50′
31° 20′	9.7160–10	9.9315–10	9.7845–10	0.2155	58° 40′
31° 30′	9.7181–10	9.9308–10	9.7873–10	0.2127	58° 30′
31° 40′	9.7201–10	9.9300–10	9.7902–10	0.2098	58° 20′
31° 50′	9.7222–10	9.9292–10	9.7930–10	0.2070	58° 10′
32° 0′	9.7242–10	9.9284–10	9.7958–10	0.2042	58° 0′
32° 10′	9.7262–10	9.9276–10	9.7986–10	0.2014	57° 50′
32° 20′	9.7282–10	9.9268–10	9.8014–10	0.1986	57° 40′
32° 30′	9.7302–10	9.9260–10	9.8042–10	0.1958	57° 30′
32° 40′	9.7322–10	9.9252–10	9.8070–10	0.1930	57° 20′
32° 50′	9.7342–10	9.9244–10	9.8097–10	0.1903	57° 10′
33° 0′	9.7361–10	9.9236–10	9.8125–10	0.1875	57° 0′
33° 10′	9.7380–10	9.9228–10	9.8153–10	0.1847	56° 50′
33° 20′	9.7400–10	9.9219–10	9.8180–10	0.1820	56° 40′
33° 30′	9.7419–10	9.9211–10	9.8208–10	0.1792	56° 30′
33° 40′	9.7438–10	9.9203–10	9.8235–10	0.1765	56° 20′
33° 50′	9.7457–10	9.9194–10	9.8263–10	0.1737	56° 10′
34° 0′	9.7476–10	9.9186–10	9.8290–10	0.1710	56° 0′
34° 10′	9.7494–10	9.9177–10	9.8317–10	0.1683	55° 50′
34° 20′	9.7513–10	9.9169–10	9.8344–10	0.1656	55° 40′
34° 30′	9.7531–10	9.9160–10	9.8371–10	0.1629	55° 30′
34° 40′	9.7550–10	9.9151–10	9.8398–10	0.1602	55° 20′
34° 50′	9.7568–10	9.9142–10	9.8425–10	0.1575	55° 10′
35° 0′	9.7586–10	9.9134–10	9.8452–10	0.1548	55° 0′
35° 10′	9.7604–10	9.9125–10	9.8479–10	0.1521	54° 50′
35° 20′	9.7622–10	9.9116–10	9.8506–10	0.1494	54° 40′
35° 30′	9.7640–10	9.9107–10	9.8533–10	0.1467	54° 30′
35° 40′	9.7657–10	9.9098–10	9.8559–10	0.1441	54° 20′
35° 50′	9.7675–10	9.9089–10	9.8586–10	0.1414	54° 10′
36° 0′	9.7692–10	9.9080–10	9.8613–10	0.1387	54° 0′
	log cos	log sin	log ctn	log tan	Angle

Angle	log sin	log cos	log tan	log ctn	
36° 0′	9.7692−10	9.9080−10	9.8613−10	0.1387	54° 0′
36° 10′	9.7710−10	9.9070−10	9.8639−10	0.1361	53° 50′
36° 20′	9.7727−10	9.9061−10	9.8666−10	0.1334	53° 40′
36° 30′	9.7744−10	9.9052−10	9.8692−10	0.1308	53° 30′
36° 40′	9.7761−10	9.9042−10	9.8718−10	0.1282	53° 20′
36° 50′	9.7778−10	9.9033−10	9.8745−10	0.1255	53° 10′
37° 0′	9.7795−10	9.9023−10	9.8771−10	0.1229	53° 0′
37° 10′	9.7811−10	9.9014−10	9.8797−10	0.1203	52° 50′
37° 20′	9.7828−10	9.9004−10	9.8824−10	0.1176	52° 40′
37° 30′	9.7844−10	9.8995−10	9.8850−10	0.1150	52° 30′
37° 40′	9.7861−10	9.8985−10	9.8876−10	0.1124	52° 20′
37° 50′	9.7877−10	9.8975−10	9.8902−10	0.1098	52° 10′
38° 0′	9.7893−10	9.8965−10	9.8928−10	0.1072	52° 0′
38° 10′	9.7910−10	9.8955−10	9.8954−10	0.1046	51° 50′
38° 20′	9.7926−10	9.8945−10	9.8980−10	0.1020	51° 40′
38° 30′	9.7941−10	9.8935−10	9.9006−10	0.0994	51° 30′
38° 40′	9.7957−10	9.8925−10	9.9032−10	0.0968	51° 20′
38° 50′	9.7973−10	9.8915−10	9.9058−10	0.0942	51° 10′
39° 0′	9.7989−10	9.8905−10	9.9084−10	0.0916	51° 0′
39° 10′	9.8004−10	9.8895−10	9.9110−10	0.0890	50° 50′
39° 20′	9.8020−10	9.8884−10	9.9135−10	0.0865	50° 40′
39° 30′	9.8035−10	9.8874−10	9.9161−10	0.0839	50° 30′
39° 40′	9.8050−10	9.8864−10	9.9187−10	0.0813	50° 20′
39° 50′	9.8066−10	9.8853−10	9.9212−10	0.0788	50° 10′
40° 0′	9.8081−10	9.8843−10	9.9238−10	0.0762	50° 0′
40° 10′	9.8096−10	9.8832−10	9.9264−10	0.0736	49° 50′
40° 20′	9.8111−10	9.8821−10	9.9289−10	0.0711	49° 40′
40° 30′	9.8125−10	9.8810−10	9.9315−10	0.0685	49° 30′
40° 40′	9.8140−10	9.8800−10	9.9341−10	0.0659	49° 20′
40° 50′	9.8155−10	9.8789−10	9.9366−10	0.0634	49° 10′
41° 0′	9.8169−10	9.8778−10	9.9392−10	0.0608	49° 0′
41° 10′	9.8184−10	9.8767−10	9.9417−10	0.0583	48° 50′
41° 20′	9.8198−10	9.8756−10	9.9443−10	0.0557	48° 40′
41° 30′	9.8213−10	9.8745−10	9.9468−10	0.0532	48° 30′
41° 40′	9.8227−10	9.8733−10	9.9494−10	0.0506	48° 20′
41° 50′	9.8241−10	9.8722−10	9.9519−10	0.0481	48° 10′
42° 0′	9.8255−10	9.8711−10	9.9544−10	0.0456	48° 0′
42° 10′	9.8269−10	9.8699−10	9.9570−10	0.0430	47° 50′
42° 20′	9.8283−10	9.8688−10	9.9595−10	0.0405	47° 40′
42° 30′	9.8297−10	9.8676−10	9.9621−10	0.0379	47° 30′
42° 40′	9.8311−10	9.8665−10	9.9646−10	0.0354	47° 20′
42° 50′	9.8324−10	9.8653−10	9.9671−10	0.0329	47° 10′
43° 0′	9.8338−10	9.8641−10	9.9697−10	0.0303	47° 0′
43° 10′	9.8351−10	9.8629−10	9.9722−10	0.0278	46° 50′
43° 20′	9.8365−10	9.8618−10	9.9747−10	0.0253	46° 40′
43° 30′	9.8378−10	9.8606−10	9.9772−10	0.0228	46° 30′
43° 40′	9.8391−10	9.8594−10	9.9798−10	0.0202	46° 20′
43° 50′	9.8405−10	9.8582−10	9.9823−10	0.0177	46° 10′
44° 0′	9.8418−10	9.8569−10	9.9848−10	0.0152	46° 0′
44° 10′	9.8431−10	9.8557−10	9.9874−10	0.0126	45° 50′
44° 20′	9.8444−10	9.8545−10	9.9899−10	0.0101	45° 40′
44° 30′	9.8457−10	9.8532−10	9.9924−10	0.0076	45° 30′
44° 40′	9.8469−10	9.8520−10	9.9949−10	0.0051	45° 20′
44° 50′	9.8482−10	9.8507−10	9.9975−10	0.0025	45° 10′
45° 0′	9.8495−10	9.8495−10	0.0000	0.0000	45° 0′
	log cos	log sin	log ctn	log tan	Angle

45°—Logarithms of Trigonometric Functions—54°   III

Angle	sin	cos	tan	ctn	sec	csc	
0° 0′	0.0000	1.0000	0.0000	—	1.000	—	90° 0′
0° 10′	0.0029	1.0000	0.0029	343.8	1.000	343.8	89° 50′
0° 20′	0.0058	1.0000	0.0058	171.9	1.000	171.9	89° 40′
0° 30′	0.0087	1.0000	0.0087	114.6	1.000	114.6	89° 30′
0° 40′	0.0116	0.9999	0.0116	85.94	1.000	85.95	89° 20′
0° 50′	0.0145	0.9999	0.0145	68.75	1.000	68.76	89° 10′
1° 0′	0.0175	0.9998	0.0175	57.29	1.000	57.30	89° 0′
1° 10′	0.0204	0.9998	0.0204	49.10	1.000	49.11	88° 50′
1° 20′	0.0233	0.9997	0.0233	42.96	1.000	42.98	88° 40′
1° 30′	0.0262	0.9997	0.0262	38.19	1.000	38.20	88° 30′
1° 40′	0.0291	0.9996	0.0291	34.37	1.000	34.38	88° 20′
1° 50′	0.0320	0.9995	0.0320	31.24	1.001	31.26	88° 10′
2° 0′	0.0349	0.9994	0.0349	28.64	1.001	28.65	88° 0′
2° 10′	0.0378	0.9993	0.0378	26.43	1.001	26.45	87° 50′
2° 20′	0.0407	0.9992	0.0407	24.54	1.001	24.56	87° 40′
2° 30′	0.0436	0.9990	0.0437	22.90	1.001	22.93	87° 30′
2° 40′	0.0465	0.9989	0.0466	21.47	1.001	21.49	87° 20′
2° 50′	0.0494	0.9988	0.0495	20.21	1.001	20.23	87° 10′
3° 0′	0.0523	0.9986	0.0524	19.08	1.001	19.11	87° 0′
3° 10′	0.0552	0.9985	0.0553	18.07	1.002	18.10	86° 50′
3° 20′	0.0581	0.9983	0.0582	17.17	1.002	17.20	86° 40′
3° 30′	0.0610	0.9981	0.0612	16.35	1.002	16.38	86° 30′
3° 40′	0.0640	0.9980	0.0641	15.60	1.002	15.64	86° 20′
3° 50′	0.0669	0.9978	0.0670	14.92	1.002	14.96	86° 10′
4° 0′	0.0698	0.9976	0.0699	14.30	1.002	14.34	86° 0′
4° 10′	0.0727	0.9974	0.0729	13.73	1.003	13.76	85° 50′
4° 20′	0.0756	0.9971	0.0758	13.20	1.003	13.23	85° 40′
4° 30′	0.0785	0.9969	0.0787	12.71	1.003	12.75	85° 30′
4° 40′	0.0814	0.9967	0.0816	12.25	1.003	12.29	85° 20′
4° 50′	0.0843	0.9964	0.0846	11.83	1.004	11.87	85° 10′
5° 0′	0.0872	0.9962	0.0875	11.43	1.004	11.47	85° 0′
5° 10′	0.0901	0.9959	0.0904	11.06	1.004	11.10	84° 50′
5° 20′	0.0929	0.9957	0.0934	10.71	1.004	10.76	84° 40′
5° 30′	0.0958	0.9954	0.0963	10.39	1.005	10.43	84° 30′
5° 40′	0.0987	0.9951	0.0992	10.078	1.005	10.128	84° 20′
5° 50′	0.1016	0.9948	0.1022	9.788	1.005	9.839	84° 10′
6° 0′	0.1045	0.9945	0.1051	9.514	1.006	9.567	84° 0′
6° 10′	0.1074	0.9942	0.1080	9.255	1.006	9.309	83° 50′
6° 20′	0.1103	0.9939	0.1110	9.010	1.006	9.065	83° 40′
6° 30′	0.1132	0.9936	0.1139	8.777	1.006	8.834	83° 30′
6° 40′	0.1161	0.9932	0.1169	8.556	1.007	8.614	83° 20′
6° 50′	0.1190	0.9929	0.1198	8.345	1.007	8.405	83° 10′
7° 0′	0.1219	0.9925	0.1228	8.144	1.008	8.206	83° 0′
7° 10′	0.1248	0.9922	0.1257	7.953	1.008	8.016	82° 50′
7° 20′	0.1276	0.9918	0.1287	7.770	1.008	7.834	82° 40′
7° 30′	0.1305	0.9914	0.1317	7.596	1.009	7.661	82° 30′
7° 40′	0.1334	0.9911	0.1346	7.429	1.009	7.496	82° 20′
7° 50′	0.1363	0.9907	0.1376	7.269	1.009	7.337	82° 10′
8° 0.	0.1392	0.9903	0.1405	7.115	1.010	7.185	82° 0′
8° 10′	0.1421	0.9899	0.1435	6.968	1.010	7.040	81° 50′
8° 20′	0.1449	0.9894	0.1465	6.827	1.011	6.900	81° 40′
8° 30′	0.1478	0.9890	0.1495	6.691	1.011	6.765	81° 30′
8° 40′	0.1507	0.9886	0.1524	6.561	1.012	6.636	81° 20′
8° 50′	0.1536	0.9881	0.1554	6.435	1.012	6.512	81° 10′
9° 0′	0.1564	0.9877	0.1584	6.314	1.012	6.392	81° 0′
	cos	sin	ctn	tan	csc	sec	Angle

Angle	sin	cos	tan	ctn	sec	csc	
9° 0′	0.1564	0.9877	0.1584	6.314	1.012	6.392	81° 0′
9° 10′	0.1593	0.9872	0.1614	6.197	1.013	6.277	80° 50′
9° 20′	0.1622	0.9868	0.1644	6.084	1.013	6.166	80° 40′
9° 30′	0.1650	0.9863	0.1673	5.976	1.014	6.059	80° 30′
9° 40′	0.1679	0.9858	0.1703	5.871	1.014	5.955	80° 20′
9° 50′	0.1708	0.9853	0.1733	5.769	1.015	5.855	80° 10′
10° 0′	0.1736	0.9848	0.1763	5.671	1.015	5.759	80° 0′
10° 10′	0.1765	0.9843	0.1793	5.576	1.016	5.665	79° 50′
10° 20′	0.1794	0.9838	0.1823	5.485	1.016	5.575	79° 40′
10° 30′	0.1822	0.9833	0.1853	5.396	1.017	5.487	79° 30′
10° 40′	0.1851	0.9827	0.1883	5.309	1.018	5.403	79° 20′
10° 50′	0.1880	0.9822	0.1914	5.226	1.018	5.320	79° 10′
11° 0′	0.1908	0.9816	0.1944	5.145	1.019	5.241	79° 0′
11° 10′	0.1937	0.9811	0.1974	5.066	1.019	5.164	78° 50′
11° 20′	0.1965	0.9805	0.2004	4.989	1.020	5.089	78° 40′
11° 30′	0.1994	0.9799	0.2035	4.915	1.020	5.016	78° 30′
11° 40′	0.2022	0.9793	0.2065	4.843	1.021	4.945	78° 20′
11° 50′	0.2051	0.9787	0.2095	4.773	1.022	4.876	78° 10′
12° 0′	0.2079	0.9781	0.2126	4.705	1.022	4.810	78° 0′
12° 10′	0.2108	0.9775	0.2156	4.638	1.023	4.745	77° 50′
12° 20′	0.2136	0.9769	0.2186	4.574	1.024	4.682	77° 40′
12° 30′	0.2164	0.9763	0.2217	4.511	1.024	4.620	77° 30′
12° 40′	0.2193	0.9757	0.2247	4.449	1.025	4.560	77° 20′
12° 50′	0.2221	0.9750	0.2278	4.390	1.026	4.502	77° 10′
13° 0′	0.2250	0.9744	0.2309	4.331	1.026	4.445	77° 0′
13° 10′	0.2278	0.9737	0.2339	4.275	1.027	4.390	76° 50′
13° 20′	0.2306	0.9730	0.2370	4.219	1.028	4.336	76° 40′
13° 30′	0.2334	0.9724	0.2401	4.165	1.028	4.284	76° 30′
13° 40′	0.2363	0.9717	0.2432	4.113	1.029	4.232	76° 20′
13° 50′	0.2391	0.9710	0.2462	4.061	1.030	4.182	76° 10′
14° 0′	0.2419	0.9703	0.2493	4.011	1.031	4.134	76° 0′
14° 10′	0.2447	0.9696	0.2524	3.962	1.031	4.086	75° 50′
14° 20′	0.2476	0.9689	0.2555	3.914	1.032	4.039	75° 40′
14° 30′	0.2504	0.9681	0.2586	3.867	1.033	3.994	75° 30′
14° 40′	0.2532	0.9674	0.2617	3.821	1.034	3.950	75° 20′
14° 50′	0.2560	0.9667	0.2648	3.776	1.034	3.906	75° 10′
15° 0′	0.2588	0.9659	0.2679	3.732	1.035	3.864	75° 0′
15° 10′	0.2616	0.9652	0.2711	3.689	1.036	3.822	74° 50′
15° 20′	0.2644	0.9644	0.2742	3.647	1.037	3.782	74° 40′
15° 30′	0.2672	0.9636	0.2773	3.606	1.038	3.742	74° 30′
15° 40′	0.2700	0.9628	0.2805	3.566	1.039	3.703	74° 20′
15° 50′	0.2728	0.9621	0.2836	3.526	1.039	3.665	74° 10′
16° 0′	0.2756	0.9613	0.2867	3.487	1.040	3.628	74° 0′
16° 10′	0.2784	0.9605	0.2899	3.450	1.041	3.592	73° 50′
16° 20′	0.2812	0.9596	0.2931	3.412	1.042	3.556	73° 40′
16° 30′	0.2840	0.9588	0.2962	3.376	1.043	3.521	73° 30′
16° 40′	0.2868	0.9580	0.2994	3.340	1.044	3.487	73° 20′
16° 50′	0.2896	0.9572	0.3026	3.305	1.045	3.453	73° 10′
17° 0′	0.2924	0.9563	0.3057	3.271	1.046	3.420	73° 0′
17° 10′	0.2952	0.9555	0.3089	3.237	1.047	3.388	72° 50′
17° 20′	0.2979	0.9546	0.3121	3.204	1.048	3.356	72° 40′
17° 30′	0.3007	0.9537	0.3153	3.172	1.049	3.326	72° 30′
17° 40′	0.3035	0.9528	0.3185	3.140	1.049	3.295	72° 20′
17° 50′	0.3062	0.9520	0.3217	3.108	1.050	3.265	72° 10′
18° 0′	0.3090	0.9511	0.3249	3.078	1.051	3.236	72° 0′
	cos	sin	ctn	tan	csc	sec	Angle

Angle	sin	cos	tan	ctn	sec	csc	
18° 0′	0.3090	0.9511	0.3249	3.078	1.051	3.236	72° 0′
18° 10′	0.3118	0.9502	0.3281	3.047	1.052	3.207	71° 50′
18° 20′	0.3145	0.9492	0.3314	3.018	1.053	3.179	71° 40′
18° 30′	0.3173	0.9483	0.3346	2.989	1.054	3.152	71° 30′
18° 40′	0.3201	0.9474	0.3378	2.960	1.056	3.124	71° 20′
18° 50′	0.3228	0.9465	0.3411	2.932	1.057	3.098	71° 10′
19° 0′	0.3256	0.9455	0.3443	2.904	1.058	3.072	71° 0′
19° 10′	0.3283	0.9446	0.3476	2.877	1.059	3.046	70° 50′
19° 20′	0.3311	0.9436	0.3508	2.850	1.060	3.021	70° 40′
19° 30′	0.3338	0.9426	0.3541	2.824	1.061	2.996	70° 30′
19° 40′	0.3365	0.9417	0.3574	2.798	1.062	2.971	70° 20′
19° 50′	0.3393	0.9407	0.3607	2.773	1.063	2.947	70° 10′
20° 0′	0.3420	0.9397	0.3640	2.747	1.064	2.924	70° 0′
20° 10′	0.3448	0.9387	0.3673	2.723	1.065	2.901	69° 50′
20° 20′	0.3475	0.9377	0.3706	2.699	1.066	2.878	69° 40′
20° 30′	0.3502	0.9367	0.3739	2.675	1.068	2.855	69° 30′
20° 40′	0.3529	0.9356	0.3772	2.651	1.069	2.833	69° 20′
20° 50′	0.3557	0.9346	0.3805	2.628	1.070	2.812	69° 10
21° 0′	0.3584	0.9336	0.3839	2.605	1.071	2.790	69° 0′
21° 10′	0.3611	0.9325	0.3872	2.583	1.072	2.769	68° 50′
21° 20′	0.3638	0.9315	0.3906	2.560	1.074	2.749	68° 40′
21° 30′	0.3665	0.9304	0.3939	2.539	1.075	2.729	68° 30′
21° 40′	0.3692	0.9293	0.3973	2.517	1.076	2.709	68° 20′
21° 50′	0.3719	0.9283	0.4006	2.496	1.077	2.689	68° 10′
22° 0′	0.3746	0.9272	0.4040	2.475	1.079	2.669	68° 0′
22° 10′	0.3773	0.9261	0.4074	2.455	1.080	2.650	67° 50′
22° 20′	0.3800	0.9250	0.4108	2.434	1.081	2.632	67° 40′
22° 30′	0.3827	0.9239	0.4142	2.414	1.082	2.613	67° 30′
22° 40′	0.3854	0.9228	0.4176	2.394	1.084	2.595	67° 20′
22° 50′	0.3881	0.9216	0.4210	2.375	1.085	2.577	67° 10′
23° 0′	0.3907	0.9205	0.4245	2.356	1.086	2.559	67° 0′
23° 10′	0.3934	0.9194	0.4279	2.337	1.088	2.542	66° 50′
23° 20′	0.3961	0.9182	0.4314	2.318	1.089	2.525	66° 40′
23° 30′	0.3987	0.9171	0.4348	2.300	1.090	2.508	66° 30′
23° 40′	0.4014	0.9159	0.4383	2.282	1.092	2.491	66° 20′
23° 50′	0.4041	0.9147	0.4417	2.264	1.093	2.475	66° 10′
24° 0′	0.4067	0.9135	0.4452	2.246	1.095	2.459	66° 0′
24° 10′	0.4094	0.9124	0.4487	2.229	1.096	2.443	65° 50′
24° 20′	0.4120	0.9112	0.4522	2.211	1.097	2.427	65° 40′
24° 30′	0.4147	0.9100	0.4557	2.194	1.099	2.411	65° 30′
24° 40′	0.4173	0.9088	0.4592	2.177	1.100	2.396	65° 20′
24° 50′	0.4200	0.9075	0.4628	2.161	1.102	2.381	65° 10′
25° 0′	0.4226	0.9063	0.4663	2.145	1.103	2.366	65° 0′
25° 10′	0.4253	0.9051	0.4699	2.128	1.105	2.352	64° 50′
25° 20′	0.4279	0.9038	0.4734	2.112	1.106	2.337	64° 40′
25° 30′	0.4305	0.9026	0.4770	2.097	1.108	2.323	64° 30′
25° 40′	0.4331	0.9013	0.4806	2.081	1.109	2.309	64° 20′
25° 50′	0.4358	0.9001	0.4841	2.066	1.111	2.295	64° 10′
26° 0′	0.4384	0.8988	0.4877	2.050	1.113	2.281	64° 0′
26° 10′	0.4410	0.8975	0.4913	2.035	1.114	2.268	63° 50′
26° 20′	0.4436	0.8962	0.4950	2.020	1.116	2.254	63° 40′
26° 30′	0.4462	0.8949	0.4986	2.006	1.117	2.241	63° 30′
26° 40′	0.4488	0.8936	0.5022	1.991	1.119	2.228	63° 20′
26° 50′	0.4514	0.8923	0.5059	1.977	1.121	2.215	63° 10′
27° 0′	0.4540	0.8910	0.5095	1.963	1.122	2.203	63° 0′
	cos	sin	ctn	tan	csc	sec	Angle

Angle	sin	cos	tan	ctn	sec	csc	
27° 0′	0.4540	0.8910	0.5095	1.963	1.122	2.203	63° 0′
27° 10′	0.4566	0.8897	0.5132	1.949	1.124	2.190	62° 50′
27° 20′	0.4592	0.8884	0.5169	1.935	1.126	2.178	62° 40′
27° 30′	0.4617	0.8870	0.5206	1.921	1.127	2.166	62° 30′
27° 40′	0.4643	0.8857	0.5243	1.907	1.129	2.154	62° 20′
27° 50′	0.4669	0.8843	0.5280	1.894	1.131	2.142	62° 10′
28° 0′	0.4695	0.8829	0.5317	1.881	1.133	2.130	62° 0′
28° 10′	0.4720	0.8816	0.5354	1.868	1.134	2.118	61° 50′
28° 20′	0.4746	0.8802	0.5392	1.855	1.136	2.107	61° 40′
28° 30′	0.4772	0.8788	0.5430	1.842	1.138	2.096	61° 30′
28° 40′	0.4797	0.8774	0.5467	1.829	1.140	2.085	61° 20′
28° 50′	0.4823	0.8760	0.5505	1.816	1.142	2.074	61° 10′
29° 0′	0.4848	0.8746	0.5543	1.804	1.143	2.063	61° 0′
29° 10′	0.4874	0.8732	0.5581	1.792	1.145	2.052	60° 50′
29° 20′	0.4899	0.8718	0.5619	1.780	1.147	2.041	60° 40′
29° 30′	0.4924	0.8704	0.5658	1.767	1.149	2.031	60° 30′
29° 40′	0.4950	0.8689	0.5696	1.756	1.151	2.020	60° 20′
29° 50′	0.4975	0.8675	0.5735	1.744	1.153	2.010	60° 10′
30° 0′	0.5000	0.8660	0.5774	1.732	1.155	2.000	60° 0′
30° 10′	0.5025	0.8646	0.5812	1.720	1.157	1.990	59° 50′
30° 20′	0.5050	0.8631	0.5851	1.709	1.159	1.980	59° 40′
30° 30′	0.5075	0.8616	0.5890	1.698	1.161	1.970	59° 30′
30° 40′	0.5100	0.8601	0.5930	1.686	1.163	1.961	59° 20′
30° 50′	0.5125	0.8587	0.5969	1.675	1.165	1.951	59° 10′
31° 0′	0.5150	0.8572	0.6009	1.664	1.167	1.942	59° 0′
31° 10′	0.5175	0.8557	0.6048	1.653	1.169	1.932	58° 50′
31° 20′	0.5200	0.8542	0.6088	1.643	1.171	1.923	58° 40′
31° 30′	0.5225	0.8526	0.6128	1.632	1.173	1.914	58° 30′
31° 40′	0.5250	0.8511	0.6168	1.621	1.175	1.905	58° 20′
31° 50′	0.5275	0.8496	0.6208	1.611	1.177	1.896	58° 10′
32° 0′	0.5299	0.8480	0.6249	1.600	1.179	1.887	58° 0′
32° 10′	0.5324	0.8465	0.6289	1.590	1.181	1.878	57° 50′
32° 20′	0.5348	0.8450	0.6330	1.580	1.184	1.870	57° 40′
32° 30′	0.5373	0.8434	0.6371	1.570	1.186	1.861	57° 30′
32° 40′	0.5398	0.8418	0.6412	1.560	1.188	1.853	57° 20′
32° 50′	0.5422	0.8403	0.6453	1.550	1.190	1.844	57° 10′
33° 0′	0.5446	0.8387	0.6494	1.540	1.192	1.836	57° 0′
33° 10′	0.5471	0.8371	0.6536	1.530	1.195	1.828	56° 50′
33° 20′	0.5495	0.8355	0.6577	1.520	1.197	1.820	56° 40′
33° 30′	0.5519	0.8339	0.6619	1.511	1.199	1.812	56° 30′
33° 40′	0.5544	0.8323	0.6661	1.501	1.202	1.804	56° 20′
33° 50′	0.5568	0.8307	0.6703	1.492	1.204	1.796	56° 10′
34° 0′	0.5592	0.8290	0.6745	1.483	1.206	1.788	56° 0′
34° 10′	0.5616	0.8274	0.6787	1.473	1.209	1.781	55° 50′
34° 20′	0.5640	0.8258	0.6830	1.464	1.211	1.773	55° 40′
34° 30′	0.5664	0.8241	0.6873	1.455	1.213	1.766	55° 30′
34° 40′	0.5688	0.8225	0.6916	1.446	1.216	1.758	55° 20′
34° 50′	0.5712	0.8208	0.6959	1.437	1.218	1.751	55° 10′
35° 0′	0.5736	0.8192	0.7002	1.428	1.221	1.743	55° 0′
35° 10′	0.5760	0.8175	0.7046	1.419	1.223	1.736	54° 50′
35° 20′	0.5783	0.8158	0.7089	1.411	1.226	1.729	54° 40′
35° 30′	0.5807	0.8141	0.7133	1.402	1.228	1.722	54° 30′
35° 40′	0.5831	0.8124	0.7177	1.393	1.231	1.715	54° 20′
35° 50′	0.5854	0.8107	0.7221	1.385	1.233	1.708	54° 10′
36° 0′	0.5878	0.8090	0.7265	1.376	1.236	1.701	54° 0′
	cos	sin	ctn	tan	csc	sec	Angle

Angle	sin	cos	tan	ctn	sec	csc	
36° 0′	0.5878	0.8090	0.7265	1.376	1.236	1.701	54° 0′
36° 10′	0.5901	0.8073	0.7310	1.368	1.239	1.695	53° 50′
36° 20′	0.5925	0.8056	0.7355	1.360	1.241	1.688	53° 40′
36° 30′	0.5948	0.8039	0.7400	1.351	1.244	1.681	53° 30′
36° 40′	0.5972	0.8021	0.7445	1.343	1.247	1.675	53° 20′
36° 50′	0.5995	0.8004	0.7490	1.335	1.249	1.668	53° 10′
37° 0′	0.6018	0.7986	0.7536	1.327	1.252	1.662	53° 0′
37° 10′	0.6041	0.7969	0.7581	1.319	1.255	1.655	52° 50′
37° 20′	0.6065	0.7951	0.7627	1.311	1.258	1.649	52° 40′
37° 30′	0.6088	0.7934	0.7673	1.303	1.260	1.643	52° 30′
37° 40′	0.6111	0.7916	0.7720	1.295	1.263	1.636	52° 20′
37° 50′	0.6134	0.7898	0.7766	1.288	1.266	1.630	52° 10′
38° 0′	0.6157	0.7880	0.7813	1.280	1.269	1.624	52° 0′
38° 10′	0.6180	0.7862	0.7860	1.272	1.272	1.618	51° 50′
38° 20′	0.6202	0.7844	0.7907	1.265	1.275	1.612	51° 40′
38° 30′	0.6225	0.7826	0.7954	1.257	1.278	1.606	51° 30′
38° 40′	0.6248	0.7808	0.8002	1.250	1.281	1.601	51° 20′
38° 50′	0.6271	0.7790	0.8050	1.242	1.284	1.595	51° 10′
39° 0′	0.6293	0.7771	0.8098	1.235	1.287	1.589	51° 0′
39° 10′	0.6316	0.7753	0.8146	1.228	1.290	1.583	50° 50′
39° 20′	0.6338	0.7735	0.8195	1.220	1.293	1.578	50° 40′
39° 30′	0.6361	0.7716	0.8243	1.213	1.296	1.572	50° 30′
39° 40′	0.6383	0.7698	0.8292	1.206	1.299	1.567	50° 20′
39° 50′	0.6406	0.7679	0.8342	1.199	1.302	1.561	50° 10′
40° 0′	0.6428	0.7660	0.8391	1.192	1.305	1.556	50° 0′
40° 10′	0.6450	0.7642	0.8441	1.185	1.309	1.550	49° 50′
40° 20′	0.6472	0.7623	0.8491	1.178	1.312	1.545	49° 40′
40° 30′	0.6494	0.7604	0.8541	1.171	1.315	1.540	49° 30′
40° 40′	0.6517	0.7585	0.8591	1.164	1.318	1.535	49° 20′
40° 50′	0.6539	0.7566	0.8642	1.157	1.322	1.529	49° 10′
41° 0′	0.6561	0.7547	0.8693	1.150	1.325	1.524	49° 0′
41° 10′	0.6583	0.7528	0.8744	1.144	1.328	1.519	48° 50′
41° 20′	0.6604	0.7509	0.8796	1.137	1.332	1.514	48° 40′
41° 30′	0.6626	0.7490	0.8847	1.130	1.335	1.509	48° 30′
41° 40′	0.6648	0.7470	0.8899	1.124	1.339	1.504	48° 20′
41° 50′	0.6670	0.7451	0.8952	1.117	1.342	1.499	48° 10′
42° 0′	0.6691	0.7431	0.9004	1.111	1.346	1.494	48° 0′
42° 10′	0.6713	0.7412	0.9057	1.104	1.349	1.490	47° 50′
42° 20′	0.6734	0.7392	0.9110	1.098	1.353	1.485	47° 40′
42° 30′	0.6756	0.7373	0.9163	1.091	1.356	1.480	47° 30′
42° 40′	0.6777	0.7353	0.9217	1.085	1.360	1.476	47° 20′
42° 50′	0.6799	0.7333	0.9271	1.079	1.364	1.471	47° 10′
43° 0′	0.6820	0.7314	0.9325	1.072	1.367	1.466	47° 0′
43° 10′	0.6841	0.7294	0.9380	1.066	1.371	1.462	46° 50′
43° 20′	0.6862	0.7274	0.9435	1.060	1.375	1.457	46° 40′
43° 30′	0.6884	0.7254	0.9490	1.054	1.379	1.453	46° 30′
43° 40′	0.6905	0.7234	0.9545	1.048	1.382	1.448	46° 20′
43° 50′	0.6926	0.7214	0.9601	1.042	1.386	1.444	46° 10′
44° 0′	0.6947	0.7193	0.9657	1.036	1.390	1.440	46° 0′
44° 10′	0.6967	0.7173	0.9713	1.030	1.394	1.435	45° 50′
44° 20′	0.6988	0.7153	0.9770	1.024	1.398	1.431	45° 40′
44° 30′	0.7009	0.7133	0.9827	1.018	1.402	1.427	45° 30′
44° 40′	0.7030	0.7112	0.9884	1.012	1.406	1.423	45° 20′
44° 50′	0.7050	0.7092	0.9942	1.006	1.410	1.418	45° 10′
45° 0′	0.7071	0.7071	1.0000	1.000	1.414	1.414	45° 0′
	cos	sin	ctn	tan	csc	sec	Angle

Deg.	Radians	Deg.	Radians	Deg.	Radians	Deg.	Radians	Deg.	Radians
0°	0.000 000	20°	0.349 066	40°	0.698 132	60°	1.047 198	80°	1.396 263
1	0.017 453	21	0.366 519	41	0.715 585	61	1.064 651	81	1.413 717
2	0.034 907	22	0.383 972	42	0.733 038	62	1.082 104	82	1.431 170
3	0.052 360	23	0.401 426	43	0.750 492	63	1.099 557	83	1.448 623
4	0.069 813	24	0.418 879	44	0.767 945	64	1.117 011	84	1.466 077
5	0.087 266	25	0.436 332	45	0.785 398	65	1.134 464	85	1.483 530
6	0.104 720	26	0.453 786	46	0.802 851	66	1.151 917	86	1.500 983
7	0.122 173	27	0.471 239	47	0.820 305	67	1.169 371	87	1.518 436
8	0.139 626	28	0.488 692	48	0.837 758	68	1.186 824	88	1.535 890
9	0.157 080	29	0.506 145	49	0.855 211	69	1.204 277	89	1.553 343
10	0.174 533	30	0.523 599	50	0.872 665	70	1.221 730	90	1.570 796
11	0.191 986	31	0.541 052	51	0.890 118	71	1.239 184	91	1.588 250
12	0.209 440	32	0.558 505	52	0.907 571	72	1.256 637	92	1.605 703
13	0.226 893	33	0.575 959	53	0.925 025	73	1.274 090	93	1.623 156
14	0.244 346	34	0.593 412	54	0.942 478	74	1.291 544	94	1.640 609
15	0.261 799	35	0.610 865	55	0.959 931	75	1.308 997	95	1.658 063
16	0.279 253	36	0.628 319	56	0.977 384	76	1.326 450	96	1.675 516
17	0.296 706	37	0.645 772	57	0.994 838	77	1.343 904	97	1.692 969
18	0.314 159	38	0.663 225	58	1.012 291	78	1.361 357	98	1.710 423
19	0.331 613	39	0.680 678	59	1.029 744	79	1.378 810	99	1.727 876
100°	1.745 329	200°	3.490 659	300°	5.235 988	400°	6.981 317	500°	8.726 646

Minutes to Radians   Vb

Min.	Radians	Min.	Radians	Min.	Radians	Min.	Radians	Min.	Radians
1′	0.000 291	13′	0.003 782	25′	0.007 272	37′	0.010 763	49′	0.014 254
2	0.000 582	14	0.004 072	26	0.007 563	38	0.011 054	50	0.014 544
3	0.000 873	15	0.004 363	27	0.007 854	39	0.011 345	51	0.014 835
4	0.001 164	16	0.004 654	28	0.008 145	40	0.011 636	52	0.015 126
5	0.001 454	17	0.004 945	29	0.008 436	41	0.011 926	53	0.015 417
6	0.001 745	18	0.005 236	30	0.008 727	42	0.012 217	54	0.015 708
7	0.002 036	19	0.005 527	31	0.009 018	43	0.012 508	55	0.015 999
8	0.002 327	20	0.005 818	32	0.009 308	44	0.012 799	56	0.016 290
9	0.002 618	21	0.006 109	33	0.009 599	45	0.013 090	57	0.016 581
10	0.002 909	22	0.006 400	34	0.009 890	46	0.013 381	58	0.016 872
11	0.003 200	23	0.006 690	35	0.010 181	47	0.013 672	59	0.017 162
12	0.003 491	24	0.006 981	36	0.010 472	48	0.013 963	60	0.017 453

To convert **tenths of minutes** to radians, shift the decimal point one place to the left in the entries for 1′ through 9′.

Radians to Degrees and Minutes   Vc

n	n radians	$\dfrac{n}{10}$ radians	$\dfrac{n}{100}$ radians	$\dfrac{n}{1000}$ radians	$\dfrac{n}{10{,}000}$ radians
1	57° 17.75′	5° 43.77′	0° 34.38′	3.44′	0.34′
2	114° 35.49′	11° 27.55′	1° 8.75′	6.88′	0.69′
3	171° 53.24′	17° 11.32′	1° 43.13′	10.31′	1.03′
4	229° 10.99′	22° 55.10′	2° 17.51′	13.75′	1.38′
5	286° 28.73′	28° 38.87′	2° 51.89′	17.19′	1.72′
6	343° 46.48′	34° 22.65′	3° 26.26′	20.63′	2.06′
7	401° 4.23′	40° 6.42′	4° 0.64′	24.06′	2.41′
8	458° 21.97′	45° 50.20′	4° 35.02′	27.50′	2.75′
9	515° 39.72′	51° 33.97′	5° 9.40′	30.94′	3.09′

461

x	$\sin x$	$\cos x$	$\tan x$	$\operatorname{ctn} x$	e^x	e^{-x}	x
0.00	0.0000	1.0000	0.0000	—	1.000	1.0000	**0.00**
0.01	0.0100	1.0000	0.0100	100.00	1.010	0.9900	0.01
0.02	0.0200	0.9998	0.0200	49.99	1.020	0.9802	0.02
0.03	0.0300	0.9996	0.0300	33.32	1.030	0.9704	0.03
0.04	0.0400	0.9992	0.0400	24.99	1.041	0.9608	0.04
0.05	0.0500	0.9988	0.0500	19.98	1.051	0.9512	0.05
0.06	0.0600	0.9982	0.0601	16.65	1.062	0.9418	0.06
0.07	0.0699	0.9976	0.0701	14.26	1.073	0.9324	0.07
0.08	0.0799	0.9968	0.0802	12.47	1.083	0.9231	0.08
0.09	0.0899	0.9960	0.0902	11.081	1.094	0.9139	0.09
0.10	0.0998	0.9950	0.1003	9.967	1.105	0.9048	**0.10**
0.11	0.1098	0.9940	0.1104	9.054	1.116	0.8958	0.11
0.12	0.1197	0.9928	0.1206	8.293	1.127	0.8869	0.12
0.13	0.1296	0.9916	0.1307	7.649	1.139	0.8781	0.13
0.14	0.1395	0.9902	0.1409	7.096	1.150	0.8694	0.14
0.15	0.1494	0.9888	0.1511	6.617	1.162	0.8607	0.15
0.16	0.1593	0.9872	0.1614	6.197	1.174	0.8521	0.16
0.17	0.1692	0.9856	0.1717	5.826	1.185	0.8437	0.17
0.18	0.1790	0.9838	0.1820	5.495	1.197	0.8353	0.18
0.19	0.1889	0.9820	0.1923	5.200	1.209	0.8270	0.19
0.20	0.1987	0.9801	0.2027	4.933	1.221	0.8187	**0.20**
0.21	0.2085	0.9780	0.2131	4.692	1.234	0.8106	0.21
0.22	0.2182	0.9759	0.2236	4.472	1.246	0.8025	0.22
0.23	0.2280	0.9737	0.2341	4.271	1.259	0.7945	0.23
0.24	0.2377	0.9713	0.2447	4.086	1.271	0.7866	0.24
0.25	0.2474	0.9689	0.2553	3.916	1.284	0.7788	0.25
0.26	0.2571	0.9664	0.2660	3.759	1.297	0.7711	0.26
0.27	0.2667	0.9638	0.2768	3.613	1.310	0.7634	0.27
0.28	0.2764	0.9611	0.2876	3.478	1.323	0.7558	0.28
0.29	0.2860	0.9582	0.2984	3.351	1.336	0.7483	0.29
0.30	0.2955	0.9553	0.3093	3.233	1.350	0.7408	**0.30**
0.31	0.3051	0.9523	0.3203	3.122	1.363	0.7334	0.31
0.32	0.3146	0.9492	0.3314	3.018	1.377	0.7261	0.32
0.33	0.3240	0.9460	0.3425	2.919	1.391	0.7189	0.33
0.34	0.3335	0.9428	0.3537	2.827	1.405	0.7118	0.34
0.35	0.3429	0.9394	0.3650	2.740	1.419	0.7047	0.35
0.36	0.3523	0.9359	0.3764	2.657	1.433	0.6977	0.36
0.37	0.3616	0.9323	0.3879	2.578	1.448	0.6907	0.37
0.38	0.3709	0.9287	0.3994	2.504	1.462	0.6839	0.38
0.39	0.3802	0.9249	0.4111	2.433	1.477	0.6771	0.39
0.40	0.3894	0.9211	0.4228	2.365	1.492	0.6703	**0.40**
0.41	0.3986	0.9171	0.4346	2.301	1.507	0.6637	0.41
0.42	0.4078	0.9131	0.4466	2.239	1.522	0.6570	0.42
0.43	0.4169	0.9090	0.4586	2.180	1.537	0.6505	0.43
0.44	0.4259	0.9048	0.4708	2.124	1.553	0.6440	0.44
0.45	0.4350	0.9004	0.4831	2.070	1.568	0.6376	0.45
0.46	0.4439	0.8961	0.4954	2.018	1.584	0.6313	0.46
0.47	0.4529	0.8916	0.5080	1.969	1.600	0.6250	0.47
0.48	0.4618	0.8870	0.5206	1.921	1.616	0.6188	0.48
0.49	0.4706	0.8823	0.5334	1.875	1.632	0.6126	0.49
0.50	0.4794	0.8776	0.5463	1.830	1.649	0.6065	**0.50**
x	$\sin x$	$\cos x$	$\tan x$	$\operatorname{ctn} x$	e^x	e^{-x}	x

x	$\sin x$	$\cos x$	$\tan x$	$\operatorname{ctn} x$	e^x	e^{-x}	x
0.50	0.4794	0.8776	0.5463	1.830	1.649	0.6065	**0.50**
0.51	0.4882	0.8727	0.5594	1.788	1.665	0.6005	0.51
0.52	0.4969	0.8678	0.5726	1.747	1.682	0.5945	0.52
0.53	0.5055	0.8628	0.5859	1.707	1.699	0.5886	0.53
0.54	0.5141	0.8577	0.5994	1.668	1.716	0.5827	0.54
0.55	0.5227	0.8525	0.6131	1.631	1.733	0.5769	0.55
0.56	0.5312	0.8473	0.6269	1.595	1.751	0.5712	0.56
0.57	0.5396	0.8419	0.6410	1.560	1.768	0.5655	0.57
0.58	0.5480	0.8365	0.6552	1.526	1.786	0.5599	0.58
0.59	0.5564	0.8309	0.6696	1.494	1.804	0.5543	0.59
0.60	0.5646	0.8253	0.6841	1.462	1.822	0.5488	**0.60**
0.61	0.5729	0.8196	0.6989	1.431	1.840	0.5434	0.61
0.62	0.5810	0.8139	0.7139	1.401	1.859	0.5379	0.62
0.63	0.5891	0.8080	0.7291	1.372	1.878	0.5326	0.63
0.64	0.5972	0.8021	0.7445	1.343	1.896	0.5273	0.64
0.65	0.6052	0.7961	0.7602	1.315	1.916	0.5220	0.65
0.66	0.6131	0.7900	0.7761	1.288	1.935	0.5169	0.66
0.67	0.6210	0.7838	0.7923	1.262	1.954	0.5117	0.67
0.68	0.6288	0.7776	0.8087	1.237	1.974	0.5066	0.68
0.69	0.6365	0.7712	0.8253	1.212	1.994	0.5016	0.69
0.70	0.6442	0.7648	0.8423	1.187	2.014	0.4966	**0.70**
0.71	0.6518	0.7584	0.8595	1.163	2.034	0.4916	0.71
0.72	0.6594	0.7518	0.8771	1.140	2.054	0.4868	0.72
0.73	0.6669	0.7452	0.8949	1.117	2.075	0.4819	0.73
0.74	0.6743	0.7385	0.9131	1.095	2.096	0.4771	0.74
0.75	0.6816	0.7317	0.9316	1.073	2.117	0.4724	0.75
0.76	0.6889	0.7248	0.9505	1.052	2.138	0.4677	0.76
0.77	0.6961	0.7179	0.9697	1.031	2.160	0.4630	0.77
0.78	0.7033	0.7109	0.9893	1.0109	2.181	0.4584	0.78
0.79	0.7104	0.7038	1.0092	0.9908	2.203	0.4538	0.79
0.80	0.7174	0.6967	1.030	0.9712	2.226	0.4493	**0.80**
0.81	0.7243	0.6895	1.050	0.9520	2.248	0.4449	0.81
0.82	0.7311	0.6822	1.072	0.9331	2.270	0.4404	0.82
0.83	0.7379	0.6749	1.093	0.9146	2.293	0.4360	0.83
0.84	0.7446	0.6675	1.116	0.8964	2.316	0.4317	0.84
0.85	0.7513	0.6600	1.138	0.8785	2.340	0.4274	0.85
0.86	0.7578	0.6524	1.162	0.8609	2.363	0.4232	0.86
0.87	0.7643	0.6448	1.185	0.8437	2.387	0.4190	0.87
0.88	0.7707	0.6372	1.210	0.8267	2.411	0.4148	0.88
0.89	0.7771	0.6294	1.235	0.8100	2.435	0.4107	0.89
0.90	0.7833	0.6216	1.260	0.7936	2.460	0.4066	**0.90**
0.91	0.7895	0.6137	1.286	0.7774	2.484	0.4025	0.91
0.92	0.7956	0.6058	1.313	0.7615	2.509	0.3985	0.92
0.93	0.8016	0.5978	1.341	0.7458	2.535	0.3946	0.93
0.94	0.8076	0.5898	1.369	0.7303	2.560	0.3906	0.94
0.95	0.8134	0.5817	1.398	0.7151	2.586	0.3867	0.95
0.96	0.8192	0.5735	1.428	0.7001	2.612	0.3829	0.96
0.97	0.8249	0.5653	1.459	0.6853	2.638	0.3791	0.97
0.98	0.8305	0.5570	1.491	0.6707	2.664	0.3753	0.98
0.99	0.8360	0.5487	1.524	0.6563	2.691	0.3716	0.99
1.00	0.8415	0.5403	1.557	0.6421	2.718	0.3679	**1.00**
x	$\sin x$	$\cos x$	$\tan x$	$\operatorname{ctn} x$	e^x	e^{-x}	x

x	$\sin x$	$\cos x$	$\tan x$	$\operatorname{ctn} x$	e^x	e^{-x}	x
1.00	0.8415	0.5403	1.557	0.6421	2.718	0.3679	**1.00**
1.01	0.8468	0.5319	1.592	0.6281	2.746	0.3642	1.01
1.02	0.8521	0.5234	1.628	0.6142	2.773	0.3606	1.02
1.03	0.8573	0.5148	1.665	0.6005	2.801	0.3570	1.03
1.04	0.8624	0.5062	1.704	0.5870	2.829	0.3535	1.04
1.05	0.8674	0.4976	1.743	0.5736	2.858	0.3499	1.05
1.06	0.8724	0.4889	1.784	0.5604	2.886	0.3465	1.06
1.07	0.8772	0.4801	1.827	0.5473	2.915	0.3430	1.07
1.08	0.8820	0.4713	1.871	0.5344	2.945	0.3396	1.08
1.09	0.8866	0.4625	1.917	0.5216	2.974	0.3362	1.09
1.10	0.8912	0.4536	1.965	0.5090	3.004	0.3329	**1.10**
1.11	0.8957	0.4447	2.014	0.4964	3.034	0.3296	1.11
1.12	0.9001	0.4357	2.066	0.4840	3.065	0.3263	1.12
1.13	0.9044	0.4267	2.120	0.4718	3.096	0.3230	1.13
1.14	0.9086	0.4176	2.176	0.4596	3.127	0.3198	1.14
1.15	0.9128	0.4085	2.234	0.4475	3.158	0.3166	1.15
1.16	0.9168	0.3993	2.296	0.4356	3.190	0.3135	1.16
1.17	0.9208	0.3902	2.360	0.4237	3.222	0.3104	1.17
1.18	0.9246	0.3809	2.427	0.4120	3.254	0.3073	1.18
1.19	0.9284	0.3717	2.498	0.4003	3.287	0.3042	1.19
1.20	0.9320	0.3624	2.572	0.3888	3.320	0.3012	**1.20**
1.21	0.9356	0.3530	2.650	0.3773	3.353	0.2982	1.21
1.22	0.9391	0.3436	2.733	0.3659	3.387	0.2952	1.22
1.23	0.9425	0.3342	2.820	0.3546	3.421	0.2923	1.23
1.24	0.9458	0.3248	2.912	0.3434	3.456	0.2894	1.24
1.25	0.9490	0.3153	3.010	0.3323	3.490	0.2865	1.25
1.26	0.9521	0.3058	3.113	0.3212	3.525	0.2837	1.26
1.27	0.9551	0.2963	3.224	0.3102	3.561	0.2808	1.27
1.28	0.9580	0.2867	3.341	0.2993	3.597	0.2780	1.28
1.29	0.9608	0.2771	3.467	0.2884	3.633	0.2753	1.29
1.30	0.9636	0.2675	3.602	0.2776	3.669	0.2725	**1.30**
1.31	0.9662	0.2579	3.747	0.2669	3.706	0.2698	1.31
1.32	0.9687	0.2482	3.903	0.2562	3.743	0.2671	1.32
1.33	0.9711	0.2385	4.072	0.2456	3.781	0.2645	1.33
1.34	0.9735	0.2288	4.256	0.2350	3.819	0.2618	1.34
1.35	0.9757	0.2190	4.455	0.2245	3.857	0.2592	1.35
1.36	0.9779	0.2092	4.673	0.2140	3.896	0.2567	1.36
1.37	0.9799	0.1994	4.913	0.2035	3.935	0.2541	1.37
1.38	0.9819	0.1896	5.177	0.1931	3.975	0.2516	1.38
1.39	0.9837	0.1798	5.471	0.1828	4.015	0.2491	1.39
1.40	0.9854	0.1700	5.798	0.1725	4.055	0.2466	**1.40**
1.41	0.9871	0.1601	6.165	0.1622	4.096	0.2441	1.41
1.42	0.9887	0.1502	6.581	0.1519	4.137	0.2417	1.42
1.43	0.9901	0.1403	7.055	0.1417	4.179	0.2393	1.43
1.44	0.9915	0.1304	7.602	0.1315	4.221	0.2369	1.44
1.45	0.9927	0.1205	8.238	0.1214	4.263	0.2346	1.45
1.46	0.9939	0.1106	8.989	0.1113	4.306	0.2322	1.46
1.47	0.9949	0.1006	9.887	0.1011	4.349	0.2299	1.47
1.48	0.9959	0.0907	10.983	0.0910	4.393	0.2276	1.48
1.49	0.9967	0.0807	12.35	0.0810	4.437	0.2254	1.49
1.50	0.9975	0.0707	14.10	0.0709	4.482	0.2231	**1.50**
x	$\sin x$	$\cos x$	$\tan x$	$\operatorname{ctn} x$	e^x	e^{-x}	x

x	$\sin x$	$\cos x$	$\tan x$	$\operatorname{ctn} x$	e^x	e^{-x}	x
1.50	0.9975	0.0707	14.10	0.0709	4.482	0.2231	**1.50**
1.51	0.9982	0.0608	16.43	0.0609	4.527	0.2209	1.51
1.52	0.9987	0.0508	19.67	0.0508	4.572	0.2187	1.52
1.53	0.9992	0.0408	24.50	0.0408	4.618	0.2165	1.53
1.54	0.9995	0.0308	32.46	0.0308	4.665	0.2144	1.54
1.55	0.9998	0.0208	48.08	0.0208	4.711	0.2122	1.55
1.56	0.9999	0.0108	92.62	0.0108	4.759	0.2101	1.56
1.57	1.0000	0.0008	1255.8	0.0008	4.807	0.2080	1.57
1.58	1.0000	−0.0092	−108.65	−0.0092	4.855	0.2060	1.58
1.59	0.9998	−0.0192	−52.07	−0.0192	4.904	0.2039	1.59
1.60	0.9996	−0.0292	−34.23	−0.0292	4.953	0.2019	**1.60**
1.61	0.9992	−0.0392	−25.49	−0.0392	5.003	0.1999	1.61
1.62	0.9988	−0.0492	−20.31	−0.0492	5.053	0.1979	1.62
1.63	0.9982	−0.0592	−16.87	−0.0593	5.104	0.1959	1.63
1.64	0.9976	−0.0691	−14.43	−0.0693	5.155	0.1940	1.64
1.65	0.9969	−0.0791	−12.60	−0.0794	5.207	0.1920	1.65
1.66	0.9960	−0.0891	−11.18	−0.0894	5.259	0.1901	1.66
1.67	0.9951	−0.0990	−10.047	−0.0995	5.312	0.1882	1.67
1.68	0.9940	−0.1090	−9.121	−0.1096	5.366	0.1864	1.68
1.69	0.9929	−0.1189	−8.349	−0.1198	5.419	0.1845	1.69
1.70	0.9917	−0.1288	−7.697	−0.1299	5.474	0.1827	**1.70**
1.71	0.9903	−0.1388	−7.137	−0.1401	5.529	0.1809	1.71
1.72	0.9889	−0.1487	−6.652	−0.1503	5.585	0.1791	1.72
1.73	0.9874	−0.1585	−6.228	−0.1606	5.641	0.1773	1.73
1.74	0.9857	−0.1684	−5.854	−0.1708	5.697	0.1755	1.74
1.75	0.9840	−0.1782	−5.520	−0.1811	5.755	0.1738	1.75
1.76	0.9822	−0.1881	−5.222	−0.1915	5.812	0.1720	1.76
1.77	0.9802	−0.1979	−4.953	−0.2019	5.871	0.1703	1.77
1.78	0.9782	−0.2077	−4.710	−0.2123	5.930	0.1686	1.78
1.79	0.9761	−0.2175	−4.489	−0.2228	5.989	0.1670	1.79
1.80	0.9738	−0.2272	−4.286	−0.2333	6.050	0.1653	**1.80**
1.81	0.9715	−0.2369	−4.100	−0.2439	6.110	0.1637	1.81
1.82	0.9691	−0.2466	−3.929	−0.2545	6.172	0.1620	1.82
1.83	0.9666	−0.2563	−3.771	−0.2652	6.234	0.1604	1.83
1.84	0.9640	−0.2660	−3.624	−0.2759	6.297	0.1588	1.84
1.85	0.9613	−0.2756	−3.488	−0.2867	6.360	0.1572	1.85
1.86	0.9585	−0.2852	−3.361	−0.2975	6.424	0.1557	1.86
1.87	0.9556	−0.2948	−3.242	−0.3085	6.488	0.1541	1.87
1.88	0.9526	−0.3043	−3.130	−0.3194	6.554	0.1526	1.88
1.89	0.9495	−0.3138	−3.026	−0.3305	6.619	0.1511	1.89
1.90	0.9463	−0.3233	−2.927	−0.3416	6.686	0.1496	**1.90**
1.91	0.9430	−0.3327	−2.834	−0.3528	6.753	0.1481	1.91
1.92	0.9396	−0.3421	−2.746	−0.3641	6.821	0.1466	1.92
1.93	0.9362	−0.3515	−2.663	−0.3755	6.890	0.1451	1.93
1.94	0.9326	−0.3609	−2.584	−0.3869	6.959	0.1437	1.94
1.95	0.9290	−0.3702	−2.509	−0.3985	7.029	0.1423	1.95
1.96	0.9252	−0.3795	−2.438	−0.4101	7.099	0.1409	1.96
1.97	0.9214	−0.3887	−2.370	−0.4219	7.171	0.1395	1.97
1.98	0.9174	−0.3979	−2.306	−0.4337	7.243	0.1381	1.98
1.99	0.9134	−0.4070	−2.244	−0.4456	7.316	0.1367	1.99
2.00	0.9093	−0.4161	−2.185	−0.4577	7.389	0.1353	**2.00**
x	$\sin x$	$\cos x$	$\tan x$	$\operatorname{ctn} x$	e^x	e^{-x}	x

Natural Logarithms of Numbers

N	$\ln N$	$\ln \frac{1}{10} N$	$\ln \frac{1}{100} N$	N	$\ln N$	$\ln \frac{1}{10} N$	$\ln \frac{1}{100} N$
0	—	—	—	50	3.9120	1.6094	−0.6931
1	0.0000	−2.3026	−4.6052	51	3.9318	1.6292	−0.6733
2	0.6931	−1.6094	−3.9120	52	3.9512	1.6487	−0.6539
3	1.0986	−1.2040	−3.5066	53	3.9703	1.6677	−0.6349
4	1.3863	−0.9163	−3.2189	54	3.9890	1.6864	−0.6162
5	1.6094	−0.6931	−2.9957	55	4.0073	1.7047	−0.5978
6	1.7918	−0.5108	−2.8134	56	4.0254	1.7228	−0.5798
7	1.9459	−0.3567	−2.6593	57	4.0431	1.7405	−0.5621
8	2.0794	−0.2231	−2.5257	58	4.0604	1.7579	−0.5447
9	2.1972	−0.1054	−2.4079	59	4.0775	1.7750	−0.5276
10	2.3026	0.0000	−2.3026	60	4.0943	1.7918	−0.5108
11	2.3979	0.0953	−2.2073	61	4.1109	1.8083	−0.4943
12	2.4849	0.1823	−2.1203	62	4.1271	1.8245	−0.4780
13	2.5649	0.2624	−2.0402	63	4.1431	1.8405	−0.4620
14	2.6391	0.3365	−1.9661	64	4.1589	1.8563	−0.4463
15	2.7081	0.4055	−1.8971	65	4.1744	1.8718	−0.4308
16	2.7726	0.4700	−1.8326	66	4.1897	1.8871	−0.4155
17	2.8332	0.5306	−1.7720	67	4.2047	1.9021	−0.4005
18	2.8904	0.5878	−1.7148	68	4.2195	1.9169	−0.3857
19	2.9444	0.6419	−1.6607	69	4.2341	1.9315	−0.3711
20	2.9957	0.6931	−1.6094	70	4.2485	1.9459	−0.3567
21	3.0445	0.7419	−1.5606	71	4.2627	1.9601	−0.3425
22	3.0910	0.7885	−1.5141	72	4.2767	1.9741	−0.3285
23	3.1355	0.8329	−1.4697	73	4.2905	1.9879	−0.3147
24	3.1781	0.8755	−1.4271	74	4.3041	2.0015	−0.3011
25	3.2189	0.9163	−1.3863	75	4.3175	2.0149	−0.2877
26	3.2581	0.9555	−1.3471	76	4.3307	2.0281	−0.2744
27	3.2958	0.9933	−1.3093	77	4.3438	2.0412	−0.2614
28	3.3322	1.0296	−1.2730	78	4.3567	2.0541	−0.2485
29	3.3673	1.0647	−1.2379	79	4.3694	2.0669	−0.2357
30	3.4012	1.0986	−1.2040	80	4.3820	2.0794	−0.2231
31	3.4340	1.1314	−1.1712	81	4.3944	2.0919	−0.2107
32	3.4657	1.1632	−1.1394	82	4.4067	2.1041	−0.1985
33	3.4965	1.1939	−1.1087	83	4.4188	2.1163	−0.1863
34	3.5264	1.2238	−1.0788	84	4.4308	2.1282	−0.1744
35	3.5553	1.2528	−1.0498	85	4.4427	2.1401	−0.1625
36	3.5835	1.2809	−1.0217	86	4.4543	2.1518	−0.1508
37	3.6109	1.3083	−0.9943	87	4.4659	2.1633	−0.1393
38	3.6376	1.3350	−0.9676	88	4.4773	2.1748	−0.1278
39	3.6636	1.3610	−0.9416	89	4.4886	2.1861	−0.1165
40	3.6889	1.3863	−0.9163	90	4.4998	2.1972	−0.1054
41	3.7136	1.4110	−0.8916	91	4.5109	2.2083	−0.0943
42	3.7377	1.4351	−0.8675	92	4.5218	2.2192	−0.0834
43	3.7612	1.4586	−0.8440	93	4.5326	2.2300	−0.0726
44	3.7842	1.4816	−0.8210	94	4.5433	2.2407	−0.0619
45	3.8067	1.5041	−0.7985	95	4.5539	2.2513	−0.0513
46	3.8286	1.5261	−0.7765	96	4.5643	2.2618	−0.0408
47	3.8501	1.5476	−0.7550	97	4.5747	2.2721	−0.0305
48	3.8712	1.5686	−0.7340	98	4.5850	2.2824	−0.0202
49	3.8918	1.5892	−0.7133	99	4.5951	2.2925	−0.0101
50	3.9120	1.6094	−0.6931	100	4.6052	2.3026	0.0000

Factorials and Their Logarithms

For $n! = p \cdot 10^k$, k is the integral part of $\log n!$

n	p to four digits	$\log n!$	n	p to four digits	$\log n!$	n	p to four digits	$\log n!$
1	1.	0.0000	21	5.109	19.7083	41	3.345	49.5244
2	2.	0.3010	22	1.124	21.0508	42	1.405	51.1477
3	6.	0.7782	23	2.585	22.4125	43	6.042	52.7811
4	2.4	1.3802	24	6.204	23.7927	44	2.658	54.4246
5	1.20	2.0792	25	1.551	25.1906	45	1.196	56.0778
6	7.20	2.8573	26	4.033	26.6056	46	5.503	57.7406
7	5.040	3.7024	27	1.089	28.0370	47	2.586	59.4127
8	4.032	4.6055	28	3.049	29.4841	48	1.241	61.0939
9	3.629	5.5598	29	8.842	30.9465	49	6.083	62.7841
10	3.629	6.5598	30	2.653	32.4237	50	3.041	64.4831
11	3.992	7.6012	31	8.223	33.9150	51	1.551	66.1906
12	4.790	8.6803	32	2.631	35.4202	52	8.066	67.9066
13	6.227	9.7943	33	8.683	36.9387	53	4.275	69.6309
14	8.718	10.9404	34	2.952	38.4702	54	2.308	71.3633
15	1.308	12.1165	35	1.033	40.0142	55	1.270	73.1037
16	2.092	13.3206	36	3.720	41.5705	56	7.110	74.8519
17	3.557	14.5511	37	1.376	43.1387	57	4.053	76.6077
18	6.402	15.8063	38	5.230	44.7185	58	2.351	78.3712
19	1.216	17.0851	39	2.040	46.3096	59	1.387	80.1420
20	2.433	18.3861	40	8.159	47.9116	60	8.321	81.9202

Trigonometric Functions of Some Particular Angles

θ	θ in radians	$\sin \theta$	$\cos \theta$	$\tan \theta$	$\operatorname{ctn} \theta$	$\sec \theta$	$\csc \theta$
0°	0	0	1	0	—	1	—
15°	$\pi/12$	0.2618	0.2588	0.9659	0.2679	3.7321	1.0353	3.8637
30°	$\pi/6$	0.5236	0.5	0.8660	0.5774	1.7321	1.1547	2
45°	$\pi/4$	0.7854	0.7071	0.7071	1	1	1.4142	1.4142
60°	$\pi/3$	1.0472	0.8660	0.5	1.7321	0.5774	2	1.1547
75°	$5\pi/12$	1.3090	0.9659	0.2588	3.7321	0.2679	3.8637	1.0353
90°	$\pi/2$	1.5708	1	0	—	0	—	1
105°	$7\pi/12$	1.8326	0.9659	−0.2588	−3.7321	−0.2679	−3.8637	1.0353
120°	$2\pi/3$	2.0944	0.8660	−0.5	−1.7321	−0.5774	−2	1.1547
135°	$3\pi/4$	2.3562	0.7071	−0.7071	−1	−1	−1.4142	1.4142
150°	$5\pi/6$	2.6180	0.5	−0.8660	−0.5774	−1.7321	−1.1547	2
165°	$11\pi/12$	2.8798	0.2588	−0.9659	−0.2679	−3.7321	−1.0353	3.8637
180°	π	3.1416	0	−1	0	—	−1	—
195°	$13\pi/12$	3.4034	−0.2588	−0.9659	0.2679	3.7321	−1.0353	−3.8637
210°	$7\pi/6$	3.6652	−0.5	−0.8660	0.5774	1.7321	−1.1547	−2
225°	$5\pi/4$	3.9270	−0.7071	−0.7071	1	1	−1.4142	−1.4142
240°	$4\pi/3$	4.1888	−0.8660	−0.5	1.7321	0.5774	−2	−1.1547
255°	$17\pi/12$	4.4506	−0.9659	−0.2588	3.7321	0.2679	−3.8637	−1.0353
270°	$3\pi/2$	4.7124	−1	0	—	0	—	−1
285°	$19\pi/12$	4.9742	−0.9659	0.2588	−3.7321	−0.2679	3.8637	−1.0353
300°	$5\pi/3$	5.2360	−0.8660	0.5	−1.7321	−0.5774	2	−1.1547
315°	$7\pi/4$	5.4978	−0.7071	0.7071	−1	−1	1.4142	−1.4142
330°	$11\pi/6$	5.7596	−0.5	0.8660	−0.5774	−1.7321	1.1547	−2
345°	$23\pi/12$	6.0214	−0.2588	0.9659	−0.2679	−3.7321	1.0353	−3.8637
360°	2π	6.2832	0	1	0	—	1	—

d/n	1	2	3	4	5	6	7	8	n	9	10	11	12	13	14	15	d/n
0.1	0.1	0.2	0.3	0.4	0.5	0.6	0.7	0.8	0.1	0.9	1.0	1.1	1.2	1.3	1.4	1.5	0.1
0.2	0.2	0.4	0.6	0.8	1.0	1.2	1.4	1.6	0.2	1.8	2.0	2.2	2.4	2.6	2.8	3.0	0.2
0.3	0.3	0.6	0.9	1.2	1.5	1.8	2.1	2.4	0.3	2.7	3.0	3.3	3.6	3.9	4.2	4.5	0.3
0.4	0.4	0.8	1.2	1.6	2.0	2.4	2.8	3.2	0.4	3.6	4.0	4.4	4.8	5.2	5.6	6.0	0.4
0.5	0.5	1.0	1.5	2.0	2.5	3.0	3.5	4.0	0.5	4.5	5.0	5.5	6.0	6.5	7.0	7.5	0.5
0.6	0.6	1.2	1.8	2.4	3.0	3.6	4.2	4.8	0.6	5.4	6.0	6.6	7.2	7.8	8.4	9.0	0.6
0.7	0.7	1.4	2.1	2.8	3.5	4.2	4.9	5.6	0.7	6.3	7.0	7.7	8.4	9.1	9.8	10.5	0.7
0.8	0.8	1.6	2.4	3.2	4.0	4.8	5.6	6.4	0.8	7.2	8.0	8.8	9.6	10.4	11.2	12.0	0.8
0.9	0.9	1.8	2.7	3.6	4.5	5.4	6.3	7.2	0.9	8.1	9.0	9.9	10.8	11.7	12.6	13.5	0.9

d/n	16	17	18	19	20	21	22	23	n	24	25	26	27	28	29	30	d/n
0.1	1.6	1.7	1.8	1.9	2.0	2.1	2.2	2.3	0.1	2.4	2.5	2.6	2.7	2.8	2.9	3.0	0.1
0.2	3.2	3.4	3.6	3.8	4.0	4.2	4.4	4.6	0.2	4.8	5.0	5.2	5.4	5.6	5.8	6.0	0.2
0.3	4.8	5.1	5.4	5.7	6.0	6.3	6.6	6.9	0.3	7.2	7.5	7.8	8.1	8.4	8.7	9.0	0.3
0.4	6.4	6.8	7.2	7.6	8.0	8.4	8.8	9.2	0.4	9.6	10.0	10.4	10.8	11.2	11.6	12.0	0.4
0.5	8.0	8.5	9.0	9.5	10.0	10.5	11.0	11.5	0.5	12.0	12.5	13.0	13.5	14.0	14.5	15.0	0.5
0.6	9.6	10.2	10.8	11.4	12.0	12.6	13.2	13.8	0.6	14.4	15.0	15.6	16.2	16.8	17.4	18.0	0.6
0.7	11.2	11.9	12.6	13.3	14.0	14.7	15.4	16.1	0.7	16.8	17.5	18.2	18.9	19.6	20.3	21.0	0.7
0.8	12.8	13.6	14.4	15.2	16.0	16.8	17.6	18.4	0.8	19.2	20.0	20.8	21.6	22.4	23.2	24.0	0.8
0.9	14.4	15.3	16.2	17.1	18.0	18.9	19.8	20.7	0.9	21.6	22.5	23.4	24.3	25.2	26.1	27.0	0.9

d/n	31	32	33	34	35	36	37	38	n	39	40	41	42	43	44	45	d/n
0.1	3.1	3.2	3.3	3.4	3.5	3.6	3.7	3.8	0.1	3.9	4.0	4.1	4.2	4.3	4.4	4.5	0.1
0.2	6.2	6.4	6.6	6.8	7.0	7.2	7.4	7.6	0.2	7.8	8.0	8.2	8.4	8.6	8.8	9.0	0.2
0.3	9.3	9.6	9.9	10.2	10.5	10.8	11.1	11.4	0.3	11.7	12.0	12.3	12.6	12.9	13.2	13.5	0.3
0.4	12.4	12.8	13.2	13.6	14.0	14.4	14.8	15.2	0.4	15.6	16.0	16.4	16.8	17.2	17.6	18.0	0.4
0.5	15.5	16.0	16.5	17.0	17.5	18.0	18.5	19.0	0.5	19.5	20.0	20.5	21.0	21.5	22.0	22.5	0.5
0.6	18.6	19.2	19.8	20.4	21.0	21.6	22.2	22.8	0.6	23.4	24.0	24.6	25.2	25.8	26.4	27.0	0.6
0.7	21.7	22.4	23.1	23.8	24.5	25.2	25.9	26.6	0.7	27.3	28.0	28.7	29.4	30.1	30.8	31.5	0.7
0.8	24.8	25.6	26.4	27.2	28.0	28.8	29.6	30.4	0.8	31.2	32.0	32.8	33.6	34.4	35.2	36.0	0.8
0.9	27.9	28.8	29.7	30.6	31.5	32.4	33.3	34.2	0.9	35.1	36.0	36.9	37.8	38.7	39.6	40.5	0.9

d/n	46	47	48	49	50	51	52	53	n	54	55	56	57	58	59	60	d/n
0.1	4.6	4.7	4.8	4.9	5.0	5.1	5.2	5.3	0.1	5.4	5.5	5.6	5.7	5.8	5.9	6.0	0.1
0.2	9.2	9.4	9.6	9.8	10.0	10.2	10.4	10.6	0.2	10.8	11.0	11.2	11.4	11.6	11.8	12.0	0.2
0.3	13.8	14.1	14.4	14.7	15.0	15.3	15.6	15.9	0.3	16.2	16.5	16.8	17.1	17.4	17.7	18.0	0.3
0.4	18.4	18.8	19.2	19.6	20.0	20.4	20.8	21.2	0.4	21.6	22.0	22.4	22.8	23.2	23.6	24.0	0.4
0.5	23.0	23.5	24.0	24.5	25.0	25.5	26.0	26.5	0.5	27.0	27.5	28.0	28.5	29.0	29.5	30.0	0.5
0.6	27.6	28.2	28.8	29.4	30.0	30.6	31.2	31.8	0.6	32.4	33.0	33.6	34.2	34.8	35.4	36.0	0.6
0.7	32.2	32.9	33.6	34.3	35.0	35.7	36.4	37.1	0.7	37.8	38.5	39.2	39.9	40.6	41.3	42.0	0.7
0.8	36.8	37.6	38.4	39.2	40.0	40.8	41.6	42.4	0.8	43.2	44.0	44.8	45.6	46.4	47.2	48.0	0.8
0.9	41.4	42.3	43.2	44.1	45.0	45.9	46.8	47.7	0.9	48.6	49.5	50.4	51.3	52.2	53.1	54.0	0.9

d/n	61	62	63	64	65	66	67	68	n	69	70	71	72	73	74	75	d/n
0.1	6.1	6.2	6.3	6.4	6.5	6.6	6.7	6.8	0.1	6.9	7.0	7.1	7.2	7.3	7.4	7.5	0.1
0.2	12.2	12.4	12.6	12.8	13.0	13.2	13.4	13.6	0.2	13.8	14.0	14.2	14.4	14.6	14.8	15.0	0.2
0.3	18.3	18.6	18.9	19.2	19.5	19.8	20.1	20.4	0.3	20.7	21.0	21.3	21.6	21.9	22.2	22.5	0.3
0.4	24.4	24.8	25.2	25.6	26.0	26.4	26.8	27.2	0.4	27.6	28.0	28.4	28.8	29.2	29.6	30.0	0.4
0.5	30.5	31.0	31.5	32.0	32.5	33.0	33.5	34.0	0.5	34.5	35.0	35.5	36.0	36.5	37.0	37.5	0.5
0.6	36.6	37.2	37.8	38.4	39.0	39.6	40.2	40.8	0.6	41.4	42.0	42.6	43.2	43.8	44.4	45.0	0.6
0.7	42.7	43.4	44.1	44.8	45.5	46.2	46.9	47.6	0.7	48.3	49.0	49.7	50.4	51.1	51.8	52.5	0.7
0.8	48.8	49.6	50.4	51.2	52.0	52.8	53.6	54.4	0.8	55.2	56.0	56.8	57.6	58.4	59.2	60.0	0.8
0.9	54.9	55.8	56.7	57.6	58.5	59.4	60.3	61.2	0.9	62.1	63.0	63.9	64.8	65.7	66.6	67.5	0.9

d/n	76	77	78	79	80	81	82	83	n	84	85	86	87	88	89	90	d/n
0.1	7.6	7.7	7.8	7.9	8.0	8.1	8.2	8.3	0.1	8.4	8.5	8.6	8.7	8.8	8.9	9.0	0.1
0.2	15.2	15.4	15.6	15.8	16.0	16.2	16.4	16.6	0.2	16.8	17.0	17.2	17.4	17.6	17.8	18.0	0.2
0.3	22.8	23.1	23.4	23.7	24.0	24.3	24.6	24.9	0.3	25.2	25.5	25.8	26.1	26.4	26.7	27.0	0.3
0.4	30.4	30.8	31.2	31.6	32.0	32.4	32.8	33.2	0.4	33.6	34.0	34.4	34.8	35.2	35.6	36.0	0.4
0.5	38.0	38.5	39.0	39.5	40.0	40.5	41.0	41.5	0.5	42.0	42.5	43.0	43.5	44.0	44.5	45.0	0.5
0.6	45.6	46.2	46.8	47.4	48.0	48.6	49.2	49.8	0.6	50.4	51.0	51.6	52.2	52.8	53.4	54.0	0.6
0.7	53.2	53.9	54.6	55.3	56.0	56.7	57.4	58.1	0.7	58.8	59.5	60.2	60.9	61.6	62.3	63.0	0.7
0.8	60.8	61.6	62.4	63.2	64.0	64.8	65.6	66.4	0.8	67.2	68.0	68.8	69.6	70.4	71.2	72.0	0.8
0.9	68.4	69.3	70.2	71.1	72.0	72.9	73.8	74.7	0.9	75.6	76.5	77.4	78.3	79.2	80.1	81.0	0.9

d/n	91	92	93	94	95	96	97	98	n	99	100	101	102	103	104	105	d/n
0.1	9.1	9.2	9.3	9.4	9.5	9.6	9.7	9.8	0.1	9.9	10.0	10.1	10.2	10.3	10.4	10.5	0.1
0.2	18.2	18.4	18.6	18.8	19.0	19.2	19.4	19.6	0.2	19.8	20.0	20.2	20.4	20.6	20.8	21.0	0.2
0.3	27.3	27.6	27.9	28.2	28.5	28.8	29.1	29.4	0.3	29.7	30.0	30.3	30.6	30.9	31.2	31.5	0.3
0.4	36.4	36.8	37.2	37.6	38.0	38.4	38.8	39.2	0.4	39.6	40.0	40.4	40.8	41.2	41.6	42.0	0.4
0.5	45.5	46.0	46.5	47.0	47.5	48.0	48.5	49.0	0.5	49.5	50.0	50.5	51.0	51.5	52.0	52.5	0.5
0.6	54.6	55.2	55.8	56.4	57.0	57.6	58.2	58.8	0.6	59.4	60.0	60.6	61.2	61.8	62.4	63.0	0.6
0.7	63.7	64.4	65.1	65.8	66.5	67.2	67.9	68.6	0.7	69.3	70.0	70.7	71.4	72.1	72.8	73.5	0.7
0.8	72.8	73.6	74.4	75.2	76.0	76.8	77.6	78.4	0.8	79.2	80.0	80.8	81.6	82.4	83.2	84.0	0.8
0.9	81.9	82.8	83.7	84.6	85.5	86.4	87.3	88.2	0.9	89.1	90.0	90.9	91.8	92.7	93.6	94.5	0.9

d/n	106	107	108	109	110	111	n	112	113	114	115	116	117	d/n
0.1	10.6	10.7	10.8	10.9	11.0	11.1	0.1	11.2	11.3	11.4	11.5	11.6	11.7	0.1
0.2	21.2	21.4	21.6	21.8	22.0	22.2	0.2	22.4	22.6	22.8	23.0	23.2	23.4	0.2
0.3	31.8	32.1	32.4	32.7	33.0	33.3	0.3	33.6	33.9	34.2	34.5	34.8	35.1	0.3
0.4	42.4	42.8	43.2	43.6	44.0	44.4	0.4	44.8	45.2	45.6	46.0	46.4	46.8	0.4
0.5	53.0	53.5	54.0	54.5	55.0	55.5	0.5	56.0	56.5	57.0	57.5	58.0	58.5	0.5
0.6	63.6	64.2	64.8	65.4	66.0	66.6	0.6	67.2	67.8	68.4	69.0	69.6	70.2	0.6
0.7	74.2	74.9	75.6	76.3	77.0	77.7	0.7	78.4	79.1	79.8	80.5	81.2	81.9	0.7
0.8	84.8	85.6	86.4	87.2	88.0	88.8	0.8	89.6	90.4	91.2	92.0	92.8	93.6	0.8
0.9	95.4	96.3	97.2	98.1	99.0	99.9	0.9	100.8	101.7	102.6	103.5	104.4	105.3	0.9

d/n	118	119	120	121	122	123	n	124	125	126	127	128	129	d/n
0.1	11.8	11.9	12.0	12.1	12.2	12.3	0.1	12.4	12.5	12.6	12.7	12.8	12.9	0.1
0.2	23.6	23.8	24.0	24.2	24.4	24.6	0.2	24.8	25.0	25.2	25.4	25.6	25.8	0.2
0.3	35.4	35.7	36.0	36.3	36.6	36.9	0.3	37.2	37.5	37.8	38.1	38.4	38.7	0.3
0.4	47.2	47.6	48.0	48.4	48.8	49.2	0.4	49.6	50.0	50.4	50.8	51.2	51.6	0.4
0.5	59.0	59.5	60.0	60.5	61.0	61.5	0.5	62.0	62.5	63.0	63.5	64.0	64.5	0.5
0.6	70.8	71.4	72.0	72.6	73.2	73.8	0.6	74.4	75.0	75.6	76.2	76.8	77.4	0.6
0.7	82.6	83.3	84.0	84.7	85.4	86.1	0.7	86.8	87.5	88.2	88.9	89.6	90.3	0.7
0.8	94.4	95.2	96.0	96.8	97.6	98.4	0.8	99.2	100.0	100.8	101.6	102.4	103.2	0.8
0.9	106.2	107.1	108.0	108.9	109.8	110.7	0.9	111.6	112.5	113.4	114.3	115.2	116.1	0.9

d/n	130	131	132	133	134	135	n	136	137	138	139	140	141	d/n
0.1	13.0	13.1	13.2	13.3	13.4	13.5	0.1	13.6	13.7	13.8	13.9	14.0	14.1	0.1
0.2	26.0	26.2	26.4	26.6	26.8	27.0	0.2	27.2	27.4	27.6	27.8	28.0	28.2	0.2
0.3	39.0	39.3	39.6	39.9	40.2	40.5	0.3	40.8	41.1	41.4	41.7	42.0	42.3	0.3
0.4	52.0	52.4	52.8	53.2	53.6	54.0	0.4	54.4	54.8	55.2	55.6	56.0	56.4	0.4
0.5	65.0	65.5	66.0	66.5	67.0	67.5	0.5	68.0	68.5	69.0	69.5	70.0	70.5	0.5
0.6	78.0	78.6	79.2	79.8	80.4	81.0	0.6	81.6	82.2	82.8	83.4	84.0	84.6	0.6
0.7	91.0	91.7	92.4	93.1	93.8	94.5	0.7	95.2	95.9	96.6	97.3	98.0	98.7	0.7
0.8	104.0	104.8	105.6	106.4	107.2	108.0	0.8	108.8	109.6	110.4	111.2	112.0	112.8	0.8
0.9	117.0	117.9	118.8	119.7	120.6	121.5	0.9	122.4	123.3	124.2	125.1	126.0	126.9	0.9

d/n	142	143	144	145	146	147	n	148	149	150	151	152	153	d/n
0.1	14.2	14.3	14.4	14.5	14.6	14.7	0.1	14.8	14.9	15.0	15.1	15.2	15.3	0.1
0.2	28.4	28.6	28.8	29.0	29.2	29.4	0.2	29.6	29.8	30.0	30.2	30.4	30.6	0.2
0.3	42.6	42.9	43.2	43.5	43.8	44.1	0.3	44.4	44.7	45.0	45.3	45.6	45.9	0.3
0.4	56.8	57.2	57.6	58.0	58.4	58.8	0.4	59.2	59.6	60.0	60.4	60.8	61.2	0.4
0.5	71.0	71.5	72.0	72.5	73.0	73.5	0.5	74.0	74.5	75.0	75.5	76.0	76.5	0.5
0.6	85.2	85.8	86.4	87.0	87.6	88.2	0.6	88.8	89.4	90.0	90.6	91.2	91.8	0.6
0.7	99.4	100.1	100.8	101.5	102.2	102.9	0.7	103.6	104.3	105.0	105.7	106.4	107.1	0.7
0.8	113.6	114.4	115.2	116.0	116.8	117.6	0.8	118.4	119.2	120.0	120.8	121.6	122.4	0.8
0.9	127.8	128.7	129.6	130.5	131.4	132.3	0.9	133.2	134.1	135.0	135.9	136.8	137.7	0.9

d/n	154	155	156	157	158	159	n	160	161	162	163	164	165	d/n
0.1	15.4	15.5	15.6	15.7	15.8	15.9	0.1	16.0	16.1	16.2	16.3	16.4	16.5	0.1
0.2	30.8	31.0	31.2	31.4	31.6	31.8	0.2	32.0	32.2	32.4	32.6	32.8	33.0	0.2
0.3	46.2	46.5	46.8	47.1	47.4	47.7	0.3	48.0	48.3	48.6	48.9	49.2	49.5	0.3
0.4	61.6	62.0	62.4	62.8	63.2	63.6	0.4	64.0	64.4	64.8	65.2	65.6	66.0	0.4
0.5	77.0	77.5	78.0	78.5	79.0	79.5	0.5	80.0	80.5	81.0	81.5	82.0	82.5	0.5
0.6	92.4	93.0	93.6	94.2	94.8	95.4	0.6	96.0	96.6	97.2	97.8	98.4	99.0	0.6
0.7	107.8	108.5	109.2	109.9	110.6	111.3	0.7	112.0	112.7	113.4	114.1	114.8	115.5	0.7
0.8	123.2	124.0	124.8	125.6	126.4	127.2	0.8	128.0	128.8	129.6	130.4	131.2	132.0	0.8
0.9	138.6	139.5	140.4	141.3	142.2	143.1	0.9	144.0	144.9	145.8	146.7	147.6	148.5	0.9

d/n	166	167	168	169	170	171	n	172	173	174	175	176	177	d/n
0.1	16.6	16.7	16.8	16.9	17.0	17.1	0.1	17.2	17.3	17.4	17.5	17.6	17.7	0.1
0.2	33.2	33.4	33.6	33.8	34.0	34.2	0.2	34.4	34.6	34.8	35.0	35.2	35.4	0.2
0.3	49.8	50.1	50.4	50.7	51.0	51.3	0.3	51.6	51.9	52.2	52.5	52.8	53.1	0.3
0.4	66.4	66.8	67.2	67.6	68.0	68.4	0.4	68.8	69.2	69.6	70.0	70.4	70.8	0.4
0.5	83.0	83.5	84.0	84.5	85.0	85.5	0.5	86.0	86.5	87.0	87.5	88.0	88.5	0.5
0.6	99.6	100.2	100.8	101.4	102.0	102.6	0.6	103.2	103.8	104.4	105.0	105.6	106.2	0.6
0.7	116.2	116.9	117.6	118.3	119.0	119.7	0.7	120.4	121.1	121.8	122.5	123.2	123.9	0.7
0.8	132.8	133.6	134.4	135.2	136.0	136.8	0.8	137.6	138.4	139.2	140.0	140.8	141.6	0.8
0.9	149.4	150.3	151.2	152.1	153.0	153.9	0.9	154.8	155.7	156.6	157.5	158.4	159.3	0.9

d/n	178	179	180	181	182	183	n	184	185	186	187	188	189	d/n
0.1	17.8	17.9	18.0	18.1	18.2	18.3	0.1	18.4	18.5	18.6	18.7	18.8	18.9	0.1
0.2	35.6	35.8	36.0	36.2	36.4	36.6	0.2	36.8	37.0	37.2	37.4	37.6	37.8	0.2
0.3	53.4	53.7	54.0	54.3	54.6	54.9	0.3	55.2	55.5	55.8	56.1	56.4	56.7	0.3
0.4	71.2	71.6	72.0	72.4	72.8	73.2	0.4	73.6	74.0	74.4	74.8	75.2	75.6	0.4
0.5	89.0	89.5	90.0	90.5	91.0	91.5	0.5	92.0	92.5	93.0	93.5	94.0	94.5	0.5
0.6	106.8	107.4	108.0	108.6	109.2	109.8	0.6	110.4	111.0	111.6	112.2	112.8	113.4	0.6
0.7	124.6	125.3	126.0	126.7	127.4	128.1	0.7	128.8	129.5	130.2	130.9	131.6	132.3	0.7
0.8	142.4	143.2	144.0	144.8	145.6	146.4	0.8	147.2	148.0	148.8	149.6	150.4	151.2	0.8
0.9	160.2	161.1	162.0	162.9	163.8	164.7	0.9	165.6	166.5	167.4	168.3	169.2	170.1	0.9

Symbol	Value	Common Logarithm
π	3.1415 9265	0.4971 4987
e = Napierian base	2.7182 8183	0.4342 9448
γ = Euler's constant	0.5772 1566	9.7613 3811–10
$M = \log e$	0.4342 9448	9.6377 8431–10
$1/M = \ln 10$	2.3025 8509	0.3622 1569
$1/e$	0.3678 7944	9.5657 0552–10
$\sqrt{e}$	1.6487 2127	0.2171 4724
$1/\sqrt{e}$	0.6065 3066	9.7828 5276–10
$180/\pi$ = degrees in 1 radian	57.2957 7951	1.7581 2263
$\pi/180$ = radians in 1 degree	0.0174 5329	8.2418 7737–10
$\pi/10800$ = radians in 1 minute	0.0002 9088 8209	6.4637 2612–10
$\pi/648000$ = radians in 1 second	0.0000 0484 8137	4.6855 7487–10
$\pi/6$	0.5235 9878	9.7189 9862–10
$\pi/4$	0.7853 9816	9.8950 8988–10
$\pi/3$	1.0471 9755	0.0200 2862
$\pi/2$	1.5707 9633	0.1961 1988
π^2	9.8696 0440	0.9942 9975
π^3	31.0062 7668	1.4914 4962
π^4	97.4090 9103	1.9885 9949
$1/\pi$	0.3183 0989	9.5028 5013–10
$1/\pi^2$	0.1013 2118	9.0057 0025–10
$1/\pi^3$	0.0322 5153	8.5085 5038–10
$1/\pi^4$	0.0102 6598	8.0114 0051–10
$\sqrt{\pi}$	1.7724 5385	0.2485 7494
$\sqrt[3]{\pi}$	1.4645 9189	0.1657 1662
$\sqrt[3]{\pi^2}$	2.1450 2940	0.3314 3325
$1/\sqrt{\pi}$	0.5641 8958	9.7514 2506–10
$1/\sqrt[3]{\pi}$	0.6827 8406	9.8342 8338–10
$\sqrt{2\pi}$	2.5066 2827	0.3990 8993
$1/\sqrt{2\pi}$	0.3989 4228	9.6009 1007–10
$\sqrt{2/\pi}$	0.7978 8456	9.9019 4006–10
$\sqrt[3]{\pi/6}$	0.8059 9598	9.9063 3287–10

Certain Values with Greater Accuracy

$$\pi = 3.1415\ 9265\ 3589\ 7932\ 3846\ 2643\ 3832\ 7956$$
$$\log \pi = 0.4971\ 4987\ 2694\ 1338\ 5435\ 1268\ 2882\ 9090$$
$$\ln \pi = 1.1447\ 2988\ 5849\ 4001\ 7414\ 3427\ 3513\ 5306$$
$$e = 2.7182\ 8182\ 8459\ 0452\ 3536\ 0287\ 4713\ 5266$$
$$M = 0.4342\ 9448\ 1903\ 2518\ 2765\ 1128\ 9189\ 1661$$
$$1/M = 2.3025\ 8509\ 2994\ 0456\ 8401\ 7991\ 4546\ 8436$$
$$\log M = 9.6377\ 8431\ 1300\ 5367\ 8912\ 2967\ 4986\ 4511\text{–}10$$

ANSWERS

The answers to the odd-numbered exercises only are given here. The answers to the even-numbered exercises are available in a separate pamphlet, furnished only with the consent of the instructor.

Section 1–2. Pages 4 and 5

1. (a) 3, -3, $\sqrt[3]{27}$, $\sqrt[3]{-8}$, $\sqrt[4]{16}$;
   (b) 3, -3, $\frac{1}{3}$, $\frac{4}{3}$, $\sqrt[3]{27}$, $\sqrt[3]{-8}$, $\sqrt[3]{\frac{27}{8}}$, $\sqrt[4]{16}$;
   (c) $\sqrt{3}$, 3π, $\sqrt[3]{25}$;
   (d) all.
3. (a) True; (b) true; (c) false; *a rational number*; (d) true.
5. (a) Integers greater than 1; (b) integers; (c) positive integers; (d) positive rational numbers.
7. (a) Positive real numbers; (b) real numbers; (c) positive real numbers; (d) positive real numbers.
9. (a) 2; (b) no; m/n exists if $n \neq 5$.

Section 1–3. Page 7

3. (a) Positive, 1; (b) positive, 6; (c) negative, 4; (d) positive, 2; (e) positive, 5; (f) negative, 3; (g) negative, 4; (h) positive, 4; (i) negative, $5 - \pi$.
5. (a) 3; (b) 5; (c) 0; (d) 16; (e) -16; (f) -16; (g) 4; (h) 0.
7. $+10$, -20, -32, -1, $+2$.

Section 1–4. Pages 8 and 9

1. (a) $3 < 5$; (b) $-3 > -5$; (c) $-5 < 2$; (d) $2 > 0$; (e) $0 > -2$; (f) $-1 > -2$.
3. (a) $-.100$, $-.030$, $-.004$, $+.027$, $+.053$; (b) $-.004$, $+.027$, $-.030$, $+.053$, $-.100$.
5. (a) $-\sqrt{6}$, $-\frac{2}{3}$, 0, 1.62, 3, $\frac{22}{7}$; (b) -5, $-\sqrt{13}$, -3, $\sqrt{10}$, 4, 6.
7. (a) $x > a$; (b) $x < b$; (c) $a < x < b$; (d) $x < a$ or $x > b$.
9. (a) At origin or to right (positive side) of origin; (b) at origin; (c) to right of origin; (d) to left of origin.
11. (a) The origin and P_1; (b) points to left (negative side) of origin or to right of P_1; (c) points between origin and P_1; (d) the origin; (e) points to left of origin; (f) points to right of origin.

Section 1–5. Pages 12 and 13

1. 4.   3. -8.   5. -12.   7. 12.   9. 3.   11. -4.   13. $-\frac{3}{5}$.   15. $\frac{32}{25}$.
17. $-\frac{32}{9}$.   19. $-xy + xz$.   21. $x - 8$.   23. -16.   25. $-\frac{8}{25}$.
27. (a) $5x + (-2)$; (b) $4 + (-y)$; (c) $2 + (-5 - \sqrt{2})$; (d) $a + (-b + c)$.
29. (a) True; (b) true; (c) true; (d) false.
31. (a) Of unlike sign; (b) at least one of them zero; (c) of like sign.

Section 1–6. Pages 16 and 17

1. 3^5.   3. x^7.   5. $1/x^4$.   7. 3^{10}.   9. 2^2.   11. x^2.   13. 289.   15. 5329.
17. 941,192.   19. a^{10}.   21. $8u^3$.   23. $-x^5$.   25. $-x^{10}$.   27. x^7y^5.
29. $a^{12}b^8$.   31. x^{12}.   33. $-\frac{64}{27}$.   35. -2.   37. a^2/b^2.   39. w^3/v^2.   41. x^{a+b}.
43. b^xa^x.   45. 2^{20}.   47. -2^4.   49. $1/2^1$.   53. Yes.
55. (a) $a > 1$ and $m > 1$; (b) $a = 1$ or $m = 1$; (c) $a < 1$ and $m > 1$.
57. (a) 11_2, 110_2, 1011_2, 10100_2; (b) 2, 5, 11, 27.

Section 1–7. Pages 18 and 19

1. $\frac{1}{8}$. **3.** -8. **5.** 1. **7.** 0. **9.** $\frac{1}{8}$. **11.** 128. **13.** $\frac{1}{6561}$. **15.** $\frac{1}{8}$.
17. $1/3^{12}$. **19.** $1/3^{12}$. **21.** $1/3^{12}$. **23.** $\frac{1}{4}$. **25.** $\frac{64}{6561}$. **27.** 2. **29.** 1. **31.** x.
33. $1/a^2$. **35.** b^3/c^2. **37.** $8b^6/a^3$. **39.** $-\frac{1}{5}d/c^3$. **41.** x^2y^4/z^6. **43.** $-x$.
45. 1. **47.** y^7. **49.** $1/a^4$. **51.** x^2. **53.** b^2.

Section 1–8. Pages 20 and 21

1. $3.24 \cdot 10^2$. **3.** $4.6 \cdot 10^4$. **5.** $9.2 \cdot 10^{-4}$. **7.** $6.34 \cdot 10^6$. **9.** 67,600.
11. $4.05224 \cdot 10^{11}$. **13.** 0.001 849. **15.** 0.000 232 6. **17.** 240,000 miles.
19. 93,000,000 miles. **21.** 25,000 miles per hour. **23.** 10,000,000,000.
25. 0.000 000 000 001 60 erg. **27.** $2.095 \cdot 10^8$ persons.
29. $1.92 \cdot 10^{19}$ miles; 19,200,000,000,000,000,000 miles.

Section 1–9. Pages 23 to 25

1. (a) 3.0; (b) 2.97. **3.** (a) 3.5; (b) 3.45. **5.** (a) 0.0015; (b) 0.00149.
7. (a) 210, i.e., $2.1 \cdot 10^2$; (b) 210, i.e., $2.10 \cdot 10^2$. **9.** $1.09 \cdot 10^{-3}$ foot. **11.** $8.00 \cdot 10^6$.
13. $1.61 \cdot 10^{10}$ miles. **15.** $2.36 \cdot 10^{-5}$ inch. **17.** 0.9. **19.** 4.0. **21.** 5.90.
23. 3.0. **25.** 15,000. **27.** 630, i.e., $6.3 \cdot 10^2$. **29.** 10.01. **31.** 592.
33. 118.1. **35.** 10.3. **37.** 76.24. **39.** (a) 0.5776; (b) 0.58.
41. (a) 21,952,000,000; (b) 22,000,000,000. **43.** (a) 0.000 034 48; (b) 0.000 034.
45. (a) 555.6; (b) 560. **47.** (a) 0.01370; (b) 0.01370. **49.** $4 \cdot 10^{-7}$.

Section 2–1. Pages 28 and 29

1. (a) 640; (b) $\frac{135}{4}$; (c) -80. **3.** (a) -17; (b) 79; (c) $-\frac{13}{16}$; (d) $\frac{33}{2}$. **5.** (a) $\frac{1}{64}$; (b) 0.
7. (a) $3x^4$, $3xyzw$, $2x^2y^2/z$; (b) $3x + 4$, $ax + b$; (c) $3a^2 - 2a + 1$, $ax^2 + bx + c$,
$3x^2 - 5xy + 6y^2$; (d) $3x + 4$, $3x^4$, $3xyzw$, $3a^2 - 2a + 1$, $ax + b$, $ax^2 + bx + c$,
$3x^2 - 5xy + 6y^2$, $x^2 - y^2 + x - y + 2$.
9. $2xy^2$, $3xy^2$, πxy^2. **11.** (a) $5x^4y^5$; (b) x^4y^5; (c) $-4x^4y^5$; (d) $6x^4y^5$; (e) $3ax^4y^5$; (f) $\frac{3}{2}x^4y^5$.
13. (a) 5; (b) 3; (c) 5; (d) 7; (e) 7. **19.** Impossible.

Section 2–2. Page 30

1. $2x - y + z$. **3.** $3x + 4$. **5.** $x - 6$. **7.** $\frac{3}{2}$. **9.** $\frac{1}{2}$. **11.** $-5x + 7$. **13.** 3.
15. $-x^2 - 11xy + 8y^2$. **17.** $(a + b) - (x - y)$. **19.** $(3a + 2b) - (3x - 2y)$.
21. 5. **23.** 1. **25.** -12. **27.** $1/x$. **29.** $81x^{8n}$. **31.** $3x^{-8n}$.

Section 2–3. Pages 32 and 33

1. $4x^2 - 3x^2 - 2x - 12$. **3.** $-3y^3 - 9y^2 + 2y - 6$. **5.** $a^3 + a^2 - 2a + 2b^2 - 4$.
7. $3a + 3a^2 - 3a^4$. **9.** $2z^3w^3 + 6z^4w^2 - 8z^5w$. **11.** $\frac{2}{3}x^2yz^5 - \frac{4}{3}x^3y^3z^4 + 2x^4yz^7$.
13. $x^2 + 3x - 10$. **15.** $a^2 - 14a + 48$. **17.** $15x^2 + 14x - 8$. **19.** $6 - 13n + 6n^2$.
21. $c^2 + 2cd + d^2$. **23.** $x^2 + 4xy + 4y^2$. **25.** $9a^2 - 25b^2$. **27.** $9 - x^2$.
29. $6r^2 + 5rs - 6s^2$. **31.** $\frac{1}{4}y^2 - \frac{11}{24}y + \frac{1}{4}$. **33.** $4u^2 + v^2 - 4uv + 20u - 10v + 25$.
35. $6x^3 + x^2 + 9x + 5$. **37.** $a^3x^3 - b^3$. **39.** $-2x^4 - x^3 + 7x^2 - 21x + 9$.
41. $3a^3 - 7a^2 - 18a - 8$. **43.** $2x^2 - 10y^2 - 12z^2 - xy - 2xz + 23yz$.
45. (a) $-x^2 - 4x + 9$; (b) $x^2 + 4x - 9$. **47.** (a) $2x^2 - 4xy$; (b) $4xy - 2x^2$.
49. Change the sign of each term of the answer to (a).

Section 2–4. Pages 35 and 36

1. $3x^2y$. **3.** $-6y^3z^2$. **5.** $4x^2 - 3y$. **7.** $\frac{2}{3}v - 1 + \frac{2}{5u}$. **9.** $a^2 + 2a - 3$.

11. $y + 2 + \dfrac{2}{3y - 1}$. **13.** $4x - 1 - \dfrac{1}{3x + 2}$. **15.** $x^2 - 2 + \dfrac{2x - 1}{x^2 - 1}$.

17. $5a - 2 + \dfrac{-31a + 11}{3a^2 + 5a + 5}$. **19.** $x^2 + x + 1$. **21.** $x^3 - 3x^2 + 9x - 27$.

23. $\frac{2}{7}$. **25.** $\frac{20}{3}$.

Section 2–5. Page 38

1. (a) 11, 31; (b) 9, 10, 12, 30, 32.
3. Every other even number has 2 as a factor and so is composite.
5. $10x - 6x^2$.   **7.** $4 - 9x^2$.   **9.** $4y^2 - 16a^2$.   **11.** $n^2 + 8n + 16$.
13. $9a^2 + 48ab + 64b^2$.   **15.** $8x^2 + 8xy + 2y^2$.   **17.** $x^2 + 3x - 10$.
19. $5x^2 - 3xy - 2y^2$.   **21.** $6a^2 - 13ab^2 + 6b^4$.   **23.** $\frac{1}{18}a^2 - \frac{1}{8}b^2$.
25. $-6r^2 - 5rs + 6s^2$.   **27.** $x^4 - 2x^2y^2 + y^4$.   **29.** $a^3 - 8b^3$.
31. $x^2 + 4y^2 + 9 + 4xy + 6x + 12y$.   **33.** $27x^3 - 54x^2 + 36x - 8$.
35. $x^2 + 4x + 4 - a^2$.   **37.** $x^4 + 2x + x^{-2}$.   **39.** $x^{2n} + 6x^n + 9$.
41. (a) 96; (b) 399; (c) 8.99; (d) 875; (e) 99.91; (f) 0.039975.

Section 2–6. Pages 41 to 43

1. $3x(1 + 2y)$.   **3.** $(a - b)(x + y)$.   **5.** $(x + 2y)(x -- 2y)$.
7. $(5x + 4y)(5x - 4y)$.   **9.** $(a - b + c)(a - b - c)$.   **11.** $(a + 2b)^2$.
13. $(2u - 3v)^2$.   **15.** $(7 + 2y)^2$.   **17.** $(3 + x)(9 - 3x + x^2)$.
19. $(5a - 2b)(25a^2 + 10ab + 4b^2)$.   **21.** $(a - 2)(a - 3)$.   **23.** $(x - 8)(x - 2)$.
25. $(7 - c)(1 - c)$.   **27.** $(3x - 2)(x - 2)$.   **29.** $(3x - 4a)(2x + a)$.
31. $(a - 1)(b - 1)$.   **33.** $(a + b)(a - b + 1)$.   **35.** $(x + y - z)(x - y + z)$.
37. $(a + 4)(2a^2 - 3)$.   **39.** $(3x + 4)(2x - 5)$.   **41.** $\frac{1}{100}(6m + 7n)(6m - 7n)$.
43. $(x^2 + y^2)(x + y)(x - y)$.   **45.** $(x + 2)(x - 1)(x^2 - 2x + 4)(x^2 + x + 1)$.
47. $(4x^2 + 3yz^3)^2$.   **49.** $(x^n + 2)(x^n + 1)$.   **51.** $(x - 1)(x - 2)(5x - 7)$.
53. $(a^2 + a + 5)(a^2 - a + 5)$.   **55.** $4(x^2 + 2bx + 2b^2)(x^2 - 2bx + 2b^2)$.
57. $2^2 \cdot 3^2 \cdot 7x$.   **59.** $2^4 \cdot 3 \cdot 5x^2y^3$.   **61.** $2^3 \cdot 3^2 \cdot 7^2abx^3y^3z^2$.   **63.** $2(x + 3)(x - 3)$.
65. $(a + b)(a - b)^2$.   **67.** $2(3z + 2)^2(4z - 3)(3z - 2)$.   **71.** 41; also others.

Section 2–7. Pages 45 to 47

1. (a) $\dfrac{24}{6x + 18}$; (b) $\dfrac{-12}{-3x - 9}$; (c) $\dfrac{4}{x + 3}$; (d) $\dfrac{12x}{3x^2 + 9x}$.

3. (a) $\dfrac{a^3b + a^2b^2 + ab^3}{a^2b + ab^2}$; (b) $\dfrac{a^3 - b^3}{a^2 - b^2}$.   **5.** $x = -3$.   **7.** No real values.   **9.** $-\frac{3}{2}$.

11. $-\frac{7}{8}$.   **13.** $-\dfrac{ab}{c}$.   **15.** $\dfrac{pq}{r}$.   **17.** $\dfrac{1}{1}$, i.e., 1.   **19.** $-\dfrac{ab^3}{c^2}$.   **21.** $\dfrac{3}{12}$.

23. $\dfrac{6x + 10}{12}$.   **25.** $\dfrac{2x^2y}{18xy}$.   **27.** $\dfrac{12b}{18xy}$.   **29.** $\dfrac{18xy}{18xy}$.   **31.** $\dfrac{1}{2x}$.   **33.** $\dfrac{y^2}{4x}$.

35. $\dfrac{4y^3}{9x^3}$.   **37.** $-\frac{9}{2}x$.   **39.** $-\dfrac{1}{x + y}$.   **41.** $\dfrac{x - y}{x + y}$.   **43.** $\dfrac{1}{y^2 + x^2}$.

45. $\dfrac{a - b}{a^2 + ab + b^2}$.

47. Incorrect in first two steps; see last two warnings in text.

Section 2–8. Pages 50 to 52

1. $3x + 2y$.   **3.** b^3.   **5.** $\dfrac{2b^2}{ab^2}, \dfrac{3ab}{ab^2}, \dfrac{15}{ab^2}$.   **7.** $\dfrac{(x - y)^2}{x^2 - y^2}, \dfrac{(x + y)(x^2 + y^2)}{x^2 - y^2}, \dfrac{3}{x^2 - y^2}$.

9. $\dfrac{4a - 32b}{a^2 - 4b^2}$.   **11.** $\dfrac{5x - 5y}{6}$.   **13.** $\dfrac{4}{a + 1}$.   **15.** $\dfrac{5x^2 + x - 12}{6x(x + 3)(x - 3)}$.

17. $\dfrac{-x^3 - 5x^2 - x + 1}{x^3(x + 1)}$.   **19.** 0.

21. (a) $\dfrac{3(4 - 2x^2 - 2xt - t^2)}{(2 - x^2 - 2xt - t^2)(2 - x^2)}$; (b) $\dfrac{3(2xt + t^2)}{(2 - x^2 - 2xt - t^2)(2 - x^2)}$;

    (c) $\dfrac{-3(2xt + t^2)}{(2 - x^2 - 2xt - t^2)(2 - x^2)}$.

23. $\frac{2}{9}$.   **25.** $\frac{z}{x+y}$.   **27.** $\frac{32}{15}ab$.   **29.** $\frac{r}{s^2t}$.   **31.** $\frac{1}{x-1}$.   **33.** $\frac{x^2(x^2+y^2)}{y(x+y)^2}$.

35. $-\frac{x^2+x+2}{x-1}$.   **37.** $-\frac{8}{7}$.   **39.** $3-x$.   **41.** $\frac{xy}{x+y}$.   **43.** $\frac{a+b}{a^2b(b-a)}$.

45. $\frac{x}{x+2y}$.

Section 2–8.   Miscellaneous Exercises.   Pages 52 to 55

1. $\frac{x+5}{6}$.   **3.** $\frac{a+1}{a-3}$.   **5.** $\frac{z^3+3z^2-6z-27}{3z(z+3)}$.   **7.** $-\frac{1}{a+b}$.   **9.** $\frac{u+v+w}{u-v+w}$.

11. $\frac{4x+3}{x-4}$.   **13.** $\frac{3a-2b}{2a-3b}$.   **15.** $\frac{x^2+y^2}{x+y}$.   **17.** $\frac{1}{3}$.   **19.** $\frac{x^2}{(1-x^2)^2}$.

21. $-\frac{6x+4}{x^2}$.   **23.** $\frac{125}{x^3}$.   **25.** $\frac{y^2-3}{y^2-1}$.   **27.** $\frac{x+1}{x-1}$.   **29.** $\frac{y-x}{xy}$.

31. $\frac{ab}{a^2-ab+b^2}$.   **33.** $6 \cdot 10^4$.   **35.** $5.0 \cdot 10^{-4}$.   **37.** $3.00 \cdot 10^3$.   **39.** 0.217.

41. 0.00013 or 0.0001333.   **43.** 14.   **45.** 204.   **47.** $\frac{3x-2}{-4x+3}$.

49. (a) 144; (b) $110\frac{1}{4}$; (c) 90,000.   **51.** 15,200; 20,600; 23,000; 24,400; 25,200.
53. (a) 583.9 days; (b) 779.9 days; (c) 779.9 days; (d) $\frac{4}{3}p$.
55. (a) 24 pounds on the moon, 406 pounds on Jupiter, 96 pounds on the other planet;
(b) 0.16 x pounds on the moon, 2.71 x pounds on Jupiter, 0.64 x pounds on the other planet.

Section 3–2.   Pages 58 and 59

1. (a) 1, 2, 4, 9; $-1, -2, -4, -9$; (b) $\frac{1}{2}, \frac{1}{4}, \frac{1}{12}$; $-\frac{1}{2}, -\frac{1}{4}, -\frac{1}{12}$; (c) 11, 20, 26; $-11, -20, -26$; (d) $3 \cdot 10^2, 6 \cdot 10^5, 4 \cdot 10^2, 9 \cdot 10^{-3}$; $-3 \cdot 10^2, -6 \cdot 10^5, -4 \cdot 10^2, -9 \cdot 10^{-3}$.
3. (a) 2; (b) 4; (c) $\frac{1}{5}$; (d) 0.2; (e) $3 \cdot 10^5$.   **5.** $\frac{1}{5}$.   **7.** $\frac{3}{4}$.   **9.** 0.5, i.e., $\frac{1}{2}$.
11. -0.2, i.e., $-\frac{1}{5}$.   **13.** (a) 36; (b) 2.449; (c) 216; (d) 1.817.
15. (a) 0.36; (b) 0.7746; (c) 0.216; (d) 0.8434.
17. (a) 136,900; (b) 19.235; (c) 50,653,000; (d) 7.179.
19. (a) 13.69; (b) 1.9235; (c) 50.653; (d) 1.5467.
21. (a) 0.7225; (b) 0.9220; (c) 0.614125; (d) 0.9473.
23. (a) $1.936 \cdot 10^{-5}$; (b) 0.06633; (c) $8.5184 \cdot 10^{-8}$; (d) 0.16386.
25. (a) $7.84 \cdot 10^{12}$; 1673.3; (c) $2.1952 \cdot 10^{19}$; (d) 140.95.
27. (a) $8.464 \cdot 10^{-11}$; (b) 0.0030332; (c) $7.78688 \cdot 10^{-16}$; (d) 0.020954.
29. 18.36, 18.44; agree to better than 2 significant digits.
31. True.   **33.** False.   **35.** $1.8 \cdot 10^2$ inches.   **37.** $2.1 \cdot 10^3$ meters.

Section 3–3.   Pages 61 to 63

1. 4.   **3.** 4.   **5.** 2.   **7.** $\frac{1}{3}$.   **9.** 4.   **11.** 4.   **13.** 243.   **15.** $\frac{2}{5}$.
17. $-\frac{1}{1024}$.   **19.** 0.04.   **21.** 4.   **23.** 3.606.   **25.** $\frac{1}{15}$.   **27.** $\frac{1}{64}$.   **29.** 2.

31. 0.16   **33.** x^2.   **35.** $x^{\frac{1}{2}}$.   **37.** $\frac{1}{a^4}$.   **39.** $3b^3$.   **41.** $\frac{1}{x^{\frac{3}{2}}}$.   **43.** $a^{\frac{1}{6}}$.   **45.** $\frac{1}{z^{\frac{3}{4}}}$.

47. $-x^{\frac{1}{5}}$.   **49.** $\frac{1}{x^{\frac{1}{12}}}$.   **51.** $-x^3y$.   **53.** $\frac{x^4z^{\frac{2}{3}}}{y^{\frac{2}{3}}}$.   **55.** $a^{\frac{1}{3}}$.   **57.** $\frac{1}{5}x^6$.   **59.** 5x.

61. $\frac{1}{x^2} - \frac{2}{xy} + \frac{1}{y^2}$.   **63.** $\frac{r^2s^2}{r^2+s^2}$.   **65.** $r - 2 + \frac{1}{r}$.   **67.** $x - y$.   **69.** $\frac{x+1}{x^{\frac{1}{2}}}$.

71. x^{4n^2-9}.   **73.** $y^{\frac{a^2-a-2}{a}}$.   **75.** $\frac{1}{3000}$.   **77.** 50.   **79.** x^{a+3}.   **81.** x^{a^2-a-2}.

83. b^{2x}.   **85.** $a^{\frac{1}{}}$.   **87.** y^{k^2+k}.   **89.** x^{3b}.   **91.** $a^{2n} - b^{2n}$.   **93.** 2^{6x+1}.

95. $x^{8a} - 6x^{4a}y^{5b} + 9y^{10b}$.   **97.** y^{6n^2}.   **99.** x^{m^2+mn}.   **101.** $\frac{4^{2n}-1}{3^{2n}}$.

Section 3–4.   Pages 64 and 65

1. $\sqrt[3]{6}$.   **3.** $\sqrt[3]{x^2}$.   **5.** $2a^2\sqrt{2a}$.   **7.** $2\sqrt{x} - \sqrt{3y}$.   **9.** $\frac{1}{5}\sqrt{5}$.   **11.** $\frac{\sqrt{xy}}{y}$.

13. $5^{\frac{4}{3}}$.   **15.** $2x^{\frac{3}{4}}$.   **17.** $x^{\frac{1}{4}}y^{\frac{2}{5}}$.   **19.** $(a^2 - x^2)^{\frac{1}{2}}$.   **21.** $2\sqrt{2}$.   **23.** $6\sqrt[3]{2}$.

25. $-2\sqrt[3]{4}$.   **27.** $4\cdot10^4$.   **29.** $\frac{3}{10}\sqrt[3]{20}$.   **31.** $\frac{1}{5}\sqrt{15}$.   **33.** $-\frac{1}{3}\sqrt[3]{15}$.

35. $2x^2y\sqrt{3x}$.   **37.** $\frac{\sqrt[3]{6x^2z^2}}{2x}$.   **39.** $\frac{3x^4}{y^4}\sqrt{y}$.   **41.** $\sqrt[9]{4}$.   **43.** $\sqrt{6x^n}$.   **45.** $x\sqrt[6]{x^5}$.

47. $\sqrt[30]{x^{10}y^2z}$.   **49.** $\sqrt{75}$.   **51.** $\sqrt[3]{a^3b}$.   **53.** $\sqrt{\frac{9c^3}{d^2}}$.   **55.** $\sqrt[6]{a^3}$, $\sqrt[6]{b^2}$, $\sqrt[6]{c}$.

57. $\sqrt[6]{\frac{5}{4}}$, $\sqrt[6]{\frac{16}{9}}$, $\sqrt[6]{\frac{27}{8}}$.   **59.** $\sqrt[12]{3^{12}a^3}$, $\sqrt[12]{3^6a^6}$, $\sqrt[12]{\frac{a^4}{2^{12}}}$.   **61.** 56.92.   **63.** 5.130.

65. 85.37.   **67.** 0.6640.
69. (a) 1.8^- seconds; (b) $2\frac{1}{2}$ seconds; (c) 7.9^+ seconds.
71. (a) $1.5\cdot10^5$ centimeters per second; (b) $1.3^-\cdot10^5$ centimeters per second.

Section 3–5.   Pages 67 to 69

1. $8\sqrt{3}$; 13.86.   **3.** $14\sqrt{2}$; 19.80.   **5.** $\frac{1.9}{4}\sqrt[3]{4}$; 7.538.   **7.** $36\sqrt{3}$; 62.35.

9. $\sqrt{2}$; 1.414.   **11.** $\frac{1}{3}\sqrt{6}$; 0.816.   **13.** $-\frac{1}{2}$; -0.5.   **15.** 73.

17. (a) $\sqrt{5}$; (b) $\sqrt{3}$; (c) $\sqrt{3}$; (d) $\sqrt{6}$; (e) $\sqrt{2}$.   **19.** $(a - ab - b^2)\sqrt{a}$.

21. $\left(\frac{1}{y} - \frac{2}{x^2} - \frac{3x}{4}\right)\sqrt{2xy}$.   **23.** $\frac{5}{4}\sqrt{10}$.   **25.** x.   **27.** 147.   **29.** $\frac{3.2}{5}\sqrt[3]{2}$.

31. $10\sqrt{2} - 10\sqrt{5}$.   **33.** $\frac{1}{2}\sqrt{2} - \frac{2}{9}\sqrt{3}$.   **35.** $\frac{8}{5}$.   **37.** $xy - x\sqrt{xy}$.   **39.** $\frac{1}{3}y\sqrt{x}$.

41. $\frac{1}{3xy}$.   **43.** $\sqrt[6]{a^2b}$.   **45.** -13.   **47.** $18x^2 + 20y^2 - 22xy\sqrt{3}$.   **49.** 4.

51. $\frac{9}{5} - \frac{2}{5}\sqrt{14}$.   **53.** $\frac{12x^2 + 13xy\sqrt{3} + 9y^2}{16x^2 - 27y^2}$.   **55.** $2\sqrt{2}$.

57. $\frac{-3x + y}{x^2 - y^2}\sqrt{x^2 + y^2}$.   **59.** $1.203\cdot10^7$ cycles per second ("12.03 megacycles").

Section 3–6.   Pages 70 and 71

1. 4.   **3.** -5.   **5.** $\frac{1}{6}$.   **7.** $-\frac{16}{15}$.   **9.** $-\frac{5}{3}$.   **11.** $\frac{8}{3}$.   **13.** 3.   **15.** $-\frac{1}{6}$.

17. $3\sqrt{5}$.   **19.** $\frac{3}{5}\sqrt{5}$.   **21.** $-d/c$.   **23.** d^2/c.   **25.** $1 + \sqrt{5}$.   **27.** $\frac{13}{18}$.

29. (a) $R = (1 + 0.01n)W$; (b) $\frac{W}{R} = \frac{1}{1 + 0.01n}$; (c) $\frac{G}{W} = \frac{n}{100}$; (d) $\frac{G}{R} = \frac{0.01n}{1 + 0.01n}$;
(e) $N = 0.01nW - 5$.

Section 3–7.   Pages 72 and 73

1. (a) No; (b) yes; (c) yes.   **3.** $-\frac{16}{3}$.   **5.** bc^2.   **7.** 2.38.   **9.** 2.38.

11. $\frac{7}{120}$.   **13.** $a^2 - b^2$.   **15.** (a) $\frac{2.0}{3}$; (b) $\frac{1}{24}$; (c) bc/a; (d) c.

23. 260 miles, i.e., $2.6\cdot10^2$ miles.   **25.** 48 ft.

Section 3–8.   Page 75

7. 19.2.   **9.** 61,200.   **11.** 4.59.   **13.** 1.29.   **15.** 0.253.   **17.** 4.14.

19. 21.11.   **21.** 0.532.   **23.** 2.19.   **25.** 270.   **27.** -0.289.

Section 3–9.   Pages 78 and 79

1. $-i$.   **3.** i.   **5.** 1.   **7.** $-i$.   **9.** $3 - 4i$.   **11.** $-2 - 2i$.   **13.** $12 + 5i$.

15. 1.   **17.** $3 + i\sqrt{2}$.   **19.** $-6 + 2i\sqrt{3}$.   **21.** $-4i$.   **23.** $-\frac{15}{2}i\sqrt{3}$.

25. $2 + 2i$.   **27.** $(3\sqrt{3} - 15\sqrt{2})i$.   **29.** $2\sqrt{3} + 4i\sqrt{2}$.   **31.** $-100i$.

33. -45. **35.** $-9 - 40i$. **37.** $1 - 2i\sqrt{6}$. **39.** $24 + 13i\sqrt{5}$. **41.** $11 - 7i$.
43. $-3 + 4i$. **45.** 256. **47.** $38 - 64i$. **49.** $\frac{37}{5} - \frac{46}{5}i\sqrt{2}$.

Section 4–1. Pages 82 and 83

1. The independent variable is n; all integers n such that $0 \leq n \leq 2500$.
5. $y = 7 - x$. **7.** $y = \frac{5}{2} - \frac{3}{2}x$. **9.** $y = \frac{2}{3}x + \frac{5}{3}$. **11.** $A = \frac{1}{16}p^2$; $p > 0$.
13. $C = \frac{17}{3}x$; x a positive integer. **15.** $A = T/t$; $t > 0$.
17. In cubic inches, $V = 4x(7 - x)^2$; in square inches, $S = 196 - 4x^2$; $0 < x < 7$.
19. In square feet, $A = 200x - \frac{3}{2}x^2$; $0 < x < 133\frac{1}{3}$.

Section 4–2. Pages 85 and 86

1. (a) 3; (b) 23; (c) $\frac{7.5}{4}$; (d) 5; (e) $c^2 - 3c + 5$. **3.** (a) -16; (b) -37; (c) $-11 + \sqrt{5}$.
5. (a) 4; (b) $7 + \sqrt{3}$; (c) $-\frac{1}{2} - \frac{7}{4}\sqrt{2}$; (d) $y^3 + 3y^2 - 4y - 2$.
7. (a) $\frac{74}{25}$; (b) 608.69. **9.** (a) $-5x^2$; (b) $-35x^2$.
11. (a) -13; (b) 58; (c) -63; (d) 0; (e) 25; (f) 75; (g) $x^2 + 10xy + 3y^2$.
13. (a) 3; (b) $-\frac{7}{31}$; (c) $\dfrac{2(64 - x^3)}{x(x^3 - 16)}$; (d) $\dfrac{x^2(x^6 + 64)}{2(x^6 + 256)}$.
15. (a) 0; (b) $\frac{3}{2} + \frac{3}{2}i$; (c) $\frac{18}{17} - \frac{9}{34}i$; (d) $\frac{87}{17} + \frac{69}{17}i$.
17. (a) $t^2 + 4t$; (b) $a^2 - 4a$; (c) $a^2 - 2a - 3$; (d) $2a - 3$; (d) 32.
19. $V = f(l, w, h) = lwh$; $S = g(l, w, h) = 2(lw + lh + wh)$.
21. $l = f(A, w) = \dfrac{43,560A}{w}$.
23. (a) $23,000$; (b) $c = f(m) = 0.062m + 590$, $2000 = f(23,000)$; (c) 0.062 is cost in dollars per mile for items depending on mileage, such as gasoline, oil, and some kinds of repairs; 590 is annual cost in dollars for fixed items like insurance and (possibly) depreciation.

Section 4–3. Pages 87 and 88

1. $x = \frac{1}{3}(y - 4)$. **3.** $x = 5 - y$. **5.** $x = \frac{3}{2}y$. **7.** Inverse does not exist.
9. $x = \sqrt[3]{y}$. **11.** $x = \sqrt[4]{y}$. **13.** (a) $m = \dfrac{1}{0.062}(c - 590) \approx 16c - 9500$; (b) 16 is the miles per dollar spent for items depending on mileage; 9500 is the number of miles at this rate to cover fixed annual expenses.
15. (a) $r = \dfrac{C}{2\pi}$; (b) $d = \dfrac{C}{\pi}$; (c) $A = \dfrac{C^2}{4\pi}$. **17.** $b = \dfrac{2A}{h}$.
19. (a) $r = \dfrac{\sqrt{\pi S}}{2\pi}$; (b) $V = \dfrac{S}{6\pi}\sqrt{\pi S}$.

Section 4–4. Pages 90 to 92

1. I. **3.** IV. **5.** No quadrant. **7.** No quadrant. **9.** III. **11.** IV.
17. Fourth vertex $(-8, -5)$; center $(-3, -1)$.
19. On a line parallel to, and 5 units below, the x-axis.
21. On a line parallel to, and 3 units to the right of, the y-axis.
23. On a line parallel to, and 1 unit below, the x-axis.
25. On the x-axis. **27.** Above the x-axis.
29. In the second quadrant. **31.** In the third quadrant.
33. In the first quadrant on a line parallel to and 3 units to the right of the y-axis.
35. On a line through the origin bisecting the second and fourth quadrants.
37. (a) IV; (b) II; (c) II; (d) I; (e) IV; (f) II.
39. Positive in quadrants I and III; negative in quadrants II and IV.

Section 4–5. Pages 93 and 94

1. (a) 25; (b) 6; (c) $2\sqrt{13}$; (d) $7\sqrt{2}$.   **5.** (b) $\sqrt{13}$.   **7.** $d = 5t\sqrt{130}$.
9. $d \approx \sqrt{(600)^2 + (1012.7t)^2}$.

Section 4–6. Pages 97 to 99

43. $(0, 1), (2, 1)$.   **45.** $(2, 6)$.   **47.** $(-1.6, -1.5), (1.6, -1.5)$.   **53.** 15.8.

Section 4–7. Pages 100 and 101

1. 3.   **3.** -3.   **5.** 2.   **7.** $\frac{1}{2}$.   **9.** 6.   **11.** 0.   **13.** 1.   **15.** c.   **17.** 2.
19. $\frac{3}{2}$.   **21.** $\frac{4}{3}$.   **23.** $-\frac{8}{3}$.   **25.** 0.   **27.** $3x - 1$.   **29.** $4x - 6$.   **31.** $\frac{3}{2}x + \frac{2}{3}$.
33. $-3x + 12$.   **35.** $-\frac{1}{3}x - 1$.   **37.** $\frac{3}{4}x - \frac{13}{6}$.
39. (a) $x + 2$, $x - 1$, $2x + 3$, $3x - 5$, $4 - 3x$, $-2x - 5$; (b) x^2, $-\frac{1}{2}x^2$, $4 - x^2$, $x^2 + 2x$, $3x - x^2$, $x^2 + 3x + 2$, $x^2 - 4x - 5$, $3 + x - x^2$, $5 + x - x^2$, $x^2 - 4x + 4$, $\frac{1}{2}(1 + 3x + x^2)$, $\frac{5}{3} + \frac{4}{3}x - 2x^2$.
41. (a) $(0, b)$; (b) $(1, a + b)$; (c) a.

Section 4–8. Page 103

5. 40.7.   **7.** 972.   **9.** 0.259.   **11.** 77.8.   **13.** 0.363.
17. (a) $f(1) = -1$, $f(3) = -3$; (b) by substitution, $f(2) = -3$; by interpolation, $f(2) = -2$; (c) answers disagree because x_1 and x_3 are so far apart that the graph departs substantially from a straight line between them.

Section 4–9. Pages 104 and 105

1. $-6, 2$.   **3.** 1.   **5.** $-2, 3$.   **7.** No real zeros.   **9.** $-2.1, -0.2, 2.3$.
11. $-1.5, 1.5$.   **13.** Minimum at $x = 2$.   **15.** Maximum at $x = 2.5$.
17. Maximum at $x = -1.4$, minimum at $x = 1.4$.
19. (a) In cubic inches, $V = 4x(4 - x)^2$; (b) 1.3 inches by 5.4 inches by 5.4 inches. [A precise method gives 1.3 inches by 5.3 inches by 5.3 inches.]
21. 21 miles per hour.
23. (a) In cubic inches, $D = (e + 2)^3 - e^3 = 6e^2 + 12e + 8$; (b) edges 10 inches and 12 inches.
25. (a) $2n$, $2n + 2$, $2n + 4$, $4(3n^2 + 6n + 5)$; (b) $6, 8, 10$.
27. In square inches, $S = 2\pi r^2 + \dfrac{108\pi}{r}$; base radius 3 inches, altitude 6 inches.

Section 4–11. Pages 109 to 112

1. $E = kA^4$.   **3.** $s = kt^2 = \frac{1}{2}gt^2$.   **5.** $I = \dfrac{kE}{R}$.   **7.** $N = \dfrac{S}{P}$.   **9.** $T = \dfrac{kD}{R} = \dfrac{D}{R}$.

11. (a) $f = k\sqrt{t}$; (b) $f = \dfrac{k}{l}$; (c) $f = \dfrac{k}{\sqrt{m}}$.   **13.** $F = \dfrac{kms^2}{r}$.   **19.** (a) $y = \frac{3}{16}x^2$; (b) 27.

21. (a) $y = \frac{1}{12}x\sqrt{z}$; (b) $8\sqrt{3}$.   **23.** 400 cubic centimeters.   **25.** $4\frac{1}{2}°$.
27. (a) S is multiplied by 8; (b) x must be multiplied by $\sqrt[3]{2}$.
29. (a) S is multiplied by $\frac{1}{4}$; (b) x must be multiplied by $\frac{1}{2}\sqrt{2}$.
31. $864,000$ miles.   **33.** 1080 pounds.

Section 4–11. Miscellaneous Exercises. Pages 112 to 114

1. (b) 2 hours 54 minutes after leaving home.
3. (a) 6.6 miles, 9.8 miles, 11.8 miles; (b) 6.6 miles, 9.8 miles, 11.7 miles.

5. 59^+ seconds.   **7.** **(b)** 45 miles per hour.
9. In cubic feet, $V = \frac{1}{4}x(48 - x^2)$; 4 feet by 4 feet by 2 feet.   **11.** Equal.

13. $2\sqrt{h^2 + \left(\dfrac{30}{h} - 6\right)^2} + 6$.   **15.** 30 square inches.

Section 5–1. Pages 117 and 118

1. (a) 3; (b) 7; (c) 8.   **9.** Impossible.   **11.** Identity.   **13.** Equation.
15. Identity.   **17.** Identity.   **19.** Equation.   **21.** Identity.
23. Equation (impossible).   **25.** $2m = m + 7$.   **27.** $x = y - 4$.   **29.** $x^3 = x - 7$.
31. $\sqrt{(x - 2)^2 + (y + 1)^2} = 3$.

Section 5–2. Pages 119 to 121

1. (a) No; (b) yes.   **3.** (a) No; (b) no.   **5.** (a) No; (b) yes.   **7.** No.   **9.** Yes.

11. $-\frac{5}{2}$.   **13.** $\frac{1}{12}$.   **15.** $-\frac{6}{5}$.   **17.** 0.   **19.** 16.   **21.** $-\frac{8}{3}$.   **23.** $\dfrac{q}{p - r}$.

25. -2.   **27.** 2.   **29.** No solution.   **31.** All values of x.   **33.** $-\frac{1}{64}$.

35. $-\frac{4}{41}$.   **37.** 3.   **39.** 0.   **41.** 6.   **43.** $\dfrac{C}{2\pi}$.   **45.** $\dfrac{3V}{\pi r^2}$.   **47.** $\dfrac{P + c}{n} + p_1$.

Section 5–3. Pages 122 and 123

1. 5.   **3.** -4.   **5.** 2.6.   **7.** $-2.6, 2.6$.   **9.** $-4, 3$.   **11.** $-0.7, 2$.
13. $-1.3, 2.3$.   **15.** No real roots.   **17.** 1.2.   **19.** -1.3.   **21.** $-3.3, -0.8, 1.1$.
23. $-1.7, 1.1$.   **27.** (b) 54.5 miles; (c) 72 miles.

Section 5–4. Pages 126 and 127

1. Equivalent; (a) subtract 2 from both members; (b) add 2 to both members.
3. Not equivalent; second equation lacks root -3 of first equation.
5. Not equivalent; second equation lacks root $-\sqrt{3}$ of first equation.
7. (a) Equivalent; (b) contains an extraneous root; (c) contains an extraneous root.
9. -2.   **11.** No root.   **13.** No root.   **15.** $\frac{1}{2}$.   **17.** $-\frac{1}{4}$.   **19.** $-\frac{4}{5}$.
21. No root.   **23.** $-2, 2$.   **25.** 8.

Section 5–5. Pages 129 to 132

1. \$13,000.   **3.** $35°, 5°, 140°$.   **5.** 36.   **7.** 30.
9. 98,400 yards (about 56 statute miles).
11. In dollars, $C = 2.00 + 0.09n$; 42 cubic feet.
13. \$2.   **15.** 5 miles.   **17.** $2\frac{1}{4}$ quarts.   **19.** $33\frac{1}{3}$ pounds.   **21.** \$2.
23. (a) $4720\frac{5}{6}$ feet from the gun; (b) $4583\frac{1}{3}$ feet from the gun; (c) $4456\frac{5}{6}$ feet from the gun.

Section 5–6. Pages 134 to 136

1. $x^2 - 4x + 8 = 0$.   **3.** $2x^2 = 0$.   **5.** $x^2 + (r - s)x - t = 0$.
7. Not possible.   **9.** $\pm\frac{4}{3}$.   **11.** $\pm 4\sqrt{2}$.   **13.** $\pm 4i$.   **15.** $\pm\frac{13}{9}$.   **17.** $\pm\frac{1}{3}\sqrt{15}$.

19. $\pm\frac{2}{3}i\sqrt{3}$.   **21.** $\pm\dfrac{1}{g}\sqrt{2gs}$.   **23.** $\pm\frac{3}{2}$.   **25.** $\pm\dfrac{2c}{3a}$.   **27.** $\pm i\sqrt{11}$.

29. $\pm\dfrac{2}{3a}\sqrt{9a^2 - 4b^2}$.   **31.** $\pm i\sqrt{6}$.   **33.** $0, -4$.   **35.** $\pm\frac{5}{3}$.   **37.** $-3, -1$.
39. $-3, 4$.   **41.** $\frac{2}{3}, 2$.   **43.** $-\frac{1}{2}a, \frac{3}{2}a$.   **45.** $0, 0, 0, 0, \pm 9$.   **47.** $-\frac{1}{3}, \frac{1}{5}$.
49. $3b - 5c, 3b + 5c$.   **51.** $0, \pm 1, \pm 2$.   **53.** $-\frac{5}{2}, \frac{7}{2}$.
55. 7.07 inches by 7.07 inches by 16 inches.
57. (a) 5 inches; (b) 18.7 feet; (c) 0.472 feet.   **59.** 46^+ feet per second.   **61.** 2.
63. (a) $E_b = -100E_c$; (b) -2.5.

Section 5–7. Pages 137 and 138

1. 9. **3.** $\frac{1}{9}$. **5.** 8. **7.** $\frac{5}{36}a^2$. **9.** $-1, 9$. **11.** $-3 \pm 2\sqrt{3}$; $-6.46, 0.46$.

13. $\frac{1}{2}(1 \pm \sqrt{5})$; $-0.62, 1.62$. **15.** $(-1 \pm \sqrt{7})a$; $-3.65a, 1.65a$.

17. $\frac{1}{8}(-3 \pm \sqrt{89})$; $-1.55, 0.80$. **19.** $\frac{1}{3} \pm \frac{2}{3}i\sqrt{5}$; $0.33 \pm 1.49i$. **21.** $\dfrac{1 \pm \sqrt{1 - b^2}}{a}$.

23. $\dfrac{-p \pm \sqrt{p^2 - 4kq}}{2k}$. **25.** $\sqrt{3}\sqrt{[x - (-2)]^2 - 4}$. **27.** $2\sqrt{4 - [x - (-1)]^2}$.

29. $\sqrt{\frac{45}{4} - (x - \frac{7}{2})^2}$.
31. $(y - 4)^2 = 2 \cdot \frac{3}{4}[x - (-2)]$; vertex $(-2, 4)$, axis $y - 4 = 0$.
33. $(y - \frac{1}{2})^2 = 2 \cdot \frac{1}{4}[x - (-\frac{2}{3})]$; vertex $(-\frac{2}{3}, \frac{1}{2})$, axis $y - \frac{1}{2} = 0$.
35. $(x - \frac{1}{2})^2 + (y - \frac{3}{2})^2 = 3^2$; center $(\frac{1}{2}, \frac{3}{2})$, radius 3.

Section 5–8. Pages 140 to 142

1. 1, 5. **3.** $2 \pm i\sqrt{3}$; $2 \pm 1.73i$. **5.** $-\frac{1}{5}(1 \pm \sqrt{11})$; $-0.86, 0.46$.
7. $-\frac{1}{3}\sqrt{3}, \frac{2}{3}\sqrt{3}$; $-0.58, 1.15$. **9.** $1 - 2i, -1 - 2i$.

11. $\frac{1}{20}(-3 \pm \sqrt{89})$; $-0.62, 0.32$. **13.** $-\frac{1}{4}, \frac{9}{20}$. **15.** $-\frac{1}{3}a, 3a$. **17.** $\dfrac{a}{1 - b}, \dfrac{a}{1 + b}$.

19. $-4, 6$. **21.** 7. **23.** $-y \pm 3$. **25.** $\frac{1}{2}(1 - z \pm \sqrt{-3z^2 - 2z - 19})$.
27. (a) $-8, 9$; (b) 0, 1; (c) $\frac{1}{4}, \frac{3}{4}$; (d) $\frac{1}{2}(1 \pm i\sqrt{11})$.
29. (a) 14, 16; (b) 7, 32; (c) 8, 28. **31.** 84 square inches. **33.** 1.90^- inches.
35. (a) 0.78 second and 3.22 seconds after it is thrown; (b) 4 seconds after it is thrown.
37. 16^- seconds.

Section 5–9. Page 144

1. 11. **3.** 16. **5.** No roots. **7.** 11. **9.** $-3, -2$. **11.** $\frac{5}{2}$. **13.** 2.
15. $\pm\sqrt{2}, \pm i$. **17.** $\pm\frac{1}{2}, \pm\sqrt{7}$. **19.** $9, \frac{1}{16}$. **21.** $-2, -1$. **23.** $\frac{63}{64}$.
25. $-3, -2, 1, 2$. **27.** 0. **29.** $\frac{3}{2}$. **31.** $-6, 1$. **33.** $(3, -11)$ or $(3, 13)$.

Section 5–9. Miscellaneous Exercises. Pages 144 to 147

1. $-2, -1$. **3.** $2 \pm \sqrt{6}$; $-0.45, 4.45$. **5.** 0, 1. **7.** (a) 8; (b) 2.
9. (a) 8, 9; (b) 9, 10. **11.** $\dfrac{v_0 \pm \sqrt{v_0^2 - 2gs + 2gs_0}}{g}$. **13.** 8, 9, 10. **15.** 60 years old.
17. 10. **21.** (a) 3,160,000; (b) $10^4(1100 - 4x)$. **23.** $8{:}43\frac{7}{11}$ o'clock.
25. 256^- miles per hour. **27.** Car 56 miles per hour, truck 48 miles per hour.
29. 120. **31.** (a) 3 feet; (b) 12 feet. **33.** 24,000 miles.

Section 6–1. Pages 149 and 150

1. (a) 2.3; (b) 0.4; (c) 1.1; (d) 3.3; (e) 0.3; (f) 1.7.
3. (a) 2.5; (b) 0.7; (c) 1.6.
5. (a) 4.540; (b) 0.1672; (c) 1.371; (d) 0.9030.
17. $A = A_0(0.99)^t$.
19. (a) $400{,}000{,}000\,(1.02)^{n-1959}$; (b) 1994 A.D.

Section 6–2. Pages 152 and 153

1. $\log_{10} 10{,}000 = 4$. **3.** $\log_{10} 0.01 = -2$. **5.** $\log_2 8 = 3$. **7.** $\log_{16} 2 = \frac{1}{4}$.
9. $\log_{27} 9 = \frac{2}{3}$. **11.** $\log_{\frac{1}{8}} \frac{1}{64} = 2$. **13.** $\log_7 \frac{1}{49} = -2$. **15.** $\log_{\frac{25}{9}} \frac{27}{125} = -\frac{3}{2}$.
17. $\log_r t = s$. **19.** $7^2 = 49$. **21.** $8^{\frac{4}{3}} = 16$. **23.** $27^{-\frac{2}{3}} = \frac{1}{9}$. **25.** $13^0 = 1$.
27. $a^b = c$. **29.** 2. **31.** $\frac{5}{4}$. **33.** $-\frac{1}{3}$. **35.** 0. **37.** 2. **39.** $\frac{1}{2}$.
41. 0.00001. **43.** 128. **45.** $\frac{1}{2}$. **47.** 6. **49.** 2. **51.** $-\frac{1}{4}$. **53.** $-\frac{16}{25}$.

Section 6–3.   Pages 154 and 155

1. (a) 0.90; (b) 0.40; (c) 0.11; (d) −0.15.
3. (a) 0.6; (b) −0.6; (c) 2.1; (d) −0.3; (e) 3.1.   **5.** (a) 2; (b) −4; (c) 2; (d) −1.2.
7. (a) 25; (b) 0.04; (c) 5; (d) 0.2; (e) 1; (f) 3125.   **9.** −12.   **11.** 4.1.

Section 6–4.   Pages 158 and 159

1. $\log_3 p + \log_3 q$.   **3.** $3 + \log x$.   **5.** $\frac{2}{5}\log_7 3$.   **7.** $c\log_b x + d\log_b y$.

9. $\frac{1}{3}\ln 3 + \frac{5}{6}\ln 7$.   **11.** $\log_c (a/b)$.   **13.** $\log (u^5/v^{\frac{1}{5}})$.   **15.** $\log_3 \dfrac{5^{\frac{3}{4}}}{2^{\frac{2}{3}}17^{\frac{1}{2}}}$.

17. $\log (5\sqrt{3})$.   **25.** $\frac{2}{5}$.   **27.** $-\frac{2}{3}$.   **29.** −10.   **31.** $\frac{-8}{55}$.   **33.** $\frac{89}{24}$.
35. (a) 0.7781; (b) 0.9030; (c) 0.6990.

Section 6–5.   Pages 162 and 163

	Characteristic	Mantissa		Characteristic	Mantissa
1.	2	.5612	**9.**	−2, i.e., 8 − 10	.3417
3.	0	.32081	**11.**	−5, i.e., 5 − 10	.9729
5.	9 − 10, i.e., −1	.7843	**13.**	1	.8377
7.	4 − 10, i.e., −6	.4444	**15.**	1	.3197

17. 1.   **19.** 3.   **21.** 8 − 10.   **23.** 5 − 10.   **25.** 0.   **27.** 9 − 10.
29. 4.   **31.** −14, i.e., 6 − 20.   **33.** 0.5563.   **35.** 1.9020.   **37.** 8.9943 − 10.
39. 4.9031.   **41.** 7.9212 − 10.   **43.** (a) Yes; (b) no; (c) yes; (d) yes; (e) no; (f) yes.
45. 503.8.   **47.** 5.038.   **49.** 0.05038.   **51.** 0.000 000 000 050 38.   **53.** 0.05038.
55. 31.2.   **57.** 8.59.   **59.** 0.0560.   **61.** 502.   **63.** 9,890,000,000.   **65.** 0.00446.
67. 0.4771.   **69.** 6.31.
71. (a) 9.9031 − 10; (b) 9.8751 − 10 from log 0.75, 9.8750 − 10 from (log 3 − log 4), differing because of rounding off.

Section 6–6.   Page 165

9. 0.6301.   **11.** 8.8183 − 10.   **13.** 2.6014.   **15.** 9.1778 − 10.
17. 9.9003 − 10.   **19.** 1.0565.   **21.** 6.8354 − 10.   **23.** 4.8456.   **25.** 40.08.
27. 804.4.   **29.** 3.598.   **31.** 0.8544.   **33.** 0.002 512.   **35.** 0.03841.

Section 6–7.   Pages 167 and 168

1. 378.3.   **3.** 50.34.   **5.** 0.04100.   **7.** 119.0.   **9.** 0.08420.   **11.** 21.92.
13. 0.000 137 7.   **15.** 0.04514.   **17.** 12,270.   **19.** 20,350.   **21.** 0.07152.
23. 1537.   **25.** 11,430,000.   **27.** 0.04984.   **29.** 0.000 000 035 32.   **31.** 2.088.
33. 394.5.   **35.** 412.0.   **37.** 2.651.   **39.** 1.329.   **41.** 8.600.   **43.** 9.980 feet.
45. (a) 0.556 foot; (b) 1.25 feet.

Section 6–8.   Page 170

1. −.   **3.** +.   **5.** −.   **7.** −20,090.   **9.** 2.251.   **11.** 341,600.
13. 0.1341.   **15.** 0.3229.   **17.** 1.101.   **19.** 0.2709.   **21.** 0.001 516.
23. −0.05679.   **25.** 0.434.   **27.** −1.535.   **29.** 3.462.   **31.** 0.4467.

Section 6–9.   Pages 171 and 172

3. 0.8329.   **5.** −0.4943.   **7.** 0.   **9.** 8.8393.   **11.** 0.2780.   **13.** 2.333.
15. 12.18.   **17.** 1.465.   **19.** 0.7841.   **21.** 49.8.   **23.** (a) 0.2310; (b) after 9.970 hours.

Section 6–10.   Pages 175 and 176

7. 12 billion barrels.

Section 6–10. Miscellaneous Exercises. Pages 176 and 177

1. 5. **3.** $\frac{3}{2}$. **5.** $-\frac{5}{2}$. **7.** 0. **9.** 2.603. **11.** 49.1. **13.** 9. **15.** 1.
17. 1071. **19.** 0.1476. **21.** −0.1210. **23.** (a) 1.25; (b) 0.0391.
25. 24.8 pounds. **39.** 2.5 units.

Section 7–1. Page 181

1. 114° 35.49′. **3.** −181° 33.86′. **5.** 40° 2.99′. **7.** 150°. **9.** −270°.
11. $\frac{5}{2}\pi$ rad. **13.** $-\frac{1}{2}\pi$ rad. **15.** $\frac{7}{6}\pi$ rad. **17.** $\frac{1}{4}\pi$ rad.
19. (a) 1.221178 rad.; (b) 1.22118 rad. **21.** (a) −1.425934 rad.; (b) −1.426 rad.
23. (a) 2.922845 rad.; (b) 2.92284 rad.

Section 7–2. Pages 187 and 188

	sine	cosine	tangent	cotangent	secant	cosecant
1.	+	+	+	+	+	+
3.	−	+	−	−	+	−
5.	−	−	+	+	−	−
7.	+	−	−	−	−	+
9.	−	+	−	−	+	−
11.	$\frac{1}{2}$	$\frac{1}{2}\sqrt{3}$	$\frac{1}{3}\sqrt{3}$	$\sqrt{3}$	$\frac{2}{3}\sqrt{3}$	2
13.	$\frac{1}{2}\sqrt{2}$	$-\frac{1}{2}\sqrt{2}$	−1	−1	$-\sqrt{2}$	$\sqrt{2}$
15.	$\frac{1}{2}$	$-\frac{1}{2}\sqrt{3}$	$-\frac{1}{3}\sqrt{3}$	$-\sqrt{3}$	$-\frac{2}{3}\sqrt{3}$	2
17.	$-\frac{1}{2}\sqrt{3}$	$\frac{1}{2}$	$-\sqrt{3}$	$-\frac{1}{3}\sqrt{3}$	2	$-\frac{2}{3}\sqrt{3}$
19.	$-\frac{1}{2}\sqrt{2}$	$\frac{1}{2}\sqrt{2}$	−1	−1	$\sqrt{2}$	$-\sqrt{2}$
21.	$\frac{1}{2}\sqrt{3}$	$-\frac{1}{2}$	$-\sqrt{3}$	$-\frac{1}{3}\sqrt{3}$	−2	$\frac{2}{3}\sqrt{3}$
23.	$\frac{1}{2}\sqrt{2}$	$-\frac{1}{2}\sqrt{2}$	−1	−1	$-\sqrt{2}$	$\sqrt{2}$
25.	1	0	undefined	0	undefined	1
27.	0	1	0	undefined	1	undefined
29.	0	−1	0	undefined	−1	undefined

31. 30°, 150°. **33.** 150°, 210°. **35.** 135°, 315°. **37.** 45°, 225°.
39. 225°, 315°. **41.** 30°. **43.** 135°. **45.** 90°. **47.** $\sqrt{3}x - y = 3\sqrt{3} - 4$.
49. $x + y + 1 = 0$. **51.** $y + 1 = 0$.
55. (a) No change; (b) no change; (c) no change.

Section 7–3. Pages 190 and 191

1. 0.9712. **3.** 1.828. **5.** 0.5573. **7.** 1.324. **9.** 0.5842. **11.** 4.933.
13. Table IV, 0.6134; Table VI, 0.613. **15.** Table IV, 13.73; Table VI, 13.8.
17. Table IV, 0.9323; Table VI, 0.9323. **19.** 10° 30′. **21.** 49° 10′. **23.** 34° 27′.
25. 50° 23′. **27.** 21° 6′. **29.** 74° 38′. **31.** 19° 28′. **33.** 75° 58′.
35. 70° 32′. **37.** $1 + \frac{1}{2}\sqrt{3}$, i.e., 1.8660. **39.** $\frac{9}{16}$. **41.** 5.252. **43.** 0.000 874 8.
45. $\sin x \leqq x \leqq \tan x$.
47. Cosine of any second quadrant angle is negative.

Section 7–4. Pages 193 and 194

1. $\sin x = \pm\sqrt{1 - \cos^2 x}$.

3. $\text{ctn } x = \pm\dfrac{\cos x}{\sqrt{1 - \cos^2 x}} = \pm\dfrac{\cos x}{1 - \cos^2 x}\sqrt{1 - \cos^2 x}$.

5. (a) and (b) $\sin x = -\frac{12}{13}$, $\tan x = \frac{12}{5}$, $\text{ctn } x = \frac{5}{12}$, $\sec x = -\frac{13}{5}$, $\csc x = -\frac{13}{12}$.

7. $\sin \theta$. **9.** $\cos \beta$. **11.** $-\dfrac{\sin^3 u}{\cos u}$. **13.** $\dfrac{1}{\sin^4 \psi}$. **15.** $\sin \theta + \cos \theta$.

17. $-\sin s$. **19.** $\cos^2 x - \sin^2 x$; that is, $1 - 2\sin^2 x$. **33.** r^2. **35.** 1.

Section 7–5. Pages 199 and 200

1. (a) $\tan(\alpha + \beta) = \dfrac{\tan \alpha + \tan \beta}{1 - \tan \alpha \tan \beta}$; **(b)** $\operatorname{ctn}(\alpha - \beta) = \dfrac{\operatorname{ctn} \alpha \operatorname{ctn} \beta + 1}{\operatorname{ctn} \beta - \operatorname{ctn} \alpha}$;

(c) $\operatorname{ctn}(\alpha + \beta) = \dfrac{\operatorname{ctn} \alpha \operatorname{ctn} \beta - 1}{\operatorname{ctn} \beta + \operatorname{ctn} \alpha}$.

3. (a) $\frac{1}{4}\sqrt{2}(1 + \sqrt{3})$; **(b)** $\frac{1}{4}\sqrt{2}(1 + \sqrt{3})$; **(c)** $\sqrt{3} - 2$; **(d)** $-\sqrt{2}(1 + \sqrt{3})$.

5. (a) $\frac{36}{85}$; **(b)** $-\frac{13}{85}$.   **7.** $\cos 3z$.   **9.** $\sin x$.   **11.** $\dfrac{\sin(x + y)}{\sin(x - y)}$.

13. $\sin(x + y + z) =$
$\sin x \cos y \cos z + \cos x \sin y \cos z + \cos x \cos y \sin z - \sin x \sin y \sin z$.

15. $\cos \frac{1}{2}(A + B) + \cos \frac{1}{2}(A - B) = 2 \cos \frac{1}{2}A \cos \frac{1}{2}B$.

Section 7–6. Pages 201 and 202

1. $\sin 227° = -\sin 47°$.   **3.** $\cos 280° = \cos 80°$.   **5.** $\tan 145° = -\tan 35°$.
7. $\sec 253° = -\sec 73°$.   **9.** $\sin 110° = \cos 20°$.   **11.** $\tan 115° = -\operatorname{ctn} 25°$.
13. -0.1363.   **15.** -0.2616.   **17.** 0.5979.   **19.** 1.360.   **21.** -1.152.
23. -2.880.   **25.** $9.6758 - 10$.   **27.** -0.8624.   **29.** -0.7123.

Section 7–7. Pages 203 and 204

1. (a) No; **(b)** no; **(c)** yes.   **3. (a)** No; **(b)** no; **(c)** yes.

5. (a) Yes; period 2π; frequency $\dfrac{1}{2\pi}$, i.e., about 0.16; amplitude 1; **(b)** yes; **(c)** no.

7. (a) Yes; period undefined [sometimes called "period zero"]; frequency undefined; amplitude 0; **(b)** yes; **(c)** no.

9. (a) Yes; period 2π; frequency $\dfrac{1}{2\pi}$, i.e., about 0.16; amplitude $\sqrt{2}$, i.e., 1.414; **(b)** no; **(c)** no.

Section 7–8. Pages 207 and 208

1. (a) $\frac{2}{3}\pi$; **(b)** 2; **(c)** $\dfrac{3}{2\pi}$, i.e., about 0.48.   **3. (a)** 4π; **(b)** 3; **(c)** $\dfrac{1}{4\pi}$, i.e., about 0.080.

5. (a) 2π; **(b)** 1; **(c)** $\dfrac{1}{2\pi}$, i.e., about 0.16.   **7. (a)** 2π; **(b)** 2; **(c)** $\dfrac{1}{2\pi}$, i.e., about 0.16.

9. (a) $\frac{1}{2}\pi$; **(b)** not defined ("∞"); **(c)** $\dfrac{2}{\pi}$, i.e., about 0.64.

11. (a) $\frac{1}{3}\pi$; **(b)** not defined; **(c)** $\dfrac{3}{\pi}$, i.e., about 0.95.

13. (a) π; **(b)** $\frac{2}{3}$; **(c)** $\dfrac{1}{\pi}$, i.e., about 0.32.

15. Not periodic.

17. (a) 4π; **(b)** not defined; **(c)** $\dfrac{1}{4\pi}$, i.e., about 0.080.

19. (a) $\dfrac{\pi}{218,000,000}$ second; **(b)** $\dfrac{218,000,000}{\pi}$, i.e., about 69,400,000 cycles per second.

Section 7–9. Page 209

1. (a) $\frac{1}{12}$; **(b)** 3; **(c)** 0.   **3. (a)** $\frac{1}{4}$; **(b)** 2; **(c)** $\frac{1}{6}$.   **5. (a)** $\frac{2}{3}$; **(b)** 2; **(c)** $\frac{1}{6}$.
7. (a) 6π; **(b)** $\frac{1}{8}$; **(c)** 0.   **9. (a)** 2π; **(b)** 4; **(c)** 1.   **11.** Not simple harmonic motion.
13. Simple harmonic motion with y-scale shifted.
15. Not simple harmonic motion; height of peaks varies.

Section 7–10.   Page 211

1. 0.2588.   **3.** −0.2588.   **5.** −0.7071.   **7.** $4\cos^3\alpha - 3\cos\alpha$.

9. $\pm\sqrt{\tfrac{1}{2}(1 \pm \sqrt{\tfrac{1}{2}(1 + \cos 4x)})}$, any combination of + and − signs.

11. $\pm\sqrt{\dfrac{2}{1 + \cos 2\alpha}}$.   **13.** $2\sin\theta\cos\theta\,(3 - 16\sin^2\theta\cos^2\theta)$.

15. $\pm\dfrac{\sqrt{2} \pm \sqrt{1 + \cos 64B}}{\sqrt{1 - \cos 64B}}$, any combination of + and − signs.

17. $\frac{120}{169}$, i.e., 0.7101.   **19.** $-\frac{119}{169}$, i.e., −0.7041.   **21.** $\frac{3}{13}\sqrt{13}$, i.e., 0.8322.

23. $-\frac{2}{13}\sqrt{13}$, i.e., −0.5548.   **25.** $-\frac{3}{2}$, i.e., −1.500.   **27.** $-\frac{2}{13}\sqrt{13}$, i.e., −0.5548.

29. $\csc\theta$.   **31.** $2\csc 2y$.   **33.** $\cos 2x$.   **35.** $\frac{1}{4}\sin^2 x$.

Section 7–11.   Miscellaneous Exercises.   Pages 213 and 214

1. $\frac{576}{625}$.   **3.** $\frac{4}{5}$.   **5.** $\frac{2}{5}\sqrt{6}$.   **7.** $\frac{3}{5}$.   **9.** $\frac{39}{25}$.   **11.** $-\frac{24}{25}$.

13. (a) and (b) $\tan(\alpha + \beta) = \dfrac{\tan\alpha + \tan\beta}{1 - \tan\alpha\tan\beta}$.   **15.** $\tan 2\theta = \dfrac{2\tan\theta}{1 - \tan^2\theta}$.

17. $\cos 8x + \sin 8x$.   **19.** $2\sec^2 x$.   **43.** $x^2 + y^2 = 16$.

Section 8–1.   Page 217

1. $2i$, i.e., $0 + 2i$.   **3.** $0 - 5x^2i$.   **5.** $0 + (\frac{1}{2}x\sqrt{2}/y^2)i$.   **7.** $0 - i$.   **9.** $1 - i$.

11. $4 - 2xy^2z^3i$.   **13.** $1 + \frac{15}{2}i$.   **15.** $-\frac{15}{2} + 0i$.   **17.** $x = 3, y = -5$.

19. $x = 1, y = 4$.

21. $x = -1, y = 1$; $x = -1, y = -1$; $x = 3, y = -1$; $x = 3, y = 1$.

Section 8–2.   Page 219

1. $8 - 3i$.   **3.** $-4 - 2i$.   **5.** $0 + i$.   **7.** $2 - 9i$.   **9.** $-10 + 0i$.

11. $0 - 50i\sqrt{6}$.   **13.** $-15 - 16i$.   **15.** $7 - 24i$.   **17.** $8 + 0i$.   **19.** $-18 + 0i$.

21. $-\frac{13}{2} - \frac{3}{2}i\sqrt{3}$.   **23.** $0 - 80i$.   **25.** $-\frac{10}{17} + \frac{11}{17}i$.   **27.** $-\frac{1}{7} - \frac{2}{7}i\sqrt{5}$.

29. True.   **31.** True.   **33.** True.   **35.** $(a, b) - (c, d) = (a - c, b - d)$.

37. $(a, b) \div (c, d) = \left(\dfrac{ac + bd}{c^2 + d^2}, \dfrac{bc - ad}{c^2 + d^2}\right)$.

Section 8–3.   Pages 222 and 223

9. $\sqrt{2}(\cos 45° + i\sin 45°)$.   **11.** $8(\cos 300° + i\sin 300°)$.

13. $2(\cos 150° + i\sin 150°)$.   **15.** $\frac{3}{2}(\cos 90° + i\sin 90°)$.

17. $1(\cos 180° + i\sin 180°)$.   **19.** $\frac{1}{3}(\cos 210° + i\sin 210°)$.   **21.** $3 + 3i\sqrt{3}$.

23. $1 - i\sqrt{3}$.   **25.** $5i$.   **27.** -1.   **29.** $-1.3894 + 1.4386i$.

31. (a) $a + bi$, $a + ci$, $b \neq c$.

33. (a) $r(\cos\theta + i\sin\theta)$, $r(\cos[-\theta] + i\sin[-\theta])$.

35. (a) $0 + 0i$.   **37.** $-k^2 + 0i$, $k \neq 0$; argument 180°.

Section 8–4.   Page 224

1. $5 + 4i$.   **3.** $-4 + \frac{3}{2}i$.   **5.** $-2 - 2i$.   **7.** $\frac{7}{2} + 2i$.

9. (a) $-50 - 20i$; (b) $10\sqrt{61}$ pounds, 129° 49′; 80 pounds, 270°; $10\sqrt{29}$ pounds, 201°47′.

Section 8–5.   Page 226

1. $-10 + 10i\sqrt{3}$.   **3.** $-2\sqrt{3} - 2i$.   **5.** $3\sqrt{3} + 3i$.   **7.** $-\frac{3}{2}i\sqrt{2}$.

9. $8\sqrt{3} - 8i$.   **11.** $-10 + 10i$.   **13.** $-\frac{1}{4}\sqrt{2} - \frac{1}{4}i\sqrt{2}$.   **15.** $4 + 4i\sqrt{3}$.

Section 8–6. Pages 227 and 228

1. (a) $9(\cos 90° + i \sin 90°)$; (b) $9i$.   **3.** (a) $9(\cos \frac{2}{3}\pi + i \sin \frac{2}{3}\pi)$; (b) $-\frac{9}{2} + \frac{9}{2}i\sqrt{3}$.
5. (a) $32(\cos 210° + i \sin 210°)$; (b) $-16\sqrt{3} - 16i$.
7. (a) $\cos 60° + i \sin 60°$; (b) $\frac{1}{2} + \frac{1}{2}i\sqrt{3}$.
9. (a) $-64 + 64i\sqrt{3}$; (b) $-i$; (c) $64\sqrt{3} + 64i$; (d) $-\frac{1}{4} - \frac{1}{4}i\sqrt{3}$; (e) $16 - 16i\sqrt{3}$.

Section 8–7. Page 230

1. (a) $8(\cos 120° + i \sin 120°)$, $8(\cos 300° + i \sin 300°)$; (b) $-4 + 4i\sqrt{3}$, $4 - 4i\sqrt{3}$.
3. (a) $2(\cos 7° \ 30' + i \sin 7° \ 30')$, $2(\cos 67° \ 30' + i \sin 67° \ 30')$,
    $2(\cos 127° \ 30' + i \sin 127° \ 30')$, $2(\cos 187° \ 30' + i \sin 187° \ 30')$,
    $2(\cos 247° \ 30' + i \sin 247° \ 30')$, $2(\cos 307° \ 30' + i \sin 307° \ 30')$;
    (b) $1.983 + 0.2610i$, $0.7654 + 1.848i$, $-1.218 + 1.587i$, $-1.983 - 0.2610i$,
    $-0.7654 - 1.848i$, $1.2176 - 1.587i$.
5. (a) $\sqrt[4]{2}(\cos 157° \ 30' + i \sin 157° \ 30')$, $\sqrt[4]{2}(\cos 337° \ 30' + i \sin 337° \ 30')$;
    (b) $-1.10 + 0.455i$, $1.10 - 0.455i$.
7. (a) $\cos 90° + i \sin 90°$, $\cos 270° + i \sin 270°$; (b) i, $-i$.
9. (a) $\cos 0° + i \sin 0°$, $\cos 60° + i \sin 60°$, $\cos 120° + i \sin 120°$, $\cos 180° + i \sin 180°$,
    $\cos 240° + i \sin 240°$, $\cos 300° + i \sin 300°$; (b) 1, $\frac{1}{2} + \frac{1}{2}i\sqrt{3}$, $-\frac{1}{2} + \frac{1}{2}i\sqrt{3}$, -1,
    $-\frac{1}{2} - \frac{1}{2}i\sqrt{3}$, $\frac{1}{2} - \frac{1}{2}i\sqrt{3}$.
11. $\cos \theta + i \sin \theta$, where $\theta = 0°$, $72°$, $144°$, $216°$, $288°$.
13. 4, $-2 + 2i\sqrt{3}$, $-2 - 2i\sqrt{3}$.
15. $\frac{1}{2}\sqrt[4]{18} + \frac{1}{2}i\sqrt[4]{2}$, $-\frac{1}{2}\sqrt[4]{2} + \frac{1}{2}i\sqrt[4]{18}$, $-\frac{1}{2}\sqrt[4]{18} - \frac{1}{2}i\sqrt[4]{2}$, $\frac{1}{2}\sqrt[4]{2} - \frac{1}{2}i\sqrt[4]{18}$.
17. $2\sqrt[4]{2}\,(\cos \theta + i \sin \theta)$, where $\theta = 67° \ 30'$, $247° \ 30'$.

Section 8–7. Miscellaneous Exercises. Page 231

1. $6 + (2 - 4\sqrt{3})i$.   **3.** $(8 + 8\sqrt{3}) + (8 - 8\sqrt{3})i$.   **5.** $-16 + 16i$.
7. $1.366 + 0.3659i$, $-1 + i$, $-0.3659 - 1.366i$.   **9.** 7.77.   **11.** 17.04.   **13.** True.
15. True.   **17.** True.   **19.** True.   **21.** True.

Section 9–1. Pages 234 and 235

1. $A = 37°$, $B = 53°$, $b = 4.0$.   **3.** $A = 48° \ 11'$, $B = 41° \ 49'$, $a = 4.472$.
5. $A = 33° \ 10'$, $B = 56° \ 50'$, $c = 6.118$.   **7.** $A = 75° \ 39'$, $B = 14° \ 21'$, $a = 0.1044$.
9. $B = 61° \ 0'$, $a = 2.424$, $b = 4.373$.   **11.** $A = 78° \ 34'$, $a = 0.2254$, $b = 0.04559$.
13. $B = 55° \ 0'$, $b = 9.997$, $c = 12.20$.   **15.** $A = 57° \ 42'$, $b = 19.7$, $c = 36.9$.
17. Foot, 6.84 feet; top, 18.8 feet.   **19.** $53°$.   **21.** 39 feet.   **23.** $54° \ 44'$.
25. (a) 2929 miles; (b) 1394 miles.

Section 9–2. Pages 238 and 239

1. $11°$ east of south, 408 miles per hour.   **3.** 10.4 knots north, 6.00 knots east.
5. (a) $86°$ west of north; (b) 449 knots.   **7.** 80 tons.
9. 2.27 pounds, downward to the right $39.0°$ from vertical [rounded from $39° \ 3'$].

Section 9–3. Pages 243 to 245

1. $A = 105°$, $b = 14.63$, $c = 10.35$.   **3.** $B = 15°$, $a = 8.484$, $b = 4.391$.
5. $C = 96° \ 50'$, $b = 50.42$, $c = 55.79$.   **7.** $C = 58° \ 9'$, $a = 0.07183$, $c = 0.06164$.
9. $A = 93° \ 34'$, $B = 56° \ 26'$, $a = 5.988$ or $A = 26° \ 26'$, $B = 123° \ 34'$, $a = 2.671$.
11. No triangle.   **13.** $A = 90°$, $C = 60°$, $c = 1.732$.   **15.** No triangle.
17. Reduces to $(1a)$, $(1b)$ of § 9–1.   **19.** No difference.   **21.** (a) Yes; (b) yes.
23. (a) $49° \ 18'$; (b) 1453 feet.   **25.** (a) 17,000 yards; (b) 8700 yards, i.e., 26,000 feet.
27. $13°$ toward the sun.   **29.** $19° \ 17'$.   **31.** (a) No; (b) $3.6°$ [rounded from $3° \ 35'$].

Section 9–4. Pages 246 to 248

1. 2.070. **3.** 41° 25′. **5.** 6.245. **7.** $a = \sqrt{37} \approx 6.083$, $B = 25° 17′$, $C = 34° 42′$.
9. $b = 0.0161$, $A = 38.3°$, $C = 111.7°$ [rounded from 38° 16′, 111° 44′].
11. $A = 28° 57′$, $B = 46° 34′$, $C = 104° 29′$.
13. $A = 90°$, $B = 61° 56′$, $C = 28° 4′$. **15.** $A = 102° 34′$, $B = 33° 4′$, $C = 44° 25′$.
17. 4.310 (cos 72° 7′ + i sin 72° 7′). **21.** 6.4 miles.
23. 294 knots, 4° north of west. **25.** (a) 17°; (b) 2.0 miles.

Section 9–5. Pages 250 and 251

1. (a) $\frac{1}{2}\pi$, i.e., 1.571, inches; $\frac{3}{2}\pi$, i.e., 4.712, square inches; 0.054 square inch.
(b) $\frac{1}{4}\pi$, i.e., 0.7854, meter; $\frac{1}{4}\pi$, i.e., 0.7854, square meter; 0.0200 square meter.
(c) 3π, i.e., 9.425, miles; 6π, i.e., 18.85, square miles; 13.193 square miles.
(d) $\frac{25}{12}\pi$, i.e., 6.545, feet; $\frac{125}{24}\pi$, i.e., 16.36, square feet; 4.289 square feet.
(e) 0.830 centimeter; 0.681 square centimeter; 0.0286 square centimeter.
(f) 0.04868 mile; 0.001039 square mile; 0.0002109 square mile.
(g) 0.332 yard; 0.0332 square yard; 0.0133 square yard.
(h) 151.5 centimeters; 3030 square centimeters; 3511 square centimeters.
(i) 523.6 meters; 26,180 square meters; 30,510 square meters.
(j) 0.1745 kilometer; 0.8726 square kilometer; 0.000 square kilometer.
3. (a) 1000 yards; (b) 10 yards; (c) 17.453 yards; (d) 0.291 yard; (e) 0.00485 yard.
5. (a) 2.819; (b) 0.08660. **7.** 66 radians per second.
9. 0.000 000 199 radian per second; 66,700 miles per hour. **11.** 11°.
13. 11.18 square centimeters.

Section 9–5. Miscellaneous Exercises. Pages 251 and 252

1. $C = 45°$, $a = 6.122$, $b = 1.830$.
3. No triangle.
5. $A = 104° 29′$, $B = 28° 53′$, $C = 46° 34′$.
7. $b = 15.9$, $A = 140.9°$, $C = 9.1°$.
9. $a = 37.26$, $A = 111° 19′$, $C = 38° 41′$, or $a = 6.040$, $A = 8° 41′$, $C = 141° 19′$.
13. 173.9 pounds downward at 13° 18′ to the vertical.
15. 5° north of east; 360 knots, i.e., $3.6 \cdot 10^2$ knots.
17. 145° to the side of the course.
19. $6\pi - \frac{9}{2}\sqrt{3}$, i.e., 11.06.

Section 10–1. Pages 257 and 258

1. $3x - y - 2 = 0$; $a = 3$, $b = -1$, $c = -2$.
3. $mx - y + (k - mh) = 0$; $a = m$, $b = -1$, $c = k - mh$.
5. $8x - 2 = 0$; $a = 8$, $b = 0$, $c = -2$.
7. $y^2 - x^2 - 2y = 0$; quadratic. **9.** $x^2 + y^2 = 0$; pure quadratic.
11. $xy = 0$; pure quadratic. **13.** (a) -3; (b) $\frac{3}{2}$. **15.** (a) -3; (b) 2.
17. (a) $- c/a$; (b) $- c/b$. **19.** Straight line. **21.** Straight line. **23.** Circle.
25. Hyperbola. **27.** Parabola. **29.** Straight line. **31.** Circle.

Section 10–2. Page 261

1. $(2, -1)$; consistent and independent. **3.** $(5, 3)$; consistent and independent.
5. $(-2.6, 3.4)$; consistent and independent.
7. $(-1.8, -3.7)$; consistent and independent. **9.** No solution; inconsistent.
11. Unlimited number of solutions; consistent and dependent.
13. $u = 200$, $v = 4$; consistent and independent.
15. $(2, -1)$; consistent and dependent. **17.** No solution; inconsistent.

Section 10–3. Pages 264 to 267

1. $(2, -1)$. **3.** $(5, 3)$. **5.** $(-\frac{13}{5}, \frac{17}{5})$. **7.** $(-\frac{20}{11}, -\frac{41}{11})$. **9.** No solution.
11. Unlimited number of solutions, of the form $(x, \frac{1}{2}x - \frac{3}{2})$. **13.** $u = 200, v = 4$.

15. $(\frac{23}{17}, \frac{1}{17})$. **17.** $(-\frac{1}{7}, \frac{13}{7})$. **19.** $\left(\dfrac{c - b}{a - 1}, \dfrac{ac - b}{a - 1}\right)$.

21. $\left(\dfrac{m_1 a - m_2 c - b + d}{m_1 - m_2}, \dfrac{bm_2 - dm_1 + [c - a]m_1 m_2}{m_2 - m_1}\right)$. **23.** $r = -4, s = -1$.

25. $u = 3, v = 2$. **27.** $(\frac{1}{4}, 2)$. **29.** $(-\frac{14}{5}, \frac{2}{5})$. **31.** $x = 2, y = -1$.
33. No real values.
37. (a) 10; (b) any value other than 10.
39. (a) $r = -4, s = -14$; (b) $r = -4, s \neq -14$; (c) $r \neq -4$, s any value.
41. 7, 10. **43.** 32°, 58°. **45.** 34 nickels, 90 pennies.
47. \$1.20 for first 15 words, 5 cents for each additional word.
49. $m = -\frac{4}{3}, b = \frac{17}{3}$. **51.** $R = 0.0012T + 0.40$. **53.** (a) $4\frac{1}{2}, 7\frac{1}{2}$; (b) $\frac{1}{14}, \frac{1}{10}$.
55. 40 cubic centimeters of 10% acid, 80 cubic centimeters of 4% acid.
57. $x = c \sin \alpha + d \cos \alpha, y = c \cos \alpha - d \sin \alpha$.

Section 10–4. Pages 268 and 269

1. $(4, 1, 3)$. **3.** $u = 1, v = 4, w = 0$. **5.** $(1, -\frac{3}{2}, \frac{1}{2})$. **7.** $(\frac{2}{3}, -\frac{1}{3}, 1)$.
9. $(\frac{28}{3}, \frac{14}{3}, -2)$. **11.** $x = -1, y = -2, z = 1, w = 3$. **13.** 96°, 48°, 36°.
15. 315 nickels, 180 dimes, 60 quarters.
17. (a) $a = -1, b = -3, c = 6, y^2 = -x^2 - 3x + 6$; (b) $a = 2, b = -3, c = 1$, $y^2 = 2x^2 - 3x + 1$.

Section 10–5. Page 270

1. $(3, -2), (-1.3, 4.5)$. **3.** $(-3.7, -3.4), (4.9, 1.0)$.
5. $(1.3, 2.3), (2.6, -2.6), (-2.3, -1.3), (-1.6, 1.6)$.
7. $(3.5, -2.0), (3.5, -2.0), (0, 4), (0, 4)$. **9.** No real solution.
11. $(4.8, -1.5), (1.5, -4.8), (-4.8, 1.5), (-1.5, 4.8)$.

Section 10–6. Pages 274 to 276

1. $(4, -2), (-2, 4)$. **3.** $(-\frac{3}{2}, -5)$.
5. $(4, \sqrt{33}), (4, -\sqrt{33}), (-4, \sqrt{33}), (-4, -\sqrt{33}); (4, 5.74), (4, -5.74), (-4, 5.74), (-4, -5.74)$.
7. $(\sqrt{5}, 1), (-\sqrt{5}, 1), (i\sqrt{10}, 4), (-i\sqrt{10}, 4); (2.24, 1), (-2.24, 1), (3.16i, 4), (-3.16i, 4)$.
9. $(-1, 2), (1, -2), (-\sqrt{3}, \sqrt{3}), (\sqrt{3}, -\sqrt{3}); (-1, 2), (1, -2), (-1.73, 1.73), (1.73, -1.73)$.
11. $(1, 3), (-1, -3), (3, 1), (-3, -1)$. **13.** $(-4, 5), (-\frac{3}{2}, -\frac{1}{2})$.
15. $(\sqrt{3}, -5\sqrt{3}), (-\sqrt{3}, 5\sqrt{3}); (1.73, -8.66), (-1.73, 8.66)$.
17. $(1, 4), (-1, -4), (2\sqrt{2}, \sqrt{2}), (-2\sqrt{2}, -\sqrt{2}); (1, 4), (-1, -4), (2.83, 1.41), (-2.83, -1.41)$.
19. $(2i, 0), (2i, 0), (-2i, 0), (-2i, 0)$.
21. $(-1, 2), (1, -2), (\frac{2}{7}\sqrt{42}, \frac{5}{21}\sqrt{42}), (-\frac{2}{7}\sqrt{42}, -\frac{5}{21}\sqrt{42}); (-1, 2), (1, -2), (1.85, 1.54), (-1.85, -1.54)$.
23. $x = 3, y = -2$, or $x = -3, y = 2$. **25.** 9, 13. **27.** 5 inches, 9 inches.
29. 25 feet by 40 feet. **31.** $\frac{1}{3}, \frac{1}{2}$.

Section 10–6. Miscellaneous Exercises. Pages 276 to 279

1. $(1, 2), (4, -4)$. **3.** $(2\sqrt{3}, i\sqrt{6}), (2\sqrt{3}, -i\sqrt{6}), (-2\sqrt{3}, i\sqrt{6}), (-2\sqrt{3}, -i\sqrt{6})$.
5. $(\sqrt{6}, i\sqrt{3}), (\sqrt{6}, -i\sqrt{3}), (-\sqrt{6}, i\sqrt{3}), (-\sqrt{6}, -i\sqrt{3})$. **7.** $(25, 4)$.

9. $(\frac{1}{2}, 1)$, $(\frac{1}{2}, -1)$, $(-\frac{1}{2}, 1)$, $(-\frac{1}{2}, -1)$.

11. $(\frac{3}{5}\sqrt{10}, -\frac{1}{5}\sqrt{10})$, $-\frac{3}{5}\sqrt{10}, \frac{1}{5}\sqrt{10})$, $(\frac{2}{3}\sqrt{3}, -\frac{2}{3}\sqrt{3})$, $(-\frac{2}{3}\sqrt{3}, \frac{2}{3}\sqrt{3})$.

13. $(x + y)^3 = 8xy$.   **15.** 145.   **17.** $s_0 = 10{,}650$ feet, $v_0 = -50$ feet per second.

19. $\frac{7}{3}x^2 - 4x + \frac{11}{3}$.   **21.** $a = 100{,}500$, $b = -505$, $c = -5$.

23. 88 inches, 198 inches.   **25.** 100+ feet.   **27.** $2x^2 - 3x + 5$.

29. (a) 1 hour; (b) $\frac{1}{4}$ mile per hour; (c) and (d) indeterminate (i.e., not determined by the given data).

31. Yes; 25 of P, 40 of Q, 6 of R.

Section 10–7.   Page 281

1—12. See answers for § 10–4.

13. $u = 200$, $v = 4$.   **15.** $x = 2$, $y = -1$.   **17.** No solution.

Section 10–8.   Page 282

1. (a) 3; (b) 1; (c) no; (d) not applicable, since matrix is not square.

3. (a) 3; (b) 3; (c) yes; (d) 2, 16, 0.

Section 10–9.   Pages 285 and 286

1. $x = 2$, $y = -1$.

3—12. See answers for § 10–4.

13. $x = -\frac{10}{19}$, $y = \frac{63}{19}$.   **15.** $x = \frac{1}{2}$, $y = -\frac{3}{4}$, $z = 2$.

17. $x = 1$, $y = -1$, $z = 2$, $w = 0$.   **19.** $x = -1$, $y = 2$, $z = 1$, $u = -2$, $v = 3$.

Section 10–10.   Pages 287 and 288

1. $r = 1$, $s = 2$.   **3.** $x = \frac{1}{2}$, $y = -\frac{3}{2}$.   **5.** $u = 3$, $v = 1$.   **7.** No solution.

9. $x = 1$, $y = 0$, $z = 0$.

Section 11–1.   Page 290

1. (a) $\begin{bmatrix} 3 & 1 \\ -2 & 0 \end{bmatrix}$, $\begin{bmatrix} 3 & 1 \\ \frac{1}{2} & 2 \end{bmatrix}$, $\begin{bmatrix} -2 & 0 \\ \frac{1}{2} & 2 \end{bmatrix}$; (b) $\begin{bmatrix} 3 \\ -2 \end{bmatrix}$, $\begin{bmatrix} 1 \\ 0 \end{bmatrix}$, $\begin{bmatrix} 3 \\ \frac{1}{2} \end{bmatrix}$, $\begin{bmatrix} 1 \\ 2 \end{bmatrix}$, $\begin{bmatrix} -2 \\ \frac{1}{2} \end{bmatrix}$, $\begin{bmatrix} 0 \\ 2 \end{bmatrix}$;

(c) not applicable.

3. (a) $\begin{bmatrix} a_{11} & a_{12} \\ a_{21} & a_{22} \end{bmatrix}$, $\begin{bmatrix} a_{11} & a_{13} \\ a_{21} & a_{23} \end{bmatrix}$, $\begin{bmatrix} a_{12} & a_{13} \\ a_{22} & a_{23} \end{bmatrix}$, $\begin{bmatrix} a_{11} & a_{12} \\ a_{31} & a_{32} \end{bmatrix}$, $\begin{bmatrix} a_{11} & a_{13} \\ a_{31} & a_{33} \end{bmatrix}$, $\begin{bmatrix} a_{12} & a_{13} \\ a_{32} & a_{33} \end{bmatrix}$,

$\begin{bmatrix} a_{21} & a_{22} \\ a_{31} & a_{32} \end{bmatrix}$, $\begin{bmatrix} a_{21} & a_{23} \\ a_{31} & a_{33} \end{bmatrix}$, $\begin{bmatrix} a_{22} & a_{23} \\ a_{32} & a_{33} \end{bmatrix}$; (b) $\begin{bmatrix} a_{11} \\ a_{21} \end{bmatrix}$, $\begin{bmatrix} a_{12} \\ a_{22} \end{bmatrix}$, $\begin{bmatrix} a_{13} \\ a_{23} \end{bmatrix}$, $\begin{bmatrix} a_{11} \\ a_{31} \end{bmatrix}$, $\begin{bmatrix} a_{12} \\ a_{32} \end{bmatrix}$,

$\begin{bmatrix} a_{13} \\ a_{33} \end{bmatrix}$, $\begin{bmatrix} a_{21} \\ a_{31} \end{bmatrix}$, $\begin{bmatrix} a_{22} \\ a_{32} \end{bmatrix}$, $\begin{bmatrix} a_{23} \\ a_{33} \end{bmatrix}$; (c) 3; a_{11}, a_{22}, a_{33}.

Section 11–2.   Pages 292 and 293

1—8. See the corresponding answers for § 10–3, where these systems are solved algebraically.

9. -2.   **11.** $4a - 3b$.   **13.** $x^2y - xy^2$.   **15.** $\log 8$.   **17.** $\sec \theta - \csc \theta$.

18—25. See the corresponding answers for § 10–3.

27. -6, 1.

Section 11–3.   Page 295

1—10. See the corresponding answers for § 10–4.

11. $(0, 0, 0)$.

Section 11–4.   Page 297

1. 1.   **3.** 0.   **5.** 4.   **7.** 2.   **9.** 6.   **11.** 10.   **13.** (a) 2; (b) 2.   **15.** (a) 6; (b) 6.

19. $-1 + 0 + 8 - 6 - 0 - 1$, which equals 0.

Section 11–5. Pages 301 and 302

15. $\begin{vmatrix} x & y & z \\ 2x & 4y & 5z \\ x & y & z \end{vmatrix} + \begin{vmatrix} x & y & z \\ 2x & 4y & 5z \\ 3a & 3b & 3c \end{vmatrix} = 3 \begin{vmatrix} x & y & z \\ 2x & 4y & 5z \\ a & b & c \end{vmatrix}.$

Section 11–6. Page 305

1. For **(a)**, **(b)**, **(c)**, **(d)**: 134.   **3.** For **(a)**, **(b)**, **(c)**: −6.

Section 11–7. Pages 308 and 309

1. −22.   **3.** −42.   **5.** 130.   **7.** −21.   **9.** −144.   **11.** 288.   **13.** $(b - a)^3$.
15. $x^3(x + 10)$.   **17.** $4 \pm \sqrt{19}$.   **19.** 18.   **23.** $2x - 3y + 12 = 0$.   **25.** $4x + 3y = 0$.

Section 11–8. Pages 312 and 313

1. $x = \frac{26}{23}, y = -\frac{15}{23}$.   **3.** $r = \frac{2}{3}, s = -\frac{3}{2}$.   **5.** $A = -2, B = -1, C = -\frac{3}{2}$.
7. $x = -\dfrac{1}{a}, y = \dfrac{1}{b}, z = \dfrac{3}{2c}$.   **9.** $x = -2, y = 1, z = 2, w = 3$.
11. $x = -1, y = -2, z = 1, w = 3$.   **13.** $x = 1, y = -1, z = 2, w = 0$.
15. $x = -1, \ y = 2, \ z = 1, \ u = -2, \ v = 3$.

Section 11–9. Pages 314 and 315

1. 2.   **3.** 1.   **5.** 1.   **7.** 3.   **9.** 2.   **11.** 1.   **13.** 3.

Section 11–10. Pages 318 and 319

1—10. See answers for § 10-10.
11. $x = 2y + 3$, y has any value.   **13.** $u = 200, v = 4$.   **15.** $x = 2, y = -1$.
17. No solution.   **19.** $x = 0, y = 0$.   **21.** $x = 2, y = -1$.   **23.** No solution.
25. $x = \frac{1}{11}z, y = -\frac{7}{11}z$, z has any value.   **27.** $x = 0, y = 0, z = 0$.
29. $x = -\frac{5}{7}z - \frac{11}{7}w, \ y = -\frac{3}{7}z + \frac{6}{7}w$, z and w have any values.

Section 12–1. Pages 324 and 325

1. Positive; real, unequal, rational.   **3.** Negative; imaginary.
5. Positive; real, unequal, irrational.   **7.** Positive; real, unequal, rational.
9. Positive; real, unequal, irrational.   **11.** Zero; imaginary, equal.
13. Real, unequal.   **15.** Real, unequal.   **17.** Real, equal.   **19.** −2, 2.
21. −1, −4.   **23.** −8.   **25.** 36.   **27.** 16.
29. **(a)** $b = -5$; **(b)** $b > -5$; **(c)** $b < -5$.
31. **(a)** $b = \pm 4$; **(b)** $-4 < b < 4$; **(c)** $b < -4$ or $b > 4$.
33. $x^2 - \sqrt{3}\,x = 0$; 3; roots real and unequal.
35. $x^2 + (-6 + 4i)x + (5 - 12i) = 0$; 0; roots equal.
37. **(b)** $(x + 3)^2 - 9$; **(c)** lowest, $(-3, -9)$; **(d)** minimum −9.
39. **(b)** $(x + \frac{5}{2})^2 - \frac{1}{4}$; **(c)** lowest, $(-\frac{5}{2}, -\frac{1}{4})$; **(d)** minimum −$\frac{1}{4}$.
41. **(b)** $-(x - 2)^2 + 7$; **(c)** highest, $(2, 7)$; **(d)** maximum 7.
45. **(a)** 1.5 seconds; **(b)** 36 feet.
47. **(a)** Same; **(b)** second discriminant is 36 times first discriminant.

Section 12–2. Pages 327 and 328

1. 3; −6.   **3.** 3; 0.   **5.** k; $3 - 4k$.   **7.** $x^2 - 7x + 12 = 0$.
9. $x^2 - x - 2 = 0$.   **11.** $9x^2 - 6x + 1 = 0$.   **13.** $x^2 + 2x = 0$.
15. $x^2 + 9 = 0$.   **17.** $x^2 - 4x + 1 = 0$.   **19.** $x^2 - c^2 = 0$.

21. $2x^2 - x + 1 = 0$.   **23.** $9x^2 + 24x + 28 = 0$.   **25.** $(6x - 5)(3x + 4)$.
27. $\frac{1}{3}(3x - 2 + \sqrt{19})(3x - 2 - \sqrt{19})$.   **29.** (a) $-\frac{11}{3}$; (b) 3; (c) -4; (d) $\pm 2\sqrt{2}$.
31. (a) $-\frac{14}{9}$; (b) 10; (c) $-\frac{3}{2}$; (d) $-\frac{9}{4}$.   **33.** (a) 36; (b) 32.
35. (a) $-\frac{3}{2}$; (b) $\frac{1}{2}$; (c) 1; (d) $-\frac{1}{2}$.   **37.** (a) ± 2; (b) $\pm 2i$.
39. (a) $25y^2 - 25y + 6 = 0$; (b) $15y^2 + 16y + 4 = 0$; (c) $7y^2 - 5y = 8$.   **43.** No.

Section 12–3.   Page 330

1. Absolute.   **3.** Conditional (impossible).   **5.** Conditional.   **7.** Conditional.
9. Conditional.   **11.** Conditional.   **13.** Conditional.   **15.** Conditional.
17. Absolute.   **19.** Absolute.   **21.** Conditional.   **23.** Absolute.
25. Conditional.   **27.** Absolute.   **29.** $x < 0$ and $y > 0$.   **31.** $x > -2$.
33. $-1 < y < 4$.   **35.** $x < 5$ and $y > 3$.
37. (a) Conditional; (b) and (c) nothing is shown (except that the inequality is not impossible); (d) conditional; (e) conditional; (f) absolute.

Section 12–4.   Pages 332 and 333

31. Conditional.   **33.** Absolute.   **35.** Conditional.   **37.** Absolute.   **39.** Conditional.
47. (a) Area triangle $OPR = \frac{1}{2}\sin\theta\cos\theta$; area sector $OQR = \frac{1}{2}\theta$;
area triangle $OQS = \frac{1}{2}\tan\theta = \dfrac{\sin\theta}{2\cos\theta}$.

Section 12–5.   Page 336

1. $x > 4$.   **3.** $x > 3$.   **5.** $z < -3$.   **7.** $y < -1$ or $y > 1$.
9. All real values of t.   **11.** $-5 < x < -1$.   **13.** No real values of x.
15. $x < -\frac{5}{2} - \frac{1}{2}\sqrt{37}$ or $x > -\frac{5}{2} + \frac{1}{2}\sqrt{37}$.   **17.** $x > 3$.   **19.** $x < -1$ or $x > 0$.
21. $x < -1$ or $-1 < x < 0$.   **23.** All real values of y.
25. $x < -2$ or $0 < x < 1$ or $1 < x < 3$.   **27.** $x < -4$ or $x > 3$.
29. $x < -2$ or $0 < x < 2$.   **31.** $-3 < x < -2$ or $x > 1$.   **33.** $x \leqq \frac{5}{2}$.
35. $-1 \leqq x \leqq 0$.

Section 12–6.   Pages 338 to 340

59. (a) $x > \frac{1}{2}$.   **61.** (a) $-\frac{2}{3} < x < 2$.   **63.** (a) $x \leqq -2$ or $x \geqq 2$.
65. (a) No values of x.
67. Positive if $x > 3$; negative if $x < 2$ or $2 < x < 3$.
69. Positive if $x > 3$; negative if $x < 2$ or $2 < x < 3$.
71. Positive if $2 < x < 3$ or $x > 5$; negative if $x < 2$ or $3 < x < 5$.
73. Positive if $x < -5$ or $-5 < x < -2$ or $-2 < x < 0$ or $x > 3$; negative if $0 < x < 3$.
75. $8.7 \leqq S \leqq 33.4$.   **77.** (b) Diameter $2\frac{1}{2}$ inches.

Section 12–7.   Pages 342 and 343

1. (a) 4; (b) -6; (c) -20; (d) 110.   **3.** -8.   **5.** (a) 6; (b) $\frac{298}{81}$.   **7.** No.
9. $x + 2 = 0$.   **11.** $x^3 - x^2 - x - 1 = 0$.   **13.** 4.   **15.** 4.   **17.** $k = -6, m = 11$.

Section 12–8.   Pages 346 and 347

1. $x^3 - 4x^2 + x + 6 = 0$.   **3.** $x^2 + 3x - 10 = 0$.
5. $x^4 - 3x^3 - 3x^2 + 11x - 6 = 0$.   **7.** $4x^3 + 4x^2 - 7x + 2 = 0$.
9. $x^3 - 4x^2 + 2x + 4 = 0$.   **11.** $5x^3 - 32x^2 + 82x - 28 = 0$.
13. $5x^5 - 14x^4 + 68x^3 - 168x^2 + 96x = 0$.
15. $8x^4 - 4x^3 - 21x^2 + 12x - 9 = 0$.   **17.** $16x^4 - 32x^3 + 24x^2 - 8x + 1 = 0$.
19. $x^4 - 16x^3 + 100x^2 - 288x + 324 = 0$.
21. $x^7 - 3x^6 + 5x^5 - 7x^4 + 7x^3 - 5x^2 + 3x - 1 = 0$.   **23.** $A = \frac{1}{4}, B = \frac{7}{4}$.
25. $A = 6, B = 1$.   **27.** $A = -1, B = -2, C = 1$.   **29.** $(x + 1)(x^2 - x + 1)$.

Section 12–9.   Page 349

1. $-3i$.   **3.** $1 - 4i$.   **5.** $-i\sqrt{5}$.   **7.** $\frac{1}{2}(1 + i)$.   **9.** Not determined.

11. $-\sqrt{3}$.   **13.** $-\frac{4}{3}\sqrt{15}$.   **15.** $\dfrac{1 + 3\sqrt{2}}{5}$.   **17.** Not determined.

19. $x^3 - 5x^2 + x + 7 = 0$.   **21.** $12x^4 - 12x^3 + 5x^2 + 4x - 3 = 0$.

23. $x^4 + 34x^2 + 361 = 0$.   **25.** $-\frac{3}{2}, \pm i\sqrt{2}$.   **27.** $-\frac{1}{2}, 1, -\frac{1}{2} \pm \frac{1}{2}i\sqrt{3}$.

29. $1 \pm i, \pm\sqrt{2}$.   **31.** No.

Section 12–10.   Pages 351 to 353

1. $3x^4 + 6x^3 + 7x^2 + 14x + 28$; 60.   **3.** $2x - 13$; 51.   **5.** $z^2 - 3z - 8$; -22.

7. $3x^4 + 3x^3 + 3x^2 + 5x + 10$; 10.   **9.** $-x^2 + 2x - 1$; 3.

11. $9x^3 - 12x^2 + 7x + \frac{16}{3}$; $\frac{27}{9}$.   **13.** $2x^2 + 0.7x - 0.51$; -1.719.

15. $2x^3 - x^2 - 1$; x.   **17.** (a) 9; (b) 0.   **19.** (a) $\frac{34}{9}$; (b) $-\frac{23}{9}$.   **21.** 4.488.

23. $2x^3 + x^2 + x - 20 = 0$.   **25.** $2y^2 + 2y + 14 = 0$, i.e., $y^2 + y + 7 = 0$.

27. (a) 1230 microseconds, i.e., 0.001 230 second; (b) 630 microseconds, i.e., 0.000 630 0 second.

Section 12–11.   Pages 355 and 356

1. $\pm1, \pm2, \pm3, \pm6, \pm9, \pm18$.   **3.** $\pm1, \pm5, \pm\frac{1}{3}, \pm\frac{5}{3}$.

5. $\pm1, \pm5, \pm\frac{1}{2}, \pm\frac{5}{2}, \pm\frac{1}{3}, \pm\frac{5}{3}, \pm\frac{1}{4}, \pm\frac{5}{4}, \pm\frac{1}{6}, \pm\frac{5}{6}, \pm\frac{1}{12}, \pm\frac{5}{12}$.

7. $-3, \frac{1}{2}(-5 \pm \sqrt{17})$; $-3, -4.56, -0.44$.   **9.** $-4, -1, \frac{1}{2}$.

11. $-3, -2, \frac{1}{2}(1 \pm i\sqrt{3})$; $-3, -2, 0.50 \pm 0.87i$.   **13.** $-\frac{5}{2}, -2, 0, 1$.

15. $-1, -1, -1, \pm i\sqrt{3}$; $-1, -1, -1, \pm1.73i$.

17. (a) $(x - 1)(3x - 1)(x^2 + 1)$; (b) $(x - 1)(3x - 1)(x + i)(x - i)$.

19. (a) $(v - 1)(3v^2 - 2v - 4)$; (b) $\frac{1}{3}(v - 1)(3v - 1 + \sqrt{13})(3v - 1 - \sqrt{13})$.

21. (a) $\frac{1}{3}(3x + 1)(x^2 - x + 3)$; (b) $\frac{1}{12}(3x + 1)(2x - 1 - i\sqrt{11})(2x - 1 + i\sqrt{11})$.

23. $-4, 1, 3$.   **25.** (b) $-1, \frac{1}{2}, \frac{1}{2}$.   **27.** 7 inches.

Section 12–12.   Pages 360 and 361

NOTE.   The answers to Exercises 1 and 3 are not unique, but are the natural answers under the instructions.

1. 3; -4.   **3.** 6; -2.   **9.** 0.67.   **11.** (a) -3.29; (b) 0.71; (c) 2.58.   **13.** 1.53.

15. (a) 1.31; (b) -1.13 by linear interpolation, -1.14 correct to two decimal places.

19. 0.889.   **21.** 3.91.   **23.** 0.51.

Section 12–12.   Miscellaneous Exercises.   Pages 361 and 362

1. (b) $x < -4$ or $x > 1$; (c) 25.   **3.** (b) $x \neq -2$; (c) 0.   **5.** Yes.

7. (a) $2, \frac{5}{2}, 3$; (c) $x < 2$ or $\frac{5}{2} < x < 3$.

9. (a) $x^3 - (r_1 + r_2 + r_3)x^2 + (r_1r_2 + r_1r_3 + r_2r_3)x - r_1r_2r_3$.

11. (a) $x^n - (r_1 + r_2 + \cdots + r_n)x^{n-1} + (r_1r_2 + r_1r_3 + \cdots + r_1r_n + r_2r_3$

  $+ \cdots + r_2r_n + r_3r_4 \cdots + r_3r_n + \cdots + r_{n-1}r_n)x^{n-2}$

  $+ \cdots + (-1)^k$ (sum of terms of form $r_1r_2 \cdots r_k)x^{n-k}$

  $+ \cdots + (-1)^n r_1r_2 \cdots r_n$.

13. $-\frac{1}{3}$.   **15.** Not applicable, not a polynomial equation.

Section 13–1.   Pages 364 and 365

1. $n = \dfrac{\log y - \log c}{\log x} = \dfrac{\log (y/c)}{\log x}$.   **3.** $t = \dfrac{\ln c - \ln r}{k} = -\dfrac{1}{k}\ln\dfrac{r}{c}$.   **5.** -3.

7. $-4, -1$.   **9.** $-\frac{2}{3}, 2$.   **11.** 2.3168.   **13.** 0.5991.

15. -9.32 [by another method, -9.34].   **17.** 2.188.   **19.** 0.6931.   **21.** 0.
23. $\frac{1}{2}(e^{-y} - e^y)$.   **25.** $-\frac{L}{R}\ln\left(1 - \frac{RI}{E}\right)$.   **27.** (a) 0.2310; (b) after 9.970 hours.
29. $b = 2$, $c = 5$, or $b = -2$, $c = -5$.

Section 13–2.   Page 367

1. $\{\frac{4}{3}\pi + 2k\pi, \frac{5}{3}\pi + 2k\pi\}$.   **3.** $\{\frac{1}{4}\pi + k\pi\}$.   **5.** $\{\frac{1}{3}\pi + 2k\pi, \frac{5}{3}\pi + 2k\pi\}$.
7. $\{2.215 + 2k\pi, 4.069 + 2k\pi\}$.   **9.** $\{\frac{1}{6}\pi + k\pi, \frac{5}{6}\pi + k\pi\}$.   **11.** $\{\frac{1}{4}\pi + k\pi\}$.
13. $\{\frac{1}{3}k\pi\}$.   **15.** $\{\frac{7}{6}\pi + 2k\pi, \frac{11}{6}\pi + 2k\pi, \frac{1}{12}\pi + \frac{1}{6}k\pi\}$.
17. $\{\frac{1}{8}\pi + \frac{1}{4}k\pi, \frac{1}{24}\pi + \frac{1}{4}k\pi, \frac{5}{24}\pi + \frac{1}{4}k\pi\}$.   **19.** $\{\frac{1}{2}\pi + k\pi, \frac{1}{6}\pi + 2k\pi, \frac{5}{6}\pi + 2k\pi\}$.
21. $\{\frac{1}{12}\pi + k\pi, \frac{5}{12}\pi + k\pi\}$.   **23.** $\{1.196 + 2k\pi, 5.087 + 2k\pi\}$.
25. $\{\frac{1}{2}\pi + k\pi, \frac{1}{6}\pi + 2k\pi, \frac{5}{6}\pi + 2k\pi\}$.
27. $\{\frac{2}{3}\pi + 2k\pi, \frac{4}{3}\pi + 2k\pi, 1.231 + 2k\pi, 5.052 + 2k\pi\}$.
29. $x = \frac{1}{3}\pi + 2k\pi, y = \frac{3}{2}; x = \frac{5}{3}\pi + 2k\pi, y = \frac{3}{2}$.
31. $\theta = \frac{1}{2}\pi + 2k\pi, r = 0$.   **33.** $\{\frac{1}{6}\pi + \frac{2}{3}k\pi\}$.

Section 13–3.   Page 368

1. 1.1, 2.8, 6.4.   **3.** 0.5.   **5.** 0, 0.9,   **7.** $-4.5, -2.1, 4.9$.   **9.** -1.1.
11. 0.9 foot.

Section 13–5.   Page 372

1. $-\frac{1}{4}\pi \leq t \leq \frac{1}{4}\pi$.   **3.** $0 \leq t \leq \frac{1}{3}\pi$.   **5.** $-\frac{1}{4} < t < \frac{1}{4}$.
7. $-\frac{1}{3}\pi \leq t < -\frac{1}{6}\pi$ or $0 \leq t < \frac{1}{6}\pi$.   **9.** $-\pi \leq t \leq \pi$.   **11.** $\frac{2}{3}\pi$.   **13.** $\frac{5}{3}\pi$.
15. $-\frac{1}{400}\pi$.

Section 13–6.   Pages 374 and 375

1. $\frac{1}{6}\pi$.   **3.** $-\frac{1}{6}\pi$.   **5.** π.   **7.** $-\frac{1}{4}\pi$.   **9.** $\frac{1}{2}\pi$.   **11.** 1.930.   **13.** x.
  y.   **17.** $\sqrt{1 - x^2}$.
  x is in first or second quadrant, $x + 2n\pi$; if x is in third or fourth quadrant,
$-x + 2n\pi$; where in each case n is an integer such that the answer is between 0 and π.
21. $x/\sqrt{1 + x^2}$.   **23.** $-\frac{5}{13}$.   **25.** $\frac{4}{5}$.   **27.** $\frac{1}{2}\pi$.

Section 13–6.   Miscellaneous Exercises.   Page 375

1. $\frac{1}{18}\pi, \frac{5}{18}\pi, \frac{13}{18}\pi, \frac{17}{18}\pi, \frac{25}{18}\pi, \frac{29}{18}\pi$.   **3.** $\frac{1}{6}\pi, \frac{5}{6}\pi, \frac{3}{2}\pi$.   **5.** $\frac{2}{3}\pi$.   **7.** $\frac{1}{4}\pi, \frac{3}{4}\pi, \frac{5}{4}\pi, \frac{7}{4}\pi$.
9. $\frac{3}{8}\pi, \frac{5}{8}\pi, \frac{9}{8}\pi, \frac{13}{8}\pi$.   **11.** 0.   **13.** $\frac{1}{2}e^3$, i.e., 10.04.   **15.** No solutions.
17. No solutions.   **19.** $-5.7, -4.0, 4.0, 5.7$, etc.   **21.** $\frac{3}{4}\pi, \frac{7}{4}\pi$.

Section 14–1.   Pages 377 and 378

1. (a) $1, \frac{1}{2}, \frac{1}{3}, \frac{1}{4}, \frac{1}{5}$; (b) $\frac{1}{15}$; (c) $\frac{1}{k}$; (d) $\frac{1}{n + 1}$.
3. (a) 4, 9, 16, 25, 36; (b) 256; (c) $(k + 1)^2$; (d) $(n + 2)^2$.
5. (a) $\frac{1}{2}, \frac{4}{3}, \frac{9}{4}, \frac{16}{5}, \frac{25}{6}$; (b) $\frac{225}{16}$; (c) $\frac{k^2}{k + 1}$; (d) $\frac{(n + 1)^2}{n + 2}$.
7. (a) $\frac{1}{\log \frac{3}{2}}, -\frac{1}{\log \frac{5}{2}}, \frac{1}{\log \frac{7}{2}}, -\frac{1}{\log \frac{9}{2}}, \frac{1}{\log \frac{11}{2}}$; (b) $\frac{1}{\log \frac{31}{2}}$; (c) $\frac{(-1)^{k+1}}{\log (k + \frac{1}{2})}$; (d) $\frac{(-1)^n}{\log (n + \frac{3}{2})}$.
9. $3 + 5 + 7 + 9 + 11$.   **11.** $1 + \sqrt{2} + \sqrt{3} + 2$.   **13.** $y^{-10} + y^{-15}$.
15. $\frac{1}{2} + \frac{2}{3} + \frac{3}{4} + \cdots + \frac{n}{n + 1}$.   **17.** $1 + x + x^2 + \cdots + x^k$.   **19.** 3^{n-1}.
21. $(-1)^n e^{-nx}$.   **25.** 3, 6, 12, 24, 48.   **27.** $4, -11, 19, -41, 79$.
29. $1 \cdot 3 \cdot 5 \cdot 7 \cdot 9 \cdot 11$.   **31.** $\frac{1}{2} \cdot \frac{3}{4} \cdot \frac{5}{6} \cdot \frac{7}{8} \cdot \frac{9}{10} \cdot \frac{11}{12} \cdot \frac{13}{14}$.

Section 14–2. Pages 380 and 381

1. 15, 19, 23, 27, 31.   **3.** $-3, -8, -13, -18, -23$.   **5.** 24, 29.   **7.** Not an A. P.
9. $(4a + 3b), (5a + 4b)$.   **11.** 6.   **13.** $-2\frac{1}{3}$.   **15.** $-14\frac{1}{3}$.   **17.** $-\frac{63}{2}; \frac{17}{2} - \frac{5}{2}n$.
19. (a) $\frac{18}{5}$; (b) $-16\frac{4}{5}$.   **21.** $(5t - 4u), (4t - 3u), (3t - 2u)$.   **23.** $4\frac{3}{5}, 5\frac{1}{5}, 5\frac{4}{5}, 6\frac{2}{5}$.
25. (a) $\frac{1}{2}(x + y)$; (b) $6\frac{7}{8}$; (c) $\frac{11}{2} + 3\sqrt{2}$.   **27.** No.   **29.** Yes.   **31.** \$1300.

Section 14–3. Pages 383 and 384

1. 19; 96.   **3.** $-54; -392$.   **5.** $22/a; 253/a$.   **7.** $d = 5, s_n = 188$.
9. $a_1 = 0, d = \frac{1}{4}$.   **11.** $n = 20, d = \frac{1}{19}(y - x)$.   **13.** (a) 49; (b) 1025.
15. (a) 7350; (b) 4530.   **17.** 63.   **19.** 50 cents.
21. $a_1 = a_n - (n - 1)d; s_n = \frac{1}{2}n[2a_n - (n - 1)d]$.   **23.** 408.   **25.** -3477.

Section 14–4. Pages 386 and 387

1. 5, 10, 20, 40, 80.   **3.** 81, -27, 9, -3, 1.   **5.** 16, 32.   **7.** 48, -96.
9. $\frac{1}{243}, \frac{1}{729}$.   **11.** Not a G. P. or an A. P.   **13.** $10^{-11}, 10^{-13}$.   **15.** 243.
17. $1/a^{14}$.   **19.** Thirteenth.   **21.** $\frac{1}{2}$.   **23.** ± 1.   **25.** -1.
27. (a) $\frac{243}{8}, \frac{81}{4}, \frac{27}{2}, 9$; (b) $\frac{32}{27}, -\frac{16}{9}, \frac{8}{3}, -4$; (c) 486, -162, 54, -18.
29. $\frac{1}{4}, \frac{1}{16}, \frac{1}{64}$ or $-\frac{1}{4}, \frac{1}{16}, -\frac{1}{64}$.   **31.** (a) $\pm\sqrt{pq}$; (b) $\pm 3pq^2$.   **35.** Impossible.
37. (a) No; (b) and (c) yes, for n a positive integer and $a_1 \neq 0, a_n \neq 0$, except that if only real numbers are considered and n is even then in (b) a_1 and a_n must have the same sign.
39. (a) No; (b) yes, let $c = 0$.   **41.** 64.
43. \$1343 by 4 place tables, \$1344 by more accurate tables.

Section 14–5. Pages 388 and 389

1. 160; 315.   **3.** 8; $\frac{511}{32}$.   **5.** $-0.000\,000\,02; -0.022\,222\,22$.   **7.** $a_1 = 256, a_n = 8$.
9. $r = 6, n = 4$.   **11.** $n = 11, s_n = \frac{2047}{16}$.   **13.** $s_n = \dfrac{a_n(1 - r^n)}{r^{n-1}(1 - r)}$.

Section 14–6. Pages 390 and 391

1. $\frac{9}{2}$.   **3.** $\frac{16}{9}$.   **5.** 26.   **7.** $\tan^2 0.1$.   **11.** $\frac{2}{3}$.   **13.** $\frac{122}{37}$.   **15.** $\frac{12}{5}$.
17. 217 inches, i.e., 18 feet 1 inch.   **19.** Never overtakes.

Section 14–6. Miscellaneous Exercises. Pages 391 to 393

1. 36.   **3.** \$1228.80.   **5.** (a) 166,833; (b) 1092.   **7.** 2 or 14.   **9.** 579.
11. (a) $C = 30 + \frac{59}{40}d + \frac{1}{40}d^2$; (b) 85 feet.   **13.** (a) $2\frac{10}{27}$ feet; (b) $78\frac{4}{27}$ feet; (c) 90 feet.
15. $9.22 \cdot 10^{11}$ tons.   **17.** (a) $\frac{1}{14}, \frac{1}{16}$; (b) not an H. P.; (c) not an H. P.; (d) not an H. P.

Section 14–8. Pages 398 and 399

1. False, fails for $n = 1$.
3. Proposition correct but (I) omitted from proposed proof.
5. False, (II) fails at $k = 15$.

Section 15–2. Pages 402 to 404

1. $AB, AC, AD, AE, AF, BC, BD, BE, BF, CD, CE, CF, DE, DF, EF$.
3. 48.   **5.** 66.   **7.** 70 pairs.   **9.** 720.   **11.** (a) 216; (b) 120; (c) 108; (d) 27.
13. (a) 1; (b) 4; (c) 256; (d) 24.   **15.** (a) $2^{10,000}$; (b) 10^{3001}.

Section 15–3.   Page 405

1. 56.   **3.** $\frac{12}{5}$.   **5.** $\frac{4}{57}$.   **7.** $-\frac{19}{124}$.   **9.** $n + 2$.

11. $(3r - 1)(3r - 2) \cdots (r + 2)(r + 1)r$.   **13.** $\frac{1}{120}$.   **15.** $\dfrac{2m}{2m + 1}$.

Section 15–4.   Pages 406 and 407

1. (a) 30; (b) 29,760; (c) 720; (d) 24,024; (e) 2520.   **3.** 120.   **5.** 336.
7. (a) 480; (b) 120.

Section 15–5.   Pages 408 and 409

1. 60,480.   **3.** (a) 60; (b) 15,600.   **5.** (a) 24; (b) 360.   **7.** 8640.
9. (a) $\dfrac{20!}{(4!)^5}$; (b) $\dfrac{19!}{3!\,(4!)^4}$; (c) $\dfrac{18!}{2!\,(4!)^4}$; (d) $\dfrac{5 \cdot 18!}{2!\,(4!)^4}$.
11. 3,628,800.   **13.** $\frac{1}{4}P(6, 4)$, i.e., 90.

Section 15–6.   Pages 411 and 412

1. (a) 15; (b) 4960; (c) 1; (d) 1001; (e) 120.   **3.** 1820.   **5.** 120.   **7.** 142,506.
9. 1540.   **11.** 140.   **13.** (a) 924; (b) 34,650.   **15.** 35.

Section 15–7.   Pages 415 and 416

1. $210a^6x^4$.   **3.** $-5005b^6z^9$.   **5.** $4368x^{22}a^{10}$.   **7.** $252a^5b^5$.   **9.** $112,266a^5x^6$.
11. $-126e^x$.   **13.** $436,296x^7$.   **15.** $x^4 + 4x^3y + 6x^2y^2 + 4xy^3 + y^4$.
17. $a^6 - 6a^5c + 15a^4c^2 - 20a^3c^3 + 15a^2c^4 - 6ac^5 + c^6$.
19. $128x^7 + 1344x^6y + 6048x^5y^2 + 15,120x^4y^3 + 22,680x^3y^4 + 20,412x^2y^5 + 10,206xy^6$
   $+ 2187y^7$.
21. 127.   **23.** (a) 5; (b) 31.

Section 15–8.   Pages 418 and 419

1. $x^7 + 7x^6y + 21x^5y^2 + 35x^4y^3 + 35x^3y^4 + 21x^2y^5 + 7xy^6 + y^7$.
3. $512a^9 - 2304a^8x + 4608a^7x^2 - 5376a^6x^3 + 4032a^5x^4 - 2016a^4x^5 + 672a^3x^6 -$
   $144a^2x^7 + 18ax^8 - x^9$.
5. $64 + 192\dfrac{x}{a} + 240\dfrac{x^2}{a^2} + 160\dfrac{x^3}{a^3} + 60\dfrac{x^4}{a^4} + 12\dfrac{x^5}{a^5} + \dfrac{x^6}{a^6}$.
7. $a^8b^{-8} - 8a^6b^{-6} + 28a^4b^{-4} - 56a^2b^{-2} + 70 - 56a^{-2}b^2 + 28a^{-4}b^4 - 8a^{-6}b^6 + a^{-8}b^8$.
9. $x^{26} + 13x^{24}a^2 + 78x^{22}a^4 + 286x^{20}a^6 + \cdots$.
11. $x^4 + 12x^{\frac{11}{3}}y^{\frac{1}{3}} + 66x^{\frac{10}{3}}y^{\frac{2}{3}} + 220x^3y + \cdots$.
13. $x^{103} - 206x^{102} + 21,012x^{101} - 1,414,808x^{100} + \cdots$.
15. 1.0222.   **17.** 676.52.   **19.** 0.99501.
21. $a^4 + 4a^3b + 6a^2b^2 + 4ab^3 + b^4 - 4a^3c - 12a^2bc - 12ab^2c - 4b^3c + 6a^2c^2 +$
   $12abc^2 + 6b^2c^2 - 4ac^3 - 4bc^3 + c^4$.
23. $\cdots -560e^{-\frac{10}{3}x} + 120e^{-4x} - 16e^{-\frac{14}{3}x} + e^{-\frac{16}{3}x}$.
25. 23.
27. $a^{\frac{1}{3}} - a^{-\frac{2}{3}}x^6 - a^{-\frac{5}{3}}x^{12} - \frac{5}{3}a^{-\frac{8}{3}}x^{18} + \cdots$.
29. $a^n - \frac{1}{2}a^{-n}y^{2n} - \frac{1}{8}a^{-3n}y^{4n} - \frac{3}{16}a^{-5n}y^{6n} + \cdots$.
31. $1 + 1 + \frac{1}{2}(1 - h) + \frac{1}{6}(1 - h)(1 - 2h) + \cdots$.
33. 0.99499.   **35.** 5.0990.   **37.** 2.0908.   **39.** 3.9998.

Section 15–8. Miscellaneous Exercises. Pages 419 to 421

1. (a) 380; (b) 190.   **3.** 487,635.   **5.** 270.   **7.** 120.   **9.** 35.   **11.** 1200.
13. 4,761,000.   **15.** 25,920.   **17.** (a) 30; (b) 2.   **19.** 12.
21. (a) $\dfrac{52!}{13!\,39!}$, i.e., $6.349 \cdot 10^{11}$; (b) $\dfrac{47!}{8!\,39!}$, i.e., $3.145 \cdot 10^{8}$; (c) 1.   **23.** 20.

Section 15–9. Pages 425 and 426

1. (a) c, o, l_1, l_2, e_1, g, e_2; (b) 2; (c) $\frac{2}{7}$; (d) $\frac{5}{7}$.
3. (a) $\frac{1}{4}$; (b) $\frac{3}{4}$.   **5.** 3 to 2 in favor.   **7.** (a) $\frac{3}{4}$; (b) $\frac{2}{13}$.   **9.** $\frac{1}{4}$.
11. (a) \$0.50; (b) \$0.30; (c) \$0.40.   **13.** $\frac{1}{22}$.   **15.** Odd, 25 to 24.
17. 2 chocolate, $\frac{1}{5}$; 3 chocolate, $\frac{9}{20}$; 4 chocolate, $\frac{3}{5}$; 5 chocolate, $\frac{1}{2}$.

Section 15–10. Pages 430 and 431

1. (a) 3, 4, 5, 6, 6, 7, 8, 9, 10, 12, 12, 12, 14, 15, 16, 18, 20, 21, 24, 28; (b) 6; (c) $\frac{3}{10}$.
3. $\frac{1}{2}$.   **5.** (a) 0.176; (b) 0.149⁻.   **7.** (a) $\frac{1}{100}$; (b) \$0.55; (c) $\frac{1}{32}$; (d) \$0.54⁺.
9. A: $\frac{1}{2}$; B: $\frac{1}{4}$; C: $\frac{1}{4}$.   **11.** (a) 0.9801; (b) 0.5475.   **13.** (a) 4; (b) $\frac{2304}{3125}$, i.e., about 0.74.
15. (a) $\frac{125}{7776}$; (b) $\frac{625}{3888}$; (c) $\frac{125}{1944}$.   **17.** $\frac{1}{4}$.

Section 15–11. Pages 433

1. 0.52.
3. 1960: cattle 0.527, sheep 0.153, hogs 0.304, horses and mules 0.0160; 1890: cattle 0.352, sheep 0.261, hogs 0.282, horses and mules 0.106.
5. (a) 0.103; (b) 0.0950; (c) 10; (d) 10.
7. (a) E, 0.131; T, 0.105; A, 0.082; O, 0.080; N, 0.071; R, 0.068; I, 0.063; S, 0.061.

Section 15–11. Miscellaneous Exercises. Pages 434 and 435

1. (a) $\frac{1}{5}$; (b) 10.   **3.** 0.044.   **5.** $\frac{2}{9}$.   **7.** (a) $\frac{1}{9}$; (b) $\frac{5}{18}$.   **9.** (a) $\frac{71}{75}$; (b) $\frac{4}{25}$.
11. $\frac{4}{9}$.   **13.** (a) $\frac{3}{8}$; (b) $\frac{1}{2}$; (c) 75.
15. $(\frac{1}{2})^{10}[C(10, 4) + C(10, 3) + C(10, 2) + C(10, 1) + 1]$, i.e., 0.377⁻.
17. (a) $(\frac{2}{5})^3 + 3(\frac{2}{5})^2 \cdot \frac{3}{5}$, i.e., 0.352; (b) 0.0573.

Section A–1. Page 438

1. 64.   **3.** 128.   **5.** 6.05.   **7.** 6930.   **9.** 0.0293.   **17.** 77,700.

Section A–2. Page 440

1. 198,900.   **3.** 0.605⁻.   **5.** 32.   **7.** 0.257.   **9.** 4.65⁺.   **11.** −0.0784.
13. 0.01340.   **15.** 0.0518.

Section A–3. Page 442

1. 67,600.   **3.** 0.00192.   **5.** 2.17.   **7.** 68.7.   **9.** 4.54.   **11.** 0.000 228.
109. 9.679 − 10.

Section A–4. Page 444

1. 0.656.   **3.** 0.0663.   **5.** (a) 0.466; (b) 1.907.   **7.** (a) 0.883; (b) 0.375.

INDEX

The numbers refer to pages